AFRICA
BIBLIOGRAPHY

AFRICA
BIBLIOGRAPHY
1992

works published on Africa in 1992

compiled by
Christopher H. Allen
University of Edinburgh

with assistance from Katherine Allen

in association with the
International African Institute
London

EDINBURGH UNIVERSITY PRESS

© Edinburgh University Press 1994

Edinburgh University Press
22 George Square, Edinburgh

Typeset in Lasercomp Plantin by ROM-Data, Falmouth, Cornwall, and printed in Great Britain by Page Bros, Norwich.

A CIP record for this book is available from the British Library.

ISSN 0266-6731
ISBN 0 7486 0483 9

CONTENTS

FOREWORD

African Books Collective
Its Contribution to African Publishing

Mary Jay

Introduction

Today, in the late twentieth century, the decision to publish African authors is still largely – though not wholly – taken outside the continent. If we accept the universality of human knowledge and experience, and the desirability of international exchange, does this matter?

The functions of national publishing are manifold. But there are three main beneficial functions. First, the ability of a nation to preserve, develop and communicate its identity, its culture and its heritage is central. In so far as a publishing house has this wider context as the backdrop to its publishing decisions, then those decisions can only be realistically taken within that country. Decisions taken outside the country are bound to be piecemeal, with commercial considerations paramount. An agenda set from outside the continent ultimately denies Africa the right to speak for itself. Second, literacy, books and the reading habit are central to an educated citizenry capable of taking control of their own destiny. And the type of book in this context matters. No national education system should be a fortress and it is surely the right of people in education to benefit from the free flow of intellectual ideas and material. But the crucial word here is 'flow'.

If the flow is disproportionately one-way into Africa, the likelihood is that the citizens at all levels of government – in its broadest sense – will have experienced an education system and a culture with a diluted and distorted sense of the role and development path for their own country. The much documented and most obvious example of this was during the colonial period, when educational curricula were centred, particularly in history, on a Eurocentric colonial interpretation. The role of national publishing in an educational context is not confined to the type of material available; it concerns quantity too. Whilst content matters, so does accessibility. Where national resources are scarce, libraries few in number and under-funded, bookshops few and books often prohibitive in price to the vast majority, and distribution to rural areas virtually non-existent, then irrespective of the content or origin of books, education will suffer or not be available in any meaningful sense.

It is difficult to generalise about the state of the publishing industry in Africa today, since very different conditions may prevail from one country to another and between different groups of countries – each with their own distinctive cultures, traditions, and book trade structures which have developed along different lines and at different paces. Broadly, what follows applies to the sub-Saharan anglophone countries.

Despite the domination, by the 1960s, of the ex-Africa multinationals, indigenous publishing established itself quite remarkably from around that time. The economic problems which have beset the continent in the 1980s and 1990s, however, took their toll, with the result that publishing has been severely cut back. Infrastructures have deteriorated, with particularly poor transport and communications; printing facilities are often poor with, frequently, high tariffs on essential printing equipment; retail outlets and distribution facilities are lacking or inadequate; there is a lack of access to investment capital; and chronic debt problems, and foreign exchange constraints have taken a stranglehold. Educational publishing in some countries is still disproportionately represented by the British and French multinationals, leaving the residual problems for indigenous publishers of access to the backbone of the textbook market. And in other countries, such as Kenya, governments themselves have a monopoly of the textbook market. These economic problems have compounded the problems arising from social conditions: the wide diversity of languages, the high levels of illiteracy, an emphasis on functional reading only, and the inadequacy of libraries. Many parts of Africa suffer a severe book famine. So whilst indigenous publishers established firm footholds in the 1960s and 1970s and were set to face the still formidable challenges, their task became herculean from the 1980s. Through the 1980s, whilst the scale of development was small there was, paradoxically, new innovative enterprise, with books of the highest quality on occasions being produced. These initiatives have been largely in the private sector, and disappointingly few African governments have been supportive of this vital industry. Domination of the textbook market by multinationals in partnership with governments, high tariffs on imported materials, and bureaucracy preventing books crossing borders, are simply the most obvious manifestations. In the 1990s, the light which had been kept alive is increasingly looking to common solutions on a co-operative basis, and innovative ways to overcome the problems.

African publishing: collective solutions

African publishers have come together to form two major organisations to tackle different aspects of their common problems.

The African Publishers Network (APNET) was established in February 1992. Pan-African in scope, its membership is national publishers' associations, and it aims to support communication across borders in Africa, encourage inter-African trading and joint ventures, support the establishment of national publishers' associations where none exist, run training programmes, create a resource centre, and engage in research and lobbying, amongst other activities.

African Books Collective Ltd. was established in 1989 to address one of the many problems mentioned above: the enduring problem for African publishers of the lack of distribution networks – either nationally, regionally, or internationally. If sufficient books can be sold, then a flourishing industry can start to be built. Internationally, there has been great demand, particularly from libraries, for African publications. A small number of commercial distributors, largely serving Europe and the USA, have provided a valuable service, particularly in the acquisition of government documents, 'grey' literature and other ephemera. But for those books bought locally in Africa by dealers, the publisher does not benefit from foreign exchange earnings. For the publisher, trying to process orders direct from overseas, the scale of the bureaucracy in handling export orders and the difficulties of handling small orders often meant the orders went unprocessed. And so, in 1985, a core group of eleven like-minded African publishers came together to see whether they could tackle jointly what they could not tackle individually.

African Books Collective (ABC)

Objectives

At that initial meeting, the publishers decided to set up a distribution organisation, wholly owned by themselves, to undertake joint promotion and distribution in Europe, North

America, and in Commonwealth countries outside Africa. The proposal was met with widespread enthusiasm, and four years of preparatory work, consultation exercises in the African book community, and fund-raising ensued. The objectives were primarily to market and distribute member publishers' English-language books in the main markets outside Africa, in the wider context of the dissemination of African culture and heritage, allowing Africa to speak for itself, and contributing to the international exchange of scholarship, and international understanding. Increased exposure of the wealth of their output would encourage African authors to publish on their own continent and, by earning foreign currency, the publishers would have increased resources to invest in their firms and increase their output.

Council of Management

Eighteen African publishers founded the company, and it is governed by a Council of Management, comprising elected members from the founding group, and constituted on a broad regional basis. Countries currently represented on the Council are Kenya, Nigeria (2 members), Senegal, South Africa, and Tanzania. The Council of Management is responsible for all policy matters, including the future development and role of ABC. The Council has met formally twice, part-funded by the Commonwealth Foundation. Continuous consultation takes place in the interim, and the Council of Management is provided with regular information, analysis and feedback. It is difficult to raise funding to convene the meetings, but funding is currently being sought to hold a full meeting in 1994.

Structure

Each founder member contributed £1,000 *in hard currency* towards the start-up costs – no mean achievement in the light of the constraints prevailing, but one which the publishers believed was crucial in order to demonstrate their commitment to the objectives of ABC. The unique nature of ABC itself, besides being owned and governed by the publishers themselves, lies in its non-profit making nature, enabling the net returns to publishers to be more preferential than is usually available under conventional commercial distribution arrangements. For founder member publishers, ABC retains approximately one-third of net receipts from sales as a contribution towards its operating costs. Member publishers receive sales reports and remittances and £ sterling and US Dollar remittances twice-yearly, on the basis of net proceeds from sales. Their stocks are sent to the UK on consignment terms and remain their property until sold. They receive regular analysis and feedback to contribute to their publishing decisions. Because of its trading activities, ABC has been unable to register as a charity with the UK Charities Commission, despite its non-profit making nature. It is a company limited by guarantee, and the members of the Council of Management are the members of the company. Two UK-based directors bear the legal liability.

Funding

In the light of the non-profit making nature of ABC, and the preferential terms for publishers, donor funding was sought from the outset to support the enterprise. This funding was sought for part-funding of capital and set-up costs, and to meet the shortfall of income over expenditure. The initiative fell squarely within the kind of approach which donors were rightly newly favouring – self-help, benefits to education and literacy within Africa and promotion of awareness outside. It is generally accepted amongst the international community that, for example, the right approach to food shortages in Africa is to fund projects leading to self-sustaining development of agriculture and whilst it is imperative to provide aid at times of famine or severe shortage, this must go hand in hand with support for a flourishing agriculture sector. The same could be said to apply to books and publishing: yet ABC too often met the attitude that it was asking for money to be put into the pockets of commercial publishers. The need was, and remains, for support which recognises that considerable investment is needed over a sustained time-span, until such time as the volume of turnover closes the shortfall. A definition surely of 'sustainable development'.

Three donors responded from the outset with support and encouragement: the Ford Foundation, the Swedish International Development Authority (SIDA), and the Norwegian Agency for International Development (NORAD). With this funding, ABC started operations on a small scale in 1990. The eighteen publishers took the view that too much talk had been expended over too many years at too many conferences, and some practical action must be taken by themselves to start to tackle one part of their problems.

Membership

Membership is open to all African publishers, although the Council of Management reserves the right to decide on the suitability of applications. The suitability of the list for joint promotion with existing members, among other factors, is of prime concern in deciding on new membership applications. New full members may join for a fee of £500, and are entitled to 60% of net returns; associate members do not pay a membership fee, and receive 55% of net returns; and publishers with only one or two titles for distribution may use the services of ABC without a fee, and receive 50% of net returns.

From an initial eighteen founder member publishers in 1989, membership has now more than doubled and has grown to forty-one publishers, from twelve African countries. ABC receives a steady stream of enquiries and applications for membership, which are evaluated against a common set of criteria. A large number have not been accepted for membership, primarily on the grounds of the incompatibility of the list for suitable joint promotion, but there remains a long waiting list of other publishers who are keen to join. In the light of the limited resources available, and rapid expansion in 1992 and 1993, ABC is unlikely to be admitting any further new members in 1994. But it is hoped to expand gradually as resources permit.

Of the current members, over half are African university presses, and other non-profit making academic bodies and research institutes with publishing programmes. The breakdown of membership by country is as follows: Botswana 1, Ghana 4, Kenya 2, Malawi 1, Mauritius 1, Namibia 1, Nigeria 15, Senegal 2, South Africa 2, Tanzania 4, Zambia 1 and Zimbabwe 7. Both South African publishers have been 'oppositional', that is, not collaborating with the apartheid structures and regime which are only now beginning to break down.

Services

Centralised billing and shipping is provided from one service point, with orders invoiced and shipped within a few days from receipt of order. ABC's orders processing operations are due to be fully computerised in 1994, and this will lead to even more rapid turnaround of orders in the future. Specialist services are also provided: a 'new title information on cards' bibliographic service; standing order and 'blanket' plans for libraries; and a showroom facility in central Oxford displaying (but not selling over the counter) copies of all titles stocked. The displays include member publishers' titles not stocked (mostly older backlist) but for which orders can be forwarded to publishers for direct processing.

Staff and premises

ABC's offices are located in the Jam Factory at 27 Park End Street, Oxford. The offices are located outside Africa, because the work of the organisation is to access the markets of the UK, Europe, the USA and other markets outside Africa. It is worth emphasising that, even if problems of communication and infrastructure did not exist in Africa, ABC would still be located somewhere in the markets being targeted – in the same way as a UK or US publisher has offices and distributors in overseas territories. Initially two small rooms were occupied: one used as an office and the other for the showroom display. At the beginning of 1992, ABC expanded into a bigger office suite in the same building, comprising two offices and a showroom. The current complement of staff is two full-time people: an office administrator and promotions assistant; and three part-timers: warehousing manager/shipping; orders processing/customer services; and bookkeeper/credit controller. Occasional part-time staff are employed for administrative support, and relief staff at the warehouse. Two part-time consultants are employed for overall project management, including consultancy and management services, policy guidance, financial planning, and supervision of day-to-day operations.

Warehousing premises are maintained in Burford, some twenty miles from Oxford. Former livestock byres, the 1,800 sq. ft. building has been converted and upgraded by the landlord, although the charming Cotswold building and the cobbled floors are not the usual picture conjured up by the word 'warehouse'. After careful consideration, ABC decided not to entrust warehousing to an outside service organisation, but to retain full control of its distribution service and its credit and cash collection. The warehouse now holds a stock inventory of over 108,000 units.

Promotion and marketing

The number of titles stocked has more than tripled since the start of trading in May 1990, and over 1,100 titles from forty-one member publishers are currently distributed. Some 200 new titles are added to the stock inventory every year, and each title needs individual attention.

The main methods of promotion are extensive direct mail catalogue campaigns and participation in exhibits (described below). Additionally, each title is entered into major bibliographic data bases; title information cards are prepared for all newly-published books, each card providing a short blurb plus full acquisitions data, and these are then mailed direct to key customers; individual flyers are produced and selectively mailed, on particularly outstanding or highly topical titles; and review copies are mailed to the most important African studies periodicals, library journals and other media. Trade promotion is undertaken in the U.K., with visits to key trade outlets, etc. Trade accounts are maintained with some 300 customers, but this market remains very difficult to penetrate and ABC has met with only limited success and the overall turnover from this market is still a small proportion of the total. ABC is producing, from 1993, a complete annual stocklist, and also issues an occasional *ABC Newsline* newsletter. Taking all promotion activities into account, and including also administrative, sales reporting, and warehousing costs, it has been estimated that it costs ABC, pro-rata, a total of about £300 to take on a new title. For backlist titles it is slightly less.

Diversity
Each title taken on needs individual attention and nurturing. With the growth in the number of titles handled, the diversity of the lists has increased and widened, and this brings its own problems. Books distributed include a wide spectrum of academic and scholarly publications

(covering subjects ranging from Adult Education to Zoology); bibliographies and reference resources; a strong list of over 200 titles of African creative writing (fiction, drama, poetry, and critical studies on African literature); a substantial number of children's books; plus general titles on African life and culture. Children's and folklore titles need very different marketing and targeting from that, for example, required for scholarly and academic titles; within the category of scholarly titles, the different disciplines – such as medicine or law – require different marketing.

Mainstreaming
In addition to handling this diversity, ABC has a mission to 'mainstream' African books – to 'de-exotify' them so that they are regarded and treated in the same way as books from the UK, USA or anywhere else. Why, for example, should major booksellers in the UK say that they can't stock our African literature – novels, poetry, drama – because it doesn't fit anywhere or 'there is nowhere to put it'. Why should it not sit on the shelves with the literature of Latin American magic realism, Australian fiction, and indeed the literature from the North? With one or two notable exceptions, bookshops' response is that it is a specialist interest, and would get 'lost' in the main literature shelves, could only go in its own little ghetto somewhere out of the way, and in any case,'there is no demand'. Despite Africa having three winners of the Nobel Prize for Literature, and a winner of the Booker Prize, most of the great canon of African literature is still marginalised in this way – as in so many others – from the mainstream world cultures.

A major part of the effort to mainstream, is attempting to tap into the vast potential of the US public and school library markets, and making it clear – worldwide – that African books from ABC, warehoused in the UK and available for immediate supply, are as easy to acquire as those from a UK publisher. Some 64% of ABC sales are currently in the USA. And of total sales, about 70% are to libraries – academic, institutional, and public. The scale of the task is huge: for example major US publishers mail ten times the quantities of catalogues that ABC do. It is, however, clear that this is a major development potential for ABC, in particular for the categories of children's, folklore, African heritage and (some) general titles. US public library systems have suffered budget cuts in recent years, and there has been much public lamenting. There is, however, a paradox which makes the outlook rather less depressing than might at first appear. First the number of public libraries is vast, and thus the market left after budget cutbacks still holds great potential. Second, the cuts have been reductions in budgets, rather than freezing of all new purchases. And third, and most interestingly, of the resources available, a greater percentage of the whole is being devoted to the purchase of 'multicultural' materials. This arises from the drive in US library systems to make their libraries more responsive to and reflective of the communities in which they are located. And reinforcing this trend, some libraries are now receiving grants specifically for the purchase of multicultural materials.

At the start of trading, ABC enjoyed some excellent orders from a small number of UK local authority libraries, which recognised that books from Africa were important and relevant for all young people living in a multicultural and multiracial society, including those of African heritage. But alas, the severity of cutbacks in UK public library funding has meant that almost nothing is now acquired by them: the funds simply do not exist. The London Borough of Camden, for example, has just suffered a cut of £54,000 from its annual budget, including a reduction of £20,000 for the purchase of new books.[1]

Given that part of the mission of ABC is to change perceptions about African books the politics of language is important. 'Multicultural' has long been used in the UK as meaning

---

[1] *The Bookseller*, 20 August 1993, p.13.

all cultures. The word became commonplace in the US only a few years ago, but was probably more generally used to mean non-Anglo-Saxon culture, in particular, black and hispanic communities. Now, whilst not discredited, the word has been overtaken by 'cultural diversity' as being more specifically about different and equal cultures and terms such as 'culturally inclusive' have been spawned. ABC has been happy to use whatever term is currently used and understood to mean mainstreaming African culture, but it is hard to keep up! Whatever the words are used, many US publishers are newly concentrating on publishing books for the large black population in the US, whose annual purchasing power for books is currently estimated at $180 million. ABC therefore also has the hurdle of getting the message across that its books are *from* Africa, by African authors, and communicate the African experience and heritage; and that this is quite distinct from books published in the USA by American authors, including black authors, for and about the black experience in America.

Catalogues
ABC catalogues are mailed using the Hans Zell Publishers mailing lists, built up over many years. Hans Zell acts as the senior Consultant to ABC and, through him, ABC has free access to the mailing lists. Additionally, ABC is building up some of its own new specialist lists.

Two main catalogues are issued twice-yearly, and the print runs are usually around 7,000. New (and some backlist) titles are listed with full bibliographic data, and a descriptive blurb. In 1992, a new series of subject catalogues was started. The first one covered all African Languages & Literature titles; and subsequent catalogues have covered Politics, Economics & Development; Anthropology, Sociology, and Women's Studies; Medicine & Health Sciences; History & Archaeology; Religion & Theology and Philosophy; and African Law. Subject catalogues are targeted to individual scholars on the mailing lists, and since all titles stocked in the subject area are included, this is very much more convenient for them. It also avoids the expense of mailing all main catalogues to scholars of one discipline only. Individual flyers are issued on particularly important titles, from time to time.

Two glossy four-colour catalogues in substantial print runs have been produced listing children's and folklore titles, African heritage and history, and general titles on African culture such as art, music, cookery, etc. Targeted at the public library systems worldwide, and particularly in the USA, these catalogues present a core range of books for libraries actively developing collections in this field.

Exhibits
The other main arm of promotion is participation in exhibits and book fairs. ABC has exhibited at meetings of the (US) African Studies Association, the American Libraries Association (ALA), the Black Caucus of the ALA, the Zimbabwe International Book Fair, the London International Book Fair, and the Gothenburg Book Fair. In addition, ABC has participated in joint exhibits at book fairs and scholarly meetings. In 1993, ABC was included in joint exhibits at the Royal African Society annual meeting in Oxford, the Feminist Book Festival in London, the Royal Society of Tropical Medicine & Hygiene annual meeting in Edinburgh, the 7th General Conference of the European Association of Development Research and Training Institutions (EADI) in Berlin, and the Vitabu Vya Afrika event at the Africa Centre in London.

Other activities

Whilst ABC's main mission remains the promotion of its member publishers' titles outside

Africa, the original Mission Statement from the 1985 founding meeting stated that there were two other related areas which the publishers would wish to tackle in due course – an intra-African flow of books, and distribution of French language material. The intention was to establish the main trading mission on a firm and financially secure foothold, before addressing other areas.

Intra-African Book Support Scheme

The most exciting innovation, and departure from ABC's main mission, came only 15 months after the start of trading. In August 1991 the Intra-African Book Support Scheme (IABSS) was launched.

As is well known and documented, there is very little trade in books *between* African countries. The problems which affect national and international distribution also apply regionally. Books from Ghana are not seen in Botswana, and books from Namibia are not seen in Nigeria. Indeed the incidence of books crossing neighbouring borders is still negligible. Problems of infrastructure, communication, and foreign exchange constraints, amongst others, inhibit such movements. And this brings losses in more than an economic sense. If the lack of communication of African culture, from Africa to the rest of the world, is to be deplored; then so too is the failure of one culture in Africa to communicate its heritage to another African culture. One of the factors in the cohesion of the continent must be this interchange.

The scheme was launched as a joint project of ABC and the Ranfurly Library Service (now re-named Book Aid International), Britain's largest book aid charity and an independent voluntary organisation which works in partnership with people and organisations in over 70 developing countries to provide relevant books for their needs. For RLS, the scheme enabled them 'for the first time . . . to make a positive contribution to addressing the root cause of the book famine in Africa, by supporting the African publishing industry'. And for ABC, the scheme enabled the task of an intra-African flow of books to be tackled very much sooner than anticipated, while maintaining the existing structure of the organisation.

Charity Projects (UK), which raises money through the Comic Relief appeal, made a grant of £50,000 to RLS for the purchase of ABC books for supply to selected African major academic libraries which had been unable to purchase African books published outside their own country because of the chronic foreign exchange constraints. One library in each of twelve African countries was a recipient. Each selected titles from ABC catalogues, and RLS shipped the books through free shipping facilities. DANIDA, the Danish Government's Coordinating Committee for Cultural Cooperation with Developing Countries, funded ABC directly to supply the same libraries with one copy of each new ABC-distributed title thereafter. The libraries filled out Standing Order profile forms stipulating the types of books they wished to receive. And this generous funding has continued since 1991.

When the scheme was launched, the ABC membership stood at twenty publishers, who benefited from the Charity Projects funding. As new funding is secured, all subsequent member publishers titles are also included in donations.

With the launch of IABSS, a significant component of *African-published* material has been included in a book donation scheme, perhaps for the first time. The scheme enables students and scholars from one part of Africa to gain access to African publishing from other parts of the continent; addresses the 'book famine' in Africa; and promotes an intra-African flow of books. It is recognised that there is a certain irony in books being shipped to the UK from all parts of Africa, only to be shipped back again! However, the reality is that it is simple, practical and efficient to operate the scheme in this way; and that it would be very difficult to organise within Africa in current conditions. It is clearly desirable, however, that one day the scheme should be administered from within Africa, but when the day comes that books from all over Africa can be warehoused at one point, the likelihood is that the scheme itself will no longer be necessary.

The Children's Book Support Scheme was launched in March 1992 as a component of IABSS. With general funding from the Ministry for Development Cooperation of the Netherlands Government, the scheme was similarly organised, but addressed the needs of children's libraries in Africa. Up to 188 copies of 99 different children's books, from thirteen ABC member publishers, were supplied to children's libraries, rural community centres, orphanages and primary schools in eight African countries. A total of over 13,000 units were supplied through RLS, who arranged shipping to National Library Services and other distributors (with which they have already established long term links) which then provided effective distribution networks both to and within each of the recipient countries. A further grant has been made to the CBSS by the Dutch Government for 1993.

In 1991 and 1992 the three parts of IABSS contributed remittances to member publishers of some £66,000 in hard currency.

The Swedish Agency for Research Cooperation with Developing Countries (SAREC) has provided a grant in 1993 direct to ABC, towards the development of IABSS. Three of the libraries in the original scheme have been allocated additional funding for selecting books from ABC, and two additional libraries – in Eritrea and Mozambique – have been funded to make selections. This funding has been renewed for 1994–1996.

From an expression of the ideal in 1985, the hope of promoting an intra-African flow of books has become a reality. The benefits to member publishers themselves have been great, contributing to greater publishing activity, and they are all very keen to secure funding to extend the scheme further. For ABC itself, the approximately one-third of net income retained from the sales has made a significant contribution to core-funding, enabling the minimum necessary complement of staff to be employed, and contributing to overheads. Whilst the need for core-funding is paramount (since this is not the favoured funding of donor organisations), considerable energy is being devoted to trying to secure further funding for IABSS, which itself makes a contribution to ABC's own self-generated revenue.

French-language material

As originally intended, ABC stocks only English-language material. But the publishers believed it would be right to stock books in the other languages of Africa when the firm base of English-language distribution was established. For African language material, it was recognised that the market was very small, and could not be embarked on as other than a loss-making operation. And thus no consideration should be given to this until such time in the future as the profitability of the trading operation could subsidise African language distribution. It was not thought that the potential for Portuguese language distribution was great, but that there would be potential for French language distribution. The publishers had in mind here also the desirability of breaking down the 'anglophone' and 'francophone' divisions. One of the founder members was the Council for the Development of Economic & Social Research in Africa (CODESRIA), based in Senegal, and with a publishing arm presenting research findings in books produced in both English and French. ABC distributes their English language titles. In 1993, Environmental Development Action in the Third World (ENDA), also based in Senegal, joined ABC. These two prestigious research institutions provide a bridge, and symbolise the importance of breaking down the artificial barriers inherited from the colonial spheres of power and continuing influence. But as to actual distribution of French language material, the time has not come, and may not do so. Due to inherited colonial structures, and the very different models of 'independence' in the English and French/Belgian ex-colonies, the publishing structures are very different, and selling of francophone African books is governed by different market forces. The ties in the francophone countries with publishing in France are still very strong, and few francophone African publishers are genuinely autonomous. Additionally, the traditional pattern in the francophone countries has been for distribution to be handled independently in France. Added to this, the major problem confronting anglophone publishers are the fluctuating, and deteriorating, exchange rates; whereas the francophone countries have the bulwark of the CFA system which is tied to the French franc.

ABC's own first publication

Working in the wider context of dissemination of information about African books and writing, and support for autonomous African publishing, ABC engages in related supportive activities. To further these objectives, material will occasionally be published. The first publication, in June 1993, was the *African Publishers Networking Directory and 'Names & Numbers' 1993/94* (ISBN 0952126907). A reference guide and networking tool for publishers and the book communities in Africa – and for Africana librarians and other interested in the book industries and book development in Africa – the 64pp. directory provides full names and addresses, telephone, and fax/telex numbers of the major and/or most active book publishers in Africa today. Other listings include African book trade organisations supporting African publishing, assistance programmes, book charities active in Africa, and more. The directory is free to African publishers, librarians, booksellers, and African writers. A charge of £10/$20 is made to others, as a contribution towards subsidising its free availability within Africa.

Sales

ABC's sales have steadily increased, and with the benefit of IABSS, reached some £160,000 in 1992, of which about £100,000 in hard currency was remitted back to African publisher members. ABC is currently trading with almost 400 booksellers and library suppliers, over 500 library accounts, and some 300 individual book buyers, in 69 countries. Nonetheless, with worldwide recession, current market conditions are very different to those prevailing in the planning stages in the mid-1980s, and the somewhat optimistic scenarios have, not surprisingly, failed to materialise. The business plans' aim to keep increases in overheads to no more than 7½% annually, has been difficult to achieve in the light of the rapid expansion in membership and in the inventory. ABC is currently on target for a year-to-year growth rate in turnover of about 30% (excluding IABSS sales), although this is likely to become increasingly difficult in current market conditions. Annual turnover in the region of currently £130,000–£160,000 might be considered modest, but it has been generated from scratch, and such a level of export sales and hard currency earnings has never before been achieved by African publishers.

Future needs

ABC's major expenditures and overheads are for personnel; rent for office and warehouse premises; and substantial investment in promotion and marketing each year to promote the stock inventory of over a thousand titles, (plus some 200 new titles annually). At the current level of annual recurrent expenditure (without provision for any further capital expenditures), ABC would need to generate sales of at least £470,000/$740,000 to match expenditures and reach break-even point. With a list of relatively low-priced books with an average retail price of around £8.50/$13, such turnover figures – even with the support of the most aggressive and extensive promotion – cannot be achieved at this time.

It remains an ultimate goal to achieve self-sufficiency, but from the experience of three years' trading, it is clear that any hope of early self-sufficiency is unrealistic. ABC faces the same difficult market conditions as all publishers, but given its non-profit making nature, its wider objectives, and its consequent structure, it does not have recourse to the options open to commercial publishers. With current trading conditions, brought about by the recession, these available commercial responses include shorter print runs and very substantial price rises, or the decision that it is not commercially viable to publish a title which in better conditions might have been taken on. But such options fly in the face of the objectives of ABC. Thus the need for donor funds to make up for substantial shortfalls between self-generated income retained by ABC on the one hand, and annual recurrent expenditure on the other, will remain.

There is little room for manoeuvre to cut overheads, and whilst ABC will continue to operate with strictly business-like efficiency, maintaining tight control on expenditure, and maximising all sales potentials, self-sufficiency cannot realistically be expected in the foreseeable future.

Donor funding

In 1992 direct grants were received from five agencies, in addition to separate support for IABSS. Unesco's grant represented 4.3% of total 1992 annual expenditure, CODE (Canada) 6%, DANIDA 10%, SIDA 11.2%, and generous support from the Rockefeller Foundation for promotion and marketing, including exhibit participation, represented some 40%. These agencies have renewed support for 1993, and additionally SAREC has made a direct grant.

Donor organisations have recognised, in principle, the need for long-term support for ABC. At the inception of ABC, the publishers were working in something of a void, with approaches by donors to some extent fragmented, and with only a small number concentrating on African publishing as such. There has, however, been a transformation over recent years, with the establishment of an informal group of donors working together in the context of support for African publishing, and known as the 'Bellagio Group'. This Group arose from a conference organized by the Rockefeller Foundation – at their conference centre in Bellagio, Italy – on publishing development in the Third World, including Africa.[2] Four of the African publishers at the conference were also members of ABC's Council of Management, and the ABC concept was placed firmly in the wider picture of appropriate and coordinated approaches to support for African publishing. The publishers now have the security of this context and understanding, and the understanding too that it will be many years hence before ABC can hope to break even, despite an encouraging and steady growth in sales and turnover of some 30% annually. But as the Group as such does not guarantee collective support for ABC, the daunting prospect of annual grant decisions is still being faced. With the scale of activities and trading now undertaken, and the responsibilities to publisher members and staff, the concern is now to try and secure longer commitments than one-year funding. SIDA, SAREC and CODE have already recognised this need for secure planning, and have made two- and three-year grants.

ABC's success to date

African Books Collective has achieved a considerable measure of success over a short period of time, but this success cannot be evaluated in terms of sales figures alone. Whilst the

---

[2] The papers presented at this conference were published in *Publishing and Development in the Third World*, ed. Philip G. Altbach (London: Hans Zell Publishers, 1992).

African Books Collective initiative represents a significant reversal of historical trading directions, ABC is doing a great deal more than merely selling books. It is actively promoting and disseminating African scholarship, African writing, and African cultural identity, and also contributing towards a better understanding of the ethnic, cultural and religious diversity of Africa – which in turn promotes a positive image of Africa. Moreover, ABC's activities have led to enhanced opportunities for publishing and writing in Africa.

The main concrete achievements in 1993 have covered activities at the heart of the main objectives, and in furtherance of wider objectives. Seven new member publishers were admitted, 220 new titles were actively promoted, and eighty new backlist titles taken on. 60–65% of net income received was remitted to member publishers at six-monthly intervals, in hard currency, helping member publishers to survive and grow under the current difficult trading conditions. Extensive promotion and marketing activities have been undertaken, including a variety of catalogue mailings to some 32,000 recipients. Promotion and displays have been provided for African-published books at exhibits at major library, booktrade, and professional and academic meetings. African-published books have been supplied to African academic and public libraries through the IABSS. The *African Publishers Networking Directory* was compiled, published, and distributed free to the African book community. And ABC organised a roundtable on African publishing at the (US) African Studies Association's 36th annual meeting in Boston.

Member publishers have recently evaluated how the formation of ABC has affected their publishing programmes, and amongst positive points they have made are the following direct quotations, illustrating their awareness of its tangible benefits:

'. . . ABC is turning out to be a lot more important as a distribution outlet than I ever imagined . . . we are now able to confidently assure our authors of international promotion and distribution. And I am glad to say that the mention of ABC has increased their confidence in our ability to provide this service.'

Henry Chakava, Managing Director, East African Educational Publishers, Nairobi

'The ABC letter enclosing our cheques for Period V were very pleasing and provided a great relief in an otherwise harsh economic environment. ABC earnings have contributed in no small way to our rising annual output . . . it is also clear that our books have received greater exposure to the international markets . . . authors who are now receiving payment in hard currency for royalties for their titles sold by ABC are very happy and now feel encouraged to write'.

Victor Nwankwo, Managing Director, Fourth Dimension Publishing Co., Enugu, Nigeria

'Since joining ABC our export sales have increased by about 200% while the export promotion and distribution costs have decreased by about 53%. The increased export sales revenue, which is paid in hard currency, has facilitated increased royalty payments to our authors and stimulated greater publishing activity in our books. There is no doubt that the ABC service has increased the overseas exposure and review coverage of our publications, and this development has made our existing authors happier, and has also attracted a greater number of potential authors.'

Prof. Olatunde Olatunji, Chairman, Ibadan University Press, Ibadan

'Trading with ABC has benefitted our company in Ghana . . . now we have enough funds to employ two more hands . . . the regular remittances from ABC are enabling us to expand our publishing programme'.

Woeli Dekutsey, Woeli Publishing Services, Accra

Conclusion

African Books Collective, whilst primarily a marketing and distribution enterprise, has been described as a 'turning of the tide' for African publishing, and the start of a reversal of historical trading patterns. Wide support and understanding is sought for ABC's work, and the active participation of all those who can encourage the acquisition of African books – whether librarians, academics, institutions of learning, booksellers, schools, or community organisations. There is much work to be done in the future. Membership can be expanded; more services offered to publishers, including further help in facilitating and acting for them in rights negotiations; and in due course it will make sense to have a distribution outlet in North America. The Council of Management will be meeting in 1994 to consider current and future work. The hope is that with continued, and possibly new, support of donor organisations, the publishers will have the capacity to carry the work forward.

INTRODUCTION

Scope and coverage

This bibliography records publications on Africa of interest to students of Africa, principally in the social and environmental sciences, humanities and arts. Some items from the medical, biological and natural sciences are included, and some more technical material from the major categories is excluded; in each case the criterion used is potential relevance to a reader from a social science/arts background. Thus material on AIDS (incidence, impact, and control) is included, but not that on a number of other diseases; and material on meteorology is normally excluded, but not that on climatic history or rainfall. The whole continent and associated islands are covered, but not the African diaspora. The 1992 edition aims to include material published in 1992, together with items from 1991 and 1990 not previously listed. The editor is always very glad to hear of any items omitted so that they may be included in subsequent editions. African government publications, and works of creative literature are not listed.

The principal sources of data for this issue are the book acquisitions and periodicals of Edinburgh University Library and the National Library of Scotland; use has also been made of other university libraries, notably that of the School of Oriental and African Studies and Northwestern University, and of

material received by the International African Institute. Wherever possible, the periodicals listed in the next section have been scanned for the whole of the relevant period; only those issues yielding entries are however listed, and other periodicals will have been scanned without being listed (a list of journals not carrying Africanist material would, after all, be rather long).

Arrangement

The arrangement of the bibliography is by region and country, with a preliminary section for the continent as a whole. Within each section items are arranged by subject, in the order listed below; where an item might appear under more than one heading, this is indicated by cross-reference (see the 'see also' list immediately under each subject heading), or the subject index will guide users to it.

The subject fields have been changed somewhat from previous years, to reflect the expansion of certain fields - like gender studies - or the difficulty in other cases of making clear distinctions between fields. These changes are (in alphabetical order):

Agriculture (socio-economic aspects) is now combined with Rural Development, to creat a new category, Rural Economy.

(Physical) Anthropology and Social and Cultural Anthropology are now combined, under the heading Anthropology.

Archaeology and Prehistory now appear under the heading History: early, thus locating these entries in sequence with other historical items.

A new category has been introduced, of Current Affairs, for items on very recent events, that are essentially descriptive and/or journalistic; such material formerly appeared under Politics.

Another new category, Gender, has been introduced to cover material on gender, gender relations, and women's studies (though not every item that discusses women is included under this heading).

The History entries have had their periodic coverage altered to correspond to centuries; the new headings are: History, early; History, C6-18th; History, C19th; and History, C20th. These periods have been used as a rough guide only, and items covering more than one period have usually been entered under the most recent.

Industry/Trade/Commerce has lost those entries concerned with international trade; these have been combined with material from Economics/Economic Development that concern external links (e.g. aid, regional cooperation), to form a new category: International Economic Relations.

A new category, International Relations, has been introduced, covering external relations, foreign policy etc. This material formerly appeared under Politics, and generated a great many index entries.

Politics now excludes current affairs and international relations, but includes Public Administration/Government.

Psychology is now included under Medical (formerly Medicine and Related Sciences/Psychiatry) or Sociology

Public Administration/Government is now included under Politics.

Rural Development has absorbed Agriculture (socio-economic aspects) to become Rural Economy.

Sociology now exists as a distinct category, and includes criminology.

Entry types

The bibliography contains three types of entry: periodical articles, books and pamphlets, and chapters. Periodical entries give the conventional bibliographic information. Book entries give author, title, place, publisher, and pagination (but not ISBN numbers, or price). Entries for chapters in books largely not on African topics give full bibliographic information for the volume concerned. Where, however, a book contains many relevant chapters it is listed separately, and the chapter entry includes only a short version of the title, the name(s) of the editor(s), and the entry number of the book itself.

Indexes

The bibliography has author and subject indexes, which use the entry number to indentify the relevant items. Since multiple authors are listed separately only when there are two of them (otherwise the first author is listed, followed by 'et al'), not every author of a given piece will appear in the author index.

The detailed subject index should be seen as supplementing the arrangement by subject fields. Where an item is sufficiently described by the subject heading, it will *not* appear in the subject index. The index is basically of the key-word type, and will often reflect the vocabulary of the original entry, modified to group together similiar items. Most items have a country designation, for ease of use, except for entries of general interest. Since indexing will always reflect to some degree the idiosyncracies of the indexer, readers are urged to scan broadly, and particularly to check headings in the vicinity of that deemed most relevant.

Subject headings

Agriculture, scientific
Anthropology
Architecture
Arts
Current Affairs
Demography
Economy – Development
Economic and Social History
Education
Environment
Finance
Food
Gender
Geography, human
Geography, physical
Health and Welfare Services
History, general
History, early
History, C6-18th
History, C19th
History, C20th
Industry and Trade
International Economic Relations
International Relations
Labour and Manpower
Language
Law
Library – Documentation
Literature
Media
Medical
Natural Resources
Planning
Politics
Religion, Philosophy
Rural Economy
Science and Technology
Sociology
Social Welfare
Urban Studies

PERIODICALS LIST

ACTA GEOGRAPHICA
1991 85

ACTA JURIDICA
1991

ADMINISTRATION, GESTION,
  FORMATION
1990 20, 30/31

AFRICA (EDINBURGH)
1992 62, 1-4

AFRICA (ROME)
1991 46, 3-4
1992 47, 1-2

AFRICA (SÃO PAULO)
1989/90 12/13
1991/92 14/15

AFRICA 2000
1991 6, 15

AFRICA CONTEMPORARY
  RECORD 1988/89
1992

AFRICA DEVELOPMENT
1990 15, 3/4
1991 16, 1-4

AFRICA INSIGHT
1991 21, 3-4
1992 22, 1-2

AFRICA MEDIA REVIEW
1991 5, 3
1992 6, 1-3

AFRICA QUARTERLY
1990 30, 1/2-3/4
1991 31, 1/2

AFRICA RECOVERY
1992 6, 1-3

AFRICA THEOLOGICAL
  JOURNAL
1991 20, 3

AFRICAN AFFAIRS
1992 91, 362-365

AFRICAN BOOK PUBLISHING
  RECORD
1992 18, 2

AFRICAN CHRISTIAN STUDIES
1991 7, 1-3

AFRICAN DEVELOPMENT
  PERSPECTIVES YEARBOOK
1990/91 2,

AFRICAN DEVELOPMENT
  REVIEW
1991 3, 1-2

AFRICAN JOURNAL OF
  INTERNATIONAL AND
  COMPARATIVE LAW
1990 2, 1-4

AFRICAN JOURNAL OF
  SCIENCE AND
  TECHNOLOGY, SERIES C,
  GENERAL
1991 2, 1

AFRICAN JOURNAL OF
  SOCIOLOGY
  1989/1990 3, 2

AFRICAN LANGUAGES AND
  CULTURES
  1991 4, 1, 2

AFRICAN LITERATURE
  ASSOCIATION (ALA)
  BULLETIN
  1992 18, 1

AFRICAN LIVESTOCK
  RESEARCH
  1992 1, 1

AFRICAN MUSIC
  1991 7, 1

AFRICAN RESEARCH AND
  DOCUMENTATION
  1991 56

AFRICAN REVIEW
  1989 16, 1/2

AFRICAN REVIEW OF MONEY
  FINANCE AND BANKING
  1992 1

AFRICAN STUDIES REVIEW
  1991 34, 3
  1992 35, 1

AFRICAN STUDY MONOGRAPHS
  1991 12, 1-4

AFRICAN STUDY
  MONOGRAPHS:
  SUPPLEMENTARY ISSUE
  1991 15

AFRICAN URBAN STUDIES
  1990 1
  1992 2

AFRICHE
  1990 2, 7
  1992 3, 13,15

AFRIKA FOCUS
  1991 7, 3, 4

AFRIKA JAHRBUCH 1991

AFRIKA SPECTRUM
  1991 26, 2, 3
  1992 27, 1, 2

AFRIKA UND ÜBERSEE
  1991 74, 2

AFRIQUE 2000
  1990 3
  1991 4, 5
  1992 8-11

AFRIQUE CONTEMPORAINE
  1992 161-164

AGENDA
  1991 10-13

AGRICULTURAL HISTORY
  REVIEW
  1992 40, 2

AHFAD JOURNAL
  1991 8, 2
  1992 9, 1

AL-QANTARA
  1992 13, 1

AMERICAN ANTHROPOLOGIST
  1991 93, 4

AMERICAN HISTORICAL
  REVIEW
  1992 97, 2

AMERICAN JOURNAL OF
  AGRICULTURAL ECONOMICS
  1992 74, 2

AMERICAN PRESBYTERIANS
  1991 69, 1

ANNALES
  1991 46, 6

ANNALES AEQUATORIA
1991 12

ANNALES DE GEOGRAPHIE
1992 563,

ANNALS
1992 519-524

ANTROPOLOGISCHE
VERKENNINGEN
1992 11, 1

APPLIED ECONOMICS
1991 23, 12
1992 24, 1, 6

APPLIED GEOGRAPHY
1992 12, 1

APPLIED GEOGRAPHY AND
DEVELOPMENT
1990 36-38
1992 39

ARAB HISTORICAL REVIEW
FOR OTTOMAN STUDIES
1992 5/6

ARABICA
1992 39, 1

ARCHIVES EUROPEENE DE
SOCIOLOGIE
1991 32, 2

AREA
1992 24, 4

ARISE
1991 3

ARMED FORCES AND SOCIETY
1992 18, 2, 19, 1

ARQUIVO
1991 9, 10

ASIA JOURNAL OF THEOLOGY
1992 6, 1

ASIEN AFRIKA LATEINAMERIKA
1991 19, 2, 4, 6
1991 Special issue

AU COEUR DE L'AFRIQUE
1991 59, 1-3

AZANIA
1992 27

BANKER 1992

BIOTROPICA
1992 24, 2B

BOLESWA EDUCATIONAL
RESEARCH JOURNAL
1990 7

BOLLETTINO DELLA SOCIETA
GEOGRAFICA ITALIANA
1991 8, 7/9
1992 9, 1/3

BOTSWANA NOTES AND
RECORDS
1991 23,

BRITISH JOURNAL OF MIDDLE
EAST STUDIES
1991 18, 1-2
1992 19, 1-2

BRITISH JOURNAL OF THE
SOCIOLOGY OF EDUCATION
1991 13, 4

BRITISH YEARBOOK OF
INTERNATIONAL LAW
1990 61

BULLETIN DE L'INSTITUT
FONDAMENTAL D'AFRIQUE
NOIRE. SERIE B, SCIENCES
HUMAINES
1986/1987 46, 3/4

BULLETIN DES SEANCES
1990 36, 2-4

BULLETIN OF FRANCOPHONE
    AFRICA
    1992 1

BULLETIN OF THE
    INTERNATIONAL
    COMMITTEE ON URGENT
    ANTHROPOLOGICAL AND
    ETHNOLOGICAL RESEARCH
    1990/91 32/33

BUNDA JOURNAL OF
    AGRICULTURAL RESEARCH
    1990 2

CADERNOS DE HISTORIA
    1990 8

CAHIERS D'ETUDES
    AFRICAINES
    1991 31, 1/2, 4

CAHIERS D'OUTRE-MER
    1991 44, 176
    1992 45, 177

CAHIERS D'URBAMA
    1991 5

CAHIERS DE L'ORIENT
    1991 23-26
    1992 27

CAHIERS DES RELIGIONS
    AFRICAINES
    1989 23, 45/46

CAHIERS DES SCIENCES
    HUMAINES
    1990 26, 4
    1991 27, 1-4
    1992 28, 1

CAHIERS DU CEDAF
    1991 No. 4

CAHIERS DU COMMUNISME
    1991 67, 4-9
    1992 68, 4, 10, 11

CAHIERS IVOIRIENS DE
    RECHERCHE ECONOMIQUE
    ET SOCIALE
    1990

CANADIAN GEOGRAPHER
    1991 35, 2

CANADIAN JOURNAL OF
    DEVELOPMENT STUDIES
    1991 12, 1
    1992 13, 1-3

CENTRAL AFRICAN JOURNAL
    OF MEDICINE
    1991 37, 3, 4

CHAMBER OF MINES JOURNAL
    1992 34, 1

CHOICES
    1992 1, 3

CITIES
    1991 7, 3
    1991 8, 1-4
    1992 9, 1-4

CLIMATIC CHANGE
    1991 19, 1-4
    1992 20, 4

COMMONWEALTH : ESSAYS
    AND STUDIES
    1991 14, 1, 2

COMMONWEALTH JUDICIAL
    JOURNAL
    1991 9, 2

COMMONWEALTH NOVEL IN
    ENGLISH
    1990 3, 2
    1991 4, 1-2
    1992 5, 1

COMMUNITY DEVELOPMENT
    JOURNAL
    1992 27, 1-4

COMPARATIVE AND
INTERNATIONAL LAW
JOURNAL OF SOUTHERN
AFRICA
1991 24, 1-3
1992 25, 1

COMPARATIVE ECONOMIC
STUDIES
1991 33, 3

COMPARATIVE EDUCATION
REVIEW
1992 36, 3, 4

COMPARATIVE POLITICAL
STUDIES
1991 24, 4

COMPARATIVE STUDIES IN
SOCIETY AND HISTORY
1992 34, 1

CONVERGENCE
1991 24, 1-2

COOPERATION AND
CONFLICT
1991 26, 1

COVERT ACTION QUARTERLY
1992 43

CRIMINOLOGIST
1992 16, 3

CRITIQUE OF
ANTHROPOLOGY
1992 12, 1

CUADERNOS
1991 6, 2, 3, 4, 7/8

CURRENT BIBLIOGRAHY ON
AFRICAN AFFAIRS
1991/92 23, 1-3

CURRENT HISTORY
1992 91, 565

DAEDALUS
1991 120, 3

DASP-HEFTE
1991 6, 30/31

DEMOGRAPHY
1992 29, 4

DERDE WERELD
1992 11, 2

DESERTIFICATION CONTROL
BULLETIN
1990 18

DEVELOPING ECONOMIES
1991 29, 2

DEVELOPMENT AND CHANGE
1992 23, 2

DEVELOPMENT POLICY
REVIEW
1992 10, 1-3

DEVELOPMENT SOUTHERN
AFRICA
1992 9, 2

DIALOGUE
1991 146-149

DIE ERDE
1991 122, 2, 4

DIE WELT DES ISLAMS
1991 31, 2

DISARMAMENT
1991 14, 3

DISASTERS
1992 16, 1-4

DISCOVERY AND
INNOVATION
1991 3, 2-4
1992 4, 1-2

DROIT ET CULTURES
1991 21
1992 23

EAST AFRICAN MEDICAL
JOURNAL
1990 67, 12
1991 68, 1-10

EASTERN AFRICA ECONOMIC
REVIEW
1990 6, 1,2

EASTERN AFRICAN SOCIAL
SCIENCE RESEARCH REVIEW
1990/91 6,2 & 7/1

EASTERN AND SOUTHERN
AFRICA GEOGRAPHICAL
JOURNAL
1991 2, 1
1992 3, 1

EASTERN ANTHROPOLOGIST
1991 44, 2

ECHO
1989-90 14/15
1992 17/18

ECO
1991 10

ECONOMIA
1991 4

ECONOMIA INTERNAZIONALE
1990 43, 4
1992 45, 2

ECONOMIC AND POLITICAL
WEEKLY
1992 27, 20/21

ECONOMIC DEVELOPMENT
AND CULTURAL CHANGE
1991 40, 1-4

ECONOMICS
1992 45,

ECONOMICS OF EDUCATION
REVIEW
1990 9, 4

EDUCATION AND SOCIETY
1992 10, 1

EDUCATION WITH
PRODUCTION
1991 8, 1

EDUCATIONAL DEVELOPMENT
1992 12, 1

EDUCATIONAL STUDIES IN
MATHEMATICS
1991 22, 4

ELECTORAL STUDIES
1992 11, 4

ELEMENTARY SCHOOL
JOURNAL
1991 92, 1

ENGLISH IN AFRICA
1991 18, 2

ENVIRONMENT
1990 20, 3

ENVIRONMENT AND
PLANNING A
1992 24, 9

ENVIRONMENT AND
URBANIZATION
1989 1, 2
1990 2, 2
1991 3, 1, 2

ESPRIT
1992 180

ESTUDIOS AFRICANOS
1990 5, 8/9

ETHIOPIAN JOURNAL OF
EDUCATION
1989 11, 1

ETHIOPIAN MEDICAL JOURNAL
1991 29, 3

ETHIOPIQUES
1991 7, 2
1992 55

ETUDES
GERMANO-AFRICAINES
1991 9

ETUDES INTERNATIONALES
1991 22, 4
1992 23, 2

ETUDES MALIENNES
1991 44

ETUDES OCEAN INDIEN
1991 13

EUROMONEY Dec. 1991

EUROPEAN ECONOMIC REVIEW
1991 35, 5

EUROPEAN JOURNAL OF
DEVELOPMENT RESEARCH
1992 4, 1, 2

EXECUTIVE
1991

EXTRA
1991 6, 7

FASETTE
1991 10, 2

FEMINIST ISSUES
1991 11, 4

FINANCE AND DEVELOPMENT
1992 29, 2, 4

FOCUS ON AFRICA
1992 3, 1, 3

FOOD POLICY
1992 17, 1-3

FOOD, NUTRITION AND
AGRICULTURE
1991 1, 1

FOREST AND CONSERVATION
HISTORY
1991 35, 4

FRANCOFONIA
1991 20

FRENCH REVIEW
1991 64, 3, 5

GENEVA-AFRICA
1992 30, 1, 2

GEOGRAPHICAL EDUCATION
MAGAZINE
1991 14, 1, 2

GEOGRAPHICAL REVIEW
1992 82, 1

GEOGRAPHISCHE RUNDSCHAU
1992 44, 7/8, 9

GEOGRAPHY
1992 77, 3

GEOGRAPHY RESEARCH FORUM
1992 12

GEOJOURNAL
1992 27, 4

GEOKIN
1990 1/2
1991 2, 1, 2

GEOMETHODICA
1990 15, 17

GEOPOLITIQUE AFRICAINE
1991 14
1992 15, 1

GLOBAL ECOLOGY AND
BIOGEOGRAPHY LETTERS
1992 2, 1

GOVERNMENT AND
   OPPOSITION
   1991 26, 2
   1992 27, 4

HAMDARD ISLAMICUS
   1991 14, 1, 4

HERITAGE OF ZIMBABWE
   1991 10

HIGHER EDUCATION
   1991 23, 4

HISTORICAL RESEARCH
   1991 64, 155

HISTORY IN AFRICA
   1992 19

IBLA
   1991 168

IMBONEZAMURYANGO
   1991 20

INDEX ON CENSORSHIP
   1992 21, 1-10

INDIA QUARTERLY
   1990 46, 4
   1992 48, 3

INDIAN GEOGRAPHICAL
   JOURNAL
   1990 65, 1

INDIAN JOURNAL OF
   ECONOMICS
   1991 71, 3
   1992 72, 3

INDIAN JOURNAL OF
   INDUSTRIAL RELATIONS
   1991 27, 2

INDIAN JOURNAL OF PUBLIC
   ADMINISTRATION
   1991 37, 1

INDUSTRIAL REVIEW
   (ZIMBABWE)
   1991

INDUSTRY AND DEVELOPMENT
   1991 30
   1992 31

INFORMATION TRENDS
   1992 5, 1

INTERNATIONAL AND
   COMPARATIVE LAW
   QUARTERLY
   1990 39, 3
   1991 40, 1-3
   1992 41, 1, 2

INTERNATIONAL EDUCATION
   1991 20, 2

INTERNATIONAL JOURNAL OF
   AFRICAN HISTORICAL
   STUDIES
   1992 25, 1

INTERNATIONAL JOURNAL OF
   COMPARATIVE AND APPLIED
   CRIMINAL JUSTICE
   1991 15, 2

INTERNATIONAL JOURNAL OF
   EDUCATIONAL
   DEVELOPMENT
   1991 11, 1-3
   1992 12, 2

INTERNATIONAL JOURNAL OF
   LAW AND THE FAMILY
   1991 5, 1, 3

INTERNATIONAL JOURNAL OF
   MIDDLE EAST STUDIES
   1992 24, 1-3

INTERNATIONAL JOURNAL OF
   OFFENDER THERAPY AND
   COMPARATIVE
   CRIMINOLOGY
   1991 35, 1

INTERNATIONAL JOURNAL OF
SOCIOLOGY AND SOCIAL
POLICY
1991 11, 6/8

INTERNATIONAL JOURNAL OF
UNIVERSITY ADULT
EDUCATION
1991 30, 3

INTERNATIONAL LABOUR
REVIEW
1991 130, 1-6

INTERNATIONAL RELATIONS
1991 10, 3

INTERNATIONAL REVIEW OF
MISSION
1992 81, 322

INTERNATIONAL STUDIES
1992 29, 2, 3

INTERNATIONAL STUDIES IN
THE SOCIOLOGY OF
EDUCATION
1991 1

INTERNATIONAL STUDIES
QUARTERLY
1992 36, 1, 3

INTERNATIONALE
SPECTATOR
1991 45, 10
1992 46, 6

INTERNATIONALES
AFRIKAFORUM
1992 28, 1-3

ISLAM AND CHRISTIAN
MUSLIM RELATIONS
1991 2, 2

ISLAM ET SOCIETES AU SUD
DU SAHARA
1991 5

ISLAMOCHRISTIANA
1991 17

ISSUE
1992 20, 1, 2

ITAN: BENSU JOURNAL OF
HISTORICAL STUDIES
1990 1

ITINERARIO
1991 15, 2

JANA NA LEO
1991 24

JEBAT
1990 18

JOURNAL (NAMIBIA
SCIENTIFIC SOCIETY)
1990 42,

JOURNAL FOR
CONTEMPORARY HISTORY
1990 15, 1-3
1991 16, 1, 2

JOURNAL FOR THE HISTORY
OF ARABIC SCIENCE
1991 9, 1/2

JOURNAL INSTITUTE OF
MUSLIM MINORITY AFFAIRS
1991 12, 1, 2

JOURNAL OF AFRICAN
ECONOMIES
1992 1, 1

JOURNAL OF AFRICAN
HISTORY
1992 33, 1-3

JOURNAL OF AFRICAN LAW
1990 34, 1, 2

JOURNAL OF AFRICAN
RELIGION AND PHILOSOPHY
1991 2, 1

JOURNAL OF AGRICULTURAL
ECONOMICS
1991 42, 2

JOURNAL OF AMERICAN
HISTORY
1992 79, 2

JOURNAL OF
ANTHROPOLOGICAL
RESEARCH
1991 47, 4

JOURNAL OF APPLIED ECOLOGY
1991 28, 1

JOURNAL OF ARID
ENVIRONMENTS
1991 20, 3
1992 22, 3, 4

JOURNAL OF ASIAN AND
AFRICAN AFFAIRS
1992 3, 2

JOURNAL OF ASIAN AND
AFRICAN STUDIES
1992 27, 1/2, 3/4

JOURNAL OF BIOSOCIAL
SCIENCE
1991 23, 4
1992 24, 1-4

JOURNAL OF BLACK STUDIES
1992 23 , 1

JOURNAL OF COMMON
MARKET STUDIES
1992 30, 2

JOURNAL OF
COMMONWEALTH AND
COMPARATIVE POLITICS
1992 30, 1-3

JOURNAL OF
COMMONWEALTH
LITERATURE
1992 27, 1

JOURNAL OF COMMUNIST
STUDIES
1992 8, 2

JOURNAL OF COMPARATIVE
FAMILY STUDIES
1992 23, 3

JOURNAL OF
CONSTITUTIONAL AND
PARLIAMENTARY STUDIES
1990 24, 1-4

JOURNAL OF CONTEMPORARY
AFRICAN STUDIES
1991 10, 1, 2

JOURNAL OF CONTEMPORARY
HISTORY
1992 27, 1-4

JOURNAL OF CRIMINAL
JUSTICE
1991 19, 6

JOURNAL OF DEVELOPING
AREAS
1991 26, 1-4
1992 27, 1

JOURNAL OF DEVELOPING
SOCIETIES
1992 8, 1

JOURNAL OF DEVELOPMENT
ECONOMICS
1991 37, 1/2
1992 38, 2
1992 39, 2

JOURNAL OF DEVELOPMENT
STUDIES
1990 27, 1
1991 28, 1-4

JOURNAL OF EAST AFRICAN
RESEARCH AND
DEVELOPMENT
1991 21

JOURNAL OF ECONOMIC
   STUDIES
   1992 19, 1-3

JOURNAL OF EDUCATIONAL
   THOUGHT
   1991 26, 3

JOURNAL OF
   ENVIRONMENTAL
   MANAGEMENT
   1992 34, 4; 35, 3

JOURNAL OF ETHIOPIAN
   STUDIES
   1990 23
   1991 24

JOURNAL OF IMPERIAL AND
   COMMONWEALTH HISTORY
   1992 22, 1-3

JOURNAL OF INTERNATIONAL
   DEVELOPMENT
   1991 3, 4
   1992 4, 1

JOURNAL OF INTERNATIONAL
   DEVELOPMENT
   1992 4, 1-6

JOURNAL OF INTERNATIONAL
   FOOD & AGRIBUSINESS
   MARKETING
   1991 3, 4

JOURNAL OF ISLAMIC STUDIES
   1990 1, 1
   1992 3, 1

JOURNAL OF LEGAL PLURALISM
   AND UNOFFICIAL LAW
   1990 29,
   1990/1991 30/31

JOURNAL OF MARRIAGE AND
   THE FAMILY
   1992 54, 2

JOURNAL OF MODERN

AFRICAN STUDIES
   1991 29, 4
   1992 30, 1-4

JOURNAL OF PEASANT STUDIES
   1991 19, 1

JOURNAL OF PUBLIC
   ECONOMICS
   1992 48, 1

JOURNAL OF REFUGEE STUDIES
   1992 5, 3/4

JOURNAL OF RESEARCH
   1991 1,

JOURNAL OF SEX RESEARCH
   1991 28, 3

JOURNAL OF SOCIAL
   DEVELOPMENT IN AFRICA
   1992 7, 1, 2

JOURNAL OF SOCIAL STUDIES
   (DHAKA)
   1992 58

JOURNAL OF SOUTHERN
   AFRICAN STUDIES
   1991 17, 4
   1992 18, 1-4

JOURNAL OF THE AFRICAN
   ASSOCIATION FOR LITERACY
   AND ADULT EDUCATION
   1990 5, 2-4

JOURNAL OF THE MAURITIUS
   INSTITUTE OF EDUCATION
   1991/1992 12

JOURNAL OF TRANSPORT
   ECONOMICS AND POLICY
   1992 26, 3

JOURNAL OF TROPICAL
   PEDIATRICS
   1991 37, 6
   1992 38, 1, 5

JOURNAL OF WORLD TRADE
1991 25, 1

KENYA PAST AND PRESENT
1990 22
1991 23
1992 24

KENYA UNDERWRITER
1990 18

L'AGRONOMIE TROPICALE
1990 45, 4

L'ECONOMIE DE LA REUNION
1990 47-49
1991 52, 53
1992 58

L'EGYPTE CONTEMPORAINE
1990 81, 419-422

LABOUR AND SOCIETY
1991 16, 3

LABOUR, CAPITAL AND
SOCIETY
1991 24, 1

LAND REFORM (FAO)
1990 1/2

LAND USE POLICY
1991 8, 4
1992 9, 1-3

LAW AND POLICY IN
INTERNATIONAL BUSINESS
1991 22, 3

LEGAL FORUM
1991 3, 3, 4

LESOTHO EPIDEMIOLOGICAL
BULLETIN
1990 5, 1

LEVANTE
1991 33, 4

LIBERIAN STUDIES JOURNAL
1992 17, 1, 2

LIBRARY AND ARCHIVAL
SECURITY
1992 11, 2

LOCAL GOVERNMENT STUDIES
1992 18, 3

MAGHREB-MACHREK
1990 127
1991 133, 134
1992 135-137

MAJI MAJI
1990 47

MAKTABA
1991 11, 2

MAN
1992 27, 1-4

MARANG
1991 9

MARCHES TROPICAUX ET
MEDITERRANEENS
1992 48, 2420, 2421, 2428, 2435

MATATU
1992 9

MATERIAUX ARABES ET
SUDARABIQUES
1991 3

MATOY
1991 3, 4

MEDICINE AND LAW
1991 10, 4

MIDDLE EAST JOURNAL
1992 46, 3

MIDDLE EAST REPORT
1992 22, 6

MIDDLE EASTERN STUDIES
1992 28, 2

MINERVA
1991 29, 1

MINING AND ENGINEERING
1991 56, 8

MOHLOMI
1990 6

MONDES EN DEVELOPPEMENT
1990 18, 71
1991 19, 73, 75/76

MONDES ET CULTURES
1990 50, 1
1991 51, 1-4

MUQARNAS
1991 8

NAIROBI LAW MONTHLY
1991 33-41

NETHERLANDS REVIEW OF
DEVELOPMENT STUDIES
1990/1991 3

NEUE ZEITSCHRIFT FÜR
MISSIONSWISSENSCHAFT
1992 48, 1, 2

NEW LEFT REVIEW
1992 195, 196

NEW THEATRE QUARTERLY
1992 8, 31

NIGERIAN JOURNAL OF
INTERNATIONAL AFFAIRS
1991 17, 1, 2

NIGERIAN JOURNAL OF THE
HUMANITIES
1990 7

NOMADIC PEOPLES
1991 29

NORDIC JOURNAL OF AFRICAN
STUDIES
1992 1, 1

NORTHEAST AFRICAN STUDIES
1989 11, 3
1990 12, 1-3

NOUVELLE REVUE DE SCIENCE
MISSIONNAIRE
1992 48, 1

NUTRITION RESEARCH
1991 11, 9

NWSA JOURNAL
1991 3, 1

NYTT FRÅN NODISKA
AFRIKAINSTITUTET
1991 28

OCCASIONAL RESEARCH
PAPERS
1990 34,

OKIKE
1990 30

OPEN HOUSE
INTERNATIONAL
1991 16, 1, 3

OPTIMA
1992 38, 3

ORBIS
1992 36, 1

ORITA
1991 23, 1, 2

OXFORD ECONOMIC
PAPERS
1992 44, 1

PARLIAMENTARIAN
1991 72, 4
1992 73, 4

PENANT
1991 101, 807
1992 102, 808, 809

PERIPHERIE
1992 47/48

PERSPECTIVES IN
EDUCATION
1992 13, 2

PEUPLES MEDITERRANEENS
1991 54/55, 58/59

PHILIPPINE GEOGRAPHICAL
JOURNAL
1990 34, 4

PHILIPPINE JOURNAL OF
PUBLIC ADMINISTRATION
1991 35, 3

PISTES ET RECHERCHES
1990 5, 2/3

POLICE STUDIES
1991 14, 2

POLICING AND SOCIETY
1991 1, 4

POLITICAL GEOGRAPHY
QUARTERLY
1992 11, 1-5

POLITIKON
1991 19, 1

POLITIQUE AFRICAINE
1992 45-48

POPULATION STUDIES
1992 46, 1-3

PROBLEMS OF COMMUNISM
1992 41, 1-3

PROSPECTS
1992 22, 81, 82

PSYCHOPATHOLOGIE
AFRICAINE
1990/1991 23, 2

PUBLIC ADMINISTRATION
AND DEVELOPMENT
1991 11, 5
1992 12, 1-5

PUBLIC ENTERPRISE
1991 11, 4

QUARTERLY JOURNAL OF
ADMINISTRATION
1990/1991 25, 1

QUEST
1990 4, 2
1991 5, 1-3
1992 6, 1

RACE AND CLASS
1992 34, 1, 2

RECHTSTHEORIE
1991 12

REFUGEES
1992

RELIGION
1990 20, 4

RELIGION IN MALAWI
1991 3

RES
1990/91 19/20

RES PUBLICA
1991 33, 2

RESEARCH AND
EXPLORATION
1991 7, 1

RESEARCH IN AFRICAN
LITERATURES
1992 23, 1-4

RESEARCH REVIEW
1990 6, 2

RESOURCES
1990 1, 3
1991 2, 1

REVIEW [OF THE]
INTERNATIONAL
COMMISSION OF JURISTS
1991 47

REVIEW OF AFRICAN
POLITICAL ECONOMY
1992 53-55

REVIEW OF RADICAL
POLITICAL ECONOMY
1991 23, 3/4

REVISTA DE AFRICA Y MEDIO
ORIENTE
1991 3, 1

REVISTA INTERNACIONAL DE
ESTUDOS AFRICANOS
1990 12/13

REVISTA TRIMESTRALE DI
DIRITTO PUBBLICO
1991 41, 2

REVUE ALGERIENNE DES
SCIENCES JURIDIQUES,
ECONOMIQUES ET
POLITIQUES
1991 29, 1/2

REVUE BURKINABE DE
DROIT
1991 19/20, 21

REVUE CONGOLAISE DE
DROIT
1991 9

REVUE DE GEOGRAPHIE DU
CAMEROUN
1991 10, 2

REVUE DE L'UNIVERSITE DU
BURUNDI. SERIE SCIENCES
HUMAINES
1990 7

REVUE DES DEUX MONDES
Dec. 1990
Feb. 1991

REVUE DES ETUDES
ISLAMIQUES
1990 58

REVUE DU DROIT PUBLIC
1991 107, 6
1992 108, 1

REVUE DU MONDE
MUSULMAN ET DE LA
MEDITERRANEE
1990 58
1991 59/60

REVUE ECONOMIQUE
1991 42, 5

REVUE FRANÇAISE D'HISTOIRE
D'OUTRE-MER
1992 79, 294-296

REVUE FRANÇAISE DE DROIT
CONSTITUTIONNEL
1990 1, 3

REVUE INTERNATIONALE DE
DROIT COMPARE
1991 43, 4

REVUE INTERNATIONALE DE
DROIT COMPARE
1991 43, 3

REVUE JURIDIQUE ET
POLITIQUE
1991 45, 2-4
1992 46, 1-4

REVUE TIERS MONDE
1992 33, 129-132

REVUE TUNISIENNE DE
GEOGRAPHIE
1991 19/20

RIVISTA DI STUDI
POLITICA
INTERNAZIONALE
1992 49, 3

RIVISTA DI STUDI
POLITICI
INTERNAZIONALE
1991 48, 3

ROUND TABLE
1991 319, 320

RURAL PROGRESS
1991 10, 2

SADCC ENERGY
1990 8, 20-22

SAVANNA
1991 12, 1

SAVINGS AND DEVELOPMENT
1991 15, 4
1992 16, 1-4

SCANDANAVIAN JOURNAL OF
DEVELOPMENT
ALTERNATIVES
1992 11, 1-4

SCIENCE, TECHNOLOGY AND
DEVELOPMENT
1992 10, 1, 2

SCOTTISH GEOGRAPHICAL
MAGAZINE
1992 106, 1

SENRI ETHNOLOGICAL
STUDIES
1992 31, 34

SIAS REVIEW
1991 11

SMALL ENTERPRISE
DEVELOPMENT
1991 2, 2
1992 3, 2

SOCIAL SCIENCE AND
MEDICINE
1991 33, 9-12
1992 34, 1-12

SOCIALIST REGISTER
1992

SOCIETY
1990 14, 15

SOCIOLOGICA RURALIS
1992 32, 2/3

SOCIOLOGUS
1991 41, 2

SORONDA
1991 11

SOUTH AFRICA
INTERNATIONAL
1991/1992 22, 2-4
1992 23, 1

SOUTH AFRICAN
ARCHAEOLOGICAL
BULLETIN
1992 47, 155

SOUTH AFRICAN
HUMAN RIGHTS
AND LABOUR LAW
YEARBOOK
1990 1

SOUTH AFRICAN JOURNAL OF
AFRICAN LANGUAGES
1992 12, 2

SOUTH AFRICAN JOURNAL OF
ETHNOLOGY
1991 14, 4
1992 15, 1

SOUTH AFRICAN JOURNAL OF
   SOCIOLOGY
   1991 22, 4

SOUTH AFRICAN JOURNAL ON
   HUMAN RIGHTS
   1991 7, 3
   1992 8, 1

SOUTH AFRICAN YEARBOOK
   OF INTERNATIONAL LAW
   1990/1991 16,

SOUTHERN AFRICA POLITICAL
   & ECONOMIC MONTHLY
   1990 3, 12
   1991 4, 3/4, 5

SOUTHERN AFRICA REPORT
   Jan. 1992

SOUTHERN AFRICAN
   ECONOMIST
   1991 4, 1

SOUTHWESTERN UNIVERSITY
   LAW REVIEW
   1992 21, 1

STANFORD JOURNAL OF
   INTERNATIONAL LAW
   192 29, 1

STUDENT LAW REVIEW
   1991 1

STUDIA
   1991 50

STUDIA AFRICANA
   1992 3

STUDIES IN COMPARATIVE
   INTERNATIONAL
   DEVELOPMENT
   1990-91 25, 4

STUDIES IN THIRD WORLD
   SOCIETIES
   1991 46

SUDANIC AFRICA
   1991 2

SURVEY OF JEWISH AFFAIRS
   1991

SYSTEMES DE PENSEE EN
   AFRIQUE NOIRE
   1991 11

TAAMULI
   1991 NS 2, 1/2

TALOHA
   1992 11

TANZANIA JOURNAL OF
   ECONOMICS
   1990 2, 1

TANZANIA JOURNAL OF
   PAEDIATRICS
   1991 2, 2

TANZANIAN ECONOMIC
   TRENDS
   1989/90 2, 3/4

TECHNIQUES ET
   CULTURE
   1991 17/18

THEATRE SUD
   1990 1

THEORIA
   1990 75, 76
   1991 77, 78
   1992 79, 80

THIRD WORLD FIRST
   1991 2, 2/3

THIRD WORLD PLANNING
   REVIEW
   1991 14, 1-4

TIZAME
   1990 2

TRANSACTIONS OF THE
ZIMBABWE SCIENTIFIC
ASSOCIATION
1991 65,

TRANSAFRICA FORUM
1991 7, 4, 8, 1-3
1992 9, 1

TRANSAFRICAN JOURNAL OF
HISTORY
1991 20

TRANSFORMATION
1991 16
1992 17

TYDSKRIF VIR
RASSE-AANGELEENTHEDE
1991 42, 3/4

UBUREZI UBUHANGA
N'UMUCO
1990 23

UFAHAMU
1990 18, 3
1991 19, 1

UNIVERSITY OF DAR ES
SALAAM LAW JOURNAL
1991 8

URBAN STUDIES
1992 29, 1-7

VERFASSUNG UND RECHT IN
UBERSEE
1991 24, 4
1992 25, 1-3

VIERTELJAHRESBERICHTE
1992 127

WALIA
1991 13

WHYDAH
1990/92 2, 9

WORK IN PROGRESS
1992 82-84

WORLD BANK ECONOMIC
REVIEW
1991 5, 3
1992 6, 2

WORLD ECONOMY
1992 15, 5

WORLD TODAY
1992 48, 1-12

ZAIRE-AFRIQUE
1991 258-60
1992 261-268

ZAMBEZIA
1991 18, 1, 2

ZAMBEZIA
1990 17, 1

ZAMBIA JOURNAL OF
HISTORY
1991 4

ZAMBIAN JOURNAL OF
AGRICULTURAL
SCIENCE
1990

ZAMBIAN JOURNAL OF
APPLIED EARTH
SCIENCES
1990 4, 1
1991 5, 1, 2

ZEITSCHRIFT FUR
AFRIKASTUDIEN
1991 11/12
1992 13/14

ZEITSCHRIFT FUR
AUSLANDLISCHES
OFFENTLICHES RECHT UND
VOLKERECHT
1992 52, 1

ZEITSCHRIFT FUR
  ETHNOLOGIE
  1990 115
  1991 116

ZEITSCHRIFT FUR MISSION
  1991 17, 4
  1992 18, 1

ZEITSCHRIFT FUR
  MISSIONSWISSENSCHAFT
  UND
  RELIGIONSWISSENSCHAFT
  1992 76, 1

ZEITSCHRIFT FUR WIRT-
  SCHAFTLICHTSGEOGRAPHIE
  1991 36, 1/2

ZIMBABWE JOURNAL OF
  EDUCATIONAL RESEARCH
  1990 2, 3
  1991 3, 2, 3
  1992 4, 1

ZIMBABWE LIBRARIAN
  1991 23, 1

ZIMBABWE SCIENCE NEWS
  1991 25, 7/9

AFRICA

General

1 **Bujra, A S,** Foreign financing of research and the development of African social science, *Discovery and innovation*, 3, 3 (1991) 13–21

2 **Coquery-Vidrovitch, C,** Trente années perdues, ou étape d'une longue évolution?, *Afrique contemporaine*, 164 (1992) 5–17

3 **Crjeticanin, B,** Identité culturelle et développement en Afrique, in Irele A (ed), *African education and identity (entry 268),* 209–213

4 **d'Almeida-Topor, H, Reisz, J,** (eds), *Rencontres franco-allemandes sur l'Afrique.* Paris: Harmattan, 1992, 144pp

5 **Dozon, J P,** D'un tombeau à l'autre, *Cahiers d'études africaines,* 31, 1/2 (1991) 135–57

6 **Falola, T,** Thirty years of African research and publication, *Geneva-Africa*, 30, 2 (1992) 193–97

7 **Gatter, F T, Hinz, M O,** (eds), *Gegenwartsbewältigung und Zukunftsperspektiven in Afrika.* Frankfurt: Verlag für Interkulturelle Kommunikation, 1991, 205pp

8 **Gaud, M,** Etonnante Afrique, *Afrique contemporaine*, 164 (1992) 264–74

9 **Gordon, A A, Gordon, D L,** (eds), *Understanding contemporary Africa.* Boulder: Reinner, 1992, 243pp

10 **Hino, S,** African urban studies in Japan, *African urban studies*, 1, (1990) 115–157

11 **Hoering, U, Wichterich, C,** *Kein Zustand dauert ewig: Afrika in den neunziger Jahren.* Gottingen: Lamuv, 1991, 256pp

12 **Kloos, P,** Into Africa: Dutch anthropology and the changing colonial situation, *Antropologische Verkenningen,* 11, 1 (1992) 49–64

13 **Lima, J D S,** Africa ocidental: situaçïo político-econômica, *Africa (São Paulo),* 14/15 (1991/92) 163–76

14 **Ly, B,** Les sciences sociales en Afrique: problèmes de recherche et de formation, *Africa development,* 15, 3/4 (1990) 185–207

15 **Mazrui, A A,** Africa and other civilisations; conquest and counterconquest, in Harbeson J W & Rothchild, D (eds), *Africa in world politics (entry 625),* 69–91

16 **Melber, H,** "Ganz oben thronen wir"...: zur Kontinuität und Renaissance kolonialen Denkens im deutschen Afrika-Bild, *Zeitschrift für Afrikastudien,* 13/14 (1992) 43–53

17 **Muzzati, M,** Etudes africaines et études africanistes, in Irele A (ed), *African education and identity (entry 268),* 387–90

18 **Ndegwa, S N,** The search for relevance in African studies: an African student's perspective, *Issue,* 20, 2 (1992) 42–45

19 **Pagès, M,** Images écrites de l'Afrique, *Afrique contemporaine,* 164 (1992) 245–52

20 **Pieterse, J N,** *White on Black:*
images of Africa and Blacks in
Western popular culture. New
Haven: Yale UP, 1992, 259pp
21 **Romero, P W,** (ed), *Women's*
voices on Africa: a century of travel
writings. Princeton: Weiner, 1992,
280pp
22 **Sala-Molins, L,** L'identité
africaine: jeux de masque, *Afrique*
2000, 8 (1992) 105–111
23 **Silva-Castro, J,** Les études
africaines en Méxique, in Irele A
(ed), *African education and identity*
(entry 268), 383–86
24 **Sottas, B,** L'Afrique - un
continent oublié? État et
perspectives des études africaines
en Suisse, *Geneva-Africa,* 30, 2
(1992) 177–92
25 **Svob-Dokic, N,** The state of
African studies in Yugoslavia, in
Irele A (ed), *African education and*
identity (entry 268), 391–96

Agriculture, scientific

26 **Dipeolu, O O, et al,** Current
concepts and approach to control
of livestock ticks in Africa,
Discovery and innovation, 4, 2
(1992) 35–44
27 **Linneman, A R,** *Bambara*
groundnut (Vigna subterranea)
literature: a revised and updated
bibliography. Wageningen: Dept. of
Tropical Crop Science,
Wageningen Agricultural
University, 1992, 124pp
28 **McCorkle, C M,**
Mathias-Mundy, E,
Ethnoveterinary medicine in Africa,
Africa, 62, 1 (1992)
59–93
29 **Touré, S M, Mortelmans, J,**
Impact de la trypanosomose
animale africaine (TAA), *Bulletin*
des séances, 36, 2 (1990) 239–257
30 **Wilson, R T,** *Small ruminant*

production and the small ruminant
genetic resource in tropical Africa.
Rome: FAO, 1991, 231pp

Anthropology

see also: 202, 770, 976, 993
31 **Ardener, S,** (ed), *Persons and*
powers of women in diverse cultures.
Oxford: Berg, 1992, 219pp
32 **Berndt, C, Chilver, E M,**
Phyllis Kaberry (1910–1977):
fieldworker among friends, in
Ardener S (ed), *Persons and powers*
(entry 31), 29–37, 59–60
33 **Burton, J W,** Representing
Africa: colonial anthropology
revisited, *Journal of Asian and*
African studies, 27, 3/4 (1992)
181–201
34 **Castelli, E,** Le collezioni
etnografiche africane della Società
Geografica Italiana, *Bollettino della*
Società Geografica Italiano, 9, 1/3
(1992) 165–175
35 **Charsley, S,** Dreams in African
churches, in Jedrej M C & Shaw, R
(eds), *Dreaming, religion and society*
(entry 42), 153–76
36 **Copans, L,** L'anthropologie
française au pluriel: impressions
africanistes, *Politique africaine,* 45
(1992) 129–34
37 **de Rosny, E,** *L'Afrique des*
guérisons. Paris: Karthala, 1992,
223pp
38 **Durham, D, Fernandez, J W,**
Tropical dominions: the figurative
struggle over domains of belonging
and apartness in Africa, in
Fernandez J W (ed), *Beyond*
metaphor: the theory of tropes in
anthropology (Stanford: Stanford
UP, 1991), 190–210
39 **Finnegan, R,** Reflecting back on
'Oral literature in Africa': some
reconsiderations after 21 years,
South African journal of African
languages, 12, 2 (1992) 39–47
40 **Goody, J,** Icönes et iconoclasms

en Afrique, *Annales*, 46, 6 (1991) 1235–52

41 Jacobson-Widding, A, van Beek, W E, *The creative communion: African folk models of fertility and regeneration of life.* Uppsala: Uppsala University, 1990, 351pp

42 Jedrej, M C, Shaw, R, Introduction: dreaming, religion and society in Africa, in Jedrej M C & Shaw, R (eds), *Dreaming, religion and society (entry 42)*, 1–20

43 Journet, O, et al, *Grossesse et petite enfance en Afrique noire et à Madagascar.* Paris: Harmattan, 1992, 136pp

44 Lawuyi, O B, Towards an anthropological agenda in Africa: social relativism and beyond, *European journal of development research*, 4, 1 (1992) 40–58

45 Leite, F, Bruxos et magos, *Africa (São Paulo)*, 14/15 (1991/92) 69–80

46 Moss, J, Wilson, G, *Peoples of the world: Africa and the Sahara.* Detroit: Gale Research, 1991, 443pp

47 Peek, P M, African divination systems: non-normal modes of cognition, in Peek P M (ed), *African divination (entry 48)*, 193–212

48 Peek, P M, (ed), *African divination systems: ways of knowing.* Bloomington: Indiana UP, 1991, 230pp

49 Peek, P M, The study of divination, present and past, in Peek P M (ed), *African divination (entry 48)*, 1–22

50 Rosny, E, *L'Afrique des guérisons.* Paris: Karthala, 1992, 208pp

51 Siegel, B, Family and kinship, in Gordon A & D (eds), *Understanding contemporary Africa (entry 9)*, 175–200

Arts

52 Bender, W, *La musique africain contemporaine.* Paris: Harmattan, 1992, 246pp

53 Binet, J, La vision des artistes, *Afrique contemporaine*, 164 (1992) 197–210

54 Courtney-Clarke, M, *African canvas: the art of African women.* New York: Rizzoli, 1990, 204pp

55 Diawara, M, *African cinema: politics and culture.* Bloomington: Indian UP, 1992, 192pp

56 Drewal, M T, The state of research on performance in Africa, *African studies review*, 34, 3 (1991) 1–64

57 Erlmann, V, (ed), *Populäre Musik in Afrika.* Berlin: Staatliche Museen Preussischer Kulturbesitz, 1991, 312pp

58 Gadjigo, S, Africa through African eyes, *Research in African literatures*, 23, 4 (1992) 97–105

59 Gandibert, P, *L'art africain contemporain.* Paris: Cercle d'art, 1991, 175pp

60 Gbotokuma, Z, Cultural identity and underdevelopment in subsaharan Africa, in *Voices from Africa 4 (entry 1064)*, 17–29

61 Gromyko, A A, The traditonal art of tropical Africa: sculptures and masks, in Irele A (ed), *African education and identity (entry 268)*, 141–51

62 Hourantier, M J, L'acteur négro-africain d'hier et d'aujourd'hui, *Théâtre sud*, 1 (1990) 113–122

63 Jewsiewicki, B, Le primitivisme, le post-colonialisme, les antiquités 'nègres' et la question nationale, *Cahiers d'études africaines*, 31, 1/2 (1991) 191–213

64 Kennedy, J, *New currents, ancient rivers: contemporary African artists in a generation of change.* Blue Ridge Summit:

Smithsonian Institution Press, 1992, 204pp

65 **Konare, A,** Les dramaturges négro-africains et l'histoire: une pédagogie de la responsabilité, *Ethiopiques,* 7, 2 (1991) 115–31

66 **Lihamba, A,** Popular theatre in Africa, in *Voices from Africa 4 (entry 1064),* 53–64

67 **Mabiala Mantuba Ngoma,** Arts et traditions orales en Afrique noire: essai méthodologique, *Annales aequatoria,* 12, (1991) 111–123

68 **Mbabuike, M C,** Africa: art, culture and interpretation, *Studies in Third World societies,* 46, (1991) 65–81

69 **Middleton, R,** The politics of cultural expression: African music and the world market, in Allen T & Thomas, A (eds), *Poverty and development in the1990s* (Oxford: OUP, 1992), 362–78

70 **Monga, C,** L'identité mutante: authenticité, permanances et ruptures dans les cultures africaines, *Afrique 2000,* 9 (1992) 81–97

71 **Mwansa, D,** Critique of popular theatre in Africa: definitions, focuses, and lessons, *Journal for the African Association for Literacy and Adult Education,* 5, 3 (1991) 25–39

72 **Okita, S I,** African culture and the search for identity, in Irele A (ed), *African education and identity (entry 268),* 176–83

73 **Schmidt, N J,** Recent films by subsaharan African filmmakers, 5, *African literature association (ALA) bulletin,* 18, 1 (1992) 7–11

74 **Shiri, K,** *Directory of African film-makers and films.* Trowbridge: Flicks Books, 1992, 194pp

75 **Stanley, J L,** *The arts of Africa: an annotated bibliography. Volume 2: 1988.* Atlanta: African Studies Association, 1992, 521pp

76 **Vieyra, P S,** *Réflexions d'une*

cinéaste africain. Brussels: OCIC, 1990, 205pp

Current affairs

77 **Chamley, S, et al,** Africa: what chance for democracy?, *Index on censorship,* 21, 4 (1992) 7–25

78 **Hoffmeier, R,** Afrika 1991: das Jhar im Überblick, *Afrika Jahrbuch 1991,* 7–18

Demography

79 **Abdel-Hakim, S,** (ed), *Studies in Asian and African demography: CDC annual seminar, 1990.* Cairo: Cairo Demographic Centre, 1991, 1051pp

80 **Ela, J M,** Les enjeux démographiques en Afrique noire: les dessous d'un discours, *Afrique 2000,* 8 (1992) 73–89

81 **Gbenyon, K, Locoh, T,** Mortality differences in childhood by sex in SSA, in van der Walle E et al (eds), *Mortality and society (entry 771),* 230–52

82 **Gbesemete, K P, Jonsson, D,** A cross-national analysis on determinants of life-expectancy in Africa, *Scandinavian journal of development alternatives,* 11, 3/4 (1992) 195–209

83 **Gordon, A A,** Population growth and urbanisation, in Gordon A & D (eds), *Understanding contemporary Africa (entry 9),* 123–49

84 **Hill, A,** Trends in childhood mortality in subsaharan mainland Africa, in van der Walle E et al (eds), *Mortality and society (entry 771),* 1–31

85 **Pison, G,** Twins in SSA: frequency, social status and mortality, in van der Walle E et al (eds), *Mortality and society (entry 771),* 253–78

86 **Schwartz, J,** Le démographique,

Afrique contemporaine, 161 (1992) 43–56

87 Segal, A, Africa's population dynamics: great problems for the future, *Africa contemporary record 1988/89,* (1992) A87–96

88 Tabutin, B, Akoto, E, Socio-economic and cultural differentials in the mortality of SSA, in van der Walle E et al (eds), *Mortality and society (entry 771),* 32–64

89 Vallin, J, Theries of mortality decline and the African situation, in van der Walle E et al (eds), *Mortality and society (entry 771),* 405–36

Economy - Development

see also: 351, 362, 543, 907, 987

90 Abdulai, Y S, *Africa's external debt: an obstacle to economic recovery.* Vienna: OPEC, 1990, 25pp

91 Adedeji, A, *Preparing Africa for the twenty-first century: agenda for the 1990s.* Addis Ababa: UNECA, 1991, 107pp

92 Adedeji, A, The role of popular participation in meeting the challanges of recovery and development in Africa: democratization of development process, *Journal of African Association for Literacy and Adult Education,* 5, (1990) 1–13

93 Adedeji, A, *Structural adjustment for socio-economic recovery and transformation: the African alternative. Selected statements.* Addis Ababa: UNECA, 1990, 123pp

94 African Centre for Monetary Studies, *Debt-conversion schemes in Africa.* London: Currey, 1992, 143pp

95 Agbaje, A, In search of building blocks: the state, civil society, action and grassroots development in Africa, *Africa quarterly,* 30, 3/4 (1990) 24–40

96 Alibert, J, Le temps

d'ajustement: chères ambiguités, *Afrique contemporaine,* 164 (1992) 109–119

97 Amin, S, Ideology and development in SSA, in Anyang' Nyong'o P (ed), *30 years of independence (entry 101),* 40–46

98 Anglarill, N B, Les modèles de développement en Afrique: la fin d'un mythe?, *Africa (São Paulo),* 14/15 (1991/92) 91–118

99 Anthony, A E, African domestic structure, deepening crisis and the current adjustment programme, *Africa development,* 16, 1 (1991) 73–93

100 Anunobi, F O, *Implications of conditionality, the IMF and Africa.* Lanham: UP of America, 1991, 338pp

101 Anyang' Nyong'o, P, (ed), *30 years of independence in Africa: the lost decades?* Nairobi: Academy Science Publishers, 1992, 254pp

102 Avramovic, D, Africa's debts and economic recovery, *African development review,* 3, 2 (1991) 41–64

103 Ayittey, G B N, Why structural adjustment failed in Africa, *Transafrica forum,* 8, 2 (1991) 43–65

104 Babu, A M, The struggle for post-uhuru Africa, in Anyang' Nyong'o P (ed), *30 years of independence (entry 101),* 9–24

105 Banyaku Luape Epotu, *Aperçu sur les études sociales de développment: discours critique et panoramique.* Kinshasa: Presses universitiare du Zaire, 1990, 138pp

106 Bass, H H, Democracy and popular participation as productive factors or constitutive elements of a new development vision?, *African development perspectives yearbook,* 2, (1990/91) 207–220

107 Beckman, B, Empowerment or repression? The World Bank and the politics of African adjustment,

Africa development, 16, 1 (1991)
45–72

108 **Bevan, D, et al,** Consequences
of external shocks in African-type
economies, in Milner C & Rayner,
A J (eds), *Policy adjustment (entry
184)*, 7–29

109 **Böhmer, J,** *Die
Verschuldungskrise in Schwarzafrika:
Ausmass, Ursachen und Ansatzpukte
für eine Lösung.* Berlin: Freie
Universität, Fachbereich
Wirtschaftwissenschaft, 1990, 39pp

110 **Borenane, N,** Prospects for
Africa for an alternative to the
dominant Afro-pessimism, in
Anyang' Nyong'o P (ed), *30 years
of independence (entry 101)*, 47–61

111 **Brandt, H,**
*Struckturanpassungpolitik und
landwirtschatliche Erzeuerprise in
subsaharischen Afrika.* Berlin:
Deuteches Institut für
Entwicklunspolitik, 1992, 52pp

112 **Callaghy, T M,** Africa and the
world economy: caught between a
rock and a hard place, in Harbeson
J W & Rothchild, D (eds), *Africa in
world politics (entry 625)*, 39–68

113 **Cammann, L,** (ed), *Traditional
marketing systems.* Bonn: Deutsche
Stiftung fur internationale
Entwiclung, 1992, 204pp

114 **Chatel, B,** Les specificités de la
dette africaine, *Afrique
contemporaine,* 164 (1992) 120–42

115 **Chawla, K I,** Debt crisis in
subsaharan countries, *Africa
quarterly,* 30, 3/4 (1990) 41–64

116 **Chhibber, A, Fischer, S,**
*Economic reform in subsaharan
Africa.* Washington: World Bank,
1991, 334pp

117 **Chirwa, C L,** Africa's bilateral
debt, *African development review,* 3,
2 (1991) 149–54

118 **Chitiga-Machingauta, R M,**
Networking among NGOs in
Africa, in NGLS (ed), *Voices from
Africa 2 (entry 195)*, 65–69

119 **Cockcroft, L,** The past record
and future potential of foreign
investment, in Stewart F et al
(eds), *Alternative development
strategies (entry 223)*, 336–67

120 **Conable, B R,** *Reflections on
Africa.* Washington: World Bank,
1991, 31pp

121 **Coquery-Vidrovitch, C,**
L'informel dans les villes africaines:
essai d'analyse historique et sociale,
in Coquery-Vidrovitch C &
Nedelec, C (eds), *Tiers Monde:
l'informel en question?* (Paris:
Harmattan, 1991), 171–96

122 **Cornia, A G, et al,** Overview of
an alternative long-term
development strategy, in Cornia A
G et al (eds), *Africa's recovery (entry
124)*, 159–90

123 **Cornia, A G, van der Hoeven,
R, et al,** The supply side: changing
production structures and
accelerating growth, in Cornia A G
et al (eds), *Africa's recovery (entry
124)*, 191–226

124 **Cornia, G A, et al,** *Africa's
recovery in the 1990s.* Basingstoke:
Macmillan, 1992, 375pp

125 **Dag Hammarskjöld
Foundation,** *The state and the crisis
in Africa: in search of a second
liberation.* Uppsala: the Foundation,
1992, 32pp

126 **Davidson, B,** Africa: the
politics of failure, *Socialist register
1992,* 212–26

127 **Debreuille, M,** *De l'or du noir à
l'argent du blanc.* Paris: Harmattan,
1992, 224pp

128 **Delancey, V,** The economies of
Africa, in Gordon A & D ((eds)),
*Understanding contemporary Africa
(entry 9)*, 87–121

129 **Diarra, A,** (ed), *Westafrika
zwischen autochtoner Kultur und
Modernisierung.* Frankfurt: Lang,
1991, 291pp

130 **Dihm, M,** Remarks on the role
of unrecorded transborder trade in

subsaharan Africa, in Cammann L (ed), *Traditional marketing systems (entry 113)*, 139–45

131 **Doumou, A,** L'état africain à l'épreuve de la contrainte extérieur, *Africa development*, 15, 3/4 (1990) 21–46

132 **Elbadawi, I A,** *Have World Bank supported adjustment programs improved economic performance in subsaharan Africa?* Washington: World Bank, 1992, 60pp

133 **Elbadawi, I A, et al,** *Why structural adjustment has not succeeded in subsaharan Africa.* Washington: World Bank, 1992, 96pp

134 **el-Biblawi, H A Z,** *African countries' debt problem: the differentials.* Cairo: African Society, 1990, 35pp

135 **Eriksen, T L,** *Afrikas krise: finnes det alternativer til Verdensbanken diagnose og medesin?* Oslo: NORAD, 1990, 289pp

136 **Etukudo, A,** From skepticism to confidence: African employers' organisations as partners in development, *International labour review*, 130, 1 (1991) 113–26

137 **Ferroni, M, Kanbur, R,** *Poverty-conscious restructuring of public expenditure.* Washington: World Bank, 1990, 21pp

138 **Forje, J F,** The role of research and research institutes in Africa's economic recovery and development, in NGLS (ed), *Voices from Africa 4 (entry 1064)*, 103–109

139 **Fosu, A K,** Capital instability and economic growth in subsaharan Africa, *Journal of development studies*, 28, 1 (1991) 74–85

140 **Fosu, A K,** Political instability and economic growth: evidence from subsaharan Africa, *Economic development and cultural change*, 40, 4 (1992) 829–41

141 **Freud, C,** La zone franc est-elle le bouc-émissare de l'échec de développment?, *Cahiers d'études africaines*, 31, 1/2 (1991) 159–74

142 **Frimpong-Ansah, J H, Ingham, B,** (eds), *Saving for economic recovery in Africa.* London: Currey, 1992, 210pp

143 **Gadzey, A T K,** The state and capitalist transformation in subsaharan Africa: a development model, *Comparative political studies*, 24, 4 (1991) 455–87

144 **Gaud, M,** Complexité africain et développement, *Afrique contemporaine*, 163 (1992) 3–16

145 **Gibbon, P,** The World Bank and African poverty, *Journal of modern African studies*, 30, 2 (1992) 193–220

146 **Gleave, M B (ed),** The African condition: an overview, in Gleave M B (ed), *Tropical African development (entry 147)*, 1–24

147 **Gleave, M B, (ed),** *Tropical African development; geographical perspectives.* Harlow: Longman, 1992, 366pp

148 **Golansky, M,** Prospects of African economic development, in Irele A (ed), *African education and identity (entry 268)*, 261–64

149 **Gordon, A,** Capitalist reforms in subsaharan Africa: some questions and answers, *Geneva-Africa*, 30, 1 (1992) 35–53

150 **Gordon, D F,** Conditionality in policy-based lending in Africa: USAID experience, in Mosley P (ed), *Development finance and policy reform* (New York: St Martins Press, 1992), 25–53

151 **Green, R H,** *Reduction of absolute poverty: a priority structural adjustment.* Brighton: Sussex University, IDS, 1991, 40pp

152 **Harris, G, Kusi, N,** The impact of the IMF on government expenditures: a study c f African LDCs, *Journal of international*

development, 4, 1 (1992) 73–85

153 **Harris, G, Newman, K,** The impact of the IMF on government expenditures: a study of African LDCs, *Journal of international development*, 4, 1 (1992) 73–85

154 **Helleiner, G K,** Structural adjustment and long-term development in subsaharan Africa, in Stewart F et al (eds), *Alternative development strategies (entry 223)*, 48–78

155 **Hodder, B W,** Future prospects, in Gleave M B (ed), *Tropical African development (entry 147)*, 347–59

156 **Hoogvelt, A, et al,** The World Bank and Africa: a case of mistaken identity, *Review of African political economy*, 54 (1992) 92–96

157 **Hugon, P,** Les politiques d'appui au secteur informel en Afrique, in Coquery-Vidrovitch C & Nedelec, C (eds), *Tiers Monde: l'informel en question?* (Paris: Harmattan, 1991), 55–69

158 **Hugon, P,** Trente ans de pensée africaine sur le développement, *Afrique contemporaine*, 164 (1992) 211–23

159 **Husain, I, Underwood, J,** The debt of subsaharan Africa: problems and solutions, *African development review*, 3, 2 (1991) 65–98

160 **Hutchful, E,** The debt crisis and its implications for democratisation in Latin America and Africa, *Africa development*, 15, 3/4 (1990) 133–48

161 **Ihonvbere, J O,** The African crisis, the Popular Charter and prospects for recovery in the 1990s, *Zeitschrift für Afrikastudien*, 11/12 (1991) 25–41

162 **ILO,** *The urban informal sector in Africa in retrospect and prospect: an anotated bibliography.* Geneva: ILO, 1991, 86pp

163 **Isamah, A N,** Culture, work and the development process, in *Voices from Africa 4 (entry 1064)*, 31–39

164 **Jespersen, E,** External shocks, adjustment policies and economic and social performance, in Cornia A G et al (eds), *Africa's recovery (entry 124)*, 9–50

165 **Kane, T,** Grassroots development: what role for voluntary organisations?, in NGLS (ed), *Voices from Africa 2 (entry 195)*, 9–16

166 **Kappel, R,** Strukturanpassungmassnahmen und der sozialer Dimensionen der Enwicklung in Afrika, *Afrika Jahrbuch 1991*, 57–55

167 **Kennett, D, Lumumba-Kasongo, T,** (eds), *Structural adjustment and the crisis in Africa.* Lewiston: Mellen, 1992, 147pp

168 **Killick, T,** *Explaining Africa's post-independence development experience.* London: ODI, 1990, 22pp

169 **Kiss, J,** *Sentenced to debt. African debt crisis - facts, causes and remedies.* Budapest: Institute for World Economics, 1991, 64pp

170 **Ki-Zerbo, J,** *La natte des autres, pour un développement endogène en Afrique.* Paris: Karthala, 1992, 494pp

171 **Koffi, B E,** 1980–1990: du Plan d'action du Lagos a la déclaration d'Abuja, *Afrique 2000*, 9 (1992) 59–72

172 **Koulibaly, M,** *Le liberalisme: nouveau départ pour l'Afrique.* Paris: Harmattan, 1992, 223pp

173 **Krueger, A O, et al,** (eds), *The political economy of agricultural pricing policy, vol. 3: Africa and the Mediterranean.* Baltimore: Johns Hopkins University Press, 1991, 340pp

174 **Lancaster, C,** The Lagos Three: economic regionalism in

subsaharan Africa, in Harbeson J W & Rothchild, D (eds), *Africa in world politics (entry 625)*, 249–67

175 **Lane, C E, Page, S,** *Differences in economic performance between Franc Zone and other African countries.* London: ODI, 1991, 43pp

176 **Lele, U, Adu-Nyako, K,** Integrated strategy approach for poverty alleviation: a paramount priority for Africa, *African development review*, 3, 1 (1991) 1–29

177 **Lobé Awané, M,** Réflexions sur l'avenir de la Zone Franc, *Afrique 2000*, 11 (1992) 67–71

178 **Lyakurwa, W M,** External debt problems of subsaharan Africa in the context of structural adjustment, *Tanzania journal of economics*, 2, 1 (1990) 33–51

179 **Matin, K M,** *Openness and economic performance in subsaharan Africa: evidence from time-series cross-country analysis.* Washington: World Bank, 1992, 38pp

180 **McPherson, M F,** Has socialism really failed?, *Comparative economic studies*, 33, 3 (1991) 153–66

181 **Mengisteab, K, Logan, B I,** Africa's debt crisis: are structural adjustment programmes relevant?, *Africa development*, 16, 1 (1991) 95–113

182 **Merlin, P,** *L'espoir pour l'Afrique noire.* Paris: Presence Africaine, 1991, 477pp

183 **Mibuy, A O,** La dimension antropologica del desarrollo, *Africa 2000*, 15 (1991) 10–13

184 **Milner, C, Rayner, A J, (eds),** *Policy adjustment in Africa.* Basingstoke: Macmillan, 1992, 249pp

185 **Mistry, P S,** African debt revisited: procrastination or progress?, *African development review*, 3, 2 (1991) 99–148

186 **Mkandawire, T,** 30 years of African independence: the economic experience, in Anyang' Nyong'o P (ed), *30 years of independence (entry 101)*, 86–102

187 **Mkandawire, T,** The crisis in economic development theory, *Africa development*, 15, 3/4 (1990) 209–40

188 **Morrissey, W O,** Bilateral aid to Africa and structural adjustment loans: conflict or consensus?, in Milner C & Rayner, A J (eds), *Policy adjustment (entry 184)*, 133–47

189 **Nabudere, D W,** Africa's development experience under the Lomé conventions, in Anyang' Nyong'o P (ed), *30 years of independence (entry 101)*, 145–74

190 **Narman, A,** Population, education and the labour market in SSA, in Hammarskjold M et al (eds), *Population and the development crisis in the South (Lund: PROP Publications, 1992)*, 107–114

191 **Ndiaye, M,** Domestic impediments to popular participation in the African economic and social recovery and development process, *Journal of the African Association for Literacy and Adult Education*, 5, (1990) 41–56

192 **Ndulu, B,** Enhancing income distribution and rationalising consumption patterns, in Cornia A G et al (eds), *Africa's recovery (entry 124)*, 227–45

193 **Nguema, I,** La démocratie, l'Afrique et le développement, *Revue juridique et politique*, 46, 2 (1992) 129–62

194 **Niandou Souley, A,** Economic crisis and democratisation in Africa, in Caron B et al (eds), *Democratic transition in Africa (entry 817)*, 379–85

195 **Non-Governmental Liaison Service (ed),** *Voices from Africa 2: NGOs and grassroots development.* Geneva: NGLS, 1990, 114pp

196 Ofstad, A, *Afrikas konomiske krise: finnes det grunnlag for reformer?* Bergen: Chr. Michelsens Institute, 1992, 15pp

197 Ofuatey-Kodjoe, W, African international political economy: an assessment of the current literature, in Murphy C N & Tooze, R (eds), *The new international political economy* (Boulder: Lynne Reinner, 1991), 171–89

198 Onimode, B, *A future for Africa: beyond the politics of adjustment.* London: Earthscan/Institute for African Alternatives, 1992, 177pp

199 Osipov, Y, Cherkasov, Y, Independent African countries in search of an alternative to the models of peripheral modernisation, in Irele A (ed), *African education and identity (entry 268),* 271–76

200 Penouil, M, Secteur informel et crises africaines, *Afrique contemporaine,* 164 (1992) 70–80

201 Please, S, Beyond structural adjustment in Africa, *Development policy review,* 10, 3 (1992) 289–307

202 Pottier, J, The role of ethnography in project appraisal, in Pottier J (ed), *Practising development: social science perspectives* (London: Routledge, 1992), 13–34

203 Ramanadham, V V, (ed), *Privatisation: a global view.* London: Routledge, 1992, 610pp

204 Riddell, J B, The new face of imperialism and Africa's poverty, *Journal of modern African studies,* 30, 4 (1992) 721–25

205 Riddell, J B, Things fall apart: structural adjustment programmes in subsaharan Africa, *Journal of modern African studies,* 30, 1 (1992) 53–68

206 Rifrac, S, Un continent malade du capitalisme, *Cahiers du communisme,* 67, 7/8 (1991) 64–68

207 Roch, J, De nouveaux consommateurs?, *Afrique contemporaine,* 164 (1992) 59–69

208 Rosenke, W, Siepelmeyer, T, (eds), *Afrika: der vergessene Kontinent? Zwischen selektiver Weltmarktintegration und ökologische Katastrophen.* Munster: Unrast, 1991, 257pp

209 Rudebeck, L, Conditions of people's development in postcolonial Africa, in Galli R (ed), *Rethinking the Third World* (New York: Crane Russak, 1991), 29–87

210 Rweyemamu, J F, *Third World options: power, security and the hope for another development.* Dar es Salaam: Tanzania Publishing House, 1992, 225pp

211 Salih, M A, Traditional markets and the shrinking role of the African state, in Cammann L (ed), *Traditional marketing systems (entry 113),* 188–99

212 Salvatore, D, Tavlas, G S, et al, Modelling African development prospects, in Milner C & Rayner, A J (eds), *Policy adjustment (entry 184),* 31–60

213 Satpathy, A, The role of the World Bank in subsaharan Africa in the 1980s, *Africa quarterly,* 31, 1/2 (1991) 59–75

214 Seidman, A, Anang, F, (eds), *Twenty-first century Africa: towards a new vision of self-sustainable development.* Trenton: Africa World Press, 1992, 330pp

215 Sejanamane, M M, From neo-colonialism to colonialism: the political implications of structural adjustment programmes, *NUL journal of research,* 1, (1991) 1–22

216 Shams, F, Subsaharan Africa's dilemma of indebtedness, *Journal of Asian and African affairs,* 3, 2 (1992) 192–204

217 Shaw, T M, Africa in the 1990s: beyond continental crises to sustainable development: structural adjustment, civil society and non-governmental organisations,

African development perspectives yearbook, 2, (1990/91) 193–206

218 **Simmons, R,** An error-correction approach to demand for money in five African developing countries, *Journal of economic studies,* 19, 1 (1992) 29–47

219 **Simson, U,** Zur Entwicklungsproblematik Schwarzafrikas: Plädoyer für eine realistische Sichtweise, *Afrika spectrum,* 26, 2 (1991) 145–154

220 **Sottas, B,** *Afrika entwickeln und modernisieren: Paradigmen, Identitätsbildung und kleinabäuerliche Uberlebenstrategie.* Frieburg: Universitätsverlag Freiburg Schweiz, 1992, 322pp

221 **Stewart, D B,** Economic growth and the defence burden in Africa and Latin America: simulations from a dynamic model, *Economic development and cultural change,* 40, 1 (1991) 189–207

222 **Stewart, F,** Short-term policies for long-term development, in Cornia A G et al (eds), *Africa's recovery (entry 124),* 312–33

223 **Stewart, F, et al,** (eds), *Alternative development strategies in subsaharan Africa.* Basingstoke: Macmillan, 1992, 486pp

224 **Stewart, F, Lall, S, et al,** Alternative development strategies: an overview, in Stewart F et al (eds), *Alternative development strategies (entry 223),* 3–47

225 **Tandon, Y,** Participatory development as a dimension in Africa's development and transformation efforts, *Journal of the African Association for Literacy and Adult Education,* 5, (1990) 57–66

226 **Tarr, S B,** Underming the political logic of African governments' poor economic policies, *Geneva-Africa,* 30, 1 (1992) 9–34

227 **Thisen, J K,** The design of structural adjustment programmes:

the African Alternative Framework, *Africa development,* 16, 1 (1991) 115–64

228 **Toye, J,** Interest group politics and the implementation of adjustment policies in Subsaharan Africa in Gibbon P & Bangura, Y (eds), *Authoritarianism, democracy and adjustment (entry 850),* 106–26

229 **Toye, J,** Interest group politics and the implementation of adjustment policies in subsaharan Africa, *Journal of international development,* 4, 2 (1992) 183–197

230 **Turok, B,** Towards a democratic coalition against SAP, in Anyang' Nyong'o P (ed), *30 years of independence (entry 101),* 131–44

231 **UNCTAD,** *UNCTAD's contribution to the implementation of the United Nations programme of action for African economic recovery and development.* Geveva: UNCTAD, 1991, 31pp

232 **UNCTAD,** *United Nations programme of action for African economic recovery and development 1986–1990: UNCTAD's intergovernmental input into the General Assembly's final review and appraisal of the implementation of the programme of action in 1991.* Geveva: UNCTAD, 1991, 2 vols, 15, 71pp

233 **van der Hoeven, R,** External dependence and long-term development, in Cornia A G et al (eds), *Africa's recovery (entry 124),* 272–95

234 **von Freyhold, K Tetzlaff, R,** (eds), *Die 'afrikanische Krise' und die Krise der Entwicklungspolitik.* Munster: Lit, 1991, 323pp

235 **Wagao, J H,** Economic aspects of the crisis in Africa, in Anyang' Nyong'o P (ed), *30 years of independence (entry 101),* 103–130

236 **Weeks, J,** Economic crisis and household survival strategies in

subsaharan Africa, *Africa (São Paulo)*, 12/13 (1989/90) 56–77

237 Weidmann, K, *Die EG-Entwicklungspolitik in Afrika: Hungerhilfe oder Elitenförderung.* Baden Baden: Nomos, 1991, 333pp

238 Yahaya, S, State intervention versus the market: a review of the debate, *Africa development,* 16, 3/4 (1991) 55–74

Economic and social history

see also: 1089

239 Awak'Ayom, L'esclavage des Noirs africains dans les colonies françaises et la Révolution française de 1789, *Zaïre-Afrique,* 265, (1992) 287–310

240 Berbier, J P, La CCCE: cinquante ans de relations franco-africains, *Afrique contemporaine,* 162 (1992) 60–68

241 Berry, S, Hegemony on a shoestring: indirect rule and access to agricultural land, *Africa,* 62, 3 (1992) 327–55

242 d'Almedia-Topor, H, et al, *Les transports en Afrique: XIXième-XXième siècles.* Paris: Harmattan, 1992, 364pp

243 d'Almeida-Topor, H, et al, (eds), *Les jeunes en Afrique. I: évolution et rôle (XIXè-XXè siècles).* Paris: Harmattan, 1992, 260pp

244 d'Almeida-Topor, H, et al, (eds), *Les jeunes en Afrique. 2: la politique et la ville.* Paris: Harmattan, 1992, 280pp

247 Legoux, P, Marelle, A, *Les mines et la recherche minière en Afrique occidentale française: histoire et témoignages.* Paris: Harmattan, 1991, 361pp

248 Miller, J G, Muslim slavery and slaving: a bibliography, in Savage E (ed), *The human commodity (entry 252),* 249–71

249 Morgan, W T M, Tropical

African colonial experience, in Gleave M B (ed), *Tropical African development (entry 147),* 25–49

250 Nwanunobi, C O, *African social institutions.* Lagops: University of Nigeria Press, 1992, 258pp

251 Quaghebeur, M, (ed), *Papier blanc, encre noir: cent ans de culture francophone en Afrique centrale (Zaire, Rwanda et Burundi).* Brussels: Labor, 1992, 2 vols, 690pp

252 Savage, E, (ed), *The human commodity: perspectives on the trans-saharan slave trade.* London: Cass, 1992, 279pp

253 Smith, A B, *Pastoralism in Africa: origins and development ecology.* London: Hurst, 1992, 288pp

254 Vaughan, M, *Curing their ills: colonial power and African illness.* Oxford: Polity, 1991, 224pp

255 Wigboldus, J S, Precolonial development of technology in tropical Africa: updating a review, *Techniques et culture,* 17/18, (1991) 399–410

Education

see also: 1068, 3614

256 Agyakawa, K O, *African taboos and science education.* Edinburgh: Edinburgh University, Centre of African Studies, 1992, 23pp

257 American Association for the Advancement of Science, *Science in Africa: innovations in higher education.* Washington: the Association, 1992, 107pp

258 Awori, T, Mamba, G, How to unleash the talents and energies of African people to contribute effectively to the process of development and transformation, *Journal of the African Association for Literacy and Adult Education,* 5, (1990) 24–40

259 Babarinde, K, Ogunyemi, B,

Institutional framework for democratic transition in Africa: the educational imperative, in Caron B et al (eds), *Democratic transition in Africa (entry 817)*, 111–27

260 **Baryeh, E A,** Training mechanical engineers for rural development, *African journal of science and technology. Series C, general*, 2, 1 (1991) 1–6

261 **Billetoft, J,** *Vocational training and education in subsaharan Africa: adjusting to new realities.* Copenhagen: CDR, 1990, 35pp

262 **Célestin, J B,** *L'emploi et la formation dans un contexte de crise économique: le cas de l'Afrique d'expression francaise.* Geneva: ILO, 1992, 108pp

263 **Celis, G R,** *La faillité de l'enseignement blanc en Afrique noire.* Paris: Harmattan, 1991, 167pp

264 **Committee for Academic Freedom in Africa,** The World Bank and education in Africa, *Race and class*, 34, 1 (1992) 51–60

265 **Eisemon, T O, Davis, C H,** Can the quality of scientific training and research in Africa be improved by training?, *MInerva*, 29, 1 (1991) 1–26

266 **Fine, J C,** *A strategy for graduate training in economics for Africans.* Nairobi: Initiatives, 1990, 82pp

267 **Girdwood, A,** *The function and financing of African universities.* Edinburgh: Edinburgh University, Centre of African Studies, 1992, 53pp

268 **Irele, A,** (ed), *African education and identity: proceedings of the International Congress of African Studies, Ibadan 1985.* Oxford: Zell, 1992, 447pp

269 **Kaba, I D, Rayapen, L C A,** (eds), *Relevant education for Africa.* Yaoundé: 'Professors World Peace Academy', 1990, 243pp

270 **Koudawo, F,** *La formation des cadres africains en Europe de l'Est depuis 1918.* Paris: Harmattan, 1992, 224pp

271 **Lungu, G F,** Pragmatism or crude utility: a critique of the education with production movement in contemporary Africa, *Quest*, 5, 2 (1991) 74–89

272 **Mazrui, A A,** Towards diagnosing and treating cultural dependency: the case of the African university, *International journal of educational development*, 12, 2 (1992) 95–111

273 **Miyamoto, M,** Writing and civilisation: a view from African culture, *Senri ethnological studies*, 34 (1992) 9–21

274 **Mugaju, J B,** The burden of education on economic developmentin Africa: an assessment, *Transafrican journal of history*, 20 (1991) 110–24

275 **Muhisa, T,** Pluralistic education in subsaharan Africa: an overview, *Prospects*, 22, 82 (1992) 159–70

276 **Mukras, M S,** *Graduate training in economics in anglophone Africa (except Nigeria).* Nairobi: Initiatives, 1991, 42pp

277 **Mungala, A M,** Education africain et identité, in Irele A (ed), *African education and identity (entry 268)*, 131–38

278 **Munyantwali, E,** Analyse des différentes forces qui jouent un rôle dans la planification de l'éducation en Afrique, *Uburezi ubuhanga n'umuco*, 23 (1990) 57–70

279 **Mwamwenda, T S, Mwamwenda, B B,** African's cognitive development and schooling, *International journal of educational development*, 11, 2 (1991) 129–34

280 **Ocitti, J P,** *An introduction to indigenous education in subsaharan Africa: a select annotated*

bibliography. The Hague: CESO, 1991, 70pp

281 **Otaala, B,** Alternative approaches to daycare in Africa: integration of health and early childhood education, *BOLESWA Educational research journal,* 7, (1990) 58–74

282 **Pegatienan, H J,** *Graduate training in economics in francophone west and central Africa.* Nairobi: Initiatives, 1990, 19pp

283 **Peil, M,** Leadership of anglophone universities, in Irele A (ed), *African education and identity (entry 268),* 79–87

284 **Rwomire, A,** Education and development: African perspectives, *Prospects,* 22, 82 (1992) 227–40

285 **Saint, W S,** *Universities in Africa: strategies for stabilisation and revitalisation.* New York: World Bank, 1992, 140pp

286 **Samoff, J,** The intellectual/financial complex of foreign aid, *Review of African political economy,* 53 (1992) 60–75

287 **Savage, M,** Nourishing innovation in science education in Africa: the experience of the African Forum for Children's Literacy in Science and Technology, *Science, technology and development,* 10, 2 (1992) 246–64

288 **Thompson, J D,** Volunteers in adult education: what do they give? what do they get in return?, *Journal of the African Association for Literacy and Adult Education,* 5, 4 (1991) 31–38

289 **Urch, G F,** *Education in subsaharan Africa: a source-book.* New York: Garland, 1992, 192pp

290 **Wallace, I,** Agricultural education as a learning system in Africa: enhancing effectiveness through innovation and the formal/non-formal interface, *Educational development,* 12, 1 (1992) 51–64

291 **Westley, D,** Language and education in Africa: a select bibliography, 1980–1990, *Comparative education review,* 36, 3 (1992) 355–67

Environment

see also: 208, 1012, 1062

292 **Abiola, K,** Un point de vue sur l'écologie et la société en Afrique, in Irele A (ed), *African education and identity (entry 268),* 353–57

293 **Anhuf, D, Frankenberg, P,** Die naturnahen Vegetationszone Westafrikas, *Die Erde,* 122, 4 (1991) 243–265

294 **Ayeni, B,** Man, the city and the environment, in Irele A (ed), *African education and identity (entry 268),* 337–52

295 **Ayensu, E S,** Beyond the crisis in African agriculture: balancing conservation and development, in Obasanjo O & d'Orville, H (eds), *Agricultural production and food security (entry 1040),* 119–27

296 **Biot, R, Lambert, R, et al,** *What's the problem? An essay on land degradation, science and development in subsaharan Africa.* Norwich: School of Development Studies, University of East Anglia, 1992, 42pp

297 **Blackwell, J M, et al,** *Environment and development in Africa: selected case studies.* Washington: World Bank, 1991, 127pp

298 **Boutrais, J,** L'élevage en Afrique tropicale: une activité dégradante?, *Afrique contemporaine,* 161 (1992) 109–125

299 **Brabant, P,** La dégradation des terres en Afrique, *Afrique contemporaine,* 161 (1992) 90–108

300 **Bruhns, B I,** (ed), *Okologische Zerstörungen in Afrika und alternative Strategien.* Munster: Lit, 1992, 251pp

301 **Fair, D,** Africa's rain forests: preserving Africa's rich heritage, *Africa insight,* 22, 2 (1992) 134–41

302 **Gaud, M,** Environnement, développement et coopération: quelques réflexions, *Afrique contemporaine,* 161 (1992) 265–279

303 **Ghai, D,** *Conservation, livelihood and democracy: social dynamics of environmental changes in Africa.* Geneva: UNRISD, 1992, 23pp

304 **Ghai, D,** The social dynamics of environmental change in Africa, *Whydah,* 2, 9 (1990/92) 1,3–8

305 **Gillon, Y,** Empreinte humaine et facteurs du milieu dans l'histoire écologique de l'Afrique tropicale, *Afrique contemporaine,* 161 (1992) 30–41

306 **Harsch, E,** Africa presses for its priorities to be put on the global environment agenda, *Africa recovery,* 6, 1 (1992) 1, 26–28

307 **Hjort af Ornas, A,** Environment and secure livelihoods: research and development issues for African drylands, in Hjort af Ornas A (ed), *Security in African drylands (entry 1025),* 1–19

308 **Mahalu, C R,** The OAU Council of Ministers' resolution on dumping of nuclear and industrial waste in Africa and the Basel Convention of 1989, *African journal of international and comparative law,* 2, 1 (1990) 61–71

309 **Matheson, A,** Environmental problems: toxic waste, water supplies and poaching, *Africa contemporary record 1988/89,* (1992) A67–73

310 **Moss, R P,** Environmental constraints on development in tropical Africa, in Gleave M B (ed), *Tropical African development (entry 146),* 50–92

311 **Nyang'oro, J E,** Africa's environmental problem, in Gordon A & D (eds), *Understanding contemporary Africa (entry 9),* 151–73

312 **Omari, C K,** Traditional African land ethics, in Engel J R & J G (eds), *Ethics of environment and development* (London: Pinter, 1990), 167–75

313 **Omo-Fadaka, J,** Communalism: the moral factor in African development, in Engel J R & J G (eds), *Ethics of environment and development* (London: Pinter, 1990), 176–82

314 **Perrings, C,** *Incentives for the ecologically sustainable use of human and natural resources in the drylands of subsaharan Africa: a review.* Geneva: ILO, 1991, 50pp

315 **Pourtier, R,** Migrations et dynamique de l'environnement, *Afrique contemporaine,* 161 (1992) 167–177

316 **Reij, C,** *Indigenous soil and water conservation in Africa.* London: IIED, 1991, 35pp

317 **Sharp, R, Koné, M,** *A future rooted in Africa's soil: environment, development and the search for sustainability.* New York: United Nations, 1992, 12pp

318 **Showers, K B, Malahlela, G M,** *Historical environmental impact analysis: a tool for analysis of past interventions in landscapes.* New York: Social Science Research Council, Project on African agriculture, 1992, 26pp

319 **Soumastre, S,** Les déchets industriels et l'Afrique, *Afrique contemporaine,* 161 (1992) 254–265

320 **Stocking, M,** *Land degradation and rehabilitation: research in Africa 1980–1990.* London: IIED, 1992, 31pp

321 **Suliman, M,** Climate change and environmental conflicts in Africa, *African development perspectives yearbook,* 2, (1990/91) 309–327

322 **Wegemund, R, et al,** (eds),
*Afrika: Überleben in einer ökologisch
gefährdeten Unwelt.* Munster: Lit,
1992, 326pp
323 **Woodhouse, P,** Social and
environmental change in SSA, in
Bernstein H et al (eds), *Rural
livelihoods (entry 1004),* 165–94

Finance

324 **Adams, D W,** Building durable
rural financial markets in Africa,
*African review of money finance and
banking,* 1 (1992) 5–15
325 **Aigbokhan, B E,** The theory of
optimum currency areas and
monetary integration in Africa,
Savings and development, 16, 3
(1992) 275–86
326 **Boughton, J,** The CFA franc:
zone of fragile stability in Africa,
Finance and development, 29, 4
(1992) 34–36
327 **Callier, F,** (ed), *Financial
systems and development in Africa.*
Washington: World Bank, 1991,
279pp
328 **Cobham, D,** *Monetary
integration in Africa: a deliberately
European perspective.* St Andrews: St
Andrews University, Dept. of
Economics, 1992, 33pp
329 **Devarajan, S, Rodrik, D,** *Do
the benefits of a fixed exchange rate
outweigh their cost? The Franc Zone
in Africa.* London: Centre for
Economic Policy Research, 1991,
38pp
330 **El-Nil, Y S H,** The
prerequisites for successful
financial reform, in Roe A R et al
*Instruments of economic policy (entry
341),* 185–94
331 **Frimpong-Ansah, J H,** The
mobilisation of domestic resources
for Africa's economic recovery and
development, in Frimpong-Ansah J
H & Ingham, B (eds), *Saving for
economic recovery (entry 142),* 1–28

332 **Ingham, B,** Household savings
and credit: a long view of policy, in
Frimpong-Ansah J H & Ingham, B
(eds), *Saving for economic recovery
(entry 142),* 60–74
333 **Lipumba, N H I,** The exchange
rate in structural adjustment and
economic growth in subsaharan
Africa: policy issues, in Roe A R et
al *Instruments of economic policy
(entry 341),* 17–30
334 **M'bet, A,** Issues of
management, in Roe A R et al
*Instruments of economic policy (entry
341),* 145–55
335 **Mullei, A K,** Adaption to
composite basket pegging in
African countries, *Eastern Africa
economic review,* 6, 1 (1990) 1–9
336 **Mwege, F M,** Monetary policy
issues in an African context, in Roe
A R et al *Instruments of economic
policy (entry 341),* 62–68
337 **O D I,** *The African Development
Bank: facing new challenges.*
London: ODI, 1992, 4pp
338 **Orsmond, D W H,** The
potency of monetary and fiscal
policies in subsaharan countries: St
Louis model estimates, *African
review of money finance and banking,*
1 (1992) 17–28
339 **Roe, A R,** Africa's experience
with economic policy instruments,
in Roe A R et al *Instruments of
economic policy (entry 341),* 1–16
340 **Roe, A R,** Fiscal deficits and
internal debt management in
Africa, in Roe A R et al *Instruments
of economic policy (entry 341),*
116–26
341 **Roe, A R, et al,** (eds),
*Instruments of economic policy in
Africa.* London: Currey, 1992,
238pp
342 **SAATA,** (ed), *Aspects of
exchange rate determination.* New
York: Structural Adjustment
Advisory Teams for Africa, UNDP,
1991, 153pp

343 Spears, A, The role of financial intermediation in economic growth in subsaharan Africa, *Canadian journal of development studies,* 13, 3 (1992) 361–380

344 Wagacha, M, Savings mobilisation, financial liberalisation and economic adjustment in Africa: issues, theory and policy consequences, *Africa development,* 16, 3/4 (1991) 117–41

345 Westlake, M, et al, Sub-Sahara's slippery slope, *Banker,* Dec 1992 29–38

346 Yemidale, F M, African external debt issues and management experience, in Roe A R et al *Instruments of economic policy (entry 341),* 137–44

Food

see also: 395, 1025

347 Agricultural division, UNECA, Production subsidy and price support policies for food self-sufficiency in Africa, *Rural progress,* 10, 2 (1991) 1–26

348 Bohle, H G, (ed), *Famine and food security in Africa and Asia.* Bayreuth: Naturwissenschaftliche Gesellscahft, 1991, 312pp

349 Bothomani, I B, Chipande, G H R, Food policy and security in southern Africa, a qualified optimistic view, *Tizame,* 2 (1990) 1–10

350 Caldwell, J C, Caldwell, P, Famine in Africa: a global perspective, in van der Walle E et al (eds), *Mortality and society (entry 771),* 367–90

351 Cheru, F, Debt and famine in Africa: the years of living dangerously, *Third World first,* 2, 2/3 (1991) 2–8

352 Chole, E, (ed), *Food crisis in Africa: policy and management issues.* New Delhi: Vikas, 1990, 270pp

354 de Garine, I, (ed), *Les changements des habitudes et des politiques alimentaires en Afriques.* Paris: Publisud, 1991, 278pp

355 Duffield, M, The emergence of two-tier welfare in Africa: marginalisation or an opportunity for reform?, *Public administration and development,* 12, 2 (1992) 139–54

356 Duffield, M, *War and famine in Africa.* Oxford: Oxfam, 1992, 35pp

357 Hareide, D, *Vulnerability to famine: the alternative future project.* Oslo: Prosjekt Alternativ Framtid, 1991, 249pp

358 Harriss, B, Crow, B, Twentieth century free trade reform: food market deregulation in SSA and South Asia, in Wuyts M et al (eds), *Development policy and public action* (Oxford: OUP, 1992), 199–227

359 Levinson, F J, *Addressing malnutrition in Africa.* Washington: World Bank, 1992, 44pp

360 Macrae, J, Zwi, A B, Food as an instrument of war in contemporary African famines: a review of the evidence, *Disasters,* 16, 4 (1992) 299–321

361 Maxwell, S, *Food security in Africa.* New York: United Nations, 1992, 12pp

362 Michler, W, *Weissbuch Afrika.* Berlin: Dietz, 1991, 568pp

363 Mukerjee, H, *A study of women and agricultural technologies used in food production in Africa.* London: Intermediate Technology, 1992, 90pp

364 Nair, I M, Dietary patterns in Africa, in Obasanjo O & d'Orville, H (eds), *Agricultural production and food security (entry 1040),* 57–61

365 Nnol, O, Social stress and food security in African drylands, in Hjort af Ornas A (ed), *Security in African drylands (entry 1025),* 21–39

366 Odhiambo, T R, Managing drought and locust invasions in

Africa, *Land use policy*, 8, 4 (1991)
348–53

367 Rwomire, A, The political
economy of famine; an African
perspective, *Africa insight*, 22, 2
(1992) 142–45

368 Sijm, J, *Food security and policy
interventions in Mali.* Rotterdam:
Tinbergen Institute, 1882, 231pp

369 UNECA, Food security in
Africa, in Obasanjo O & d'Orville,
H (eds), *Agricultural production and
food security (entry 1040)*, 35–56

370 Weber, A, Reichrath, S,
*Structure, trends and factors
influencing the African grain and
food economy.* Keil: Vauk, 1990,
64pp

**371 World Bank, World Food
Programme,** *Food aid in Africa:
an agenda for the 1990s.*
Washington: World Bank, 1991,
36pp

372 Yakubu, A O, Famine in
Africa: a select and annotated
bibliography, *A current bibliography
on African affairs*, 23, 2 (1991/92)
105–127

Gender

see also: 54, 363, 481

373 AFARD, *Women as agents and
beneficiaries of development assistance.*
Dakar: Association des femmes
africaines pour la recherche sur le
développement, 1990, 152pp

374 AFARD, *Women and the mass
media in Africa.* Dakar: Association
des femmes africaines pour la
recherche sur le développement,
1992, 216pp

375 AFARD, *Women and
reproduction in Africa.* Dakar:
Association des femmes africaines
pour la recherche sur le
développement, 1992, 150pp

376 Agorsah, K E, Women in
African traditional politics, *Journal
of legal pluralism and unofficial law*,

30/31 (1990/1991) 77–86

377 Bauer, S, 'Action to assist rural
women': marketing approach for
income generating activities in four
African countries (Guinea, Niger,
Tanzania, Zimbabwe), in
Cammann L (ed), *Traditional
marketing systems (entry 113)*,
10–20

378 Bonnardel, R, Femmes, ville,
informel, en Afrique au sud du
Sahara, in Coquery-Vidrovitch C &
Nedelec, C (eds), *Tiers Monde:
l'informel en question?* (Paris:
Harmattan, 1991), 247–69

379 Bruchhaus, E M, Some
thoughts on 'village-mill projects',
*African development perspectives
yearbook*, 2, (1990/91) 651–670

380 Bushra, J, *Economic interest
groups and their relevance for women's
development.* London: ACORD,
1992, 14pp

381 Drew, A, *Female consciousness
and feminism in Africa.* Manchester:
Manchester University, Dept. of
Government, 1992, 28pp

382 Droy, I, *Femmes et développement
rurale.* Paris: Karthala, 1990, 182pp

383 Etim, E U, Debt and structural
adjustment programmes: the effects
on women in Africa, *Echo*, 17/18
(1992) 18–22

384 Gordon, A A, Women and
development, in Gordon A & D
(eds), *Understanding contemporary
Africa (entry 9)*, 201–21

385 Imam, A M, Gender analysis
and African social sciences in the
1990s, *Africa development*, 15, 3/4
(1990) 241–57

386 Koopman, J, Neoclassical
household models and models of
household production: problems in
the analysis of African agricultural
households, *Review of radical
political economy*, 23, 3/4 (1991)
148–73

387 Lachenmann, G, Frauen als
gesellschaftliche Kraft im sozialen

Wandel in Afrika, *Peripherie*, 47/48 (1992) 74–93

388 **Lado, C,** Female labour participation in agricultural production and the implications for nutrition and health in rural Africa, *Social science and medicine*, 34, 7 (1992) 789–807

389 **Laketch Dirasse,** *Reaching the top: women managers in eastern and southern Africa.* Arusha: Eastern and Southern African Management Institute, 1991, 162pp

390 **Leigh-Doyle, S,** Increasing women's participation in technical fields: a pilot project in Africa, *International labour review*, 130, 4 (1991) 427–44

391 **Longwe, S H,** From welfare to empowerment: the situation of women in development in Africa, a post-UN women's decade update and future directions, *Journal of the African Association for Literacy and Adult Education*, 3, 2 (1988) 4–15

392 **Longwe, S H,** *From welfare to empowerment: the situation of women in development in Africa.* East Lansing: Michigan State University, 1990, 25pp

393 **Mazrui, A A,** The economic woman in Africa, *Finance and development*, 29, 2 (1992) 42–43

394 **Mulindi, S A Z,** How women are affected by AIDS in Africa, *Scandinavian journal of development alternatives*, 11, 3/4 (1992) 211–216

395 **Okelo, M,** The women's viewpoint, in Obasanjo O & d'Orville, H (eds), *Agricultural production and food security (entry 1040)*, 83–86

396 **Ras-Work, B,** Female genital mutilation, in NGLS (ed), *Voices from Africa 4 (entry 1064)*, 89–96

397 **Stamp. P,** *Technology, gender and power in Africa.* West Hartford: Kumarian, 1990, 185pp

398 **Steeves, H L,** *Women, rural*

information delivery and development in subsaharan Africa. East Lansing: Michigan State University, 1990, 35pp

399 **Stlen, K A, Vaa, M,** (eds), *Gender and change in developing countries.* Oslo: Norwegian UP, 1991, 312pp

400 **Sylla, A,** Pratiques mutilantes et féminité: questions d'esthétique de la femme africain, *Bulletin de l'Institut fondamental d'Afrique noire. Série B, Sciences humaines*, 46, 3/4 (1986/1987) 305–342

401 **Tabet, P,** 'I'm the meat, I'm the knife': sexual service, migration and repression in some African societies, *Feminist issues*, 11, 4 (1991) 3–21

402 **Ulin, P,** African women and AIDS: negotiating behavioural change, *Social science and medicine*, 34, 1 (1992) 63–73

403 **UNECA,** *African women in development: annotated bibliography.* Addis Ababa: UNECA, 1991, 36pp

404 **UNECA,** Case study on increasing women's access to credit through training in management and credit techniques, *Rural progress*, 10, 2 (1991) 27–48

Geography, human

405 **Chapman, G P, Baker, K M,** (eds), *The changing geography of Africa and the Middle East.* London: Routledge, 1992, 252pp

406 **Darkoh, M B K,** (ed), *African river basins and dryland crises.* Uppsala: Uppsala University, Dept. of Human and Physical Geography, 1992, 168pp

407 **Darkoh, M B K,** Introduction: African river basins at risk, in Darkoh M B K (ed), *African river basins (entry 406)*, 1–19

408 **Gould, W T S,** Population mobility, in Gleave M B (ed),

Tropical African development (entry 147), 284–314

409 Mohammed Salih, M, African dryland crisis and river basins: an overview, in Darkoh M B K (ed), *African river basins (entry 406)*, 13–20

410 Riverson, J, et al, *Rural roads in subsaharan Africa: lessons from World Bank experience.* Washington: World Bank, 1991, 48pp

411 Stahl, M, Issues for social science research focussing on dryland dynamics in Africa, in Hjort af Ornas A (ed), *Security in African drylands (entry 1025)*, 65–80

412a Zinyama, L M, Agricultural land use theory and its application with reference to Africa, *Geographical education magazine*, 14, 2 (1991) 23–40

Geography, physical

412 Gastellu-Etchegorry, J P (ed), *Satellite remote sensing.* Washington: World Bank, 1990

413 Hamilton, A C, Taylor, D, History of climate and forests in tropical Africa during the last 8 million years, *Climatic change*, 19, 1/2 (1991) 65–78

414 Maley, J, The African rain forest vegetation and palaeoenvironments during late Quaternary, *Climatic change*, 19, 1/2 (1991) 79–98

415 Neff, J W, Africa: geographic preface, in Gordon A & D ((eds)), *Understanding contemporary Africa (entry 9)*, 7–20

416 Pointet, T, Remote sensing applied to hydrogeology through case studies, in Gastellu-Etchegorry J P (ed), *Satellite remote sensing (entry 412))*, 83–91

417 Reeve, W H, *Hammer, compass and traverse wheel: a geologist in Africa.* Ely: Pentland Press, 1992,

142pp

Health & welfare services

418 Archampong, E Q, *Medical education and national development in Africa.* Accra: Ghana Academy of Arts and Sciences, 1990, 70pp

419 Desmazières, J F, Aspects institutionels de la coopération en matière de santé, *Mondes et cultures*, 50, 1 (1990) 89–101

420 Huyghe-Mauro, A, Richez, N, La dimension sociale dans les politiques d'ajustement structurel en Afrique subsaharienne, *Mondes en développement*, 18, 71 (1990) 59–64

421 Joo, S, *Krakheiten der Armut. Perspektiven der Gesundheitsplanung in Afrika.* Berlin: Reimer, 1990, 95pp

422 Korte, R, et al, Financing health services in subsaharan Africa: options for decision makers during adjustment, *Social science and medicine*, 34, 1 (1992) 1–9

423 Macgregor, J, Towards human-centred development: primary health care in Africa, *Africa insight*, 21, 3 (1991) 145–52

424 Ogbu, O, Gallagher, M, Public expenditures and health care in Africa, *Social science and medicine*, 34, 6 (1992) 615–24

425 Soola, E O, Communication and education as vaccine against the spread of AIDS in Africa, *Africa media review*, 5, 3 (1991) 33–40

426 Turshen, M, US aid to AIDS in Africa, *Review of African political economy*, 55 (1992) 95–101

427 van der Geest, S, Is paying for health care culturally acceptable in subsaharan Africa? Money and tradition, *Social science and medicine*, 34, 6 (1992) 667–73

428 von Braun, J, Social security in subsaharan Africa: reflections on policy challenges, in Ahmed E et al (eds), *Social security in developing countries* (Oxford: Clarendon, 1991), 395–414

History, general

see also: 376

429 Ajayi, J F A, Peel, J D Y, (eds), *People and empires in African history: essays in memory of Michael Crowder.* London: Longman, 1992, 254pp

430 Ampedu, C, Das Afrikabild in der deutschen Ethnologie: eine Analyse des Werkes von Heinrich Barth, in Heise K F & Kyaw Tha Tun (eds), *Traditionelles Wissen und Modernisierung* (Gottingen: Afrikanisch-Asiaticshe Studentenförderung, 1991), 7–42

432 Büttner, T, The development of African historical studies in East Germany: an outline and selected bibliography, *History in Africa,* 19, (1992) 133–146

433 Copans, J, Entretien avec Elikia M'Bololo, *Politique africaine,* 46 (1992) 155–59

434 Coquery-Vidrovitch, C, Histoire et historiographie du politique en Afrique: la nécessité d'une relecture critique (à propos de la démocratie), *Politique africaine,* 46 (1992) 31–40

435 Fetter, B, Pitfalls in the application of demographic insights to African history, *History in Africa,* 19, (1992) 299–308

436 Forbes, E, African resistance to enslavement: the nature and the evidentiary record, *Journal of Black studies,* 23, 1 (1992) 39–59

437 Fuglestad, F, The Trevor-Roper trap or the imperialism of history: an essay, *History in Africa,* 19, (1992) 309–326

438 Harding, L, *Einführung in das Studium der afrikanischen Geschichte.* Munster: Lit, 1992, 177pp

439 Hugon, A, *L'Afrique des explorateurs: vers les sources du Nil.* Paris: Gallimard, 1991, 176pp

440 Jean, C M, *Behind the eurocentric veils: the search for African realities.* Amherst: University of Massachusetts Press, 1991, 113pp

441 M'Bokolo, E, et al, *Afrique noire: histoire et civilisations. II: xix et xx siècles.* Paris: Hatier-Aupelf, 1992, 576pp

442 Nowak, B, Jan Czekanowski and his version of oral traditions of the interlacrustine region peoples, in Pilaszewicz S & Rzewuski, E (eds), *Unwritten testimonies (entry 447),* 151–66

443 Ogot, B A, Reflections on an African experience, *Journal of African history,* 33, 3 (1992) 477–82 (review article)

444 Ogutu M A, Kenyanchui, S S, *An introduction to African history.* Nairobi: Nairobi UP, 1991, 310pp

445 Ohaegbulam, F U, *Towards an understanding of the African experience from historical and contemporary perspectives.* Lanham: University Press of America, 1990, 285pp

446 O'Toole, T, The historical context, in Gordon A & D (eds), *Understanding contemporary Africa (entry 9),* 21–49

447 Pilaszewicz, S, Rzewuski, E, (eds), *Unwritten testimonies of the African past.* Warsaw: Institute of Oriental Studies, University of Warsaw, 1991, 226pp

448 Pratt, M L, *Imperial eyes: travel writing and transculturation.* London: Routledge, 1992, 257pp

449 Thomas-Emeagwali, G, African historiography, gender and technology, in Thomas-Emeagwali G (ed), *Science and technology in Nigeria (entry 450),* 1–16

450 Thomas-Emeagwali, G, (ed), *Science and technology in African history, with case studies from*

Nigeria, Sierra Leone, Zimbabwe and Zambia. Lewiston: Mellen, 1992, 204pp

451 Wamba-dia-Wamba, E, L'autodétermination des peuples et le statut de l'histoire, *Politique africaine,* 46 (1992) 7–14

History, early

452 Frajzyngier, Z Ross, W C, Methodological issues in applying linguistics to the study of prehistory, in Pilaszewicz S & Rzewuski, E (eds), *Unwritten testimonies (entry 447),* 21–44

453 Froment, A, Origine et évolution de l'homme dans la pensée de Cheikh Anta Diop: une analyse critique, *Cahiers d'études africaines,* 31, 1/2 (1991) 29–64

454 Jacob, C, Aux confins de l'humanité: peuples et paysages africains dans le *Périple d'Hannon, Cahiers d'études africaines,* 31, 1/2 (1991) 9–27

455 Jacquot, A, Le nom de la houe dans les langues bantoues du nord-ouest: implications historiques, *Cahiers des sciences humaines,* 27, 3/4 (1991) 561–576

456 Jungraithmayr, H, Centre and periphery: Chadic linguistic evidence and its possible historical significance, in Pilaszewicz S & Rzewuski, E (eds), *Unwritten testimones (entry 447),* 61–82

History, C6–18th

457 Bontinck, F, Les Carmes Déchaux au royaume de Kongo (1584–1587), *Zaïre-Afrique,* 262, (1992) 112–123

458 Thornton, J, *Africa and the Africans in the making of the Atlantic world 1400–1680.* Cambridge: Cambridge University Press, 1992, 411pp

459 Tolmacheva, M A, Ptolemy's

east Africa in early medieval Arab geography, *Journal for the history of Arabic science,* 9, 1/2 (1991) 31–43

History, C19th

see also: 464, 989

460 Ewald, J J, Slavery in Africa and the slave traders from Africa, *American historical review,* 97, 2 (1992) 465–85

461 Intartaglia, C, Scaramella, C, Alcune lettere inedite nell'archivo della Societa Africana d'Italia, *Africa (Rome),* 47, 2 (1992) 237–62

462 Mentan, N T, Overview of French imperial ideology in Africa, *African review,* 16, 1/2 (1989) 72–81

463 Perrier, J, *Vent d'avenir: le Cardinal Lavigerie (1925–1892).* Paris: Karthala, 1992, 160pp

464 Twaddle, M (ed), *Imperialism, the state, and the Third World,* London: British Academic Press, 1992, 292pp

History, C20th

see also: 644

465 Adotevi, S S, *De Gaulle et les africains.* Paris: Chaka, 1990, 185pp

466 Ageron, C R, Michel, M, (eds), *L'Afrique noire francophone: l'heure des indépendances.* Paris: Ed. CNRS, 1992, 729pp

467 Anderson, D, Killingray, D, (eds), *Policing and decolonisation: nationalism, politics and the police.* Manchester: Manchester UP, 1992, 227pp

468 Ansprenger, F, *Politische Geschichte Afrikas im 20. Jahrhundert.* Munich: Beck, 1992, 208pp

469 Cell, J W, *Hailey: a study in British imperialism.* Cambridge: CUP, 1992, 320pp

470 Colombani, O, *Mémoires coloniaux: la fin de l'empire française d'Afrique vue par les administrateurs*

coloniaux. Paris: La Découverte, 1991, 209pp

471 **Denis, P,** *L'armée française au Sahara de Bonaparte à 1990*. Paris: Harmattan, 1991, 319pp

472 **Digre, B,** *Imperialism's new clothes: the repartition of tropical Africa, 1914–1919*. New York: Lang, 1990, 225pp

473 **Geyser, O,** The visit of British Premier Harold Macmillan to Africa in the year 1960, *Journal for contemporary history*, 15, 2 (1990) 55–73

474 **Hargreaves, J D,** Habits of mind and forces of history: France, Britain and the decolonisation of Africa, in Twaddle M (ed), *Imperialism (entry 464)*, 207–19

475 **Herzog, J, Sebald, P,** Kolonialismus "von innen" - Überlegungen zur Bedeutung der Kolonialherrschaft für die Entwicklung afrikanischer Gesellschaften, *Asien, Afrika, Lateinamerika*, 19, 4 (1991) 730–743

476 **Kent, J,** *The internationalisation of colonialism: Britain, France and Black Africa 1939–1956*. Oxford: Clarendon, 1992, 365pp

477 **Mambo, R M,** Mittelafrika: the German dream of an African empire across Africa in the late 19th and early 20th centuries: an overview, *Transafrican journal of history*, 20 (1991) 161–80

478 **Mergner, G,** Die Macht der Wahrheit und des Mitleides: zur Geschichte der europäischen Kolonial-Mentalität, *Zeitschrift für Afrikastudien*, 13/14 (1992) 29–41

479 **Reinhard, W,** *Dritte Welt Afrika*. Stuttgart: Kohlhammer, 1990, 286pp

480 **Roberts, R, Mann, K,** Law in colonial Africa, in Mann K & Roberts, R (eds), *Law in colonial Africa (entry 684)*, 3–58

481 **Strobel, M,** *European women*

and the second British enpire. Bloomington: Indiana UP, 1991, 108pp

482 **Westfall, G,** *French colonial Africa: guide to official sources*. Oxford: Zell, 1992, 224pp

483 **Woodruff, W,** The decolonisation of Africa, in his *Concise history of the modern world* (Basingstoke: Macmillan, 1991), 185–200

484 **Young, C,** Africa's heritage of colonialism, *Transafrica forum*, 7, 4 (1991) 3–20

Industry & trade

see also: 605, 997, 1081

485 **Adedeji, A,** Africa's alternative framework and a new industrial stategy for Africa, *African development perspectives yearbook*, 2, (1990/91) 56–72

486 **Assaf, G B,** UNIDO's diagnostic surveys of industrial rehabilitation needs in Africa with emphasis on agro-based industries: an intergrated programme approach, *African development perspectives yearbook*, 2, (1990/91) 111–133

487 **Assaf, G B, Hesp, P,** Profiles of key branches of agro-industries in subsaharan Africa, *Industry and development*, 30, (1991) 1–41

488 **Bagachwa, M S D, Stewart, F,** Rural industries and rural linkages in subsaharan Africa, in Stewart F et al (eds), *Alternative development strategies (entry 223)*, 145–84

489 **Bhagavan, M R, Kerekezi, S,** (eds), *Energy management in Africa*. London: Zed, 1992, 180pp

490 **Coughlin, P, Anyang' Nyong'o, P,** (eds), *Industrialisation at bay: African experiences*. Nairobi:

491 **Courtant, J J,** (ed), *Le coton en Afrique de l'Ouest et du Centre*. Paris:

Documentation Française, 1991, 353pp

492 Fair, T J D, Jones, T, *The ports of subsaharan Africa and their hinterlands: an overview.* Pretoria: Africa Institute, 1991, 98pp

493 Fosu, A K, Effect of export instability on economic growth in Africa, *Journal of developing areas,* 26, 3 (1992) 323–32

494 Gahan, E, Computers for industrial management in Africa: an overview of issues, *Industry and development,* 31 (1992) 1–65

495 Griffiths, I L, Mining and manufacturing in tropical Africa, in Gleave M B (ed), *Tropical African development (entry 147),* 223–49

496 Hardy, C, The prospects for intra-regional trade growth in Africa, in Stewart F et al (eds), *Alternative development strategies (entry 223),* 426–44

497 Helmschrott, H, et al, *Afrika südlich der Sahara: trotz Rohstoffreichtum in die Armut.* Munich: Weltforum, 1990, 215pp

498 Herbert-Copley, B, Technical change in African industry: reflections on IDRC supported research, *Canadian journal of development studies,* 13, 2 (1992) 231–249

499 Hodder, B W, Gleave, M B, Transport, trade and development in tropical Africa, in Gleave M B (ed), *Tropical African development (entry 147),* 250–83

500 Kavuluvulu, K, The informal sector: panacea, malaise, or cul-de-sac?, *Southern Africa political & economic monthly,* 3, 12 (1990) 3–14

501 Knight, J B, Public enterprises and industrialisation in Africa, in Stewart F et al (eds), *Alternative development strategies (entry 223),* 321–35

502 Kordylas, J M, Agro-technology information and

Africa-centred development, *Issue,* 20, 1 (1992) 54–60

503 Labazée, P, Présentation, *Cahiers d'études africaines,* 31, 4 (1991) 435–46

504 Labazée, P, Un terrain anthropologique à explorer: l'entreprise africaine, *Cahiers d'études africaines,* 31, 4 (1991) 533–52

505 Lall, S, Structural problems of African industry, in Stewart F et al (eds), *Alternative development strategies (entry 223),* 103–44

506 Leidholm, C, Small-scale industries in Africa: dynamic issues and the role of policy, in Stewart F et al (eds), *Alternative development strategies (entry 223),* 185–212

507 Leplaideur, A, Conflicts and alliances between the international marketing system and the traditional marketing system in Africa and Madagascar: the results of experience with rice and vegetables in six African countries, in Cammann L (ed), *Traditional marketing systems (entry 113),* 76–89

508 Lyakurwa, W M, *Trade policy and promotion in Subsaharan Africa: a review of experiences and issues.* Nairobi: Initiatives, 1991, 67pp

509 Marsden, K, African entrepreneurs - pioneers of development, *Small enterprise development,* 3, 2 (1992) 15–25

510 Moody-Stuart, G, Agribusiness, in Obasanjo O & d'Orville, H (eds), *Agricultural production and food security (entry 1040),* 87–92

511 Mwase, N, *The future of TAZARA in a post-apartheid southern Africa.* Bellville: Centre for Southern African Studies, University of the Western Cape, 1992, 28pp

512 Ndongko, W A, Commercialisation as an alternative to privatisation: prospects and problems, *Africa development*, 16, 3/4 (1991) 103–115

513 Ouane, H B, La libéralisation du commerce dans les pays africains: bilan et perspectives, *Afrique 2000*, 4, (1991) 83–93

514 Parfitt, T W, Lomé's forgotten agenda?: EEC industrial cooperation with Africa, *African development perspectives yearbook*, 2, (1990/91) 377–409

515 Ranganathan, V, Introduction, in Ranganathan V (ed), *Rural electrification (entry 1046)*, 1–16

516 Ranganathan, V, Policy recommendations and conclusions, in Ranganathan V (ed), *Rural electrification (entry 1046)*, 170–77

517 Saint-Alary, E, La transmission des chocs extérieurs au secteur manufacturier en Afrique subsaharienne, *Mondes en développement*, 19, 75/76 (1991) 43–48

518 Shaaeldin, E, New industrial strategies for Africa, *African development perspectives yearbook*, 2, (1990/91) 73–87

519 Siazon, D L, Evaluation of the first Industrial development Decade for Africa and proposals for the second, *African development perspectives yearbook*, 2, (1990/91) 88–110

520 Steel, W F, Key strategic issues for IDDA II, *African development perspectives yearbook*, 2, (1990/91) 134–143

521 Tiffin, S, Osotimehin, F, (eds), *New technologies and enterprise development in Africa*. Paris: OECD Development Centre, 1992, 212pp

522 Tvedten, I, Hersoug, B, (eds), *Fishing for development: small-scale fisheries in Africa*. Uppsala: SIAS, 1992, 227pp

523 van Dijk, M P, What relevance has the path of the NICs for Africa?, *African development*

perspectives yearbook, 2, (1990/91) 43–55

524 Wangwe, S, Building indigenous technological capacity in African industry: an overview, in Stewart F et al (eds), *Alternative development strategies (entry 223)*, 238–41

525 Wayem, J A, Country experiences with industrial adjustment lending in subsaharan Africa, *African development perspectives yearbook*, 2, (1990/91) 144–159

526 Wohlmuth, K, Towards a new industrial strategy for subsaharan Africa: an introduction, *African development perspectives yearbook*, 2, (1990/91) 3–29

527 World Bank, *Strategy for African mining*. Washington: World Bank, 1992, 95pp

International economic relations

see also: 69, 204, 240, 511, 514

528 Abbate, F, Tran-Nguyen, A N, Official debt reduction: a comparative analysis of the Toronto options, the UK proposal and the Netherlands initiative, *African development review*, 3, 2 (1991) 163–72

529 Abdelli-Pasquier, F, *La Banque arabe pour le développement en Afrique et la coopération arabo-africaine*. Paris: Harmattan, 1992, 254pp

530 Aboyade, O, *Selective closure in African economic relations*. Lagos: NIIA, 1990, 21pp

531 Abubakar, M C, Ubogu, R E, An overview of intra-African trade during the last two decades: problems and prospects, *Economica internazionale*, 43, 4 (1990) 297–314

532 Alibert, J, Les mutations du grand commerce européen, *Afrique contemporaine*, 164 (1992) 81–87

533 **Anglarill, H B,** *Africa, teorias y practicas de la cooperacion economica.* Beunos Aries: Belgrano, 1991, 527pp

534 **Anon,** GATTastrophe?: Africa's trade options after the Uruguay round, *Southern african economist,* 4, 1 (1991) 5–16

535 **Barbier, J P,** Des marchés protégés aux marchés libres, *Afrique contemporaine,* 164 (1992) 99–108

536 **Barratt-Brown, M, Tiffen, P,** *Short changed: Africa and world trade.* London: Pluto, 1992, 220pp

537 **Bondzi-Simpson, P E,** Transnational corporations in Africa: a framework for regional regulatory arrangements, in Bondzi-Simpson P E (ed), *The law and economic development in the Third World* (New York: Prager, 1992), 83–111

538 **Cedergren, J Oden, B,** *In the wake of crisis: changes in development assistance to the poorest African nations.* Stockholm: SIDA, 1881, 48pp

539 **Cesoni, M L,** Les routes des drogues: explorations en Afrique subsaharienne: état des lieux pour une approche critique, *Revue tiers monde,* 33, 131 (1992) 645–71

540 **Chikeka, C O,** *Britain, France and the new African states: a study of post-independence relationships.* Lewiston: Mellen, 1990, 244pp

541 **Collier, P,** European Monetary Union and '1992': opportunities for Africa, *World economy,* 15, 5 (1992) 633–43

542 **Coussy, J,** Inter-African integration and protection policies: unavoidable falure or missed opportunities?, in Fontaine J M (ed), *Foreign trade reforms (entry 550),* 199–220

543 **Coussy, J, et al,** *Programme d'ajustement structurel et Intégration régionale en Afrique sub-saharienne:* rapport d'étude. Paris: Ministère de la Coopération, 1991, 365pp

544 **Coussy, J, Hugon, P,** *Intégration régionale et ajustement structurel en Afrique sub-saharienne.* Paris: Documentation francaise, 1992, 306pp

545 **Davenport, M,** Africa and Project 1992, in Sideri S & Sengup[ta, J (eds), *The 1992 Single European Market in the Third World* (London: Cass, 1992), 167–95

546 **Davenport, M,** Africa and the unimportance of being preferred, *Journal of Common Market studies,* 30, 2 (1992) 233–251

547 **El Malki, H,** L'Afrique et le système international, *Africa development,* 15, 3/4 (1990) 7–19

548 **Evans, D,** Import controls and the sequencing of trade policy reform, with special reference to Africa, in Fontaine J M (ed), *Foreign trade reforms (entry 550),* 79–92

549 **Fajana, O,** *Europe 1992: implications for Africa.* Lagos: Friedrich Ebert Foundation, 1990, 40pp

550 **Fontaine, J M,** (ed), *Foreign trade reforms and development strategy.* London: Routledge, 1992, 304pp

551 **Fottorino, E,** *La piste blanche: l'Afrique sous l'emprise de la drogue.* Paris: Balland, 1991, 174pp

552 **Garson, J P,** Migration and interdependence: the migration system between France and Africa, in Kritz M M et al (eds), *International migration systems* (Oxford: Clarendon, 1992), 80–93

553 **Green, R H,** *Macroeconomic aspects of commodity aid and counterpart funding in subsaharan Africa.* Brighton: Sussex University, IDS, 1991, 44pp

554 **Greenaway, D,** Export promotion in subsaharan Africa, in Milner C (ed), *Export promotion*

strategies: theory and evidence from developing counties (London: Harvester,1990), 268–84

555 **Gulhati, R,** Why stagnation of regional trade in eastern and southern Africa, *Africa quarterly,* 30, 3/4 (1990) 1–7

556 **Habicht-Ereler, S,** (ed), *'Afrikanische Alternativen' mit Hilfe der Europäer?* Loccum: Kirchliche Verwaltungsstelle Loccum, 1991, 272pp

557 **Harris, J A,** The anatomy of the Africa multinational conglomerate enterprise strategy in international development, *African review,* 16, 1/2 (1989) 113–31

558 **Husain, I, Underwood, J,** (eds), *African external finance in the 1990s.* Washington: World Bank, 1992, 200pp

559 **Idris, A K,** International investment capital and the future of growth in Africa, *Nigerian journal of international affairs,* 17, 1 (1991) 56–79

560 **Jamal, T,** *Economic and technical cooperation between India and Africa.* Bombay: Popular, 1992, 165pp

561 **Jouve, P, de Milly, H,** *Compétivité du cacao africain: analyse du marché mondial et des principaux producteurs.* Paris: Ministère de la Coopération, 1991, 279pp

562 **Kappel, R,** Delinking Africa?: African cooperation perspectives with the European communities, *African development perspectives yearbook,* 2, (1990/91) 344–376

563 **Kisanga, E J,** *Industrial and trade cooperation in eastern and southern Africa.* Aldershor: Avebury, 1991, 262pp

564 **Klegnare, S,** Essai de prospective des conventions de Lomé, *Revue congolaise de droit,* 9 (1991) 43–60

565 **Kodjo, E,** De la nécessité de la coopération régionale en Afrique, *Afrique 2000,* 3 (1990) 25–37

566 **Konaté, M T,** L'Uruguay round: les principaux enjeux et l'Afrique, *Afrique 2000,* 4, (1991) 71–81

567 **Kouassi, R N,** Note sur l'évolution de la structure du financement extérieur de l'Afrique subsaharienne, *Africa development,* 16, 3/4 (1991) 143–62

568 **Krämer, M,** Afrika als Partner der deutschen Aussenwirtschaft, *Afrika Jahrbuch 1991,* 56–63

569 **Laishley, R,** Commodity prices deal blow to Africa, *Africa recovery,* 6, 1 (1992) 1, 8–10

570 **Langhammer, R J, et al,** *Die 'Preferential Trade Area in Eastern and Southern Africa' (PTA): ein Einstieg zur ersten grossen Freihandelzone in Schwarzafrika?* Munich: Weltforum, 1990, 167pp

571 **Lelart, M,** Le Fonds Monetaire Internationale et la dette africaine, *Mondes en développement,* 18, 71 (1990) 49–58

572 **Liniger-Goumaz, M,** *L'Afrique à refaire: vers un impôt planétaire.* Paris: Harmattan, 1992, 159pp

573 **Lopes, C,** Uma perspectiva histórica da cooperaçïo técnica em Africa, *Soronda,* 11, (1991) 39–54

574 **Lopes, C,** Une perspective historique de la cooperation technique en Afrique, in Thomas-Emeagwali G (ed), *Science and technology in African history (entry 3487),* 184–201

575 **Mackie, J,** Multiplying microlevel inputs to government structures, in Edwards M & Hulme, D (eds), *Making a difference: NGOs and development in a changing world* (London: Earthscan, 1992), 70–77

576 **Mansoor, A,** Experiences of economic integration in subsaharan Africa: lessons for a fresh start,

African development perspectives yearbook, 2, (1990/91) 420–452

577 **Martin, M,** *The crumbling facade of African debt negotiations.* Basingstoke: Macmillan, 1992, 391pp

578 **Massiera, A, Pagacz, L,** *L'Europe renforce sa coopération: Lomé IV.* Paris: Harmattan, 1992, 168pp

579 **McLean, W,** The urgency of international action in Africa, *African development review*, 3, 2 (1991) 173–78

580 **Mengisteab, K,** Export-import responses to devaluation in subsaharan Africa, *Africa development*, 16, 3/4 (1991) 26–43

581 **Monaldi, V Netter, K,** Counterpurchase: a potential instrument for debt relief in selected African countries, *Savings and development*, 15, 4 (1991) 333–348

582 **Mukonoweshuro, E G,** French commercial interests in non-francophone Africa, *Africa quarterly*, 30, 1/2 (1990) 13–21

583 **Mukonoweshuro, E G,** Japanese commercial interests in contemporary Africa, *International relations*, 10, 3 (1991) 251–65

584 **Mullei, A K,** Les différents aspects du problèmes de la dette extérieure de l'Afrique: rédefinitions du role du Club de Londres, *African development review*, 3, 2 (1991) 155–62

585 **Nash, J,** An overview of trade policy reform, with implications for subsaharan Africa, in Fontaine J M (ed), *Foreign trade reforms (entry 550)*, 46–78

586 **Ndongko, W A,** Labour migration and regional economic cooperation and integration in Africa, *Labour and society*, 16, 3 (1991) 231–49

587 **Ofstad, A, et al,** Towards a 'development contract': a new model for international agreements with African countries? Bergen: Chr Michelsen Institute, 1991, 13pp

588 **Ogunsade, F L, Gleason, P,** *IMF assistance to subsaharan Africa.* Washington: IMF, 1992, 25pp

589 **O'Quin, P,** La lassitude des bailleurs de fonds, *Afrique contemporaine*, 164 (1992) 224–44

590 **Pelletier, J,** Les grandes orientations du Ministère de la Coopération et du Développement, *Mondes et cultures*, 50, 1 (1990) 103–115

591 **Prouvez, N,** Les relations ACP-CEE dans le contexte de 1992 et de Lomé IV, *African journal of international and comparative law*, 2, 2 (1990) 249–281

592 **Raffer, K, Salih, M A M** (eds), *The least-developed and the oil-rich Arab states.* Basingstoke, Macmillan, 1992, 264pp

592a **Riddell, R C,** European aid to subsaharan Africa: performance in the 1980s and future prospects, *European journal of development research*, 4, 1 (1992) 59–80

593 **Saasa, O S,** (ed), *Joining the future: economic integration and cooperation in Africa.* Nairobi: ACTS, 1991, 168pp

594 **Sall, A,** The role of aid agencies in the role of grass-root organizations and human development in Africa: problems and perspectives, *Journal of the African Association for Literacy and Adult Education*, 5, 4 (1991) 39–46

595 **Scott, G E,** Transfers, economic structure and the vulnerability of the African economy, *Journal of developing areas*, 26, 2 (1992) 213–38

596 **Sech, B,** Optimal economic policy and the cost of Euro-credit loans, in Roe A R et al (eds) *Instruments of economic policy (entry 341)*, 169–84

597 **Severino, M,** La composante

financière de l'évolution institutionelle de nos partenaires africains de la France, *Mondes et cultures*, 50, 1 (1990) 35–57

598 Sideri, S, External financial flows: the case of Africa, *African review of money finance and banking*, 1 (1992) 89–115

599 Staewen, C, *Kulturelle und psychologische Bedingungen der Zussamenarbeit mit Afrikanem.* Munich: Weltforum, 1991, 257pp

600 Stevens, C, L'avenir des exportations africaines, *Eco*, 10 (1991) 39–49

601 Tevera, D S, What's the role of international trade in African development?, *Geographical education magazine*, 14, 1 (1991) 25–31

602 Theodoropoulos, C, Bilateral agreements on economic and technical co-operation between CMEA and African states: the experience of the 40-year period 1949–1989, *African journal of international and comparative law*, 2, 3 (1990) 456–478

603 Truett, D B, Truett, L J, Nonprimary exports of African LDCs: have trade preferences helped?, *Journal of developing areas*, 26, 4 (1992) 457–74

604 Ukpabi, C, *Doing business in Africa: myths and realities.* Amsterdam: Royal Tropical Institute, 1990, 63pp

605 UNCTAD, *Africa's commodity problems: towards a solution?* Geneva: UNCTAD, 1992, 161pp

606 Wall, T, Soviet demise brings Africa new challenges, *Africa recovery*, 6, 1 (1992) 14–17

International relations

see also: 356, 465, 836

607 Agbobli, A K, Herman Cohen parle de l'Afrique: interview du secrétaire d'État adjoint américain chargé des Affaires africaines, *Afrique 2000*, 4, (1991) 5–9

608 Ayittey, G B N, Africa in the post-communist world, *Problems of communism*, 41, 1 (1992) 207–212

609 Babu, A M, Africa's interpretation of Soviet policy since perestroika: facing the challenge, *Africa contemporary record 1988/89*, (1992) A169–75

610 Bach, D C, Euro-African relations since the end of the Cold War, in Caron B et al (eds), *Democratic transition in Africa (entry 817)*, 29–37

611 Beaux, N, *Pour une nouvelle alliance Afrique-Europe.* Paris: Futuribles, 1992, 125pp

612 Botha, P du T, The Soviet assessment of socialist orientation and the African response, in Kanet R E, et al (eds), *Soviet foreign policy in transition* (Cambridge: CUP, 1992), 180–95

613 Brüne, S, Unter Reformdruch: die französische Afrikapolitik südlich des Sahara, *Afrika Jahrbuch 1991*, 37–46

614 Capron, M, (ed), *L'Europe face au sud: les relations avec le monde arabe et africain.* Paris: Harmattan, 1991, 221pp

615 Chafer, T, French African policy: towards change, *African affairs*, 91, 362 (1992) 37–51

616 Chazan, N, LeVine, V T, Africa and the Middle East: patterns of convergence and divergence, in Harbeson J W & Rothchild, D (eds), *Africa in world politics (entry 625)*, 202–27

617 Clough, M W, *Free at last? US policy toward Africa and the end of the Cold War.* New York: Council on Foreign Relations, 1992, 143pp

618 Clough, M, The United States and Africa: the policy of cynical disengagement, *Current history*, 91, 565 (1992) 193–198

619 Darman, M, Les Americains

noirs et l'Afrique aujourd'hui: quelques points de repère, *Afrique contemporaine,* 162 (1992) 27–33

620 **Desfosses, H,** The USSR and Africa in 1988: 'new thinking' and conflict resolution, *Africa contemporary record 1988/89,* (1992) A146–63

621 **Foroutan, F,** *Regional integration in subsaharan Africa: experience and prospects.* Washington: World Bank, 1992, 42pp

622 **Fulani, S A,** L'Afrique et le désarmement nucléaire régional, *Afrique 2000,* 9 (1992) 15–26

623 **Glaser, A Smith, S,** *Ces messieurs d'Afrique. Le Paris - village du continent noir.* Paris: Calmann-Levy, 1992, 235pp

624 **Harbeson, J W, Rothchild, D (eds),** Africa in post-Cold War international politics: changing agendas, in Harbeson J W & Rothchild, D (eds), *Africa in world politics (entry 625),* 1–15

625 **Harbeson, J W, Rothchild, D,** (eds), *Africa in world politics.* Boulder: Westview, 1991, 341pp

626 **Hempstone, S,** Diplomat outlines American foreign policy in Africa, *Nairobi law monthly,* 33 (1991) 25–28

627 **Herbst, J,** The United States and Africa: issues for the future, in Harbeson J W & Rothchild, D (eds), *Africa in world politics (entry 625),* 161–78

628 **Herbst, J,** The United States in Africa 1988–89: a very good year for constructive engagement, *Africa contemporary record 1988/89,* (1992) A134–45

629 **Hocker, E C,** Nation-building or nation-destroying: foreign powers and intelligence agencies in Africa, *Ufahamu,* 18, 3 (1989/90) 35–51

630 **Hoffmeier, R,** Deutsch-afrikanisch Beziehungen, *Afrika Jahrbuch 1991,* 19–25

631 **Houndekindo, G,** Le secrétaire général de l'Organisation de l'unité africaine, *Afrique 2000,* 4, (1991) 37–54

632 **Ihonvbere, J O,** The Gulf crisis and Africa: implications for the 1990s, *International studies,* 29, 3 (1992) 307–26

633 **Johnson, J,** Aid and good governance in Africa, *Round table,* 320 (1991) 395–400

634 **Kühne, W,** After the end of the cold war, *Economics,* 45, (1992) 7–28

635 **Kum'a Ndumbe,** Afrique-Allemagne: un point de vue historique, *Afrique 2000,* 4, (1991) 11–35

636 **Legum, C,** Afro-Arab relations: the elusive search for integrated institutions, *Africa contemporary record 1988/89,* (1992) A107–114

637 **Legum, C,** British policy in Africa: a decade of Thatcherism, *Africa contemporary record 1988/89,* (1992) A124–33

638 **Light, M,** Moscow's retreat from Africa, *Journal of communist studies,* 8, 2 (1992) 21–40 (also in entry 860)

639 **Mulikita, M N,** Africa overseas: Brazil's African heritage re-examined, *Internationales Afrikaforum,* 28, 1 (1992) 55–65

640 **Okoth, P G,** The African style of foreign policy: instruments of diplomacy, *African review,* 16, 1/2 (1989) 54–71

641 **Onwuka, R I,** *The anguish of dependent regionalism in Africa.* Ile-Ife: Awolowo University Press, 1991, 49pp

642 **Otayek, R,** Le monde islamo-arabe et l'Afrique noire: désintégration par le haut, intégration par le bas?, *Maghreb Machrek,* 134 (1991) 41–53

643 **Ottaway, M,** The Soviet Union and Africa, in Harbeson J W &

Rothchild, D (eds), *Africa in world politics (entry 625)*, 228–45

644 Pean, P, *L'homme de l'ombre. Eléments d'enquête autour du Jacques Foccart.* Paris: Fayard, 1990, 593pp

645 Peters, J, *Israel and Africa: the problematic friendship.* London: British Academic Press, 1992, 210pp

646 Ravenhill, J, Africa and Europe: the dilution of a 'special relationship', in Harbeson J W & Rothchild, D (eds), *Africa in world politics (entry 625)*, 179–201

647 Rifrac, S, De La Baule à Libreville: de la 'démocratie' à la 'gestion rigoureuse', *Cahiers du Communisme*, 68, 11 (1992) 66–71

648 Rossi, G, Africa facing the end of the Cold War, *Rivista di studi politica internazionale*, 49, 3 (1992) 384–92

649 Rothchild, D, Regional peacemaking in Africa: the role of the great powers as facilitators, in Harbeson J W & Rothchild, D (eds), *Africa in world politics (entry 624)*, 284–306

650 Sada, H, La France et la sécurité africain, *Afrique 2000*, 3 (1990) 19–24

651 Segal, G, China and Africa, *Annals*, 519 (1992) 115–26

652 Wauthier, C, France's year in Africa: the more things change, *Africa contemporary record 1988/89*, (1992) A115–23

653 Webber, M, Soviet policy in subsaharan Africa; the final phase, *Journal of modern African studies*, 30, 1 (1992) 1–30

654 Wright, S, The foreign policy of Africa, in Macridis R C (ed), *Foreign policy in world politics* (Englewood Cliffs: Prentice-Hall, 1992), 330–56

655 Young, C, The heritage of colonialism, in Harbeson J W & Rothchild, D (eds), *Africa in world politics (entry 625)*, 19–38

656 Zartman, I W, Inter-African negotiations, in Harbeson J W & Rothchild, D (eds), *Africa in world politics (entry 624)*, 268–83

Labour & manpower

see also: 315

657 Adepoju, A, Binational communities and labour circulation in subsaharan Africa, in Papademetriou D G & Martin, PL (eds), *The unsettled relationship* (Westport: Greenwood, 1991), 45–64

658 Aosa, E, *Managerial involvement, training and organisational effectiveness in an African context.* Glasgow: Strathclyde University, International Business Unit, 1992, 18pp

659 Caire, G, Les problèmes se l'emploi dans l'Afrique subsaharienne, *Mondes en développement*, 18, 71 (1990) 35–47

660 Cornia, A G, de Jong, J, Policies for the revitalisation of human resource development, in Cornia A G et al (eds), *Africa's recovery (entry 124)*, 246–71

661 Gleave, M B, Human resources and development, in Gleave M B (ed), *Tropical African development (entry 147)*, 93–121

662 Henry, A, Vers un modèle du management africain, *Cahiers d'études africaines*, 31, 4 (1991) 447–73

663 Jamal, V, Wages and implications for structural adjustment: how to survive in Africa?, *African development perspectives yearbook*, 2, (1990/91) 247–257

664 JASPA, *The challenge of employment planning in Africa.* Geneva/ Addis Ababa: ILO-JASPA, 1990, 148pp

665 JASPA, *Strategies for employment creation in Africa: report of the*

regional workshop. Addis Ababa: JASPA, 1990, 135pp

666 Taylor, H, Public sector personnel management in three African countries: current problems and possibilities, *Public administration and development,* 12, 2 (1992) 193–207

Language

see also: 291, 734

667 Calvet, L-J, Le facteur urbain dans le devenir linguistique des pays africaines, le facteur linguistique dans la constitution des villes africaines, *Cahiers des sciences humaines,* 27, 3/4 (1991) 411–432

668 Djité, P G, Langues et développement en Afrique, *Afrique 2000,* 3 (1990) 97–109

669 Herbert, R K, (ed), *Language and society in Africa: the theory and practice of sociolinguistics.* Johannesburg: Witswatersrand University Press, 1992, 380pp

670 Laitin, D, *Language repertoires and state construction in Africa.* Cambridge: Cambridge University Press, 1992, 217pp

671 Sanneh, L, 'They stooped to conquer': vernacular translation and the socio-cultural factor, *Research in African literatures,* 23, 1 (1992) 95–106

672 Soyoye, F A, Adewole, L O, (eds), *In honour of Prof. Ayo Bamgbose.* Ile-Ife: Awolowo University, Dept. of African Languages, 1991, 182pp

Law

see also: 308, 774

673 Abun-Nasr, J, (ed), *Law, society and national identity in Africa.* Hamburg: Buske, 1990, 225pp

674 Ahmed, S, Context and precedents with reference to the development, division and management of Nile waters, in

Howell J P, Allan J A (eds), *The Nile (entry 1328),* 225–38

675 Ajavon, A, La protection des droits de l'homme dans les constitutions des États de l'Afrique noire francophone, *Revue juridique et politique,* 46, 1 (1992) 79–87

676 Akweenda, S, Preservation of customary rights in boundary treaties: recent practice and international law, *African journal of international and comparative law,* 2, 4 (1990) 539–557

677 Bello, M, The role of the judiciary in Commonwealth Africa, *Commonwealth judicial journal,* 9, 2 (1991) 9–17

678 Chanock, M, Paradigms, policies and property: a review of the customary law of land tenure, in Mann K & Roberts, R (eds), *Law in colonial Africa (entry 684),* 61–84

679 Dlamini, C R M, Towards a regional protection of human rights in Africa: the African Charter on Human Rights and Peoples' Rights, *The comparative and international law journal of southern Africa,* 24, 2 (1991) 189–203

680 Elias, T O, *Judicial process in the newer Commonwealth.* Lagos: University of Lagos Press, 1990, 272pp

681 Gherari, H, La Charte africaine des droits et du bien-être de l'enfant, *Etudes internationales,* 22, 4 (1991) 735–52

682 Gye-Wado, O, A comparative analysis of the institutional framework for the enforcement of human rights in Africa and western Europe, *African journal of international and comparative law,* 2, 2 (1990) 187–201

683 Jallow, H B, Hunt, P, *AIDS and the African Charter.* Banjul: African Centre for Democracy and Human Rights Studies, 1991, 28pp

684 Mann, K, Roberts, R (eds), *Law in colonial Africa.* London: Currey, 1991, 264pp

685a Meledje Djedjro, F, La révision des constitutions dans les états africains francophones, *Revue du droit public,* 108, 1 (1992) 111–34

685 Moyrand, R, Réfexions sur l'introduction de l'état de droit en Afrique noire francophone, *Revue internationale de droit comparé,* 43, 4 (1991) 853–78

686 Mutoy Mubiala, La Charte africaine des droits de l'homme et des peuples dix ans plus tard: plaidoyer pour l'institution d'une Cour Régionale, *Zaïre-Afrique,* 264, (1992) 197–202

687 Nagan, W P, African human rights process: a contextual policy-oriented approach, *Southwestern University law review,* 21, 1 (1992) 63–103

688 Ng'ong'ola, C G, The post-colonial era in in relation to land expropriation laws in Botswana, Malawi, Zambia and Zimbabwe, *International and comparative law quarterly,* 41, 1 (1992) 117–36

689 Nwabueze, B, Legal and institutional mechanisms for democratic transition, in Caron B et al (eds), *Democratic transition in Africa (entry 817),* 273–313

690 Okili, O, A review of treaties on consumptive utilisation of waters of Lake Victoria and Nile drainage basin, in Howell J P, Allan J A (eds), *The Nile (entry 1328),* 193–224

691 Selassie, A G, Ethnic identity and constitutional design for Africa, *Stanford journal of international law,* 29, 1 (192) 1–56

692 Sempasa, S L, Obstacles to international commercial arbitration in African countries, *International and comparative law quarterly,* 41, 2 (1992) 387–413

693 Thompson, B, Africa's Charter on children's rights: a normative break with cultural traditionalism, *International and comparative law quarterly,* 41, 2 (1992) 432–444

694a Tshiyembe Mwayila, Droit international humanitaire et l'avènement d'un état républicain, d'une armée nouvelle et d'une défense nationale: essai prospectif pour l'Afrique des années 2000, *Revue juridique et politique,* 46, 2 (1992) 191–200

Library - documentation

694 Altbach, P G (ed), *Publishing and development in the Third World.* Oxford: Zell, 1992, 441

695 Binns, M, The documentation of African research, *African research and documentation,* 56 (1991) 1–34

696 Lanne, B, Trente ans de *L'Afrique contemporaine, Afrique contemporaine,* 164 (1992) 253–63

697 Scheven, Y, Africana reference works: an annotated list of 1ist of 1991 titles, *African book publishing record,* 18, 2 (1992) 95–106

Literature

see also: 671, 745

698 Amuta, C, The revolutionary imperative in the contemporary African novel: Ngugi's *Petals of blood* and Armah's *The healers, Commonwealth novel in English,* 3, 2 (1990) 130–42

699 Anyidoho, K, Language and development strategy in a Pan-African literary experience, *Research in African literatures,* 23, 1 (1992) 45–63

700 Asobele, J T, La vigueur de la tradition orale africaine et ses influences sur les écrivains africains modernes, *Études germano-africaines*, 9, (1991) 19–27

701 **Awodoye, S A,** *The concept of land in the African novel.* Ibadan: Evans, 1990, 148pp

702 **Bouraoui, H,** Francophone Africa on two sides of the Sahara, *Bulletin of francophone Africa*, 1 (1992) 2–11

703 **Chukwuma, H,** *Accents in the African novel.* Enugu: New Generation Books, 1991, 95pp

704 **Cooper, B,** *To lay these secrets bare: evaluating African writing.* Cape Town: Philip, 1992, 197pp

705 **Emenyonu, E N,** (ed), *Literature and Black aesthetics.* Ibadan: Heinemann, 1990, 339pp

706 **Galle, E,** Indigenous embedments in Europhone African literature, *Commonwealth : essays and studies*, 14, 1 (1991) 16–20

707 **Ghezzi, C,** La letteratura africana in Italia: un caso a parte, *Africa (Rome)*, 47, 2 (1992) 275–86

708 **Görög-Karady, V,** (ed), *D'un conte...à un autre.* Paris CNRS: 1990, 603,

709 **Görög-Karady, V, et al,** *Bibliographie annotée: littérature orale d'Afrique noire.* Paris: Conseil international de la langue française, 1992, 367pp

710 **Harrow, K W,** (ed), *Faces of Islam in African literature.* London: Currey, 1991, 320pp.

710a **Harrow, K W,** Camara Laye, Cheikh Hamidou Kane, Tayeb Salih: three Sufi authors, in Harrow K H (ed), *Faces of Islam (entry 710)*, 262–97

711 **Hausser, M,** *Pour une poétique de la négritude. Tome 2.* Paris: Harmattan, 1992, 503pp

712 **Ikonne, C, et al,** (eds), *African literature and African historical experience.* Ibadan: Heinemann, 1991, 136pp

713 **Ikonne, C, et al,** (eds), *Children and literature in Africa.* Ibadan:

Heinemann, 1992, 219pp

714 **Isola, A,** The African writer's tongue, *Research in African literatures*, 23, 1 (1992) 17–26

715 **Joseph, G,** African literature, in Gordon A & D ((eds)), *Understanding contemporary Africa (entry 9)*, 251–81

716 **Julien, E,** *African novels and the question of orality.* Bloomington: Indiana UP, 1992, 180pp

717 **Kunene, D P,** African-language literature: tragedy and hope, *Research in African literatures*, 23, 1 (1992) 7-15

718 **Kunene, M,** Problems in African literature, *Research in African literatures*, 23, 1 (1992) 27–44

719 **Lang, G,** Through a prism darkly: 'orientalism' in European-language African writing, in Harrow K H (ed), *Faces of Islam (entry 710)*, 299–311

720 **Lindfors, B,** *Popular literatures in Africa.* Trenton: Africa World Press, 1991, 136pp

722 **Mazrui, A,** Relativism, universalism and the language of African literature, *Research in African literatures*, 23, 1 (1992) 65–72

723 **Midiohouan, G O, Dossou, M,** La nouvelle négro-africaine d'expression française pendant la période coloniale (1917–1960), *Afrique 2000*, 10 (1992) 87–108

724 **Mnthali, F,** Motif and mood in the African novel, *Marang*, 9, (1991) 54–73

725 **Mphande, L,** Ideophones and African verse, *Research in African literatures*, 23, 1 (1992) 117–29

726 **Nethersole, R (ed),** *Emerging literatures.* Bern: Lang, 1990, 197 pp

726a **Ndongo-Bidyogo, D,** Literatura y sociedad, *Africa 2000*, 15 (1991) 30–35

727 **Ngandu Nkashama, P,** *Littératures et écritures en langues*

africaines. Paris: Harmattan, 1992, 407pp

728 Nnolim, C E, *Approaches to the African novel: essays in analysis.* Port Harcourt: Saros, 1992, 208pp

729 Obiechina, E N, *Language and theme: essays on African literature.* Washington: Howard UP, 1990, 249pp

730 Obiechina, E, Parables of power and powerlessness: explorations in anglophone African fiction today, *Issue,* 20, 2 (1992) 17–25

731 Okpewho, I, *African oral literature: backgrounds, character and continuity.* Bloomington: Indiana UP, 1992, 340pp

732 Omotoso, K, Politics and African literature: a statement, *Mohlomi,* 6, (1990) 175–181

733 Owomoyela, O, Language, identity and social construction in African literatures, *Research in African literatures,* 23, 1 (1992) 83–94

734 Ruhumbika, G, The African-language policy of development: African national languages, *Research in African literatures,* 23, 1 (1992) 73–82

735 Volet, J-M, Romancières francophones d'Afrique noire: vingt ans d'activité littéraire à découvrir, *French review,* 65, 5 (1992) 765–773

736 Westley, D, *Choice of language and African literature: a bibliographic essay.* Boston: African Studies Centre, Boston University, 1990, 15pp

737 Westley, D, Choice of language and African literature: a bibliographic essay, *Research in African literatures,* 23, 1 (1992) 159–71

738 Wilentz, G, *Binding cultures: Black women writers in Africa and the diaspora.* Bloomington: Indiana

University Press, 1992, 141pp

739 Wilkinson, J, *Orpheus in Africa: fragmentation and renewal in the work of four African writers.* Rome: Bulzoni, 1990, 247pp

740 Wilkinson, J, *Talking with African writers: interviews with African poets, playwrights and novelists.* London: Currey, 1992, 220pp

741 Yewah, A O, Traditions, politics and African detective fiction, *Ufahamu,* 18, 3 (1989/90) 66–76

Media

see also: 374

742 Centre d'études sur le communication en Afrique, *Communication en Afrique à l'age post-moderne: autonomie et dépendances culturelles.* Brussels: Academia, 1992, 204pp

743 Dia, S, The many roles of communications and media in Africa, in *Voices from Africa 4 (entry 1064),* 65–78

744 Hawk, B G, (ed), *Africa's media image.* New York: Praeger, 1992, 268pp

745 Maja-Pearce, A, In pursuit of excellence: thirty years of the Heinemann African Writers' Series, *Research in African literatures,* 23, 4 (1992) 125–32

746 Martin, Robert, Building independent mass media in Africa, *Journal of modern African studies,* 30, 2 (1992) 331–40

747 Mukasa, S G, Towards pan-african cooperation in satellite communication: an analysis of the RASCOM project, *Africa media review,* 6, 2 (1992) 13–30

748 Mukasa, S G, Becker, L B, Toward an indigenized philosophy of communication: an analysis of African communication educational resources and needs,

Africa media review, 6, 3 (1992)
31–50

749 Prillaman, J, Books in
francophone Africa, in Altbach P
(ed), *Publishing and development
(entry 694))*, 199–210

750 Rathgeber, E M, African book
publishing: lessons from the 1980s,
in Altbach P (ed), *Publishing and
development (entry 694))*, 77–99

751 Tudesq, A J, *L'Afrique noire et
ses télévisions.* Paris: Anthropos,
1992, 340pp

752 Zell, H, Africa; the neglected
continent, in Altbach P (ed),
*Publishing and development (entry
694))*, 65–76

753 Zell, H, African publishing:
constraints and challenges and the
experience of African Books
Collective, in Altbach P (ed),
*Publishing and development (entry
694))*, 101–118

Medical

see also: 394, 402

754 Aaby, P, Overcrowding and
intensive exposure: major
determinants of variations in
measles mortality in Africa, in van
der Walle E et al (eds), *Mortality
and society (entry 771)*, 319–48

755 Agadzi, V K, *AIDS: the African
perspective of the killer disease.* Accra:
Ghana UP, 1990, 206pp

756 Ainsworth, M, et al, *Measuring
the impact of fatal adult illness in
subsaharan Africa: an annotated
household questionnaire.*
Washington: World Bank, 1992,
164pp

757 Barnett, T, Blaikie, P, *AIDS
in Africa.* London: Belhaven, 1992,
193pp

758 Barnett, T, Blaikie, P,
*Constructing coherence: doing research
on the impact of AIDS -
postmodernism or eclecticism.*
Norwich: University of East Anglia,

School of Development Studies,
1992, 33pp

759 Bledsoe, C H, Brandon, A,
Child fosterage and child mortality
in Subsaharan Africa: some
preliminary questions and answers,
in van der Walle E et al (eds),
Mortality and society (entry 771),
279–302

760 Caldwell, J C, et al,
Underreaction to AIDS in
subsaharan Africa, *Social science and
medecine*, 34, 11 (1992) 1169–82

761 Carael, M, Piot, P, The AIDS
epidemic in Subsaharan Africa, in
van der Walle E et al (eds),
Mortality and society (entry 771),
391–404

762 Feyisetan, B J, Adeokun, L A,
Impact of child care and disease
treatment on infant mortality, in
van der Walle E et al (eds),
Mortality and society (entry 771),
145–59

763 Gentilini, M, et al, *AIDS in
Africa: meeting the challenge through
training, education and prevention.*
York: York University, Centre for
Health Economics, 1992, 25pp

764 Hervouet, J P, Environnement
et grandes endémies: le poids des
hommes, *Afrique contemporaine*,
161 (1992) 155–167

765 Jakobveit, C, Vor die
Apokalypse? Sozioökonomische
und politische Auswirkungen von
AIDS in Afrika, *Afrika Jahrbuch
1991*, 64–72

766 Lallemand, S, et al, *Grossesse et
petite enfance en Afrique noire et à
Madagascar.* Paris: Harmattan,
1991, 136pp

767 Mbacké, C, van der Walle, E,
Socio-economic factors and use of
health services as determinants of
child mortality, in van der Walle E
et al (eds), *Mortality and society
(entry 771)*, 123–44

768 Mshigeni, K E, (ed),
Proceedings of an international

conference on traditional medical plants. Dar es Salaam: Dar es Salaam UP, 1991, 365pp

769 **Ndinya-Achola, J O,** A review of ethical issues in AIDS research, *East African medical journal,* 68, 9 (1991) 735–740

770 **Nyamwaya, D,** *African indigenous medecine: an anthropological perspective for policy makers and primary health care managers.* Nairobi: African Medical Research Foundation, 1991, 44pp

771 **van der Walle, E, et al,** (eds), *Mortality and society in subsaharan Africa.* Oxford: Clarendon, 1992, 450pp

772 **van Ginneken, J K, Teunissen, AW,** Morbidity and mortality from diarrhoeal diseases in children under age five in Subsaharan Africa, in van der Walle E et al (eds), *Mortality and society (entry 771),* 176–203

773 **Weeks, D C,** The AIDS pandemic in Africa, *Current history,* 91, 565 (1992) 208–213

Natural resources

774 **Amoussa, O H,** La protection de la faune en Afrique francophone: les limites d'une approche juridique, *Afrique contemporaine,* 161 (1992) 247–54

775 **Bassey, M W,** Renewable energy research and development in West and Central Africa, in Bhagavan M R & Karekezi, S (eds), *Energy for rural development* (London: Zed,1992), 89–107

776 **Devineau, J L, Guillaumet, J L,** Origine, nature et conservation des milieux naturels africains: le point de vue des botanistes, *Afrique contemporaine,* 161 (1992) 79–90

777 **Oesterdiekhoff, P,** *Dimensionen der Energiekrise in Afrika südich der Sahara.* Bremen: Institut für Weltwirtschaft und Internationales Management, 1991, 62pp

778 **Simpson, E B,** Energy resources, in Gleave M B (ed), *Tropical African development (entry 147),* 122–52

Planning

779 **Adams, W M,** *Wasting the earth: rivers, people and planning in Africa.* London: Earthscan, 1992, 256pp

780 **Darkoh, M B K,** Planning and land development in Africa: some reflections from the ringside, in Hjort af Ornas A (ed), *Security in African drylands (entry 1025),* 41–63

781 **de Valk, P,** State, decentralisation and participation, in de Valk P & Wekwete, K H (eds), *Decentralising (entry 5485),* 3–14

782 **de Valk, P,** Who sets the riules for decentralisation? Who wants to play the game?, in de Valk P & Wekwete, K H (eds), *Decentralising (entry 5485),* 255–68

783 **Gasper, D,** *Regional planning and planning education: implications of their changing enviroment and practice.* The Hague: ISS, 1990, 64pp

Politics

see also: 126, 193, 217, 782, 962, 990

784 **Adeyemi, B A,** Prospects for a nuclear-weapons-free zone in Africa, *Disarmament,* 14, 3 (1991) 97–111

785 **African Centre for Democracy and Human Rights Studies,** *Human rights in Africa.* Banjul: the Centre, 1991, 104pp

786 **Agbaje, A,** Culture, corruption and development, in *Voices from Africa 4 (entry 1064),* 41–52

787 **Agbaje, A,** A quarantine for the African state?, *Journal of modern African studies,* 29, 4 (1991) 723–27 (review article)

788 **Akindele, S T,** Democratic transition in Africa: a pyschological

perspective, in Caron B et al (eds), *Democratic transition in Africa (entry 817)*, 83–100

789 **Allen, C, et al,** Surviving democracy?, *Review of African political economy,* 54 (1992) 3–10

790 **Amuwo, K,** The international (and domestic) context of democratic transition in Africa: road blocks to democracy, in Caron B et al (eds), *Democratic transition in Africa (entry 817),* 3–27

791 **Anyang Nyng'o, P,** Accountability and civil society, in Doornbos M et al (eds), *Beyond conflict in the Horn (entry 1533),* 217–21

792 **Anyang' Nyong'o, P,** The one-party state and its apologists, in Anyang' Nyong'o P (ed), *30 years of independence (entry 101),* 1–8

793 **Arigbede, M O,** Popular participation by whom and how: towards a collective understanding of the concept, *Journal of African Association for Literacy and Adult Education,* 5, (1990) 14–23

794 **Ashworth, L, Fichardt, L,** Writers and human rights abuses in Africa, *Information trends,* 5, 1 (1992) 3–29

795 **Asibuo, S K,** Inertia in African public administration: an examination of some causes and remedies, *Africa insight,* 21, 4 (1991) 246–51

796 **Awua-Asamoa, M,** Implications and repercussions of the arms race in Africa, in NGLS (ed), *Voices from Africa 3 (entry 913),* 9–26

797 **Ayele, S O,** Human right in Africa: implication for democratic transition, in Caron B et al (eds), *Democratic transition in Africa (entry 817),* 101–110

798 **Baechler, J,** Des institutions démocratiques pour l'Afrique, *Revue juridique et politique,* 46, 2 (1992) 163–81

799 **Bakary, T D,** Pour une approche non-partisane de la démocratie en Afrique, *Afrique 2000,* 9 (1992) 27–35

800 **Balima, S A,** Réflexions sur l'Afrique et la démocratie, *Afrique 2000,* 11 (1992) 49–54

801 **Bangura, Y,** Authoritarian rule and democracy in Africa: a theoretical discourse, in Rudebeck L (ed), *When democracy makes sense (entry 931),* 69–104

802 **Bangura, Y,** Authoritarian rule and democracy in Africa: a theoretical discourse, in Gibbon P & Bangura, Y (eds), *Authoritarianism, democracy and adjustment (entry 850),* 39–82

803 **Bangura, Y, Gibbon, P,** Adjustment, authoritarianism and democracy in Subsaharan Africa, in Gibbon P & Bangura, Y (eds), *Authoritarianism, democracy and adjustment (entry 850),* 7–38

804 **Bashir, I L,** The new world order and socio-political transition in Africa in the 1990s and beyond, in Caron B et al (eds), *Democratic transition in Africa (entry 817),* 405–22

805 **Bayart, J F, et al,** *La politique par le bas en Afrique noire: contributions à une problématique de la démocratie.* Paris: Karthala, 1992, 268pp

806 **Bayart, J F, et al,** *La politique par le bas en Afrique noire: contributions à une problématique de la démocratie.* Paris: Karthala, 1992, 268pp

807 **Baynham, S,** Geopolitics, glasnost and Africa's second liberation: political and security implications for the continent, *Africa insight,* 21, 4 (1991) 263–68

808 **Baynham, S,** Security issues in Africa: the imperial legacy, domestic violence and the military, *Africa insight,* 21, 3 (1991) 180–89

809 **Beau, N,** Rached Ghannouchi penseur et tribun, *Cahiers de l'Orient,* 27, (1992) 45–52

810 **Beckman, B,** Empowerment or repression? The World Bank and the politics of African adjustment, in Gibbon P & Bangura, Y (eds), *Authoritarianism, democracy and adjustment (entry 850),* 83–105

811 **Beckman, B,** Whose democracy? Bourgeois versus popular democracy, in Rudebeck L (ed), *When democracy makes sense (entry 931),* 131–50

812 **Bluwey, G K,** Democracy at bay: the frustrations of African liberals, in Caron B et al (eds), *Democratic transition in Africa (entry 817),* 39–49

813 **Bratton, M, Rothchild, D,** The institutional bases of governance in Africa, in Hyden G & Bratton, M (eds), *Governance and politics (entry 864),* 263–84

814 **Bratton, M, van der Walle, N,** Toward governance in Africa: popular demands and state responses, in Hyden G & Bratton, M (eds), *Governance and politics (entry 864),* 27–55

815 **Brittain, V,** Africa: a political audit, *Race and class,* 34, 1 (1992) 41–49

816 **Cardoso, C,** Militarismo e crise econômica em Africa, *Africa (São Paulo),* 14/15 (1991/92) 119–42

817 **Caron, B, et al,** (eds), *Democratic transition in Africa.* Ibadan: CREDU, 1992, 436pp

818 **Chabal, P,** *Power in Africa: an essay in political interpretation.* Basingstoke: Macmillan, 1992 (2nd edition), 311pp

819 **Chazan, N,** Democratic fragments: Africa's quest for democracy, in Eisenstadt S N (ed), *Democracy and modernity (The Hague: Brill, 1991),* 111–41

821 **Chazan, N, et al,** *Politics and society in contemporary Africa.* Basingstoke: Macmillan, 1992 (2nd edition), 483pp

822 **Coquery-Vidrovitch, C,** L'état contemporain en Afrique: héritage et création, in Irele A (ed), *African education and identity (entry 268),* 283–92

823 **Cowell, A,** *Killing the wizards: wars of power and freedom from Zaire to South Africa.* New York: Simon and Schuster, 1992, 287pp

824 **Crook, R C, Jerve, A M, (eds),** *Government and participation: institutional development, decentralisation and democracy in the Third World.* Fantoft: Michelesen Institute, 1991, 219pp

825 **Davidson, B,** *The Black man's burden; Africa and the curse of the nation-state.* London: Currey, 1992, 355pp

826 **Decalo, S,** Back to square one: the redemocratisation of Africa, *Africa insight,* 21, 3 (1991) 153–61

827 **Decalo, S,** The process, prospects and constraints of democratisation in Africa, *African affairs,* 91, 362 (1992) 7–35

828 **Decalo, S,** Towards understanding the sources of stable civilian rule in Africa: 1960–1990, *Journal of contemporary African studies,* 10, 1 (1991) 66–83

829 **Deng, L, et al,** (ed), *Democratisation and structural adjustment in Africa in the 1990s.* Madison: University of Wisconsin-Madison, African Studies Program, 1991, 218pp

830 **Diallo, S,** *Dossiers secrets de l'Afrique contemporaine. Tome 3.* Paris: J A Livres, 1991, 185pp

831 **Diop, S,** Du parti unique aux multiple partis, ou la démocratie introuvable, *Afrique contemporaine,* 164 (1992) 145–52

832 **Djaksam, T,** Conflict and unity: towards an intellectual history of the forbears of the OAU, *India quarterly,* 46, 4 (1990) 41–90

833 **Djedjro, F M,** la révision des constitutions dans les états africaines francophones: equisse de bilan, *Revue du droit public,* Jan-Fev. (1992) 111–34

834 **Dlamini, C R M,** The violation of human rights in Africa: a lesson for South Africa?, *South African journal on human rights,* 7, 3 (1991) 291–303

835 **Dodge, C P, Raundalen, M,** *Reaching children in war.* Uppsala: SIAS, 1992, 146pp

836 **Dorronsoro Ekuta, J E,** Revolución democrática africana y nuevo orden internacional, *Africa 2000,* 6, 15 (1991) 4–9

837 **Dow, H, Baker, J,** *Popular participation and development: a bibliography on Africa and Latin America.* Toronto: Toronto University, Centre for Urban and Community Studies, 1992, 145pp

838 **du Bois de Gaudusson, J,** Trente ans d'institutions constitutionelles et politiques - points de repère et interrogations, *Afrique contemporaine,* 164 (1992) 50–58

839 **Duffield, M,** Famine, conflict and the internationalisation of public welfare, in Doornbos M et al (eds), *Beyond conflict in the Horn (entry 1533),* 49–66

840 **Dunne, P, Mohammed, N,** *Military spending in subsaharan Africa: an econometric analysis.* Leeds: Leeds University, School of Business and Economic Studies, 1992, 23pp

841 **Ekeh, P,** The constitution of civil society in African history and politics, in Caron B et al (eds), *Democratic transition in Africa (entry 817),* 187–212

842 **Entralgo, A,** Changes in Europe and changes in Africa: a cause-effect relationship?, *Revista de Africa y Medio Oriente,* 3, 1 (1991) 135–52

843 **Eteki-Otabela, M L,** La marginalisation de l'Afrique: examen des rapports état-société civile, *Africa development,* 15, 3/4 (1990) 71–103

844 **Fatton, R,** *Predatory rule: state and civil society in Africa.* Boulder: Lynne Reinner, 1992, 165pp

845 **Fischer, D A V,** Implementing a nuclear-weapons-free zone in Africa, *Disarmament,* 14, 3 (1991) 112–27

846 **Forrest, J B,** The conceptual limits to power and class in Africa, *Studies in comparative international development,* 25, 4 (1990–91) 71–85

847 **Garcin, T,** Les européens et la démocratisation africaine, *Afrique 2000,* 10 (1992) 19–26

848 **Gaulme, F,** Tribus, ethnies, frontières, *Afrique contemporaine,* 164 (1992) 43–49

849 **Gibbon, P,** Structural adjustment and pressures towards multi-partyism in Subsaharan Africa, in Gibbon P & Bangura, Y (eds), *Authoritarianism, democracy and adjustment (entry 850),* 127–66

850 **Gibbon, P et al,** (eds), *Authoritarianism, democracy and adjustment: the politics of economic reform in Africa.* Uppsala: Scandinavian Institute of African Studies, 1992, 236pp

851 **Glickman, H,** *Political leaders of contemporary Africa South of the Sahara: a biographical dictionary.* New York: Greenwood, 1992, 361pp

852 **Gordon, D L,** African politics, in Gordon A & D (eds), *Understanding contemporary Africa (entry 9),* 51–85

853 **Healey, J, Robinson, M,** *Democracy, governance and economic policy: subsaharan Africa in comparative perspective.* London: Overseas Development Institute, 1992, 188pp

854 **Heimer, F-W,** O Estado pós-colonial em Africa: uma bibliografia, *Revista internacional de estudos africanos,* 12/13, (1990) 475–500

855 **Hellinger, D,** US aid policy in Africa: no room for democracy, *Review of African political economy,* 55 (1992) 84–87

856 **Henze, P B,** Africa after communism, *Problems of communism,* 41, 1 (1992) 218–222

857 **Herbst, J,** The potential for conflict in Africa, *Africa insight,* 22, 2 (1992) 105–109

858 **Hofmeier, R Matthies, V,** (eds), *Vergesenne Krieg in Afrika.* Gottingen: Lamuv, 1992, 367pp

859 **Hughes, A,** The appeal of marxism to Africa, *Journal of communist studies,* 8, 2 (1992) 4–20 (also in *entry 860*)

860 **Hughes, A,** (ed), *Marxism's retreat from Africa.* London: Cass, 1992, 164pp

861 **Hyden, G,** The efforts to restore intellectual freedom in Africa, *Issue,* 20, 1 (1992) 5–14

862 **Hyden, G,** Governance and the study of politics, in Hyden G & Bratton, M (eds), *Governance and politics (entry 864),* 1–26

863 **Hyden, G,** The role of aid and research in the political restructuring of Africa, in Crook R C & Jerve, A M (eds), *Government and participation (entry 824),* 133–58

864 **Hyden, G, Bratton, M,** (eds), *Governance and politics in Africa.* Boulder: Lynne Reinner, 1992, 327pp

865 **Imam, A,** Democratisation processes in Africa problems and prospects, *Review of African political economy,* 54 (1992) 102–105

866 **Jenkins, J C, Kposowa, A J,** The political origins and African military coups: ethnic competition, military centrality and the struggle over the post-colonial state, *International studies quarterly,* 36, 3 (1992) 271–91

867 **Kagalkar, P C,** African socialism re-examined, *India quarterly,* 48, 3 (1992) 73–84

868 **Keller, E J,** Political change and political research in Africa: agenda for the 1990s, *Issue,* 20, 1 (1992) 50–53

869 **Kittel, B,** Tribalismus oder Machtpolitik: Plädoyer für eine heuristische Neuorientierung der Analyse des Staates in Afrika, *Zeitschrift für Afrikastudien,* 11/12 (1991) 3–24

870 **Kodjo, E,** Le nouvel ordre mondial et l'Afrique, *Afrique 2000,* 10 (1992) 5–17

871 **Kone, H,** Circulation d'information et pluralisme: quels defis pour la presse africaine?, *Africa media review,* 6, 2 (1992) 1–12

872 **Kpundeh, S J,** (ed), *Democratisation in Africa: African views, African voices.* Washington: National Academy Press, 1992, 85pp

873 **Krause, K, Rosas, A,** (eds), *Development cooperation and processes towards democracy: Nordic seminar.* Helsinki: Ministry of Foreign Affairs, 1992, 154pp

874 **Kühne, W,** Demokratisierung in Vielvölkerstaaten unter schlecten wirtschaftlichen Bedingungen - das Biespiel Afrika, *Afrika Jahrbuch 1991,* 26–26

875 **Landell-Mills, P,** Governance, cultural change and empowerment, *Journal of modern African studies,* 30, 4 (1992) 543–67

876 **Le Bouder, J P,** Ajustement structurel, saine gestion de la chose publique et démocratie, *African development review,* 3, 2 (1991) 179–88

877 **Legum, C,** The OAU in 1988: a quarter of a century of progress

and disappointment, *Africa contemporary record 1988/89*, (1992) A44–54

878 **Legum, C,** The post-communist Third World: focus on Africa, *Problems of communism*, 41, 1 (1992) 195–206

879 **Lemarchand, R,** The political economy of informal economies, *Africa insight*, 21, 4 (1991) 214–21

880 **Lemarchand, R,** Uncivil states and civil societies: how illusion became reality, *Journal of modern African studies*, 30, 2 (1992) 177–91

881 **Lindgren, G, Wallenstreen, P,** Post-colonial conflicts in Africa: the beginnings of an analysis, *Taamuli*, NS 2, 1/2 (1991) 73–103

882 **Liniger-Goumaz, M,** *Le démocrature: dictature camouflé, dictature truquée.* Paris: Harmattan, 1992, 364pp

883 **Lösch, D,** *Sozialismus in Afrika.* Hamburg: Weltarchiv, 1990, 353pp

884 **Lumumba-Kasongo, T,** *Nationalistic ideologies, their policy implications and the struggle for democracy in African politics.* Lewiston: Mellen, 1991, 139pp

885 **Lumumba-Kasongo, T,** *Nationalistic ideologies, their policy implications and the struggle for democracy in African politics.* Lewiston: Mellen, 1991, 139pp

886 **Magang, D,** A new beginning: the process of democratisation in Africa, *Parliamentarian*, 73, 4 (1992) 235–39

887 **Magyar, D F,** Military intervention and withdrawal in Africa: problems and perspectives, in Danopoulos C P (ed), *From military to civilian rule* (London: Routledge, 1992), 230–48

888 **Mamdani, M,** State and civil society in contemporary Africa: reconceptualising the birth of state nationalism and the defeat of popular movements, *Africa development*, 15, 3/4 (1990) 47–70

889 **Manor, J,** (ed), *Rethinking Third World politics.* Harlow: Longman, 1991, 283pp

890 **Mathews, K,** The OAU and political economy of human rights in Africa, *African review*, 16, 1/2 (1989) 82–97

891 **Mawhood, P,** The politics of decentralisation: Eastern Europe and Africa, in Crook R C & Jerve, A M (eds), *Government and participation (entry 824)*, 51–68

892 **M'ba, C,** Quels hommes pour conduire la transition démocratique?, *Afrique 2000*, 10 (1992) 57–66

893 **Mbembe, A,** Pouvoir et économie politique en Afrique contemporaine: une réflexion, *Afrique 2000*, 8 (1992) 51–71

894 **Medard, J F,** (ed), *Etats d'Afrique noire: formations, mecanismes et crise.* Paris: Karthala, 1992, 408pp

895 **Médard, J F,** L'etat postcolonial en Afrique noire: l'interprétation néo-patrimoniale de l'etat, *Studia Africana*, 3 (1992) 125–133

896 **Mehler, A,** *Die nachkolonialen Staaten Schwarzafrikas zwischewn Ligitimität und Repression.* Frankfurt: Lang, 1990, 229pp

897 **Metena M'nteba,** Des 'évolués' aux 'technocrates' via les 'autocrates': où va l'Afrique politique contemporaine?, *Zaïre-Afrique*, 264, (1992) 208–218

898 **Mkandawire, M,** The political economy of development with a democratic face, in Cornia A G et al (eds), *Africa's recovery (entry 124)*, 296–311

899 **Moharir, V V,** Capacity building initiative for subsaharan Africa, *Public enterprise*, 11, 4 (1991) 235–45

900 **Monkotan, J B Kuassi,** Des modes originaux d'expression

démocratique en Afrique, *Afrique 2000,* 3 (1990) 55–65

901 **Mouddour, B,** La fin d'un mythe: l'avènement du multipartisme en Afrique, *Revue juridique et politique,* 46, 1 (1992) 38–45

902 **Moyo, J,** *The politics of administration: understanding bureaucracy in Africa.* Harare: SAPES Books, 1992, 151pp

903 **Mutahaba, G, Balogun, M J,** (eds), *Enhancing managment capacity in Africa.* West Hartford: Kumarian Press, 1992, 194pp

905 **Nathan, L,** *Towards a conference on security, stability, development and cooperation in Africa.* Cape Town: Centre for Southern African Studies, University of the Western Cape, 1992, 50pp

906 **Némo, J,** L'assistance technique dans les nouveau cadre de la coopération institutionelle, *Mondes et cultures,* 50, 1 (1990) 131–44

907 **Neubert, D,** (ed), *Die Zukunft Afrikas: Überleben in der Krise.* Sankt Augustin: COMDOK, 1991, 144pp

908 **Neugebauer, C,** Mahmood Mamdani on democracy and human rights, *Zeitschrift für Afrikastudien,* 13/14 (1992) 3–8

909 **Nguema, I,** La democratie, l'Afrique et le développement, *Revue juridique et politique,* 46, 2 (1992) 129–162

910 **Nguema, I,** La démocratie, l'Afrique traditionelle et le développement, *Afrique 2000,* 10 (1992) 27–56

911 **Nobilo, M,** Problems of political stability and internal unity of African countries, in Irele A (ed), *African education and identity (entry 268),* 217–27

912 **Nolutshungu, S C,** Africa in a world of democracies: interpretation and retrieval, *Journal of Commonwealth and comparative politics,* 30, 3 (1992) 316–34

913 **Non-Governmental Liaison Service (ed),** *Voices from Africa 3: War, armed conflict, destabilisation.* Geneva: NGLS, 1991, 125pp

914 **Nouguérède, Y,** La coopération administrative et judiciare, *Mondes et cultures,* 50, 1 (1990) 59–75

915 **Ntibantunganya, S,** L'Afrique dans le débat sur la démocratisation, *Au coeur de l'Afrique,* 59, 2/3 (1991) 207–235

916 **Nweke, G A,** Political education for collective self reliance, in Irele A (ed), *African education and identity (entry 268),* 228–50

917 **Nyong'o, P A,** Democratisation processes in Africa, *Review of African political economy,* 54 (1992) 97–102

918 **Ogunbadejo, O,** Africa and nuclear systems: the contending issues, *Africa contemporary record 1988/89,* (1992) A74–86

919 **Olaitan, W,** Democracy and democratisation in Africa: not yet the glorious dawn, in Caron B et al (eds), *Democratic transition in Africa (entry 817),* 423–34

920 **Olowu, D, Smoke, P,** Determinants of success in African local governments: an overview, *Public administration and development,* 12, 1 (1992) 1–17

921 **Opolot, J S E,** Police training in the states of Africa, *Police studies,* 14, 2 (1991) 62–71

922 **Osaghae, E E,** Managing ethnic conflicts under democratic transition in Africa: the promise, the failure and the future, in Caron B et al (eds), *Democratic transition in Africa (entry 817),* 213–34

923 **Osaghae, E E,** A re-examination of the conception of ethnicity in Africa as an ideology of inter-elite competition, *Africa study monographs,* 12, 1 (1991) 43–60

924 **Osaghae, E E,** Social mobilisation as a political myth in

44

Africa

Africa, *Africa quarterly*, 30, 3/4 (1990) 8–23

925 **Patman, R,** Intelligence agencies in Africa: a preliminary assessment, *Journal of modern African studies*, 30, 4 (1992) 569–85

926 **Rake, A,** *Who's who in Africa: leaders for the 1990s.* Metuchen: Scarecrow Press, 1992, 448pp

927 **Riley, S,** Africa's 'new wind of change', *World today*, 48, 7 (1992) 116–119

928 **Rossatanga-Rignault, G,** Penser post-modernité africaine: un discours, *Afrique 2000*, 11 (1992) 73–86

929 **Rothchild, D,** The internationalisation of Africa's ethnic and racial conflicts: a learning process is under way, *Africa contemporary record 1988/89*, (1992) A97–106

930 **Rudebeck, L,** *Conditions of people's development in post-colonial Africa.* Uppsala: Akut, Uppsala University, 1990, 90pp

931 **Rudebeck, L, (ed),** *When democracy makes sense.* Uppsala: Akut, Uppsala University, 1992, 399pp

932 **Rupesinghe, K,** (ed), *Internal conflict and governance.* Basingstoke: Macmillan, 1992, 300pp

933 **Samny, A,** *Conference report: democratisation and human rights in Africa.* Fantoft: Chr. Michelsen Institute, 1992, Var pagpp

934 **Sarassoro, H C,** La corruption et l'enrichissement sans cause en Afrique aujourd'hui quel antidote?, *African journal of international and comparative law*, 2, 3 (1990) 384–422

935 **Scholze, W,** Human rights between universalism and relativism, *Quest*, 6, 1 (1992) 56–68

936 **Shivji, I G,** Reawakening of politics in Africa, *Maji Maji*, 47 (1990) 59–76

937 **Sklar, R L, Strege, M,** Finding

peace through democracy in Sahelian Africa, *Current history*, 91, 565 (1992) 224–229

938 **Sow, P A,** Manifeste pour le féderalisme en Afrqiue, *Ethiopiques*, 7, 2 (1991) 68–89

939 **Ssemugooma Bagenda, A M,** Africa's refugee problems, in NGLS (ed), *Voices from Africa 3 (entry 913)*, 81–95

940 **Stetter, E,** *Political change and democracy in Africa.* Bonn: Friedrich Ebert Foundation, 1991, 23pp

941 **Tedga, P J M,** *Ouverture démocratique en Afrique noire?* Paris: Harmattan, 1991, 251pp

942 **Tetzlaff, R,** *Demokratisierung von Herrschaft und gesellschaftliche Wandel in Afrika: Perspektivern der 90er Jahre.* Bonn: Friedrich Ebert Foundation, 1991, 70pp

943 **Tiangaye, N,** Aux sources du pluralisme politique en Afrique, *Afrique 2000*, 11 (1992) 55–66

944 **Tordoff, W,** *Government and politics in Africa.* Basingstoke: Macmillan, 1992 (2nd edition), 340pp

945 **Toulabor, C M,** Transition démocratique en Afrique, *Afrique 2000*, 4, (1991) 55–70

946 **Toye, J,** Interest group politics and the implementation of adjustment policies in subsaharan Africa, in Mosley P (ed), *Development finance and policy reform* (New York: St Martins Press, 1992), 85–104

947 **Varret, J,** La coopération militaire, *Mondes et cultures*, 50, 1 (1990) 103–30

948 **von Freyhold, M,** *Demokratie-Debatte in Afrika.* Basel: Machrichtenstelle Südliches Afrika, 1991, 36pp

949 **Wamba-dia-Wamba, E,** Beyond elite politics of democracy in Africa, *Quest*, 6, 1 (1992) 28–42

950 Weiss, D, *Internationale Unterstützung des Reformprozesses in Entwicklungsländern durch Auflagenpolitik und Politikdialog? Probleme politischer Konditionalität am Beispiel Afrikas.* Berlin: Freie Universität, Fachbereich Wirtschaftwissenschaft, 1990, 21pp

951 Welch, C E, The Organisation of African Unity and the promotion of human rights, *Journal of modern African studies,* 29, 4 (1991) 535–55

952 Welch, C E, The single party phenomenon in Africa, *Transafrica forum,* 8, 3 (1991) 85–94

953 Wiseman, J A, Early post-redemocratization elections in Africa, *Electoral studies,* 11, 4 (1992) 279–291

954 Wonyu, E, Un support juridique pour la démocratie en Afrique: la Charte africaine des droits de l'homme et des peuples, *Afrique 2000,* 8 (1992) 29–49

Religion, philosophy

see also: 35, 42, 48

955 Appiah, K A, *In my father's house: Africa in the philosophy of culture.* London: Methuen, 1992, 366pp

956 Bahemuka, J M, Social anthropology as a source of African theology, *African christian studies,* 7, 2 (1991) 69–80

957 Bediako, K, New paradigms on ecumenical cooperation: an African perspective, *International review of mission,* 81, 253 (1992) 375–79

958 Bourdillon, M F C, *Religion and society: a text for Africa.* Gweru: Mambo, 1991, 406pp

959 Bujo, B, *African christian morality at the age of inculturation.* Kampala: St Paul, 1990, 137pp

960 Bujo, B, *African theology in its social context.* Maryknoll: Orbis, 1992, 143pp

961 Daly, C, Ethiopianisme et nationalisme en Afrique noire, in Irele A (ed), *African education and identity (entry 268),* 184–208

962 de Benoist, J R, Les 'clercs' et la démocratie, *Afrique contemporaine,* 164 (1992) 178–93

963 Dopanu, F A, African traditional religion and science: some reflections, in Thomas-Emeagwali G (ed), *Science and technology in Nigeria (entry 450),* 63–76

964 Echekwube, A O, The historical-philosophical background of African traditional religion, *Orita,* 23, 1 (1991) 1–14

965 Echeverría, J R, Aspectos positivos del sincretismo: religiones tradicionales y religiones del Libro, *Cuadernos,* 6, 2 (1991) 1–15

966 Engel, L, Wie die Kirchen in Afrika ihre personellen Ressourcen für theologisch Ausbildung besser einsetzen können: Bericht über ein ÖRKKonsulation in Zomba/Malawi, *Zeischrift für Mission,* 18, 1 (1992) 21–29

967 Gifford, P, Prosperity: a new and foreign element in African Christianity, *Religion,* 20, 4 (1990) 373–388

968 Harding, L, (ed), *Afrika: Mutter und Modell der europäischen Zivilisation? Die Rehabilitierung des schwarzen Kontinents durch Cheikh Anta Diop.* Berlin: Reimer, 1990, 287pp

969 Hexham, I, African religions: some recent and less known works, *Religion,* 20, 4 (1990) 361–372

970 Ikenga-Metuh, E, The spirituality of African independent church movements, *Religion in Malawi,* 3 (1991) 4–12

971 Irele, A, Éloge de aliénation, *Bulletin des séances,* 36, 2 (1990) 169–184

972 Kawonise, S, Normative impediments to democratic transition in Africa, in Caron B et al (eds), *Democratic transition in Africa (entry 817)*, 129–40

973 **Kigongo, J K,** Ethical values in African traditional education, *Journal of African religion and philosophy*, 2, 1 (1991) 43–51

974 **Kimmerle, H,** Non-Africans on African philosophy: steps to a different dialogue, *Quest*, 6, 1 (1992) 69–77

975 **King, H,** Cooperation in contextualisation: two visionaries of the African Church - Mojola Agbeki and William Hughes of the African Institute, Colwyn Bay, in Irele A (ed), *African education and identity (entry 268)*, 152–65

976 **Lewis, J R,** Images of traditional African religions in surveys of world religions, *Religion*, 20, 4 (1990) 311–322

977 **Lokangaka Losambe,** The contribution of V.-Y. Mudimbe to the meta-theory of an Afrocentric order of discourse, *Marang*, 9, (1991) 30–39

978 **Mafeje, A,** The 'Africanist' heritage and its antinomies, *Africa development*, 15, 3/4 (1990) 159–83

979 **Mandivenga, E C,** Resurgence of Islam: implications for African spirituality and dialogue, *Religion in Malawi*, 3 (1991) 12–16

980 **Moyo, A,** Religion in Africa, in Gordon A & D (eds), *Understanding contemporary Africa (entry 9)*, 223–50

981 **Muzorewa, G H,** *An African theology of mission.* Lewiston: Mellen, 1990, 204pp

982 **Nicolas, G,** L'islam au sud du Sahara, *Cahiers de l'Orient*, 27, (1992) 125–142

983 **Nyang, S S,** *Islam, christianity and African identity.* Brattleboro: Amana Books, 1990, 106pp

984 **Nyasani, J,** The ontological significance of "I" and "we" in African philosophy, *African christian studies*, 7, 1 (1991) 53–62

985 **Ogundowole, E G,** Problems and tasks of contemporary African political philosophy, in Irele A (ed), *African education and identity (entry 268)*, 251–60

986 **Oosthuzen, G C, Hexham, I,** (eds), *Empirical studies of African independent/indigenous churches.* Lewiston: Mellen, 1992, 345pp

987 **Oyeshola, D A,** Religious obstacles to development in Africa, *Orita*, 23, 1 (1991) 35–48

988 **Pobee, J S,** *AD 2000 and after: the future of God's mission in Africa.* Accra: Asempa, 1992, 94pp

989 **Renault, F,** *Le cardinal Lavigerie: l'église, l'Afrique et la France.* Paris: Fayard, 1992, 700pp

990 **Rutayisire, P,** Les eglises chrétiennes à l'heure du pluralisme politique en Afrique, *Au coeur de l'Afrique*, 59, 2/3 (1991) 361–389

991 **Ruwaichi, T,** *The constitution of Muntu: an inquiry into the eastern Bantu's metaphysics of person.* Berne: Lang, 1990, 336pp

992 **Saah, R B,** African independent church movements, *African christian studies*, 7, 3 (1991) 46–77

993 **Shaw, R,** The invention of 'African traditional religion', *Religion*, 20, 4 (1990) 339–353

994 **Thorpe, S A,** *African traditional religions: an introduction.* Pretoria: UNISA, 1992, 139pp

995 **Triaud, J l, Hamès, C,** Repères bibliographiques 1989–1991, *Islam et sociétés au sud du Sahara*, 5 (1991) 183–91

996 **Uka, E M,** The African family and issues of women's infertility, *Africa theological journal*, 20, 3 (1991) 189–200

Rural economy

see also: 352, 356, 379, 382, 388, 410, 412, 515, 516

997 **Adelman, I, Vogel, S J,** The relevance of ADLI for subsaharan

Africa, *African development perspectives yearbook*, 2, (1990/91) 258–279

998 African Academy of Sciences, (ed), *Enhancement of agricultural research in francophone Africa.* Nairobi: Academy Science Publishers, 1991, 155pp

999 Barghouti, S, et al, (eds), *Irrigation in Subsaharan Africa: the development of public and private systems.* Washington: World Bank, 1990, 99pp

1000 Baxter, P T W, Hogg, R, (eds), *Property, poverty and people: changing rights in property and problems of pastoral development.* Manchester: Dept.of Social Anthropology & International Development Centre, Manchester University, 1990, 274pp

1001 Behnke, R H, *New directions in African range managment policy.* London: ODI, 1992, 15pp

1002 Behnke, R H, Scoones, I, *Rethinking range ecology: implications for rangeland management in Africa.* London: IIED, 1992, 43pp

1003 Bernstein, H, Agrarian structures and change in SSA, in Bernstein H et al (eds), *Rural livelihoods (entry 1004)*, 65–84

1004 Bernstein, H, et al, (eds), *Rural livelihoods: crises and responses.* Oxford: OUP, 1992, 324pp

1005 Binns, J A, Traditional agriculture, pastoralism and fishing, in Gleave M B (ed), *Tropical African development (entry 147)*, 153–91

1006 Cheater, A P, Rural development and peasant alienation, *Zambezia*, 18, 2 (1991) 89–104

1007 Chona, M, The farmer's viewpoint, in Obasanjo O & d'Orville, H (eds), *Agricultural production and food security (entry 1040)*, 71–76

1008 Classen, E M, Salin, P, *The impact of stabilisation and structural*

adjustment policies on the rural sector: case studies of CDI, Senegal, Liberia, Zambia and Morocco. Rome: FAO1991, 219,

1009 Couty, P, L'agriculture africaine en réserve. Réflexions sur l'innovation et l'intensification agricoles en Afrique tropicale, *Cahiers d'études africaines*, 31, 1/2 (1991) 65–81

1010 Crehan, K, Rural households: making a living, in Bernstein H et al (eds), *Rural livelihoods (entry 1004)*, 87–112

1011 Diemer, G, Vincent, L, Irrigation in Africa: the failure of collective memory and collective understanding, *Development policy review*, 10, 2 (1992) 131–55

1012 Dixon, J A, et al, (eds), *Dryland management: economic case studies.* London: Earthscan, 1990, 364pp

1013 Doss, C R, Olson, C, (eds), *Issues in African rural development.* Arlington: Winrock International Institute, 1991, 534pp

1014 Dowswell, C R, (ed), *Feeding the future: agricultural development strategies for Africa.* Geneva: Centre for Applied Studies in International Negotiations, 1990, 207pp

1015 Duncan, A, Howell, J, Assessing the impact of structural adjustment, in Duncan A & Howell, J (eds), *Structural adjustment and the African farmer (entry 1017)*, 1–13

1016 Duncan, A, Howell, J, Conclusion: beyond adjustment, in Duncan A & Howell, J (eds), *Structural adjustment and the African farmer (entry 1017)*, 199–208

1017 Duncan, A, Howell, J, (eds), *Structural adjustment and the African farmer.* London: Currey, 1992, 214pp

1018 Eicher, C K, African agricultural development strategies, in Stewart F et al (eds), *Alternative*

development strategies (entry 223), 79–102

1019 Erpicum, R, Quelles conditions le milieu rural pourra-t-il participer au processus de démocratisation en Afrique?, *Zaïre-Afrique*, 267, (1992) 416–420

1020 Fair, T J D, *African rural development: policy and practice in six countries.* Pretoria: Africa Institute, 1992, 78pp

1021 Fontaine, J M, Sinzingre, A, *Macro-micro linkages: structural adjustment and fertiliser policy in subsaharan Africa.* Paris: OECD Development Centre, 1991, 75pp

1022 Founou-Tchuigoua, B, La crise de la modernisation agricole, la persistance de la question paysanne et de l'industrialisation de soutien à l'agriculture: ou en est le débat?, in Anyang' Nyong'o P (ed), *30 years of independence (entry 101)*, 175–205

1023 Goetz, S J, A selectivity model of household food marketing behavior in subsaharan Africa, *American journal of agricultural economics*, 74, 2 (1992) 444–452

1024 Harrison, P, What is going right with African agriculture?, in Obasanjo O & d'Orville, H (eds), *Agricultural production and food security (entry 1040)*, 128–38

1025 Hjort af Ornäs, A, (ed), *Security in African drylands: research, development and policy.* Uppsala: Uppsala University, Dept. of Human and Physical Geography, 1992, 192pp

1026 Hoffman, V, (ed), *Beratung als Lebenshilfe: humane Konzepte für eine ländliche Entwicklung.* Weikersheim: Margraf, 1992, 310pp

1027 Hogg, R, Should pastoralism continue as a way of life?, *Disasters*, 16, 2 (1992) 131–37

1028 Idachaba, F S, The technological transformation of African agriculture - is there hope?,

Discovery and innovation, 4, 2 (1992) 16–25

1029 Ilunga wa Ilunga, *La place du transfert de technologie dans le développment agricole de l'Afrique.* Bruxelles: Bureau d'informations européenes, 1992, 127pp

1030 Jaeger, W K, *The effects of economic policies on African agriculture.* Washington: World Bank, 1992, 69pp

1031 Lele, U, Adu-Nyako, K, Approaches to uprooting poverty in Africa, *Food policy*, 17, 2 (1992) 95–108

1032 Lubana Ngiyene Amena, De quelle manière la population africaine lutte-t-elle contre la misère qui la frappe très durement depuis le milieu des années 1970?, *Géokin*, 1/2, 2/1 (1990/1991) 233–240

1033 Mackenzie, F, Development from within: the struggle to survive, in Taylor D R F & Mackenzie, F (eds), *Development from within (entry 1061)*, 1–32

1034 Mazur, R E, Titilola, S T, Social and economic dimensions of local knowledge systems in African sustainable agriculture, *Sociologica ruralis*, 32, 2/3 (1992) 264–86

1035 McMaster, D, Agricultural development, in Gleave M B (ed), *Tropical African development (entry 147)*, 192–222

1036 Mekonnen Assefa, *Index des documents microfichés au Mali.* Addis Ababa: International Livestock Centre for Africa, 1991, 238pp

1037 Minvielle, J P, La formation des prix au producteur: une méthodologie d'analyse des coûts de production agricoles en milieu non monétarisé, *Cahiers des sciences humaines*, 27, 1/2 (1991) 183–191

1038 Moock, J L, Rhoades, R E, (eds), *Diversity, farmer knowledge and sustainability.* Ithaca: Cornell UP, 1992, 278pp

1039 Mpoyo, M P V, The needs of African agriculture, in Obasanjo O & d'Orville, H (eds), *Agricultural production and food security (entry 1040)*, 93–97

1040 Obasanjo, O, d'Orville, H, (eds), *The challenges of agricultural production and food security in Africa.* Washington: Crane Russak, 1992, 186pp

1041 Odhiambo, T R, Problems and prospects, in Obasanjo O & d'Orville, H (eds), *Agricultural production and food security (entry 1040)*, 65–70

1042 Okigbo, B N, *Development of sustainable agricultural systems in Africa: roles of international agricultural research centres and national agricultural research systems.* Ibadan: International Institute of Tropical Agriculture, 1991, 66pp

1043 Onyango, T A, Traditional agriculture: the case for retaining useful indigenous techniques and practices, *Resources*, 2, 1 (1991) 33–36

1044 Oxby, C, (ed), *Assisting African livestock keepers: the experience of four projects.* London: ODI, 1991, 61pp

1045 Project for Nomadic Pastoralists in Africa, *Pastoralists at a crossroads: survival and development issues in African pastoralism.* Nairobi: the Project, 1992, 91, 89pp

1046 Ranganathan, V, (ed), *Rural electrification in Africa.* London: Zed, 1992, 182pp

1047 Riddell, R, Robinson, M, *The impact of NGO poverty alleviation projects: results of the case study evaluations.* London: ODI, 1992, 36pp

1048 Riverson, J, Gavira, H, et al, *Rural roads in subsaharan Africa.* Washington: World Bank, 1992, 62pp

1049 Roche, C, It's not size that

matters: ACORD's experience in Africa, in Edwards M & Hulme, D (eds), *Making a difference: NGOs and development in a changing world* (London: Earthscan, 1992), 180–90

1050 Rodriguez, A, Fontem, N B, *Land tenure in subsaharan Africa: a bibliography.* Ottawa: Norman Patterson School of International Affairs, 1990, 73pp

1051 Roy, S, Structural adjustment programmes, the economy and the rural sector, *Africa quarterly*, 30, 1/2 (1990) 1–12

1052 Sanmarco, L, Le monde rural sacrifié: de l'injustice au risques ecologiques, *Afrique contemporaine*, 164 (1992) 168–77

1053 Scoones, I, *Wetlands in drylands: key resources for agricultural and pastoral production in Africa.* London: IIED, 1992, 23pp

1054 Shepherd, G, (ed), *Forest policies, forest politics.* London: ODI, 1992, 72pp

1055 Shepherd, G, *Managing Africa's tropical dry forests: a review of indigenous methods.* London: ODI, 1992, 117pp

1056 Shipton, P, Goheen, M, Understanding African land-holding: power, wealth, and meaning, *Africa*, 62, 3 (1992) 307–25

1057 Smith, L D, Spooner, N J, The sequencing of structural adjustment policy instruments in the agricultural sector, in Milner C & Rayner, A J (eds), *Policy adjustment (entry 184)*, 61–79

1058 Suliman, M, Overview, in Dudley N et al (eds), *Land is life: land reform and sustainable agriculture* (London: Intermediate Technology, 1992), 83–88

1059 Swaminathan, M S, Agricultural production in Africa, in Obasanjo O & d'Orville, H (eds), *Agricultural production and food security (entry 1040)*, 11–33

1060 Taylor, D R F, Development
from within and survival in rural
Africa: a synthesis of theory and
practice, in Taylor D R F &
Mackenzie, F (eds), *Development
from within (entry 1061)*, 214–58

**1061 Taylor, D R F, Mackenzie,
F,** (eds), *Development from within:
survival in rural Africa.* London:
Longman, 1992, 284pp

1062 Toulmin, C, et al, The future
of Africa's drylands: is local
resource management the answer?,
in Holmberg J (ed), *Policies for a
small planet* (London:
Earthcsan,1992), 225–57

1063 Various authors, *Enhancement
of agricultural research in francophone
Africa: proceeedings of the
Pan-African Congress on
Agriculture and Agricultural
Research in Africa.* Nairobi:
Academy Science Publishers,
1991, 155pp

1064 Various authors, *Voices from
Africa 4: culture and development.*
Geneva: UNCTAD, 1992, 109pp

Science & technology

1064a Abdel Rahman, A,
Communication technology in
Africa: dependency or
self-reliance?, *Africa media review,*
5, 3 (1991) 11–18

**1065 African Association of
Science Editors,** *Directory of
scholarly journals published in Africa:
a preliminary survey.* Nairobi:
Academy Science Publishers, 1990,
49pp

**1066 American Association for
the Advancement of Science,**
*Science in Africa: setting research
priorities.* Washington: the
Association, 1992, 65pp

1067 Bass, T A, *Camping with the
Prince and other tales of science in
Africa.* Boston: Houghton Mifflin,
1990, 282pp

1068 Eisenmon, T O, Davis, C H,
Universities and scientific research
capacity, *Journal of Asian and
African studies,* 27, 1/2 (1992)
68–93

1069 En'sem, A, Pour la primauté
de la science et de la technologie en
Afrique, in Irele A (ed), *African
education and identity (entry 268),*
310–18

1070 Forje, J W, The role and
effectiveness of national science and
technology policy-making bodies in
Africa, *Journal of Asian and African
studies,* 27, 1/2 (1992) 12–30

1071 Forje, J W, Two decades of
science and technology in Africa:
what has been reaped?, in Irele A
(ed), *African education and identity
(entry 268),* 319–33

1072 Gaillard, J, Waast, R, The
uphill emergence of scientific
communities in Africa, *Journal of
Asian and African studies,* 27, 1/2
(1992) 41–67

1073 Hyman, E L, The design of
micro-projects and macro-policies:
examples from three appropriate
technology projects in Africa,
Journal of Asian and African studies,
27, 1/2 (1992) 134–51

1074 Kwakye, E B, Photovoltaic
solar electricity to improve quality
of rural life in Africa, *African journal
of science and technology, Series C,
General,* 2, 1 (1991) 43–53

1075 Levallois, M, La coopération
scientifique, *Mondes et cultures,* 50,
1 (1990) 77–88

1076 Lewis, S G, Samoff, J, (eds),
*Microcomputers in African
development: critical perspectives.*
Boulder: Westview, 1992, 258pp

1077 Malu wa Kalenga, Nuclear
techniques and solar energy: a
quest for sustainable development
in Africa, *Discovery and innovation,*
4, 1 (1992) 17–21

1078 Mlawa, H M, (ed), *Proceedings
of the annual workshop of researchers.*

Dar es Salaam: Eastern and Southern Africaan Technology Policy Studies Network, 1990, 55pp

1079 **Segal, A,** Appropriate technology: the African experience, *Journal of Asian and African studies,* 27, 1/2 (1992) 124–33

1080 **Singh, C,** Managing science and technology development: policy tasks ahead, *Africa quarterly,* 30, 3/4 (1990) 65–88

1081 **Tiffin, S, Osotimehin, F,** Innovation of new and emerging technology for industrial development in Africa, *Journal of Asian and African studies,* 27, 1/2 (1992) 94–113

1082 **Tiffin, S, Osotimehin, F,** *New technologies and enterprise development in Africa.* Paris: OECD Development Centre, 1992, 212pp

1083 **Vitta, P B,** Management of technology policy in subsaharan Africa: the policy researchers burden, *Journal of Asian and African studies,* 27, 1/2 (1992) 31–40

1084 **World Bank, et al,** *Fisheries and acquaculture research capabilities and needs in Africa.* Washington: World Bank, 1991, 73pp

Sociology

see also: 166, 387, 673, 958

1085 **Ainsworth, M, et al,** *Measuring the impact of fatal adult illness in subsaharan Africa: living standards measurement study.* Washington: World Bank, 1992, 164pp

1086 **Alemka, E E O,** Socioeconomic trend and human welfare in Africa, *Africa quarterly,* 31, 1/2 (1991) 1–23

1087 **Apt, N A,** Ageing in the community: trends and prospects in Africa, *Community development journal,* 27, 2 (1992) 130–39

1088 **Arthur, J A,** Development and crime in Africa: a test of modernisation theory, *Journal of criminal justice,* 19, 6 (1991) 499–513

1089 **Caldwell, J C, et al,** The family and sexual networking in subsaharan Africa: historical regional differences and present-day implications, *Population studies,* 46, 3 (1992) 385–410

1090 **Chole, E,** Expenditure patterns: a framework for inter-country comparisons, in Mohammed D (ed), *Social development in Africa (entry 1093),* 227–51

1091 **Chole, E,** Introduction: what is social development?, in Mohammed D (ed), *Social development in Africa (entry 1093),* 4–21

1092 **Makannah, T J,** *A bibliography on refugees in subsaharan Africa.* Addis Ababa: UNECA, 1992, 30pp

1093 **Mohammed, D,** (ed), *Social development in Africa: strategies, policies and programmes after the Lagos Plan.* Oxford: Zell, 1991, 257pp

1094 **Munywoki, S,** Anomie and cultural lag: impediments to development, *Journal of east African research and development,* 21, (1991) 53–69

1095 **Musanga, T,** (ed), *Criminology in Africa.* Rome: UN Interregional Crime and Justice Research Institute, 1992, 272pp

1096 **Nukunya, G K,** *Tradition and change: the case of the family.* Accra: Ghana UP, 1992, 34pp

1097 **Refugee Policy Group,** *Internally displaced persons in Africa.* Washington: the Group, 1992, 70pp

1098 **Shauro, E,** Formation of a system of new needs in African countries, in Irele A (ed), *African*

education and identity (entry 268),
277–82

1099 Standing, H, AIDS:
conceptual and methodological
issues in researching sexual
behaviour in subsaharan Africa,
Social science and medecine, 34, 5
(1992) 475–83

1100 Strarouchenko, G, Voies et
formes nouvelles du progrès social
dans les pays d'Afrique, in Irele A
(ed), *African education and identity
(entry 268)*, 265–70

1101 Vaugelade, J, Les unités
collectives dans les enquêtes
statistiques africaines: pour la
traduction et pour l'utilisation du
concept de ménage agricole,
Cahiers des sciences humaines, 27,
3/4 (1991) 389–394

Social welfare

1102 Anon, New drive to protect
Africa's children, *Africa recovery*, 6,
3 (1992) 14–17

1103 Beckley, S, Social costs of the
crisis: education, employment and
health, *Echo*, 17/18 (1992) 13–17

1104 Chan, S, *Social development in
Africa today: some radical proposals.*
Lewiston: Mellen, 1991, 118pp

1105 Gibbon, P, 'Social dimensions
of adjustment' and the problem of
poverty in Africa, *Nytt från Nodiska
Afrikainstitutet*, 28 (1991) 5–26

1106 Kouassivi, A, The roles and
responsibilities of
non-governmental organisations
(NGOs) and grassroots
communities, *Journal of the African
Association for Literacy and Adult
Education*, 5, 4 (1991) 18–30

1107 Mupedziswa, R, Africa at the
crossroads: major challenges for
social work education and practice
towards the year 2000, *Journal of
social development in Africa*, 7, 2
(1992) 19–38

1108 Okelo, J A, NGOs and

consumer issues in Africa today, in
NGLS (ed), *Voices from Africa 2
(entry 195)*, 71–82

1109 Sooth, C P, *Enstehungs- und
Entwicklungsbedingungen staatlicher
Systeme sozialer Sicherung in Afrika.*
Hamburg: Institut für
Afrika-Kunde, 1992, 200pp

Urban studies

see also: 294, 667

1110 Aeroe, A, The role of small
towns in southeast Africa, in Baker
J & Pedersen, P O (eds),
Rural-urban interface (entry 1111),
51–68

1111 Baker, J, Pedersen, P O,
(eds), *The rural-urban interface in
Africa: expansion and adaptation.*
Uppsala: SIAS, 1992, 320pp

1112 Baker, J, Pedersen, P O,
Introduction, in Baker J &
Pedersen, P O (eds), *Rural-urban
interface (entry 1111)*, 11–28

1113 Coppierters't Wallant, R,
*Jeunesse maginalisée, espoir de
l'Afrique. Un juge des enfants témoigne.*
Paris: Harmattan, 1992, 187pp

1114 Coquery, M, Secteur informel
et production de l'espace urbanisé
en Afrique, in Coquery-Vidrovitch
C & Nedelec, C (eds), *Tiers Monde:
l'informel en question?* (Paris:
Harmattan, 1991), 197–213

1115 Coussy, J, et al, *Urbanisation
et dépendance alimentaire en Afrique
sub-saharienne.* Paris: SEDES,
1991, 230pp

1116 Gleave, M B, Urbanisation, in
Gleave M B (ed), *Tropical African
development (entry 147)*, 315–46

1117 Godard, X, Teurneir, P, *Les
transport urbains en Afrique à l'heure
de l'ajustement.* Paris: Karthala,
1992, 248pp

1118 Lee-Smith, D, Stren, R E,
New perspectives on African urban
management, *Environment and
urbanization*, 3, 1 (1991) 23–36

1119 **Martin, R,** Developing the capacity for urban manangement in Africa: the technical assistance and training approach to urban development, *Cities,* 8, 2 (1991) 134–41

1120 **Ng'ethe, N, Ngau, G,** *The role of the informal sector in the development of small and intermediate sized cities.* Nairobi: Nairobi University, IDS, 1991, 73pp

1121 **Olawale, A C,** Social economy and urban agriculture, *Africa (Rome),* 47, 2 (1992) 263–67

1122 **Pourcet, G,** La ville, l'informel et l'environnement, *Afrique contemporaine,* 161 (1992) 178–187

1123 **Pourrier, R,** L'explosion urbaine, *Afrique contemporaine,* 164 (1992) 153–57

1124 **Simon, D,** *Cities, capital and development: African cities in the world economy.* London: Belhaven, 1992, 226pp

1125 **Simon, D,** Conceptualising small towns in African development, in Baker J & Pedersen, P O (eds), *Rural-urban interface (entry 1111),* 29–50

1126 **Stren, R,** African urban research since the late 1980s: responses to poverty and urban growth, *Urban studies,* 29, 3/4 (1992) 533–55

1127 **Stren, R E,** Old wine in new bottles? An overview of Africa's urban problems and the "urban management" approach to dealing with them, *Environment and urbanization,* 3, 1 (1991) 9–22

1128 **Toure, M, Fadayomi, T O,** (eds), *Migration, development and urbanisation policies in subsaharan Africa.* Dakar: Codesria, 1992, 317pp

LUSOPHONE AFRICA

General

1129 **Goncalves, J,** *The social sciences in Angola, Cape Verde, Guinea-Bissau, Mozambique and São Tome & Principe.* Dakar: Codesria, 1992, 46pp

Education

1130 **Rugema, M, Tvedten, I,** *Survey of possible expanded educational assistance to refugees from Angola and Mozambique.* Nairobi: All-Africa Conference of Churches, 1991, 114pp

Health & welfare services

No entry, see also: 1130

Politics

1131 **Meyns, P,** (ed), *Demokratie und Strukturreform im portugieisischprachigen Afrika.* Frieburg: Arnold Bergstraesser Institut, 1992, 303pp

NORTH AFRICA

Anthropology

1140 Moss, J, Wilson, G, *Peoples of the world: Middle East and North Africa.* Detroit: Gale Research, 1991, 437pp

Architecture

No entry, see also: 1141, 2506

Arts

1141 Brentjes, B, *Die Kunst der Mauren: islamische Traditionen in Nordafrika und Südspanien.* Cologne: DuMont, 1992, 282pp

Economy - Development

1142 Agbobli, A K, Le jeu de l'Europe en Méditerrannée, *Afrique 2000,* 8 (1992) 515

Economic and social history

1143 Austen, R A, The mediterranean islamic slave trade out of Africa: a tentative census, in Savage E (ed), *The human commodity (entry 252),* 214–48

1144 Collins, R O, The nilotic slave trade: past and present, in Savage E (ed), *The human commodity (entry 252),* 140–61

1145 Hunwick, J, Black Africans in the Mediterranean world: introduction to a neglected aspect of the African diaspora, in Savage E (ed), *The human commodity (entry 252),* 5–38

1146 Pennell, C R, Cannibalism in early modern North Africa, *British journal of Middle East Studies,* 18, 2 (1991) 169–85

1147 Wright, J, The Wadai-Benghazi slave route, in Savage E (ed), *The human commodity (entry 252),* 174–84

Finance

1148 Nsouli, S, et al, Striving for currency convertability in North Africa, *Finance and development,* 29, 4 (1992) 44–47

Gender

1149 Yacine, T, (ed), *Amour, phantasmes et sociétés en Afrique du Nord et au Sahara.* Paris: Harmattan, 1992, 188pp

Geography, human

1150 Barth, H, et al, *Fous du désert: les premiers explorateurs du Sahara, 1849–1887.* Paris: Phébus, 1991, 270pp

1151 Joffe, G, The changing geography of North Africa, in Chapman G P & Baker, K M (eds), *The changing geography of Africa (entry 405),* 139–64

History, C6–18th

1152 Amoulet, F, Minorité

européenne en Afrique du Nord au XVIIIième siècle, *Arab historical review for Ottoman studies,* 5/6, (1992) 11–16

1153 Mastino, A, (ed), *L'Africa romana: atti des IX convegno di studio nuovo, 13–15 dicembre 1991.* Sassari: Gallizzi, 1991, 2 vols, 1149pp

International relations

1154 Freund, W S, (ed), *La perestroika et les rapports Nord-Sud en Méditerranée.* Hamburg: Deutsches Orient-institut, 1992, 352pp

Labour & manpower

1155 Elbadawi, I A, Rocha, R de R, *Determinants of expatriate workers' remittances in North Africa and Europe.* Washington: World Bank, 1992, 56pp

Natural resources

1156 Hegazi, A, Renewable energy development in North Africa, in Bhagavan M R & Karekezi, S (eds), *Energy for rural development* (London: Zed,1992), 127–43

Politics

1157 Anderson, L, Obligation and accountability: Islamic politics in North Africa, *Daedalus,* 120, 3 (1991) 93–112

1158 Dwyer, K, *Arab voices: the human rights debate in the Middle East.* Berkeley: University of California Press, 1991, 245pp

1159 Faath, S, Mattes, H, (ed), *Demokratie und Menschenrecht in Nordafrika.* Hamburg: Wuquf, 1992, 563pp

1160 Flory, M, et al, *Les régimes politiques arabes .* Paris: PUF, 1991, 558pp

1161 Seddon, D, *Popular protest, austerity and economic liberalism in the Middle East and North Africa.* Norwich: School of Development Studies, University of East Anglia, 1992, 64pp

1162 Zartman, I W, State building and the military in Arab Africa, in Korany B et al (eds), *The many faces of national security in the Arab world* (Basingstoke: Macmillan, 1992), 239–57

Religion, philosophy

1163 Obdeijn, H, Herovert de islam noord-Afrika?, *Internationale spectator,* 46, 6 (1992) 373–380

MAGHREB

General

1164 Lacoste, C, Lacoste, Y, (eds), *L'état du Maghreb.* Paris: La Decouverte, 1991, 572pp

Anthropology

1165 Ferrié, J-N, Vers une anthropologie déconstructiviste des sociétés musulmanes du Maghreb, *Peuples méditerranéens,* 54/55, (1991) 229–246

Architecture

1166 Hamaleh, S, Creating the traditional city: a French project, in Alsayyad N (ed), *Forms of dominance* (Aldershot: Avebury, 1992), 241–59

1167 Mechta, K, (ed), *Maghreb: architecture et urbanisme - patrimoine, tradition et modernité.* Paris: Publisud, 1991, 217pp

Current affairs

1168 Bonnefous, M, *Maghreb:*

repères et rappels. Paris: CHEAM, 1990, 138pp

Demography

No entry, see also: 1193

Economic and social history

1169 Savage, E, Berbers and Blacks: Ibadi slave traffic in eighth century North Africa, *Journal of African history,* 33, 3 (1992) 351–68

Education

1170 Annabi, M, *Actes du Colloque 'L'Université et les transformations sociales', Tunis, 14–19 Mai 1990.* Tunis: Université du Tunies, Centre d'études et de recherches économiques et sociales, 1992, 142, 181pp
1171 Moatassime, A, Cultural pluralism and education in the Maghreb, *Prospects,* 22, 82 (1992) 171–84

Food

1172 Aghrout, A, The food deficits problem in the Arab Maghreb Union: present state and future perspectives, *British journal of Middle East Studies,* 19, 1 (1992) 54–67

History, early

1173 Wright, H T, et al, Datations absolues des sites archéologiques du centre de Madagascar: présentation des déterminations, *Taloha,* 11 (1992) 121–45

History, C6–18th

1174 Chiauzzi, G, et al, *Maghreb médiéval: l'apogée des la civilisation islamique dans l'occident arabe.* Aix

en Provenece: Publisud, 1991, 287pp
1175 Mahfoudh, F, L'introduction du mihrab en Ifriqiya et son évolution jusqu'au XIe siècle, *IBLA,* 168, (1991) 263–279
1176 Temimi, A, Pour des points de repère à l'étude de l'administration ottomane au Maghreb, *Arab historical review for Ottoman studies,* 5/6, (1992) 111–117
1177 Touati, H, Prestige ancestral et système symbolique sarifien dans le Maghreb central du XVIIe siècle, *Arabica,* 39, 1 (1992) 1–24

International economic relations

1178 Handouni, S, Les tentatives d'intégration des pays du Maghreb face à l'élargissement de la CEE, *Etudes internationales,* 23, 2 (1992) 319–48
1179 Sid-Ahmed, A, Maghreb, quelle intégration à la lumière des experiences dans le tiers monde?, *Revue tiers monde,* 33, 129 (1992) 67–97

International relations

1180 Marks, J, The Magreb in 1988: creating a viable unity, *Africa contemporary record 1988/89,* (1992) A55–66
1181 Marquina, A Echeverria, C, La politique de l'Espagne au Maghreb, *Maghreb-Machrek,* 137 (1992) 43–55
1182 Melasuo, T, Maghreb conflicts, socioeconomic crises, and unity, in Raffer K & Salih, M A M (ed), *The least developed and the oil-rich (entry 592),* 49–63
1183 Safir, N, Les opinions maghrébines et la guerre du Golfe: logiques de solidarité et problématique de la modernité,

Peuples méditerranéens, 58/59, (1992) 39–47

1184 Seddon, D, *Politics and the Gulf crisis: government and popular responses in the Maghreb.* Norwich: School of Development Studies, University of East Anglia, 1991, 50pp

Language

1185 Moatissime, A, *Arabisatisation et langue française au Maghreb: un aspect sociolinguistique des dilemmes du développement.* Paris: PUF, 1992, 174pp

Literature

1186 Déjeux, J, Francophone literature in the Magreb: the problem and the possibility, *Research in African literatures,* 23, 2 (1992) 5–19

1187 Dugas, G, *Bibliographie critique de la littérature judeo-maghrebine d'expression française.* Paris: Harmattan, 1992, 95pp

1188 Dugas, G, An unknown Maghrebian genre: judeo-maghrebian literature of French expression, *Research in African literatures,* 23, 2 (1992) 21–32

1189 Gontard, M, Francophone North African literature and critical theory, *Research in African literatures,* 23, 2 (1992) 33–38

1190 Kaye, J, Zoubir, A, *The ambiguous compromise: language, literature and national identity in Algeria and Morroco.* London: Routledge, 1990, 141pp

Religion, philosophy

1191 Palmisano, A L, Istituzioni religiose e sfruttamento delle risorse nell'islam maghrebino: l'esempio delle 'zawaya, *Africa (Rome),* 46, 4 (1991) 503–519

1192 Van der Walt, A J, Invloed van die Islam in die Maghreb, *South African journal of ethnology,* 15, 1 (1992) 14–19

Rural economy

1193 Amara, H A, Pression démographique et dynamique des structures agraires au Maghreb, *Mondes en développement,* 18, 71 (1990) 9–17

1194 Bisson, J, Le Sahara dans le développement des états maghrébins: I, II, *Maghreb-Machrek,* 134 (1991) 3–27 and 35 (1992) 79–106

Sociology

1195 Bedrani, S, Social development strategies in North Africa: Algeria, Tunisia and Morocco, in Mohammed D (ed), *Social development in Africa (entry 1093),* 155–210

Urban studies

1196 Brugnes, M P, (ed), *Universités et développement urbain dans le tiers monde: étude comparée des Fes (Maroc), Merida (Venezuela), Morelia (Mexico) et Sfax (Tunisie).* Paris: Ed. CNRS, 1990, 192pp

ALGERIA

Anthropology

1197 Bensalah, Y, Approche rythmique de quelques devinettes d'Ed-Dis et de Khermam (Bousâada-Algérie), *Matériaux arabes et sudarabiques,* 3, (1991) 229–263

Architecture

1198 Lamprakos, M, Le Corbusier
in Algiers: the Plan Obus as
colonial urbanism, in Alsayyad N
(ed), *Forms of dominance*
(Aldershot: Avebury, 1992),
188–210

Arts

1199 Mécherie-Saada, N, Musique
et société chez les Touaregs de
l'Ahaggar, *Revue du monde
musulman et de la Méditerranée,* 58,
(1990) 136–142

Current affairs

1200 Djeghloul, A, L'après Chadlie
a-t-il commencé?,
Maghreb-Machrek, 133 (1991)
99–103
1201 Fontaine, J, Les élections
législatives algériennes: résultats du
premier tour, *Maghreb-Machrek,*
135 (1992) 155–65
1202 Harbi, M, Algérie:
l'interruption du processus
électoral: respect ou déni de la
constitution?, *Maghreb-Machrek,*
135 (1992) 145–54
1203 Kalfleche, J M, Algéria:
tragiques contresens, *Geopolitique
africaine,* 15, 1 (1992) 9–24
1204 Kapil, A, Portrait statistique
des élections du 12 juin 1990:
chiffres-clés pour une analyse,
Cahiers de l'Orient, 23, (1991)
41–63
1205 Lamchichi, M, Algérie: la
démocratie en peril, *Revue des Deux
Mondes,* (1992) 67–76
1206 Leveau, R, Anatomie d'un
changement incertain, *Esprit,* 180
(1992) 90–94
1207 Leveau, R, L'Algérie en état
de siège, *Maghreb-Machrek,* 133
(1991) 92–99
1208 Mongin, C, Accéder à la

démocratie?, *Esprit,* 180 (1992)
161–66
1209 Prenant, A, L'Algérie en crise
face à ses contraintes, *Cahiers du
Communisme,* 68, 10 (1992) 83–92
1210 Sigaud, D, *La fracture
algérienne, 1990, carnets du route.*
Paris: Calmann-Levy, 1991, 265pp

Economy - Development

1211 Boukaraoun, H, The
privatization process in Algeria,
Developing economies, 29, 2 (1991)
89–124
1212 Boukharaoun, H, The
privatisation process in Algeria,
Developing economies, 29, 2 (1991)
89–124
1213 Laabas, B, Wilson, P R D,
Modelling savings behaviour in
centrally planned developing
countries: the case of Algeria 1963
to 1984, *Savings and development,*
16, 3 (1992) 255–73
1214 Mouhoubi, S, Bank autonomy
and economic performance: the
case of Algeria, in Roe A R et al
*Instruments of economic policy (entry
341),* 221–28
1215 Salah, M, Le
dysfonctionnement de l'entreprise
publique économique en Algérie,
Revue internationale de droit comparé,
43, 3 (1991) 627–676

Economic and social history

1216 Canteau, J, *Le feu et la pluie de
l'Atlas: vie quotidienne d'une famille
de colons français.* Paris: Harmattan,
1992, 255pp
1217 Leon, A, *Colonisation,
enseignement et education.* Paris:
Harmattan, 1991, 320pp

Education

1218 Kadri, A, Enseignement: le
système en question, *Cahiers de*

l'Orient, 23, (1991) 163–196

Finance

1219 Nemouchi, F, Offre de monnaie et développement économique en Algérie, *Revue algérienne des sciences juridiques, économiques et politiques,* 29, 1/2 (1991) 203–216

Food

1220 Pfeiffer, K, Does food security make a diference? Algeria, Egypt and Turkey in comparative persepctive, in Korany B et al (eds), *The many faces of national security in the Arab world* (Basingstoke: Macmillan, 1992), 127–44

Gender

see also: 1261, 1263
1221 Amrane, D, *Les femmes algériennes dans la guerre.* Paris: Plon, 1991, 299pp
1222 Benhassine-Miller, A, Les femmes algériennes, *Bulletin of francophone Africa,* 1 (1992) 39–48
1223 Hakiki-Talahite, F, Sous le voile...les femmes, *Cahiers de l'Orient,* 23, (1991) 123–142
1224 Hakiki-Talahite, F, Women, economic reforms and politics, in Rudebeck L (ed), *When democracy makes sense (entry 931),* 151–60
1225 Khodja, S, *A comme Algérienne.* Alger: Entreprise nationale du livre, 1991, 274pp
1226 Tlemçani, R, The rise of Algerian women: cultural dualism and multi-party politics, *Journal of developing societies,* 8, 1 (1992) 69–81

Geography, human

1227 Prenant, A, Littoral intérieur

et dynamique urbaine dans l'histoire de l'Algérie, *Cahiers d'URBAMA,* 5, (1991) 19–35

Geography, physical

1228 Carton, P, Inventory of small and medium-size irrigation schemes in Algeria using SPOT numerical data, in Gastellu-Etchegorry J P (ed), *Satellite remote sensing (entry 412a),* 59–66

History, C19th

1229 Boutaleb, A, *L'Emir Abd-el-Kader et la formation de la nation algérienne: de l'Emir Abd-el-Kader à la guerre de liberation.* Alger: Dahlab, 1990, 344pp
1230 Colonna, U, La Compagnie de Jésus en Algérie (1840–1880): l'exemple de la mission de Kabylie (1863–1880), *Maghreb-Machrek,* 135 (1992) 68–78

History, C20th

see also: 1221
1231 Clancy-Smith, J, The house of Zainab: female authority and saintly succession in colonial Algeria, in Keddie N R & Baron, B (eds), *Women in Middle Eastern history (entry 1333),* 254–74
1232 Gaspard, F, *De Dreux à Alger: Maurice Violette 1870–1960.* Paris: Harmattan, 1991, 210pp
1233 Harbi, M, et al, *Les années algériennes* ou la soft histoire médiatique?, *Peuples méditerranéens,* 58/59, (1992) 325–340
1234 Leimdorfer, F, *Discours académique et colonialism: thèmes et recherche sur l'Algérie pendant le période coloniale.* Paris: Publisud, 1992, 316pp
1235 MacMaster, N, The 'dark age'

of colonialism: Algeria 1920–54,
Bulletin of francophone Africa, 1
(1992) 106–111

1236 **Pervillé, G,** Trente ans après:
réflexions sur les accords d'Évian,
Revue française d'histoire d'outre-mer,
79, 296 (1992) 367–381

1237 **Ruedy, J,** *Modern Algeria: the
origins and development of a nation.*
Bloomington: Indiana UP, 1992,
290pp

1238 **Sorlin, P,** French opinion and
the Algerian war, *Bulletin of
francophone Africa*, 1 (1992) 49–57

Industry & trade

1239 **Abdesselam, B,** *Le gaz
algérien: stratégies et enjeux.* Alger:
Bouchene, 1990, 345pp

1240 **Chikhi, S,** Désindustrialisation
et crise de société en Algérie, *Africa
development*, 16, 2 (1991) 57–71

1241 **Hocine, R,** Privatisation in
Algeria, in Ramanadham V V (ed),
Privatisation (entry 203), 319–36

1242 **Salah, M,** Pour une
perfectibilité du fonctionnement
des sociétés commerciales, *Revue
algérienne des sciences juridiques,
économiques et politiques*, 29, 1/2
(1991) 141–164

International economic relations

1243 **Fardeheb, A,** La régulation
internationale des flux et les aspects
fondamentaux de l'evolution de
l'économie algérienne, *Revue
algérienne des sciences juridiques,
économiques et politiques*, 29, 1/2
(1991) 177–202

1244 **Kerdoun, A,** L'entreprise
conjointe en Afrique instrument de
coopération: l'exemple de la
Société forestière algéro-congolaise,
*Revue algérienne des sciences
juridiques, économiques et politiques*,
29, 1/2 (1991) 99–118

1245 **Kramer, H J,** *Geschäftspartner
Algerien.* Cologne: Bundesstelle für
Aussenhandelsinformation, 1991,
103pp

International relations

No entry, see also: 1220

Language

1246 **Djite, P G,** L'arabisation de
l'Algérie: motivations linguistique
et sociopolitique, *Afrique 2000*, 8
(1992) 91–103

1247 **Elimam, A,** Linguistique et
démocratie, *Cahiers de l'Orient*, 23,
(1991) 143–162

Law

1248 **Beke, D,** La constitution
algérienne de 1989: une passerelle
entre le socialisme et l'islamisme?,
Afrika focus, 7, 3 (1991) 241–272

1249 **Benchenebeb, A,** La formation
du lien de Kafala et les silences
législatifs, *Revue algérienne des
sciences juridiques, économiques et
politiques*, 29, 1/2 (1991) 47–53

1250 **Bendourou, O,** Le conseil
constitutionnel algérien, *Revue du
droit public*, 107, 6 (1991) 1617–40

1251 **el Hocine, H D-B,** Droit
public et droit privé: quelques
aspects de l'évolution de la
législation algérienne, *Revue
algérienne des sciences juridiques,
économiques et politiques*, 29, 1/2
(1991) 79–98

1252 **Guesmi, A,** Le contrôle de
constitutionnalité en Algérie:
réalités et perspectives, *Revue
algérienne des sciences juridiques,
économiques et politiques*, 29, 1/2
(1991) 65–78

Literature

1253 **Achour, C,** Les écrivains
algériens aux prises avec une

langue (histoire, société, création), *Bulletin of francophone Africa*, 1 (1992) 12–19

1254 Bois, M, Arabic language Algerian literature, *Research in African literatures*, 23, 2 (1992) 103–111

1255 Bonn, C, *Kateb Yacine, 'Nedjma'.* Paris: PUF, 1990, 126pp

1256 Bonn, C, Kateb Yacine, *Research in African literatures*, 23, 2 (1992) 60–70

1257 Bouzar, W, The French-language Algerian novel, *Research in African literatures*, 23, 2 (1992) 51–59

1258 Desplanques, F, The long, luminous wake of Mohammed Dib, *Research in African literatures*, 23, 2 (1992) 71–88

1259 Gafaiti, H, Rachid Boudjedra: the bard of modernity, *Research in African literatures*, 23, 2 (1992) 89–102

1260 Jones, R, Images of Algeria in the fiction of Mohammed Dib, *Bulletin of francophone Africa*, 1 (1992) 20–29

1261 Roche, A, Women's literature in Algeria, *Research in African literatures*, 23, 2 (1992) 209–15

1262 Schousboe, E, *Albert Bensoussan.* Paris: Harmattan, 1992, 132pp

1263 Tahon, M B, Women novelists and the struggle for Algeria's national liberation (1957–1980), *Research in African literatures*, 23, 2 (1992) 39–50

Media

No entry, see also: 1290

Politics

see also: 1294

1264 Adams, P, Algeria, Islam and North Africa, *South Africa international*, 23, 1 (1992) 18–25

1265 Addi, L, Peut-il exister une sociologie politique en Algérie?, *Peuples méditerranéens*, 54/55, (1991) 221–227

1266 Ali, S H, Algérie: le premier séminaire national des zaouïas, *Maghreb-Machrek*, 135 (1992) 53–67

1267 Bachir, Y C, Le multipartisme en Algérie: une nouvelle donnée constitutionnelle, *African journal of international and comparative law*, 2, 3 (1990) 440–455

1268 Bekkar, R, Taking up space in Tlemcen: the islamist occupation of urban Algeria, *Middle East report*, 22, 6 (1992) 11–15

1269 Blin, L, Algérie: les élites politiques, *Cahiers de l'Orient*, 25/26, (1992) 237–259

1270 Bourenane, N, Pouvoir d'état et société civile en Algérie, *Africa development*, 15, 3/4 (1990) 105–22

1271 Chikhi, S, *Algeria: from mass rebellion in October 1988 to workers' social protest*: Uppsala, SIAS, 23pp

1272 Chikhi, S, Algeria: from mass rebellion in October 1988 to workers' social protests, in Rudebeck L (ed), *When democracy makes sense (entry 931)*, 363–84

1273 Djeghloul, A, Le multipartisme à l'algérienne, *Maghreb-Machrek*, 127 (1990) 194–210

1274 Djerbal, D, Ait Hamou, L, Women and democracy in Algeria, *Review of African political economy*, 54 (1992) 106–111

1275 Entelis, J P, The crisis of authoritarianism in North Africa: the case of Algeria, *Problems of communism*, 41, 3 (1992) 71–81

1276 Faath, S, *Algerien: gesellscahftliche Strukturen und politische Reformen zu Beginn der neunziger Jahre.* Hamburg: Deutsches Orient-Institut, 1990, 730pp

1277 **Faraouët, A, Guyomarch, C,** Islamisme ou islamismes?, *Cahiers de l'Orient,* 27, (1992) 23–43

1278 **Howe, J,** The crisis of Algerian nationalism and the rise of Islamic integralism, *New left review,* 196 (1992) 85–100

1279 **Kapil, A,** Les partis islamistes en Algérie, *Maghreb-Machrek,* 133 (1991) 103–111

1280 **Khelladi, A,** *Les islamistes algériens face au pouvoir.* Algiers: Alfa, 1991, 203pp

1281 **Lakeral, M,** (ed), *Algérie, de l'indépendance à état d'urgence.* Paris: Harmattan, 1992, 284pp

1282 **Leca, J,** Algérie: politique et société, *Maghreb-Machrek,* 133 (1991) 89–92

1283 **Leveau, R,** *Algeria: adversaries in search of uncertain compromises.* Paris: Institute for Security Studies, West European Union, 1992, 29pp

1284 **Roberts, H,** The Algerian state and the challenge of democracy, *Government and opposition,* 27, 4 (1992) 433–54

1285 **Roy, O,** Le néofondamentalisme: des Frères musulmanes au FIS, *Esprit,* 180 (1992) 79–89

1286 **Serpa, E,** The fundamentalist reaction and the future of Algeria, *Africa insight,* 21, 3 (1991) 194–203

1287 **Tahi, M S,** The arduous democratisation process in Algeria, *Journal of modern African studies,* 30, 3 (1992) 397–419

1288 **Tridi, R,** *L'Algérie en quelques maux: autopsie d'une anomie.* Paris: Harmattan, 1992, 280pp

Religion, philosophy

see also: 1223

1289 **Babès, L,** Passion et ironie dans la cité: Annaba: du 'ribat' au réformisme, *Maghreb-Machrek,* 135 (1992) 39–52

1290 **Deheuvels, L W,** *Islam et*

pensée contemporaine en Algérie: la revue 'Al-Asâla', 1971–1981. Paris: CNRS, 1992, 310pp

1291 **Ferhat, H,** Abu l-'Abbas: contestation et sainteté, *Al-Qantara,* 13, 1 (1992) 181–199

1292 **Landousies, J,** Chrétiens et musulmans en Algérie, *Islamochristiana,* 17, (1991) 99–129

Sociology

see also: 1295

1293 **Aktouf, O,** *Algérie entre l'exil et la curée.* Paris: Harmattan, 1990, 330pp

1294 **Entelis, J P, Naylor, P C,** (eds), *State and society in Algeria: state, culture and society in Arab North Africa.* Boulder: Westview, 1992, 307pp

Urban studies

see also: 1198

1295 **Boudebaba, R,** *Urban growth and housing policy in Algeria: a case study of a migrant community in the city of Constantine.* Aldershot: Avebury, 1992, 300pp

EGYPT

Demography

1296 **Mahgoub, Y M, Hussein, M A,** *Regional urban-rural differentials of the educational impact on fertility in Egypt.* Cairo: Cairo Demographic Centre, 1992, 31pp

1297 **Osheba, I K T, Sayed, H A A,** *The fertility impact of contraceptive use in Egypt: an aggregate analysis.* Cairo: Demographic Centre, 1991, 36pp

1298 **Sayed, H A A,** *Services availability and family planning in Egypt.* Cairo: Cairo Demographic Centre, 1991, 50pp

1299 **Sayed, H A A, el Tawila, S I,**

Patterns of family life cycle and household structure in Egypt. Cairo: Cairo Demographic Centre, 1991, 95pp

1300 Zaky, H H M, *Intra-family decision interaction and complete family size: the case of Egypt.* Cairo: Cairo Demographic Centre, 1991, 17pp

Economy - Development

see also: 173

1301 Shafih, N, Modelling private investment in Egypt, *Journal of development economics,* 39, 2 (1992) 263–77

1302 Timewell, S, Egypt: one more 'final' chance, *Banker,* July 1991 40–44

Economic and social history

1303 Baron, B, The making and breaking of marital bonds in modern Egypt, in Keddie N R & Baron, B (eds), *Women in Middle Eastern history (entry 1333),* 275–91

1304 Berkey, J P, Women and islamic education in the Mamluk period, in Keddie N R & Baron, B (eds), *Women in Middle Eastern history (entry 1333),* 143–59

1305 Chesworth, P, History of water use in Sudan and Egypt, in Howell J P, Allan J A (eds), *The Nile (entry 1328),* 40–58

1306 Lutfi, H, Manners and customs of fourteenth century Cairene women: female anarchy versus male sar'i order in Muslim prescriptive treatises, in Keddie N R & Baron, B (eds), *Women in Middle Eastern history (entry 1333),* 99–121

1307 Osman, M, *Zur Entwicklung der ägyptischen Textilindustrie zwischen 1939 und 1952.* Frankfurt: Lang, 1991, 178pp

1308 Petry, C F, Class solidarity

versus gender gain: women as custodians of property in later medieval Eygpt, in Keddie N R & Baron, B (eds), *Women in Middle Eastern history (entry 1333),* 122–42

1309 Raymond, A, Architecture and urban development: Cairo during the Ottoman period (1517–1798), in Spagnolo J P (ed), *Problems of the modern Middle East in historical perspective* (Reading: Ithaca, 1992), 211–27

1310 Shaw, B D, Explaining incest: brother-sister marriage in Graeco-Roman Egypt, *Man,* 27, 2 (1992) 267–99

1311 Tignor, R L, The Suez crisis of 1956 and Egypt's foreign private sector, *Journal of imperial and Commonwealth history,* 22, 2 (1992) 274–97

1312 Winter, M, *Egyptian society under Ottoman rule, 1517–1798.* London: Routledge, 1992, 323pp

Education

1313 Dupuis, J, L'université francophone d'Alexandrie, *Monde et cultures,* 51, 1–4 (1991) 55–63

1314 Richards, A, *Higher education in Egypt.* Washington: World Bank, 1992, 40pp

Environment

1315 Abu El-Ennan, S M, et al, Dunes encroachment on the cultivated land in Egypt, *Desertification control bulletin,* 18 (1990) 1–5

Finance

1316 Timewell, S, Egypt: one down, one to go, *Banker,* July 1992 55–59

1317 Zaki, M Y, Behaviour and determinants of the currency to demand deposit ratio in Egypt,

Journal of developing areas, 26, 3
(1992) 357–70

Food

1318 **el-Kholei, O A,** Objectives
and implications of Egyptian food
policies, *L'Égypte contemporaine*, 81,
419/420 (1990) 19–58
1319 **Harik, L,** Subsidisation
policies in Egypt: neither economic
growth nor distribution,
*International journal of Middle East
studies*, 24, 3 (1992) 481–99

Gender

1320 **Badran, M,** From
consciousness to activism: feminist
politics in early twentieth century
Egypt, in Spagnolo J P (ed),
*Problems of the modern Middle East
in historical perspective* (Reading:
Ithaca, 1992), 27–48
1321 **Danielson, V,** Artists and
entrepreneurs: female singers in
Cairo during the 1920s, in Keddie
N R & Baron, B (eds), *Women in
Middle Eastern history (entry 1333)*,
292–309
1322 **Hatem, M F,** Economic and
political liberalisation in Egypt and
the demise of state feminism,
*International journal of Middle East
studies*, 24, 2 (1992) 231–51
1323 **Lane, S D, Meleis, A I,**
Roles, work, health perceptions and
health resources of women: a study
in an Egyptian Delta hamlet, *Social
science and medecine*, 33, 10 (1991)
1197–1208
1324 **Larson, B K,** Women's work
and status in rural Egypt, *NWSA
journal*, 3, 1 (1991) 38–52
1325 **Nelson, C,** Biography and
women's history: on interpreting
Doria Shafik, in Keddie N R &
Baron, B (eds), *Women in
Middle Eastern history (entry 1333)*,
310–33

1326 **Qasim Amin,** *The liberation of
women; a document in the history of
Egyptian feminism.* New York:
Columbia University Press, 1992,
128pp

Geography, human

see also: 1381
1327 **Allan, J A,** Review of evolving
water demands and national
development options, in Howell J
P, Allan J A (eds), *The Nile (entry
1328)*, 181–91
1328 **Howell, J P, Allen, J A,** (eds),
*The Nile: resource evaluation, resource
management, hydropolitics and legal
issues.* London: SOAS, Centre of
Near and Middle Eastern Studies,
1990, 245pp

Geography, physical

see also: 1509
1329 **Evans, T,** History of Nile
flows, in Howell J P, Allan J A
(eds), *The Nile (entry 1328)*, 5–39
1330 **Sutcliffe, J V, Lazenby, J B
C,** Hydrological data requirements
for planning Nile management, in
Howell J P, Allan J A (eds), *The
Nile (entry 1328)*, 107–36
1331 **Zewdie Abate,** The integrated
development of Nile Basin waters,
in Howell J P, Allan J A (eds), *The
Nile (entry 1328)*, 137–51

Health & welfare services

1332 **Azer, A, Afifi, E,** *Social
support systems for the aged in Egypt.*
Tokyo: United Nations University
Press, 1992,

History, general

1333 **Keddie, N R, Baron, B,** (ed),
*Women in Middle Eastern history:
shifting boundaries in sex and gender.*
New Haven : Yale UP, 1991,

History, early

1334 Johnson, S B, *The cobra goddess of ancient Egypt.* London: Kegan Paul, 1990, 276pp
1335 Rice, M, *Egypt's making: the origins of ancient Egypt, 5000–2000 BC.* London: Routledge, 1990, 322pp

History, C6–18th

1336 Bregeon, J N, *L'Egypte français au jour le jour, 1798–1801.* Paris: Perrin, 1991, 441pp

History, C19th

1337 Kruger, M, *'Le baton egyptien'. Der ägyptische Knüppel: die Rolle der 'ägyptischen Frage' in der deutschen Ausssenpolitik von 1875/6 bis zur 'entente cordiale'.* Frankfurt: Lang, 1991, 291pp
1338 Sonbol, A el-A, *The creation of a medical profession in Egypt, 1800–1922.* Syracuse, NY: Syracuse University Press, 1991, 177pp
1339 Toledano, E H, *State and society in mid-nineteenth century Egypt.* Cambridge: CUP, 1990, 320pp

History, C20th

see also: 1320
1340 Botman, S, *Egypt from independence to revolution, 1919–52.* Syracuse, NY: Syracuse University Press, 1991, 170pp
1341 Collins, R O, History and hydropolitics and the Nile, in Howell J P, Allan J A (eds), *The Nile (entry 1328),* 153–80
1342 Deeb, M, Continuity in modern Egyptian history: the Wafd and the Muslim Brothers, in Spagnolo J P (ed), *Problems of the modern Middle East in historical perspective* (Reading: Ithaca, 1992), 49–61

1343 Erlich, H, British internal security and Egyptian youth, in Cohen M J & Kolinsky, M (eds), *Britain and the Middle East in the 1930s* (Basingstoke: Macmillan,1992), 98–112
1344 Goldberg, E, Peasants in revolt - Egypt 1919, *International journal of Middle East studies,* 24, 2 (1992) 261–80
1345 Gordon, J, *Nasser's blessed movement: Egypt's Free Officers and the July revolution.* Oxford: OUP, 1991, 254pp
1346 Harris, P, Egypt: defence plans, in Cohen M J & Kolinsky, M (eds), *Britain and the Middle East in the 1930s* (Basingstoke: Macmillan,1992), 61–78
1347 Hopwood, D, *Egypt 1945–1990.* London: Routledge (3rd edn., revised), 1991, 207pp
1348 Jankowski, J, Eyptian regional policy in the wake of the Anglo-Egyptian Treaty of 1936: Arab alliance or islamic caliphate?, in Cohen M J & Kolinsky, M (eds), *Britain and the Middle East in the 1930s* (Basingstoke: Macmillan,1992), 81–97
1349 Mikdadi, F, *Gamal Abdel Nasser: a bibliography.* New York: Greenwood, 1991, 148pp
1350 Oren, M B, *The origins of the second Arab-Israel war: Egypt, Israel and the great powers, 1952–1958.* London: Cass, 1992, 290pp
1351 Reid, D M, Cultural imperialism and nationalism: the struggle to define and control the heritage of Arab art in Egypt, *International journal of Middle East studies,* 24, 1 (1992) 57–76
1352 Woodward, P, *Nasser.* Harlow: Longman, 1992, 176pp

Industry & trade

1353 Davies, S P, et al, Small manufacturing enterprises in Egypt,

Economic development and cultural change, 40, 2 (1991) 381–412

1354 El-Hawayan, H A W, Sullivan D, Privatisation in Egypt, in Ramanadham V V (ed), *Privatisation (entry 203)*, 337–53

International economic relations

see also: 1377

1355 Lavy, V, Sheffer, E, *Foreign aid and economic development in the Middle East: Egypt, Syria and Jordan*. New York: Praeger, 1991, 163pp

International relations

see also: 1348, 1350

1356 Lorenz, J P, *Egypt and the Arabs: foreign policy and the search for national identity*. Boulder: Westview, 1990, 184pp

1357 Sid-Ahmed, M, Le nouvel ordre régional, vu du Caire, *Maghreb-Machrek*, 136 (1992) 15–25

1358 Talhami, G H, *Palestine and the Egyptian national identity*. New York: Praeger, 1992, 177pp

Labour & manpower

1359 Khashaba, N A, Trade strategy for employment growth in Egypt 1960–1986, *L'Égypte contemporaine*, 81, 421/422 (1990) 111–140

Law

No entry, see also: 690

Literature

1360 Booth, M, Colloquial arabic poetry, politics and the press in modern Egypt, *International journal of Middle East studies*, 24, 3 (1992) 419–40

1361 Francis-Saad, M, Naguib Mahfouz: du fils du pays à l'homme universal, *Revue du monde musulman et de la Méditerrananée*, 59/60 (1991) 241–252

1362 Le Gassick, T, (ed), *Critical perspectives on Naguib Mahfouz*. Washington: Three Continents, 1991, 181pp

1363 Mikhail, M N, *Studies in the short fiction of Mahfouz and Idris*. New York: New York UP, 1992, 168pp

Media

No entry, see also: 1360

Medical

1364 Casterline, J B, et al, Infant and child mortality in rural Egypt, *Journal of biosocial science*, 24, 2 (1992) 245–60

1365 Loza, S F, et al, *Oral contraceptive compliance and continuation in Egypt*. Cairo: Cairo Demographic Centre, 1991, 24pp

1366 Rasahd, H, *A reappraisal of how oral rehydration therapy affected mortality in Egypt*. Wshington: World Bank, 1992, 26pp

Planning

No entry, see also: 1380

Politics

1367 Africa Watch, *Behind closed doors: torture and detention in Egypt*. New York: Africa Watch, 1992, 144pp

1368 Amnesty International, *Egypt: ten years of torture*. London: Amnesty International, 1991, 17pp

1369 Zubaida, S, Islam, the state and democracy: contrasting conceptions of society in Egypt,

Middle East report, 22, 6 (1992) 2–10

Allan J A (eds), *The Nile (entry 1328),* 83–92

Religion, philosophy

1370 Akhari, S, The clergy's concepts of rule in Egypt and Iran, *Annals,* 524 (1992) 92–102

1371 Ben Néfissa-Paris, S, Le mouvement associatif égyptien et l'islam: éléments d'une problématique, *Maghreb-Machrek,* 135 (1992) 19–36

1372 Cannuyer, C, *Les Coptes.* Turnhout: Brepols, 1990, 230pp

1373 Kemke, A H E, *Stiftungen im muslimischen Rechtsleben des neuzeitlichen Agypten: die schariatrechtlichen Gutachen (Fatwas) von Muhammed 'Abduh (st.1905) zum Wakf.* Frankfurt: Lang, 1991, 181pp

1374 Voll, J O, Fundamentalism in the Sunni Arab world: Egypt and the Sudan, in Marty M E (ed), *Fundamentalisms observed* (Chicago: University of Chicago Press, 1991), 345–402

Rural economy

see also: 1324

1375 Dittman, A, Oasis markets: economic interaction between permanent and periodic markets in Faiyum (Eygpt) and Kashgar (China), in Cammann L (ed), *Traditional marketing systems (entry 113),* 37–47

1376 Dyer, G, Farm size-farm productivity re-examined: evidence from rural Egypt, *Journal of peasant studies,* 19, 1 (1991) 59–72

1377 Nassar, S, Some issues of agricultural trade policies in Egypt, *L'Égypte contemporaine,* 81, 419/420 (1990) 71–106

1378 Stoner, R F, Future irrigation planning in Egypt, in Howell J P,

Sociology

1379 Khawaga, D el, Le développement communautaire copte: un mode de participation au politique?, *Maghreb-Machrek,* 135 (1992) 3–18

Urban studies

1380 Davidson, F, Lessons from implementation: the impact of an active land management policy on integrated land development in Ismailia, Egypt, in Baross P & van der Linden, J (eds), *Transformation of land supply systems in Third World cities* (Aldershot: Avebury, 1992), 277–94

1381 Deggs, M R, Doornkamp, J C, Earthquake hazard and urban development in Egypt, *Third World planning review,* 14, 4 (1991) 391–408

1382 Kardash, H, Wilkinson, N, Development within development: user extensions of five story walk-up housing in Cairo, *Open house international,* 16, 1 (1991) 9–18

1383 Steinberg, F, Cairo: informal land development and the challenge for the future, in Baross P & van der Linden, J (eds), *Transformation of land supply systems in Third World cities* (Aldershot: Avebury, 1992), 111–32

1384 Tipple, G, Wilkinson, N, Self-help transformation of government-built flats: the case of Helwan, Egypt, in Mathey K (ed), *Beyond self-help housing* (London: Mansell, 1992), 283–302

1385 Wilkinson, N, et al, Development within development: the case of Helwan New community, Cairo, *Open house*

international, 16, 3 (1991) 3–15

1386 Wilkinson, N, Kardash, H,
Development within development:
distribution of responsibilities in
aided self-help in Egypt's new city
settlements, *Third World planning
review*, 14, 3 (1991) 297–312

LIBYA

Architecture

1387 Fuller, M, Building power:
Italian architecture and urbanism
in Libtya and Ethiopia, in Alsayyad
N (ed), *Forms of dominance*
(Aldershot: Avebury, 1992), 211–39

Economy - Development

1388 Beschourner, N, Smith, A,
*Libya in the 1990s: can its resources
be salvaged?* London: Economist
Intelligence Unit, 1991, 98pp

Food

1389 Schliephake, K, Libya:
irrigation and food security in an
oil-rich desert country, *African
development perspectives yearbook*, 2,
(1990/91) 502–523

Geography, human

1390 Decraene, P, Le grand fleuve
artificiel Libyien, *Monde et cultures*,
51, 1–4 (1991) 266–77

History, C6–18th

1391 Zeltner, J C, *Tripoli: carrefour
de l'Europe et des pays du Tchad,
1500–1795.* Paris: Harmattan,
1992, 300pp

History, C20th

1392 Baldinetti, A, 'Aziz 'Ali
al-Misri: un ufficiale egiziano al

fronte libico (1911–13), *Africa
(Rome)*, 47, 2 (1992) 268–275

International relations

**1393 Foreign & Commonwealth
Office,** *Libya and the PanAm 103
bombing.* London: FCO, 1992,
10pp

1394 Lemarchand, R, Libyan
adventurism, in Harbeson J W &
Rothchild, D (eds), *Africa in world
politics (entry 625)*, 144–58

Politics

1395 Djaziri, M, Indépendance et
changement politique en Libye:
l'Islam et l'évolution de l'Etat
(1951–1990), *Canadian journal of
development studies*, 13, 3 (1992)
337–359

Rural economy

1396 Dalton, W G, Some
considerations in the sedentarisation
of nomads: the Libyan case, in
Salzman C & Galaty, J G (eds),
Nomads in a changing world
(Naples: Instituto Universitario
Orientale, 1990) 139–64

Urban studies

No entry, see also: 1387

MOROCCO

General

1397 Ennaji, M, Une science sociale
au Maroc, pour quoi faire?, *Peuples
méditerranéens*, 54/55, (1991)
213–220

Anthropology

see also: 1447

1398 Eickelmann, D F, *Knowledge*

and power in Morocco: the education
of a twentieth century notable.
Princeton: Princeton University
Press, 1992, 224pp

Architecture

1399 Rabinow, P, Colonialism,
modernity: the French in Morocco,
in Alsayyad N (ed), *Forms of
dominance* (Aldershot: Avebury,
1992), 167–82

Current affairs

1400 Ballaiche, J, Maroc: une
répression féroce au service d'une
exploitation forcenée, *Cahiers du
communisme,* 67, 9 (1991) 102–105

Economy - Development

see also: 173
1401 Brachet, P, *Corruption et
sous-développement au Maroc.* Paris:
Harmattan, 1992, 197pp

Economic and social history

1402 Shroeter, D J, Slave markets
and slavery in Moroccan urban
society, in Savage E (ed), *The
human commodity (entry 252),*
185–213

Education

No entry, see also: 1406

Environment

1403 Mirkes, M, Makrophyten als
Bio-indikatoren zur Beurteilung der
Gewässerverschmutzung im
semiariden Marokko, *Die Erde,*
122, 4 (1991) 317–333

Finance

1404 Zejli, A, L'offre de monnaie et

l'inflation au Maroc, *Savings and
development,* 16, 2 (1992) 145–158

Gender

1405 Davis, S S, Impediments to
empowerment: Moroccan women
and the agencies, *Journal of
developing societies,* 8, 1 (1992)
111–121
1406 Spratt, J E, Women and
literacy in Morocco, *Annals,* 520
(1992) 121–32

Geography, human

**1407 Müller-Hohenstein, K,
Popp, H,** *Marokko: ein islamisches
Entwicklungsland mit kolonialer
Vergangenheit.* Stuttgart: Klett,
1990, 229pp

History, general

1408 López Garcia, B, Entre
Europe et Orient: Ceuta et Melilla,
*Revue du monde musulman et de la
Méditerrananée,* 59/60 (1991)
165–180

History, C6–18th

1409 Burkhalter, S L, Listening for
silences in Almoravid history:
another reading of "The conquest
that never was", *History in Africa,*
19, (1992) 103–131
1410 Cornell, V J, Mystical doctrine
and political action in Moroccan
sufism: the role of the exemplar in
the Tariqa al-Jazuliyya, *Al-Qantara,*
13, 1 (1992) 201–231
1411 Lagardere, V, *Les almoravides
jusqu'au règne du Jusuf ben Tasfin.*
Paris: Harmattan, 1992, 240pp
1412 Sebti, A, Hagiographie du
voyage au Maroc médiéval,
Al-Qantara, 13, 1 (1992) 167–179

History, C20th

1413 Aouchar, A, *La presse marocaine dans la lutte pour l'indépendance (1933-1956).* Casablanca: Wallada, 1990, 160pp

1414 Del Pozo Manzano, E, La campaña de Ifni en la última guerra de Africa: 1957-58, *Estudios africanos,* 5, 8/9 (1990) 107-128

1415 Doumou, A, (ed), *The Moroccan state in historical perspective 1850-1985.* Dakar: Codesria, 1990, 174pp

1416 Gershovich, M, A Moroccan Saint-Cyr, *Middle Eastern studies,* 28, 2 (1992) 231-257

1417 Monjib, H, *La monarchie marocaine et la lutte pour le pouvoir.* Paris: Harmattan, 1992, 367pp

1418 Moreno Juste, A, El régimen franquista y la reactualización de la cuestión tangerina en 1952, *Estudios africanos,* 5, 8/9 (1990) 73-91

1419 Neila Hernández, J L, Las responsabilidades internacionales de la II República en Marruecos: el problema del abandonismo, *Estudios africanos,* 5, 8/9 (1990) 47-71

1420 Sánchez Ruano, F, La República morisca de Rabat-Salé, *Estudios africanos,* 5, 8/9 (1990) 139-148

1421 Sangmuah, E N, Sultan Mohammed ben Youssef's American strategy and the diplomacy of North African decolonisation, *Journal of contemporary history,* 27, 1 (1992) 129-48

1422 Tessainer y Tomasich, C-F, Por qué El Raisuni no pactó con Abd el Krim?, *Estudios africanos,* 5, 8/9 (1990) 101-106

Industry & trade

1423 British Consulate General,

Casablanca, *Morocco: pharmaceutical industry.* London: Foreign & Commonwealth Office, 1992, 30pp

1424 Eussner, A, Private industry response to structural adjustment and deregulation in Morocco, *Internationales Afrikaforum,* 28, 2 (1992) 181-195

1425 Saulniers, A H, Privatisation in Morocco, in Ramanadham V V (ed), *Privatisation (entry 203),* 293-318

International relations

1426 Souhaili, M, *The roi et la rose: Hassan II et Mitterrand - des rapports équivoques.* Paris: Harmattan, 1992, 143pp

Language

1427 McGuire, J, Forked tongues, marginal bodies: writing as translation in Khatibi, *Research in African literatures,* 23, 1 (1992) 107-116

Law

1428 Rousset, M, Maroc 1972-1992: une constitution immuable ou changeante?, *Maghreb-Machrek,* 137 (1992) 15-24

Literature

1429 Abdalaoui, M A, The Moroccan novel in French, *Research in African literatures,* 23, 4 (1992) 9-33

1430 Abdel-Jouad, H, Mohammed Khaïr-Eddine: the poet as iconoclast, *Research in African literatures,* 23, 2 (1992) 145-50

1431 Alessandra, J, Abdellatif Laabi: a writing of dissidence, *Research in African literatures,*

23, 2 (1992) 151–66

1432 Bousfiha, N, Contemporary French-language Moroccan poetry, *Research in African literatures,* 23, 2 (1992) 113–30

1433 Cazeneuve, O, Gender, age, and narrative transformations in *L'enfant de sable* by Tahar Ben Jelloun, *French review,* 64, 3 (1991) 437–450

1434 Kaye, J, Morocco's linguistic conundrum: or, why do they still write in French?, *Bulletin of francophone Africa,* 1 (1992) 91–105

1435 Marx-Scouras, D, A literature of departure: the cross-cultural writing of Driss Chraïbi, *Research in African literatures,* 23, 2 (1992) 131–44

1436 Mdarhri-Alaoui, A, Abdelkebir Khatibi: writing a dynamic identity, *Research in African literatures,* 23, 2 (1992) 167–76

Medical

1437 Aouattah, A, Maladie mentale et thérapie maraboutique au Maroc: le cas Bouia Omar, *Psychopathologie africain,* 23, 2 (1990/1991) 173–196

Politics

1438 Amnesty International, *Morocco: a pattern of political imprisonment, 'disappearances' and torture.* London: Amnesty International, 1991, 76pp

1439 Amnesty International, *Morocco: Amnesty International briefing.* London: Amnesty International, 1991, 14pp

1440 Diouri, M, *A qui appartient le Maroc?* Paris: Harmattan, 1992, 271pp

1441 Jacquemin, G, Maroc: la démocratie limitée, *Cahiers du Communisme,* 68, 10 (1992) 93–95

1442 Serfaty, A, For another kind of Morocco, *Middle East report,* 22, 6 (1992) 24–28

Rural economy

see also: 1008

1443 Bencherifa, A, *L'oasis de Figuig: persistance et changement.* Passau: Passavia Universitätsverlag, 1990, 109pp

1444 Kagermeier, A, International labour migration and its influence on self-help marketing activities: a case study from north-eastern Morocco, in Cammann L (ed), *Traditional marketing systems (entry 113),* 165–75

1445 Kydd, J, Thoyer, S, *Structural adjustment and Moroccan agriculture: an assessment of reforms in the sugar and cereals sectors.* Paris: OECD Development Centre, 1992, 87pp

1446 Pérennès, J J, Le Maroc à portée du million d'hectares irrigués: éléments pour un bilan, *Maghreb-Machrek,* 137 (1992) 25–42

Sociology

1447 Bencherifa, A, (ed), *Le Maroc: espace et société.* Passau: Passavia Universitätsverlag, 1990, 286pp

TUNISIA

Anthropology

1448 Ben Rejeb, R, propos de la transe psychothérapeutique de Sidi Da''âs: note sur la place du djinn dans les psychothérapies traditionnelles: approche psychanalytique, *IBLA,* 168, (1991) 215–221

Current affairs

1449 Article 19, *Tunisia: attacks on*

the press and government critics.
London: Article 19, 1991, 13pp

Economy - Development

1450 Ben Zakour, A, Kria, K, *Le secteur informel en Tunisie: cadre réglementaire et practique courante.* Paris: OECD Development Centre, 1992, 95pp

1451 Delamasure, D, L'économie tunisienne: de l'état-providence à l'ambition liberale, *Mondes en développement,* 18, 71 (1990) 19–33

Economic and social history

1452 Fabris, A, 'Barra a Tunisi': una rotta da Venezia per le merci e la cultura, *Levante,* 33, 4 (1991) 13–19

1453 Hitchner, R B, Mattingly, D J, Fruits of empire - the production of olive oil in Roman Africa, *Research and exploration,* 7, 1 (1991) 36–55

Environment

1454 Johnson, D E, et al, Evaluation of plant species for land restoration in central Tunisia, *Journal of arid environments,* 22, 4 (1992) 305–322

Finance

1455 Banque Centrale de Tunisie, The experience of Tunisia, in Roe A R et al (eds) *Instruments of economic policy (entry 341),* 102–106

Gender

1456 Creyghton, M L, Breast-feeding and *baraka* in northern Tunisia, in Maher V (ed) (*The anthropology of breast-feeding*), (Oxford: Berg, 1992) 37–58

Health & welfare services

1457 Camau, M, et al, *Etat de santé: besoin médical et enjeux politiques en Tunisie.* Paris: Ed. CNRS, 1990, 290pp

History, general

1458 Sebag, P, *Histoire des juifs de Tunisie.* Paris: Harmattan, 1991, 335pp

History, C6–18th

1459 Ben Sliman, F, Despotisme et violence sous les Hafsides, *IBLA,* 168, (1991) 255–262

History, C20th

1460 Cannon, B D, Safiullah, M, The function of wakalah in intra-Ottoman relations: Egypt and Tunisia in the first half of the 19th century, *Arab historical review for Ottoman studies,* 5/6, (1992) 25–29

1461 el Mechat, Samya, *Tunisie: les chemins vers l'indépendance (1945–1956).* Paris: Harmattan, 1992, 279pp

1462 Hopwood, S, *Habib Bourguiba of Tunisia.* Basingstoke: Macmillan, 1992, 159pp

Industry & trade

1463 Sethom, H, L'industrie tunisienne: bilan et perspectives, *Revue tunisienne de géographie,* 19/20 (1991) 181–222

1464 Zakour, A B, *Le secteur informel en Tunisie: cadre réglementaire et practique courante.* Paris: OECD Development Centre, 1992, 96pp

International economic relations

No entry, see also: 3548

Labour & manpower

1465 Frechiou, R, *New information technologies and employment in financial institutions in Tunisia.* Geneva: ILO, 1991, 42pp

Library - documentation

1466 Kadri, M S, Les bases d'un réseau national tunisien de lecture publique: essai d'analyse socio-culturelle, *IBLA,* 168, (1991) 235–254

Literature

1467 Bekri, T, On French-language Tunisian literature, *Research in African literatures,* 23, 2 (1992) 177–82

1468 Breteau, C H, Roth, A, De l'art poétique à Takroûna: poèmes de l'amour et de la sagesse, *Revue des études islamiques,* 58, (1990) 1–107

1469 Fontaine, J, Arabic-language Tunisian literature (1956–1990), *Research in African literatures,* 23, 2 (1992) 183–93

1470 Fontaine, J, Le centième roman tunisien: Zahrat al Sabbâr de Alia Tabaï, *IBLA,* 168, (1991) 223–234

Media

1471 Barrouhi, A, *Demain, la démocratie? Communication et politique sous Bourguiba.* Tunis: Afkar et Ich'Haar, 1990, 275pp

Politics

see also: 1471

1472 Ghilès, F, Contemporary Tunisia: can reforms succeed without political pluralism?, *Bulletin of francophone Africa,* 1 (1992) 30–38

1473 Vengroff, R, Ben Salem, H, Assessing the impact of decentralisation on governance: a comparative methodological approach and application to Tunisia, *Public administration and development,* 12, 5 (1992) 473–92

Rural economy

1474 Bou Ali, S, Dollé, V, Example of a global approach in preSaharan Tunisisan agricultural development, in Bishay A & Dregne, H (eds), *Desert development Part 1* (London: Harwood, 1991), 87–101

1475 Zussman, M, *Development and disenchantment in rural Tunisia: the Bourguiba years.* Boulder: Westview, 1992, 212pp

Sociology

see also: 1475

1476 Dhaouadi, M, Une exploration sociologique dans la personnalité tunisienne, *IBLA,* 168, (1991) 203–213

1477 Tjomsland, M, *Negotiating the 'in-between': modernising practiceds and identities in post-colonial Tunisia.* Bergen: Chr. Michelsens Institute, 1992, 201pp

Urban studies

1478 Denieuil, P N, *Les entrepreneurs du développement: l'ethno-industrialisation en Tunisie - la dynamique du Sfax.* Paris: Harmattan, 1992, 207pp

1479 Dlala, H, Les grandes moments de l'evolution démo-spatiale de la ville de Bizerte, *Revue tunisienne de géographie,* 19/20 (1991) 115–150

1480 Wright, G, *The politics of design in French colonial urbanism.* Chicago: University of Chicago Press, 1991, 389pp

NORTH EAST AFRICA

Economy - Development

1500 Degefe, B, Economic integration as an instrument to attain peace and stability on the Horn, *Northeast African studies,* 12, 2/3 (1990) 55–63

1501 Malwal, B, Prospects for peace, recovery and development in the Horn of Africa, in Doornbos M et al (eds), *Beyond conflict in the Horn (entry 1533),* 6–12

1502 Prendergast, J, *Peace, development and the people of the Horn of Africa.* Washington: Bread for the World Institute on Hunger and Development, 1992, 56pp

1503 Raffer, K Salih, M A M, (eds), *The least developed and the oil-rich Arab countries: dependence, interdependence and patronage.* Basingstoke: Macmillan, 1992, 251pp

Food

see also: 1502, 1524

1504 Article 19, *Starving in silence: a report on famine and censorship.* London: Article 19, 1990, 146pp

1505 Hubbard, M, et al, Regional food security strategies: the case of IGADD in the Horn of Africa, *Food policy,* 17, 1 (1992) 7–22

1506 Tegegne Teka, The dromedary in the East African countries: its virtues, present conditions and potentials for food production, *Nomadic peoples,* 29, (1991) 3–9

Gender

1507 Amina Mama, The need for gender analysis, in Doornbos M et al (eds), *Beyond conflict in the Horn (entry 1533),* 72–78

Geography, human

1508 Allan, J A, The changing geography of the lower Nile: Egypt and Sudan as riparian states, in Chapman G P & Baker, K M (eds), *The changing geography of Africa (entry 405),* 165–90

Geography, physical

1509 Hulme, M, Global climate change and the Nile Basin, in Howell J P, Allan J A (eds), *The Nile (entry 1328),* 59–81

Health & welfare services

1510 El-Nagar, S el-H, Children and war in the Horn of Africa, in Doornbos M et al (eds), *Beyond conflict in the Horn (entry 1533),* 15–21

History, early

1511 Sadr, K, *The development of nomadism in ancient northeast Africa.* Philadephia: University of Philadephia Press, 1991, 180pp

Industry & trade

1512 Mamyw Ayalew, The refurbishing and expanding of trade networks in the Horn of Africa, in Doornbos M et al (eds), *Beyond conflict in the Horn (entry 1533),* 94–102

International economic relations

see also: 1503

1513 Brown, R P C, et al, Debt, adjustment and donor intervention in the postwar Horn of Africa, in Doornbos M et al (eds), *Beyond conflict in the Horn (entry 1533),* 195–209

1514 Brown, R P C, et al, *Debt, adjustment and donor interventions in post-war Horn of Africa.* The Hague: ISS, 1991, 24pp

1515 Koppen, S, Some aspects of the Gulf Cooperation Council's relationship with LDACs, in Raffer K & Salih, M A M (ed), *The least developed and the oil-rich (entry 592),* 31–48

1516 Raffer, K, 'Structural adjustment' or debt relief: the case of Arab LLDCs, in Raffer K & Salih, M A M (ed), *The least developed and the oil-rich (entry 592),* 153–71

1517 Wulf, V, The effects of the Lomé Convention on the LDACs, in Raffer K & Salih, M A M (ed), *The least developed and the oil-rich (entry 592),* 64–81

International relations

see also: 1526, 1529, 1632

1518 Harbeson, J W, The international politics of identity in the Horn of Africa, in Harbeson J W & Rothchild, D (eds), *Africa in world politics (entry 625),* 119–43

1519 Makinda, S M, The Horn of Africa in the changing world climate, in Bruce R H (ed), *Prospects for peace: changes in the Indian Ocean region* (Perth: Indian Ocean Centre for Peace Studies, 1992), 235–51

1520 Makinda, S M, *Security in the Horn of Africa.* London: Institute of Strategic Studies, 1992, 80pp

1521 Schraeder, P J, The Horn of Africa: US foreign policy in an altered Cold War environment, *Middle East journal,* 46, 3 (1992) 571–93

1522 Sheth, V S, OAU and the Ethiopia-Somalia boundary dispute, *Africa quarterly,* 30, 1/2 (1990) 27–33

1523 Teshome G Wagaw, The international political ramifications of Falasha emigration, *Journal of modern African studies,* 29, 4 (1991) 557–81

Media

1524 Sorenson, J, Covering famine and war in the Horn of Africa, *Northeast African studies,* 12, 2/3 (1990) 133–145

Natural resources

1525 Tvedt, T, The management of water and irrigation: the Blue Nile, in Doornbos M et al (eds), *Beyond conflict in the Horn (entry 1533),* 79–92

Politics

see also: 1504, 1533

1526 Heinrich, W, (ed), *Entwicklungspersepktiven am Horn von Afrika.* Hamburg: Dienste in Ubersee, 1991, 158pp

1527 Mohammed, A, Beyond the conflict: peace and cooperation in the Horn, in NGLS (ed), *Voices from Africa 3 (entry 913),* 69–79

1528 Nzongola-Ntajala, G, (ed),

Conflict in the Horn of Africa.
Atlanta: African Studies
Association, 1991, 190pp

1529 Olsen, G R, Domestic and
international causes of instability in
the Horn of Africa, with special
emphasis on Ethiopia, *Cooperation
and conflict,* 26, 1 (1991) 21–31

1530 Taddia, I, At the origin of the
State/nation dilemma: Ethiopia,
Eritrea, Ogaden in 1941, *Northeast
African studies,* 12, 2/3 (1990)
157–170

Religion, philosophy

1531 Samatar, S S, (ed), *In the
shadow of conquest: Islam in colonial
northeast Africa.* Trenton: Red Sea
Press, 1992, 163pp

Rural economy

1532 Cliffe, L, Agrarian crisis and
strategies for recovery in the Horn:
a comparative regional perspective,
in Doornbos M et al (eds), *Beyond
conflict in the Horn (entry 1533),*
189–94

1533 Doornbos, M, et al, (eds),
Beyond conflict in the Horn. London:
Currey, 1992, 243pp

1534 Fre, Z, Pastoralists and
agropastoralists losing ground: a
Horn of Africa perspective, in Hjort
af Ornas A (ed), *Security in African
drylands (entry 1025),* 159–82

1535 Harbeson, J W, Post drought
adjustments among Horn of Africa
pastoralists: policy and institution
building dimensions, *Land reform,*
1/2 (1990) 15–29

1536 Mukunu Gamaledin,
Pastoralism: existing limitations,
possibilities for the future, in
Doornbos M et al (eds), *Beyond
conflict in the Horn (entry 1533),*
178–84

1537 Samatar, A I, Social classes
and economic restructuring in

pastoral Africa: Somali notes,
African studies review, 35, 1 (1992)
101–127

DJIBOUTI

General

1538 Schraeder, P J, Crustal
anniversary reflections on the
nascent field of Djibouti studies,
*Current bibliograhy on African
affairs,* 23, 3 (1991/92) 227–45

Economy - Development

1539 Wais, I, *Dschibuti:
Entwicklungsprobleme und
Perspektiven kleiner Staaten. Ein
Fallbeispiel.* Osnabruck:
Forschungsinstitut Dritte Welt,
1991, 346pp

Economic and social history

1540 Shiferaw Bekele, The
Ethiopian railway and British
finance capital, 1896–1902,
Africa (Rome), 46, 3 (1991)
351–374

International relations

1541 Koburger, C W, *Naval strategy
east of Suez: the role of Djibouti.* New
York: Praeger, 1992, 114pp

ERITREA

General

No entry, see also: 1554

Current affairs

1542 Saleh, H, Now that the war is
over, *Focus on Africa,* 3, 3 (1992)
37–40

Food

No entry, see also: 1598

Gender

see also: 1547

1543 Pezaro, A, *Normenwandel und Normkonflikte im Akkulturationsprozess: zur Orienteirung in einer fremdem Kultur am Beispiel eritreischer Flüchtingsfrauen im Sudan.* Saarbruckenm: Breitenbach, 1991, 439pp

1544 Selassie, W N, The changing position of Eritrean women: an overview of women's participation in the EPLF, in Doornbos M et al (eds), *Beyond conflict in the Horn (entry 1533)*, 67–71

Health & welfare services

1545 Habte-Selassie, E, Eritrean refugees in the Sudan: a preliminary analysis of voluntary repatriation, in Doornbos M et al (eds), *Beyond conflict in the Horn (entry 1533)*, 23–32

International relations

1546 Kendie, D, An aspect of the geo-politics of the Red Sea, *Northeast African studies,* 12, 2/3 (1990) 117–131

Law

1547 Kemink, F, *Die Tegrenna-Frauen in Eritrea: eine Untersuchung der Kodizes des Gewohnheitrechts 1890–1941.* Stuttgart: Steiner, 1991, 183pp

Politics

see also: 1530, 1650, 1658
1548 Abbay, A, The Eritrea dilemma, *Transafrica forum,* 7, 4 (1991) 35–49

1549 Becker, E Mitchell, C, *Chronology of conflict resolution initiatives in Eritrea.* Fairfax: George Mason University, Institute for Conflict Analysis and Resolution, 1991, 180pp

1550 Hizkias Assefa, An interest approach to resolution of civil wars in the Horn of Africa: lessons from the negotiations on the Eritrean conflict, in Rupesinghe K (ed), *Internal conflict (entry 932),* 169–86

1551 Papstein, R, *Eritrea: revolution at dusk.* Trenton: Red Sea Press, 1991, 169pp

1552 Pool, D, *Establishing movements' hegemony: the Eritrean Peoples Liberation Front and the cities, 1977.* Manchester: Manchester University, Dept. of Government, 1992, 49pp

Rural economy

see also: 1672
1553 Berhane Woldemichael, Rural development in a post-conflict Eritrea: problems and policy options, in Doornbos M et al (eds), *Beyond conflict in the Horn (entry 1533),* 171–77

Sociology

No entry, see also: 1875

ETHIOPIA

General

1554 Cheru, F, Pausewang, S, *Economic reconstruction and the peasants in Ethiopia.* Bergen: Michelsen Institute, 1992, 66pp

1555 Taddesse, T, Enrico Cerulli (1898–1988): in appreciation of his great Ethiopian scholarship, *Journal*

of Ethiopian studies, 23, (1990) 85–92

Agriculture, scientific

1556 Abebe Wosene, Traditional husbandry practices and major health problems of camels in the Ogaden (Ethiopia), *Nomadic peoples,* 29, (1991) 21–30

1557 Asfar Negesse, et al, Developing and early-maturing maize variety to solve seasonal food shortage, in Franzel S & van Houten, H (eds), *Research with farmers (entry 1674),* 60–68

1558 Frankel, S, Impact, institutionalisation and methodology: research with farmers, in Franzel S & van Houten, H (eds), *Research with farmers (entry 1674),* 243–64

1559 Gemechu Gedeno, et al, Agronomic improvement and new cropping patterns, in Franzel S & van Houten, H (eds), *Research with farmers (entry 1674),* 69–76

1560 Goe, M R, The Ethiopian 'maresha': clarifying design and development, *Northeast African studies,* 11, 3 (1989) 71–112

1561 Jutzi, S C, Mohammed-Salem, M A, Improving productivity on highland vertisols: the oxen-drawn broadbed maker, in Franzel S & van Houten, H (eds), *Research with farmers (entry 1674),* 97–108

1562 Kassahun Seyoum, et al, Prospects for improving coffee-based farming systems, in Franzel S & van Houten, H (eds), *Research with farmers (entry 1674),* 173–90

1563 Tanner, D G, et al, Developing technologies to improve soil fertlity, weed control and wheat varieties, in Franzel S & van Houten, H (eds), *Research with farmers (entry 1674),* 158–70

1564 Teshome Regasse, et al, Developing technologies for small-scale farmers: on-farm research in the Nazret area, in Franzel S & van Houten, H (eds), *Research with farmers (entry 1674),* 126–42

Anthropology

1565 Abbink, J, Funeral as ritual: an analysis of Me'en mortuary rites (Southwest Ethiopia), *Africa (Rome),* 47, 2 (1992) 221–336

1566 Abbink, J, Tribal formation on the Ethiopian fringe: toward a history of the 'Tishana', *Northeast African studies,* 12, 1 (1990) 21–42

1567 Bassi, M, The system of cattle redistribution among the Obbu Borana and its implications for development planning, in Baxter P T W & Hogg, R (eds), *Property, poverty and people (entry 1000),* 32–37

1568 Donham, D L, *History, power, ideology: central isues in marxism and anthropology.* Cambridge: CUP, 1990, 242pp

1569 Gufu Oba, Changing property relations among settling pastoralists: an adaptive strategy to declining pastoral resources, in Baxter P T W & Hogg, R (eds), *Property, poverty and people (entry 1000),* 38–44

1570 Hinnant, J T, Guji trance and social change: symbolic response to domination, *Northeast African studies,* 12, 1 (1990) 65–78

1571 Hultin, J, Resource-use, territory and property among the Magua Oromo, in Baxter P T W & Hogg, R (eds), *Property, poverty and people (entry 1000),* 95–109

1572 Lewis, H S, Gada, big man, 'k'allu': political succession among the eastern Mech'a Oromo, *Northeast African studies,* 12, 1 (1990) 43–64

1573 Schröder, H, (ed), *Die Oromo*

am Horn von Afrika. Ganderkesee: Hilfsorganisation der Oromo Relief Association in der Bundesrepublik Deutchland, 1991, 135pp

1574 Wagaw, T G, The acculturation of the Falashas in Israel and in Africa: a field study, in Irele A (ed), *African education and identity (entry 268),* 166–75

Architecture

No entry, see also: 1387

Current affairs

1575 Amnesty International, *Ethiopia: end of era of brutal repression.* London: Amnesty International, 1991, 58pp

1576 Brüne, S, Ideology, government and development: the People's Democratic Republic of Ethiopia, *Northeast African studies,* 12, 2/3 (1990) 189–199

1577 Eikenberg, K, Übergang wohin?: die 'Charta Äthiopiens für die Übergangsperiod', *Afrika spectrum,* 26, 3 (1991) 391–403

1578 Norwegian Institute of Human Rights, *Local and regional elections in Ethiopa 21 June 1992: report of the Norwegian observer group.* Oslo: The Institute, 199, 16pp

Demography

1579 Zewoldi, J, *Fertility behaviour of elites and their perception of the population problem in Ethiopia: a synthesis.* Addis Ababa: n.p., 1992, 80pp

Economy - Development

1580 Griffin, K, et al, *The economy of Ethiopia.* Basingstoke: Macmillan, 1992, 312pp

1581 Kebbede, G, *The state and*

development in Ethiopia. New Jersey: Humanities Press, 1992, 177pp

1582 Mekonen Tadesse, (ed), *The Ethiopian economy: structure, problems and policy issues.* Addis Ababa: n.p., 1992, 393pp

1583 Wolde Medhin, D, The 1920s: formative years in the development of modern economic thinking in Ethiopia, *Mondes en développement,* 19, 75/76 (1991) 21–30

Economic and social history

1584 Daniel Teferra, *Social history and theoretical analyses of the economy of Ethiopia.* Lewiston: Mellen, 1990, 122pp

1585 Pankhurst, R, *A social history of Ethiopia: the northern and central highlands from early medieval times to the rise of Emperor Tewodros II.* Addis Ababa: Addis Ababa University, Institute of Ethiopian Studies, 1990, 371pp

Education

see also: 3147

1586 Abtaha, S, et al, What factors shape girls' performance: evidence from Ethiopia, *International journal of educational development,* 11, 2 (1991) 107–18

1587 Elleni Tedla, Indigenous African education as a means for understanding the fullness of life: Amara traditional education, *Journal of Black studies,* 23, 1 (1992) 7–26

1588 Germa Amare, Trends in higher education in post-revolutionary Ethiopia, in Irele A (ed), *African education and identity (entry 268),* 109–25

1589 Kiros, F R, *Implementing educational policies in Ethiopia.* Washington: World Bank, 1990, 116pp

1590 Shenkut, M K, Mobilising for literacy: the Ethiopian experience, *Journal of the African Association for Literacy and Adult Education,* 5, 3 (1991) 12–16

1591 Tekeste Negash, *The crisis of Ethiopan education: some implications for nation-building.* Uppsala: Dept. of Education, Uppsala University, 1990, 112pp

1592 Tilahun, W, Thirty years of university based in-service teacher education, *Ethiopian journal of education,* 11, 2 (1990) 85–128

Environment

see also: 1666
1593 Stahl, M, Environmental rehabilitation in the northern Ethiopian highlands: constraints to people's participation, in Ghai D & Vivian, J M (eds), *Grassrooots environmental action* (London: Routledge,1992), 281–303

Finance

1594 Kidane, A, The determinants of savings in Ethiopia, in Frimpong-Ansah J H & Ingham, B (eds), *Saving for economic recovery (entry 142),* 75–84

1595 Roberts, J, Seignorage and resource mobilisation in socialist Ethiopia, *Development policy review,* 10, 3 (1992) 271–88

Food

see also: 357, 1557, 1612
1596 Abebe Haile Gabriel, *Generating marketed surplus of food through state farms: a critical evaluation of Ethiopian experience.* The Hague: ISS, 1990, 90pp

1597 Jones, B, The FFHC agricultural programme in southern Ethiopia, in Edwards M & Hulme, D (eds), *Making a difference: NGOs*

and development in a changing world (London: Earthscan, 1992), 78–88

1598 Keller, E J, Drought, war and the politics of famine in Ethiopia and Eritrea, *Journal of modern African studies,* 30, 4 (1992) 609–24

1599 Kelly, M, Entitlements, coping mechanisms and indicators of access to food: Wollo region, Ethiopia, 1987–88, *Disasters,* 16, 4 (1992) 322–38

1600 Mazzacane, V, The cost of food consumer subsidies: the case of Ethiopia, *Africa (Rome),* 46, 4 (1991) 573–587

1601 Pankhurst, A, *Resettlement and famine in Ethiopia: the villagers' experience.* Manchester: Manchester University Press, 1992, 290pp

1602 Seaman, J, Famine mortality in Ethiopia and Sudan, in van der Walle E et al (eds), *Mortality and society (entry 771),* 349–66

1603 Toole, M J, Bhatia, R, Somali refugees in Hartisheik A camp, eastern Ethiopa, *Journal of refugee studies,* 5, 3/4 (1992) 313–26

1604 Waller, J, *Fau: portrait of an Ethiopian famine.* Jefferson: McFarland, 1990, 147pp

1605 Webb, P, et al, *Famine in Ethiopia: policy implications of coping failures at national and household levels.* Stanford: International Food Policy Research Institute, 1992, 167pp

Gender

see also: 1586, 1639, 1692
1606 Dejene Aredo, *The gender division of labour in Ethiopian agriculture: a study of time allocation in private and cooperative farms in two villages.* New York: Social Science Research Council, Project on African agriculture, 1992, 39pp

1607 Laketch Dirasse, *The commoditisation of female sexuality: prostitution and socio-economics*

relations in Addis Ababa, Ethiopa.
New York: AMS Press, 1991,
168pp

1608 Pankhurst, H, *Gender,
development and identity: an
Ethiopian study.* London: Zed,
1992, 216pp

Geography, human

1609 Melasno, T, Amare Worku,
The Gerado River basin an
example of small river management
possibilities in Ethiopia, in Darkoh
M B K (ed), *African river basins
(entry 406),* 133–46

Health & welfare services

1610 Asres Kebede, Implementing
a development communication
project: a descriptive study of the
Communication Support to Health
Project in Ethiopia, *Africa media
review,* 6, 2 (1992) 57–65

1611 Kloos, H, Health impact of
war in Ethiopia, *Disasters,* 16, 4
(1992) 347–54

1612 Kloos, H, et al, The health
impact of the 1984–85 Ethiopian
resettlement programme: three case
studies, in Darkoh M B K (ed),
African river basins (entry 406),
147–65

1613 Wendmu Dejene,
Implementing a new approach to
urban health problems: the case of
Addis Ababa, *Environment and
urbanization,* 3, 2 (1991) 127–135

History, general

**1615 Crummey, D, Sishagne, S,
et al,** Oral traditions in a literate
culture: the case of christian
Ethiopia, in Pilaszewicz S &
Rzewuski, E (eds), *Unwritten
testimones (entry 447),* 137–49

1617 Quirin, J, *The evolution of the
Ethiopian jews: a history of the Beta
Israel (Falasha) to 1920.*
Philadelphia: University of
Pennsylvania Press, 192, 336pp

1618 Rubenson, S, Conflict and
environmental stress in Ethiopian
history: looking for correlations,
Journal of Ethiopian studies, 24,
(1990) 71–96

1619 Taddesse, T, Place names in
Ethiopian history, *Journal of
Ethiopian studies,* 24, (1991)
115–131

History, early

1620 Fattovich, R, Remarks on the
pre-Aksumite period in northern
Ethiopia, *Journal of Ethiopian
studies,* 23, (1990) 1–33

1621 Marrassini, P, Some
consideration on the problem of
the 'Syriac influences' on Aksumite
Ethiopia, *Journal of Ethiopian
studies,* 23, (1990) 35–46

1622 Munro-Hay, S, The rise and
fall of Aksum: chronological
considerations, *Journal of Ethiopian
studies,* 23, (1990) 47–53

1623 Phillipson, D W, Aksum in
Africa, *Journal of Ethiopian studies,*
23, (1990) 55–65

History, C19th

1624 Pankhurst, R, The political
image: the impact of the camera in
an ancient African state, in
Edwards E (ed), *Anthropology and
photography 1860–1920* (New
Haven: Yale UP, 1992), 234–41

History, C20th

1625 Gemeda, G, Subsistence,
slavery and violence in the lower
Omo valley, ca 1898–1940's,
Northeast African studies, 12, 1
(1990) 5–19

1626 Zewde, B, 'Twixt sirdar and
emperor: the Anuak in

Ethio-Sudanese relations
1902–1935, *Northeast African
studies,* 12, 1 (1990) 79–93

Industry & trade

1627 Baker, J, The Gurage of
Ethiopia: rural-urban interaction
and entrepreneurship, in Baker J &
Pedersen, P O (eds), *Rural-urban
interface (entry 1111),* 125–47
1628 Mariam, H G, Rural
electrification in Ethiopia, in
Ranganathan V (ed), *Rural
electrification (entry 1046),* 67–111

International relations

see also: 1522
1629 Baissa, L, United States
military assistance to Ethiopia,
1953–1974: a reappraissal of a
difficult patron-client relationship,
Northeast African studies, 11, 3
(1989) 51–70
1630 Calchi Novati, G, Italia e
Etiopia dopo ia guerra: una nuova
realtá, i risarcimenti e la stele rapita,
Africa (Rome), 46, 4 (1991) 479–502
1631 Tekle, A, Conditions for
peace in the Horn of Africa: the
need for spatial and political
reorganisation in Ethiopia,
Northeast African studies, 12, 2/3
(1990) 147–156
1632 Yagya, V S, Ethiopia and its
neighbors: an evolution of
relations, 1974–1989, *Northeast
African studies,* 12, 2/3 (1990)
107–116

Labour & manpower

**1633 Getachew Metaferia,
Maiganet Shifferraw,** *The
Ethiopian revolution of 1974 and the
exodus of Ethiopia's trained muman
resources.* Lewiston: Mellen, 1991,
167pp

Language

1634 Richter, R, Proverbs - an old
literary tradition in Ethiopa, in
Pilaszewicz S & Rzewuski, E (eds),
Unwritten testimones (entry 447),
181–89

Law

1635 Mantel-Niecko, J, Law that
generates instability: the case of the
Ethiopian proclamations of
September 1987, *Northeast
African studies,* 12, 2/3 (1990)
83–89
1636 Pateman, R, The Horn of
Africa: prospects for the resolution
of conflict, *Northeast African studies,*
12, 2/3 (1990) 91–106

Literature

1637 Assefa, T, Detective fiction in
Amharic, *Northeast African studies,*
11, 3 (1989) 13–33

Media

1638 Janas, J, *History of the mass
media in Ethiopia.* Warsaw:
University of Warsaw, Institute of
Oriental Studies, 1991, 83pp

Medical

1639 Assefa Hailemariam,
Fertility levels and trends in Arsi
and Shoa regions of central
Ethiopia, *Journal of biosocial science,*
23, 4 (1991) 387–400
1640 Habtamu, W, Gratification
patterns among peasants and
workers in central Ethiopia,
Ethiopian journal of education, 11, 1
(1989) 52–72
1641 Larson, C, Risk behaviours for
HIV infection: their occurrence and
determinants in Jima town,
southwestern Ethiopia, *Ethiopian*

medical journal, 29, 3 (1991)
127–139

1642 Mekonnen, A,
Organophosphate pesticide
poisoning in 50 Ethiopian patients,
Ethiopian medical journal, 29, 3
(1991) 109–118

1643 Menassie, G, The use and
values of wild plant products to the
people of Bale, *Walia,* 13 (1991)
21–28

1644 Tirussew, T, Onset, bodily
reactions, and psycho-social
consequences of menarche among
a group of Ethiopian girls,
Ethiopian journal of education, 11, 2
(1990) 1–27

1645 Yohannes, A G, et al, Child
morbidity patterns in Ethiopia,
Journal of biosocial science, 24, 2
(1992) 143–55

Politics

1646 Abbink, J, The deconstruction
of 'tribe': ethnicity and politics in
southwestern Ethiopia, *Journal of
Ethiopian studies,* 24, (1991) 1–21

1647 Becker, E Mitchell, C,
*Chronology of conflict resolution
initiatives in Ethiopia.* Fairfax:
George Mason University, Institute
for Conflict Analysis and
Resolution, 1991, 161pp

1648 Clapham, C, The socialist
experience in Ethiopia and its
demise, *Journal of communist studies,*
8, 2 (1992) 105–25 (also in *entry 860*)

1649 Clapham, C, State, society
and political institutions in
revolutionary Ethiopia, in Manor J
(ed), *Rethinking Third World Politics
(entry 889),* 242–66

1650 Clapham, C, The structure of
regional conflict in northern
Ethiopia, in Twaddle M (ed),
Imperialism (entry 464), 260–73

1651 Donham, D L, Revolution
and modernity in Maale, Ethiopia,
1974–87, *Comparative studies in*

society and history, 34, 1 (1992)
28–57

1652 Eikenberg, K, Die "Charta
Äthiopiens für die
Übergangsperiode", *Afrika
spectrum,* 26, 3 (1991) 391–403

1653 Harbeson, J W, Perspectives
on the Ethiopian transformation:
variations on common themes,
Northeast African studies, 12, 2/3
(1990) 65–82

1654 Hasselblatt, G, et al, *Das
geheime Lachen im Bambuswald:
vom Freiheitskampf der Oromo in
Äthiopien.* Stuttgart: Radius, 1990,
153pp

1655 Henze, P B, The Ethiopian
Revolution: mythology and history,
Northeast African studies, 12, 2/3
(1990) 1–17

1656 Krylov, A, Islam and
nationalism: two trends of the
separatist movement in Ethiopia,
Northeast African studies, 12, 2/3
(1990) 171–176

1657 Mengisteab Kidane, Averting
Ethiopia's disintegration,
Transafrica forum, 9, 1 (1992) 3–13

1658 Michler, W, Äthiopien 1991:
politische Neugeburt und friedliche
Lösung des Eritrea-Konflikts,
Vierteljahresberichte, 127 (1992)
71–83

1659 Pausewang, S, *Rural conditions
for democracy in Ethiopia: peasant
self-determination and the state.*
Bergen: CMI, 1991, 18pp

1660 Sherr, E, Political structure of
Ethiopia, *Northeast African studies,*
12, 2/3 (1990) 177–188

1661 Woldu, S M, Democratic
transition in Africa: a case study of
Ethiopia, in Caron B et al (eds),
*Democratic transition in Africa (entry
817),* 69–80

Religion, philosophy

1662 Abbas, H G, Le rôle du culte
de Chaikh Hussein dans l'islam des

Arssi (Éthiopie), *Islam et sociétés au Sud du Sahara*, 5 (1991) 21–42

1663 Hussein, A, The historiography of Islam in Ethiopia, *Journal of Islamic studies*, 3, 1 (1992) 15–46

1664 Pankhurst, R, The Falashas, or Judaic Ethiopians, in their Christian Ethiopian setting, *African affairs*, 91, 365 (1992) 567–82

Rural economy

see also: 1616, 1628

1665 Ayele Gebre Mariam, Livestock and economic differentiation in north east Ethiopia: the Afar case, *Nomadic peoples*, 29, (1991) 10–20

1666 Cheru, F, *Constraints for a conservation-based agricultural development policy in Ethiopia.* Bergen: CMI, 1992, 37pp

1667 Chilot Yirga, et al, Farming systems of the Kulumsa area, in Franzel S & van Houten, H (eds), *Research with farmers (entry 1674),* 145–57

1668 Dadi, L, et al, Marketing maize and tef in western Ethiopia: implications for policies following market liberalization, *Food policy,* 17, 3 (1992) 201–213

1669 Dessalegn Rahmato, *The dynamics of rural poverty: case studies from a district in southern Ethiopia.* Dakar: Codesria, 1992, 70pp

1670 Dolal, M, Pastoral resources, human displacement and state policy: the Ogadenian case, in Doornbos M et al (eds), *Beyond conflict in the Horn (entry 1533),* 185–88

1671 Fantu Cheru, *Constraints for a conservation-based agricultural development policy in Ethiopia: a baseline study in Fedis Awraja.* Bergen: Michelsen Institute, 1992, 37pp

1672 Fantu Cheru, Pausewang, S, *Economic reconstruction and the peasants in Ethiopia: two papers presented at the symposium on the Ethiopian economy, with a postscript.* Bergen: Chr. Michelsens Institute, 1992, 66pp

1673 Frankel, S, et al, Grain marketing policies and peasant production, in Franzel S & van Houten, H (eds), *Research with farmers (entry 1674),* 212–26

1674 Franzel, S, Van Houten, H, (eds), *Research with farmers: lessons from Ethiopia.* Wallingford: Commonwealth Agricultural Bureau, 1992, 303pp

1675 Gérard, D, Oasian agriculture and camel harnessed traction: a new initiative of the Afar pastoralists of the Awash valley in Ethiopia for complementary food production, *Nomadic peoples*, 29, (1991) 42–52

1676 Hailu Beyene, Constraints to increasing wheat production in the smallholder sector, in Franzel S & van Houten, H (eds), *Research with farmers (entry 1674),* 201–211

1677 Hailu Beyene, Chilot Yerga, Vertisol farming systems of North Shewa, in Franzel S & van Houten, H (eds), *Research with farmers (entry 1674),* 79–96

1678 Legesse Dadi, et al, The farming system of the Bako area, in Franzel S & van Houten, H (eds), *Research with farmers (entry 1674),* 43–59

1679 Legesse Dadi, et al, Marketing maize and tef in the Bako area: implications for the post-market-liberalisation policies, in Franzel S & van Houten, H (eds), *Research with farmers (entry 1674),* 227–40

1680 Legesse Dadi, et al, Socioeconomic constraints to increasing maize production, in Franzel S & van Houten, H (eds),

Research with farmers (entry 1674), 191–200

1681 Mekonnen Assefa, *Index to livestock literature microfiched in Ethiopia.* Addis Ababa: International Livestock Centre for Africa, 1990, 237pp

1682 Mekuria, M, et al, Farming systems research in Ethiopia: evolution, development and organisation, in Franzel S & van Houten, H (eds), *Research with farmers (entry 1674),* 28–40

1683 Mulugetta Bezzabeh, Attempts at the transformation of Ethiopia's agriculture: problems and prospects, in Doornbos M et al (eds), *Beyond conflict in the Horn (entry 1533),* 143–53

1684 Pausewang, S, Brauchen Afrikas Bauern eine neue Weltordnung? Antworten aus der Persrektive äthiopischer Bauern, *Afrika spectrum,* 27, 2 (1992) 187–205

1685 Schubert, W, *Die Landwirtschaft in Athiopien.* Berlin: Institut für Ausländlische Landwirtschaft und Agarargeschichte, 1991, 67pp

1686 Ståhl, M, Capturing the peasants through cooperatives: the case of Ethiopia, *Northeast African studies,* 12, 1 (1990) 95–122

1687 Stork, H, *Studies on the smallholder agriculture in the Haraghe Highlands, eastern Ethiopia.* Hannover: Hannover University, Institute of Horticulture Economics, 1991, 94pp

1688 Stroud, A, Mekuria, M, Ethiopia's agricultural sector: an overview, in Franzel S & van Houten, H (eds), *Research with farmers (entry 1674),* 9–27

1689 Tafesse, M, Poposed capacity building strategy for the irrigation subsector of Ethiopia, in Alaerts G J et al (eds), *A strategy for water sector capacity building* (New York:

UNDP, 1991), 139–44

1690 Tegegne Teka, Camel and the household economy of the Afar: a study of selected members of Wahlifanta Camel Herders' Society of Awssa, Ethiopia, *Nomadic peoples,* 29, (1991) 31–41

1691 Tilahu Milatun, et al, The farming systems of the Nazret area, in Franzel S & van Houten, H (eds), *Research with farmers (entry 1674),* 111–25

1692 Wudnesh Hailu, *Rural family of Ethiopia: economic activities, household analysis, and standard household type comparisons.* Hamburg: Weltarchiv, 1991, 213pp

Science & technology

1693 Drew E, et al, Development of science and technology information services in Ethiopia, *Science, technology and development,* 10, 1 (1992) 52–66

Sociology

1694 Aboud, F, et al, Intellectual, social and nutritional status of children in an Ethiopian orphanage, *Social science and medecine,* 33, 11 (1991) 1275–80

1695 Taddele Seyoum Teshale, *The life history of an Ethiopian refugee (1944–1991).* Lewiston: Mellen, 1991, 109pp

SOMALIA

Agriculture, scientific

1696 Abdurahman, O, Bornstein, Diseases of camels (Camelus dromedarius) in Somalia and prospects for better health, *Nomadic peoples,* 29, (1991) 104–112

Anthropology

1697 Pelizzari, E, *Le Mingis en Somalie: analyse d'une version de culte de possession 'Saar'.* Paris: Centre d'études africaines, EHESS, 1991, 30pp

Current affairs

1698 Djama, M, Sur la violence en Somalie: genèse et dynamique des formations armées, *Politique africaine,* 47 (1992) 147–52

1699 Harsch, E, Strengthened Somali relief effort threatened by continued fighting, *Africa recovery,* 6, 3 (1992) 6–9

1700 Marchal, R, La guerre à Mogadiscio, *Politique africaine,* 46 (1992) 120–25

1701 Omaar, R, Somalia: at war with itself, *Current history,* 91, 565 (1992) 230–234

1702 Searle, C, Agony and struggle in northern Somalia, *Race and class,* 34, 2 (1992) 23–32

1703 Segura, N, Gonzales, D, Is the 'small Somalia' in danger?, *Revista de Africa y Medio Oriente,* 3, 1 (1991) 40–47

1704 Wells, R, Biles, P, Shell-shocked, *Focus on Africa,* 3, 1 (1992) 13–18

Economy - Development

1705 Brann, G, Survival strategies and the state in Somalia, in Raffer K & Salih, M A M (ed), *The least developed and the oil-rich (entry 592),* 111–27

1706 Braun, G, The Somali development concept in crisis, *Northeast African studies,* 11, 3 (1989) 1–12

1707 Jamal, V, Somalia: the Gulf link and adjustment, in Raffer K & Salih, M A M (ed), *The least*

developed and the oil-rich (entry 592), 128–52

1708 Noor, M H, *Ursachen der Arbeitslosigkeit, Inflastion und Marktspaltung und ihre Auswirken auf die somalische Wirtschaft.* Munich: Kyrill & Method, 1991, 334pp

Economic and social history

No entry, see also: 1715

Food

see also: 1746

1709 Hjort af Ornäs, A, et al, Food production and dryland management: a Somali camel research agenda, *Nomadic peoples,* 29, (1991) 113–124

1710 Hunter, J, Somalia: politics of famine, *Covert action quarterly,* 43 (1992) 52–57

Gender

No entry, see also: 1721,1723

Geography, human

1711 Surdich, F, La spedizione Stefanini-Puccioni in Somalia (1924), *Bollettino della Società Geografica Italiana,* 9, 1/3 (1992) 125–140

Health & welfare services

1712 Klaas, A, Galaty, M, A comparison of the health sector in Kuwait and Somalia, in Raffer K & Salih, M A M (ed), *The least developed and the oil-rich (entry 592),* 229–42

1713 Ryle, J, Notes on the repatriation of Somali refugees from Ethiopia, *Disasters,* 16, 2 (1992) 160–68

1714 Zitelman, T, Refugee aid,

moral communities and resource sharing in Somalia: prelude to civil war, *Sociologus*, 41, 2 (1991) 118–38

History, C19th

1715 Joint-Daguenet, R, La côte africaine du golfe d'Aden au milieu du XIXe siècle, *Revue française d'histoire d'outre-mer*, 79, 294 (1992) 87–113

History, C20th

see also: 1626

1716 Omar, M O, *The road to zero: Somalia's road to self-destruction.* Streatham: Haan Associates, 1992, 213pp

Industry & trade

1717 Ahmed, I I, Rural electrification in Somalia, in Ranganathan V (ed), *Rural electrification (entry 1046),* 162–69

1718 Janzen, J, Somalias Küstenfischerei: gegenwärtige Situation und zukünftige Entwicklungsmöglichkeiten, *Die erde*, 122, 2 (1991) 131–143

1719 Little, P D, Traders, brokers and market 'crisis' in southern Somalia, *Africa*, 62, 1 (1992) 94–124

International relations

No entry, see also: 1522

Labour & manpower

No entry, see also: 1708

Literature

1720 Ahmed, A J, Of poets and sheikhs: Somali literature, in

Harrow K H (ed), *Faces of Islam (entry 710),* 79–89

1721 Ghattas-Soliman, S, The two-sided image of women in *Season of migration to the North*, in Harrow K H (ed), *Faces of Islam (entry 710),* 91–103

1722 Okonkwo, J I, The novelist as artist: the case of Nurrudin Farah, *Commonwealth novel in English*, 5, 1 (1992) 46–58

1723 Zainab Mohamed Jama, Fighting to be heard: Somali women's poetry, *African languages and cultures*, 4, 1 (1991) 43–53

Media

1724 Sailhan, M, Un journaliste dans le maquis somalien: les risques du métier, *Politique africaine*, 48 (1992) 117–122

Natural resources

1725 Peveling, R, Nutzungsabhängige Zusammensetzung und Verbreitung südsomalischer Grasgesellschaften und ihr Einfluß auf das Schadenspotential von Quelea Quelea, *Geomethodica*, 15, (1990) 47–65

1726 Wilhelmi, F, Methodische Probleme der Erfassung von Quelea Quelea, einem Schadvogel im Getreideanbau Süd-Somalias, *Geomethodica*, 15, (1990) 141–162

Politics

see also: 1701, 1716

1727 Adam, H, Somalia: militarism, warlordism or democracy, *Review of African political economy*, 54 (1992) 11–26

1728 Barcik, K, Normack, S, (eds), *Somalia: a historical, cultural and political analysis.* Uppsala: Life and Peace Institute, 1991, 45pp

1729 Becker, E Mitchell, C, *Chronology of conflict resolution initiatives in Somalia.* Fairfax: George Mason University, Institute for Conflict Analysis and Resolution, 1991, 89pp

1730 Bongartz, M, *Somalia im Bürgerkrieg: Ursachen und Perspektiven des innenpolitischen Konflikts.* Kamburg: Institut für Afrika-Kunde, 1991, 121pp

1731 Esa, A B, Somalia's political misfortunes: from scientific socialism to a human rights crisis, in Barcik K & Normack, S (eds), *Somalia (entry 1728),* 29–42

1732 Gegreyesus, E G, *Somalia in difficulties.* Utrecht: Federatie van Vluchtelingen Organisaties in Nederland, 1992, 156pp

1733 Lewis, I M, The recent political history of Somalia, in Barcik K & Normack, S (eds), *Somalia (entry 1728),* 4–15

1734 Osman, A A, Somalia, in NGLS (ed), *Voices from Africa 3 (entry 913),* 59–68

1735 Raafat, E M, La crise somalienne actuelle: sa nature et ses raisons, in Anyang' Nyong'o P (ed), *30 years of independence (entry 101),* 206–31

1736 Samatar, A I, Destruction of state and society in Somalia: beyond the tribal convention, *Journal of modern African studies,* 30, 4 (1992) 625–41

1737 Samatar, A I, Social decay and public institutions: the war to reconstruction in Somalia, in Doornbos M et al (eds), *Beyond conflict in the Horn (entry 1533),* 213–16

Rural economy

see also: 1717

1738 Adam, H M, Somalia: rural production organisation and prospects for reconstruction, in Doornbos M et al (eds), *Beyond conflict in the Horn (entry 1533),* 154–65

1739 Elmi, A A, Livestock production in Somalia with special emphasis on camels, *Nomadic peoples,* 29, (1991) 87–103

1740 Farah Mohamed, A Touati, J, *Sedentarisierung von Namden: Chancen und Gefahren einer Entwicklungsstrategie am Beispiel Somalias.* Saarbrucken: Brietenbach, 1991, 145pp

1741 Janzen, J, Anthropogeographische Forschung in den Bewässerungsregionen Süd-Somalias - Ziele, Methodik, Ergebnisse, *Geomethodica,* 15, (1990) 71–102

1742 Janzen, J, Dams and large-scale irrigated cultivation versus mobile livestock keeping? The Baardheere Dam project in Southern Somalia and its possible consequences for mobile animal husbandry, *Applied geography and development,* 38, (1991) 53–65

1743 Janzen, J, Mobile livestock keeping - a survival strategy for the countries of the Sahel? - the case of Somalia, *Applied geography and development,* 37, (1991) 7–20

1744 Leser, H, *Landwirtschaftsbewertungen und Landschaftsplannung in afrikanischen Entwicklungsländern: Biespiel Somalia.* Basle: Basler Afrika Bibliographen, 1990, 182pp

1745 Little, P D, Seasonality and rural-urban linkages in southern Somalia, in Baker J & Pedersen, P O (eds), *Rural-urban interface (entry 1111),* 85–101

1746 Samatar, M S, Survival strategies among the pastoralists in the district of Waule-Weyn, in Hjort af Ornas A (ed), *Security in African drylands (entry 1025),* 91–104

1747 Scholz, U, Problems of rainfed

agriculture in Southern Somalia, *Geomethodica*, 15, (1990) 47–65

1748 **Taha, A,** Trading camel milk: coping with survival in a Somalia pastoral context, in Hjort af Ornas A (ed), *Security in African drylands (entry 1025)*, 139–57

Sociology

1749 **Ehlers, P Witzge, A,** *Somalia: bakgrund och framtid.* Uppsala: SIAS, 1992, 95pp

1750 **Helander, B,** The Somali family, in Barcik K & Normack, S (eds), *Somalia (entry 1728)*, 17–28

SUDAN

General

1751 **Dominguez, Z, Pena, A,** *Sudan.* Havana: Ciencias Sociales, 1990, 232pp

Agriculture, scientific

1752 **Abu Sin, M E,** Transformation of camel breeding in the Sudan, *Nomadic peoples*, 29, (1991) 53–60

Anthropology

1753 **Braukamper, U,** *Migration und ethnische Wandel: Untersuchungen aus der östlichen Sudanzone.* Stuttgart: Steiner, 1992, 315pp

1754 **Burton, J W,** Nilotic cosmology and the divination of Atuot philosophy, in Peek P M (ed), *African divination (entry 48)*, 41–52

1755 **Faris, J C,** Photography, power and the southern Nuba, in Edwards E (ed), *Anthropology and photography 1860–1920* (New Haven: Yale UP, 1992), 211–17

1756 **Grüb, A,** *The Lotuho of southern Sudan.* Stuttgart: Steiner, 1991, 194pp

1757 **Hjort af Ornas, A Dahl, G,** *Responsible man: the Atamman Beja of northeastern Sudan.* Stockholm: Dept. of Social Anthropology, Stockholm University, 1991, 193pp

1758 **Holy, L,** Berti dream interpretation, in Jedrej M C & Shaw, R (eds), *Dreaming, religion and society (entry 42)*, 86–99

1759 **Holy, L,** *Religion and custom in a muslim society: the Berti of Sudan.* Cambridge: CUP, 1991, 243pp

1760 **Hutchinson, S,** 'Dangerous to eat'. Rethinking pollution states among the Nuer of Sudan, *Africa*, 62, 4 (1992) 490–504

1761 **Jedrej, M C,** Ingessana dreaming, in Jedrej M C & Shaw, R (eds), *Dreaming, religion and society (entry 42)*, 111–25

1762 **Prah, K K,** Anthropologists, colonial administration, and the Lutoko of eastern Equatoria, Sudan, 1952–53, *African journal of sociology*, 3, 2 (1989/1990) 70–86

1763 **Ring, M M,** Dinka stock trading and shifts in rights in cattle, in Baxter P T W & Hogg, R (eds), *Property, poverty and people (entry 1000)*, 192–205

1764 **Simonse, S,** *Kings of disaster: dualism, centralism and the scapegoat king in southeastern Sudan.* Leiden: Brill, 1992, 477pp

Arts

1765 **Coote, J,** 'Marvels of everyday vision': the anthropology of aesthetics and the cattle-keeping Nilotes, in Coote J & Shelton, A (eds), *Anthropology, art and aesthetics* (Oxford: Clarendon, 1992), 245–74

1766 **Kirker, C L,** 'This is not your time here'. Islamic fundamentalism and art in Sudan - an African artist interviewed, *Issue*, 20, 2 (1992) 5–11

Economy - Development

1767 Robison, G, Sudan: a cause for concern, *World today*, 48, 4 (1992) 61–64

1768 Brown, R P C, *Debt and private wealth: debt, capital flight and the IMF in Sudan.* Basingstoke: Macmillan, 1992, 334pp

1769 Brown, R P C, Migrants' remittances, capital flight and macroeconomic imbalance in Sudan's hidden economy, *Journal of African economies*, 1, 1 (1992) 86–108

1770 Musa, E A, Public enterprise and planned development in Africa: the case of Sudan, *Public enterprise*, 11, 4 (1991) 289–302

1771 Saad, A A, Simpson, M C, *Devaluation and structural adjustment in SSA: some evidence from the Siudanese oilseeds sub-sector.* Leeds: Leeds University, School of Business Studies, 1990, 20pp

1772 Yongo-Bure, B, The underdevelopment of the southern Sudan since independence, in Daly M W & Sikainga, A A (eds), *Civil war in the Sudan (entry 1845)*, 51–77

Economic and social history

see also: 1305

1773 Adelberger, J, Aspects of Fur culture, or Felkin revisited: Arkell's discussion of a 19th century traveller's report with six Fur prisoners at al-Fashir, *Sudanic Africa*, 2, (1991) 53–77

1774 Bjrkelo, A, Shouk, A A, A land dispute in Berber, *Sudanic Africa*, 2, (1991) 1–28

1775 Johnson, D H, Recruitment and entrapment in private slave armies: the structure of the *zara'ib*

in the southern Sudan, in Savage E (ed), *The human commodity (entry 252)*, 162–73

1776 Pelliccioni, F, Schiavitù e città nel Sudan meridionale: genesi e sviluppo dell'urbanizzazione nel XIX secolo e sue interrelazioni con la storia della <tratta>, *Bollettino della Società Geografica Italiana*, 8, 7/9 (1991) 499–523

1777 Prunier, G, Military slavery in Sudan during the Turkiyya (1820–1885), in Savage E (ed), *The human commodity (entry 252)*, 129–39

1778 Spaulding, J, The value of virginity on Echo Island, 1860–1866, *International journal of African historical studies*, 25, 1 (1992) 67–83

Education

1779 Akrat, S M, In-service education for teachers of pupils with mental handicap: a survey of practices in Africa with special reference to Sudan, *Ahfad journal*, 8, 2 (1991) 25–36

1780 Beasley, I, *Before the wind changed: people, places and education in the Sudan.* Oxford: OUP, 1992, 512pp

Environment

see also: 297, 1869

1781 Abdel-Ati, H A, Small towns under conditions of environmental stress: Sinkat, eastern Sudan, in Baker J & Pedersen, P O (eds), *Rural-urban interface (entry 1111)*, 69–84

1782 Saarainen, T, Luukkanen, O, Afforestation experiments on multipurpose tree species in the central Sudan, in Bishay A & Dregne, H (eds), *Desert development; Part 1* (London: Harwood, 1991), 435–47

Finance

1783 Ibrahim, B el-D, Some asapects of Islamic banking in LDACs: reflections on the Faisal Islamic Bank, Sudan, in Raffer K & Salih, M A M (ed), *The least developed and the oil-rich (entry 592),* 216–28

1784 Trenk, M, *Der Schatten der Verschuldung: komplexe Kreditbeziehungen des informellen Finansektors.* Saarbrucken: Brietenbach, 1991, 185pp

Food

see also: 1602

1785 Coughnegor, C M, 'Captured by' but not 'prisoners' of capitalism: strategies of limited-resource farm households in Sudan, *Journal of Asian and African studies,* 27, 3/4 (1992) 202–15

1786 de Waal, A, Starving out the South, 1984–9, in Daly M W & Sikainga, A A (eds), *Civil war in the Sudan (entry 1845),* 157–85

1787 Deng, F M, Minear, L, *The challenges of famine relief: emergency operations in the Sudan.* Washington: Brookings Institution, 1992, 165pp

1788 Dowden, R, Why the food just stopped, *Sunday review,* (6.6.1993) 14–17

1789 Hubbard, M, *Strengthening the famine prevention capability of local government in Western Sudan: learning from the Kordofan experience.* Birmingham: Birmingham University, Development Administration Group, 1990, 16pp

1790 Jaspars, S, *Are rich and poor equally vulnerable to famine in North Darfur, Sudan?* The Hague: Institute of Social Studies, 1992, 20pp

1791 Pyle, A, The resilience of households to famine in El Fasher, Sudan, 1982–89, *Disasters,* 16, 1 (1992) 19–27

1792 Spiers, B E, Famine in Africa, in Gastellu-Etchegorry J P (ed), *Satellite remote sensing (entry 412),* 115–119

1793 van Dijk, M P, Food security in the Sudan: the need for a regional strategy, in Raffer K & Salih, M A M (ed), *The least developed and the oil-rich (entry 592),* 99–110

1794 Young, H, A case study of the Chadian refugees in Western Sudan: the impact of the food assessment mission, *Journal of refugee studies,* 5, 3/4 (1992) 327–35

Gender

1795 Badri, A E, Women in management and public administration in Sudan, *Ahfad journal,* 8, 2 (1991) 5–24

1796 Grawert, E, Socio-economic linkages between agriculture and industry: are rural women involved in an 'industrialisation process'? considered from Kutum, a small town in western Sudan, *African development perspectives yearbook,* 2, (1990/91) 677–694

1797 Greunbaum, E, The islamist state and Sudanese women, *Middle East report,* 22, 6 (1992) 29–32

1798 Greunebaum, E, *Nuer women in southern Sudan: health, reproduction and work.* East Lansing: Michigan State University, 1990, 29pp

1799 Hale, S, The rise of Islam and women of the National Islamic Front of Sudan, *Review of African political economy,* 54 (1992) 27–41

1800 Ismail, E Makkri, M, *Frauen im Sudan.* Wuppertal: Hammer, 1990, 177pp

Geography, human

see also: 1327, 1328

1801 Abdel Ati, H A, The damming of the River Atbara and its downstream impact, in Darkoh M B K (ed), *African river basins (entry 406),* 21–43

1802 Osman, M, *Verwüstung die Zerstörung von Kulturland am Biespiel des Sudan.* Bremen: CON, 1990, 127pp

1803 Ruppert, H, The significance of drinking water for population migration in the Sahel Zone of the Republic of Sudan, *Applied geography and development,* 37, (1991) 39–47

Geography, physical

see also: 1330, 1331

1804 Hassan, H M, Wigton, W, Remote sensing and agricultural information for crop forecasting: Sudan experience, in Gastellu-Etchegorry J P (ed), *Satellite remote sensing (entry 412),* 121–34

Health & welfare services

see also: 2843

1805 Altigani, M, The role of the village midwives in antenatal care services in the Sudan, *Journal of tropical pediatrics,* 38, 1 (1992) 43–48

1806 Cairncross, S, Kinnear, J, Elasticity of demand for water in Khartoum, Sudan, *Social science and medecine,* 34, 2 (1992) 183–89

1807 El Musharaf, A O, The role of female doctors in the health services in Sudan, *Ahfad journal,* 8, 2 (1991) 37–57

1808 Luk, J, Relief, rehabilitation and reconstruction in the SPLM/SPLA administered areas during the transitional phase and beyond, in Doornbos M et al (eds), *Beyond conflict in the Horn (entry 1533),* 42–48

1809 Mercur, A, Mortality and morbidity in refugees camps in eastern Sudan, 1985–90, *Disasters,* 16, 1 (1992) 28–42

1810 Salim, Z A, The role of the graduate nurse of Khartoum Nursing College in nursing service, *Ahfad journal,* 8, 2 (1991) 58–84

History, early

1811 Taylor, J H, *Egypt and Nubia.* London: British Museum, 1991, 72pp

1812 Welsby, D, Daniels, C, *Soba: archeological research at a medieval capital on the Blue Nile.* London: British Institute in Eastern Africa, 1991, 381pp

1813 Zarrough, M el-D A, *The kingdom of Alwa.* Calgary: University of Calgary Press, 1991, 124pp

History, C6–18th

1814 Warburg, G R, The Turco-Egyptian Sudan: a recent historiographical controversy, *Die Welt des Islams,* 31, 2 (1991) 193–215

1815 Yusoff, K, Reflections on the relationship between Egypt and Nuba during early Mamluk period, *Jebat,* 18, (1990) 289–295

History, C19th

1816 Hanson, J, Robinson, D, *After the jihad: the reign of Ahmad al-Kabir in the Western Sudan.* East Lansing: Michigan State UP, 1992, 410pp

1817 Warburg, G R, *Historical discord on the Nile Valley.* London: Hurst, 1992, 210pp

History, C20th

see also: 1341, 1817

1818 el Amin, M N, Was there an alliance between the Watanist (Nationalist) Party, international communism and the White Flag League in the Sudan?, *British journal of Middle East studies*, 19, 2 (1992) 177–85

1819 Hanes, W T, Sir Hubert Huddleston and the independence of the Sudan, *Journal of imperial and Commonwealth history*, 22, 2 (1992) 248–73

Industry & trade

see also: 1796

1820 Hansohm, D, Linkages between agriculture and industry in Sudan, with special references to small industries, *African development perspectives yearbook*, 2, (1990/91) 546–555

1821 Hansohm, D, *Small industry development in Africa: lessons from Sudan*. Hamburg: Lit, 1992, 263pp

1822 Ibrahim, B A, Evaluation of empirical studies on handicrafts, and small scale industrial activities in Sudan, *Ahfad journal*, 9, 1 (1992) 55–77

1823 Kirscht, H, *Bootsbau in Omdurman (Sudan)*. Stuggart: Steiner, 1990, 183pp

International economic relations

No entry, see also: 1768

International relations

1824 Warburg, G R, The Sudan and Israel: an episode in bilateral relations, *Middle Eastern studies*, 28, 2 (1992) 385–396

Labour & manpower

1825 Abdalla, A K, A framework for the development of a managerial evaluation system in the Sudanese public agricultural corporation, *Public enterprise*, 11, 4 (1991) 280–88

1826 Alnagarabi, M A M, Migration from rural Sudan to oil-rich Arab countries, in Raffer K & Salih, M A M (ed), *The least developed and the oil-rich (entry 592)*, 172–83

1827 Ibrahim, S el-D, Patterns of internal wage labour migration in the Horn of Africa: the case of the Sudan, in Doornbos M et al (eds), *Beyond conflict in the Horn (entry 1533)*, 117–27

Law

see also: 690

1828 Tier, A M, Conflict of laws and legal pluralism in the Sudan, *International and comparative law quarterly*, 39, 3 (1990) 611–40

1829 Tier, A M, Islamisation of the Sudan laws and constitution, *Verfassung und Recht in Ubersee*, 25, 2 (1992) 199–219

1830 Tier, A M, Islamization of the Sudan laws and constitution: its allure and its impracticability, *Verfassung und Recht in Übersee*, 25, 2 (1992) 199–219

Literature

1831 Shoush, M I, In search of an Afro-Arab identity: the southern view of the northern Sudan as seen through the novels of Francis Deng, *British journal of Middle East studies*, 18, 1 (1991) 67–81

Media

1832 Article 19, *Country*

commentary: Sudan. London:
Article 19, 1991, 22pp

Medical

see also: 1798
1833 Omer, M I A, Child health in
the spontaneous settlements
around Khartoum, _Environment
and urbanization,_ 2, 2 (1990) 65–70

Natural resources

1834 Hassan, H W, Sudan's
National Energy Resaerch Council
and renewable energy technologies,
in Bhagavan M R & Karekezi, S
(eds), _Energy for rural development_
London: Zed, (1992) 119–23
1835 Knott, D, Hewett, R G M,
Future water development
planning in Sudan, in Howell J P,
Allan J A (eds), _The Nile (entry
1328),_ 93–106
1836 Kok, P N, Adding fuel to the
conflict: oil, war and peace in the
Sudan, in Doornbos M et al (eds),
_Beyond conflict in the Horn (entry
1533),_ 104–112

Planning

1837 Post, J, Small scale economic
activity and town planning in
Kassala, Sudan, _Third World
planning review,_ 14, 1 (1991) 53–74
1838 Tvedt, T, Non-implemented
plans as a barrier to development:
the case of the Jonglei project in the
southern Sudan, in Darkoh M B K
(ed), _African river basins (entry
406),_ 59–78

Politics

see also: 835, 1786, 1836, 1858
1839 Al-Teraifi, A-A A, Financing
regional and local government in
Sudan, _Environment and
urbanization,_ 3, 2 (1991) 136–144

1840 An-Na'im, A A,
Constitutional discourse and the
civil war in the Sudan, in Daly M
W & Sikainga, A A (eds), _Civil
war in the Sudan (entry 1845),_
97–116
1841 Becker, E Mitchell, C,
_Chronology of conflict resolution
initiatives in Sudan._ Fairfax: George
Mason University, Institute for
Conflict Analysis and Resolution,
1991, 167pp
1842 Bob, A, Islam, the State and
politics in the Sudan, _Northeast
African studies,_ 12, 2/3 (1990)
201–220
1843 Bwolo, A D, The impact of
armed conflict on the development
of Sudan, in NGLS (ed), _Voices
from Africa 3 (entry 913),_ 37–44
1844 Daly, M W, Broken bridge and
empty basket: the political and
economic background to the
Sudanese civil war, in Daly M W &
Sikainga, A A (eds), _Civil war in the
Sudan (entry 1845),_ 1–26
1845 Daly, M, Sikainga, A A,
(eds), _Civil war in the Sudan._
London: British Academic Pres,
1992, 220pp
1846 de Waal, A, Some comments
on militias in the contemporary
Sudan, in Daly M W & Sikainga, A
A (eds), _Civil war in the Sudan
(entry 1845),_ 142–56
1847 Deng, F M, Hidden agendas
for the peace process, in Daly M W
& Sikainga, A A (eds), _Civil war in
the Sudan (entry 1845),_ 186–215
1848 Garang, J, (ed. M Khalid),
The call for democracy in Sudan.
London: Kegan Paul International
(2nd edn), 1992, 292pp
1849 Johnson, D H, Prunier, G,
The foundation and expansion of
the SPLA, in Daly M W &
Sikainga, A A (eds), _Civil war in the
Sudan (entry 1845),_ 117–41
1850 Keen, D, _A political economy of
refugee flows from south-west Sudan,_

1986–1988. Geneva: UNRISD, 1992, 37pp

1851 Lako, G T, The Jonglei Canal scheme as a socieconomic factor in the civil war in the Sudan, in Darkoh M B K (ed), *African river basins (entry 406),* 45–57

1852 Marchal, R, Le Soudan entre islamisme et dictature militaire, *Maghreb-Machrek,* 137 (1992) 56–79

1853 Prunier, G, Les 'Frères' et l'armée..., *Cahiers de l'Orient,* 27, (1992) 53–70

1854 Raghavan, N, The southern Sudanese secessionist movement, in Premdas R et al (eds), *Secessionist movements in comparative perspective* (London: Pinter, 1990), 128–40

1855 Sikainga, A A, Northern Sudan: political parties and the civil war, in Daly M W & Sikainga, A A (eds), *Civil war in the Sudan (entry 1845),* 78–96

1856 Wakoson, E W, The politics of Southern self-government 1972–83, in Daly M W & Sikainga, A A (eds), *Civil war in the Sudan (entry 1845),* 27–50

1857 Wakoson, E N, Sudan's Addis Ababa Peace Treaty: why it failed, *Northeast African studies,* 12, 2/3 (1990) 19–53

Religion, philosophy

see also: 1374, 1766, 1829, 1842

1858 Hunwick, J O, (ed), *Religion and national integration in Africa: Islam, Christianity, politics in the Sudan and Nigeria.* Evanston: Northwestern UP, 1992, 176pp

1859 Karrar, A S, *The Sufi brotherhoods in the Sudan.* London: Hurst, 1992, 234pp

Rural economy

see also: 1820, 1838, 1851

1860 Abbas, B, Tilley, P, Pastoral management for protecting ecological balance in Halaib District, Red Sea Province, Sudan, *Nomadic peoples,* 29, (1991) 77–86

1861 Abdelkarim, A, *Primitive capital accumulation in the Sudan.* London: Cass, 1992, 197pp

1862 Ahmed, A G M, Rural production systems in the Sudan, in Doornbos M et al (eds), *Beyond conflict in the Horn (entry 1533),* 133–42

1863 Ahmed, T E, The effect of changes in production relations on tenants' debts: the case of the Sudan Gezira Scheme, *Public enterprise,* 11, 4 (1991) 268–79

1864 El Mangouri, H, Dryland management in the Kordofan and Darfur Provines of Sudan, in Dixon J A et al (eds), *Dryland management (entry 1012),* 86–97

1865 Elbadawi, I A, Real overvaluation, terms of trade shocks and the cost to agriculture in subsaharan Africa: the case of the Sudan, *Journal of African economies,* 1, 1 (1992) 59–85

1866 el-Dishouni, S A, Agricultural development issues in the northern region of the Sudan: cooperatives and private small-holders, in Darkoh M B K (ed), *African river basins (entry 406),* 113–119

1867 Köhler-Rollefson, I, et al, The camel pastoral system of the Southern Rashaida in eastern Sudan, *Nomadic peoples,* 29, (1991) 68–76

1868 Mohamed, T E S A, Ahmed, A G M, Camel pastoralism as a food system in the Sudan: limitations and changes, *Nomadic peoples,* 29, (1991) 61–67

1869 Mohammed Salih, M O, Environmental and social insecurity in the drylands of the Sudan, in Hjort af Ornas A (ed), *Security in African drylands (entry 1025),* 123–38

1870 Pieper, A, et al, *The sector programme for rural development: programme evaluation with special reference to Indonesia, Sudan, Rwanda, Tanzania and Nicaragua.* The Hague: Ministry of Foreign Affairs, 1992, 153pp

1871 Plusquellec, H L, *The Gezira irrigation scheme in Sudan: objectives, design and performance.* Washington: World Bank, 1990, 90pp

1872 Saad, A A, Simpson, M C, *Supply responses of peasant cultivators in the Sudan: a rational expectations model.* Leeds: Leeds University, School of Business Studies, 1991, 15pp

1873 Yongo-Bure, B, The role of small-scale rural industries in the recovery and development of the southern Sudan, in Doornbos M et al (eds), *Beyond conflict in the Horn (entry 1533),* 166–70

Sociology

1874 Hamid, G M, Livelihood patterns of displaced households in Greater Khartoum, *Disasters,* 16, 3 (1992) 230–38

1875 Sendker, L, *Eritreische Fluchting in Sudan: zwischen Assimilation und Segregation.* Hamburg: Institur für Afrika-Kunde, 1990, 292pp

Urban studies

see also: 1833

1876 Ahmad, A M, Housing submarkets for the urban poor - the case of Greater Khartoum, the Sudan, *Environment and urbanization,* 1, 2 (1989) 50–59

EAST AFRICA

General

1880 Hino, S, A bibliography on Swahili studies in Japan, *African urban studies,* 2 (1992) 139–58

1881 Hino, S, Swahili studies in Japan, *African urban studies,* 2 (1992) 77–138

Anthropology

1882 Böhmer-Bauer, K, *Nahrung, Weltbild und Gesellschaft: Ernährung und Nahrungsregein des Massai als Spiegel der gesellschaftlichen Ordung.* Saarbrucken: Brietenbach, 1990, 161pp

1883 Le Guennec-Coppens, F, *Les Swahili entre Afrique et Arabie.* Paris: Karthala, 1991, 224pp

1884 Middleton, J, *The world of the Swahili: an African mercantile civilisation.* New Haven: Yale UP, 1992, 254pp

1885 Rigby, P, *Cattle, capitalism and class: Ilparakuyo Maasai transformations.* Philadelphia: Temple University Press, 1992, 247pp

1886 Sengo, T S Y, Proverbs in an East African setting, *Matatu,* 9 (1992) 67–80

Arts

1887 Graebner, W, Sources for the study of popular culture in East Africa: a select bibliography and discography, *Matatu,* 9 (1992) 173–206

1888 Martin, S H, Brass bands and the Beni phenomenon in urban East Africa, *African music,* 7, 1 (1991) 72–81

Economy - Development

1889 Bauer, H, et al, *Armutsbekämpfung durch Hilfe under Selbsthilfe. Selbsthilfe zwischen Staat und Gesellschaft: Beispiele aus Ostafrika.* Bonn: Thenee, 1990, 32pp

1890 Beynon, J, (ed), *Market liberalisation and private sector response in eastern and southern Africa.* Oxford: International Development Centre, 1992, 35pp

1891 Chole, E, et al, (eds), *The crisis of development strategies in eastern Africa.* Addis Ababa: OSSREA, 1990, 285pp

1892 Ng'ethe, N, *In search of NGOs: towards a funding strategy to create NGO research capacity in eastern and southern Africa.* Nairobi: Nairobi University, IDS, 1991, 75pp

Economic and social history

1893 Gregory, R B, *The rise and fall of philanthropy in East Africa.* New Brunswick: Transaction, 1992, 251pp

1894 Stiles, D, The ports of East Africa, the Comores and Madagascar: their place in Indian Ocean trade from 1–1500 AD, *Kenya past and present,* 24 (1992) 27–36

Education

1895 Bogonko, S N, *Reflections on education in East Africa.* Nairobi: OUP, 1991, 326pp

1896 de Beyer, J, The incidence and impact on earnings of formal training provided by enterprises in Kenya and Tanzania, *Economics of education review,* 9, 4 (1990) 321–30

1897 Friedrich Ebert Foundation, *Challenges of workers' education in East Africa today: report on a regional seminar.* Nairobi: the Foundation, 1990, 236pp

1898 Mukras, M S, *The state of graduate training in economics in eastern and southern Africa.* Nairobi: Initiatives, 1990, 53pp

Environment

see also: 1937

1899 Ayiemba, E H O, Environmental constraints to development efforts in semiarid regions of East Africa, in Irele A (ed), *African education and identity (entry 268),* 369–80

1900 Thibon, C, Politiques de l'environnnement dans la région des Grands Lacs, *Afrique contemporaine,* 161 (1992) 230–238

Finance

1901 Malkamäki, M, *Banking the poor: informal and semi-formal financial systems serving the microenterprise.* Helsinki: Helsinki University, Institute of Development Studies, 1991, 132pp

Food

No entry, see also: 1882

Gender

No entry, see also: 1935, 1936

Geography, human

1902 Dublin, H T, Dynamics of the Serengeti-Mara woodlands: an historical perspective, *Forest and conservation history,* 35, 4 (1991) 169–78

1903 O'Connor, A M, The changing geography of eastern Africa, in Chapman G P & Baker, K M (eds), *The changing geography of Africa (entry 405),* 114–38

Health & welfare services

No entry, see also: 1934

History, general

1904 Spaulding, J L, An historical context for the study of Islam in eastern Africa, in Harrow K H (ed), *Faces of Islam (entry 710),* 23–36

History, early

1905 Knappert, J, Language and history in Africa, *Annales aequatoria,* 12, (1991) 79–109

1906 van Grunderbeek, M C, Essai de délimitation chronologiqe de l'Age de Fer ancien au Burundi, au Rwanda et dans la region des Grand Lacs, *Azania,* 27, (1992) 53–80

History, C19th

1907 Setel, P, *'A good moral tone': Victorian ideals of health and the judgement of persons in nineteenth century travel and mission accounts from East Africa.* Boston: African Studies Centre, Boston University, 1991, 18pp

History, C20th

1908 Loth, H, Koloniale und

missionarische Interessen in Deutsch-Ostafrika, *Zeitschrift für Mission,* 17, 4 (1991) 207–217

Industry & trade

1909 Bartels, L, Textiel in Oost-Afrika, in *Bontjes voor de tropen: de export van imitatieweefsels naar de tropen* (Zwolle: Waanders Uitgevers, 1991), 65–76

1910 Cameron, K M, *Into Africa: the story of the East African safari.* London: Constable, 1990, 229pp

International economic relations

1911 Agbor-Tabi, P, International law and functional integration: the East African Community revisited, *African review,* 16, 1/2 (1989) 16–27

Language

1912 Mazrui, A A, Zirimo, P, The secularization of an Afro-Islamic language: church, state, and market-place in the spread of Kiswahili, *Journal of Islamic studies,* 1, (1990) 24–53

1913 Ryanga, S, Imbalances in the modernisation and promotion of the Swahili language in East Africa: the case of Kenya and Tanzania, *Ufahamu,* 18, 3 (1989/90) 21–34

1914 Schadeberg, T C, Historical inferences from Swahili etymologies, in Pilaszewicz S & Rzewuski, E (eds), *Unwritten testimonies (entry 447),* 105–22

Library - documentation

see also: 2126

1915 Maliyamkono, T L, et al, *Research undertaken recently in eastern and southern Africa.* Dar es Salaam: Shihana, 1990, 506pp

Literature

1916 Bierstecker, A, Language, poetry and power: a reconsideration of 'Utendi wa Mwana Kupona', in Harrow K H (ed), *Faces of Islam (entry 710),* 59–77

1917 Geider, T, Early Swahili travelogues, *Matatu,* 9 (1992) 27–65

1918 Grea, E I, Trends in the East African novel in English, *Commonwealth novel in English,* 5, 1 (1992) 73–80

1919 Philipson, R, Balzac in Zanzibar: the Swahili novel as disseminator of bourgeois individualism, *Research in African literatures,* 23, 3 (1992) 85–98

1920 Shariff, I N, Islam and secularity in Swahili literature: an overview, in Harrow K H (ed), *Faces of Islam (entry 710),* 37–57

Media

1921 Maja-Pearce, A, The press in East Africa, *Index on censorship,* 21, 7 (1992) 50–89

Medical

1922 Bwayo, J J, et al, Long distance truck drivers: Pt 1. Prevalence of sexually transmitted diseases (STDs), *East african medical journal,* 68, 6 (1991) 425–429

1923 Bwayo, J J, et al, Long distance truck drivers. Pt. 2: knowledge and attitudes on sexually transmitted diseases and sexual behaviour, *East african medical journal,* 68, 9 (1991) 714–719

Religion, philosophy

1924 Azevedo, M, Prater, G S,

The minority status of Islam in East Africa: a historico-sociological perspective, *Journal institute of Muslim minority affairs*, 12, 2 (1991) 482–497

1925 Constantin, F, Afrique orientale: l'islam bloqué: inconscience ou provocation?, *Studia Africana*, 3 (1992) 164–170

1926 Hillman, E, Maasai religion and the Christian mission, *African christian studies*, 7, 2 (1991) 3–11

1927 Okullu, H, Church, state and society in East Africa, in Anyang' Nyong'o P (ed), *30 years of independence (entry 101)*, 25–39

Rural economy

1928 Barnett, T, Blaikie, P, *Simple methods for monitoring the socio-economic impact of AIDS: lessons from research in Uganda and Kenya.* Norwich: University of East Anglia, School of Development Studies, 1992, 9pp

1929 Chitere, O P, Mutiso, R, *Working with rural communities: a participatory action research.* Nairobi: Nairobi UP, 1992, 206pp

1930 Cromwell, E, *The impact of economic reform on the performance of the seed sector in eastern and southern Africa.* Paris: OECD Development Centre, 1992, 90pp

1931 Schneider, H K, Development and the pastoralists of East Africa, in Salzman C & Galaty, J G (eds), *Nomads in a changing world* (Naples: Instituto Universitario Orientale, 1990) 179–209

1932 Schwartz, L A, Kampen, J, *Agricultural extension in East Africa.* Washington: World Bank, 1991, 59pp

Sociology

see also: 1888
1933 Bujra, J, Ethnicity and class:

the case of the East African 'Asians', in Allen T & Thomas, A (eds), *Poverty and development in the1990s* (Oxford: OUP, 1992), 347–61

1934 Chole, E, Eastern Africa: government expenditure on social development, in Mohammed D (ed), *Social development in Africa (entry 1093)*, 213–26

1935 Linnebuhr, E, Kanga: popular cloths with messages, *Matatu*, 9 (1992) 81–90

1936 Omari, C K, Shaidi, L P, (eds), *Social problems in eastern Africa.* Dar es Salaam: Dar es Salaam University Press, 1991, 161pp

Urban studies

1937 Hosier, R, Energy and environmental management in eastern African cities, *Environment and planning, series A*, 24, 9 (1992) 1231–54

1938 Kironde, J M L, Creations in Dar es Salaam and extensions in Nairobi: the defiance of inappropriate building standards, *Cities*, 9, 3 (1992) 220–31

1939 Rakodi, C, Developing institutional capacity to meet the housing needs of the urban poor: experience in Kenya, Tanzania and Zimbabwe, *Cities*, 8, 3 (1991) 228–43

BURUNDI

General

see also: 2216
1940 Daniels, M, *Burundi.* Oxford: Clio, 1992, 135pp

Current affairs

1941 Amnesty International, *Burundi: sectarian security forces*

violate human rights with impunity.
London: Amnesty International,
1992, 29pp

1942 Erler, B Reyntyens, P, *Die
Ereignisse in Burundi im November
und Dezember 1991:
Untersuchungsbericht.* Bonn: n.p.,
1992, 43pp

1943 Hakizimane, D, *Burundi: le
non-dit.* Vernier: Remesha, 1991,
189pp

1944 Thibon, C, Les événements de
novembre-décembre 1991 au
Burundi, *Politique africaine,* 45
(1992) 154–58

Economy - Development

1945 Nicayenzi, Z, Evolution de la
dette publique du Burundi et son
impact sur les équilibres
macro-économique 1970–1988,
Administration, gestion, formation, 29
(1990) 23–58

1946 Ruberintwari, P, Les
programmes d'ajustement
structurel: le cas du Burundi, *Au
coeur de l'Afrique,* 59, 2/3 (1991)
311–338

Education

1947 Eisemon, T O, Schwille, J,
Primary schooling in Burundi and
Kenya: preparation for secondary
education or for self-employment?,
Elementary school journal, 92, 1
(1991) 23–40

1948 Ndimurukundo, N,
Education des adultes et
démocratie au Burundi, *Au coeur de
l'Afrique,* 59, 2/3 (1991) 285–309

Environment

No entry, see also: 1900

Gender

No entry, see also: 1950

History, C20th

1949 Harroy, J P, Verschuren, J,
Présentation du manuscrit de Jean
Ghislain: "Le brouillard sur la
Kibira: souvenirs d'un territorial au
Burundi", *Bulletin des séances,* 36, 3
(1990) 391–405

1950 Hunt, N R, Noise over
camouflaged polygamy, colonial
morality taxation, and a
woman-naming crisis in Belgian
Africa, *The journal of African history,*
32, 3 (1991) 471–494

1951 Laely, T, Le destin du
Bushingantabe: transformation
d'une structure locale d'autorité au
Burundi, *Geneva-Africa,* 30, 2
(1992) 75–98

International economic relations

1952 Greenaway, D, Milner, C R,
Policy appraisal and the structure
of protection in a low-income
developing country: problems of
measurement and evaluation in
Burundi, *Journal of development
studies,* 27, 1 (1990) 22–42

Law

1953 Makoroka, S, La coopération
judiciaire: un aspect de
l'harmonisation des droits
nationaux dans le cadre de la
C.E.P.G.L., *Revue de l'université du
Burundi. Série sciences humaines,* 7
(1990) 8–28

1954 Reyntjens, F, L'ingénierie de
l'unité nationale: quelques
singularités de la constitution
burundaise de 1992, *Politique
africaine,* 47 (1992) 141–46

Literature

1955 Havyarimana, G, *Les soleils
des indépendances* (1968)
d'Ahmadou Kourouma: innovation

par la fusion thématique et narrative, *Revue de l'université du Burundi. Série sciences humaines,* 7 (1990)

Politics

1956 Jolly, B, Présentation du projet 'amélioration des structures de l'administration publique', *Administation, gestion, formation,* 30/31 (1990) 129–148
1957 Minani, P, La liberté et la démocratie sont-elles possibles au Burundi? Une réflexion à la lumière de l'oeuvre de Montesquieu, *Au coeur de l'Afrique,* 59, 2/3 (1991) 237–262
1958 Nkengurutse, A, Historique de la réforme administrative au Burundi, *Administation, gestion, formation,* 30/31 (1990) 1990
1959 Ntabona, A, Institution des Bashingantahe à l'heure du pluralisme politique africain, *Au coeur de l'Afrique,* 59, 2/3 (1991) 263–284
1960 Ntambwiriza, Z, La stratégie d'action en matière d'amélioration des structures de l'administration, *Administration, gestion, formation,* 30/31 (1990) 149–159
1961 Ress, D, *The Burundi ethnic massacres, 1988.* Lewiston: Mellen, 1992, 126pp

Religion, philosophy

1962 Ntabona, A, Ruberintwari, Pratique religieuse dans le milieu urbain de Bujumbura, *Au coeur de l'Afrique,* 59, 1 (1991) 3–17

Rural economy

1963 Bove, R, Societa e zootecnia nel Burundi, *Africa (Rome),* 46, 4 (1991) 601–108
1964 Delor-Vandueren, A,

Degand, J, *Burundi: démographie, agriculture et environnement.* Louvain-la-Neuve: CIDEP, 1992, 74pp

Sociology

KENYA

Agriculture, scientific

1965 Barrow, E G C, Articulating local forestry knowledge in policy: the case of Turkana, *Resources,* 2, 1 (1991) 23–29
1966 Engelskjn, K, *Tsetse fly control in a Maasai pastoralist society in Nguruman, southwest Kenya.* Oslo: Noragric, 1990, 137pp
1967 Johansson, S, Luukkanen, O, Results from irrigated species and provenence trials in Bura, Kenya, in Bishay A & Dregne, H (eds), *Desert development ; Part 1* (London: Harwood, 1991), 449–63
1968 Mochoge, B O, Mwonga, S M, Difference between soil properties of land under continuous cultivation and fallow in three soil types in Kenya, *Discovery and innovation,* 3, 3 (1991) 77–83
1969 Ongaro, W A, Modern maize technology, yield variations, and efficiency differences: a case of small farms in western Kenya, *Eastern Africa economic review,* 6, 1 (1990) 11–30
1970 Scholte, P T, Leaf litter and *Acacia* pods as feed for livestock during the dry season in *Acacia-Commiphora* bushland, Kenya, *Journal of arid environments,* 22, 3 (1992) 271–276
1971 Stiles, D, Indigenous dry-land plants for Kenyan development, *Kenya past and present,* 22 (1990) 41–44

Anthropology

see also: 2054, 2059

1972 Broch-Due, V, 'Livestock speak louder than sweet words': changing property and gender relations among the Turkana, in Baxter P T W & Hogg, R (eds), *Property, poverty and people (entry 1000)*, 147–63

1973 Cohen, D W, Odhiambo, E S, *Burying SM: the politics of knowledge and the sociology of power in Africa.* London: Currey, 1992, 159pp

1974 Geider, T, *Die Figur des Oger in der traditionellen Literatur und Lebenswelt der Pokomo in Ost-Kenya.* Cologne: Koppe, 1990, 2 vols, 774pp

1975 Hogg, R, The politics of changing property relations among Isiola Boran pastoralists in northern Kenya, in Baxter P T W & Hogg, R (eds), *Property, poverty and people (entry 1000)*, 20–31

1976 Kelly, H, Commercialisation, sedentarisation, economic diversification and changing property relations among Orma pastoralists on Kenya: some possible target issues for future pastoral research, in Baxter P T W & Hogg, R (eds), *Property, poverty and people (entry 1000)*, 80–94

1977 Kratz, C, Amusement and absolution: transforming narratives during confession of social debts, *American anthropologist*, 93, 4 (1991) 826–51

1978 Oda, M, The 'Inchama' council and witchcraft among the Abakuria of western Kenya, *Senri ethnological studies*, 31 (1992) 83–103

1979 Parkin, D, Simultaniety and sequencing in the oracular speech of Kenyan diviners, in Peek P M (ed), *African divination (entry 48)*, 173–89

1980 Peatrik, A-M, Le chant des hyènes tristes; essai sur les rites funéraires des Meru du Kenya et des peuples apparentés, *Systèmes de pensée en Afrique noire*, 11, (1991) 103–130

1981 Schlee, G, Holy grounds, in Baxter P T W & Hogg, R (eds), *Property, poverty and people (entry 1000)*, 45–54

1982 Spencer, P, Time and the boundaries of the economy in Maasai, in Baxter P T W & Hogg, R (eds), *Property, poverty and people (entry 1000)*, 121–28

1983 Stiles, D, The Gabbra Jilla, *Kenya past and present*, 23 (1991) 23–34

1984 Stördas, F, Intention of implication: the effects of Turkana social organisation on ecological balances, in Baxter P T W & Hogg, R (eds), *Property, poverty and people (entry 1000)*, 137–46

1985 Swartz, M J, *The way the world is: cultural processes and social relations among the Mombasa Swahili.* Berkeley: University of California Press, 1991, 350pp

1986 Tietmeyer, E, *Gynaegamie im Wandel: die Agikuyu zwischen Tradition und Anpassung.* Munster: Lit, 1991, 225pp

Current affairs

1987 Ajulu, R, Kenya: the road to democracy, *Review of African political economy*, 53 (1992) 79–87

1988 Bourmaud, D, Kenya: démocratie et indépendance, *Politique africaine*, 47 (1992) 135–40

1989 Imanyara, G, Maina, W, What future Kenya?, *Nairobi law monthly*, 37 (1991) 19–23

1990 Makinda, S M, Kenya - out of the straitjacket, slowly, *World today*, 48, 10 (1992) 188–92

1991 M'Inoti, K, Beyond the 'emergency' in the North-eastern

Province, *Nairobi law monthly,* 41
(1992) 37–43

Demography

1992 Jensen, A N, Economic
change, marriage relations and
fertility in a rural area of Kenya, in
Stlen K A & Vaa, M (eds), *Gender
and change (entry 399),* 67–89

1993 Kalule-Sabiti, I, The effect of
nuptuality status variables on
fertility: the Kenyan experennce,
South African journal of sociology,
23, 1 (1992) 12–19

1994 Kalule-Sabiti, I,
Socio-economic factors affecting
fertility in Kenya, *South African
journal of sociology,* 23, 2 (1992)
46–52

1995 Khasiani, S A, The nature
and impact of population policy in
Kenya, *African journal of sociology,*
3, 2 (1989/90) 44–60

1996 Mirza, M N, et al, Mortality
patterns in a rural Kenyan
community, *East African medical
journal,* 67, 12 (1990) 823–829

1997 Ochollo-Ayayo, A B C, *The
spirit of a nation: an analysis of
policy, ethics and customary rules of
conduct for regulating fertility levels in
Kenya.* Nairobi: Shirikon, 1991,
210pp

1998 Tiffen, M, (ed), *Environmental
change and dryland management in
Machakos District, Kenya:
population profile.* London: ODI,
1991, 38pp

Economy - Development

1999 Adam, C, et al, Kenya, in
Adam C et al *Adjusting privatisation*
(London: Currey, 1992), 323–51

2000 Bevan, D, et al, *Controlled
open economies : a neoclassical
approach to structuralism.* Oxford:
Clarendon, 1990, 367pp

2001 Kimuyu, A P, Urbanization,

economic structure, and demand
for fuels in Kenya, *Eastern Africa
economic review,* 6, 2 (1990)
111–115

2002 Kleemeier, E, L'aide française
au Kenya: à qui profite-t-elle?,
Cahiers d'études africaines, 31, 1/2
(1991) 175–89

2003 Lehman, H P, The paradox of
state power in Africa: debt
management policies in Kenya and
Zimbabwe, *African studies review,*
35, 2 (1992) 1–34

2004 Leys, C, *Learning from the
Kenya debate.* Sheffield: Sheffield
University, Dept. of Politics, 1992,
31pp

2005 Mosley, P, How to confront
the World Bank and get away with
it: a case study of Kenya, 1980–87,
in Milner C & Rayner, A J (eds),
Policy adjustment (entry 184),
99–131

2006 Mulyungi, J, On the role of
African NGOs, in NGLS (ed),
Voices from Africa 2 (entry 195),
45–58

2007 Ottichilo, W K, *Weathering the
storm: climatic change and investment
in Kenya.* Nairobi: ACTS, 1991,
90pp

2008 Porter, D, et al, *Development
in practice: paved with good
intentions.* London: Routledge,
1991, 234pp

2009 Wilson, L S, The Harambee
movement and efficient public
good provision in Kenya, *Journal of
public economics,* 48, 1 (1992) 1–19

2010 World Bank, *Kenya:
reinvesting in stabilisation and growth
through public sector adjustment.*
Washington: World Bank, 1992,
207pp

2011 Zeleza, T, Economic policy
and performance in Kenya since
independence, *Transafrican journal
of history,* 20 (1991) 35–76

Economic and social history

see also: 2020, 2038

2012 Castro, A P, Njukiine forest: transformation of a common-property resource, *Forest and conservation history,* 35, 4 (1991) 160–68

2013 Duder, C J D, BEADOC: the British East African Disabled Officers' Colony and the white farmers of Kenya, *Agricultural history review,* 40, 2 (1992) 142–50

2014 Metts, R L, Economic development and the terms of trade: the case of Kenya Colony, 1925–1963, *Eastern Africa economic review,* 6, 1 (1990) 45–53

2015 Morton, F, *Children Ham: freed slaves and fugitive slaves on the Kenya coast, 1873–1907.* Boulder: Westview, 1990, 241pp

2016 Ochieng, W R, Maxon, R M, (eds), *An economic history of Kenya.* Nairobi: East African Educational Publishers, 1992, 460pp

2017 Odhiambo, A, From warriors to 'JoNanga': the struggle over nakedness by the Luo of Kenya, *Matatu,* 9 (1992) 11–25

2018 Sobania, N W, Social relations as an aspect of property rights - northern Kenya in the precolonial and colonial periods, in Baxter P T W & Hogg, R (eds), *Property, poverty and people (entry 1000),* 1–19

Education

see also: 2033, 2034, 2052

2019 Bennaars, G A, et al, (eds), *Social education and ethics: developing a new area of learning.* Nairobi: 'Professors World Peace Academy of Kenya', 1990, 133pp

2020 Bogonko, S N, *A history of modern education in Kenya.* Nairobi: Evans, 1992, 208pp

2021 Bogonko, Sorobea Nyachieo, The development of university

education in Kenya 1960–1989, *Journal of east African research and development,* 21, (1991) 141–168

2022 Ngau, M, The gap between promise and performance: educational policy-making and implementation in Kenya, *Ufahamu,* 18, 3 (1989/90) 3–20

2023 Otiende, J E, et al, *Education and development in Kenya: a historical perspective.* Nairobi: OUP, 1991, 176pp

2024 Sturmann, U, *Bildung, Berufsbildung ... und was dann?: angepasste Handwerkausbildung für den ländlichen Raum - die Youth Polytechnics in Kenia.* Saarbruckem: Brietenbach, 1990, 261pp

2025 Tanno, Y, *Education in Kenya: a bibliographical approach.* Tokyo: Institute of Developing Economies, 1990, 249pp

2026 van Dam, A, *Het onderwijs in Kenia.* The Hague: CESO, 1990, 67pp

Environment

see also: 1984, 1998, 2147, 2195

2027 Arum, G, et al, Paper industry, *Resources,* 1, 3 (1990) 17–20

2028 Finkel, M, Darkoh, M B K, Sustaining the arid and semi-arid (ASAL) environment in Kenya through improved pastoralism and agriculture, *Journal of east African research and development,* 21, (1991) 1–20

2029 Gichuki, F N, *Environmental change and dryland management in Machakos District, Kenya: conservation profile.* London: ODI, 1991, 94pp

2030 Holmberg, G, An economic evaluation of soil conservation in Kitui District, Kenya, in Dixon J A et al (eds), *Dryland management (entry 1012),* 56–71

2031 Kemper, K E, Widstrand, C,

Environmental sanitation in developing countries: a selected and annotated bibliography. Linkoping: Dept. of Water and Environmental Studies, Linkoping University, 1991, 83pp

2032 **Kilewe, A M, Thoams, D B,** Land degradation in Kenya: a framework for policy and planning. London: Commonwealth Secretariat, 1992, 147pp

2033 **Korir-Koech, M,** Environmental education in Kenya beyond the year 2000, Journal of east African research and development, 21, (1991) 40–52

2034 **Lee-Smith, D, Chaudhry, T,** Environmental information for and from children, Environment and urbanization, 2, 2 (1990) 27–32

2035 **Mortimore, M,** (ed), Environmental change and dryland management in Machakos District, Kenya: a profile of technological change. London: ODI, 1991, 49pp

2036 **Mortimore, M,** Environmental change and dryland management in Machakos District, Kenya: tree management. London: ODI, 1992, 37pp

2037 **Schuhmann, R,** Unweltschutz durch Strafrecht in Schwarzafrika: eine vergleichende Untersuchung anhand einer Fallstudie für Kenia. Freiburg: Max Plank Institute, 1991, 430pp

2038 **Tiffen, M, Mortimore, M,** Environment, population control and productivity in Kenya: a case study of Machakos District, Development policy review, 10, 3 (1992) 359–87

Finance

2039 **Kwasa, S O,** Mobilisation of public and private resources in Kenya from 1964 to 1987, in Frimpong-Ansah J H & Ingham, B

(eds), Saving for economic recovery (entry 142), 85–92

2040 **Mullei, A R,** The managed floating system in Kenya, in Roe A R et al (eds) Instruments of economic policy (entry 341), 43–51

2041 **Mureithi, L P, Nditiru, S K,** Information technology in Kenya's financial sector. Geneva: ILO, 1991, 27pp

2042 **Musoko, G C /Kagane, E,** Kenya's experience of interest rate policy and credit allocation, in Roe A R et al (eds) Instruments of economic policy (entry 341), 69–78

2043 **Mwega, F M, Killick, T,** Monetary policy in Kenya, 1967–88, Eastern Africa economic review, 6, 2 (1990) 117–142

2044 **Oshikoya, T W,** Interest rate liberalisation, savings investment and growth: the case of Kenya, Savings and development, 16, 3 (1992) 305–20

2045 **Sastry,** The impact of AIDS in life assurance in Africa, Kenya underwriter, 18 (1990) 14–18

Food

see also: 2175, 2179

2046 **Geuns, M, et al,** Child nutrition in the pre-harvest season in Kenya, East African medical journal, 68, 2 (1991) 93–105

2047 **Kennedy, E,** The impact of drought on production, consumption and nutrition in southwest Kenya, Disasters, 16, 1 (1992) 9–18

2048 **K'Okul, R N O,** Maternal and child health in Kenya. Uppsala: SIAS, 1992, 214pp

2049 **Leegwater, P, et al,** Dairy development and nutrition in Kilifi District, Kenya. Leiden: Afrikastudiecentrum, 1991, 134pp

2050 **Little, P D,** The elusive granary: herder, farmer and state in northern Kenya. Cambridge:

Cambridge University Press, 1992, 224pp

2051 O'Leary, M, Changing responses to drought in northern Kenya: the Rendille and Gabbra livestock producers, in Baxter P T W & Hogg, R (eds), *Property, poverty and people (entry 1000)*, 55–79

Gender

see also: 2119, 2141

2052 Cook, A S, et al, University education and career development: female agricultural students in Kenya, *International education,* 20, 2 (1991) 5–13

2053 Kiteme, K, The socioeconomic impact of the African marketwoman trade in rural Kenya, *Journal of Black studies,* 23, 1 (1992) 135–51

2054 La Fontaine, J, The persons of women, in Ardener S (ed), *Persons and powers (entry 31)*, 89–104

2055 Maas, M, *Women's social and economic projects: experiences from Coast Province.* Leiden: Afrikastudiecentrum, 1991, 67pp

2056 Maina, W, Women participation in public affairs in Kenya, *Nairobi law monthly,* 40 (1992) 34–37

2057 Mitullah, W, Hawking as a survival strategy for the urban poor in Nairobi: the case of women, *Environment and urbanization,* 3, 2 (1991) 13–22

2058 Nelson, N, The women who left and those who have stayed behind: rural-urban migration in western-central Kenya, in Chant S (ed), *Gender and migration in developing countries* (London: Belhaven, 1992), 109–138

2059 Njiro, E, Aspects of gender subordination in pre-colonial Embu society of Kenya, *Bulletin of the international committee on urgent anthropological and ethnological research,* 32/33 (1990/91) 81–92

2060 Olenja J M, Gender and agricultural production in Samia Kenya: strategies and constraints, *Journal of east African research and development,* 21, (1991) 81–92

2061 Presley, C A, *Kikuyu women, the Mau Mau rebellion and social change in Kenya.* Boulder: Westview, 1992, 213pp

2062 Silberschmidt, M, Have men become the weaker sex? Changing life situations in Kisii District, Kenya, *Journal of modern African studies,* 30, 2 (1992) 237–53

2063 Silberschmidt, M, *Women's position in the household and their use of family planning and antenatal services: a case study from Kisii District, kenya.* Copenhagen: CDR, 1991, 148pp

2064 Sörensen, A von Bülow, D, *Gender and contract farming in Kericho, Kenya.* Copenhagen: CDR, 1990, 16pp

2065 Sorensen, A, Women's organisations among the Kipsigis: change, variety and different participation, *Africa,* 62, 4 (1992) 547–66

2066 Thomas-Slayter, B, Politics, class and gender in African resource management: the case of rural Kenya, *Economic development and cultural change,* 40, 4 (1992) 809–28

2067 von Bulow, D, Bigger than men? Gender relations and their changing meanings in Kipsigis society, Kenya, *Africa,* 62, 4 (1992) 523–46

2068 von Bülow, D, *Reconsidering female subordination: Kipsigis women in Kenya.* Copenhahen: CDR, 1991, 29pp

2069 von Bülow, D, *Transgressing gender boundaries: Kipsigis women in Kenya.* Copenhahen: CDR, 1991, 19pp

2070 **Wichterich, C,** Moral, Markt, Macht: Frauergruppen in Kenia, *Peripherie,* 47/48 (1992) 7–21

Geography, human

2071 **Vorlaufer, K,** *Kenya.* Stuttgart: Klett, 1990, 261pp
2072 **Wortham, R,** *Spatial developments and religious orientation in Kenya.* Lewiston: Mellen, 1990, 365pp

Geography, physical

2073 **Sutherland, R A, et al,** Analysis of the monthly and annual rainfall climate in a semi-arid environment, Kenya, *Journal of arid environments,* 20, 3 (1991) 257–275

Health & welfare services

see also: 2063
2074 **Airey, T,** The impact of road construction on the spatial characteristics of hospital utilisation in the Meru district of Kenya, *Social science and medecine,* 34, 10 (1992) 1135–46
2075 **Bradley, J E, Meme, J,** Breastfeeding promotion in Kenya: changes in health worker knowledge, attitudes and practices, 1982–89, *Journal of tropical pediatrics,* 38, 5 (1992) 228–234
2076 **Kenya, P R,** Measles and mathematics: 'control or eradication', *East African medical journal,* 67, 12 (1990) 856–863

History, early

2077 **Horton, M,** Primitive Islam and architecture in East Africa, *Muqarnas,* 8, (1991) 103–116

History, C19th

2078 **Ogutu, M A,** Forts and

fortification in Western Kenya (Marachi and Ugenya) in the 19th century, *Transafrican journal of history,* 20 (1991) 77–96

History, C20th

see also: 2061
2079 **Berman, B, Lonsdale, J,** *Unhappy valley: conflict in Kenya and Africa.* London: Currey, 1992, 504pp
2080 **Cashmore, T H R,** A random factor in British imperialism: district administration in colonial Kenya, in Twaddle M (ed), *Imperialism (entry 464),* 124–35
2081 **Frost, R,** *Enigmatic proconsul: Sir Philip Mitchell and the twilight of Empire.* London: Radcliffe Press, 1992, 288pp
2082 **Kahiga, S,** *Dedan Kimathi: the real story.* Nairobi: Longman, 1990, 337pp
2083 **Komma, T,** Language as a ultra-human power and the authority of leaders as marginal men: rethinking Kipsigis administrative chiefs in the colonial period, *Senri ethnological studies,* 31 (1992) 105–157
2084 **Lamphear, J,** *The scattering time: Turkana responses to colonial rule.* Oxford: OUP, 1992, 336pp
2085 **Macharia, R,** *The truth about the trial of Jomo Kenyatta.* Nairobi: Longman, 1991, 316pp
2086 **Malhotra, V,** *Kenya under Kenyatta.* Delhi: Kalinga, 1990, 103pp
2087 **Maupeu, H,** *L'administration indirecte, les Méthodistes et la formation de identité Meru (Kenya 1933–1963).* Paris: Centre d'études africaines, EHESS, 1990, 35pp
2088 **Mwangi wa Githumo,** The truth about the Mau Mau movement: the most popular uprising in Kenya, *Transafrican journal of history,* 20 (1991) 1–18

2089 Throup, D, Crime, politics and the police in colonial Kenya, 1939–63, in Anderson D M & Killingray, D (eds), *Policing and decolonisation* (Manchester: Manchester UP, 1992), 127–57

Industry & trade

see also: 2027, 2049, 2110

2090 Burisch, M, Promoting rural industry: the Rural Industrial Development Programme in western Kenya, in Coughlin P & Ikiara, G K (eds), *Kenya's industrialisation dilemma (entry 2097)*, 319–34

2091 Coughlin, P, Gradual maturation of an import-export substitution industry: the textile industry, in Coughlin P & Ikiara, G K (eds), *Kenya's industrialisation dilemma (entry 2097)*, 127–52

2092 Coughlin, P, Kenyan foundries and metal engineering industries: technical possibilities v. political and bureaucrtaic obstacles, in Coughlin P & Ikiara, G K (eds), *Kenya's industrialisation dilemma (entry 2097)*, 185–208

2093 Coughlin, P, Monopoly, economies of scale, and excess capacity in the glass industry, in Coughlin P & Ikiara, G K (eds), *Kenya's industrialisation dilemma (entry 2097)*, 110–26

2094 Coughlin, P, The steel industry: contradictory policies, government inertia and private conflicts, in Coughlin P & Ikiara, G K (eds), *Kenya's industrialisation dilemma (entry 2097)*, 240–90

2095 Coughlin, P, Towards the next phase, in Coughlin P & Ikiara, G K (eds), *Kenya's industrialisation dilemma (entry 2097)*, 362–80

2096 Coughlin, P, et al, Farmers, managers and government in an integrated agro-industry: sugar and sugar cane, in Coughlin P & Ikiara,

G K (eds), *Kenya's industrialisation dilemma (entry 2097)*, 153–84

2097 Coughlin, P, Ikiara, G K, (eds), *Kenya's industrialisation dilemma.* Nairobi: Heinemann, 1991, 403pp

2098 de Wilde, T, Schreurs, S, Introducing the production of improved *jikos* in Kenya, in de Wilde T & Schreurs, S (eds), *Opening the marketplace to small enterprise* (West Hartford: Kumarian, 1991), 81–94

2099 Ikiara, G K, Policy change and the informal sector: a review, in Coughlin P & Ikiara, G K (eds), *Kenya's industrialisation dilemma (entry 2097)*, 309–18

2100 Juma, C, Investment strategy and technology policy: empirical lessons from power alcohol development, in Coughlin P & Ikiara, G K (eds), *Kenya's industrialisation dilemma (entry 2097)*, 26–56

2101 Kerre, H O, Industrialisation and the low-level production trap: the hand tools and cutlery industry, in Coughlin P & Ikiara, G K (eds), *Kenya's industrialisation dilemma (entry 2097)*, 77–89

2102 Lado, C, Rural periodic markets: a case study from North Malakisi Location, Bungoma District, Kenya, *Eastern and southern Africa geographical journal,* 2, 1 (1991) 37–55

2103 Masai, W S, Promoting an efficient transport and vehicle industry, in Coughlin P & Ikiara, G K (eds), *Kenya's industrialisation dilemma (entry 2097)*, 209–39

2104 McCormick, D, Success in urban small-scale manufacturing: implications for economic development, in Coughlin P & Ikiara, G K (eds), *Kenya's industrialisation dilemma (entry 2097)*, 335–61

2105 Mwau, G, Coughlin, P,

Industrialisation and government policy: the case of electrical cable manufacturing, in Coughlin P & Ikiara, G K (eds), *Kenya's industrialisation dilemma (entry 2097)*, 90–109

2106 **Mwega, F M,** Informal entrepreneurship in an African urban area, *Small enterprise development*, 2, 3 (1991) 33–37

2107 **Owino, P W,** The pharmaceutical industry: excess capacity, missed opportunities and planning failures, in Coughlin P & Ikiara, G K (eds), *Kenya's industrialisation dilemma (entry 2097)*, 57–76

2108 **Sinclair, M T, et al,** The structure of international tourism and tourism development in Kenya, in Harrison D (ed), *Tourism and the less developed countries* (London: Belhaven, 1992), 47–63

2109 **Sunny, G,** Kenya's industrial exports: market conditions and domestic policies, *Eastern Africa economic review*, 6, 1 (1990) 31–43

International economic relations

2110 **Biswas, A,** The role of production cooperation in India-Kenya economic relations, *Africa quarterly*, 30, 1/2 (1990) 34–49

2111 **Fontaine, J F,** Import liberalisation in Kenya, in Fontaine J M (ed), *Foreign trade reforms (entry 550)*, 249–73

2112 **Vaitsos, C,** The state and foreign business interests, in Coughlin P & Ikiara, G K (eds), *Kenya's industrialisation dilemma (entry 2097)*, 6–25

2113 **von Boguslawski, M Weise, B,** Armutbekämpfung und Entwicklungszussamenarbeit: das Beispiel agarkolonisation in Kenia, *Geographische Rundschau*, 44, 9 (1992) 520–27

International relations

2114 **Godfrey, P,** *United States of America's foreign policy towards Kenya 1952–1969*. Nairobi: Gideon S Were Press, 1992, 123pp

Labour & manpower

see also: 666

2115 **Barber, G M, et al,** Determinants of urban labour force participation in Kenya, *Eastern Africa economic review*, 6, 2 (1990) 83–94

2116 **Tostensen, A,** Between shamba and factory: industrial labour migration, in Coughlin P & Ikiara, G K (eds), *Kenya's industrialisation dilemma (entry 2097)*, 291–308

Law

see also: 2037

2117 **Bundeh, B G,** *Birds of Kamiti*. Nairobi: Heinemann, 1991, 168pp

2118 **Kibwana, K,** Issues of constitutional reform in Africa: the example of Kenya, *Nairobi law monthly*, 33 (1991) 31–38

2119 **Kibwana, K,** Women and the constitution in Kenya, *Verfassung und Recht in Ubersee*, 25, 1 (1992) 6–20

2120 **Kuria, G K,** The constitutional duty to remain politically neutral, *Nairobi law monthly*, 36 (1991) 27–33

2121 **Kuria, G K,** KANU has no right to abolish the fundamental rights of Kenyans, *Nairobi law monthly*, 39 (1991) 21–26

2122 **Maina, W,** Justice Dugdale and the Bill of Rights, *Nairobi law monthly*, 34 (1991) 27–36

2123 **M'Inoti, K,** The reluctant guard: the High Court and the decline of constitutional remedies in Kenya, *Nairobi law monthly*, 34 (1991) 17–26

2124 Ojwang, J B, Salter, D R, The legal profession in Kenya, *Journal of African law*, 34, 1 (1990) 9–26

2125 Seppäkä, P, *The history and future of the customary law in Kenya.* Helsinki: Helsinki University, IDS, 1990, 23pp

Library - documentation

2126 Hütteman, L, (ed), *Coordination of information systems and services in Kenya.* Bonn: Deutsches Stiftung für internationale Entwicklung, 1990, 214pp

2127 Okinda, S, The public image of the library/librarian: observations from Kenya and Nigeria, *Maktaba*, 11, 2 (1991) 18–27

Literature

see also: 3729

2128 Adewoye, S A, The strength of the rhetoric of oral tradition in Ngugi wa Thiong'o's *Devil on the cross*, *Commonwealth novel in English*, 5, 1 (1992) 11–19

2129 Bardolph, J, *Ngugi wa Thiong'o: l'homme et l'oeuvre.* Paris: Presence Africaine, 1991, 182pp

2130 Frederiksen, B F, City life and city texts: popular knowledge and articulation in the slums of Nairobi, in Kaarsholm P (ed), *Cultural struggle (entry 4200)*, 227–37

2131 Gikandi, S, Ngugi's conversion: writing and the politics of language, *Research in African literatures*, 23, 1 (1992) 131–44

2132 Kozain, R, Form as politics, or The tyranny of narrativity: re-reading Ngugi wa Thiong'o's *Petals of blood* , *Ufahamu*, 18, 3 (1990) 77–90

2133 Mbele, J, Language in African literature: an aside to Ngugi, *Research in African literatures*, 23, 1 (1992) 145–51

2134 Perera, S W, From Mumbi to Wanja: the emergence of the woman in Ngugi's fiction, *Commonwealth : essays and studies*, 14, 2 (1992) 69–78

2135 Schmitt, E, Graebner, W, *Sukuma wiki:* food and drink in the Nairobi novels of Meja Mwangi, *Matatu*, 9, (1992) 133–151

Media

2136 Chakava, H, Kenyan publishing, independence and independence, in Altbach P (ed), *Publishing and development (entry 694))*, 119–50

2137 Frederiksen, B F, 'Joe', the sweetest reading in Africa: documentation and discussion of a popular magazine in Kenya, *African languages and cultures*, 4, 2 (1991) 135–155

2138 Wachira, C, The story of the barracks boy: Gitobu Imanyara, the man behind the *Nairobi Law Monthly*, *Society*, 15 (1990) 6–23

Medical

2139 Kangethe, R, Dhadphale, M, Prevalence of psychiatric illness among Kenyan children, *East african medical journal*, 68, 7 (1991) 526–530

2140 Kaseje, D C O, Malaria in Kenya: prevention, control and impact on mortality, in van der Walle E et al (eds), *Mortality and society (entry 771)*, 204–29

2141 Katisivo, M N, Muthami, L N, Social characteristics and sexual behaviour of women at high risk of HIV, *East African medical journal*, 68, 1 (1991) 34–38

2142 Kigamwa, P A, Psychiatric

morbidity and referral rate among
medical in-patients at Kenyatta
National hospital, *East African
medical journal,* 68, 5 (1991)
383–388

2143 Mulindi, S A Z, Strategies for
HIV infection prevention in a
developing country: case study of
Kenya, *Scandinavian journal of
development alternatives,* 11, 1
(1992) 53–62

2144 Ojwang, S B O, Omuga, B,
Contraceptive use among women
admitted with abortion in Nairobi,
East African medical journal, 68, 3
(1991) 197–203

2145 Okumu, C V, et al, Past
reproductive and sexual
characteristics of women with tubal
infertility at Kenyatta National
Hospital, *East African medical
journal,* 67, 12 (1990) 864–872

2146 Swartz, M J, Aggressive
speech, status, and cultural
distribution among the Swahili of
Mombasa, in Jordan D K &
Swartz, M J (eds), *Personality and
the cultural construction of society*
(Birmingham: University of
Alabama Press, 1990), 116–42

Natural resources

2147 Lado, C, Problems of wildlife
management and land use in
Kenya, *Land use policy,* 9, 3 (1992)
169–84

2148 Msangi, J P, Sustainability in
exploitation development and
management of hydrological
resources of Turkana District,
*Journal of east African research and
development,* 21, (1991) 21–39

2149 Ramphall, D, *A multicriteria
approach for Third World rural energy
evaluation, with a case stiusy of
Kenya.* Bremen: University of
Bremen, Institute for World
Economics and International
Management, 1992, 30pp

2150 Rehker, J R, Wald- und
Holzwirtschaft am Mount Kenya,
Geographische Rundschau, 44, 7/8
(1992) 446–51

2151 Wiesmann, U,
Wasserentwicklungsplanung
zwischen Ressourcenschonung und
Bedürfnisorientierung -
methodische Aspekte am
Fallbeispiel Laikipia, Kenia,
Geomethodica, 17, (1992) 123–149

Politics

see also: 2056, 2207, 2755

2152 Anon, Remembering J M
Kariuki, *Nairobi law monthly,* 41
(1992) 27–36

2153 Barkan, J D, The rise and fall
of a governance regime in Kenya,
in Hyden G & Bratton, M (eds),
Governance and politics (entry 864),
167–92

2154 Cohen, J M, Foreign advisors
and capacity building: the case of
Kenya, *Public administration and
development,* 12, 5 (1992) 493–510

2155 Hornsby, C, Throup, D,
Elections and political change in
Kenya, *Journal of Commonwealth
and comparative politics,* 30, 2
(1992) 172–99

2156 Muriithi, E, Voiding
neo-one-party dictatorship in
multi-party era, *Nairobi law
monthly,* 40 (1992) 32–37

2157 Murungi, K, Prospects for
multi-party democracy in Africa,
with special reference to Kenya,
Nairobi law monthly, 34 (1991)
43–46

2158 Nuoka, M, Ouko: what
happened?, *Society,* 14 (1990) 4–10

2159 Odera Oruka, H, *Oginga
Odinga: his philosophy and beliefs.*
Nairobi: Initiatives, 1992, 166pp

2160 Oyugi, W O, The unification
of the local government system in
Kenya: an historical note, in de
Valk P & Wekwete, K H (eds),

Decentralising (entry 5485), 206–23

2161 **Ross, S D,** The rule of law and lawyers in Kenya, *Journal of modern African studies,* 30, 3 (1992) 421–442

2162 **Smoke, P,** Rural local government finance in Kenya: the case of Murang'a County Council, *Public administration and development,* 12, 1 (1992) 87–96

2163 **Smoke, P,** Small town local government finance in Kenya: the case of Karatina town council, *Public administration and development,* 12, 1 (1992) 71–85

2164 **Widner, J A,** Kenya's slow progress towards multiparty politics, *Current history,* 91, 565 (1992) 214–218

2165 **Widner, J A,** *The rise of a party-state in Kenya - from 'Harambee!' to 'Nyayo!'.* Berkeley: University of California Press, 1992, 283pp

Religion, philosophy

No entry, see also: 2072

Rural economy

see also: 1020, 2053, 2060, 2113

2166 **Bigsten, A, Ndungu, N S,** Kenya, in Duncan A & Howell, J (eds), *Structural adjustment and the African farmer (entry 1017),* 48–85

2167 **Burke, K,** Property relations in 'animals of strangers': notes on re-stocking programmes in Turkana, northwest Kenya, in Baxter P T W & Hogg, R (eds), *Property, poverty and people (entry 1000),* 129–36

2168 **Carter, M R, et al,** *Tenure security for whom? Differential impacts of land policy in Kenya.* Madison: University of Wisconsin, Land Tenure Center, 1991, 38pp

2169 **Chavangi, N A,** Household based tree planting activities for

fuelwood supply in rural Kenya, in Taylor D R F & Mackenzie, F (eds), *Development from within (entry 1061),* 148–69

2170 **Cullis, A Pacey, A,** *A development dialogue: rainwater harvesting in Turkana.* London: Intermediate Technology, 1992, 126pp

2171 **Darkoh, M B K,** Irrigation and development in Kenya's arid and semi-arid lands, in Darkoh M B K (ed), *African river basins (entry 406),* 79–95

2172 **Das, M, Kolack, S,** Hoe cultivation: the African example, in their *Technology, values and society* (New York: Lang, 1990), 63–81

2173 **Donovan, M,** Changing land-use patterns in Ndaraweta, *Resources,* 2, 1 (1991) 37–40

2174 **Evans, H E,** A virtuous circle model of rural-urban development: evidence from a Kenyan small town and its hinterland, *Journal of development studies,* 28, 4 (1992) 640–67

2175 **Fratkin, E,** Drought and development in Marsabit District, Kenya, *Disasters,* 16, 2 (1992) 119–30

2176 **Hebinck, P G M,** *The agrarian structure in Kenya: state, farmers and commodity relations.* Saarbrucken: Breitenbach, 1990, 309pp

2177 **Hedlund, H,** *Prices and fluctuations: three case studies on members' views on cooperative development.* Lusaka: Institute for African Studies, University of Zambia, 1990, 51pp

2178 **Heyer, J,** Contrasts in village-level fieldwork: India and Kenya, in Devereux S & Hoddinott, J (eds), *Fieldwork in developing countries* (Hemel Hempstead: Harvester, 1992), 200–216

2179 **Hoorweg, J, et al,** *Economic and nutritional conditions at*

settlement schemes in Coast Province.
Leiden: Afrikastudiecentrum,
1991, 193pp

2180 Johansson, S, Irrigation and
development in the Tana River
basin, in Darkoh M B K (ed),
African river basins (entry 406),
97–112

**2181 Kalikander, F, Hoekstra, D
A,** Dryland management: the
Machakos District, Kenya, in
Dixon J A et al (eds), *Dryland
management (entry 1012),* 43–56

2182 Kerven, C, *Customary
commerce: a historical reassessment of
pastoral livestock marketing in Africa.*
London: ODI, 1992, 119pp

2183 Malombe, J, *Planning for
housing in irrigation settlement
schemes in Kenya: Ahero and West
Kano Schemes.* London: ODI,
Irrigation Management Network,
1992, 19pp

2184 Mukherjee, K K,
Management of cooperative
agricultural marketing societies in
Kenya: some lessons from Indian
experience, *Africa quarterly,* 30, 3/4
(1990) 89–95

2185 Munei, P, Grazing schemes
and group ranches as models for
developing pastoral lands in Kenya,
in Baxter P T W & Hogg, R (eds),
*Property, poverty and people (entry
1000),* 110–20

2186 Mutisya, D N, Lado, C,
Some socio-economic factors
behind roadside farming in Kiambu
District, Kenya, *Journal of east
African research and development,*
21, (1991) 107–127

2187 O'Leary, M, Palsson, G,
Pastoral resources and strategies:
similarities and differences between
the Rendille and Gabra of northern
Kenya, in Hjort af Ornas A (ed),
*Security in African drylands (entry
1025),* 105–22

2188 Ondiege, P O, Local coping
strategies in Machakos district,

Kenya, in Taylor D R F &
Mackenzie, F (eds), *Development
from within (entry 1061),* 125–47

2189 Orwa, K, The impact of
capitalist modes of production on
peasant modes of production: an
overview of grain production on
Rusinga Island, *African journal of
sociology,* 3, 2 (1989/1990) 26–43

2190 Ouma, S K, *21 essays on
cooperation and development in Kenya.*
Nairobi: Shirikon, 1990, 165pp

2191 Reckers, U, *Nomadischer
Viehhalter in Kenya: die Ost-Pokot
aus human-ökologische Sicht.*
Hamburg: Institut für
Afrika-Kunde, 1992, 167pp

2192 Rubin, D S, Labour patterns
in agricultural households: a
time-use study in southwest Kenya,
in Moock J L & Rhoades, R E
(eds), *Diversity (entry 1038),* 169–88

2193 Shipton, P, Debts and
trespasses: land, mortgages and the
ancestors in western Kenya, *Africa,*
62, 3 (1992) 357–88

2194 Sottas, B, Aspects of a peasant
mode of production: exchange and
the extent of sufficiency among
smallholders in West Laikipia,
Kenya, *Journal of Asian and African
studies,* 27, 3/4 (1992) 271–95

2195 Tiffen, M, (ed), *Environmental
change and dryland management in
Machakos District, Kenya: production
profile.* London: ODI, 1991,

2196 Tiffen, M, (ed), *Environmental
change and dryland management in
Machakos District, Kenya:
institutional profile.* London: ODI,
1992, 78pp

2197 Walz, G, *Nomaden in
Nationalstaat: zur integration der
Nomaden in Kenia.* Berlin: Reimer,
1992, 232pp

Science & technology

No entry, see also: 1073

Sociology

2198 Fowler, A F, The post-school experiences and attitudes of Kenyan youth towards education, training, employment, and national development, *Education with production,* 8, 1 (1991) 47–79

2199 Francis, E, Qualitative research: collecting life histories, in Devereux S & Hoddinott, J (eds), *Fieldwork in developing countries* (Hemel Hempstead: Harvester, 1992), 86–101

2200 Gecau, K, Culture and the tasks of development in Africa: lessons from the Kenyan experience, in Kaarsholm P (ed), *Cultural struggle (item 4200),* 75–93

2201 Hoddinott, J, Fieldwork under time constraints, in Devereux S & Hoddinott, J (eds), *Fieldwork in developing countries* (Hemel Hempstead: Harvester, 1992), 73–85

2202 Matsuda, M, Soft resistance in the everyday life: a life-strategy of the Maragoli migrants in Nairobi, *Senri ethnological studies,* 31 (1992) 1–82

2203 Muita, J W G, Nduati, R W K, Battered baby syndrome at Kenyatta National Hospital, Nairobi, *East African medical journal,* 67, 12 (1990) 900–906

2204 Ojwang, S B O, Maggwa, A B N, Adolescent sexuality in Kenya, *East African medical journal,* 68, 2 (1991) 74–80

2205 Partanen, J, *Sociability and intoxication: alcohol and drinking in Kenya, Africa and the modern world.* Helsinki: Finnish Foundation for Alcohol Studies, 1991, 295pp

Social welfare

2206 Hoddinott, J, Rotten kids or manipulative parents: are children old age security in western Kenya?, *Economic development and cultural change,* 40, 3 (1992) 545–65

Urban studies

see also: 2130, 3603

2207 Bubba, N, Lamba, D, Urban management in Kenya, *Environment and urbanization,* 3, 1 (1991) 37–59

2208 Drager, S, Ausmass und Muster innerstädtischer Wohnstandortwechsel von Migranten in Mombasa - eine empirische Untersuchung am Biespiel unterschiedlicher Sozialgruppen, *Zeitschrift für Wirtschaftlichsgeographie,* 36, 1/2 (1991) 61–76

2209 Macharia, K, Slum clearance and the informal economy in Nairobi, *Journal of modern African studies,* 30, 2 (1992) 221–36

2210 Matsuda, M, A formation process of urban colony of the Maragoli migrants in Kangemi, Nairobi, *African urban studies,* 1 (1990) 27–104

2211 Mensing, F, *Die Chance des Simon K: Einblicke in ein Siedlungsprojekt an der kenianischen Küste.* Eschborn: Deutsche Gesellschaft für Technische Zusamenarbeit, 1991, 34pp

2212 Ojany, F F, Macoloo, G C, Urban centres as ecological systems: a case study of Kisumu town, Kenya, *Eastern and southern Africa geographical journal,* 2, 1 (1991) 1–21

2213 Pugh, C, Land use policies and low income housing in developing countries with reference to Kenya and India, *Land use policy,* 9, 1 (1992) 47–63

2214 Rodriguez-Torres, D, *Urban development in Nairobi, yesterday and today.* Nairobi: IFRA, 1992, 41pp

2215 Seger, M, Nairobi: Struktur und Funktion einer postcolonialen primate city, *Geographische Rundschau,* 44, 9 (1992) 528–35

RWANDA

General

2216 Rossel, H, Le Rwanda et le Burundi à la veille de leur 30e anniversaire d'indépendance, *Geneva-Africa,* 30, 2 (1992) 11–74

Agriculture, scientific

2217 Sperling, L, Farmer participation in the development of bean varieties in Rwanda, in Moock J L & Rhoades, R E (eds), *Diversity (entry 1038),* 96–112

Anthropology

2218 Birigamba, J, The role of the Banyarwanda myths, *Occasional research papers,* 34, (1990) 1–23
2219 Taylor, C C, *Milk, honey and money: changing concepts in Rwandan healing.* Washington: Smithsonian Institution Press, 1992, 257pp

Current affairs

2220 Amnesty International, *Rwanda: persecution of Tutsi minority and repression of government critics, 1990–1992.* London: Amnesty International, 1992, 33pp
2221 Körner, P, Schlichte, K, *Invasion in Rwanda.* Hamburg: Universität Hamburg, Institut für Politische Wissenschaft, 1991, 36pp
2222 Mazarredo, M C P, Rwanda: the Tutsi rebellion and its regional implications, *Revista de Africa y Medio Oriente,* 3, 1 (1991) 28–33

Demography

2223 Vankrunkelsven, J, Comment aborder le problème démographique?, *Dialogue,* 148 (1991) 57–64

Economy - Development

see also: 2261
2224 Bezy, F, *Rwanda 1962–1989: bilan socio-économique d'un régime.* Louvain-la-neuve: Institut d'études du développement, 1990, 61pp
2225 Nzisabira, J, *Participation populaire au processus de développement du Rwanda: les idées et les faits.* Louvain-la-Neuve: CIDEP, 1992, 327pp
2226 Uwizeyimana, L, La débâcle du système économique rwandais, *Uburezi ubuhanga n'umuco,* 23 (1990) 71–94

Education

2227 Munyakazi, L, Lenseignement/apprentissage du français à l'école primaire au Rwanda, *Uburezi ubuhanga n'umuco,* 23 (1990) 29–56
2228 Rutsindura, A, Enseignement et corruption, *Dialogue,* 149 (1991) 53–60

Environment

No entry, see also: 1900

Food

2229 Schnepf, R, L'alimentation du jeune enfant au Rwanda: résultats d'une enquête de l'Unicef-Kigali, *Imbonezamuryango,* 20 (1991) 14–18
2230 Uwizeyimana, L, *Périodicité des crises alimentaires au Rwanda: essai d'interprétation.* Ruhengeri: Dept. du Géographie, Université Nationale du Rwanda, 1990, 98pp

Gender

2231 Bucyedusenge, G, et al, *Le rôle de la femme dans l'agriculture rwandaise.* Kigali: Minisitère de l'agriculture, 1990, 76pp

2232 Service de l'appui à la cooperation canadienne, *Profil socio-économique de la femme rwandaise: version finale.* Kigali: Réseau des femmes oeuvrant pour le développement rural, 1991, 100pp

Health & welfare services

see also: 2843

2233 Habimana, P, Bararwandika, A, Connaissances, opinions, et comportements des parents en matière de vaccination, *Imbonezamuryango,* 20 (1991) 8–13

History, C19th

No entry, see also: 4020

History, C20th

2234 Honke, G, *Als die Weissen kamen: Ruanda und die Deutschen 1885–1919.* Wuppertal: Hammer, 1990, 164pp

2235 Rumiya, J, *Le Rwanda sous le regime du mandat Belge (1916–1931).* Paris: Harmattan, 1992, 249pp

Industry & trade

2236 Gotanegre, J F, Le tourisme au Rwanda: une émergence éphémère?, *Les cahiers d'outre-mer,* 45, 177 (1992) 21–40

Labour & manpower

2237 Uwizeyimama, L, L'équilibre ethnique et régional dans l'emploi, *Dialogue,* 146 (1991) 15–31

Law

2238 Havugimana, D, Aspects de la compétence internationale des juridictions civiles rwandaises. Pt 1, *Penant,* 101, 807 (1991) 367–375

2239 Havugimana, D, Aspects de la compétence internationale des juridictions civiles rwandaises. Pt 2, *Penant,* 102, 808 (1992) 46–74

2240 Ndagijimana, F, *L'Afrique face à ses défis: le problème des refuges rwandais.* Geneva: Arunga, 1990, 143pp

2241 Ntampaka, C, L'apport de la constitution du 10 juin 1991, *Dialogue,* 148 (1991) 39–48

Media

2242 Anon, Radioscopie de la nouvelle presse rwandaise, *Dialogue,* 147 (1991) 69–81

2243 Griet, J, Vous avez dit: 'liberté d'information'!, *Dialogue,* 147 (1991) 95–98

2244 Higiro, J M V, Plaidoyer pour une politique nationale de l'information, *Dialogue,* 147 (1991) 99–112

2245 Karemera, G, La presse rwandaise à la croisée des chemins, *Dialogue,* 147 (1991) 31–34

2246 Mutaganzwa, C, La liberté de presse, essai d'interprétation conjoncturelle, *Dialogue,* 147 (1991) 51–58

2247 Ntamahungiro, J, Se réconcilier avec le peuple, *Dialogue,* 147 (1991) 35–50

2248 Reyntjens, P, Droit à l'information, droit d'informer, *Dialogue,* 147 (1991) 17–24

2249 Sibomana, A, Pour une presse de la liberté, *Dialogue,* 147 (1991) 25–29

2250 Theunis, G, Quelle télévision

pour le Rwanda de demain?,
Dialogue, 147 (1991) 83–93
2251 Theunis, G, Bagaragaza,
L'eau de la démocratie, *Dialogue,*
147 (1991) 37–39

Politics

see also: 2242, 2243, 2245, 2246,
2247, 2248, 2249, 2251
2252 Chrétien, J P, La crise
politique Rwandaise,
Geneva-Africa, 30, 2 (1992)
121–140
2253 Chrétien, J P, Le défi de
l'intégrisme ethnique dans
l'historiographie africaine: le cas du
Rwanda et du Burundi, *Politique
africaine,* 46 (1992) 71–83
2254 Eliat, B, La défense civile,
Dialogue, 146 (1991) 32–40
2255 Funga, F, Pouvoir, ethnies, et
régions, *Dialogue,* 149 (1991) 21–42
2256 Godding, J P, La jeunesse
rurale face à l'avenir, *Dialogue,* 149
(1991) 47–52
2257 Godding, J P, Pour une
véritable décentralisation, *Dialogue,*
148 (1991) 29–37
2258 Maryomeza, T, Exigences
éthiques de l'ordre démocratique,
Dialogue, 147 (1991) 113–120
2259 Ndahimana, J, Pour une
démystification du problème
rwandais, *Dialogue,* 148 (1991)
49–55
2260 Newbury, C, Rwanda: recent
debates over governance and rural
development, in Hyden G &
Bratton, M (eds), *Governance and
politics (entry 864),* 193–219
**2261 Ngirira, M, Nzitabakuze, J
B,** *Le Rwanda à la croisée des
chemins.* Butare: Imprimerie
Nationale, 1991, 207pp
2262 Ntamahungiro, E, Les
contours du multipartisme
rwandais, *Dialogue,* 146 (1991)
41–53
2263 Thibeau, J, (ed), *Le Rwanda:*

ombres et lumieres. Brussels:
Commission Justice et Paix, 1991,
42pp
2264 Twahirwa, M, Pour une
conférence nationale au Rwanda,
Dialogue, 149 (1991) 43–46

Religion, philosophy

2265 Gatwa, T, PAS et droits de
l'homme: le rôle des églises,
Dialogue, 146 (1991) 72–82
2266 O'Donoghue, J, A Bantu
philosophy: an analysis of
philosophical thought among the
people of Rwanda, based on *La
philosophie bantu-rwandaise de l'etre,*
*Journal of African religion of
philosophy,* 2, 1 (1991) 127–64
2267 Overdulve, C M, *Le defi des
pauvres: de la fonction diaconale de
l'eglise au Rwanda.* Butare: Faculté
de Théologie Protestante Butare,
1991, 210pp

Rural economy

see also: 1870, 2231, 2260, 4084
2268 Blarel, B, et al, The
economics of farm fragmentation:
evidence from Ghana and Rwanda,
World Bank economic review, 6, 2
(1992) 233–254
2269 Harth, C, Standortgerechte
Landnutzungsmethoden zur
Lösung der Ernährungsund
Ressourcenkrise in Ruanda -
Chance oder Illusion?,
Geomethodica, 17, (1992)
43–66
2270 Munyantwari, F, Des
paysans-agriculteurs sans espoir,
Dialogue, 148 (1991) 23–28
2271 Musengimana, S, Victims of
their success: local NGOs become
the prey of northern 'developers',
in NGLS (ed), *Voices from Africa 2
(entry 195),* 39–44
2272 Reymond, C, Le paysan, le
crédit et l'usure: crédit informel et

banques populaires au Rwanda, *Geneva-Africa,* 30, 2 (1992) 99–119

2273 Rudolph, S, *Untersuchungen zum Aufbau optimaler Agroforstsysteme in Rwanda.* Frankfurt: Lang, 1991, 184pp

Sociology

see also: 2224

2274 Gashayija, P C, La problématique de l'identité culturelle, du langage, et du développement. Réflexions critiques, applicables au Rwanda, *Uburezi ubuhanga n'umuco,* 23 (1990) 7–15

2275 Ntampaka, C, La famille dans les sociétés Rwandaise et Burundaise en évolution, *Au coeur de l'Afrique,* 59, 1 (1991) 54–78

2276 Talbot, C, Prendre parti pour les pauvres, *Dialogue,* 146 (1991) 83–88

2277 Vidal, C, *Sociologie des passions: Rwanda, Côte d'Ivoire.* Paris: Karthala, 1991, 180pp

TANZANIA

Anthropology

2278 Bellagamba, A, La causalità della malattia nella cultura Hehe (Tanzania), *Africa (Rome),* 46, 4 (1991) 541–563

2279 Manyesha, H, Prayer among the Fipa, *Occasional research papers,* 34, (1990) 106–132

2280 Wada, S, Changes in the practice of circumcision among the Iraqw of Tanzania, *Senri ethnological studies,* 31 (1992) 159–172

2281 Willis, R, The great mother and the god of the lake: royal and priestly power in Ulungu, *Zambia journal of history,* 4, (1991) 21–29

Arts

No entry, see also: 2339

Current affairs

2282 Ngasongwa, J, Tanzania introduces a multi-party system, *Review of African political economy,* 54 (1992) 112–116

Demography

2283 Barke, M, Sowden, C, Population change in Tanzania 1978–88: a preliminary analysis, *Scottish geographical magazine,* 106, 1 (1992) 9–16

Economy - Development

see also: 2000, 2363, 2364, 2366, 2806, 5574

2284 Bagachwa, M S D, The nature and magnitude of the second economy in Tanzania, *Tanzanian economic trends,* 2, 3/4 (1989/90) 25–33

2285 Berberoglu, B, The state and development in Africa: focus on Tanzania, in his *The political economy of development* (Albany: SUNY Press, 1992), 135–44

2286 Booth, D, *Structural adjustment in socio-political context: some findings from Iringa region.* Dar es Salaam: Tanzania Development Research Group, 1991, 29pp

2287 Chandrasekhar, S, *Third World development experience: Tanzania.* Delhi: Daya, 1990, 84pp

2288 Doriye, J, Cross-conditionality and obligatory adjustment in the 1980s: the case of Tanzania, in Rodriguez (ed), *Cross-conditionality, banking regulation and Third World debt* (Basingstoke: Macmillan, 1992), 227–64

2289 Doriye, J, Public office and private gain: an interpretation of

the Tanzanian experience, in
Wuyts M et al (eds), *Development
policy and public action* (Oxford:
OUP, 1992), 91–113

2290 Harrison, M, Tanzania
economy 1985–1991: hopeful
signs, but, *Executive,* (1991) 9–16

2291 Hartmann, J, (ed), *Rethinking
the Arusha declaration.* Copenhagen:
CDR, 1991, 321pp

2292 Henley, J S, *Privatisation in an
African context: the case of Tanzania.*
Edinburgh: Edinburgh University,
Dept. of Business Studies, 1991,
18pp

2293 Makoba, J W, State and
institutional responses to parastatal
growth in Tanzania, *Scandinavian
journal of development alternatives,*
11, 3/4 (1992) 67–88

2294 Martinussen, H, *Okonomisk
politikk i Tanzania på 1970-pallet.*
Bergen: Norges handelshyskole,
1991, 58pp

2295 Moshi, H P B, *Zum
Entwicklungsbeitrag staatlicher
Unternehmen in den
Entwicklungsländern. Dargstellt am
Biespiel Tansania.* Baden-Baden:
Nomos, 1992, 282pp

2296 Ngasongwa, L, *Foreign-assisted
regional integrated development
projects in Tanzania: a case for
rehabilitation.* Norwich: University
of East Anglia, School of
Development Studies, 1991, 43pp

2297 Peiffer, S, *Der IWF und
Tansania.* Hamburg: Institut für
Afrika-Kunde, 1990, 233pp

2298 Roy, P, Socialism in two
countries: a study of socioeconomic
dynamics and their effect on
socialist strategies in early
post-independence years in India
and Tanzania, in Forster P G &
Maghimbi, S (eds), *Tanzanian
peasantry (entry 2395),* 94–102

2299 Rugumamu, S, Technical
cooperation as an instrument of
technology transfer: some evidence

from Tanzania, *European journal of
development research,* 4, 1 (1992)
81–96

2300 Rugumisa, S, *A review of
Tanzania's economic recovery
programme (1986–1989).* Dar es
Salaam: Tanzania Development
Research Group, 1990, 18pp

2301 Rutabanzibwa, P, Tanzania's
response to the oil crisis: impacts
and lessons, *Tanzanian economic
trends,* 2, 3/4 (1989/90) 34–70

2302 Rutayisire, L W, *An SAM for
Tanzania.* The Hague: ISS, 1991,
17, 2pp

2303 Shao, I F, et al, *Structural
adjustment in a socialist country: the
case of Tanzania.* Harare: SAPES
Books, 1992, 46pp

2304 Wagao, J H, Adjustment
policies in Tanzania, 1981–9: the
impact on growth, structure and
human welfare, in Cornia A G et al
(eds), *Africa's recovery (entry 124),*
72–92

Economic and social history

see also: 4119

2305 Bhacker, M R, *Trade and
empire in Muscat and Zanzibar: the
roots of the British dimension.*
London: Routledge, 1992, 278pp

2306 Biermann, W, *Kolonie und
City: britische Wirtschaftsstrategie
und- politik in Tanganyika,
1920–1955.* Saarbrucken:
Breitenbach, 1991, 164pp

2307 Moore, S F, From giving to
lending to selling: property
transactions reflecting historical
changes in Kilimanjaro, in Mann K
& Roberts, R (eds), *Law in colonial
Africa (entry 684),* 108–27

2308 Sheriff, A, Mosques,
merchants and landowners in
Zanzibar stone town, *Azania,* 27,
(1992) 1–20

Education

see also: 2337

2309 Bahendwa, L F, *Christian religious education in the Lutheran diocese of northwestern Tanzania.* Helsinki: Finnish Society for Missiology and Ecumenics, 1990, 388pp

2310 Elborgh, K, (ed), *Rückkehr - ohne Aussicht auf Erfölg?* Saarbrucken: Breitenbach, 1991, 181pp

2311 Itandala, B, Impact of Arusha Declaration on higher education in Tanzania, *African review,* 16, 1/2 (1989) 1–9

2312 Kalinjuma, A, The Tanzania 'Kisomo' experience: case study of an exemplary literacy project in Africa, *Journal of the African Association for Literacy and Adult Education,* 5, 3 (1991) 1–5

2313 Kweka, A N, Twenty tears with education for self-reliance, *Maji Maji,* 47 (1990) 30–58

2314 Mmari, G R V, Challenges of institutional building in the contemporary environment, *Maji Maji,* 47 (1990) 1–29

2315 Samoff, J, The facade of precision in education data and statistics: a troubling example from Tanzania, *Journal of modern African studies,* 29, 4 (1991) 669–89

2316 van Dam, A, *Het onderwijs in Tanzania.* The Hague: CESO, 1990, 65pp

Environment

see also: 297, 2031, 2424

2317 Lane, C, *Barabaig natural resource management: sustainable land use under threat of destruction.* Geneva: UNRIRD, 1990, 22pp

2318 Lane, C, The Barabaig pastoralists in Tanzania: sustainable land use in jeopardy, in Ghai D & Vivian, J M (eds), *Grassrooots environmental action* (London: Routledge,1992), 81–105

2319 Lawi, Y Q, 'Modernisation' and the de-harmonisation of the man-nature relationship: the case of the agricopastoral Iraqw of the olf Mbubu district, in Forster P G & Maghimbi, S (eds), *Tanzanian peasantry (entry 2395),* 45–57

2320 Mushala, H M, Environmental crisis and the peasantry in Tanzania, in Forster P G & Maghimbi, S (eds), *Tanzanian peasantry (entry 2395),* 236–49

2321 Strömquist, L, Environmental impact assessment of natural disasters: a case study of the recent Lake Bubati floods in northern Tanzania, *Geografiska annaler,* 74A, 2/3 (1992) 81–91

Finance

2322 Kimei, C S, A perspective on exchange rate policies and their results: the experience of Tanzania, in Roe A R et al (eds) *Instruments of economic policy (entry 341),* 31–42

2323 Mtatifikolo, F P, An economic analysis of Tanzania's tax performance experiences since the 1973 Tax Act, *Eastern Africa economic review,* 6, 2 (1990) 55–67

2324 Osoro, N E, The revenue generating potential of the Tanzanian tax system, *Tanzania journal of economics,* 2, 1 (1990) 53–62

2325 Rutayisire, L W, The experience of Tanzania, in Roe A R et al (eds) *Instruments of economic policy (entry 341),* 92–101

2326 Rwegasira, K S P, *Financial analysis and institutional lending operations management in a developing country: a critical perspective of Tanzanian banks and DFIs.* Dar es Salaam: Dar es Salaam UP, 1991, 208pp

2327 Rwegasira, K, *Problems of*

*financial analysis in institutional
lending operations: some lessons from
Tanzania.* Aldershot: Avebury,
1992, 228pp

Food

see also: 2335, 2342

2328 Latham, M C, et al, *Thoughts
for food: an evaluation of the
Tanzania Food and Nutrition Centre.*
Stockhom: SIDA, 1992, 103pp

2329 Mlozi, M R S, et al, Urban
agriculture as a survival strategy in
Tanzania, in Baker J & Pedersen, P
O (eds), *Rural-urban interface (entry
1111),* 284–94

2330 Pelletier, D L, *The uses and
limitations of information in the Iringa
Nutrition Program, Tanzania.*
Ithaca: Food and Nutrition Policy
Program, Cornell University, 1991,
79pp

2331 Tibaijuka, A K, Grappling
with urban food insecurity in the
midst of plenty: Government
launches "Operation Okoa
Mazao", *Tanzanian economic trends,*
2, 3/4 (1989/90) 13–24

2332 Yambi, O, Mlolwa, R,
*Improving nutrition in Tanzania in
the 1980s: the Iringa experience.*
Firenze: International Child
Development Centre, 1992, 49pp

Gender

see also: 2346, 2365, 2368

2333 Gerrard, S, Clans, gender and
kilns, in Stlen K A & Vaa, M (eds),
Gender and change (entry 399),
223–46

2334 Gondwe, Z S, *Female intestate
succession to land in rural Tanzania:
whither equality?* East Lansing:
Michigan State University, 1990,
27pp

**2335 Holmboe-Ottesen, G,
Wandel, M,** 'Wife, today I only
had money for pombe': gender and

food - women's bargaining power
and agricultural change in a
Tanzanian community, in Stlen K
A & Vaa, M (eds), *Gender and
change (entry 399),* 93–119

2336 Larsson, B, *Conversion to
greater freedom? Women, church and
social change in northwestern
Tanzania under colonial rule.*
Stockholm: Almqvist and Wiksell,
1991, 230pp

2337 Malekela, G, et al, *Girls'
educational opportunities and
performance in Tanzania.* Dar es
Salaam: Tanzania Development
Research Group, 1990, 34pp

2338 Mbilinyi, M B, *Big slavery:
agribusiness and the crisis in
women's employment in
Tanzania.* Dar es Salaam:
University of Dar es Salaam Press,
1991, 95pp

2339 Mekacha, R D K, Are women
devils?: the portrayal of women in
Tanzanian popular music, *Matatu,*
9 (1992) 99–113

2340 Ngaiza, M K, Koda, B, (eds),
The unsung heroines. Dar es Salaam:
Dar es Salaam UP, 1991, 232pp

2341 Nypan, A, Revival of female
circumcision: a case of
neo-traditionalism, in Stlen K A &
Vaa, M (eds), *Gender and change
(entry 399),* 39–65

**2342 Wandel, M,
Holmboe-Ottesen, G,** Women's
work in agriculture and child
nutrition in Tanzania, *Journal of
tropical pediatrics,* 38, 5 (1992)
252–255

Geography, physical

2343 Payton, R W, et al,
Landform, soils and erosion in the
northeastern Irangi hills, Kondoa,
Tanzania, *Geografiska annaler,* 74A,
2/3 (1992) 65–79

Health & welfare services

2344 Horstman, R G, *Registration of the disabled in Zanzibar: a descriptive analysis of the 1988/1989 registration of the disabled in northern region of Zanzibar.* Groningen: Population Research Centrer, Groningen University, 1991, 75pp

2345 Kilonzo, G P, Pitkänen, Y T, (eds), *Pombe: report of the alcohol research project in Tanzania, 1988–90.* Helsinki: Helsinki University, Institute of Development Studies, 1991, 100 + 56pp

2346 McCauley, A P, et al, Household decisions among the Gogo people of Tanzania: determining the roles of men, women and the community in implementing a trachoma prevention programme, *Social science and medecine*, 34, 7 (1992) 817–24

2347 TADREG, *The provision and acceptability of child immunisation services in Tanzania.* Dar es Salaam: Tanzania Development Research Group, 1992, 52pp

History, general

2348 Willis, J, The makings of a tribe: Bondei identities and histories, *Journal of African history*, 33, 2 (1992) 191–208

History, early

2349 Mapunda, B B B, The role of archaeology in development: the case of Tanzania, *Transafrican journal of history*, 20 (1991) 19–34

History, C19th

2350 Gansser, R, (ed. H Dauber), *'Nicht als Abenteuer bin ich hiergekommen...' 100 Jahre Entwicklungs-'Hilfe': Tagebücher und Brief aus Deutch-Ostafrika 1896–1902.* Frankfurt: Verlag für Interkulturelle Kommunikation, 1991, 322pp

2351 von Sicard, S, The understanding of church and mission among the Berlin missionaries in the southern highlands of Tanzania, *Africa theological journal*, 20, 3 (1991) 223–37

History, C20th

No entry, see also: 2336

Industry & trade

see also: 521

2352 Aere, A, *Rethinking industrialisation, from a national to a local perspective: a case study of the industrialisation process in Tanzania with particular emphasis on the construction industry.* Copenhagen: Centre for Development Research, 1992, 285pp

2354 Bagachwa, M S D, *Choice of technology in industry: the economics of grain-milling in Tanzania.* Ottawa: IDRC, 1991, 144pp

2355 Bagachwa, M S D, The role of the intermediate industry section in Tanzania, *African journal of sociology*, 3, 2 (1989/90) 1–25

2356 de Wilde, T, Schreurs, S, Introducing the production of glazed pottery in rural villages in Tanzania, in de Wilde T & Schreurs, S (eds), *Opening the marketplace to small enterprise* (West Hartford: Kumarian, 1991), 65–80

2357 Mbelle, A, Efficiency performance under structural adjustment programmes: the case of textile manufacturing in Tanzania, *Tanzania journal of economics*, 2, 1 (1990) 23–31

2358 Nindi, B, Agricultural

marketing reforms and the public
versus private debate in Tanzania,
in Forster P G & Maghimbi, S
(eds), *Tanzanian peasantry (entry
2395)*, 169–89

2359 van Donge, J K, Waluguru
traders in Dar es Salaam: an
analysis of the social construction
of economic life, *African affairs*, 91,
363 (1992) 181–205

2360 Wangwe, S, Building
indigenous technological capacity:
a study of selected industries in
Tanzania, in Stewart F et al (eds),
*Alternative development strategies
(entry 223)*, 265–93

2361 Zell, H, *Die
Kapitalgüterindustrie in Tanzania.*
Hamburg: Institut für
Afrika-Kunde, 1990, 263pp

International economic relations

2362 Mihyo, P B, Practical
problems in the South-South
development cooperation: some
experiences involving Tanzania,
Verfassung und Recht in Übersee, 25,
2 (1992) 220–237

2363 Othman, H, Maganya, E,
(eds), *Tanzania's debt problem and
the world economy.* Dar es Salaam:
IDS, University of Dar es Salaam,
1990, 142pp

International relations

2364 Elgström, O, *Foreign aid
negotiations: the Swedish-Tanzanian
aid dialogue.* Aldershot: Avebury,
1992, 179pp

Labour & manpower

No entry, see also: 666, 2381

Law

see also: 2334
2365 Mtengeti-Migiro, R, Legal

developments on women's rights to
inherit land under customary law in
Tanzania, *Verfassung und Recht in
Übersee*, 24, 4 (1991) 362–371

2366 Peter, C M, *Promotion and
protection of foreign investments in
Tanzania: a comment on the new
investment code.* Dar es Salaam:
Freidrich Ebert Foundation, 1990,
87pp

2367 Shaidi, L P, The rights of
street and abandoned children,
*University of Dar es Salaam law
journal*, 8, (1991) 20–23

2368 Wanitzek, U, Legally
unrepresented women petitioners
in the lower courts of Tanzania: a
case of justice denied?, *Journal of
legal pluralism and unofficial law*,
30/31 (1990/1991) 255–271

Literature

2369 Beck, R-M, Women are
devils!: a formal and stylistic
analysis of *Mwanameka, Matatu*, 9,
(1992) 115–132

Media

2370 Bgoya, W, The challenge of
publishing in Tanzania, in Altbach
P (ed), *Publishing and development
(entry 694))*, 169–89

2371 Lederbogen, U, *The African
journalist: a portrait of Tanzanian
news people and their work.* Bonn:
Friedrich Ebert Foundation, 1991,
61pp

2372 Lederbogen, U, *Watchdog or
missionary? A portrait of African news
people and their work: a case study in
Tanzania.* Frankfurt: Lang, 1992,
180pp

Medical

2373 Mpanju, W, Do Amisi, D M,
Impact of measles vaccine on the
reported incidence of measles in

Tanzania, *Tanzania jornal of paediatrics*, 2, 2 (1991) 29–33

2374 **Shija, J K,** *Surgery in Tanzania.* Dar es Salaam: Dar es Salaam University, 1991, 58pp

2375 **Urrio, T F,** Maternal deaths at Songea Regional hospital, southern Tanzania, *East African medical journal*, 68, 2 (1991) 81–87

Planning

2376 **Forster, P G,** The importance of anthropological research in rural development planning in Tanzania, in Forster P G & Maghimbi, S (eds), *Tanzanian peasantry (entry 2395)*, 31–44

2377 **Maro, P S,** The evolution and functioning of the planning system in Tanzania, in de Valk P & Wekwete, K H (eds), *Decentralising (entry 5485)*, 119–36

Politics

see also: 903, 904, 2291

2378 **Bukurura, L H,** Public participation in financing local development: the case of Tanzanian development levy, *Africa development*, 16, 3/4 (1991) 75–99

2379 **Jerve, A M, Naustdalslid, J,** *Research on local government in Tanzania.* Bergen: CMI, 1990, 27pp

2380 **Liviga, A J,** Local government in Tanzania: partners in development or administrative agent for central government?, *Local government studies*, 18, 3 (1992) 208–25

2381 **Mamuya, I,** *Structural adjustment and retrenchment in the civil service: the case of Tanzania.* Geneva: ILO, 1991, 64pp

2382 **Martin, D C,** Demokrasia ni nini? Fragments swahili du débat politique en Tanzanie, *Politique africaine*, 47 (1992) 109–34

2383 **Masanja, P,** Some notes on the Sungusungu movement, in Forster P G & Maghimbi, S (eds), *Tanzanian peasantry (entry 2395)*, 203–211

2384 **Member, Y,** *Flight to freedom: a true hijacker's story.* London: Tanzania Youth Democratic Movement, 1992, 72pp

2385 **Mukandla, R S,** Much ado about nothing: the 1990 election in Tanzania, *Taamuli*, NS 2, 1/2 (1991) 104–21

2386 **Mutahaba, G R,** Organisation for local governance: searching for an appropriate local level institutional framework innTanzania, in Crook R C & Jerve, A M (eds), *Government and participation (entry 824)*, 69–92

2387 **Norsk Institutt for by- og regiosforskning,** *Research on local government in Tanzania.* Bergen: Chr Michelsen Institute, 1992, 48pp

2388 **Shivji, I G,** Pre-conditions for a popular debate on democracy in Tanzania, *University of Dar es Salaam law journal*, 8, (1991) 6–19

2389 **Tripp, A M,** Local organisations, participation, and the state in urban Tanzania, in Hyden G & Bratton, M (eds), *Governance and politics (entry 864)*, 221–242

Rural economy

see also: 1020, 1870, 2338, 2358

2390 **Booth, D,** Why Tanzanian society is not experiencing structural adjustment: the case of Iringa, in Forster P G & Maghimbi, S (eds), *Tanzanian peasantry (entry 2395)*, 250–71

2391 **Caplan, P,** Socialism from above: the view from below, in Forster P G & Maghimbi, S (eds), *Tanzanian peasantry (entry 2395)*, 103–23

2392 Coullson, A, The contribution of economists to rural development in Tanzania, in Forster P G & Maghimbi, S (eds), *Tanzanian peasantry (entry 2395)*, 190–202

2393 Delobel, T, Metsch, R, *An analysis of the coffee based farming system of the Matengo Highlands, Mbinga District, Tanzania.* Wageningen: Wageningen Agricultural University, 1991, 32pp

2394 Ezaza, W P, Towards a strategy for agricultural development in the United Republic of Tanzania, *Eastern and southern Africa geographical journal,* 2, 1 (1991) 23–35

2395 Forster, P G, Maghimbi, S, (eds), *The Tanzania peasantry: economy in crisis.* Aldershot: Avebury, 1992, 287pp

2396 Gibogwe, V, A critical assessment of capital supply to rural small-scale industries in Tanzania, *Small enterprise development,* 2, 3 (1991) 49–53

2397 Gijsman, A, Rusami, E, *Food security, livestock and sustainability of agricultural systems in Sukumaland, Tanzania.* Wageningen: Wageningen Agricultural University, 1991, 25pp

2398 Kashuliza, A K, Agricultural credit in Tanzania: the policy and operational problems of the Cooperative and Rural Development Bank, *Savings and development,* 16, 4 (1992) 327–352

2399 Kaya, H O, *People's participation programmes and the dilemma of rural leadership in Tanzania.* Berlin: Schrieber, 1992, 102pp

2400 Kees van Donge, J, Agricultural decline in Tanzania: the case of the Uluguru mountains, *African affairs,* 91, 362 (1992) 73–94

2401 Komba, A Y, Technological factors in peasant production in Tanzania: three decades of learning by doing, in Forster P G & Maghimbi, S (eds), *Tanzanian peasantry (entry 2395)*, 74–93

2402 Lundahl, M, Msambichaka, L A, The emergence of agricultural credit in Tanzania, *Tanzania journal of economics,* 2, 1 (1990) 63–76

2403 Maghimbi, S, The abolition of peasant cooperatives and the crisis in the rural economy in Tanzania, in Forster P G & Maghimbi, S (eds), *Tanzanian peasantry (entry 2395)*, 216–35

2404 Maghimbi, S, The decline of the economy of the mountain zones of Tanzania: a case strudy of Mwanga District (North Pare), in Forster P G & Maghimbi, S (eds), *Tanzanian peasantry (entry 2395)*, 13–30

2405 Maro, P S, The impact of decentralisation on spatial equity and rural development in Tanzania, in de Valk P & Wekwete, K H (eds), *Decentralising (entry 5485)*, 137–75

2406 Merten, P, Anspruch und Wirklichkeit zielgruppenorientierter Entwicklungsplanung: das Beispiel integrierter ländlicher Regionalentwicklung im Handeni-Distrikt im Nordosten Tanzanias, *Afrika spectrum,* 26, 2 (1991) 199–220

2407 Moshi, H P B, Cooperative and agricultural development problems and policy options: the Tanzanian experience 1961–1990, in Forster P G & Maghimbi, S (eds), *Tanzanian peasantry (entry 2395)*, 58–73

2408 Ndagala, D K, Production diversification and community development in African pastoral areas, in Hjort af Ornas A (ed), *Security in African drylands (entry 1025)*, 81–90

2409 Ndaro, J M M, Local coping strategies in Dodoma district, Tanzania, in Taylor D R F & Mackenzie, F (eds), *Development from within (entry 1061),* 170–96

2410 Nkhoma-Wamunza, A, The informal sector: a strategy for survival in Tanzania, in Taylor D R F & Mackenzie, F (eds), *Development from within (entry 1061),* 196–213

2411 Omari, C K, Some notes on self-help programmes and the Pare people and their impact on social development, in Forster P G & Maghimbi, S (eds), *Tanzanian peasantry (entry 2395),* 1–12

2412 Rigby, P, Pastoralist production and socialist transformation in Tanzania, in Salzman C & Galaty, J G (eds), *Nomads in a changing world* (Naples: Instituto Universitario Orientale, 1990) 233–89

2413 Rugarabamu, R G, *Case studies on rural poverty alleviation in the Commonwealth: Tanzania.* London: Commonwealth Secretariat, 1992, 64pp

2414 Sendaro, A M, Technical stagnation, aging population and agricultural production in Tanzania: the case of Lugoba, Msata and Mboya villages in Bagamoya district, in Forster P G & Maghimbi, S (eds), *Tanzanian peasantry (entry 2395),* 151–68

2415 Shivji, I G, The roots of an agrarian crisis in Tanzania: a theoretical perspective, in Forster P G & Maghimbi, S (eds), *Tanzanian peasantry (entry 2395),* 124–50

2416 Waters, T, Lifeworld and system: of water systems and grain mill development in rural Tanzania, *African studies review,* 35, 2 (1992) 35–44

Science & technology

see also: 1082

2417 Wangwe, S M, Luvanga, N E, Technology transformation in the Third World: the case of Tanzania, *Tanzania journal of economics,* 2, 1 (1990) 3–22

Sociology

2418 Holm, M, Survival strategies of migrants to Makambako - an intermediate town in Tanzania, in Baker J & Pedersen, P O (eds), *Rural-urban interface (entry 1111),* 238–57

2419 Makoba, J W, State control of the economy and class formation in postcolonial Africa: the case of Tanzania, *Africa quarterly,* 31, 1/2 (1991) 34–46

2420 von Troil, M, Looking for a better life in town: the case of Tanzania, in Baker J & Pedersen, P O (eds), *Rural-urban interface (entry 1111),* 223–37

2421 Waters, T, A cultural analysis of the economy of affection and the uncaptured peasantry in Tanzania, *Journal of modern African studies,* 30, 1 (1992) 163–75

Social welfare

No entry, see also: 2411

Urban studies

see also: 1110, 2331

2422 Kaitilla, S, Low cost urban renewal in Tanzania: community participation in Dar es Salaam, *Cities,* 7, 3 (1991) 211–23

2423 Rakodi, C, Some issues urban development and planning in Tanzania, Zambia, and Zimbabwe, in Drakakis-Smith D (ed), *Urban and regional change (entry 4224),* 121–46

2424 Yhdego, M, Urban
environmental degradation in
Tanzania, *Environment and
urbanization*, 3, 1 (1991) 147–152

UGANDA

General

2425 Boyd, R, Grmela, S, et al,
*Brief overview of contemporary
Uganda.* Montreal: University of
Montreal, Centre for
Developing-Area Studies, 1990,
19pp

Agriculture, scientific

2426 Opio-Odongo, J M A, *Designs
on the land: agricultural research in
Uganda, 1890–1990.* Nairobi:
ACTS Press, 1992, 144pp

Anthropology

2427 Bunnya, A, The significance
of butter 'Omuzigo Omuganda' in
the Ganda culture, *Occasional
research papers*, 34, (1990) 24–48
2428 Kyamu, S P, The concept of
home among the Batoro, *Occasional
research papers*, 34, (1990) 74–82
2429 Nasseem, Z, A
historico-juridical character of the
'Nubians' of Uganda: some
reflections on a conference of
scholls of jurisprudence, *Journal of
African religion of philosophy*, 2, 1
(1991) 63–75

Arts

2430 Breitinger, E, Popular urban
theatre in Uganda: between
self-help and self-enrichment, *New
theatre quarterly*, 8, 31 (1992)
270–290
2431 Breitinger, E, Populäres
theater in Uganda: zwischen
strategien zur selbsthilfe und zur

selbstbereicherung, *Internationales
Afrikaforum*, 28, 2 (1992) 159–180

Economy - Development

2432 Friedrich Ebert Foundation,
*The management of the Uganda
economy; agenda for reforms:
proceedings of a workshop.* Kampala:
the Foundation, 1990, 36pp
2433 Green, C, Murinde, V,
Potency of budgetary and financial
policy instruments in Uganda, in
Milner C & Rayner, A J (eds),
Policy adjustment (entry 184),
149–71
2434 Kayizzi-Mugerwa, S,
Uganda: at a crossroad. Stockholm:
SIDA, 1992, 45pp
**2435 Kayizzi-Mugerwa, S,
Bigsten, A,** On structural
adjustment in Uganda, *Canadian
journal of development studies*, 13, 1
(1992) 57–76
2436 Murinde, V, Application of
stochastic simulation and policy
sensitivity techniques to a
macroeconomic model of Uganda,
Applied economics, 24, 1 (1992)
1–18

Economic and social history

2437 Kaberuka, W, *The political
economy of Uganda, 1890–1979: a
case study of colonialism amnd
underdevelopment.* New York:
Vantage, 1990, 309pp
2438 Musere, J, *African sleeping
sickness: political ecology, colonialism
and control in Uganda.* Lewiston:
Mellen, 1990, 208pp
2439 Mwambutsya, N, Precapitalist
social formation: the case of the
Banyankole of southwestern
Uganda, *Eastern African social
science research review*, 6,2 & 7/1,
(1990/91) 78–94

Education

2440 Kajubi, W G, Financing of higher education in Uganda, *Higher education,* 23, 4 (1991) 433–41

2441 Kyagulanyi, E N G, The state of geography in Uganda, *Eastern and southern Africa geographical journal,* 2, 1 (1991) 83–109

2442 Majanja-Zaali, I M, The Ugandan literacy experience, *Convergence,* 24, 1–2 (1991) 19–24

Finance

2443 Ssermogerere, G, Mobilisation of domestic financial resources in Uganda: commercial banks versus the Uganda Cooperative Savings and Credit Union, in Frimpong-Ansah J H & Ingham, B (eds), *Saving for economic recovery (entry 142),* 93–118

Food

2444 Mwaka, V M, The environment and food security in Uganda, *Eastern and southern Africa geographical journal,* 2, 1 (1991) 67–82

Gender

see also: 2487

2445 Okwe, A, Women wage workers in Uganda, *Arise,* 3 (1991) 10–13

Health & welfare services

2446 Allen, T, Upheaval, affliction and health: a Ugandan case study, in Bernstein H et al (eds), *Rural livelihoods (entry 1004),* 217–48

2447 Ankrah, E M, AIDS in Uganda: initial social work responses, *Journal of social development in Africa,* 7, 2 (1992) 53–61

2448 Williams, J P, Scaling-up via legal reform in Uganda, in Edwards M & Hulme, D (eds), *Making a difference: NGOs and development in a changing world* (London: Earthscan, 1992), 89–97

History, C20th

2449 Cohen, D W, 'A case for the Busoga': Lloyd Fallers and the construction of an African legal system, in Mann K & Roberts, R (eds), *Law in colonial Africa (entry 684),* 229–54

2450 Hansen, H B, Church and state in a colonial context, in Twaddle M (ed), *Imperialism (entry 464),* 95–123

2451 Simiyu, V G, The emergence of a sub-nation: a history of Babukusu to 1990, *Transafrican journal of history,* 20 (1991) 125–44

2452 Thompson, G, Colonialism in crisis: the Uganda disturbances of 1945, *African affairs,* 91, 365 (1992) 605–24

Industry & trade

2453 Bibangambah, J R, Macro-level constraints and the growth of the informal sector in Uganda, in Baker J & Pedersen, P O (eds), *Rural-urban interface (entry 1111),* 303–313

2454 Nyakaana, J B, A note on the diffusion and influence of the out-board motor engine on the fish industry in Uganda, *Journal of east African research and development,* 21, (1991) 133–140

2455 Rutega, S B, Privatisation in Uganda, in Ramanadham V V (ed), *Privatisation (entry 203),* 396–417

Labour & manpower

see also: 2445

2456 Barya, J J B, *Workers and the law in Uganda.* Kampala: Centre for Basic Research, 1991, 76pp

2457 Josephine, A, *Workers' struggle, the labour process and the question of control: the case of United Garment Industry Limited.* Kampala: Centre for Basic Research, 1991, 55pp

2458 Rubanga, E, Barya, J J B, *Workers' control: the struggle to take over MULCC textile factory in Kampala.* Kampala: Centre for Basic Research, 1991, 37pp

Law

see also: 2448

2459 Hansen, H B, *A long journey towards a new constitution: the Uganda experiment in constitution making.* Copenhagen: Center for Afrikastudier, Copenhagen University, 1992, 12pp

2460 Kiapi, A, African concepts of law and law reform in Uganda, *Journal of African religion of philosophy,* 2, 1 (1991) 59–62

Literature

2461 Ofuani, O A, "No sweetness here!": a stylistic commentary on Okot p'Bitek's *Song of soldier, Matatu,* 9, (1992) 153–172

2462 Okumu, C, The form of Okot p'Bitek's poetry: literary borrowing from Acoli oral traditions, *Research in African literatures,* 23, 3 (1992) 53–66

Medical

see also: 2438

2463 Kampikaho, A, Irwig, L M, Incidence and causes of maternal mortality in five Kampala hospitals, 1980–1986, *East african medical journal,* 68, 8 (1991) 624–631

2464 Seeley, J A, et al,

Community-based HIV/AIDS research - whither community participation? Unsolved problems on a research programme in rural Uganda, *Social science and medecine,* 34, 10 (1992) 1089–95

2465 Vella, V, et al, Determinants of child mortality in southwest Uganda, *Journal of biosocial science,* 24, 1 (1992) 103—12

Natural resources

2466 Paterson, J D, The ecology and history of Uganda's Budongo forest, *Forest and conservation history,* 35, 4 (1991) 179–87

Politics

see also: 835, 888, 2479

2467 Amnesty International, *Uganda: the failure to safeguard human rights.* London: Amnesty International, 1992, 88pp

2468 Furley, O, Uganda: a second-phase bid for legitimacy under international scrutiny, in Rupesinghe K (ed), *Internal conflict (entry 932),* 208–29

2469 Kabala, P K, The impact of armed conflict in Uganda: the current situation and Uganda's development needs, in NGLS (ed), *Voices from Africa 3 (entry 913),* 45–58

2470 Klaaren, J, Woolman, S, Government's efforts to protect human rights in Uganda, *Nairobi law monthly,* 35 (1991) 26–28

2471 Museveni, Y K, *What is Africa's problem? Speeches and writings on Africa.* Kampala: NRM Publications, 1992, 282pp

2472 Mutibwa, P, *Uganda since independence.* London: Hurst, 1992, 209pp

2473 Oloka-Onyango, J, *Armed conflict, political violence and the human rights monitoring of Uganda: 1971–1990.* Kampala: Centre for

Basic Research, 1991, 33pp

2474 Oloka-Onyango, J, Tinfifa, S, *Constitutionalism in Uganda: report on a survey and workshop of organised groups.* Kampala: Centre for Basic Research, 1991, 39pp

2475 Omara-Otunnu, A, The challenge of democratic pluralism in Uganda, *Issue,* 20, 1 (1992) 41–49

2476 Omara-Otunnu, A, The struggle for democracy in Uganda, *Journal of modern African studies,* 30, 3 (1992) 443–63

2477 Omara-Otunnu, A, The challenge of democratic pluralism in Uganda, *Nairobi law monthly,* 35 (1991) 29–34

2478 Ouma, S O A, Corruption in public policy and its impact on development: the case of Uganda since 1979, *Public administration and development,* 11, 5 (1991) 473–490

Religion, philosophy

2479 Natukunda-Togboa, E R, The resurgence of fundamentalism: a case study of the Alice Lakwena problem, *Journal of African religion of philosophy,* 2, 1 (1991) 76–91

2480 Njinya-Mujinya, L, Zoroastrian and Kinyakore views of good and evil: a comparative study, *Journal of African religion of philosophy,* 2, 1 (1991) 95–113

Rural economy

see also: 1049

2481 Ddungu, E, *A review of MISR-Wisconsin Land Tenure Center study on land tenure and agricultural development in Uganda.* Kampala: Centre for Basic

Research, 1991, 21pp

2482 de Coninck, J, Riddell, R, *Evaluating the impact of NGOs in rural poverty alleviation: Uganda country study.* London: ODI, 1992, 119pp

2483 Mamdani, M, Class formation and rural livelihoods: a Ugandan case study, in Bernstein H et al (eds), *Rural livelihoods (entry 1004),* 195–216

2484 Sinwogevere, E, Cassava processing and utilisation in Luwero, *Ahfad journal,* 9, 1 (1992) 5–16

2485 Ssemogerere, G, *Structural adjustment programmes and the coffee sector in Uganda, 1981–1987.* Nairobi: Initiatives, 1990, 53pp

Sociology

2486 Bazaara, N, *The state and social differentiation in Kakindo village, Masindi district, Uganda.* Kampala: Centre for Basic Research, 1991, 38pp

2487 Behrend, H, Alice Lakwena und due Holy-Spirit-Bewegung im Norden Ugandas, *Peripherie,* 47/48 (1992) 129–36

2488 Dunn, A, *The social consequences of HIV/AIDS in Uganda.* London: Save the Children Fund, 1992, 26pp

Urban studies

2489 Calas, B, Residential morphology of Kampala, *Eastern and southern Africa geographical journal,* 3, 1 (1992) 65–74

2490 Ouma, S J, *The politics of housing policy in Uganda.* Glasgow: Strathclyde University, Dept. of Government, 1992, 42pp

WEST AFRICA

Agriculture, scientific

2500 Lévéque, C, et al, (eds),
*Faune des poissons d'eaux douce et
saumâtres de l'Afrique de l'Ouest.
Tome II.* Paris: ORSTOM, 1992,
518pp

Anthropology

2501 Diaw, B J, *A Fulbe bibliography
(1976–1986).* Gothenburg: IASSA,
1991, 47pp

2502 Egblewogbe, E Y, Social
and psychological aspects of
greeting among the Ewes of West
Africa, *Research Review,* 6, 2 (1990)
8–18

2503 Schott, R, Serment et vux chez
des ethnies voltaïques (Lyela,
Bulsa, Tallensi) en Afrique
occidental, *Droit et cultures,* 14
(1987) 29–56

2504 Stoller, P, *The cinematic griot:
the ethnography of Jean Rouch.*
Chicago: Unverisity of Chicago
Press, 1992, 247pp

2505 Witte, H, Tradition and
renewal in the West African
concept of person, in Geertz A W
& Jensen, J S (ed), *Religion,
tradition, and renewal* (Aarhus:
Aarhus UP, 1991), 177–84

Architecture

2506 Aradeon, S B, Al-Sahili: the
historians' myth of architectural
technology transfer from North
Africa, in Irele A (ed), *African*

education and identity (entry 268),
295–309

Arts

2507 Pfaff, F, Five West African
film makers and their films, *Issue,*
20, 2 (1992) 31–37

2508 Picton, J, Tradition,
technology and lurex: some
comments on textile history and
design in West Africa, in
Smithsonian Museum *History
design and craft (entry 2510),* 13–52

2509 Posnansky, M, Traditional
cloth from Ewe heartland, in
Smithsonian Museum *History
design and craft (entry 2510),* 113–32

2510 Smithsonian Museum, (ed),
*History design and craft in West
African strip-woven cloth.*
Washington: the Museum, 1992,
168pp

2511 Utudjian Saint-André, E,
New modes of writing in West
African drama: prison plays from
Sierra Leone, Ghana and Nigeria,
Commonwealth: essays and studies,
14, 1 (1991) 70–77

Economy - Development

2512 Baker, K, The changing
geography of West Africa, in
Chapman G P & Baker, K M
(eds), *The changing geography of
Africa (entry 405),* 80–113

2513 Bray, M, West African
economic strategies: Franc Zone or
regional economic groupings? The

case of the CEAO and Ecowas, *Bulletin of francophone Africa*, 1 (1992) 58–73

2514 **Ekpo, A H,** Economic development under structural adjustment: evidence from selected West African countries, *Journal of social development in Africa*, 7, 1 (1992) 25–43

Economic and social history

2515 **Alpern, S B,** The European introduction of crops into West Africa in precolonial times, *History in Africa*, 19, (1992) 13–43

2516 **Brooks, G E,** *Landlords and strangers: ecology, society and trade in western Africa, 1000–1630.* Boulder: Westview, 1991, 352pp

2517 **Candotti, M,** La diffusione dei cauri nel Sudan occidentale tra l'undicesimo e il sedicesimo secolo, *Africa (Rome)*, 46, 3 (1991) 321–334

2518 **Cowen, M P, Shenton, R W,** Bankers, peasants and land in British West Africa 1905–37, *Journal of peasant studies*, 19, 1 (1991) 26–58

2519 **Eltis, D,** Precolonial western Africa and the Atlantic economy, in Solow B L (ed), *Slavery and the rise of the Atlantic system* (Cambridge, CUP, 1991), 91–119

2520 **Falola, T,** The Lebanese in colonial West Africa, in Ajayi J F A & Peel, J D Y (eds), *Peoples and empires (entry 429)*, 121–41

2521 **Henige, D, McCaskie, T C (eds),** *West African economic and social history.* Madison: University of Wisconsin African Studies Program, 1991, 232pp

2521 **Iroko, A F,** Le sel marin de la côte des Esclaves durant la période précoloniale, *Africa (Rome)*, 46, 4 (1991) 520–540

2522 **Klein, M A,** The slave trade in the Western Sudan during the nineteenth century, in Savage E (ed), *The human commodity (entry 252)*, 39–60

2523 **Lynn, M,** Bristol, West Africa and the 19th-century palm oil trade, *Historical research*, 64, 155 (1991) 359–374

2524 **Lynn, M,** Technology, trade and 'a race of native capitalists': the Krio diaspora of West and the steamship, 1852–95, *Journal of African history*, 33, 3 (1992) 421–40

2525 **Makepeace, M,** (ed), *Trade on the Guinea Coast 1657–1666: the correspondence of the British East India Company.* Madison: African Studies Program, University of Wisconsin-Madison, 1991, 158pp

2526 **van den Boogaart, E,** The trade between western Africa and the Atlantic world, 1600–1900: estimates of trends in composition and value, *Journal of African history*, 33, 3 (1992) 369–85

Education

2527 **Niane, D J,** Problèmes d'éducation et identité nationale en Afrique de l'Ouest depuis 1960, in Irele A (ed), *African education and identity (entry 268)*, 126–30

Environment

2528 **Bosc, P M,** Culture attelée et environnement: réflexions à partir d'expériences ouest-africaines, *Afrique contemporaine*, 161 (1992) 197–209

2529 **Breman, H,** Desertification control - the West African case: prevention is better than cure, *Biotropica*, 24, 2B (1992) 328–334

2530 **Ibrahim, F,** Gründe des Scheiterns der bisherigen Strategien zur Bekämpfung der Desertifikation in der Sahelzone, *Geomethodica*, 17, (1992) 71–87

2531 **Jaujay, J,** Les 'aménagistes'

face à l'environnement: l'exemple du fleuve Sénégal, *Afrique contemporaine,* 161 (1992) 217–224

2532 Krings, T, Ecofarming in Africa: experiences in east Africa - possibilities and models in the Sudan zone, *Applied geography and development,* 36, (1990) 45–60

2533 Martin, C, *The rainforests of West Africa: ecology, threats, conservation.* Basle: Birkhauser, 1991, 235pp

2534 Roose, E, La CGES, nouvelle strategié de lutte anti-érosive: application à l'amenagement de terroir en zone sudano-sahélienne d'Afrique occidentale, in *World Forestry Congress (Paris 1991), 2nd Proceedings,* 194–202

2535 Verdeaux, F, Sociétés de pêcheurs et environnement: savoirs et appropriation halieutique du milieu, *Afrique contemporaine,* 161 (1992) 125–144

Finance

2536 Medhora, R, Reserve pooling the West African Monetary Union, *Economia internazionale,* 45, 2 (1992) 209–22

2537 Medhora, R, The West African Monetary Union: institutional arrangements and the links with France, *Canadian journal of development studies,* 13, 3 (1992) 151–179

2538 N'Guessan, T, Un modèle de comportement bureaucratique de la Banque centrale: le cas de la BCEAO, *Revue économique,* 42, 5 (1991) 901–15

Food

see also: 2586

2539 Savané, M A, (ed), *Populations et gouvernments face aux problèmes alimentaires: regards sur des zones de l'Afrique de l'Ouest.* Geneva: UNRISD, 1992, 389pp

Gender

2540 Denzer, L, Gender and decolonisation: a study of three women in West African public life, in Ajayi J F A & Peel, J D Y (eds), *Peoples and empires (entry 429),* 217–36

2541 Wilentz, G, *Binding cultures: Black women writers in Africa and the diaspora.* Bloomington: Indiana UP, 1992, 141pp

Geography, physical

2542 Achard, F, Blasco, F, Use of remote sensing in survey, management and economic development of tropical rainforests, in Gastellu-Etchegorry J P (ed), *Satellite remote sensing (entry 412),* 135–47

2543 Ringrose, S, Matheson, W, The use of landsat MSS imagery to determine the aerial extent of woody vegetation cover change in the west-central Sahel, *Global ecology and biogeography letters,* 2, 1 (1992) 16–25

2544 Tappan, G G, et al, Seasonal vegetation monitoring with AVHRR data for grasshopper and locust control in West Africa, in Gastellu-Etchegorry J P (ed), *Satellite remote sensing (entry 412),* 153–64

Health & welfare services

2545 Hill, A G, Making better use of demographic data and health statistics in primary health care, in van der Walle, E, et al (eds), *Mortality and society (entry 771),* 65–98

History, general

2546 Bühnen, S, Place names as an historical source: an introduction with examples from Southern Senegambia and Germany, *History in Africa,* 19, (1992) 45-101

2547 Fage, J D, A supplement to *A guide to original sources for precolonial Western Africa* : corrigenda et addenda, *History in Africa,* 19, (1992) 201-236

2548 Robinson, D, An approach to Islam in West African history, in Harrow K H (ed), *Faces of Islam (entry 710),* 107-29

2549 Winsnes, S A, The jaundic'd eye: bias in the Danish sources for West African history, in Henige D & McCaskie, T C (eds), *West African economic and social history (entry 2521),* 217-25

History, C6–18th

2550 Conrad, D C, Searching for history in the Sunjata epic: the case of Fakoli, *History in Africa,* 19, (1992) 147-200

2551 Dieterlen, G, Sylla, D, *L'empire du Ghana: le Wagadou et les traditions de Yéréré.* Paris: Karthala, 1992, 257pp

2552 Law, R, The Atlantic slave trade in Yoruba historiography, in Falola T (ed), *Yoruba historiography (entry 3205),* 123-34

2553 Mane, M, Le Kaabu: une des grandes entités du patrimoine historique Guinéo-Séné-Gambien, *Ethiopiques,* 7, 2 (1991) 101-114

2554 Walinski, G, The image of the riuler as presented in the traditoin abour Sundjata, in Pilaszewicz S & Rzewuski, E (eds), *Unwritten testimones (entry 447),* 215-26

History, C19th

2555 Birkett, D, *Mary Kingsley: imperial adventurer.* Basingstoke: Macmillan, 1992, 200pp

History, C20th

2556 Aurich, S, Einige Reaktionen auf das Vordringen französischer Militärexpeditionen in den Gebieten zwischen oberem Ubangi, Schari und Tschad (1899–1902), *Asien, Afrika, Lateinamerika,* 19, 6 (1991) 1022–1036

Industry & trade

2557 Moseley, K P, West African industry and the debt crisis, *Journal of international development,* 4, 1 (1992) 1-27

2558 Mosley, K P, West African industry and debt crisis, *Journal of international development,* 4, 1 (1992) 1-27

2559 Neiland, A Vernumbe, I, *Artisanal fisheries of the Chad Basin in Africa: an information crisis.* Portsmouth: Portsmouth Polytechnic, Centre for Marine Resource Economics, 1990, 74pp

2560 van der Vloet, G, Weven in West-Afrika, in *Bontjes voor de tropen: de export van imitatieweefsels naar de tropen* (Zwolle: Waanders Uitgevers, 1991), 83–89

International economic relations

2561 Ariyo, A, Tariff harmonisation, government revenue and economic integration within ECOWAS: some reflections, *Development policy review,* 10, 2 (1992) 155-74

2562 Bierschenk, T, et al, Langzeitfolgen der Entwicklungshilfe: empirische Untersuchungen im ländlichen Westafrika, *Afrika spectrum,* 26, 2 (1991) 155-180

2563 Golisch, A, Messner, F, The

new international environment as a new chance for economic cooperation: the ECOWAS-perspective, *African development perspectives yearbook*, 2, (1990/91) 453–464

2564 Hanish, R, (ed), *Der Kakaoweltmarkt: Weltmarktintegrierte Entwicklung und nationale Steuerungspolitik der Produzentenländer. Band 2: Afrika.* Hamburg: Dueutches Übersee Institut, 1991, 509pp

2565 Nwachukwu, I O S, (ed), *Nigeria and the ECOWAS since 1985: towards a dynamic regional integration.* Enugu: Fourth Dimension, 1991, 258pp

2566 Ouali, K S, (ed), *Intégration et développement.* Paris: Economica, 1990, 350pp

2567 Thompson, B, Legal problems of economic integration in the West African sub-region, *African journal of international and comparative law*, 2, 1 (1990) 85–102

2568 Ziadré Tiero, D, *Entwicklungspolitische Möglichkeiten und Probleme regionaler okonomische Integration postkolonialer Staaten: das Biespiel von UDAO und UDEAO.* Frankfurt: Verlag für Interkulturelle Kommunikation, 1991, 205pp

Labour & manpower

2569 Arthur, J A, International labor migration patterns in West Africa, *African studies review*, 34, 3 (1991) 65–87

2570 Makinwa-Adebusoye, P, The West African migration system, in Kritz M M et al (eds), *International migration systems* (Oxford: Clarendon, 1992), 63–79

Law

see also: 2567

2571 Arthur, J A, Development of

penal policy in British West Africa: exploring the colonial dimension, *International journal of comparative and applied criminal justice*, 15, 2 (1991) 187–206

2572 Pinho, A T de, Les États d'Afrique de l'ouest et la mise en uvre des dispositions de la Convention des Nations Unies sur le droit de la mer en matière de pêche, *Penant*, 102, 808/809 (1992) 5–18 and 156–181

Literature

see also: 2541

2573 Asfar, G, Amadou Hampate Ba and the Islamic dimension of West African oral literature, in Harrow K H (ed), *Faces of Islam (entry 710)*, 141–50

2574 Johnson, L A, Crescent and conscoiusness: Islamic orthodoxies and the West African novel, in Harrow K H (ed), *Faces of Islam (entry 710)*, 239–60

Media

2575 van de Werk, J K, Challenge and reality in West African publishing, in Altbach P (ed), *Publishing and development (entry 694)*, 191–98

Natural resources

2576 Janssen, V, *Wasser oder Leben: ein bericht aus Afrika und der reichen Welt.* Bonn: Dietz, 1990, 166pp

2577 Krings, T, Methodische Probleme bei der Umsetzung von Agroforstwirtschaftsprojekten in den westlichen Sahelländern Afrikas, *Geomethodica*, 17, (1992) 95–116

2578 Okali, D U U, Sustainable use of West African moist forest lands, *Biotropica*, 24, 2B (1992) 335–344

Politics

2579 Clauzel, J, L'évolution des structures de l'administration territoriale dans quelques états de l'Afrique francophone au sud du Sahara, *Monde et cultures,* 51, 1–4 (1991) 208–25

2580 Fair, D, West Africa's river basin organisations, *Africa insight,* 21, 4 (1991) 257–62

Rural economy

2581 Bloomfield, E M, Lass, R A, *Impact of structural adjustment and adoption of technology on competitiveness of major cocoa producing countries.* Paris: OECD Development Centre, 1992, 91pp

2582 Brautigan, D, Land rights and agricultural development in West Africa: a case study of two Chinese projects, *Journal of developing areas,* 27, 1 (1992) 21–32

2583 Frantz, C, West African pastoralism: transformation and resistance, in Salzman C & Galaty, J G (eds), *Nomads in a changing world* (Naples: Instituto Universitario Orientale, 1990) 293–337

2584 Krings, T, Kulturbaumparke in den Agrarlandschaften Westafrikas - eine Form autochthoner Agroforstwirtschaft, *Die Erde,* 122, 2 (1991) 117–129

2585 Lae, R, *Les pêcheries artisanals lagunaires ouest-africaines.* Paris: ORSTOM, 1992, 202pp

2586 Lavigne Delville, P, Irrigation, émigration et sécurité alimentaire sur le fleuve Sénégal, *Cahiers des sciences humaines,* 27, 1/2 (1991) 105–116

2587 Lavigne Delville, P, *La rizière et la valise: irrigation, migration et stratégies paysannes dans la vallée du fleuve Sénégal.* Paris: Syros-Alternatives, 1991, 231pp

2588 Lawry, S W, Stienbarger, D M, *Tenure and alley farming in the humid zone of West Africa: final report of research in Cameroon, Nigeria and Togo.* Madison: University of Wisconsin, Land Tenure Center, 1991, 63pp

2589 Terry, E R, Rice in West Africa: the role of WARDA, in Obasanjo O & d'Orville, H (eds), *Agricultural production and food security (entry 1040),* 111–116

Science & technology

2590 Kani, A, Mathematics in the central Bilad al-Sudan, in Thomas-Emeagwali G (ed), *Science and technology in Nigeria (entry 450),* 17–36

2591 Udo Nebbio, J E, Science, technology and development in ECOWAS, *Journal of Asian and African studies,* 27, 1/2 (1992) 114–23

Sociology

2592 Haight, B M, A comparison of Muslims as minorities in the Volta region, Ghana, the Côte d'Ivoire and among the Yoruba of Nigeria in west Africa, *Journal of the Institute of Muslim Minority Affairs,* 12, 2 (1991) 449–463

2593 Lachenmann, G, *Social movements and civil society in West Africa.* Berlin: German Development Institute, 1992, 98pp

2594 van Hear, N, *Consequences of the forced mass repatriation of migrant communities: recent cases from West Africa and the Middle East.* Geneva: UNRISD, 1992, 38pp

SAHEL

Agriculture, scientific

2595 Breman, H, de Ridder, N,

*Manuel sur les pâturages des pays
sahéliens.* Paris: Karthala, 1991,
485pp

2596 Hveem, B, et al, *Rapport
d'étape: plantes sauvages.* Oslo:
Senter for utvikling og milj, 1992,
22 parts, var pp

Anthropology

2597 Romey, A, *Histoire, mémoire, et
sociétés. L'exemple de N'goussa: oasis
berbèrephone du Sahara (Ouargla).*
Paris: Harmattan, 1992, 174pp

Economic and social history

2598 Mahadi, A, The aftermath of
the jihad in the central Sudan as a
major factor in the volume of the
trans-saharan slave trade in the
nineteenth century, in Savage E
(ed), *The human commodity (entry
252),* 111–28

2599 McDougall, E A, Salt,
Saharans and the trans-saharan
slave trade: nineteenth century
developments, in Savage E (ed),
The human commodity (entry 252),
61–88

Environment

No entry: see also: 2613

Food

2600 Buchanan-Smith, M, et al,
*A guide to famine early warning and
food information systems in the Sahel
and Horn of Africa.* Brighton:
Sussex University, IDS, 1991,
98pp

2601 Davies, S, et al, *Early warning
in the Sahel and the Horn of Africa:
the state of the art - a review of the
literature.* Brighton: Sussex
University, IDS, 1991, 160pp

Geography, physical

2602 Barisano, E, Monitoring of
renewable natural resources and
crop forecasting in Sahelian
countries, in Gastellu-Etchegorry J
P (ed), *Satellite remote sensing (entry
412),* 103–114

History, C20th

see also: 471

Medical

2603 Will, M R, *Un institut régional
africain vient au jour.* Saarbrucken:
Brietenbach, 1991, 357pp

Natural resources

see also: 2602

2604 Guèye, I, Laban, P, *From
woodlots to village land management
in the Sahel.* London: IIED, 1992,
21pp

2605 Sircoulon, J, Évolution des
climats et des ressources en eau,
Afrique contemporaine, 161 (1992)
57–76

Politics

2606 Bourgeot, A, L'enjeu politique
de l'histoire: vision idéologique des
événements touaregs (1990–1992),
Politique africaine, 48 (1992) 129–35

2607 Champaud, J, Le Sahel et la
démocratie, *Politique africaine,* 47
(1992) 3–8

Rural economy

2608 Bosc, P M, et al, *Le
développement agricole au Sahel.
Tome 3: terrains et innovations.*
Montpellier: Centre de coopération
internationale en recherche
agronomique pour le
développment, 1992, 297pp

2609 Brown, E P, Nooter, R, *Sucessful small-scale irrigation in the Sahel.* Washington: World Bank, 1992, 65pp

2610 Catellanet, C, *L'irrigation villageoise: gérer les petits périmetres irrigués au Sahel.* Paris: Ministère de la Coopération, 1992, 368pp

2611 Dollé, V, Livestock raising: an important element of the production system of oases, in Bishay A & Dregne, H (eds), *Desert development ; Part 1* (London: Harwood, 1991), 531–43

2612 Havelange, F, *Liberér la parole paysanne au Sahel.* Paris: Harmattan, 1991, 126pp

2613 Leisinger, K M, (ed), *Überleben im Sahel: eine ökologische und entwicklungspolitsche Herausforderung.* Basle: Birkhäuser, 1992, 202pp

2614 Shanmugaratnam, N, et al, *Resource managment and pastoral institution building in the west African Sahel.* New York: World Bank, 1992, 77pp

2615 Yung, J M, et al, *Le développement agricole au Sahel. Tome IV: défis, recherches et innovations au Sahel.* Montpellier: Centre de coopération internationale en recherche agronomique pour le dévelopement, 1992, 383pp

Science & technology

2616 Madon, G, Foyers améliorés ou substitution?, *Afrique contemporaine,* 161 (1992) 209–217

Sociology

2617 Bessis, S, (ed), *Les enfants du Sahel.* Paris: Harmattan, 1992, 175pp

FRANCOPHONE WEST AFRICA

Arts

2618 Camara, S, *Gens de la parole: essai sur la condition et le rôle des griots dans la société malinké.* Paris: Karthala, 1992, revised edition, 376pp

2619 Drame, A, Senn-Borloz, A, Jeliya: etre griot et musicien aujourd'hui. Paris: Harmattan, 1992, 366pp

Finance

2620 Diagne, A, Politique monetaire et environnement économique. Les travaux de recherche sur l'UMOA: un aperçu, *Africa development,* 16, 3/4 (1991) 6–26

2621 Kouadio, D M, Leuthold, R M, Optimal cross-hedging alternatives for the CFA franc, *African development review,* 3, 1 (1991) 35–46

History, C20th

2622 Clauzel, J, L'administration coloniale française et les sociétés nomades dans l'ancienne Afrique occidentale francaise, *Politique africaine,* 46 (1992) 99–116

2623 Coquery-Vidrovitch, C, Goerg, O, (eds), *L'Afrique occidentale au temps des Français. Colonisateurs et colonisés, c.1860–1960.* Paris: Decouverte, 1992, 459pp

2624 Dicko, A A, *Journal d'un defaite: autour du référendum du 28 Septembre 1958 en Afrique Noire.* Paris: Harmattan, 1992, 127pp

2625 Mbaye, S, *Histoire des institutions coloniales françaises en l'Afrique de l'Ouest (1816–1960).*

Dakar: Direction des archives du
Sénégal, 1991, 339pp

International relations

2626 O'Brien, D C, The show of
state in a neocolonial twilight:
francophone Africa, in Manor J
(ed), *Rethinking Third World Politics
(entry 889)*, 145–65

Language

2627 Chaudenson, R,
Plurilinguisme et développement
en Afrique subsaharienne
francophone: les problèmes de la
communication, *Cahiers des sciences
humaines,* 27, 3/4 (1991) 305–313

Literature

2628 Wynchank, A, New paths for
Francophone West African novels,
in Nethersole R (ed), *Emerging
literatures (entry 726)*, 71–79

Politics

2629 Claudot-Hawad, H, Bandits,
rebelles et partisans: vision plurielle
des événements touaregs,
1990–1992, *Politique africaine,* 46
(1992) 143–49

BENIN

Current affairs

2630 Daloz, J P, L'itinéraire du
pionnier: sur l'évolution politique
béninoise, *Politique africaine,* 46
(1992) 132–37

Economy - Development

see also: 2646
2631 Dossou, R, Benin struggles for
market-led recovery, *Africa
recovery,* 6, 3 (1992) 18–23

2632 Houdard, G, et al, Bénin,
*Marchés tropicaux et
méditerranéens,* 48, 2420 (1992)
768–801
2633 Lutz, C, Spatial arbitrage
between rural and urban maize
markets in Benin, in Cammann L
(ed), *Traditional marketing systems
(entry 113)*, 90–100
2634 van den Boogerd, L, et al, *Le
secteur informel à Kandi, République
de Bénin: description de la situation
actuelle et recommandations pour le
programme d'appui
PADEC-KANDI.* Parakou: IRI
BONSE, 1991, 87pp
2635 van Tilburg, A, Competition
between rural and urban maize
markets in South Benin, in
Cammann L (ed), *Traditional
marketing systems (entry 113)*,
101–112
2636 Vittin, T, Bénin: le défi de la
gestion, *Politique africaine,* 48
(1992) 136–39

Economic and social history

2637 Law, R, The gold trade of
Whydah in the seventeenth
century, in Henige D & McCaskie,
T C (eds), *West African economic
and social history (entry 2521)*,
105–118
2638 Law, R, Posthumous questions
for Karl Polanyi: price inflation in
pre-colonial Dahomey, *Journal of
African history,* 33, 3 (1992)
387–420
2639 Roussé-Grosseau, C, *Mission
catholique et choc des modèles culturels
en Afrique: l'exemple du Dahomey
(1861–1928).* Paris: Harmattan,
1992, 390pp

Gender

2640 Albert, I, De nouvelles
pratiques alimentaires dans les
groupements féminins du Bénin

côtier, *Revue tiers monde*, 33, 132 (1992) 861–72

Geography, human

2641 Vennetier, P, Aménagements littoraux et évolution d'un système lagunaire: étude de cas au Bénin, *Les cahiers d'outre-mer*, 44, 176 (1991) 321–332

History, general

2642 Soumonni, E A, Dahomean Yorubaland, in Falola T (ed), *Yoruba historiography (entry 3205)*, 65–74

History, C19th

2643 Bonfils, J, La Mission Catholique en République du Bénin: la vicariat apostolique du Dahomey, de 1862 à 1870 et de la côte du Bénin de 1870 à 1883, *Nouvelle revue de science missionnaire*, 48, 1 (1992) 35–54
2644 Revelli, M (ed), Quattro anno nel Dahomey: barni del diario di missione di padre Francesco Borghero (1861–1864), *Afriche*, 3, 15 (1992) 1–49

History, C20th

2645 Asiwaju, A I, Law in African borderlands: the lived experience of the Yoruba astride the Nigeria/Dahomey border, in Mann K & Roberts, R (eds), *Law in colonial Africa (entry 684)*, 224–38

International economic relations

2646 Elwert, G, Elwert-Kretschmer, K, *Mit den Augen der Beniner: eine andere Evaluation von 25 Jahren DED in Benin.* Berlin: Deutscher Entwicklungdienst, 1991, 171pp

2647 Elwert-Kretschmer, K, Elwert, G, Mit den Augen der Béniner: eine evaluation von 25 jahren DED in Bénin, *Afrika spectrum*, 26, 3 (1991) 335–350
2648 Igue, J O, Soule, B G, *L'état entrepôt au Bénin: commerce informel ou solution à la crise?* Paris: Karthala, 1992, 210pp

Law

2649 Cabanis, A, Martin, M L, Nore sur la constitution béninoise du 2 décembre 1990, *Revue juridique et politique*, 46, 1 (1992) 28–37
2650 Matthews, J L, *Republic of Benin.* Dobbs ferry : Oceana, 1990, 45pp

Media

2651 Vittin, T E, Crise, renouveau démocratique et mutations du paysage médiatique au Bénin, *Afrique 2000*, 9 (1992) 37–57

Medical

2652 Tall, E K, L'anthropologue et le psychiatre face aux médecines traditionnelles: récit d'une expérience, *Cahiers des sciences humaines*, 28, 1 (1992) 67–81

Politics

2653 Allen, C, 'Democratic renewal' in Africa: two essays on Benin. Edinburgh: Edinburgh University, Centre of African Studies, 1992, 48pp
2654 Allen, C, 'Goodbye to all that'. The short and sad story of socialism in Benin, *Journal of communist studies*, 8, 2 (1992) 62–81 (also in *entry 860*)
2655 Allen, C, Restucturing an

authoritarian state: 'democratic renewal' in Benin, *Review of African political economy*, 54 (1992) 42–58

2656 Laleye, O M, Urban local govenrment finance in Benin: the case of Cotonou Urban District 1, *Public administration and development*, 12, 1 (1992) 53–70

Religion, philosophy

No entry, see also: 2639

Rural economy

see also: 2640

2657 Bierschenk, T, Forster, R, Rational herdsmen: economic strategies of the agro-pastoral Fulani of northern Bénin, *Applied geography and development*, 38, (1991) 110–125

2658 den Ouden, J H B, *Nous faisons le commerce: analyse anthropologique des entrepreneurs et des entreprises dans un village Adja, Bénin.* Wageningen: Development Sociology Dept., Wageningen Agricultural University, 1991, 61pp

2659 Haan, L, et al, From symbiosis to polarization? Peasants and pastoralists in Northern Benin, *Indian geographical journal*, 65, 1 (1990) 51–65

2660 Liebchen, A, *Überlebensstrategien eines kleinbäuerlichen Dorfes des Bariba am Rande der Sahelzone in Norden Benins.* Berlin: Free University, 1991, 90pp

Sociology

2661 Kohnert, D, Sozio-kulturelle Kurzanalyse, *Afrika spectrum*, 26, 3 (1991) 405–414

BURKINA FASO

Anthropology

2662 Blegna, D, *Les masques dans la société Marka de Fobiri et ses environs: origines, culte, art.* Stuttgart: Steiner, 1990, 262pp

2663 Dacher, M, *Prix des épouses, valeur des soeurs, & Les representations de la maladie.* Paris: Harmattan, 1992, 203pp

2664 Ilboudu, P, *Croyances et pratiques religieuses traditionelles des Mossi.* Stuttgart: Steiner, 1990, 256pp

2665 Izard, M, *L'odyssée du pouvoir: un royaume africain. Etat, société, destin individuel.* Paris: CID, 1992, 156pp

2666 Meyer, P, Divination among the Lobi of Burkina Faso, in Peek P M (ed), *African divination (entry 48)*, 91–100

2667 Omvlee, J, *Mediumieke divinatie bij de Bobo in Burkina Faso.* Utrecht: Dept. of Cultural Anthropology, Utrecht University, 1992, 129pp

2668 Poda, E, Image du mort, effigie de l'ancêtre, *Systèmes de pensée en Afrique noire*, 11, (1991) 91–101

Arts

2669 Luning, S, *Mossi maskers in musea: dode voorwerpen of levende wezens.* Leiden: Leiden University, 1991, 76pp

2670 Pacéré, T F, *Le language des tam-tams et des masques en Afrique.* Paris: Harmattan, 1992, 342pp

2671 Zimmer, W, *Répétoire du théatre burkinabe.* Paris: Harmattan, 1992, 139pp

Economy - Development

see also: 2690

2672 Hörburger, R, (ed), *Burkina*

Faso: *Unterentwicklung und Selbshelife in einem Sahel-Land.* Frankfurt: Brandes & Apsel, 1990, 228pp

2673 **Savadogo, K, Wetta, C,** The impact of self-imposed adjustment: the case of Burkina Faso, 1983–9, in Cornia A G et al (eds), *Africa's recovery (entry 124)*, 53–71

2674 **Sawadogo, A,** The state counter-attacks: clearly defined priorites for Burkina Faso, in NGLS (ed), *Voices from Africa 2 (entry 195)*, 59–64

Environment

2675 **Lindskog, P, Mando, A,** *The relationship between research institutes and NGOs in the field of soil and water conservation in Burkina Faso.* London: IIED, 1992, 17pp

2676 **Roose, E, Rodrigues, L,** *Aménagement des terroirs au Yatenga. Quatres années de CGES: bilan et perspectives.* Montpellier: ORSTOM, 1990, 40pp

2677 **Wardman, A, Salas, L G,** The implementation of anti-erosion techniques in in the Sahel: a case study from Kaya, Burkina Faso, *Journal of developing areas*, 26, 1 (1991) 65–80

Gender

see also: 2687

2678 **Brun, T,** The assessment of total energy expenditure of female famers under field conditions, *Journal of biosocial science*, 24, 3 (1992) 325–33

Health & welfare services

2679 **Körngen, H,** *Heilen in der Dorfgemeinschaft: Analphabeten als Dorfgesundheitshelfer im burkinischen Sahel.* Berlin: Reimer, 1990, 250pp

History, general

see also: 2665

2680 **Banaon, K E,** *Poterie et société chez les Nuna de Tierkou.* Stuttgart: Steiner, 1990, 186pp

2681 **Millogo, K A,** *Kokana: essai d'histoire structurale.* Stuttgart: Steiner, 1990, 231pp

History, C6–18th

2682 **Samtouma, I,** *La métallurgie ancienne du fer dans la région de Koumbri (Yatenga, Burkina Faso).* Stuttgart: Steiner, 1990, 176pp

Industry & trade

2683 **Bayala, A B,** La formation des prix au Burkina Faso, *Revue burkinabè de droit*, 21 (1992) 61–70

Language

2684 **Some, P A,** *Significat et société: le cas de Dagara du Burkina Faso.* Paris: Harmattan, 1992, 270pp

Law

2685 **Bado, L,** La directive en droit public burkinabè depuis la Révolution d'août: le cas particulier du Coordonnateur National des Structures Populaires (C.N.S.P.), ex Secrétaire Général National des Comités de Défense de la Révolution (S.G.N.C.D.R.), *Revue burkinabè de droit*, 19/20, (1991) 27–43

2686 **Schott, R,** La loi contre la religion?: sur le rapport du droit et de la religion dans le changement social à partir d'exemples de l'Afrique de l'Ouest, *Droit et cultures*, 21 (1991) 16–31

2687 **Steinbrich, S,** The social and legal position of Lyela women (Burkina Faso), *Journal of legal*

pluralism and unofficial law, 30/31
(1990/1991) 139–164

Politics

2688 Bado, L, Le régime
constitutionnel et politique de la
IVe République burkinabè, *Revue
burkinabè de droit,* 21 (1992) 9–22

2689 Blanc, F P, (ed),
*Administration et société au Burkina
Faso.* Toulouse: Presse de l'IEP,
1991, 187pp

2690 Jalade, M, L'évolution
institutionelle et économique du
Burkina Faso, *Monde et cultures,* 51,
1–4 (1991) 161–66

2691 Kiemde, P, Le bicaméralisme
en Afrique et au Burkina Faso,
Revue burkinabè de droit, 21 (1992)
23–50

2692 Otayek, R, Burkina Faso: la
'rectification' démocratique, *Studia
Africana,* 3 (1992) 11–26

2693 Otayek, R, The democratic
'rectification' in Burkina Faso,
Journal of communist studies, 8, 2
(1992) 82–104 (also in *entry 860*)

2694 Robinson, P T, Grassroots
legitimation of military governance
in Burkina Faso and Niger: the
core contradictions, in Hyden G &
Bratton, M (eds), *Governance and
politics (entry 864),* 143–65

2695 Schmitz, E, *Politische
Herrschaft in Burkina Faso: von der
Unabhängigkiet bis zum Sturz
Thomas Sankaras, 1960–1987.*
Freiburg: Arnold Bergstraeseer
Institute, 1990, 377pp

Religion, philosophy

see also: 2686
2696 Van Duc, J, Le pèlerinage des
Voltaïques / Burkinabe aux lieux
saints de l'islam, passé-présent:
orientation générale de thèse, *Islam
et sociétés au Sud du Sahara,* 5,
(1991) 165–177

Rural economy

2697 Bigot, Y, Raymond, G,
*Traction animale et motorisation en
zone contonnière de l'Afrique de
l'Ouest: Burkina Faso.*
Montpellier: CIPAD, 1991,
95pp

**2698 Ouedraogo, B L, Le Balle,
Y,** *Entraide villageoise et
développement: groupements paysans
au Burkina Faso.* Paris: Harmattan,
1990, 177pp

2699 Schwedersky, T,
*Mitgliederpartizipation in dörflichen
Selbshilfeorganisationen. Das Beispiel
des 'groupements villageois' in der
Region von Hounde, Burkina
Faso.* Aachen: Heredot, 1990,
380pp

CHAD

Anthropology

2700 Tubiana, M J, Problèmes
posés par l'arrivée massive de
nomades dans une zone occupée
par des sédentaires, et par la
naissance de groupements d'un
type nouveau, in Baxter P T W &
Hogg, R (eds), *Property, poverty and
people (entry 1000),* 217–28

Current affairs

2701 Ramirez, C, Another violent
change in Chad, *Revista de
Africa y Medio Oriente,* 3, 1 (1991)
33–40

Economic and social history

No entry, see also: 3672

Health & welfare services

2702 Foltz, A M, Foltz, W J, The
politics of health reform in Chad,
in Perkins D H & Roemer, M

(eds), *Reforming economic systems in developing countries* (Cambridge, Mass.: Harvard Institute for International Development, 1991), 137–57

History, C20th

2703 Le Rumeur, G, *Méhariste et chef de poste au Tchad.* Paris: Harmattan, 1991, 189pp

International relations

2704 Massaquoi, B J, Conflict resolution: the OAU and Chad, *Transafrica forum,* 7, 4 (1991) 83–97

Law

2705 Moyrand, A, Les nouvelles institutions politiques du Tchad: la Charte nationale du 1er mars 1991, *Revue juridique et politique,* 45, 3/4 (1991) 282–91

Politics

2706 Hassan Abbakar, M, *Un tchadien à l'aventure.* Paris: Harmattan, 1992, 121pp
2707 Lydie-Doual, T, Chad: civil war and development prospects, in NGLS (ed), *Voices from Africa 3 (entry 913),* 27–35

Religion, philosophy

2708 Magnant, J P, (ed), *L'islam au Tchad.* Talence: CEAN, Bordeaux University, 1992, 150pp

Rural economy

2709 Pairault, J, Boum (Tchad) après trente ans, *Afrique contemporaine,* 164 (1992) 88–96

COTE D'IVOIRE

Anthropology

2710 Gottleib, A, *Under the Kapok tree: identity and difference in Beng thought.* Bloomington: Indiana UP, 1992, 184pp
2711 Launay, R, *Beyond the stream: Islam and society in a West African town.* Berkeley: University of California Press, 1992, 258pp
2712 Schürkens, U, Veränderung der sozialen Ungleichheit in einem Entwicklungsland von der vorkolonialen bis zur heutigen Zeit: ein theoretisches Konzept und seine empirische Überprüfung, *Zetschrift für Ethnologie,* 115, (1990) 199–208

Economy - Development

2713 Chamley, C, Côte d'Ivoire: the failure of structural adjustment, in Thomas V et al (eds), *Restructuring economies in distress: policy reform and the World Bank* (Oxford: OUP, 1992), 287–308
2714 Deaton, A, Saving and income smoothing in Côte d'Ivoire, *Journal of African economies,* 1, 1 (1992) 1–24
2715 Faure, Y A, Le quatrième plan d'ajustement structurel de la Côte-d'Ivoire: de la technique économique à l'économie politique, *Canadian journal of development studies,* 13, 3 (1992) 411–431
2716 Gilguy, C, Côte d'Ivoire: quelle relève par le secteur privé?, *Marchés tropicaux et méditerranéens,* 48, 2435 (1992) 1805–1844
2717 Glewwe, P, Targeting assistance to the poor: efficient allocation of transfers when household income is not observed, *Journal of development economics,* 38, 2 (1992) 297–321

2718 Hillen, P, (ed), *Im Schatten des Wachstums: Arbeits- und Lebensbedingungen in der Côte d'Ivoire.* Saarbrucken: Breitenbach, 1990, 380pp

2719 Kakwani, N C, *Poverty and economic growth: with application to Côte d'Ivoire.* Washington: World Bank, 1990, 55pp

2720 Kourouma, M, Les aspects fiscaux des conventions pétroliéres en Côte-d'Ivoire, *Revue juridique et politique,* 46, 2 (1992) 201–218

2721 Rueda-Sabater, E, Stone, A, *Côte d'Ivoire: private sector dynamics and constraints.* Washington: World Bank, 1992, 48pp

2722 Schneider, H, et al, *Adjustment and equity in Côte d'Ivoire.* Paris: OECD Development Centre, 1992, 153pp

2723 Weekes-Vagliani, W, *Analyse des variables socio-culturelles et l'ajustement en Côte d'Ivoire.* Paris: OECD Development Centre, 1990, 59pp

Environment

2724 Bakker, R R, *Analyse van factoren, die de humane gezondheidstoestand bepalen, in een veranderend eco-systeem in de Taî regio (Ivoorkust).* Wageningen: Wageningen Agricultural University, 1992, 123pp

2725 Mitja, D, *Influence de la culture itinérante sur la végétation d'une savane humide de Côte d'Ivoire.* Paris: ORSTOM, 1992, 270pp

Finance

2726 Niamkey, A M, Monnaie, inflation et croissance en Côte d'Ivoire, *Africa development,* 16, 3/4 (1991) 45–54

2727 Sarassoro, H C, L'escompte de chèque en Côte d'Ivoire (étude de droit bancaire), *African journal of*

international and comparative law, 2, 2 (1990) 202–233

Food

2728 Akindès, F, Restauration populaire et sécurité alimentaire à Abidjan, *Cahiers des sciences humaines,* 27, 1/2 (1991) 169–179

2729 Odounfa, A, Akindes, F, La population sous-alimentée d'Abidjan: crise économique, solidarité familiale et politique alimentaire, *Cahiers des sciences humaines,* 27, 1/2 (1991) 217–234

2730 Perrault, P T, La sécurité alimentaire en Côte d'Ivoire: un essai de mesure, *Cahiers ivoiriens de recherche économique et sociale,* Special issue (1990) 67–75

Gender

2731 Haddad, L, Hoddinott, J, *Gender aspects of household expenditures and resource allocation in the Côte d'Ivoire.* Oxford: Oxford University, Institute of Economics and Statistics, 1991, 56pp

2732 Weekes-Vagliani, W, Structural adjustment and gender in Côte d'Ivoire, in Afshar H & Dennis, C (eds), *Women and adjustment policies in the Third World* (Basingstoke: Macmillan, 1991), 117–49

Geography, human

2733 Berron, H, Le littoral lagunaire de Côte d'Ivoire: milieu physique, peuplement et modifications anthropiques, *Les cahiers d'outre-mer,* 44, 176 (1991) 345–363

Health & welfare services

2734 Thomas, D, et al, *Public policy and anthropometric outcomes in the*

CDI. New haven: Yale University, Economic Growth Center, 1991, 37pp

History, general

2735 Perrot, C H, La lecture des difficultés démographiques à travers celle des génealogies: perspectives méthodologiques à travers le cas Anyi (Côte d'Ivoire), in Henige D & McCaskie, T C (eds), *West African economic and social history (entry 2521)*, 189–94

History, C20th

2736 Groff, D, The dynamics of collaboration and the role of law in French West Africa: the case of Kwame Kangah of Assikasso (Côte d'Ivoire), 1898–1922, in Mann K & Roberts, R (eds), *Law in colonial Africa (entry 684)*, 146–66

2737 Lawler, N E, *Soldiers of misfortune: Ivorien tirailleurs of World War II*. Athens, Ohio: Ohio UP, 1992, 267pp

Industry & trade

see also: 2759, 5445

2738 Bredeloup, S, Des négociants au long cours s'arrêtent à Dimbokro (Côte d'Ivoire), *Cahiers d'études africaines*, 31, 4 (1991) 475–86

2739 Mytelka, L, Ivoirian industry at the crossrods, in Stewart F et al (eds), *Alternative development strategies (entry 223)*, 243–64

2740 Navaretti, G B, Joint ventures and autonomous industrial development: the of the Côte d'Ivoire, in Stewart F et al (eds), *Alternative development strategies (entry 223)*, 402–25

International economic relations

2741 Zike, M, *La rebellion ivoirienne contre les multinationals*. Abidjan: Ami, 1991, 185pp

International relations

2742 Yao, B K, Le dialogue Yamoussoukro-Pretoria: un aperçu, *Afrique 2000*, 9 (1992) 5–13

Labour & manpower

2743 Kouamé, A, La sous-utilisation des ressources humaines et ses causes: quelques hypothèses dur le cas ivoirien, *Labour, capital and society*, 24, 1 (1991) 110–33

Law

2744 Kourouma, M, Contribution à l'étude des accords de siège entre la Côte d'Ivoire et les organisations internationales, *Revue juridique et politique*, 46, 1 (1992) 97–115

2745 Kourouma, M, Éléments juridiques du diagnostic de l'informatisation de l'administration ivoirienne, *Penant*, 102, 809 (1992) 197–214

2746 Togba, Z, Parti unique et contrôle juridictionnel des élections législatives en Côte d'Ivoire: les cas de l'arrêt Béganan Bogui de la Cour suprème, *Revue juridique et politique*, 45, 2 (1991) 156–71

Literature

2747 Laverdière, L, Africano et cristiano: la relgione, Dio e, sullo sfondo, i missionari nell'opera di Bernard Dadie, *Afriche*, 13 (1992) 3–32

Medical

see also: 2724

2748 Vidal, L, SIDA et
représentations de la maladie:
éléments de réflexion sur la
séropositivité et sa prise en charge,
Cahiers des sciences humaines, 28, 1
(1992) 83–98

Politics

see also: 2579

2749 Bakary, T D, Mouvement
sociaux et changement politique en
Côte d'Ivoire, *Géopolitique africaine,*
14, (1991) 1–17

2750 Bakary Akin, T D, *Côte
d'Ivoire: une succession impossible?*
Paris: Harmattan, 1991, 207pp

2751 Bakary-Akin, T, *La démocratie
par le haut en Côte d'Ivoire.* Paris:
Harmattan, 1992, 320pp

2752 Bartolomei, J,
Neocostituzionalismo nell'Africa
francofona subsaharaiana:
l'esperieza ivoriana di
democrazia orientata, *Revista
trimestrale di diritto pubblico,* 41, 2
(1991) 70–80

2753 Conte, B, Lavenue, J J, La
Côte d'Ivoire un an après les
confrontations electorales de 1990:
hypothèses et hypothèques, *Revue
juridique et politique,* 46, 1 (1992)
1–27

2754 Crook, R, State, society and
political institutions in Côte
d'Ivoire and Ghana, in Manor J
(ed), *Rethinking Third World Politics
(entry 889),* 213–41

2755 Medard, J F, The historical
trajectories of the Ivoirian and
Kenyan states, in Manor J (ed),
*Rethinking Third World Politics
(entry 889),* 185–212

2756 Nguessan-Zoukou, L, *Régions
et régionalisation in CDI.* Paris:
Harmattan, 1990, 179pp

2757 Widner, J A, The 1990

election in Côte d'Ivoire, *Issue,* 20,
1 (1992) 31–40

Rural economy

see also: 1008

2758 Boutillier, J L, Le système de
production des Koulango de
Nassian en situation d'enclavement
(fin des années 1960), *Cahiers
ivoiriens de recherche économique et
sociale,* Special issue (1990) 87–123

2759 Fiege, K, *Bäuerliche
Exportproduktion in der Côte d'Ivoire:
fallstudien zu wirschatlichen und
sozialen Auswirkungen der Faffee-
und Kakaoproduktion.* Hamburg:
Institute für Afrika-Kunde, 1991,
409pp

**2760 Fricke, W,
Kochendörfer-Lucius, G,** The
influence of transportation
infrastructure on the regional
pattern of agriculture in West
Africa, using as an example the
impact of the minor road network
in the Dan Hills region of the Ivory
Coast, *Applied geography and
development,* 39, (1992) 30–47

2761 Harre, D, *Le riz en Côte
d'Ivoire: origine et performance des
secteurs de transformation artisanal et
industriel.* Paris: Solagaral, 1992,
88pp

2762 M'bet, A, Savings
determinants and mobilisation in
subsaharan Africa: the case of Côte
d'Ivoire, in Frimpong-Ansah J H &
Ingham, B (eds), *Saving for
economic recovery (entry 142),*
160–80

2763 Peltre-Wurtz, J, Steck, B,
*Les charrues de la Bagoué: gestion
paysanne d'une opération cotonnière
en CDI.* Paris: ORSTOM, 1991,
303pp

2764 Ruf, F, Les crises cacoyères: la
malédiction des âges d'or?, *Cahiers
d'études africaines,* 31, 1/2 (1991)
83–134

2765 Zoungrana, P, Les 'soubresauts' de la politique rizicole en Côte d'Ivoire, *Cahiers ivoiriens de recherche économique et sociale,* Special issue (1990) 7–28

Sociology

see also: 2277, 2712

2766 Glewwe, P, *Estimating the determinants of household welfare in Côte d'Ivoire.* Washington: World Bank, 1990, 50pp

2767 Trouvé, J, *Eléments pour l'approche des indicateurs sociaux en Côte d'Ivoire.* Geneva: UNRISD, 1990, 47pp

Urban studies

2768 Touré, A, Lifestyles and evolving cultural values, in *Voices from Africa 4 (entry 1064),* 9–16

GAMBIA

Economy - Development

2769 Hadjimichael, M T, et al, *Gambia: economic adjustment in a small open economy.* Washington: IMF, 1992, 43pp

2770 McPherson, M F, *The politics of economic reform in the Gambia.* Cambridge, Mass.: Harvard Institute for International Development, 1991, 41pp

2771 McPherson, M F, Radelet, S C, Economic reform in the Gambia: policies, politics, foreign aid, and luck, in Perkins D H& Roemer, M (eds), *Reforming economic systems in developing countries* (Cambridge, Mass.: Harvard Institute for International Development, 1991), 115–36

Finance

2772 Ceesay, M A, Financial liberalisation and exchange rate degulation: the Gambia's experience, in Roe A R et al (eds) *Instruments of economic policy (entry 341),* 195–203

Gender

see also: 2778, 2781

2773 Carney, J A, Peasant women and economic transformation in the Gambia, *Development and change,* 23, 2 (1992) 67–90

2774 Skramstad, H, *The fluid meaning of female circumcision in a multiethnic context in Gambia: disttribution of knowledge and linkages to sexuality.* Bergen: Michelsen Institute, 1990, 21pp

2775 Skramstad, H, *'Kvinner i utvikling' i Gambia: nye kjnnsrelasjoner med hjelp fra Verdensbanken?* Bergen: CMI, 1992, 25pp

2776 Skramstad, H, *Prostitute as metaphor in gender construction: a Gambian setting.* Bergen: Michelsen Institute, 1990, 25pp

History, C6–18th

2777 Hill, M H, Towards a chronology of the publications of Francis Moore's *Travels into the inland parts of Africa...,* *History in Africa,* 19, (1992) 353–368

International relations

No entry, see also: 3549

Rural economy

see also: 2582, 2773

2778 Carney, J, *Contract farming and female rice growers in the Gambia.* London: ODI, Irrigation

Management Network, 1992, 19pp

2779 Sumberg, J, Gilbert, E, Agricultural mechanisation in the Gambia: drought, donkeys and minimum tillage, *African livestock research,* 1, 1 (1992) 1–10

2780 Webb, J L A, Ecological and economic change along the middle reaches of the Gambia river, 1945–1984, *African affairs,* 91, 365 (1992) 543–65

2781 Webb, P, When projects collapse: irrigation failure in the Gambia from a household perspective, *Journal of international development,* 3, 4 (1991) 339–53

Sociology

see also: 3491, 3492

2782 Brown, N, Beach boys as culture brokers in Bakau Town, Gambia, *Community development journal,* 27, 4 (1992) 361–70

GHANA

Anthropology

see also: 2502

2784 Akutsu, S, The demise and the enthronement of the Asantehene: political aspects of Asante kingship, *Senri ethnological studies,* 31 (1992) 503–534

2785 Avorgbedor, D K, Some contributions of 'halo' music to research theory and pragmatics in Ghana, *Bulletin of the international committee on urgent anthropological and ethnological research,* 32/33 (1990/91) 61–80

2786 Fink, H, *Religion, disease and healing in Ghana: a case study of traditional Dormaa medecine.* Muncih: Trickster Wissenschaft, 1990, 361pp

2787 McCaskie, T C, People and animals: constructing the Asante

experience, *Africa,* 62, 2 (1992) 221–47

2788 Platvoet, J G, 'Renewal' by retrospection: the Asante Anokye traditions, in Geertz A W & Jensen, J S (ed), *Religion, tradition, and renewal* (Aarhus: Aarhus UP, 1991), 149–76

Arts

2789 Warren, D M, Andrews, J K, *Akan arts and aesthetics: elements of change in a Ghanaian indigenous knowledge system.* Ames, Iowa: Iowa State University, Technology and Social Change Program, 1990, 53pp

Economy - Development

see also: 173, 2866

2790 Agbobli, A K, La renaissance économique ghanéenne, *Afrique 2000,* 4, (1991) 113–123

2791 Ahiakpor, J C, Rawlings, economic policy, and the poor: consistency or betrayal?, *Journal of modern African studies,* 29, 4 (1991) 583–600

2792 Akuoko-Frimpong, H, *Rebalancing the public and private sectors in developing countries: the case of Ghana.* Paris: OECD Development Centre, 1990, 70pp

2793 Bank of Ghana, The Ghanaian experience, in Roe A R et al *Instruments of economic policy (entry 341),* 205–13

2794 Boateng, E O, et al, A poverty profile for Ghana, 1987–1988, *Journal of African economies,* 1, 1 (1992) 25–58

2795 Frimpong-Ansah, J H, *The vampire state in Africa: the political economy of decline in Ghana.* London: Currey, 1992, 205pp

2796 Green, D M, Structural adjustment and politics in Ghana, *Transafrica forum,* 8, 2 (1991) 67–89

2797 Grömping, R, (ed), *Ghana: ändern sich die Zieten? Wirtschaftliche Abhängigkeit und Selbshilfe.* Berlin: Das Arabische Buch, 1990, 167pp

2798 Jebuni, C D, et al, *Exchange rate policy and macroeconomic performance in Ghana.* Nairobi: Initiatives, 1991, 29pp

2799 Kapur, I, *Ghana: adjustment and growth, 1983–91.* Washington: IMF, 1991, 69pp

2800 King, R, Samaan, K, *Assessment of institutional capacity for implementing district development projects in Dangme West district, Ghana.* Dortmund: SPRING Centre, University of Dortmund, 1992,

2801 Kraus, J, The political economy of stabilisation and structural adjustment in Ghana, in Rothchild D (ed), *Ghana (entry 2809),* 119–55

2802 Kusi, N, Ghana: can the adjustment reforms be sustained?, *Africa development,* 16, 3/4 (1991) 181–206

2803 Kusi, N K, Macroeconomic adjustments, economic growth and the balance of payments in Ghana, 1983–88, *Journal of international development,* 4, 5 (1992) 541–559

2804 Kyerime, S S, Exchange rate, price and output interrelationships in Ghana: evidence from vector autoregression, *Applied economics,* 23, 12 (1991) 1801–1810

2805 Leechor, C, Ghana: ending chaos, in Thomas V et al (eds), *Restructuring economies in distress: policy reform and the World Bank* (Oxford: OUP, 1992), 309–31

2806 McLaren, J, Balance of payments volatility and food security: the 'portfolio' approach applied to Ghana and Tanzania, *Eastern Africa economic review,* 6, 2 (1990) 95–109

2807 Rimmer, D, *Staying poor: Ghana's political economy*

1950–1990. Oxford: Pergamon, 1992, 243pp

2808 Roe, A, Schneider, H, *Adjustment and equity in Ghana.* Paris: OECD Development Centre, 1992, 160pp

2809 Rothchild, D, (ed), *Ghana: the political economy of economic recovery.* Boulder: Lynne Reinner, 1991, 284pp

2810 Rothchild, D, Ghana and structural adjustment: an overview, in Rothchild D (ed), *Ghana (entry 2809),* 3–17

2811 Tangri, R, The politics of government-business relations in Ghana, *Journal of modern African studies,* 30, 1 (1992) 97–111

2812 Tay, F D, *Sparen, Investition und finanzielle Intermediation im Kontext der Unterentwicklung: zum Problem der institutionalisierung der Kapitalbildung in Entwicklungsländern, dargestellt am Biespiel Ghanas.* Bochum: Universität Bochum, Institut für Entwicklungsforschung und Entwicklungspolitik, 1990, 370pp

2813 Toye, J, World Bank policy-conditioned loans: how did they work in Ghana in the 1980s?, in Milner C & Rayner, A J (eds), *Policy adjustment (entry 184),* 81–97

2814 Woodward, D, The impact of devaluation on poverty in Ghana, in his *Debt, adjustment and poverty in developing countries, Vol. 2* (London: Pinter, 1992), 305–25

Economic and social history

2815 Coquery-Vidrovitch, C, Villes africaines anciennes: une civilisation mercantile pré-négrière dans l'Ouest africain, XVI et XVII siècles, *Annales,* 46, 6 (1991) 1389–410

2816 Dumett, R E, Traditional slavery in the Akan region in the nineteenth century: sources, issues

and interpretations, in Henige D &
McCaskie, T C (eds), *West African
economic and social history (entry
2521)*, 7–22

2817 Fieldhouse, D, War and the
origins of the Gold Coast Cocoa
Marketing Board, 1939–40, in
Twaddle M (ed), *Imperialism (entry
464)*, 153–82

2818 Maier, D J E, Military
acquisition of slaves in Asante, in
Henige D & McCaskie, T C (eds),
*West African economic and social
history (entry 2521)*, 119–32

2819 McCaskie, T C, Nananom
Mpow of Mankessim: an essay in
Fante history, in Henige D &
McCaskie, T C (eds), *West African
economic and social history (entry
2521)*, 133–50

2820 vam Dantzig, A, The
Akanists: a West African Hansa, in
Henige D & McCaskie, T C (eds),
*West African economic and social
history (entry 2521)*, 205–216

Education

see also: 2870

2821 Cobbe, J, The political
economy of education reform in
Ghana, in Rothchild D (ed), *Ghana
(entry 2809)*, 101–115

2822 Delage, P B, Canadian
assistance for institution building:
case study of the Ghana-Guelph
project, 1970–1978, *Journal of
developing areas*, 26, 1 (1991) 81–94

2823 Glewwe, P, *Schooling, skills and
the returns to government investment
in education: an exploration using
data from Ghana.* Washington:
World Bank, 1991, 56pp

2824 Kotey, N, Student loans in
Ghana, *Higher education*, 23, 4
(1991) 451–59

2825 Lavy, V, *Investment in human
capital: schooling supply constraints in
rural Ghana.* Washington: World
Bank, 1992, 36pp

Environment

2826 Boaten, A A, Asante: the
perception and the utilisation of the
environment before the twentieth
century, *Research review*, 6, 2
(1990) 19–28

2827 Dorm-Adzobu, C,
Environmental activities in Ghana:
national concepts, experiences and
perspectives, *African development
perspectives yearbook*, 2, (1990/91)
328–338

2828 Mensah, J, Whitney, H A,
Some Third World environmental
perceptions and behaviours
concerning urban waste: a
survey of Techiman, Ghana,
Canadian geographer, 35, 2 (1991)
156–165

2829 Uhlig, C, (ed), *Fragen der
Unweltpolitik in Entwicklungsländern.*
Bochum: Universität Bochum,
Institut für Entwicklungsforschung
und Entwicklungspolitik, 1991,
109pp

Finance

2830 Kallon, K M, An econometric
analysis of money demands in
Ghana, *Journal of developing areas*,
26, 4 (1992) 475–88

2831 Obben, J, Performance of the
Ghanaian rural banks: a
canonical correlation analysis,
Savings and development, 16, 2
(1992) 183–197

2832 Sowa, N K, *Monetary control in
Ghana 1957–1988.* London: ODI,
1991, 47pp

Food

see also: 2806, 2836

2833 Dei, G J S, The indigenous
responses of a Ghanaian rural
community to seasonal food supply
cycles and the socio-environmental
stresses of the 1980s, in Taylor D

R F & Mackenzie, F (eds), *Development from within (entry 1061)*, 58–81

2834 Devereux, S, 'Observers are worried': learning the language and counting the people in northeastern Ghana, in Devereux S & Hoddinott, J (eds), *Fieldwork in developing countries* (Hemel Hempstead: Harvester, 1992), 43–56

2835 Kyereme, S S, Thorbecke, E, Factors affecting food poverty in Ghana, *Journal of development studies*, 28, 1 (1991) 39–52

Gender

see also: 2889

2836 Ameyaw, S, *The dynamics of female entrepreneurship in indigenous food markets: a case study of Techiman, Ghana.* East Lansing: Michigan State University, 1990, 25pp

2837 Brydon, L, Ghanaian women in the migration process, in Chant S (ed), *Gender and migration in developing countries* (London: Belhaven, 1992), 91–108

2838 Higgins, P A, Alderman, H, *Labour and women's nutrition: a study of energy expenditure, fertility and nutritional status in Ghana.* Washington: World Bank, 1992, 41pp

2839 Kost, T K, Callenius, C, *Ghanaische Frauen erzählen aus irhen Alltag.* Hamburg: Institut für Afrika Kunde, 1992, 214pp

2840 Pheneba-Sakyi, Y, Determinants of current contraceptive use among Ghanaian women at highest risk of pregnancy, *Journal of biosocial science*, 24, 4 (1992) 463–75

Geography, physical

2841 Ofori-Sarpong, E, Rainfall reliability over Ghana, *Journal of east African research and development*, 21, (1991) 93–106

2842 Rossi, G, Évolution d'un front deltaïque et actions anthropiques: le cas du delta de la Volta (Ghana), *Les cahiers d'outre-mer*, 44, 176 (1991) 333–343

Health & welfare services

see also: 418

2843 McNamara, R, et al, *Family planning programs in subsaharan Africa: case studies from Ghana, Rwanda and the Sudan.* Washington: World Bank, 1992, 23pp

2844 Quaye, R, The political economy of health and medical care: the Ghanaian experience, *Scandinavian journal of development alternatives*, 11, 1 (1992) 5–25

2845 van Burik, J R, et al, *Hospitals on the move: an investigative study on hospital building in Ghana.* Delft: Bouwkunde, 1990, 294pp

2846 Yankah, K, Traditional lore in population communication: the case of the Akan in Ghana, *Africa media review*, 6, 1 (1992) 15–24

History, general

see also: 2788

2847 Goody, E, Goody, J, Creating a text: alternative interpretations of Gonja drum history, *Africa*, 62, 2 (1992) 266–70

History, C19th

2848 Kouame, R A, L'hégémonie Asante sur l'Abron Gyaman, 1740–1875: plus d'un siècle de domination et de resistence, *Africa (Rome)*, 47, 2 (1992) 173–83

2849 McCaskie, T C, Empire state: Asante and the historians, *Journal*

of African history, 33, 3 (1992)
467–76 (review article)
2850 **Wilks, I,** On mentally mapping
Greater Asante: a study of time and
motion, *Journal of African history,*
33, 2 (1992) 175–90

History, C20th

see also: 3646
2851 **Baku, K,** *Kobina Sekyi of
Ghana: an annotated bibliography of
his writings.* Boston: African Studies
Centre, Boston University, 1991,
11pp
2852 **Birmingham, D,** *Kwame
Nkrumah.* London: Sphere Books,
1990, 129pp
2853 **Casely-Hayford, A,
Rathbone, R,** Politics, families
and freemasonry in the colonial
Cold Coast, in Ajayi J F A & Peel, J
D Y (eds), *Peoples and empires
(entry 429),* 143–60
2854 **Israel, A M,** Ex-servicemen at
the crossroads: protest and politics
in postwar Ghana, *Journal of
modern African studies,* 30, 2 (1992)
359–68
2855 **Rathbone, R,** Political
intelligence and policing in Ghana
in the 1940s and 1950s, in
Anderson D M & Killingray, D
(eds), *Policing and decolonisation*
(Manchester: Manchester UP,
1992), 84–126
2856 **Verlet, M,** Dire, savoir,
pouvoir: deux épisodes des
trajectoires politiques ghanéennes,
Cahiers des sciences humaines, 27,
3/4 (1991) 457–476

Industry & trade

2857 **Boapeah, S N, Poppe, M,**
*Strengthening spatial circuits of small
scale industries for district
development: a case study of Dagme
West district, Ghana.* Dortmund:
SPRING Centre, University of

Dortmund, 1992, 120pp
2858 **Burrows, S,** The role of
indigenous NGOs in the
development of small town
enterprises in Ghana, in Baker J &
Pedersen, P O (eds), *Rural-urban
interface (entry 1111),* 187–99
2859 **Fontaine, J M,** Bias overkill?
Removal of anti-export bias and
manufacturing investment: Ghana
1983–89, in Adhikari R et al (eds),
*Industrial and trade policy reform in
developing countries* (Manchester:
Manchester UP, 1992), 120–34
2860 **Gyimah-Bondi, E,** State
enterprises divestiture: recent
Ghanaian experiences, in Rothchild
D (ed), *Ghana (entry 2809),*
193–208
2861 **Nugent, P,** Educating
Rawlings: the evolution of
government strategy toward
smuggling, in Rothchild D (ed),
Ghana (entry 2809), 69–84
2862 **Powell, J,** Kumasi University's
involvement in grassroots industrial
development, *Small enterprise
development,* 2, 2 (1991) 35–43

International economic relations

2863 **Anyemedu, K,** Export
diversification under the Economic
Recovery Programme, in
Rothchild D (ed), *Ghana (entry
2809),* 209–20
2864 **Martin, M,** Negotiating
adjustment and external finance:
Ghana and the international
community, 1982–1989, in
Rothchild D (ed), *Ghana (entry
2809),* 235–63

International relations

2865 **Dumor, E K,** *Ghana, OAU
and southern Africa: an African
response to apartheid.* Accra: Ghana
University Press, 1991, 290pp
2866 **Shahid, A S,** *Development and*

foreign policy: Ghana's experience 1966–69. Delhi: Kalinga, 1991, 190pp

Labour & manpower

2867 **Herbst, J,** Labour in Ghana under structural adjustment: the politics of acquiescence, in Rothchild D (ed), *Ghana (entry 2809)*, 173–92

Law

see also: 2686

2868 **Agbosu, L K,** Land registration in Ghana: past, present and future, *Journal of African law,* 34, 2 (1990) 104–27

2869 **Asibuo, S K,** The revolutionary administration of justice and public accountability in Ghana, *Philippine journal of public administration,* 35, 3 (1991) 253–263

Library - documentation

2870 **Alemna, A,** Library security, book theft and mutilation: a study of university libraries in Ghana, *Library and archival security,* 11, 2 (1992) 23–35

Medical

2871 **Glewwe, P,** *Estimating the determinants of cognitive achievement in low-income countries: the case of Ghana.* Washington: World Bank, 1992, 74pp

Natural resources

2872 **Addo, S T,** Distribution of the main domestic fuel item in Ghana: ramifications and deductions, *Philippine geographical journal,* 34, 4 (1990) 163–170

Politics

see also: 2754, 2809, 2867, 5513

2873 **Chazan, N,** Liberalisation, governance and political space in Ghana, in Hyden, G & Bratton, M (eds), *Governance and politics (entry 864)*, 121–41

2874 **Chazan, N,** The political transformation of Ghana under the PNDC, in Rothchild D (ed), *Ghana (entry 2809)*, 21–47

2875 **Crook, R C,** Decentralisation and participation in Ghana and Cote d'Ivoire, in Crook R C & Jerve, A M (eds), *Government and participation (entry 824)*, 93–118

2876 **Hansen, E,** *Ghana under Rawlings: early years.* Lagos: Malthouse Press, 1991, 157pp

2877 **Haynes, J,** One-party state, no-party state, multi-party state? 35 years of democracy, authoritarianism and development in Ghana, *Journal of communist studies,* 8, 2 (1992) 41–62 (also in *entry 860*)

2878 **Jeffries, R,** Leadership commitment and political opposition to structural adjustment in Ghana, in Rothchild D (ed), *Ghana (entry 2809)*, 157–71

2879 **Jeffries, R,** Urban popular attitudes towards the Economic Recovery Programme and the PNDC government in Ghana, *African affairs,* 91, 363 (1992) 207–26

2880 **Kodzi, K,** *Worse than South Africa: hypocrisy in African politics.* London: Moreto, 1991, 205pp

2881 **Ninsin, K A,** The PNDC ands the problem of legitimacy, in Rothchild D (ed), *Ghana (entry 2809)*, 49–67

2882 **Ninsin, K A, Drah, F K,** (eds), *Ghana's transition to constitutional rule.* Accra: Ghana University Press, 1991, 124pp

2883 **Owusu, M,** Democracy and

156

West Africa

Africa: a view from the village, *Journal of modern African studies,* 30, 3 (1992) 369–96

2884 **Shillington, K,** *Ghana and the Rawlings factor.* Basingstoke: Macmillan, 1992, 192pp

Religion, philosophy

see also: 3658

2885 **Christian Council of Ghana,** *The Church and Ghana's search for a new democratic system.* Accra: Presbyterian Press, 1990, 35pp

2886 **Pobee, J S,** *Religion and politics in Ghana.* Accra: Asempa, 1991, 150pp

2887 **Pobee, J S,** *Religion and politics in Ghana: a case study of the Acheampong period, 1972–78.* Accra: Ghana UP, 1992, 25pp

Rural economy

2888 **Dei, G J S,** A Ghanaian town revisited: changes and continuities in local adaptive strategies, *African affairs,* 91, 362 (1992) 95–120

2889 **Dei, G J S,** *Hardships and survival in rural West Africa: a case study of a Ghananian community.* Dakar: Codesria, 1991, 142pp

2890 **Jacobeit, C,** Reviving cocoa: policies and perspectives on structural adjustment in Ghana's key agricultural sector, in Rothchild D (ed), *Ghana (entry 2809),* 221–32

2891 **Kasanga, R K,** *Agricultural land administration and social differentiation: a case of the Tono, Vea and Fumbisi belts of northeastern Ghana.* New York: Social Science Research Council, Project on African agriculture, 1992, 40pp

2892 **Manuh, T,** Survival in rural Africa: the salt cooperatives in Ada district, Ghana, in Taylor D R F & Mackenzie, F (eds), *Development from within (entry 1061),* 102–24

2893 **Mikell, G,** Equity issues in

Ghana's rural development, in Rothchild D (ed), *Ghana (entry 2809),* 85–100

2894 **Pearce, R,** Ghana, in Duncan A & Howell, J (eds), *Structural adjustment and the African farmer (entry 1017),* 14–47

2895 **Pickett, J, Shaeeldin, E,** *Comparative advantage in agriculture in Ghana.* Paris: OECD Development Centre, 1990, 40pp

2896 **Songsore, J,** The cooperative credit union movement in northwestern Ghana: development agent or agent of incorporation?, in Taylor D R F & Mackenzie, F (eds), *Development from within (entry 1061),* 82–101

2897 **Vyakarnam, S, Fiafor, J,** Cultural issues in enterprise development: a case study of rural Ghana, *Small enterprise development,* 2, 3 (1991) 37–41

2898 **Wekiyo, I,** Shea butter extraction, *Ahfad journal,* 9, 1 (1992) 17–27

Sociology

see also: 3491, 3492

2899 **Abotchie, C,** The impact of marriage on economic criminality in Ghana, *Criminologist,* 16, 3 (1992) 50–59

Urban studies

2900 **Diko, J, Tipple, A G,** Migrants build at home: long distance housing development by Ghanaians in London, *Cities,* 9, 4 (1992) 288–94

2901 **Hofmann, E,** Veränderungen in den Zugangmöglichkeiten en zu Boden und Wohnraum und ihre Auswirkungen auf die Migrationsstruckturen in Kumasi/Ghana, *Zeitschrift für Wirtschaftlichsgeographie,* 36, 1/2 (1991) 49–60

2902 Korbie, D, Family-houses in Ghanaian cities: to be or not to be?, *Urban studies,* 29, 7 (1992) 1159–72

2903 Malpezzi, S, et al, *Costs and benefits of rent control: a case study in Ghana.* Washington: World Bank, 1990, 139pp

2904 Tipple, A G, Willis, K G, Why should Ghanaians build houses in urban areas? An introduction to private sector housing supply in Ghana, *Cities,* 9, 1 (1992) 60–74

GUINEA

Economy - Development

2905 Boissier, A, Guinea: a long road to recovery, *Africa recovery,* 6, 1 (1992) 20–24

Economic and social history

2906 Dioubate, Y, *Pauvreté et marché du travail à Conkary (République du Guinée).* Geneva: International Institute for Labour Studies, 1992, 91pp

Environment

2907 Botte, R, Les rapports Nord-Sud, la traite négrière et le Fuuta Jaloo à la fin du XVIII siècle, *Annales,* 46, 6 (1991) 1411–35

Environment

2908 Bertrand, F, L'originalité des mangroves de Guinée dans le monde tropical humide, *Les cahiers d'outre-mer,* 44, 176 (1991) 365–378

History, C19th

2909 Pilaszewicz, S, On the veracity of oral tradition as a historical source: the case of Samori Ture, in Pilaszewicz S & Rzewuski, E (eds), *Unwritten testimones (entry 447),* 167–80

Industry & trade

2910 Lambert, A, Les hommes d'affaires guinéens, *Cahiers d'études africaines,* 31, 4 (1991) 487–508

Labour & manpower

2911 Diallo, M, et al, *Guinée: pour une nouvelle syndicalisme en Afrique.* Paris: Harmattan, 1992, 158pp

Law

2912 Roy, P, La Guinée à l'aube de l'État de droit (la loi fondamentale du 31 décembre 1990), *Penant,* 102, 809 (1992)

Literature

2913 Sellin, E, Islamic elements in Camara Laye's *L'enfant noir,* in Harrow K H (ed), *Faces of Islam (entry 710),* 227–36

Politics

see also: 2579

2914 de Raulin, A, La constitution guinéenne du 23 décembre 1990, *Revue juridique et politique,* 46, 2 (1992) 182–190

GUINEA-BISSAU

Anthropology

2915 Scantamburlo, L, *Etnologia dos Bijagos da Ilha de Bubaque.* Lisbon: Instituto de Investigaçïo Cientifica Tropical, 1991, 109pp

Economy - Development

2916 Aguilar, R, Zejan, M,
Guinea-Bissau: a fresh start.
Goteborg: Gothenburg University,
Dept. of Economics, 1991, 73pp
2917 Padovani, F, O Programa de
Ajustamento na Guiné-Bissau e a
dicussïo do modelo, *Soronda,* 11,
(1991) 55–64
2918 Tvedten, I, Programas de
ajustamento estrutural e
implicaçoes locais: o caso dos
pescadores artesanais na
Guiné-Bissau, *Soronda,* 11, (1991)
65–80

Economic and social history

2919 Brooks, G E, Bolama: centro
de interesses imperialistas
africanos, europeus, euro-africanos
e americanos, *Soronda,* 11, (1991)
5–38

Gender

2920 Kipp, E, et al, *Mindjeres:
vrouwen in het Westafrikaanse land
Guinee-Bissau.* Bolsward: Het Witte
Boekhuis, 1991, 103pp

Politics

2921 Forrest, J B, *Guinea-Bissau:
power, conflict and renewal in a west
African nation.* Boulder: Westview,
1992, 165pp
2922 Rudebeck, L, Politics and
structural adjustment in a West
African village, in Rudebeck L (ed),
*When democracy makes sense (entry
931),* 267–84

Rural economy

2923 Alvesson, M, Zeján, M,
Guiné-Bissau: o impacto do
Programa de Ajustamento
Estrutural sobre o bem-estar dos

pequenos proprietários rurais,
Soronda, 11, (1991) 81–103

LIBERIA

Anthropology

see also: 2932
2924 David, M S, 'To be Kwii is
good': a personal account of
research in a Kpelle village,
Liberian studies journal, 17, 2 (1992)
203–15
2925 Sevareid, P, I know money, I
don't know human beings: a Mano
house palaver, *Liberian studies
journal,* 17, 1 (1992) 105–119

Arts

see also: 2933

Current affairs

2926 Brehun, L, *Liberia: the war of
horror.* Legon: Adwinsa, 1991,
156pp
2927 Pulido, C, et al, Liberia:
simple recommendations for
internationalizing a conflict, *Revista
de Africa y Medio Oriente,* 3, 1
(1991) 23–28

Economic and social history

2928 Corby, R A, Cuttington
University College, Liberia: years at
Cape Palmas, 1889–1901, *Liberian
studies journal,* 17, 1 (1992) 1–24
2929 McDaniel, A, Extreme
mortality in nineteenth century
Africa: the case of Liberian
immigrants, *Demography,* 29, 4
(1992) 581–94
2930 Plotzki, E P, The Bong mine
venture, *Liberian studies journal,* 17,
1 (1992) 66–78
2931 Suter, C, Liberia: an enclave
economy at the exterme periphery,
in his *Debt cycles in the world*

economy (Boulder: Westview, 1992), 145–59

Gender

2932 Moran, M H, *Civilised women: gender and prestige in southeastern Liberia.* Ithaca: Cornell UP, 1990, 189pp

2933 Schmidt, C, Group expression and performance among the Kpelle women's associations of Liberia, in Herdon M & Ziegler, S (eds), *Music, gender and culture* (New York: Peters, 1990), 131–42

Health & welfare services

2934 Stephens, C, Back to basics: a community-based environmental health project in West Point, Monrovia, Liberia, *Environment and urbanization,* 3, 1 (1991) 140–146

History, general

2935 Tonkin, E, *Narrating our pasts: the social construction of oral history.* Cambridge: CUP, 1992, 171pp

History, C19th

No entry, see also: 3617

History, C20th

2936 Smyke, R, Nathaniel Varney Massaquoi (1905–1962): a biographical essay, *Liberian studies journal,* 17, 1 (1992) 46–65

Industry & trade

2937 Farmer, G R, Liberian Enterprises Ltd., "...something that will help the people of Liberia", *Liberian studies journal,* 17, 2 (1992) 216–34

International relations

see also: 2942, 3293

2938 Gershoni, Y, The formation of Liberia's boundaries, part 1: agreements, *Liberian studies journal,* 17, 1 (1992) 25–45

2939 Gershoni, Y, The formation of Liberia's boundaries, part 2: the demarcation process, *Liberian studies journal,* 17, 2 (1992) 177–202

2940 Nwokedi, E, *Regional integration and regional security: Ecomog, Nigeria and the Liberian crisis.* Bordeaux: Institut d'études politiques, Université de Bordeaux, 1992, 19pp

Literature

2941 Brown, R H, A short analysis of Bai T Moore's poetry and prose writings, *Liberian studies journal,* 17, 1 (1992) 94–14

Media

2942 Holmes, P A, The Voice of America in Liberia: the end of the road, *Liberian studies journal,* 17, 1 (1992) 79–93

Politics

2943 Kefft, S K, *The dialectics of secret society power in states.* Atlantic Highlands:

Religion, philosophy

see also: 3628

2944 Gifford, P, Liberia's never-die Christians, *Journal of modern African studies,* 30, 2 (1992) 349–58

Rural economy

No entry, see also: 1008

Sociology

2945 Ruiz, H A, Liberia: the
honeymoon is over, *Refugees,* 8
(1992) 30–34

MALI

Agriculture, scientific

see also: 2596
2946 Adesina, A A, Village-level
studies and sorghum technology
development in West Africa: a case
study in Mali, in Moock J L &
Rhoades, R E (eds), *Diversity (entry
1038)* 147–68
2947 Kremer, A R, Pests and
donors in Mali, 1985–90, *Disasters,*
16, 3 (1992) 207–16

Anthropology

2948 Jespers, P, Parler aux morts,
parler aux ancêtres, *Systèmes de
pensée en Afrique noire,* 11, (1991)
181–205
2949 Mateos González, C, Los
Dogones: mito y realidad,
Cuadernos, 6, 4 (1992) 1–16
2950 Müller, F V, *Flexibel aus
Tradition: Strategien wirtschaftlichen
und sozialen Handelns im mittleren
Nigertal (Mali).* Munich: Trickster,
1990, 155pp

Architecture

2951 Maas, P, Mommersteeg, G,
Djenne: chef-d'oeuvre architectural.
Amsterdam: Kit, 1992, 224pp

Arts

2952 Brett-Smith, S, Empty space:
the architecture of Dogon cloth,
Res, 19/20, (1990/91) 162–177
2953 Gruner, D, Töpferei der
Malinke, in Lüdtke H & Vossen, R
(eds), *Töpfereiforschung -*

*archäologisch, ethnologisch,
volkskundusch* (Bonn: Habelt,
1991), 93–103

Current affairs

2954 Bertrand, M, Un an de
transition politique: de la révolte à
la troisième République, *Politique
africaine,* 47 (1992) 9–22
2955 Le Roy, E, Mali: la Troisième
République face à la méfiance des
ruraux, *Politique africaine,* 46
(1992) 138–42

Demography

2956 Cazes, M-H, Dynamique
démographique et évolutive d'un
isolat: les Dogon de Boni, *Études
maliennes,* 44, (1991) 57–64
2957 Hertrich, V, Omissions,
double-comptes, erreurs sur les
âges: les résultats d'une enquête
renouvelée en pays bwa (Mali),
Études maliennes, 44, (1991) 21–38
2958 Petit, V, Vandewalle, H,
Méthodologie et premiers résultats
du recensement de
l'arrondissement de Sangha (pays
Dogon - Mali), *Études maliennes,*
44, (1991) 39–50

Economy - Development

2959 Berthélemy, J C, *L'expérience
de l'allégement de la dette du Mali.*
Paris: OECD Development Centre,
1992, 37pp
2960 Gilguy, C, et al, Le Mali,
Marchés tropicaux et méditerranéens,
48, 2428 (1992) 1319–1357
2961 Lê Châu, Politiques
économiques et crises durant des
trente années d'indépendance,
Politique africaine, 47 (1992) 31–42
2962 Raghavan, M, Les ONG au
Mali, *Politique africaine,* 47 (1992)
91–100

Education

2963 Cisse, S, *L'enseignement islamique en Afrique noire.* Paris: Harmattan, 1992, 220pp

2964 Gérard, E, Entre état et populations: l'école et l'éducation en devenir, *Politique africaine,* 47 (1992) 59–69

2965 Pairault, C, Les langages d'une éducation pour la santé, *Cahiers des sciences humaines,* 27, 3/4 (1991) 343–354

Finance

2966 Bauman, E, Dia, A, Parle-moi d'argent ou le théâtre Koteba au service de la Bank of Africa-Mali, *Cahiers des sciences humaines,* 27, 3/4 (1991) 403–409

Food

see also: 3013

2967 Benini, A A, Armed conflict, access to markets and food crisis warning: a note from Mali, *Disasters,* 16, 3 (1992) 240–48

2968 Cekan, J, Seasonal coping strategies in central Mali: five villages during the 'soudure', *Disasters,* 16, 1 (1992) 66–73

2969 Oshaug, A, et al, *Rapport d'étape: sécurité alimentaire/femmes.* Oslo: Senter for Utvikling og milj, 1992, 7 parts,

2970 Phelinas, P, La stratégie alimentaire entre la famine et l'autosuffisance, *Politique africaine,* 47 (1992) 43–50

2971 Phelinas, P, Libéralisation du commerce des grains et sécurité alimentaire au Mali: les limites du marché, le nouveau rôle de l'État, *Cahiers des sciences humaines,* 27, 1/2 (1991) 65–72

2972 Schmidt-Wulffen, W-D, Food supply assured by market economy? The example of Mali,

Applied geography and development, 37, (1991) 91–106

Gender

see also: 3014

2973 Broetz, G, *'Uns bleibt nur der Hunger'. Zur Handlungsrationalität von Frauen in Mali.* Hamburg: Institute für Afrika-Kunde, 1992, 243pp

2974 Creevey, L, Supporting small-scale enterprises for women farmers in the Sahel, *Journal of international development,* 3, 4 (1991) 35–86

2975 Toulmin, C, *Cattle, women and wells: managing household survival in the Sahel.* Oxford: Clarendon, 1992, 295pp

2976 Vaa, M, Work, livelihoods and family responsibilities in urban poverty, in Stlen K A & Vaa, M (eds), *Gender and change (entry 399)* 121–46

Geography, human

2977 Wagner, H G, A road building project in the Sahel region of Mali (Gourma) as an instrument of development - spatial-economic effects upon traditional subsistance economies, *Applied geography and development,* 36, (1990) 31–44

Health & welfare services

2978 Brunet-Jailly, J, Santé, une occasion manquée: le Mali et 'l'initiative de Bamako', *Afrique contemporaine,* 162 (1992) 3–18

2979 Diarra, A, *Children's health in Mali and the prerequistes for promotion.* Helsinki: Helsinki University, IDS, 1991, 99pp

History, early

2981 Bolland, R, et al, *Tellem*

textiles: archaeological finds from burial caves in Mali's Bandiagara Cliff. Amsterdam: Royal Tropical Institute, 1991, 320pp

2982 **Huysecom, E,** Fanfannyégène: un abri-sous-roche à occupation néolithique au Mali - la fouille, le materiel archéologique. Stuttgart: Steiner, 1990, 79pp

2983 **Raimbault, M, Sanogo, K,** (eds), Recherches archéologiques au Mali. Paris: Karthala, 1991, 563pp

History, C6–18th

2984 **Bolland, R,** Clothing from burial caves in Mali, 11th-18th century, in Smithsonian Museum History design and craft (entry 2510) 53–81

History, C19th

2985 **Grevoz, D,** Les acannoneries de Tomboutou: les français à la conquête de la cité mythique 1870–1894. Paris: Harmattan, 1992, 183pp

2986 **Roberts, R,** The case of Faama Mademba Sy and the ambiguities of legal jurisdiction in early colonial French Soudan, in Mann K & Roberts, R (eds), Law in colonial Africa (entry 684) 185–201

2987 **Saint-Martin, Y-J,** Je vous écris de Ségou: lettres d'Eugène-Abdon Mage, Revue française d'histoire d'outre-mer, 79, 294 (1992) 5–51

Industry & trade

2988 **Maharux, A,** Politiques d'industrialisation, Politique africaine, 47 (1992) 70–78

Language

2989 **D'Ans, A M, et al,** Langues et

métiers modernes ou modernisés au Mali (santé et travail du fer). Paris: Didier Erudition, 1992, 213pp

Library - documentation

2990 **Brassuer, G, Diop, B D,** Se documenter sur le Mali, Politique africaine, 47 (1992) 101–107

2991 **Harmon, S A,** The Malian National Archives at Kaluba: access and applicability, History in Africa, 19, (1992) 441–444

Literature

2992 **Devey, M,** Amadou Hampâté Bâ: l'écrivain de l'oralité, Afrique 2000, 10 (1992) 123–33

2993 **Jouanny, R,** (ed), Lecture d l'oeuvre d'Hampaté Ba. Paris: Harmattan, 1992, 99pp

Media

2994 **Keita, M K,** Réflexion sur la presse écrite, Politique africaine, 47 (1992) 79–90

Medical

see also: 2965

2995 **Bellis, G, Yalkue, Y,** Aspects de la pathologie des Dogon de Sangha, Études maliennes, 44, (1991) 51–56

2996 **Coppo, P, et al,** Perceived morbidity and health behaviour in a Dogon community, Social science and medecine, 34, 11 (1992) 1227–35

2997 **Fargues, P, Nassour, O,** Seasonal variation in urban mortality: the case of Bamako, 1974 to 1985, in van der Walle E et al (eds), Mortality and society (entry 771) 99–122

2998 **Malgras, D,** Arbres et arbustes guérisseurs des savannes amliennes. Paris: Karthala, 1992, 476pp

Natural resources

2999 Djobo, H, et al,
Décentralisation, gouvernance et gestion des resources naturelles renouvelables: options locales dans la République du Mali. Paris: OECD, 1991, 160pp

Politics

3000 Bernus, E, Etre Touareg au Mali*Politique africaine,* 47 (1992) 23–30
3001 Diallo, T D, *Gérer le transition démocratique au Mali.* Bamako: Editions imprimeries du Mali, 1990, 136pp
3002 Diarrah, C O, *Vers la 3ème république du Mali.* Paris: Harmattan, 1992, 236pp
3003 Hall, R E, et al, *L'organisation des services publiques, la participation populaire et la décentralisation: options locales pour l'organisation et la production des services publiques dans la République du Mali.* Paris: OECD, 1991, 78pp
3004 Konaté, M, *Mali: ils ont assassiné l'espoir - réflexions sur le drame d'un peuple.*

Rural economy

see also: 1029, 2974, 3053
3005 Akasaka, M, Small urban center and the development of periodic markets in rural Mali, *African urban studies,* 2, (1992) 1–42
3006 Anhut, R, *Grenzen entwicklungspolitischer Intervention: der politikdialog in der Entwicklungsstrategien.* Wiesbaden: Deutscher Universitäts-Verlag, 1990, 194pp
3007 Baumann, E, Le pécheur, le colonisateur et l'état indépendant, *Politique africaine,* 47 (1992) 51–58
3008 Bourgeot, A, Pastoralism and development in Mali, in Salzman C & Galaty, J G (eds), *Nomads in a changing world* (Naples: Instituto Universitario Orientale, 1990) 383–92
3009 Diawara, G, *Irrigation and the Soninke people: organisational and management problems, current situation and prospects.* London: ODI, Irrigation Management Network, 1992, 25pp
3010 Haidara, A K Y, *Ländliche Entwicklung und die 'Tön'-Strategie in Mali.* Hamburg: Institut für Afrika-Kunde, 1992, 319pp
3011 Hijkoop, J, et al, *Une lutte de longue haleine...: aménagments anti-érosifs et gestion de terrior.* Bamako: Institut d'économie rurale, 1991, 155pp
3012 Krings, T, *Agrarwissen bäuerlicher Gruppen in Mali, Westafrika: Standortgerechte Elemente in den Landnutzungssystemen der Senoufo, Bwa, Dogon und Somono.* Berlin: Reimer, 1991, 301pp
3013 Miaga, A, et al, *The harvesting of wild-growing grain crops in the Gourma region of Mali.* London: IIED, 1991, 13pp
3014 Schulz, D, *'Ni wari t'i bolo' oder 'Wenn Du kein Geld hast': Handlungsspielräume von Bäuerinnen in der Sahelzone.* Mainz: Titus Grab, 1990, 142pp
3015 van Duivenbooden, N, et al, (eds), *Competing for limited resources: the case of the fifth region of Mali. Report 2: plant, livestock and fish production.* Wageningen: Centre for Agrobiological Research, Wageningen Agricultural University, 1991, 242, 55pp
3016 Veeneklaas, F R, et al, *Competing for limited resources: the case of the fifth region of Mali. Report 4: development scenarios.* Wageningen: Centre for Agrobiological Research,

Wageningen Agricultural
University, 1991, 144, 37pp

Science & technology

3017 Keita, M, Rolle und Funktion
der Wissenschaft und der
internationales
Wissenschaftskooperation in
Process des Gesellschaftswandels in
Afrika: der Fallbeispiel Mali, in
Heise K F & Kyaw Tha Tun (eds),
*Traditionelles Wissen und
Modernisierung* (Gottingen:
Afrikanisch-Asiaticshe
Studentenförderung, 1991), 112–36

Sociology

3018 Bagayogo, S, L'hospitalité
dans l'aire culturelle mandingue,
Études maliennes, 44, (1991) 3–20

Urban studies

see also: 2976
3019 van Westen, A C M, Land
supply for low income housing,
Bamako, Mali: its evolution and
performance, in Baross P & van der
Linden, J (eds), *Transformation of
land supply systems in Third World
cities* (Aldershot: Avebury, 1992),
81–110

MAURITANIA

Economy - Development

see also: 1503
3020 Lassalle, P, Sugier, J B,
*Rituels et développement ou le jardin
du Soufi.* Paris: Harmattan, 1992,
175pp

Education

3021 Hirth, M, *Traditionelle Bildung
und Erziehung in Mauretanien: zum
entwicklungspolitischen Potential der*

maurischen mahadra. Franfurt:
Lang, 1991, 368pp

Industry & trade

3022 Audibert, J, *MIFERMA: une
aventure humaine et industrielle en
Mauritanie.* Paris: Harmattan,
1991, 216pp

International economic relations

No entry, see also: 1515, 1516, 1517

International relations

see also: 3550
3023 Pazzanita, A G, Mauritania's
foreign policy: the search for
protection, *Journal of modern
African studies,* 30, 2 (1992)
281–304

Law

3024 Villasante-de Beauvais, M,
Hiérarchies statutaires et conflits
fonciers dans l'Assaba contemporain
(Mauritanie): rupture ou
continuité?, *Revue du monde
musulman et de la Méditerrananée,*
59/60 (1991) 181–210

Library - documentation

3025 Cortese, D, et al, *Mauritania.*
Oxford: Clio, 1992, 165pp

Literature

3026 Martin Granel, N, et al,
*Guide de la littérature mauritanienne:
une anthologie méthodique.* Paris:
Harmattan, 1992, 204pp

Politics

see also: 3578
3027 Marchesin, P, *Tribus, ethnies
et pouvoir en Mauritanie.* Paris:

Karthala, 1992, 437pp

Rural economy

3028 Hutchinson, C F, Integration of the remote sensing and farming systems research in West Africa, in Bishay A & Dregne, H (eds), *Desert development ; Part 1* (London: Harwood, 1991), 59–68

Sociology

see also: 3598
3029 Lefort, F Bader, C, *Mauritanie: la vie reconciliée.* Paris: Fayard, 1991, 238pp

NIGER

Anthropology

see also: 2504, 3053
3030 de Latour, E, *Les temps de pouvoir.* Paris: CID, 1992, 208pp
3031 Oxby, C, The 'living milk' runs dry: the decline of a form of joint ownership and matrilineal inheritance among the Twareg (Niger), in Baxter P T W & Hogg, R (eds), *Property, poverty and people (entry 1000)*, 222–28
3032 Ramir, S, *Les pistes de l'oubli: Touaregs su Niger.* Paris: Felin, 1991, 179pp
3033 White, C, Changing animal ownership and access to land among the Wodaabe (Fulani) of central Niger, in Baxter P T W & Hogg, R (eds), *Property, poverty and people (entry 1000)*, 240–54

Arts

3034 Issa, M, *Oumarou Ganda, cinéaste nigérien: un regard du dedans sur la société en transition.* Dakar: Enda, 1991, 80pp

Economy - Development

see also: 3042
3035 Joumard, I, et al, *The impact of laws and regulations on micro and small enterprises in Niger and Swaziland.* Paris: OECD Development Centre, 1992, 92pp
3036 Riedel, J, *Sozio-kulturelle Herausforderungen für die Entwicklungspolitik: die Republik Niger.* Munich : Weltforum, 1990, 457pp
3037 Tinguiri, K L, Stabilisation without structural adjustment: the case of Niger, 1982–9, in Cornia A G et al (eds), *Africa's recovery (entry 124)*, 53–71

Economic and social history

3038 Gregoire, E, *The Alhazai of Maradi: traditional Hausa merchants in a changing sahelian city.* Boulder: Lynne Reinner, 1992, 185pp
3039 Weiss, R, *Wandel des Agrarsystems und Ernärungssicherung in Niger.* Hamburg: Institut für Afrika-Kunde, 1990, 209pp

Environment

3040 Bargel, G, *Desertifikationbekämpfung und soziale Organisation: möglichkeiten und Grenzen der Implementierung technischer Massnahmen zum Erosionsschutz im Niger.* Berlin: Technical University, 1990, 39pp

Food

No entry, see also: 3039

Geography, physical

3041 Sivakumar, M V K, Climate change and implications for agriculture in Niger, *Climatic change*, 20, 4 (1992) 297–312

Industry & trade

No entry, see also: 504

International economic relations

see also: 3280

3042 Vourc'h, A, Boukar Massa,
V, *L'expérience de l'allégement de la*
dette du Niger. Paris: OECD
Development Centre, 1992, 30pp

Law

see also: 3035

3043 Maidoka, A, La constitution
nigérienne de 24 septembre 1989,
Revue juridique et politique, 45, 2
(1991) 113–32
3044 Maidoka, A, La nouvelle
organisation des pouvoirs publics
nigériens: l'acte fondamental no.
21, *Revue juridique et politique,* 46, 1
(1992) 46–53
3045 Tankoano, A, La révision de
la constitution du 24 septembre
1989 et l'évolution du régime
politique nigérien,
Revue juridique et politique, 46, 1
(1992) 54–78

Natural resources

3046 Baumhauer, R, Hagedorn,
H, Problems of groundwater
capture in the Kawar (Niger),
Applied geography and development,
36, (1990) 99–109
3047 Schenker, A,
Goumandayoke, M, Water-point
rehabilitation and management in
the pastoral zone of Niger, West
Africa, in Bishay A & Dregne, H
(eds), *Desert development ; Part 1*
(London: Harwood, 1991), 339–58

Politics

see also: 2694
3048 Ibrahim, J, From popular

exclusion to popular participation:
democratic transition in Niger, in
Caron B et al (eds), *Democratic*
transition in Africa (entry 817),
51–68
3049 Martin, F, *Le Niger du Prés.*
Diori: chronologie 1960–1974. Paris:
Harmattan, 1991, 421pp

Religion, philosophy

3050 Grégoire, E, Accumulation
marchande et propagation de
l'islam en milieu urbain: le cas de
Maradi (Niger), *Islam et sociétés au*
Sud du Sahara, 5 (1991) 43–55

Rural economy

see also: 2182
3051 de Coninck, J, Tinguiri, K L,
Niger, in Duncan A & Howell, J
(eds), *Structural adjustment and the*
African farmer (entry 1017), 158–98
3052 Schenker, A,
Goumandayoke, M, Future
strategies for marginal agropastoral
subsistence economies in
subsaharan Africa: Niger
experiences, in Bishay A & Dregne,
H (eds), *Desert development ;*
Part 1 (London: Harwood, 1991),
569–85
3053 Seddon, D, Anthropology and
appraisal: the preparation of two
IFAD pastoral development
project, in Pottier J (ed), *Practising*
development: social science perspectives
(London: Routledge, 1992),
71–109
3054 Sutter, J W, Commercial
strategies, drought and monetary
pressure: Wodaabe nomads of
Tanout arrondissement, Niger, in
Salzman C & Galaty, J G (eds),
Nomads in a changing world
(Naples: Instituto Universitario
Orientale, 1990) 339–82

Sociology

3055 Djirmey, A, et al, Lutte et identité culturelle au Niger, *Politique africaine,* 45 (1992) 142–48

NIGERIA

General

3056 Bergstresser, H, *Nigeria.* Munich: Beck, 1991, 126pp

Agriculture, scientific

see also: 3152
3057 Adegbehin, J O, et al, Resources of the mangrove with special reference to the coastal areas of Nigeria: their utilization and management perspective, *Discovery and innovation,* 3, 2 (1991) 37–45
3058 Ezenwa, M I S, Important considersations for choice of species for the scattered farm tree agroforestry model in the sudano-sahelian area of Nigeria, *Savanna,* 12, 1 (1991) 65–72
3059 Goldsmith, A A, *Building agricultural institutions: transferring the land-grant model to India and Nigeria.* Boulder: Westview, 1990, 270pp
3060 Okagbue, R N, Microbiology and traditional methods of food processing in Nigeria, in Thomas-Emeagwali G (ed), *Science and technology in Nigeria (entry 450),* 37–46
3061 Osunade, M A A, Identification of crop soils by small farmers of south-western Nigeria, *Journal of environmental management,* 35, 3 (1992) 193–203
3062 Thomas-Emeagwali, G, Lasisi, R O, Change in cassava processing technology in Nigeria, in Thomas-Emeagwali G (ed),

Science and technology in Nigeria (entry 450), 47–61

Anthropology

see also: 3238, 3317
3063 Abasiattai, M B, *The Ibibio: an introduction to the land, the people and their culture.* Calabar: Wusen Printing Press, 1991, 604pp
3064 Babatunde, E D, *A critical study of Bini and Yoruba value systems of Nigeria in change.* Lewiston: Mellen, 1992, 288pp
3065 McKenzie, P, Dreams and visions from nineteenth century Yoruba religion, in Jedrej M C & Shaw, R (eds), *Dreaming, religion and society (entry 42),* 126–34
3066 Nicolas, G, Recompositions sacrificiales au Nigeria contemporain, *Archives européene de sociologie,* 32, 2 (1991) 299–326
3067 Nwokocha, C C A, La cola simbolo di amore e du inta per gli Ibo, *Afriche,* 2, 7 (1990) 1–33
3068 Ojoade, J O, Proverbs as repositories of traditional medical practice in Nigeria, in Thomas-Emeagwali G (ed), *Science and technology in African history (entry 450),* 1–21
3069 Okebalama, C N, The hunter in Ubàkala Igbo life, *African languages and cultures,* 4, 2 (1991) 177–187
3070 Omojola, B, Kiriboto music in Yoruba culture, *Bulletin of the international committee on urgent anthropological and ethnological research,* 32/33 (1990/91) 121–142
3071 Osunwole, S, Witchcraft and sorcery: Yoruba beliefs and medecine, *Orita,* 23, 2 (1991) 73–82
3072 Ray, K, Dreams of grandeur: the call to the office in northcentral Igbo religious leadership, in Jedrej M C & Shaw, R (eds), *Dreaming, religion and society (entry 42),* 55–70

3073 Weingarten, S, *Zur materiellen Kultur der Befölkerung des Jos-Plateaus.* Stuttgart: Steiner, 1990, 258pp

Arts

3074 Euba, A, *Yoruba drumming: the dundun tradition.* Altendorg: Gräbner, 1990, 548pp

3075 Hagher, I H, (ed), *The practice of community theatre in Nigeria.* Lagos: Lobi Consortium, 1990, 111pp

3076 Hagher, I H, *The Tiv Kwagh-hir: a popular Nigerian puppet theatre.* Ibadan: Shaneson, 1990, 224pp

3077 Layiwola, D, The radical alternative and the dilemma of the intellectual dramatist in Nigeria, *Ufahamu,* 19, 1 (1991) 64–79

3078 Ogundele, S O, Aspects of Tiv pottery: present and past, *African study monographs,* 12, 3 (1991) 119–31

3079 Perani, J, The cloth connection: patrons and producers of Hausa and Nupe prestige strip-weave, in Smithsonian Museum *History design and craft (entry 2510),* 95–112

3080 Sauer, M E, Nigeria and India: the use of film for development - whispers in a crowd, *Africa media review,* 6, 1 (1992) 25–33

3081 Ukpokodu, I P, *Socio-political theatre in Nigeria.* Lewiston: Mellen, 1992, 300pp

Current affairs

3082 Saro-Wiwa, K, *Similia: essays on anomic Nigeria.* Port Harcourt: Saros, 1991, 200pp

Demography

3083 Dimkpa-Harry, S,

Probabilistic analysis of fertility and fecundity: an application to Tombia in Rivers State, Nigeria, *African study monographs,* 12, 3 (1991) 161–66

3084 Feyisetan, B J, Bankole, A, Mate selection and fertility in northern Nigeria, *Journal of comparative family studies,* 22, 3 (1991) 273–92

Economy - Development

see also: 3472, 3496

3085 Adeoye, A O, Of economic masquerades and vulgar economy: a critique of the structural adjustment program in Nigera, *Africa development,* 16, 1 (1991) 23–44

3086 Agbaje, A, Adjusting state and market in Nigeria: the paradoxes of orthodoxy, *Afrika spectrum,* 27, 2 (1992) 123–137

3087 Agbese, P O, Moral economy and the expansion of the privatisation constituency in Nigeria, *Journal of Commonwealth and comparative politics,* 30, 3 (1992) 335–57

3088 Ajaikaiye, D O, *Public enterprise policies in Nigeria (a macroeconomic impact analysis).* Ibadan: NISER, 1990, 87pp

3089 Akinlo, A E, Export instability and savings behaviour in Nigeria: a simultaneous equation approach, *Indian journal of economics,* 72, 285 (1991) 203–211

3090 Anyanwu, J, President Babangida's structural adjustment programme and inflation in Nigeria, *Journal of social development in Africa,* 7, 1 (1992) 5–24

3091 Anyiwe, M A, The incidence of socio-economic burden of the Nigerian structural adjustment programme, *Indian journal of economics,* 72, 285 (1991) 133–150

3092 Babalola, A, BAT and the

penetration of capital into Oyo State, *Review of African political economy,* 53 (1992) 96–101

3093 **Bangura, Y,** Structural adjustment and deindustrialisation in Nigeria: 1986–1988, *Africa development,* 16, 2 (1991) 5–32

3094 **Blanden, M,** For sale signs go up in Lagos, *Banker,* Oct 1992 22–28

3095 **Davies, A E H,** The IMF in the Nigerian economy: pressures and responses, *India quarterly,* 46, 4 (1990) 91–114

3096 **Dayomi, A, Alokan, O,** The economic context of democratic transition in Africa: the case of Nigeria, in Caron B et al (eds), *Democratic transition in Africa (entry 817),* 359–77

3097 **Ekpo, A H, Ndebbio, J E U,** The economics of public enterprise in Nigeria: implications for recovery and development, *Public enterprise,* 11, 4 (1991) 258–67

3098 **Ezeala-Harrison, F,** An empirical framework for the efficiency-wage model: use of micro-data for Nigeria, *Journal of economic studies,* 19, 3 (1992) 18–35

3099 **Fadahunsi, A,** Devaluation: impact on employment, inflation, growth and development, in Olukoshi A O (ed), *Structural adjustment in Nigeria (entry 3111),* 33–53

3100 **Forrest, T,** The advance of African capital: the growth of NIgerian private enterprise, in Stewart F et al (eds), *Alternative development strategies (entry 223),* 368–401

3101 **Ibi Ajayi, S,** *Macroeconomic approach to external debt: the case of Nigeria.* Nairobi: Initiatives, for African Economic Research Consortium, 1991, 66pp

3102 **Kuye, O A,** Problems and prospects of Nigeria's privatisation and commercialisation programme,

Quarterly journal of administration, 25, 1 (1990/1991) 49–73

3103 **Mbachu, O,** Strains and economic demand of structural adjustment programme in Nigeria: some implications, *Africa (Rome),* 46, 3 (1991) 427–439

3104 **Mosley, P,** Policy-making without facts: a note on the assessment of structural adjustment policies in Nigeria, 1985–1990, *African affairs,* 91, 363 (1992) 227–40

3105 **Mustapha, A R,** Structural adjustment and multiple modes of livelihood in Nigeria, in Gibbon P & Bangura, Y (eds), *Authoritarianism, democracy and adjustment (entry 850),* 188–216

3106 **Ogbe, N E,** *Evaluation of Nigeria's debt-relief experience (1985–1990).* Paris: OECD Development Centre, 1992, 49pp

3107 **Ogbonna, D O,** The role of the energy sector in achieving stable development in Nigeria, *Savanna,* 12, 1 (1991) 34–51

3108 **Okolie, A C,** Economic crisis, structural adjustment, and prospects for political stability in Nigeria's Third Republic, *Ufahamu,* 19, 1 (1991) 44–63

3109 **Okonkwo, I C,** The political economy of privatisation in Nigeria, *Public enterprise,* 11, 4 (1991) 303–13

3110 **Olowu, D, et al,** (eds), *Local institutions and national development in Nigeria.* Ile-Ife: Awolowu UP, 1991, 142pp

3111 **Olukoshi, A O,** (ed), *The politics of structural adjustment in Nigeria.* London: Currey, 1992, 144pp

3112 **Olukoshi, A O,** General introduction: from crisis to adjustment in Nigeria, in Olukoshi A O (ed), *Structural adjustment in Nigeria (entry 3111),* 1–13

3113 **Omo-Bare, I,** Economic

development in Nigeria: an examination of public policy under military and civilian led regimes, *Scandinavian journal of development alternatives*, 11, 3/4 (1992) 91–109

3114 **Onah, F E,** Privatization and commercialization: the Nigerian experience, *African development perspectives yearbook*, 2, (1990/91) 619–631

3115 **Orugbani, A,** The debt trap and the current crisis in Nigeria: an historical analysis, *India quarterly*, 46, 4 (1990) 55–80

3116 **Robertson, J W,** The process of trade reform in Nigeria and the pursuit of structural adjustment, in Milner C & Rayner, A J (eds), *Policy adjustment (entry 184)*, 173–95

3117 **Wilfert, A,** *Vom 'Oilboom' zum 'SAP': die Entwicklung der wirtschaftspolitischen Rahmenbedingungen in Nigeria.* Bayreuth: Bayreuth University, 1990, 69pp

Economic and social history

3118 **Abubakar, N,** Metallurgy in northern Nigeria: Zamfara metal industry in the nineteenth century, in Thomas-Emeagwali G (ed), *Science and technology in African history (entry 450)*, 55–77

3119 **Adebayo, A G,** The production and export of hides and skins in colonial northern Nigeria, 1900–1945, *Journal of African history*, 33, 2 (1992) 273–300

3120 **Adebayo, A G,** Taming the nomads: the colonial state, the Fulani pastoralists and the production of clarified butter fat (CBF) in Nigeria, *Transafrican journal of history*, 20 (1991) 190–212

3121 **Andulkadie, M S,** Textile technology in nineteenth century Igalaland, central Nigeria, in

Thomas-Emeagwali G (ed), *Science and technology in Nigeria (entry 450)*, 135–44

3122 **Babalola, E O,** The significance of traditional African and Christian marriage in the islamisation of Yorubaland, *Africa theological journal*, 20, 3 (1991) 201–209

3123 **Bell-Gam, W I,** *Development of coastal and estuarine settlements in the Niger Delta: the case of Bonny Local Government Area.* Berne: Lang, 1990, 454pp

3124 **Christelow, A,** Theft, homicide, and oathing in early twentieth century Kano, in Mann K & Roberts, R (eds), *Law in colonial Africa (entry 684)*, 205–23

3125 **Guyer, J I,** *British, colonial and postcolonial food regulation, with reference to Nigeria: an essay in formal sector anthropology.* Boston: African Studies Centre, Boston University, 1991, 18pp

3126 **Mann, K,** The rise of Taiwo Olowo: law, accumulation and mobility in early colonial Lagos, in Mann K & Roberts, R (eds), *Law in colonial Africa (entry 684)*, 85–107

3127 **Njoku, O N,** Colonialism and the decline of the traditional metal industry of the Igbo, Nigeria, *Itinerario*, 15, 2 (1991) 59–78

3128 **Nzemeke, A D,** Local patronage and commercial enterprise in Lagos 1850–1861, *Africa (Rome)*, 47, 1 (1992) 105–114

3129 **O'Hear, A,** The introduction of weft float motifs to strip weaving in Ilorin, in Henige D & McCaskie, T C (eds), *West African economic and social history (entry 2521)*, 175–88

3130 **Olukoju, A,** Elder Dempster and the shipping trade of Nigeria during the First World War, *Journal of African history*, 33, 2 (1992) 255–71

3131 **Oshin, O,** Historical roots of the rural development problem, in Olanrewaju S A & Falola, T (eds), *Rural development problems in Nigeria (entry 3476)*, 19–42

3132 **Thomas-Emeagwali, G, Idress, AA,** Glass-making technology in Nupeland, central Nigeria; some questions, in Thomas-Emeagwali G (ed), *Science and technology in African history (entry 450)*, 129–45

Education

see also: 3190, 3199

3133 **Ajayi, K, Ajayi, T,** *New perspectives in Nigerian education.* Ibadan: Vantage, 1990, 200pp

3134 **Atteh, S O,** A comparative analysis of Nigerian educational policies for national integration, 1842–1990, *Scandinavian journal of development alternatives,* 11, 3/4 (1992) 137–173

3135 **Boehm, U,** *Vocational training in Nigeria: project planning study.* Bremen: Universität Bremen, Nord-Süd Forum, 1992, 48pp

3136 **Chuta, E J,** Student loans in Nigeria, *Higher education,* 23, 4 (1991) 443–49

3137 **Fafunwa, A B,** *History of education in Nigeria.* Ibadan: Nigerian Publishers Services, 1991, 320pp

3138 **Fafunwa, A B,** *Up and on! A Nigerian teacher's odyssey.* Ikeja: John West, 1990, 299pp

3139 **Godonoo, P,** The perceived role of literacy and its attendant problems in Nigeria, *Ufahamu,* 19, 1 (1991) 80–91

3140 **ibn Junaid, M, Lewis, I,** The educational process in Africa: questions in consideration of the nomadic Fulani of Nigeria, in Irele A (ed), *African education and identity (entry 268)*, 67–78

3141 **Ikhariale, M A,** The institution of the Visitor, in English and overseas universities: problem of its use in Nigeria, *International and comparative law quarterly,* 40, 3 (1991) 699–716

3142 **Kemi, O,** Academic performance as a function of preschool education: a study of private and public primary schools in Nigeria, *Ethiopian journal of education,* 11, 2 (1990) 129–159

3143 **Nkpa, N,** Science teaching in Nigerian institutions, in Thomas-Emeagwali G (ed), *Science and technology in Nigeria (entry 450)*, 77–105

3144 **Ojo, J D,** *Law and university administration in Nigeria.* Lagos: Malthouse, 1990, 200pp

3145 **Okedara, J T, Okedara, C A,** Mother-tongue literacy in Nigeria, *Annals,* 520 (1992) 91–102

3146 **Olaloye, A O, Ogunrinola, I O,** Short run demand function for university education in Nigeria, *Tanzania journal of economics,* 2, 1 (1990) 77–84

3147 **Omole, M A L,** Mass literacy campaigns in Nigeria: learning from the Ethiopian experience, *Journal of the African Association for Literacy and Adult Education,* 5, 3 (1991) 17–24

3148 **Omotara, B A,** The dynamics of medical students' career and medical speciality choices: a Maiduguri Medical School study, *East african medical journal,* 68, 7 (1991) 547–554

3149 **Urwick, J, Junaidu, S U,** The effects of school physical facilities on the processes of education: a qualitative study of Nigerian primary schools, *International journal of educational development,* 11, 1 (1991) 19–30

Environment

see also: 3370

172

West Africa

3150 **Aina, T A, Salau, A T,** (eds), *The challenge of sustainable development in Nigeria.* Ibadan: Nigerian Environmental Study Action Team, 1992, 248pp

3151 **Ariyo, J A,** (ed), *Environmental issues.* Zaria: Ahmadu Bello University, Dept. of Geography, 1992, 53pp

3152 **Ehui, S K, et al,** Economic analysis of soil erosion effects in alley-cropping. no-till and bush-fallow systems in southwest Nigeria, in Moock J L & Rhoades, R E (eds), *Diversity (entry 1038),* 225–45

3153 **Goldman, A,** Resource degradation, agricultural change and sustainability in farming systems in southeast Nigeria, in Moock J L & Rhoades, R E (eds), *Diversity (entry 1038),* 246–72

3154 **Neiland, A Vernumbe, I,** *Fisheries development and resource usage conflict: a case study of deforestation associated with the Lake Chad Fishery in Nigeria.* Portsmouth: Portsmouth Polytechnic, Centre for Marine Resource Economics, 1990, 23pp

3155 **Ologe, K O,** (ed), *Sustainable development in Nigeria's dry belt: problems and prospects.* Ibadan: Nigerian Environmental Study Action Team, 1991, 112pp

3156 **Saro-Wiwa, K,** *Genocide in Nigeria: the Ogoni tragedy.* Port Harcourt: Saros, 1992, 103pp

Finance

3157 **Agu, C C,** Analysis of the determinants of the Nigerian banking system's profits and profitability performance, *Savings and development,* 16, 4 (1992) 353–370

3158 **Agu, C,** *The financial sector in Nigeria: overview and reform in economic adjustment programmes.*

Bangor: University College of North Wates, Institute of European Finance, 1992, 29pp

3159 **Aigbokhan, B E,** The Naira exchange rate depreciation and domestic inflation, *Indian journal of economics,* 71, 283 (1991) 507–16

3160 **Akintola-Arikawe, J O,** *Central development banking and Nigerian maufacturing: the role of the National Industrial Development Bank in regional development perspective.* Lagos: University of Lagos Press, 1990, 209pp

3161 **Alawode, A A,** Financial deregulation and the effectiveness of bank supervision in Nigeria, *Savings and development,* 16, 1 (1992) 101–13

3162 **Central Bank of Nigeria,** The Nigerian experience, in Roe A R et al (ed) *Instruments of economic policy (entry 341),* 156–68

3163 **Ibe, A C,** Ownership structure and performance in the banking industry in Nigeria, *Savings and development,* 16, 3 (1992) 243–54

3164 **Jimoh, A,** The monetary approach to balance of payments evidence from Nigeria, *Eastern Africa economic review,* 6, 1 (1990) 69–75

3165 **Nwankwo, G O,** *Money and capital markets in Nigeria today.* Lagos: University of Lagos Press, 1991, 75pp

3166 **Ojo, J A T,** *Financial sector management and Nigeria's economic transformation problem.* Lagos: University of Lagos Press, 1992, 49pp

3167 **Osuntogun, A, et al,** The impact of specialised small-holder credit programmes on farmer-beneficiaries: a case study of the First Bank of Nigeria Community Loan Scheme in Oyo State of Nigeria, *African review of money finance and banking,* 1 (1992) 75–87

3168 Taiwo, I O, A flow-of-funds approach to savings mobilisation using nigerian data, *Savings and development,* 16, 2 (1992) 169–182

Food

3169 Abidoye, R, Randle, O, Comparative nutritional assessment of children in military and private schools in Nigeria, *Nutrition research,* 11, 9 (1991) 989–99

3170 Bentley, M E, et al, Development of a nutritionally adequate and culturally appropriate weaning food in Kwara State, Nigeria; an interdisciplinary approach, *Social science and medecine,* 33, 10 (1991) 1103–1111

3171 Gefu, J O, Part-time farming as an urban survival strategy, in Baker J & Pedersen, P O (eds), *Rural-urban interface (entry 1111),* 295–302

3172 Okuneye, P A, The problem of declining food production, in Olanrewaju S A & Falola, T (eds), *Rural development problems in Nigeria (entry 3476),* 56–82

Gender

see also: 3229, 3339, 3359

3173 Akande, J, et al, *The contribution of women to national development in Nigeria.* Lagos: University of Lagos, 1990, 102pp

3174 Akande, M, Enhancing the performance of women's multiple roles: a case study of Isoya Rural Development Programme, Ile-Ife, Nigeria, *Community development journal,* 27, 1 (1992) 60–68

3175 Anyanwu, J C, Women's access to credit facilities from commercial banks in Nigeria: challenges for the 1990s, *Savings and development,* 16, 4 (1992) 421–440

3176 Awe, B, (ed), *Nigerian women in historical perspective.* Benin City: Sankore, 1992, 167pp

3177 Chhachhi, A, Pittin, R, *Multiple identities, multiple strategies: confronting state, capital and patriarchy.* The Hague: Institute of Social Studies, 1991, 42pp

3178 Crumbley, D H, Impurity and power: women in Aladura churches, *Africa,* 62, 4 (1992) 505–22

3179 Dennis, C, The christian churches and women's experience of structural adjustment in Nigeria, in Afshar H & Dennis, C (eds), *Women and adjustment policies in the Third World* (Basingstoke: Macmillan, 1991), 179–204

3180 Hollos, M, Migration, education, and the status of women in Southern Nigeria, *American anthropologist,* 93, 4 (1991) 852–870

3181 Ibie, N O, Media/cultural imperialism and Nigerian women: whose culture, which imperialism?, *Journal of social development in Africa,* 7, 2 (1992) 39–52

3182 Koster, R, *Hausa vrouwen en Islam.* Leiden: Onderzoek en Dokumentatiecentrum Vrouwen en Autonomie, 1990, 77pp

3183 Mack, B B, Women and slavery in nineteenth century Hausaland, in Savage E (ed), *The human commodity (entry 252),* 89–110

3184 Okonjo, K, *Nigerian women's participation in national politics.* East Lansing: Michigan State University, 1991, 46pp

3185 Okunna, C S, Female faculty in journalism education in Nigeria: implications for the status of women in society, *Africa media review,* 6, 1 (1992) 47–58

3186 Okunna, C S, Sources of development information among rural women in Nigeria: a case study, *Africa media review,* 6, 3 (1992) 65–77

3187 Olurode, L, (ed), *Women and social change in Nigeria.* Festac City, Lagos State: Unity, 1990, 161pp

3188 Oruwari, Y, The changing role of women in families and their housing needs: a case study of Port Harcourt, Nigeria, *Environment and urbanization*, 3, 2 (1991) 6–12

3189 Owens-Ibie, N, Domestic miscommunication as a development constraint: a study of wife-beating among selected junior workers, *Africa media review*, 6, 1 (1992) 35–47

3190 Pittin, R, *Selective education: issues of gender, class and ideology in northern Nigeria.* The Hague: Institute of Social Studies, 1990, 42pp

3191 Thomas-Emeagwali, G, The intersection of gender and technology in Nigeria, in Thomas-Emeagwali G (ed), *Science and technology in Nigeria (entry 450)*, 161–70

Geography, human

3192 Chokor, B A, Mene, S A, An assessment of preference for landscapes in the developing world: case study of Warri, Nigeria, and environs, *Journal of environmental management*, 34, 4 (1992) 237–256

3193 Okafor, S I, Distributive effects of location: government hospitals in Ibadan, *Area*, 24, 4 (1992) 128–35

Geography, physical

3194 Balogun, E E, *Scientific challenges and the importance of weather prediction in Nigeria.* Ile-Ife: Awolowo University Press, 1991, 42pp

3195 Olaniran, O J, Evidence of climatic change in Nigeria based on annual series of rainfall of different daily amounts, 1919–1985,

Climatic change, 19, 3 (1991) 319–340

Health & welfare services

see also: 3193

3196 Alubo, S O, Health services and military messianism in Nigeria (1983–1990), *Journal of social development in Africa*, 7, 1 (1992) 45–65

3197 Black, M, *From handpumps to health: the evolution of water and sanitation programmes in Bangladesh, India and Nigeria.* New York: United Nations Childrens Fund, 1990, 133pp

3198 Olokesusi, A O, The rural health care delivery problem, in Olanrewaju S A & Falola, T (eds), *Rural development problems in Nigeria (entry 3476)*, 134–56

History, general

see also: 450, 3487

3199 Abubakar, T, (ed), *The essential Mahmud: selected writings of Mahmud Modibbo Tukur.* Zaria: Ahmadu Bello UP, 1990, 421pp

3200 Achi, B, Biologically based warfare in precolonial Nigeria, in Thomas-Emeagwali G (ed), *Science and technology in African history (entry 3487)*, 23–31

3201 Adeoye, A O, Understanding the crisis in modern Nigerian historiography, *History in Africa*, 19, (1992) 1–11

3202 Afolayan, F, Towards a history of eastern Yorubaland, in Falola T (ed), *Yoruba historiography (entry 3205)*, 75–87

3203 Danmole, H O, Arabic historiography on the Yoruba, in Falola T (ed), *Yoruba historiography (entry 3205)*, 89–104

3204 Erim, E O, Songs as sources of history, *Itan: Bensu journal of historical studies*, 1 (1990) 36–44

3205 Falola, T, (ed), *Yoruba historiography.* Madison: University of Wisconsin, African Studies Program, 1991, 214pp

3206 Falola, T, The minor works of T.O. Avoseh, *History in Africa,* 19, (1992) 237–262

3207 Farias, P F de Moraes, History and consolation: royal Yorùbá bards comment on their craft, *History in Africa,* 19, (1992) 263–297

3208 Jansen, H G P, Dairy consumption in northern Nigeria: implications for development policies, *Food policy,* 17, 3 (1992) 214–226

3209 Lawuyi, O B, Studies on traditional religion, in Falola T (ed), *Yoruba historiography (entry 3205),* 43–49

3210 Pawlak, N, Historical inferences to be drawn from the Hausa names of plants, in Pilaszewicz S & Rzewuski, E (eds), *Unwritten testimonies (entry 447),* 97–103

History, early

3211 Agbaje-Williams, B, Archaeology and Yoruba studies, in Falola T (ed), *Yoruba historiography (entry 3205),* 5–29

3212 Anozie, F N, Twenty-six tears of archaeology in Bendel state, *Nigerian journal of the humanities,* 7 (1990) 38–44

3213 Longtau, S R, Linguistic evidence on the origins of the peoples: the case of the Tarok people of Plateau State (Nigeria), *Afrika und Übersee,* 74, 2 (1991) 191–204

History, C6–18th

3214 Barkindo, B M, The royal pilgrimage tradition of the Saifawa of Kanem and Borno, in Ajayi J F A & Peel, J D Y (eds), *Peoples and empires (entry 429),* 1–20

3215 Webster, J B, Pre-dynastic Uromi: a model - I, *Itan: Bensu journal of historical studies,* 1 (1990) 1–12

History, C19th

3216 Achi, B, Military technology in Nigeria before 1900, in Thomas-Emeagwali G (ed), *Science and technology in Nigeria (entry 450),* 145–58

3217 Amadi, I R, Human rights in pre-colonial Igbo society of Nigeria: an analysis, *Africa (Rome),* 46, 3 (1991) 403–410

3218 Apata, Z O, Ilorin-Lagos relations in the nineteenth century: a study of British imperial struggle in Yorubaland, *Transafrican journal of history,* 20 (1991) 145–60

3219 Atanda, J A, The Fulani jihad and the collapse of the Old Oyo empire, in Falola T ((ed)), *Yoruba historiography (entry 3205),* 105–121

3220 Barber, K, Oriki and the changing perception of greatness in nineteenth-century Yorubaland, in Falola T (ed), *Yoruba historiography (entry 3205),* 31–41

3221 Brenner, L, The jihad debate between Sokoto and Borno: an historical analysis of islamic political discourse in Nigeria, in Ajayi J F A & Peel, J D Y (eds), *Peoples and empires (entry 429),* 21–43

3222 Danmole, H D, Integration in a Nigerian society in the nineteenth century: the Ilorin example, *Africa (São Paulo),* 12/13 (1989/90) 25–42

3223 Doortmont, M R, Samuel Johnson (1846–1901): missionary, diplomat, and historian, in Falola T (ed), *Yoruba historiography (entry 3205),* 167–82

3224 Elegbede-Fernandez, A D,

Lagos: a legacy of honour. Ibadan: Spectrum, 1992, 203pp

3225 Erhagbe, E O, *The Nupe invasion of Etsakoland: its impact on the socio-political development of the Etsako clans, c.1860–1897.* Boston: African Studies Centre, Boston University, 1991, 16pp

3226 Falola, T, The Yoruba wars of the nineteenth century, in Falola T (ed), *Yoruba historiography (entry 3205),* 183–206

3227 Falola, T, Law, R, (eds), *Warfare and diplomacy in precolonial Nigeria: essays in honour of Robert Smith.* Madison: University of Wisconsin, African Studies Program, 1991, 221pp

3228 Faluyi, K, The economics of the Sokoto jihad, *Hamdard islamicus,* 14, 1 (1991) 29–42

3229 Idrees, A A, Gogo Habiba of Bida: the rise and demise of a nineteenth century Nupe merchant princess and politician, *African study monographs,* 12, 1 (1991) 1–9

3230 Idress, I D, Ilorin factor in the 19th century Nupe politics: a study in the inter-emirate relations within Sokoto Caliphate, Nigeria, *Transafrican journal of history,* 20 (1991) 181–89

3231 Last, M, 'Injustice ' and legitimacy in the early Sokoto Caliphate, in Ajayi J F A & Peel, J D Y (eds), *Peoples and empires (entry 429),* 45–57

3232 Lawuyi, O B, The Obatala factor in Yoruba history, *History in Africa,* 19, (1992) 369–375

3233 Mills, S, *Discourse of difference: an analysis of women's travel writing and colonialism.* London: Routledge, 1991, 232pp

3234 Mohammed, D, *Zungeru: the forgotten capital of northern Nigeria.* Oworonsoki: Bolukun, 1991, 149pp

3235 Mwauwa, A O, The foundation of the Aro Confederacy:

a theoretical analysis of state formation in southeastern Nigeria, *Itan: Bensu journal of historical studies,* 1 (1990) 93–108

3236 Oyebode, A, Treaties and the colonial enterprise: the case of Nigeria, *African journal of international and comparative law,* 2, 1 (1990) 17–36

3237 Rosenberg, D M, Ibo resistance to British colonial power, *Ufahamu,* 19, 1 (1991) 3–21

History, C20th

see also: 2645, 3176

3238 Apter, A, *Black critics and kings.* Chicago: Universituy of Chicago Press, 1992, 280pp

3239 Boutet, R, *L'effroyable guerre du Biafra.* Paris: Harmattan, 1992, 191pp

3240 Furlong, P J, Azikiwe and the National Church of Nigeria and the Cameroons: a case study of the political use of religion in African nationalism, *African affairs,* 91, 364 (1992) 433–52

3241 Harneit-Sievers, A, *Zwischen Depression und Dekolonisation: afrikanische Händler und Politik in süd-Nigeria 1935–1954.* Saarbrucken: Breitenbach, 1991, 432pp

3242 Jaja, S O, (ed), *Opobo since 1879; a documentary record.* Ibadan: Ibadan University Press, 1991, 506pp

3243 Labinjoh, J, *Modernity and tradition in the politics of Ibadan (1900–1975).* Ibadan: Fountain, 1991, 225pp

3244 Mba, N E, *Ayo Rosiji, man with vision.* Ibadan: Spectrum, 1992, 209pp

3245 Mbadiwe, K O, *Rebirth of a nation.* Enugu: Fourth Dimension, 1991, 306pp

3246 McClintock, N C, *Kingdoms in the sand and sun: an African path to*

independence. London: Radcliffe Press, 1992, 200pp

3247 Nwauwa, A O, On Aro colonial primary source material: a critique of the historiography, *History in Africa,* 19, (1992) 377–385

3248 Nzemeke, A D, Contradictions between policy and practise on the road to Nigerian independence: Britain and the West African Students Union, 1930–1945, *Africa (Rome),* 46, 4 (1991) 593–600

3249 Olajumoke, R, *The spring of a monarch: the epic struggle of King Adeyina Oyekan II of Lagos.* Lagos: Lawebod Nigeria, 1990, 260pp

3250 Richards, P, Landscapes of dissent - Ikale and Ilaje country 1870–1950, in Ajayi J F A & Peel, J D Y (eds), *Peoples and empires (entry 429),* 161–83

3251 Sodipo, H, *A dynasty of 'missioners'.* Ibadan: Spectrum, 1992, 126pp

3252 Zachernuk, P S, The Lagos intelligentsia and the idea of progress, ca. 1860–1960, in Falola T (ed), *Yoruba historiography (entry 3205),* 157–65

Industry & trade

see also: 3079, 3160, 3462

3253 Ademisokun-Turton, D, Rural industrialisation in Nigeria: an overview, *African development perspectives yearbook,* 2, (1990/91) 609–618

3254 Adubifa, A, *Technology policy in Nigeria: a critical appraisal of the industry sector.* Ibadan: NISER, 1990, 201pp

3255 Bashir, I L, Odowu, O, (eds), *Policy issues in small-scale industrial development in Nigeria.* Jos: Jos University, Centre for Development Studies, 1991, 177pp

3256 Erinosho, L, Bello-Imam, I

B, *Perspectives on small-scale food processing and distribution industries in Nigeria.* Ibadan: Vantage, 1991, 144pp

3257 Ikpeze, N, New industrial policies and perspectives for manufacturing in Nigeria, *African development perspectives yearbook,* 2, (1990/91) 585–608

3258 Ilori, M O, A bibliographic and policy review of technological development in food processing industries of Nigeria, *Science, technology and development,* 10, 1 (1992) 67–79

3259 Jolayemi, J K, A multiattribute utility and cash-flow procedure for evaluating and selecting local raw materials for Nigerian agro-based industries, *Discovery and innovation,* 3, 2 (1991) 29–36

3260 Lee, K S, Anas, A, Costs of deficient infrastructure: the case of Nigerian manufacturing, *Urban studies,* 29, 7 (1992) 1071–92

3261 Obeleagu-Nzelibe, C G, *Management of small-scale business in Nigeria.* Enugu: Fourth Dimension, 1990, 168pp

3262 Obi, A W, Prospects for small-scale industries development under a structural adjustment programme: the case of Nigeria, *Africa development,* 16, 2 (1991) 33–56

3263 Ochia, K, Internal trip characteristics of urban market traders in a Nigerian commercial town: an analysis using a multiple linear regression model, *Third World planning review,* 14, 1 (1991) 39–52

3264 Ohiorhenuan, J F E, Poloamina, I D, Building indigenous technological capacity in African industry: the Nigerian case, in Stewart F et al (eds), *Alternative development strategies (entry 223),* 294–317

3265 Olukoshi, A O, Structural adjustment and Nigerian industry, in Olukoshi A O (ed), *Structural adjustment in Nigeria (entry 3111),* 54–74

3266 Osoba, A M, The missing middle: new chances and programmes of developing the small-scale industries in Nigeria, *African development perspectives yearbook,* 2, (1990/91) 632–643

3267 Ramanadham, V V, Privatisation in Nigeria, in Ramanadham V V (ed), *Privatisation (entry 203),* 354–72

3268 Shea, P S, Textile technology in Nigeria: some practical manifestations, in Thomas-Emeagwali G (ed), *Science and technology in Nigeria (entry 450),* 107–33

3269 Tasmuno, T N, Aderinwale, A, *Abebe: portrait of a Nigerian leader.* Abeokuta: Africa Leadership Forum, 1991, 163pp

3270 Umeh, P O C, et al, *Increasing productivity in Nigeria: proceedings of the First National Conference on Productivity, 1st-3rd December 1987.* Lagos: Macmillan, 1991, 586pp

3271 Uniamikogbo, S O, The state of the capital goods industry in a developing economy; the case of Nigeria, *Indian journal of economics,* 72, 3 (1992) 319–34

3272 Willer, H, Rösch, P-G, Gescheiterte Unternehmen - Konsequenz des Strukturanpassungsprogramms in Nigeria?, *Afrika spectrum,* 27, 2 (1992) 139–158

3273 Yahaya, S, The Dutch disease and the development of the manufacturing sector in Nigeria: 1970–85, *African development review,* 3, 1 (1991) 68–89

3274 Yahaya, S, State versus market: the privatisation programme of the Nigerian state, in Olukoshi A O (ed), *Structural adjustment in Nigeria (entry 3111),* 16–32

3275 Yakubu, A O, Indigenisation of foreign business in Nigeria: a select bibliography, *Current bibliograhy on African affairs,* 23, 1 (1991/92) 1–18

International economic relations

3276 Aboyade, O, *Selective closure in African economic relations.* Lagos: NIIA, 1991, 21pp

3277 Ajayi, S I, *An economic anaysis of capital flight from Nigeria.* Washington: World Bank, 1992, 76pp

3278 Business International Ltd, *Making profits in Nigeria: opportunities and operating conditions.* London: Economist Intelligence Unit, 1991, 152pp

3279 Falegan, B, *Nigeria's external debt problem.* Ibadan: Fountain, 1992, 293pp

3280 Grégoire, E, Les chemins de la contebande: étude des réseaux commerciaux en pays hausa, *Cahiers d'études africaines,* 31, 4 (1991) 509–32

3281 Njoku, J E, Ofiabulu, E C, The effect of the structural adjustment program on the output, prices and exports of major agricultural export crops in Nigeria, *Journal of international food & agribusiness marketing,* 3, 4 (1991) 69–84

3282 Ogwu, U J, Olukoshi, A, *The economic diplomacy of the Nigerian state.* Ibadan: Vantage, 1992, 237pp

3283 Oyejide, T A, The impact of priced-based and quantity-based import control measures in Nigeria, in Fontaine J M (ed), *Foreign trade reforms (entry 550),* 237–48

International relations

3284 Akinterinwa, B A, Fortress

Europe: problems and prospects for Franco-Nigerian relations, *Journal of Asian and African affairs,* 3, 2 (1992) 123–45

3285 Bukarambe, B, Nigeria and independant Namibia: an outlook of their emerging relations, *Nigerian journal of international affairs,* 17, 1 (1991) 1–26

3286 Eke, K K, *Nigeria's foreign policy under two military governments, 1966–1979.* Lewiston: Mellen, 1990, 192pp

3287 Nwolise, O C B, Blacks in the diaspora: a case of neglected catalysts in the achievement of Nigerian foreign policy goals, *Journal of Black studies,* 23, 1 (1992) 117–34

3288 Obiozor, G A, (ed), *Basic issues in Nigerian foreign policy: IBB's foreign policy pronouncements (1986–1991).* Lagos: NIIA, 1992, 88pp

3289 Obiozor, G A, (ed), *Nigerian foreign policy in perspective: Admiral Augustus Aikhomu's foreign policy statements from 1987–1992.* Lagos: NIIA, 1992, 142pp

3290 Obiozor, G, *Nigerian participation in the United Nations.* Enugu: Fourth Dimension, 1991, 249pp

3291 Obiozor, G, *Uneasy friendship: Nigerian-American relations.* Enugu: Fourth Dimension, 1992, 247pp

3293 Vogt, M A, Nigeria's participation in the ECOWAS monitoring group Ecomog, *Nigerian journal of international affairs,* 17, 1 (1991) 101–122

Labour & manpower

3294 Adesina, J O, Workers in Nigeria's social development experience: a critique of current mythologies, *Africa development,* 16, 2 (1991) 95–119

3295 Affinnih, Y H, *Occupational commitment and the mystique of*

self-employment among Lagos (Nigeria) port and dock workers. Lewiston: Mellen, 1992, 198pp

3296 Andrae, G, Urban workers as farmers: agro-links and livelihood of Nigerian textile workers in the crisis of the 1980s, in Baker J & Pedersen, P O (eds), *Rural-urban interface (entry 1111),* 200–22

3297 Bangura, Y, Beckman, B, African workers and structural adjustment: a Nigerian case study, in Olukoshi A O (ed), *Structural adjustment in Nigeria (entry 3111),* 75–96

3298 Fajana, S, Factors affecting productivity of labour: a study of managerial employees in Nigeria's public enterprises, *Public enterprise,* 11, 4 (1991) 246–57

3299 Fapohunda, O J, *Retrenchment and redeployment in the public sector of the Nigerian economy.* Geneva: ILO, 1991, 56pp

3300 Jega, A, Professions associations in structural adjustment, in Olukoshi A O (ed), *Structural adjustment in Nigeria (entry 3111),* 97–111

3301 Johnnie, P B, Towards workers' survival in a recessionary economy: an examination of the public sector in Nigeria, *Indian journal of industrial relations,* 27, 2 (1991) 86–94

3302 Meagher, K, Yunusa, M B, *Limits to labour absorption: conceptual and historical background to adjustment in Nigeria's urban informal sector.* Geneva: UNRISD, 1991,

3303 Owoye, O, Incomes policies, inflation and strikes in Nigeria, 1950–1985: an empirical investigation, *Applied economics,* 24, 6 (1992) 587–592

Language

3304 Jowitt, D, *Nigerian English*

usage: an introduction. Lagosq: Longman, 1991, 277pp

Law

see also: 3387

3305 Abun-Nasr, J M, Le droit islamique entre 'traditionalisme' et droit occidental au Nigéria, *Droit et cultures,* 21 (1991) 51–57

3306 Adeyika, A G, Intellectual property rights in developing countries: NIgeria's Copyright Decree, 1988, in Bondzi-Simpson P E (ed), *The law and economic development in the Third World* (New York: Praeger, 1992), 43–81

3307 Ajetunmobi, M A, The place of Islamic law in the Constitution of the Federal Republic of Nigeria, 1989, *Hamdard islamicus,* 14, 1 (1991) 67–82

3308 Beveridge, F C, Taking control of foreign investment: a case study of indigenisation in Nigeria, *International and comparative law quarterly,* 40, 2 (1991) 302–33

3309 Ikhariale, M A, The independence of the judiciary under the Third Republican constitution of Nigeria, *Journal of African law,* 34, 2 (1990) 145–58

3310 Okagbue, I, Private prosecutions in Nigeria: recent developments and some proposals, *Journal of African law,* 34, 1 (1990) 53–66

3311 Olowofoyeku, A A, Habeus corpus, judicial liability and the Nigerian constitution, *International and comparative law quarterly,* 40, 1 (1991) 49–65

3312 Quashigah, K, The federal principle in the 1989 constitution of Nigeria: its securement, *Journal of constitutional and parliamentary studies,* 24, 1–4 (1990) 28–52

Library - documentation

see also: 2217

3313 Adelberger, J, The National Archives - Kaduna (NAK), Nigeria, *History in Africa,* 19, (1992) 435–439

Literature

3314 Amadiume, I, Class and gender in *Anthills of the Savannah* - a critique, *Okike,* 30, (1990) 147–157

3315 Anohu, V A, Chinua Achebe: cultural transfers and the foreign reader, *Okike,* 30, (1990) 121–127

3316 Anyadike, C, Achebe and the truth of fiction, *Okike,* 30, (1990) 75–82

3317 Azuonye, C, Morphology of the Igbo folktale; its ethnographic, historiographic and aesthetic implications, *Africa (São Paulo),* 12/13 (1989/90) 117–36

3318 Bryce, J, Conflict and contradiction in women's writing on the Nigerian Civil War, *African languages and cultures,* 4, 1 (1991) 29–42

3319 Chuta, S C, *Things fall apart* and the Acts of the Apostles: identification of parallels in church growth, *Okike,* 30, (1990) 43–52

3320 Dunton, C, *Make man talk true: Nigerian drama in English since 1970.* Oxford: Zell, 1992, 215pp

3321 Durnoha, I, The Igbo novel and the literary communication of Igbo culture, *African study monographs,* 12, 4 (1991) 185–200

3322 Ebeogu, A, The spirit of agony: war poetry from Biafra, *Research in African literatures,* 23, 4 (1992) 35–49

3323 Emenyonu, E N, A literary reading of Chinua Achebe's *Anthills of the Savannah* and Chinelo Achebe's *The last laugh and other stories, Okike,* 30, (1990) 135–144

3324 **Emenyonu, E N,** *Studies in the Nigerian novel.* Ibadan: Heinemann, 1991, 142pp

3325 **Enekwe, O O,** Interview with Chinua Achebe, *Okike,* 30, (1990) 129–133

3326 **Ezeigbo, T A,** War, history, aesthetics, and the thriller tradition in Eddie Iroh's novels, *African languages and cultures,* 4, 1 (1991) 65–76

3327 **Furniss, G,** Hausa poetry on the Nigerian Civil War, *African languages and cultures,* 4, 1 (1991) 21–28

3328 **Garcia do Nascimento, L,** Religiosity among Igbo people, *Africa (São Paulo),* 12/13 (1989/90) 181–87

3329 **Harding, F,** Soyinka and power: language and imagery in *Madmen and specialists, African languages and cultures,* 4, 1 (1991) 87–98

3330 **Inyama, N F,** Parallel illumination in Chinua Achebe's *A man of the people, Okike,* 30, (1990) 104–112

3331 **Izevbaye, D,** History's eye-witness: vision and representation in the works of Chinua Achebe, *Okike,* 30, (1990) 21–38

3332 **Maja-Pearce, A,** *A mask dancing: Nigerian novelists of the eighties.* Oxford: Zell, 1992, 198pp

3333 **ni Chreachain, F,** How the present shapes the past: Festus Iyayi's *Heroes* - the Nigerian civil war revisited, *Journal of Commonwealth literature,* 27, 1 (1992) 48–57

3334 **Nnolim, C,** (ed), *Critical essays on Ken Saro-Wiwa's 'Sozaboy; a novel in rotten English'.* Port Harcourt: Saros, 1992, 128pp

3335 **Nwachukwu-Agbada, J O J,** Because of humanity: the ring of patriotic anguish in Wole Soyinka's poetry, *Commonwealth: essays and studies,* 14, 2 (1992) 79–88

3336 **Nwachukwu-Agbada, J O J,** The short story as a repository of the social histories of two Third World cultures: Samuel Selvon and Chinua Achebe, *Okike,* 30, (1990) 87–95

3337 **Nwahunanya, C,** The aesthetics of Nigerian war fiction, *Commonwealth novel in English,* 3, 2 (1990) 194–207

3338 **Nwahunanya, C,** Social tragedy in Achebe's rural novels: a contrary view, *Commonwealth novel in English,* 4, 1 (1991) 1–13

3339 **Nwankwo, C,** Power and the new African woman in Chinua Achebe's *Anthills of the savannah, Commonwealth novel in English,* 4, 2 (1991) 1–9

3340 **Nwodo, C S,** Objective and subjective values in Achebe's *Things fall apart, Okike,* 30, (1990) 56–67

3341 **Ogunjimi, B,** The herd insinct and class literature in Nigeria today, *Issue,* 20, 2 (1992) 12–16

3342 **Ogunsina, B,** *The development of the Yoruba novel.* Ile-Ife: Awolowo University, Dept. of African Languages, 1992, 191pp

3343 **Ojinmah, U,** *Chinua Achebe: new perspectives.* Ibadan: Spectrum, 1991, 128pp

3344 **Rajeshwar, M,** *The intellectual and society in the work of Wole Soyinka.* New Delhi: Prestige, 1990, 95pp

3346 **Saro-Wiwa, K,** The language of African literature: a writer's testimony, *Research in African literatures,* 23, 1 (1992) 153–57

3347 **Séverac, A,** The verse of Soyinka's plays: *A dance of the forests, Research in African literatures,* 23, 3 (1992) 41–51

3348 **Wright, D,** Soyinka past and present, *Journal of modern African studies,* 30, 4 (1992) 715–719

3349 **Wright, D,** Stock-taking

Soyinkana, 1986–1988, *Research in African literatures*, 23, 4 (1992) 107–116

Media

see also: 3181

3350 Amienyi, O P, The actual contribution of mass media use to integrative tendency in Nigeria, *Africa media review*, 6, 2 (1992) 31–46

3351 Nwankwo, V U, Publishing in Nigeria today, in Altbach P (ed), *Publishing and development (entry 694)*, 151–68

3352 Ogbondah, C W, British colonial authoritarianism, African military dictatorship and the Nigerian press, *Africa media review*, 6, 3 (1992) 1–18

3353 Okere, L C, Nigerian press and the expulsion of West African aliens 1983, *International studies*, 29, 3 (1992) 327–38

3354 Orewere, B, Possible implications of modern mass media for traditional communication in a Nigerian rural setting, *Africa media review*, 5, 3 (1991) 53–65

3355 Oso, L, The commercialisation of the Nigerian press: development and implications, *Africa media review*, 5, 3 (1991) 41–51

3356 Ozoh, H C, An analysis of the pattern of media use by teachers in a Nigerian education district, *Africa media review*, 5, 3 (1991) 1–10

3357 Pate, U A, Reporting African countries in the Nigerian press: perspectives in international news, *Africa media review*, 6, 1 (1992) 59–70

3358 Sani, A A, Dr Rupert M East and the beginnings of *Gaskiya ta fi kwabo, Savanna*, 12, 1 (1991) 17–20

Medical

see also: 3148, 3490

3359 Adewunmi, A, Gureje, O, Puerperal psychiatric disorders in Nigerian women, *East African medical journal*, 68, 10 (1991) 775–781

3360 Adikwu, M U, Osondu, B O, Four years of Essential Drugs List in Nigeria, *Social science and medecine*, 33, 9 (1991) 1005–1010

3361 Ahmed, M H, A two year prospective study of manic disorder and its symptomatology in northern Nigeria, *East African medical journal*, 68, 10 (1991) 782–788

3362 Ahonsi, B A, Development implications of early mortality factors in Nigeria, *Journal of social development in Africa*, 7, 1 (1992) 67–85

3363 Cogswell, M E, et al, Sociodemographic and clinical factors affecting recognition of childhood diarrhea by mothers in Kwara State, Nigeria, *Social science and medecine*, 33, 10 (1991) 1209–16

3364 Iloeje, S O, Rutter's behaviour scale (B2) for children (teachers scale): validation and standardization for use on Nigerian children, *Journal of tropical pediatrics*, 38, 5 (1992) 235–239

3365 Moloye, O, Herbal medicine in Nigeria: the case of Bendel State, *Studies in Third World societies*, 46, (1991) 193–205

3366 Moloye, O, Herbal practice and social well-being in Nigeria: an anthropological perspective, *Studies in Third World societies*, 46, (1991) 169–191

3367 Odebiyi, A I, Impact of AIDS on the patterns of AIDS-related risk and preventative behaviours among married men in a Nigerian town, *Scandinavian journal of development alternatives*, 11, 2 (1992) 5–14

3368 Thomas-Emeagwali, G, The control of water-based diseases in colonial Northern Nigeria, in Thomas-Emeagwali G (ed), *Science and technology in African history (entry 3487)*, 41–54

3369 Wright, E A, Low birthweight in the plateau region of Nigeria, *East African medical journal*, 67, 12 (1990) 894–899

Natural resources

3370 Areola, O, *Ecology of natural resources in Nigeria.* Aldershot: Avebury, 1991, 258pp

3371 Neiland, A, Vernumbe, I, *The impact of damming, drought and over-exploitation on the conservation of marketable stocks of the River Benue, Nigeria.* Portsmouth: Portsmouth Polytechnic, Centre for Marine Resource Economics, 1990, 7pp

3372 Osemeobo, G J, Religious practices and biotic conservation in Nigeria, *Geojournal*, 27, 4 (1992) 331–38

Planning

3373 Fadare, O, Wahab, K A, Constraints to effective physical planning and development control administration in Oyo State: a research note, *Quarterly journal of administration*, 25, 1 (1990/1991) 75–84

Politics

see also: 903, 904, 3184, 3199, 3353, 3437, 3489, 5032, 5033

3374 Adetula, V, The political economy of democratic transition in Nigeria 1985–1991, in Caron B et al (eds), *Democratic transition in Africa (entry 817)*, 331–48

3375 Ojabbohunmi, G A, *Institutionalisation of policy analysis in developing countries with special reference to Nigeria.* The Hague: ISS, 1990, 79pp

3376 Agbese, P O, Sanitizing democracy in Nigeria, *Transafrica forum*, 9, 1 (1992) 41–55

3377 Agbese, P O, Kieh, G K, Military disengagement from African politics: the Nigerian experience, *Afrika Spectrum*, 27, 1 (1992) 4–23

3378 Ajayi, S A, *Perspectives: the Nigerian Customs and Excise Department.* Ibadan: Joe-Tolalu, 1990, 138pp

3379 Amuwo, K, Socio-economic development and the Nigerian state: a partial critique of the Nigerian civil, *Quarterly journal of administration*, 25, 1 (1990/1991) 33–48

3380 Awazurike, C, Nigeria: soldiers, intellectuals and democratisation, *Transafrica forum*, 8, 1 (1991) 29–41

3381 Awofeso, A, *M K O Abiola: the make whole again.* Lagos: Update Commiunications, 1990, 414pp

3382 Aziegbe, S, The political transition programme and the future of democracy in Nigeria, in Caron B et al (eds), *Democratic transition in Africa (entry 817)*, 389–404

3383 Bajowa, O, *Spring of a life: an autobiography.* Ibadan: Spectrum, 1992, 151pp

3384 Barua, P B, Ethnic conflict in the military of developing nations: a comparative analysis of India and Nigeria, *Armed forces and society*, 19, 1 (1992) 123–37

3385 Bello-Imam, I B, *Local government finance in Nigeria.* Ibadan: Vantage, 1990, 316pp

3386 Bergstresser, H, Zum demokratisierungsprozess in

Nigeria: die Gouverneurs-Wahlen 1991, *Afrika Spectrum*, 27, 1 (1992) 81–87

3387 Davies, A E, Ideological debate: capitalism or socialism in Nigeria?, *Africa (São Paulo)*, 14/15 (1991/92) 143–62

3388 Dlakwa, H D, Salient features of the 1988 civil service reforms in Nigeria, *Public administration and development*, 12, 3 (1992) 297–311

3389 Ekwe-Ekwe, H, *Issues in Nigerian politics since the fall of the of the Second Republic 1984–1990.* Lewiston: Mellen, 1992, 98pp

3390 Etuk, E, *The Nigerian public service: in search of creative excellence.* Ibadan: Spectrum, 1992, 257pp

3391 Falola, T, Precolonial origins of the national question in Nigeria: the Yoruba identity as a case study, *Africa (São Paulo)*, 12/13 (1989/90) 3–24

3392 Gboyega, B, *Local government in Nigeria.* Akure: Ajomoro, 1991, 201pp

3393 Guyer, J I, *Representation without taxation: an essay on democracy in rural Nigeria.* Boston: African Studies Centre, Boston University, 1991, 29pp

3394 Hock, K, Wie religiös sind die 'Religiösen Unruhen'?: fallbeispiele aus dem Bauchi-State, Nigeria, *Afrika Spectrum*, 27, 1 (1992) 43–58

3395 Ibeanu, O O, Class interest and public policy in Nigeria: an analysis of governments' policies on agriculture and housing, *African review*, 16, 1/2 (1989) 29–39

3396 Ibrahim, J, The state, accumulation and democratic forces in Nigeria, in Rudebeck L (ed), *When democracy makes sense (entry 931)*, 105–29

3397 Ibrahim, J, The transition to civilian rule: sapping democracy, in Olukoshi A O (ed), *Structural adjustment in Nigeria (entry 3111)*, 129–40

3398 Ige, B, *Detainee's diary.* Ibadan: Nigerian Publishers Services, 1992, 262pp

3399 Igwe, A, *Nnamdi Azikiwe: the philosopher of our time.* Enugu: Fourth Dimension, 1992, 286pp

3400 Ihonvbere, J O, Adjustment, political transition, and the organization of military power in Nigeria, *Ufahamu*, 19, 1 (1991) 22–43

3401 Ihonvbere, J O, A critical evaluation of the failed 1990 coup in Nigeria, *Journal of modern African studies*, 29, 4 (1991) 601–26

3402 Ihonvbere, J O, Structural adjustment and Nigeria's democratic transition, *Transafrica forum*, 8, 3 (1991) 61–83

3403 Ilesanmi, M O, Religion and politics in independent Nigeria, *Orita*, 23, 1 (1991) 49–70

3404 Lawuyi, O B, Ethnicity, political leadership and the search for a stable Nigerian society, *Scandinavian journal of development alternatives*, 11, 3/4 (1992) 127–135

3405 Loimeier, R, Die dynamik religiöser Unruhen in nord-Nigeria, *Afrika Spectrum*, 27, 1 (1992) 59–80

3406 Momoh, A, The philosophical and ideological foundations to the transition to civil rule in Nigeria, in Caron B et al (eds), *Democratic transition in Africa (entry 817)*, 141–65

3407 Nwabueze, B O, *Military rule and constitutionalism in Nigeria.* Ibadan: Spectrum, 1992, 368pp

3408 Nwago, N, *The vote.* Ibadan: Spectrum, 1992, 203pp

3409 Nzelibe, C G O, (ed), *Current issues in public and local government administration.* Enugu: Fourth Dimension, 1991, 352pp

3410 Obudumu, K, The Nigerian military and leadership succession: a materialist examination of the economic foundation of Nigeria's Third Republic, in Caron B et al (eds), *Democratic transition in Africa (entry 817)*, 237–56

3411 O'Donovan I, Management and change in northern Nigerian local government, *Public administration and development,* 12, 4 (1992) 355–71

3412 Ogbemudia, S O, *Years of challenge.* Idaban: Heinemann, 1991, 271pp

3413 Okolocha, C, Political cleavages and transition to democracy in Nigeria, in Caron B et al (eds), *Democratic transition in Africa (entry 817),* 167–83

3414 Olowu, D, *The Nigerian federal system.* Ibadan: Evans, 1992, 280pp

3415 Olowu, D, Urban local government finance in Nigeria: the case of Lagos municipal area, *Public administration and development,* 12, 1 (1992) 19–38

3416 Olowu, D, Urban local government finance in Nigeria: the case of Onitsha local government, *Public administration and development,* 12, 1 (1992) 39–52

3417 Osia, K, Leadership and followership: Nigeria's problems of governance, *Scandinavian journal of development alternatives,* 11, 3/4 (1992) 175–194

3418 Otite, A, The ruling elite and the role of government in Nigerian political economy, *Scandinavian journal of development alternatives,* 11, 3/4 (1992) 111–118

3419 Owolabi, A, The military and democratic transition: an analysis of the transition programmme of the Babangida administration, in Caron B et al (eds), *Democratic transition in Africa (entry 817),* 257–70

3420 Oyovbaire, S, (ed), *Foundations of new Nigeria: the IBB era.* n.p.: Precision Press, 1991, 74pp

3421 Pacheco, O, Military disengagement in Nigeria: the planned transition to civilian rule in 1993, *Journal of contemporary African studies,* 10, 2 (1991) 44–56

3422 Salamone, F A, Playing at nationalism: Nigeria, a nation of 'ringers', *Geneva-Africa,* 30, 1 (1992) 55–75

3423 Shagaya, J N, *The Internal Affairs Ministry: an overview.* Lagos: Alfa Communications, 1990, 175pp

3424 Suberu, R T, Federalism and the transition to democratic governance in Nigeria, in Caron B et al (eds), *Democratic transition in Africa (entry 817),* 315–29

3425 Suberu, R T, Problems of federation in the Second Nigerian Republc and prospects for the future, *Africa (Rome),* 47, 1 (1992) 29–56

3426 Tongo, A, Sambo, I A, *Adamu Tafawa Balewa: biography and selected speeches.* Ibadan: Spectrum, 1992, 151pp

3427 Udogu, E I, In search of political stability and survival: towards Nigeria's Third Republic, *Scandinavian journal of development alternatives,* 11, 3/4 (1992) 5–28

3428 Williams, D C, Accomodation in the midst of crisis? Assessing governance in Nigeria, in Hyden G & Bratton, M (eds), *Governance and politics (entry 864),* 97–119

3429 Williams, D C, Assessing future democratic accountability in Nigeria: investigative tribunals and Nigerian political culture, *Scandinavian journal of development alternatives,* 11, 3/4 (1992) 51–65

Religion, philosophy

see also: 1858, 3179, 3251, 3394, 3405

3430 Ajetunmobi, M A, Islamic scholars of Ilorin and their place in Yorubaland, *Journal, Institute of muslim minority affairs,* 12, 1 (1991) 135–147

3431 **Alokan, A,** *The Christ Apostolic Church: CAC 1928–1988.* Lagos: Ibukunola, 1991, 382pp

3432 **Babalola, E O,** The impact of African traditional religion and culture upon the Aladura churches, *Asia journal of theology,* 6, 1 (1992) 130–140

3433 **Blanckmeister, B,** Islam, tradition und ökonomie aus der sicht nordnigerianischer unternehmer, *Afrika Spectrum,* 27, 1 (1992) 25–42

3434 **Boyd, J, Maishanu, H M,** *Sir Siddiq Abubakar III: Sarkin Musulmi.* Ibadan: Spectrum, 1991, 152pp

3435 **Gumi, A, Tsiga, I A,** *Where I stand.* Ibadan: Spectrum, 1992, 220pp

3436 **Gundert-Hock, S,** Frauen in unabhängigen afrikanischen Kirchen: ein Vorbild für die:"Mainstream churches"?, *Zeitschrift für Missionswissenschaft und Religionswissenschaft,* 76, 1 (1992) 33–47

3437 **Hunwick, J,** An African case study of political Islam: Nigeria, *Annals,* 524 (1992) 143–55

3438 **Mbon, F M,** *Brotherhood of the Cross and the Star: a new religious movement in Nigeria.* Frankfurt: Lang, 1992, 350pp

3439 **Ogungbemi, S,** A critical examination of the origin of man in Yoruba metaphysics, *Journal of African religion and philosophy,* 2, 1 (1991) 17–22

3440 **Olayiwola, D O,** Religious pluralism and functionalism among the Ijesa-Yoruba of Nigeria, *Asia journal of theology,* 6, 1 (1992) 141–153

3441 **Olupona, J K,** (ed), *Religion and peace in multi-faith Nigeria.* Ile-Ife: Awolowo UP, 1992, 203pp

3442 **Soyinka, W,** *The credo of being and nothingness.* Ibadan: Spectrum, 1991, 35pp

Rural economy

see also: 2182, 3131, 3153, 3174, 3253

3443 **Alkali, R A,** The World Bank: financing rural development and the politics of debt in Nigeria, *Africa development,* 16, 3/4 (1991) 163–79

3444 **Arene, C J,** Loan repayment and technical assistance among small-holder maize farmers in Nigeria, *African review of money finance and banking,* 1 (1992) 63–74

3445 **Ariyo, J A, Ogbonna, D O,** The effects of land speculation on agricultural production among peasants in Kachia local government area of Kaduna State, Nigeria, *Applied geography,* 12, 1 (1992) 31–46

3446 **Barbier, E B, et al,** *Economic valuation of wetland benefits: the Hadejia-Jama'are flood plain, Nigeria.* London: IIED, 1991, 41pp

3447 **Braun, M, Fricke, W, et al,** The double function of periodic markets in densely populated rural areas of Uyo, SE Nigeria, in Cammann L (ed), *Traditional marketing systems (entry 113),* 62–69

3448 **Chidebulu, S A,** *Hired labour on smallholder farms in Nigeria: a study of southeastern Nigeria.* Morriton: Winrock International Institute, 1990, 24pp

3449 **Dibua, J I,** Government's agricultural policy and rural development in Nigeria: the case of Bendel State 1964–68, *African review,* 16, 1/2 (1989) 40–53

3450 **Eboh, E C, et al,** Nigerian village money lenders and their usurious interest rates: an analysis of intervening factors, *Savings and development,* 15, 4 (1991) 361–372

3451 **Ebong, M O,** (ed), *Mobilisation of resources for rural development in Nigeria.* Calabar: Wusen Printing Press, 1991, 304pp

3452 **Eyoh, D L,** Reforming peasant production in Africa: power and technological change in two Nigerian villages, *Development and change,* 23, 2 (1992) 37–66

3453 **Eyoh, D L,** Structures of intermediation and change in African agriculture: a Nigerian case study, *African studies review,* 35, 1 (1992) 17–39

3454 **Faforiji, R A,** Fiscal incentives for rural development, in Olanrewaju S A & Falola, T (eds), *Rural development problems in Nigeria (entry 3476),* 157–73

3455 **Gefu, J O,** *Pastoralist perspectives in Nigeria: the Fulbe of Udubo Grazing Reserve.* Uppsala: Scandinavian Institute of African Studies, 1992, 106pp

3456 **Giwa, A T, Ahmed, S,** A select bibliography of the postgraduate theses of the Faculty of Agriculture of Admadu Bello University, Zaria, Nigeria (1978–1990), *Savanna,* 12, 1 (1991) 77–81

3457 **Guyer, J I,** Small change: indivdual farm work and collective life in a western Nigerian savanna town, 1969–88, *Africa,* 62, 4 (1992) 465–89

3458 **Imoudu, P B, Onosakponome, E,** Bank loan requirement and availability for Nigerian small farmers: a comparative analysis of experiences, *African review of money finance and banking,* 1 (1992) 49–61

3459 **Jansen, H G P,** Dairy consumption in northern Nigeria: implications for development policies, *Food policy,* 17, 3 (1992) 214–226

3460 **Kolawole, A,** The impact of drought in Lake Chad and its influence upon the South Chad Irrigation Project, Nigeria, in Darkoh M B K (ed), *African river basins (entry 406),* 121–32

3461 **Mawuli, A, Khwaja, G A,** Some aspects of employment in the peasant economy of northern Nigeria: a case study, *Journal of east African research and development,* 21, (1991) 70–80

3462 **Mbata, J N,** Economics of cottage industries in the rural areas of Rivers State, Nigeria: a case study of cassava grating industry, *Discovery and innovation,* 4, 1 (1992) 45–51

3463 **Mbata, J N, Ebbe, N B,** A comparative study of the supervised and non-supervised agricultural credit scheme as a tool for agricultural development in Rivers State, Nigeria, *Discovery and innovation,* 3, 4 (1991) 29–35

3464 **Mofunanya, B E,** The mobilisation of rural savings in Nigeria: famers' attitudes to 'formal' and 'informal' institutions, in Frimpong-Ansah J H & Ingham, B (eds), *Saving for economic recovery (entry 142),* 152–59

3465 **Mohamed Salih, M A,** *Pastoralists and planners: local knowledge and resource management in Gidan Magajia grazing reserve, northern Nigeria.* London: IIED, 1992, 37pp

3466 **Mustapha, A R,** Structural adjustment and agrarian change in Nigeria, in Olukoshi A O (ed), *Structural adjustment in Nigeria (entry 3111),* 112–28

3468 **Njoku, J E,** *Determinants of adoption of improved oil-palm production technologies in Imo State, Nigeria.* Morriton: Winrock International Institute, 1990, 17pp

3469 **Nwosu, A C,** The rural industrialisation problem, in Olanrewaju S A & Falola, T (eds), *Rural development problems in Nigeria (entry 3476),* 83–112

3470 **Nwosu, N I A,** The state and rural development in Nigeria, *Ufahamu,* 18, 3 (1989/90) 52–65

3471 Okoji, M A, A regional survey of labor problems in Nigerian peasant agriculture, *Philippine geographical journal,* 34, 4 (1990) 181–193

3472 Olagbaju, J O, Adeseun, G O, The problem of declining agricultural export production, in Olanrewaju S A & Falola, T (eds), *Rural development problems in Nigeria (entry 3476),* 43–55

3473 Olagoke, M A, *Efficiency of resource use in rice production systems in Anambra State, Nigeria.* Morriton: Winrock International Institute, 1990, 24pp

3474 Olanrewaju, S A, Overview of the rural development problem, in Olanrewaju S A & Falola, T (eds), *Rural development problems in Nigeria (entry 3476),* 1–18

3475 Olanrewaju, S A, The rural transportation problem, in Olanrewaju S A & Falola, T (eds), *Rural development problems in Nigeria (entry 3476),* 113–33

3476 Olanrewaju, S A, Falola, T, (eds), *Rural development problems in Nigeria.* Aldershot: Avebury, 1992, 183pp

3477 Olanrewaju, S A, Falola, T, The prospects for rural development, in Olanrewaju S A & Falola, T (eds), *Rural development problems in Nigeria (entry 3476),* 174–83

3478 Osunade, M A A, Evaluation of fallow lands by small farmers of southwestern Nigeria, *Scandinavian journal of development alternatives,* 11, 2 (1992) 49–60

3479 Otite, O, Okali, C, (eds), *Readings in Nigerian society and rural economy.* Ibadan: Heinemann, 1990, 478pp

3480 Sirak Teklu, (ed), *Index to livestock literature on Nigeria.* Addis Ababa: International Livestock Centre for Africa, 1992, 279pp

3481 Umebali, E E, An economic analysis of farmers multi-purpose co-operative societies in eastern part of Nigeria, *Eastern Africa economic review,* 6, 2 (1990) 77–82

3482 Williams, D C, Measuring the impact of land reform policy in Nigeria, *Journal of modern African studies,* 30, 4 (1992) 587–608

3483 Williams, T O, Comparative advantage of crop-livestock production systems in southwest Nigeria and the technical research implications, in Moock J L & Rhoades, R E (eds), *Diversity (entry 1038),* 189–204

Science & technology

see also: 3143

3484 Ihonvbere, J, Obstacles to the development of science and technology in contemporary Nigeria, in Thomas-Emeagwali G (ed), *Science and technology in African history (entry 3487),* 165–82

3485 Kani, A, Mathematics in pre-colonial central Sudan, in Thomas-Emeagwali G (ed), *Science and technology in African history (entry 3487),* 33–39

3486 Olaoye, R O, Policy options on technology in contemporary Nigeria, in Thomas-Emeagwali G (ed), *Science and technology in Nigeria (entry 450),* 171–80

3487 Thomas-Emeagwali, G, (ed), *The historical development of science and technology in Nigeria.* Lewiston: Mellen, 1992, 180pp

Sociology

see also: 3187

3488 Akpala, C O, Bolaji, A B O, Drug abuse among secondary school students in Sokoto, Nigeria, *Psychopathologie africaine,* 23, 2 (1990/1991) 197–204

3489 Daloz, J P, *Le Nigéria: société*

et politique (bibliographie annotée). Talence: CEAN, Bordeaux University, 1992, 115pp

3490 Emeha, E A, Nigerians coping with stress: age, sex and religious variations, *Orita,* 23, 2 (1991) 108–22

3491 Fadayomi, T O, The history of social development in Gambia, Ghana, Nigeria, in Mohammed D (ed), *Social development in Africa (entry 1093),* 109–34

3492 Fadayomi, T O, Social development strategies in Gambia, Ghana, Nigeria, in Mohammed D (ed), *Social development in Africa (entry 1093),* 135–50

3493 Gage-Brandon, A J, The polygny-divorce relationship: a case study of Nigeria, *Journal of marriage and the family,* 54, 2 (1992) 285–92

3494 Guyer, J I, *Changing nuptiality in a Nigerian community: observations from the field.* Boston: African Studies Centre, Boston University, 1990, 14pp

3495 Igbinovia, P E, Begging in Nigeria, *International journal of offender therapy and comparative criminology,* 35, 1 (1991) 21–33

3496 Lawuyi, T, Falola, T, The instability of the naira and social payment among the Yoruba, *Journal of Asian and African studies,* 27, 3/4 (1992) 216–28

3497 Ogbuagu, S C, Changing burial practices in Nigeria: some evidence from the obituaries, *Savanna,* 12, 1 (1991) 21–33

3498 Ogunlesi, A O, Nigerian juvenile offenders: a case controlled study, *Medicine and law,* 10, 4 (1991) 369–74

3499 Okonjo, K, Aspects of continuity and change in mate selection among the Igbo West of the river Niger, *Journal of comparative family studies,* 23, 3 (1992) 339–60

3500 Oloyede, O, Surviving an economic recession: 'game play' in a Nigerian factory, *Review of African political economy,* 55 (1992) 44–56

3501 Otite, O, *Ethnic pluralism and ethnicity in Nigeria.* Ibadan: Shaneson, 1990, 200pp

3502 Sokari-George, E, et al, Rural electrification: a study of socio-economic and fertility change in Rivers State, Nigeria, *African study monographs,* 12, 4 (1991) 167–84

Urban studies

3503 Agbola, T, Oshogbo, *Cities,* 9, 3 (1992) 249–60

3504 Arimah, B C, Hedonic prices and the demand for housing attributes in ... Ibadan, Nigeria, *Research in African literatures,* 23, 5 (1992) 639–51

3505 Zubiru, M, *Shelter for all by the year 2000? Implementing a low cost housing programme for Nigeria.* Glasgow: Strathclyde University, Centre for Planning, 1991, 33pp

SENEGAL

Agriculture, scientific

3506 Corneir-Salem, M C, *Gestion et évolution des espaces aquatiques: la Casamance.* Paris: ORSTOM, 1992, 584pp

Anthropology

3507 Dilley, R, Dreams, inspiration and craftwork among Tukolor weavers, in Jedrej M C & Shaw, R (eds), *Dreaming, religion and society (entry 42),* 71–86

3508 Diouf, M, La personnalité sérère à travers les âges: les valeurs de civilisation à l'épreuve du temps, *Ethiopiques,* 55 (1992) 8–19

3509 Fassin, D, *Pouvoir et maladie*

en Afrique: anthropologie sociale dans la banlieue de Dakar. Paris: PUF, 1992, 360pp

3510 **Faye, A,** Tradition et modernité: le dilemne culturel du Seereer contemporain, *Ethiopiques,* 55 (1992) 132–36

3511 **Le Pichon, A, Baldé, S,** *Le troupeau des songes: le sacrifice du fils et l'enfant prophète dans les traditions des peuls du Fouladou.* Paris: Maison des Sciences de l'Homme, 1990, 273pp

3512 **Linares, O F,** *Power, prayer and production: the Jola of Casamance, Senegal.* Cambridge: CUP, 1992, 258pp

3513 **Mark, P,** *The wild bull and the sacred forest: form, meaning and change in Senegambian initiation masks.* Cambridge: CUP, 1992, 170pp

3514 **Ndiaye, O S,** Diversité et unicité sérères: l'exemple de la région de Thies, *Ethiopiques,* 55 (1992) 120–31

3515 **Ndour, B B,** Ndiaganiao: une entité socio-culturelle dans le Diegueme, *Ethiopiques,* 55 (1992) 108–115

Arts

3516 **Diop, A O,** *Le théatre traditionel au Sénégal.* Dakar: Nouvelles Editions Africaines, 19990, 48pp

3517 **Sembene Ousman, Firinne ni Chreachain,** 'If I were a woman, I'd never marry an African', *African affairs,* 91, 363 (1992) 241–47

Economy - Development

3518 **Berg, E,** *Adjustment postponed: economic policy reform in Senegal in the 1980s.* Bethesda: USAID, 1990, 253pp

3519 **Diouf, M,** La crise de l'ajustement, *Politique africaine,* 45 (1992) 62–85

3520 **D'Sech, B,** Privatisation or removal of market imperfections: a challenge for Senegal, in Roe A R et al (ed) *Instruments of economic policy (entry 341),* 214–21

3521 **Guillamont, P, Guillamont-Jeanneney, S,** La conséquences sociales de l'ajustement en Afrique selon la politique de change, *Politique africaine,* 45 (1992) 101–21

3522 **Lee, E, et al,** *Ajustement, emploi et développement au Sénégal.* Geneva: ILO, 1992, 125pp

3523 **Thiam, P D,** *Stratégies d'interface, intégration économique et développement.* Frankfurt: Lang, 1991, 249pp

Economic and social history

3524 **Boone, C,** *Merchant capital and the roots of state power in Senegal 1930–1985.* Cambridge: CUP, 1992, 299pp

3525 **Chastanet, M,** Crise et régulation en pays Soninké (Sénégal) depuis le milieu du XIXe siècle, *Cahiers des sciences humaines,* 27, 1/2 (1991) 131–145

3526 **Marfaing, L,** *Evolution du commerce au Sénégal, 1820–1930.* Paris: Harmattan, 1991, 313pp

3527 **Schmitz, J,** Histoire savante et formes spatio-généalogiques de la mémoire (Haalpulaar de la vallée du Sénégal), *Cahiers des sciences humains,* 26, 4 (1990) 531–552

Food

3528 **Christiansen, S,** Models for food security in the dry regions of Senegal, in Hjort af Ornas A (ed), *Security in African drylands (entry 1025),* 183–92

3529 **Jolly, C M, Diop, O,** Food preferences and ethnicity: policy implications for Senegal, *Journal of international food & agribusiness marketing,* 3, 3 (1991) 83–102

3530 Thieba, D, Associations paysannes, sécurité alimentaire et commerce céréalier au Sénégal, *Cahiers des sciences humaines,* 27, 1/2 (1991) 97–103

Gender

3531 Heath, D, *Class and gender: social uses of space in urban Senegal.* East Lansing: Michigan State University, 1990, 15pp

3532 Sy, M, Les migrations féminines au Sénégal, *Echo,* 14/15 (1989–90) 10–15

Geography, physical

3533 Hanan, N P, et al, Assessment of desertification around deep wells in the Sahel using satellite imagery, *Journal of applied ecology,* 28, 1 (1991) 173–186

History, C6–18th

3534 Diouf, M, L'information historique: l'exemple du Siin, *Ethiopiques,* 55 (1992) 51–55

3535 Girard, J, *L'or du Bambouk. Une dynamique de civilisation ouest-africaine: du royaume de Gabou à la Casamance.* Geneva: Chène-Bourg, 1992, 347pp

3536 Ndiaye, F, La saga du peuple sérère et l'histoire du Sine, *Ethiopiques,* 55 (1992) 38–44

3537 Ngom, B, La question gelwaar et la formation du royaume du Sine, *Ethiopiques,* 55 (1992) 23–37

3538 Sackur, A, The French Revolution and race relations in Senegal, 1780–1810, in Ajayi J F A & Peel, J D Y (eds), *Peoples and empires (entry 429),* 69–87

3539 Thiam, M B, Diaw, A T, La porte de Fata: un hiatus historico-géographique dans le troisième cycle du mythe gelwar, *Ethiopiques,* 55 (1992) 45–50

History, C19th

3540 Sarr, D, Roberts, R, The jurisdiction of Muslim tribunals in colonial Senegal, 1857–1932, in Mann K & Roberts, R (eds), *Law in colonial Africa (entry 684),* 131–45

History, C20th

3541 Dieng, A A, *Blaise Diagne: député noir de l'Afrique.* Paris: ed Chaka, 1990, 187pp

3542 Konaté, A, *La cri du mange-mil: mémoires d'un préfet sénégalais.* Paris: Harmattan, 1991, 237pp

3543 Vaillant, J G, *Black, French and African: a life of Leopold Sedar Senghor.* Cambridge, Mass.: Harvard UP, 1990, 388pp

Industry & trade

see also: 3548

3544 Chambas, G, Geourjeon, A, The new industrial policy in Senegal: a highly controversial reform, in Adhikari R et al (eds), *Industrial and trade policy reform in developing countries* (Manchester: Manchester UP, 1992), 135–49

3545 Ebin, V, A la recherche du nouveaux 'poissons': stratégies commerciales mourides par temps de crise, *Politique africaine,* 45 (1992) 86–99

3546 Geist, H, Rural weekly markets in the Thiès region: observations on the grain market of the Senegalese groundnut basin, *Applied geography and development,* 36, (1990) 78–98

3547 Geourjon, A M, Import liberalisation and the new industrial

policy in Senegal, in Fontaine J M
(ed), *Foreign trade reforms (entry
550)*, 221–36

International economic relations

3548 **Barbier, J P, Véron, J B,** *Les
zones franches industrielles
d'exportation (Haiti, Maurice,
Sénégal, Tunisie)*. Paris: Karthala,
1991, 166pp

International relations

3549 **Sall, E,** *Sénégambie: territoires,
frontières, espace et reseaux sociales.*
Bordeaux: Institut d'études
politiques, Université de Bordeaux,
1992, 28pp
3550 **Santoir, C,** Le conflit
mauritano-sénégalais: la genése: le
cas des Peul de la haute vallée du
Sénégal, *Cahiers des sciences
humains,* 26, 4 (1990) 553–576

Language

3551 **Balde, A,** Etudes de
linguistique et developpment
socio-économique en Afrique,
Africa (São Paulo), 12/13
(1989/90) 78–116
3552 **Juillard, C,** Comportements et
attitudes de la jeunesse face au
multilinguisme en Casamance
(Sénégal), *Cahiers des sciences
humaines,* 27, 3/4 (1991) 433–456

Law

3553 **Eichelsheim, J,** Urban
expansion and old local land tenure
systems around the city of
Ziguinchor, Senegal, *Netherlands
review of development studies,* 3,
(1990/1991) 31–47
3554 **Hesseling, G,** *Pratiques
foncières à l'ombre du droit:
l'application du droit foncière urbain à
Zinguinchor, Sénégal.* Leiden:

Afrikastudiecentrum, 1992, 214pp
3555 **Hesseling, G,** Urban land
conflicts and the administration of
justice in Ziguinchor, Senegal,
*Netherlands review of development
studies,* 3, (1990/1991) 13–29

Literature

3556 **Boyd-Buggs, D,** Mouridism
in Senegalese fiction, in Harrow K
H (ed), *Faces of Islam (entry 710),*
201–14
3557 **Cham, M B,** Islam in
Senegalese literature and fim, in
Harrow K H (ed), *Faces of Islam
(entry 710),* 163–86
3558 **Glinga, W,** *Litteratur in
Senegal.* Berlin: Reimer, 1990,
632pp
3559 **Kluback, W,** Poetic
companions: Paul Claudel and
Leopold Sedar Senghor, *Journal of
African religion and philosophy,* 2, 1
(1991) 114–20
3560 **Larrier, R,** Correspondance et
création littéraire: Mariama Bâ's
Une si longue lettre, French review,
64, 5 (1991) 747–753
3561 **Makward, E,** Women,
tradition and religion in Sembene
Ousmane's work, in Harrow K H
(ed), *Faces of Islam (entry 710),*
187–99
3562 **Ndoye, A K,** La relation
éducative Thierno-Samba Diallo
dans *L'aventure ambigue,
Ethiopiques,* 7, 2 (1991) 28–39
3563 **Ngandu Nkashama, P,**
*Négritude et poétique: une lecture de
l'oeuvre critique de Léopold Sédar
Senghor.* Paris: Harmattan, 1992,
158pp
3564 **Petroni, L,** Senghor, sensuel
et plurivalent poète civil: identité,
émotion, universalité, *Francofonia,*
20, (1991) 21–37
3565 **Sadji, A B,** L'oeuvre de David
Diop tiraillée entre la tradition
linguistique francophone et le

nationalisme révolutionnaire africain, *Études germano-africaines*, 9, (1991) 83–90

3566 **Tchého, I C,** The image of Islam in selected tales of Birago Diop, in Harrow K H (ed), *Faces of Islam (entry 710)*, 215–26

Media

3567 **Article 19,** *Country commentary: Senegal*. London: Article 19, 1992, 17pp

Medical

3568 **Leroy, O, Garenne, M,** The two most dangerous days of life: a study of neonatal tetanus in Senegal (Niakhar), in van der Walle E et al (eds), *Mortality and society (entry 771)*, 160–75

Politics

see also: 896, 2579

3569 **Bathily, A,** *Mai 68 à Dakar: ou la révolte universitaire et le démocratie*. Paris: Harmattan, 1992, 191pp

3570 **Coulon, C,** La démocratie sénégalaise: bilan d'une expérience, *Politique africaine*, 45 (1992) 3–8

3571 **Coumba Diop, M,** *Sénégal, trajectoires d'un état*. Dakar: Codesria, 1992, 500pp

3572 **Diouf, A,** Sénégal: vers une réelle démocratie, *Revue des deux mondes*, (1992) 148–153

3573 **Hughes, A,** The collapse of the Senegambian Federation, *Journal of Commonwealth and comparative politics*, 30, 2 (1992) 200–222

3574 **Ly, A,** *Les regroupements politiques au Sénégal (1956–1970)*. Dakar: Codesria, 1992, 448pp

3575 **Ndiaye, F, et al,** *Visages publiques au Sénégal: 10 personnalités*

politiques parlent. Paris: Harmattan, 1990, 258pp

3576 **O'Brien, D C,** Le 'contrat social' sénégalais à l'épreuve, *Politique africaine*, 45 (1992) 9–20

3577 **Wegemund, R,** Der Casamance-Konflikt, *Afrika spectrum*, 26, 3 (1991) 374–390

3578 **Wegemund, R,** *Politisierte Ethnizität in Mauritanien und Senegal*. Hamburg: Institut für Afrika-Kunde, 1991, 190pp

3579 **Young, C, Kante, B,** Governance, democracy, and the 1988 Senegalese elections, in Hyden G & Bratton, M (eds), *Governance and politics (entry 864)*, 57–74

Religion, philosophy

see also: 3512

3580 **Gomez-Perez, M,** Associations islamiques à Dakar, *Islam et sociétés au Sud du Sahara*, 5 (1991) 5–19

3581 **Ka, T,** Vie et doctrine d'Ahmad Saghir Mbaye, le soufi de Louga (Sénégal), 1864–1946, *Bulletin de l'institut fondamental d'Afrique noire. Série B, Sciences humaines*, 46, 3/4 (1986/1987) 284–304

3582 **Lepoittevin, C, Mendy, J,** Sénégalais chrétiens et musulmans en dialogue: un effort de réponse commune aux défis du monde contemporaine, *Islamochristiana*, 17, (1991) 169–194

3583 **Ndiaye, T,** Eléments de philosophie existentielle à travers les proverbs sérères, *Ethiopiques*, 55 (1992) 101–107

3584 **Thiaw, I L,** La religiosité des Seereer, avant et pendant leur islamisation, *Ethiopiques*, 55 (1992) 59–86

3585 **Wamba-dia-Wamba, E,** Homage to the great African

savant, Cheikh Anta Diop, *Quest*,
5, 2 (1991) 63–72

Rural economy

see also: 1008, 3512

3586 Ba, H, Nuttall, C, Village
associations on the riverbanks of
Senegal: the new development
actors, in NGLS (ed), *Voices from
Africa 2 (entry 195)*, 83–104

3587 Busaker, D, *L'analyse
socio-économique des systèmes
d'exploitation agricole et de la gestion
de terroir dans le Bas-Saloum,
Sénégal.* Berlin: Technische
Universität, 1990, 225pp

3588 Dia, I, Fall, B, *The
contribution of different types of
sociocultural studies to irrigation
projects: the Kaskas experience.*
Wageningen: Wageningen
Agricultural University, Dept. of
Irrigation, 1990, 32pp

3589 Diemer, G, Huibers, F P,
*Farmer-managed irrigation in the
Senegal River valley: implications for
the current design method. End of
project report.* Wageningen:
Wageningen Agricultural
University, Dept. of Irrigation and
Soil and Water Conservation,
1991, 89pp

3590 Diop, A B, Les paysans du
bassin arachidier: conditions de vie
et comportements de survie,
Politique africaine, 45 (1992) 39–61

3591 Golan, E H, *Land tenure reform
in Senegal: an economic study from
the peanut basin.* Madison:
University of Wisconsin, Land
Tenure Center, 1990, 137pp

3592 Guèye, M B, *Cooperation
between Senegalese NGOs and
national research structures:
constraints and perspectives.* London:
IIED, 1992, 36pp

3593 Lachenmann, G,
*Bauernorganisation und
Selbshilfebewegung in Senegal: die*

*Stärkung der mittleren Ebene im
Strukturwandel.* Berlin: Deutches
Institut für Entwicklungspolitik,
1990, 248pp

3594 Lecomte, B, Senegal: the
young farmers of Walo and the new
agricultural policy, *Review of
African political economy*, 55 (1992)
87–95

3595 Woodhouse, P, Ndiaye, I,
*Structural adjustment and irrigated
food farming in Africa: the
'disengagement' of the state in the
Senegal River valley.* Milton
Keynes: Open University,
Developppment Policy and
Practice Group, 1990, 37pp

3596 Yade, M, *Optimierung der
Verorgung des senegalesischen
Marktes mit Reis.* Kiel: Vauk, 1990,
228pp

Sociology

see also: 3524

3597 Charles, K, Migration et
espace culturel sérère: l'exemple de
la jeunesse sérère de Dakar-Pikine,
Ethiopiques, 55 (1992) 116–119

3598 Santoir, C, Les Peul 'refusés',
les Peul mauritaniens réfugiés au
Sénégal (Département de Matam),
Cahiers des sciences humains, 26, 4
(1990) 577–603

3599 Sene, B, Eléments pour la
définition d'un programme
d'action sociale, *Ethiopiques*, 55
(1992) 139–45

Urban studies

see also: 3509

3600 Diouf, M, Fresques murales et
écriture de l'histoire: le *set/setal* à
Dakar, *Politique africaine*, 46 (1992)
41–54

3601 Navarro, R, 'Irrégularité
urbaine' et genèse de l'africanité
urbaine au Cap-Vert, in
Coquery-Vidrovitch C & Nedelec,

C (eds), *Tiers Monde: l'informel en question?* (Paris: Harmattan, 1991), 215–37

3602 **Salem, G,** Crise urbaine et controle social à Pikine: bornes-fontaines et clientelisme, *Politique africaine,* 45 (1992) 21–38

3603 **Vorlaufer, K,** Urbanisierung und Stadt-Land-Bezeihungen von Migranten in Primat- und Sekundärstädten Afrikas: Dakar/Senegal und Mombasa/Kenya, *Zeitschrift für Wirtschaftlichsgeographie,* 36, 1/2 (1991) 77–108

SIERRA LEONE

Anthropology

3604 **Shaw, R,** Dreaming as accomplishment: power, the individual and Temne divination, in Jedrej M C & Shaw, R (eds), *Dreaming, religion and society (entry 42),* 36–54

3605 **Shaw, R,** Splitting truths from darkness: epistemological aspects of Temne divination, in Peek P M (ed), *African divination (entry 48),* 137–52

3606 **Waldie, K,** 'Cattle and conctrete': changing property relationships and property interests among the Fula cattle herders around Kababal, northeast Sierra Leone, in Baxter P T W & Hogg, R (eds), *Property, poverty and people (entry 1000),* 229–39

Arts

3607 **Edwards, J P,** The sociological significance and uses of Mende country cloth, in Smithsonian Museum *History design and craft (entry 2510),* 133–68

Current affairs

3608 **Sylver, V,** Strasser, *Focus on Africa,* 3, 3 (1992) 5–8

3609 **Tosterin, M,** Settling scores, *Focus on Africa,* 3, 1 (1992) 25–29

Economy - Development

3610 **Weeks, J,** *Development strategy and the economy of Sierra Leone.* Basingstoke: Macmillan, 1992, 191pp

Economic and social history

3611 **Zack-Williams, A,** Diamond mining in Sierra Leone 1930–1980, in Thomas-Emeagwali G (ed), *Science and technology in African history (entry 3487),* 101–27

Education

3612 **Bledsoe, C,** The cultural transformation of western education in Sierra Leone, *Africa,* 62, 2 (1992) 182–202

3613 **Bockarie, S A,** School-community integration: a concept in teacher education as proposed by the Bunumbu reform in Sierra Leone, *International journal of educational development,* 11, 3 (1991) 255–58

3614 **Hildebrand, K H,** *'Bookish' knowledge or empowering capacities? Education and social development in subsaharan Africa with a case study of Sierra Leone.* Frankfurt: Verlag für Interkulturelle Kommunikation, 1991, 104pp

3615 **Kargbo, R F,** *Educational assistance and school development in Sierra Leone.* Frankfurt: Lang, 1991, 261pp

History, general

No entry, see also: 450

History, C6–18th

3616 Braidwood, S J, *The Black poor and white philanthropists. London's Blacks: foundations of the Sierra Leone settlements.* Liverpool: Liverpool University Press, 199??, 288pp

History, C19th

3617 Abasiattai, M B, The search for independence: New World Blacks in Sierra Leone and Liberia, 1787–1847, *Journal of Black studies,* 23, 1 (1992) 107–116

3618 Sillah, M-B, Edward Blyden and Islam in Sierra Leone: a study of African intellectual response to British colonialism, *Hamdard islamicus,* 14, 4 (1991) 23–42

3619 Wyse, A J G, The place of Sierra Leone in African diaspora studies, in Ajayi J F A & Peel, J D Y (eds), *Peoples and empires (entry 429),* 107–20

Industry & trade

3620 Lahair, B, Salt processing in Sierra Leone, *Ahfad journal,* 9, 1 (1992) 28–54

Law

3621 Thompson, B, Child abuse in Sierra Leone: normative disparities, *International journal of law and the family,* 5, 1 (1991) 13–23

Library - documentation

3622 Binns, M, Binns, J A, *Sierra Leone.* Oxford: Clio, 1992, 235pp

Medical

3623 Bell, L V, *Mental and social disorder in subsaharan Africa: the case of Sierra Leone 1787–1990.*

New York: Greenwood, 1991, 206pp

Natural resources

3624 Hewapathirane, D U, Swampland resources of Sierra Leone: factors affecting their development, *Eastern and southern Africa geographical journal,* 3, 1 (1992) 51–63

Politics

3625 Kandeh, J D, Politicization of ethnic identities in Sierra Leone, *African studies review,* 35, 1 (1992) 81–99

3626 Kandeh, J K, Sierra Leone: contradictory class functionality of the 'soft' state, *Review of African political economy,* 55 (1992) 30–43

3627 Kline, B, Siera Leone: civil-military republic, in Danopoulos C P (ed), *From military to civilian rule* (London: Routledge, 1992), 214–29

Religion, philosophy

3628 Bah, M A, The status of Muslims in Sierra Leone and Liberia, *Journal of the Institute of Muslim Minority Affairs,* 12, 2 (1991) 464–481

Rural economy

see also: 2582

3629 Bah, O M, Community participation in rural water supply development in Sierra Leone, *Community development journal,* 27, 1 (1992) 30–41

3630 Hewapathirane, D U, The use of swamp lands for rice farming in Sierra Leone, *Eastern and southern Africa geographical journal,* 2, 1 (1991) 111–127

3631 Knickle, K, *Integrating*

*small-scale irrigation development
with the existing agricultural system: a
case study of smallholder swamp rice
schemes in Sierra Leone.* London:
ODI, Irrigation Management
Network, 1992, 28pp

Sociology

3632 Thayer, J S, A dissenting view
of Creole culture in Sierra Leone,
Cahiers d'études africaines, 31, 1/2
(1991) 215–30

TOGO

Anthropology

see also: 2502
3633 Blier, R, Diviners as alienists
and annunciators among the
Batammaliba of Togo, in Peek P M
(ed), *African divination (entry 47),*
73–90
3634 De la Torre, I, *Le vodu en
Afrique de l'Ouest: rites et traditions -
le cas des sociétés Guen-Mina (sud
Togo).* Paris: Harmattan, 1991,
175pp
3635 Dugast, S, "Ouvrir la bouche
de l'ancêtre": le processus
d'ancestralisation à travers
quelques séquences des rites
funéraires chez les Bassar du
Nord-Togo, *Systèmes de pensée en
Afrique noire,* 11, (1991) 131–180
3636 Kossi, K E, *La structure
socio-politique et son articulation avec
la pensée religuese chez le Aja-Tado
du sud-est Togo.* Stuttgart: Steiner,
1990, 320pp
3637 Smadja, M, Les affaires du
mort, *Systèmes de pensée en Afrique
noire,* 11, (1991) 57–89
**3638 Van Rouveroy van Nieuwaal,
E A B,** Sorcellerie et justice
coutumière dans une société
togolaise: une quantité
négligeable?, *Journal of legal
pluralism and unofficial law,* 29,

(1990) 137–162

Economy - Development

3639 Gozo, K M, Dravie, A A,
*L'état et le secteur non-structuré au
Togo.* Addis Ababa: PECTA, 1990,
56pp

Economic and social history

3640 Reitsma, H, de Haan, L,
Northern Togo and the world
economy, *Political geography
quarterly,* 11, 5 (1992) 475–84
3641 Schürkens, U, Le travail au
Togo sous mandat de la France
(1919–1941), *Revue français
d'histoire d'outre-mer,* 79, 295
(1992) 227–240

Education

see also: 3651
3642 Paul, J J, Technical secondary
education in Togo and Cameroun -
research note, *Economics of
education review,* 9, 4 (1990)
405–410
3643 Ulferts, H, *Les femmes au Togo:
leur access à l'éducation et à la
formation.* Bremen: Universität
Bremen, Nord-Süd Forum, 1992,
36pp

Gender

No entry, see also: 3643, 3653

History, C20th

3644 Agbobli, A K, *Sylvanus
Olympio: un destin tragique.* Paris:
Harmattan, 1992, 189pp
3645 Erbar, R, *Ein 'Platz an der
Sonne'? Die Verwaltungs- und
Wirtschaftgeschichte der deutschen
Kolonie Togo 1884–1914.* Stuttgart:
Steiner, 1991, 350pp
3646 Kent, J, The Ewe question,

1945–56: French and British
reactions to nationalism in West
Africa, in Twaddle M (ed),
Imperialism (entry 464), 183–206
3647 Schuerkens, U,
L'administration française au Togo
et l'utilisation de la notion de
coutume, *Droits et cultures,* 23
(1992) 213–30

Industry & trade

3648 Bergeron, I, Privatisation
through leasing: the Togo steel
case, in Ramamurti R & Vernon,
R (eds), *Privatisation and control
of state-owned enterprises* (Washington:
World Bank, 1991), 153–75
3649 Etienne-Nugue, J, *Artisanats
traditionnels en Afrique noire: Togo.*
Paris: Harmattan, for Institut
Culturel Africain, 1992, 222pp
3650 Larson, T J, Six-day markets
of the Kabiye of north Togo, *South
African journal of ethnology,* 14, 4
(1991) 115–121

Language

3651 Lange, M-F, Le choix des
langues enseignées à l'école au
Togo: quels enjeux politiques?,
Cahiers des sciences humaines, 27,
3/4 (1991) 477–495

Law

3652 Adjamagbo-Johnson, K, La
propriété à l'épreuve de la
législation foncière et agraire,
Penant, 102, 809 (1992)
215–233
3653 Baerends, E A, Woman is
king, man a mere child: some notes
on the socio-legal position of
women among the Anufom in
northern Togo, *Journal of legal
pluralism and unofficial law,* 30/31
(1990/1991) 33–75
3654 Massina, P, Plaidoyer pour le

fonctionnement de la juridiction
administrative au Togo, *Revue
burkinabè de droit,* 19/20, (1991)
7–25

Literature

3655 Riesz, J, et al, (eds), *Le champ
littéraire togolais.* Altendorf:
Gräbner, 1991, 199pp

Politics

see also: 805
3656 Bassah, A, Coup d'oeil sur la
nouvelle administration territoriale
togolaise, *Revue juridique et
politique,* 45, 3/4 (1991) 335–45
3657 Dogbé, Y E, *Le renouveau
démocratique au Togo.* Lome:
Akpagnon, 1991, 84pp

Religion, philosophy

3658 Barbier, J C, El-Hadj Bukari
dit 'Modjolobo' ou le guerre des
fétiches à Sokodé, *Islam et sociétés
au Sud du Sahara,* 5 (1991) 73–102

Rural economy

3659 Antheaume, B, Pontie, G,
les planteurs-rénovateurs de cacao
du Litimé (centre-ouest du Togo):
l'innovation technique à marche
forcée, *Cahiers des sciences humaines,*
26, 4 (1990) 655–677
3660 Schadek, H P,
*Entwicklungsmöglichkeiten
kleinbäuerlicher Betreibssysteme in der
Zentralregion Togos.* Kiel: Vauk,
1992, 353pp

Urban studies

see also: 1114
3661 Marguerat, Y, *Lomé, les étapes
de la croissance: une brève histoire de
la capitale du Togo.* Lome: Haho,
1992, 64pp

3662 Schilter, C, *L'agriculture urbaine à Lomé.* Paris: Karthala, 1991, 334pp

3663 Schilter, C, L'agriculture urbain: une activité créatrice d'emplois, en économie de survie (le cas de Lomé), *Cahiers des sciences humaines,* 27, 1/2 (1991) 159–168

WESTERN SAHARA

International relations

3664 Berramdame, A, *La Sahara Occidentale: enjeu magrébin.* Paris: Karthala, 1992, 357pp

Politics

3665 Moha, E, *Le Sahara occidental: ou la guerre salle de Boumedienne.* Paris: Picollec, 1990, 189pp

3666 Rössel, K, *Wind, Sand und (Mercedes-) Sterne: Westsahara - der vergessene Kampf für die Freiheit.* Unkel/ Rhein: Horlemann, 1991, 413pp

WEST CENTRAL AFRICA

Anthropology

3670 Ballif, N, *Les Pygmées de la grand forêt.* Paris: Harmattan, 1992, 240pp

Economy - Development

3671 Kitchen, R, Problems of regional integration in Africa: UDEAC, in Milner C & Rayner, A J (eds), *Policy adjustment (entry 184),* 221–37

Economic and social history

3672 Mollion, P, *Sur les pistes de l'Oubangui-Chari au Tchad, 1890–1930: la drame du portage en Afrique centrale.* Paris: Harmattan, 1992, 272pp

Finance

3673 Banque des Etats de l'Afrique Centrale, The experience of the central African states, in Roe A R et al (eds) *Instruments of economic policy (entry 341),* 107–115

Geography, human

3674 Atsimadja, F A, The changing geography of central Africa, in Chapman G P & Baker, K M (eds), *The changing geography of Africa (entry 405),* 52–79

CAMEROUN

General

3675 Salmon, P, Symoens, J J, (eds), *La recherche en sciences humaines au Cameroun.* Brussels: Académie Royale des Sciences d'Outre-Mer, 1991, 145pp

Anthropology

see also: 31, 32

3676 Christensen, T G, *An African tree of life.* Maryknoll: Orbis, 1990, 184pp

3677 Curley, R, Private dreams and public knowledge in a Camerounian independent church, in Jedrej M C & Shaw, R (eds), *Dreaming, religion and society (entry 42),* 135–52

3678 Dognin, R, L'arbre peul, *Cahiers des sciences humaines,* 26, 4 (1990) 505–529

3679 Ifeka, C, The mystical and political powers of Queen Mothers, kings and commoners in Nso', Cameroon, in Ardener S (ed), *Persons and powers (entry 31),* 135–57

3680 Ombolo, J P, *Sexe et société en Afrique noire: l'anthopologie sexuelle Beti. Essai analytique, critique et comparatif.* Paris: Harmattan, 1991, 395pp

3681 van Beek, W E A, The dirty smith: smell as a social frontier among the Kapsiki/Higi of north Cameroon and northeastern

Nigeria, *Africa,* 62, 1 (1992) 38–58

3682 Wazaki, H, The political structure of the Bamoun kingdom in Cameroon and the urban-rural relationship, *Senri ethnological studies,* 31 (1992) 303–371

Demography

3683 Defo, B C, Mortality and attrition processes in longditudinal studies in Africa: an appraisal of the IFORD studies, *Population studies,* 46, 2 (1992) 327–48

Economy - Development

3684 Derrick, J, Cameroon: from oil boom to recession, *Africa recovery,* 6, 2 (1992) 16–21

3685 Essombe Edimo, J-R, Désengagement de l'Etat et réhabilitation des entreprises parapubliques au Cameroun, *Mondes en développement,* 19, 75/76 (1991) 67–73

3686 Gauthier, M, *A social accounting matrix for Cameroon.* Ithaca: Food and Nutrition Policy Program, Cornell University, 1991, 44pp

3687 Jua, N, Cameroon: jump-starting an economic crisis, *Africa insight,* 21, 3 (1991) 162–71

3688 Kambou, G, Devarajan, S, Over, M, The economic impact of AIDS in an African country: simulations with a computable general equilibrium model of Cameroon, *Journal of African economies,* 1, 1 (1992) 109–30

3689 Tedga, P J M, *Entreprise publiques, état et crise au Cameroun: faillité d'un système.* Paris: Harmattan, 1990, 303pp

Economic and social history

3690 Dongmo, J-L, Conflits agriculteurs-éleveurs pour la terre sur le versant oriental des monts Bamboutos (ouest-Cameroun), *Revue de géographie du Cameroun,* 10, 2 (1991) 117–129

3691 Essomba, J M, *Civilisation de fer er sociétés en Afrique centrale.* Paris: Harmattan, 1992, 699pp

3692 Herbert, E W, Lost-wax casting in the Cameroun grassfields, in Henige D & McCaskie, T C (eds), *West African economic and social history (entry 2521),* 69–80

3693 Jenkins, P, In the eye of the beholder: an exercise in the interpretation of two photographs taken in Cameroun early this century, in Henige D & McCaskie, T C (eds), *West African economic and social history (entry 2521),* 93–103

3694 Shimada, Y, Formation de la civilisation 'complexe' islam et vêtements en Afrique sub-saharienne: étude de cas de l'Adamawa, *Senri ethnological studies,* 31 (1992) 373–422

3695 Vincent, J F, Données nouvelles sur la fondation et le peuplement de la chefferie de Marva (Nord Cameroun), *Senri ethnological studies,* 31 (1992) 481–501

Education

see also: 3642

3696 Mbala Owono, R, *Scolarisation et dispartités socioéconomiques dans le Province de l'Est au Cameroun.* Yaounde: CEPER, 1990, 95pp

3697 Sikounmo, H, *L'école du sous-développement: gros plan sur l'enseignement secondaire en Afrique.* Paris: Harmattan, 1992, 290pp

3698 Syndicat nationale des enseignants du supérieur, *La dérive de l'université au Cameroun/The university in Cameroon: an institution in disarray.*

Yaoundé: SYNES, 1992, 94, 79pp

3699 Tafah-Edokat, E O, The pure human capital investment model: a test and application using LDC data, *Scandinavian journal of development alternatives,* 11, 1 (1992) 63–79

Environment

3700 Hallaire, A, Les montagnards du nord du Cameroun et leur environnement, *Afrique contemporaine,* 161 (1992) 144–155

3701 Ngoufo, R, Conservation de la nature et développement rural dans le cadre du projet Korup (sud-ouest Cameroun), *Revue de géographie du Cameroun,* 10, 2 (1991) 99–115

Finance

3702 Ndongko, W A, The experience of Cameroon, in Roe A R et al *Instruments of economic policy (entry 341),* 79–88

Food

see also: 3754

3703 Froment, A, Koppert, G, Une évaluation biologique du développement économique est-elle possible?, *Cahiers des sciences humaines,* 27, 1/2 (1991) 193–204

Gender

see also: 3679

3704 Chilver, E M, Women cultivators, cows and cash crops in Cameroon, in Ardener S (ed), *Persons and powers (entry 31),* 105–33

3705 Kondé, E, *The use of women for the empowerment of men in African nationalist politics: the 1958 'anlu' in Cameroon.* Boston: African Studies

Centre, Boston University, 1990, 16pp

3706 Lewis, B, Farming women, public policy and the women's ministry: a case study from Cameroon, in Staudt K (ed), *Women, international development, and politics* (Philadelphia: Temple UP, 1990), 180–200

Geography, physical

3707 Walker, A B, et al, Seismic monitoring of Lake Nyos, Cameroon, following the gas release disaster of August 1986, in McCall G J H et al (eds), *Geohazards, natural and man-made* (London: Chapman & Hall, 1992), 65–79

History, early

3708 Essomba, J M, (ed), *L'archéologie au Cameroun.* Paris: Karthala, 1992, 384pp

3709 Marliac, A, *De la préhistorie à la historie au Cameroun septentrional.* Paris: ORSTOM, 12991, 944pp

History, C19th

3710 Eguchi, P K, 'The Europeans are not good': a Fulbe 'mbooku' poem of protest, *Senri ethnological studies,* 31 (1992) 465–480

3711 Midel, M, *Fulbe und Deutsche in Adamawa (Nord-Kamerun) 1809–1916: auswirkungen afrikanischer und kolonialier Eroberung.* Frankfurt: Lang, 1990, 360pp

History, C20th

see also: 3705

3712 Eckert, A, *Die Duala und die Kolonialmächte: eine Untersuchung zu Widerstand, Protest und Protonationalismus in Kamerun vor*

dem Zweiten Weltkrieg. Munster:
Lit, 1991, 347pp

3713 Eyinga, A, *L'UPC: une révolution manquée?* Paris: Chaka, 1991, 191pp

3714 Mohammadou, E, Le soulèvement mahdiste de Goni Waday dans la Haute-Bénoué (juillet 1907), *Senri ethnological studies,* 31 (1992) 423–464

3715 Ngueukam Tientcheu, A, Ruben Um Nyobé: le héros national camerounais, *Afrique 2000,* 5 (1991) 75–87

3716 Oyono, D, *Colonie ou mandat international? La politique française au Cameroun de 1919 à 1946.* Paris: Harmattan, 1992, 221pp

3717 Rohde, E, *Chefferie Bamileke: Tradition, Herrschaft und Kolonialsystem.* Munster: Lit, 1990, 263pp

Industry & trade

3718 Hagel, T, *Die Privatisierung des Düngmittelsektors in Kamerun.* Hamburg: Institut für Afrika-Kunde, 1992, 122pp

3719 Hillebrand, E, et al, *Le secteur informel au Cameroun: importance et perspectives.* Yaounde: Friedrich Ebert Foundation, 1991, 50pp

3720 Richman, A, de Wilde, T, Marketing of small-scale maize mills in Cameroon, in de Wilde T & Schreurs, S (eds), *Opening the marketplace to small enterprise* (West Hartford: Kumarian, 1991), 25–45

International economic relations

see also: 1244

3721 Amin, J A, *The Peace Corps in Cameroon.* Kent: Kent State University Press, 1992, 240pp

3722 Devarajan, S, Rodrik, D, Pro-competition effects of trade reform: results from a CGE model of Cameroon, *European economic review,* 35, 5 (1991) 1157–84

3723 Messing, W, *Geschäftspartner Kamerun.* Cologne: Bundesstelle für Aussenhandelsinformation, 1992, 70pp

Labour & manpower

3724 Boisvert, J, Kamdem, E, La formation permanente en gestion au Cameroun, *Afrique 2000,* 10 (1992) 67–85

Language

see also: 3748

3725 Cook, A, Cameroun: l'étonnant bilinguisme, *Bulletin of francophone Africa,* 1 (1992) 74–82

Law

3726 Mbome, F, Les expériences de révision constitutionnelle au Cameroun, *Penant,* 102, 808 (1992) 19–45

3727 Olinga, A D, Cameroun: vers un présidentialisme démocratique: réflexions sur la révision constitutionelle du 23 avril 1991, *Revue juridique et politique,* 46, 4 (1992) 419–29

Literature

3728 Breitinger, E, Kamerun: literaten kämpfen gegen die zensur, *Internationales Afrikaforum,* 28, 3 (1992) 255–265

3729 Drame, K, *The novel as transformation myth: a study of the novels of Mongo Beti and Ngugi wa Thiong'o.* Syracuse, NY: Syracuse University, Maxwell School of Citizenship and Public Affairs, 1990, 122pp

Media

3730 Churchill, E M, The right to

inform and the 1990 press law in Cameroon, *Africa media review*, 6, 3 (1992) 19–29

3731 Mehler, A, *Presse und politischer Aufbruch in Kamerun: Kommentertie Presseschau für das Jahr 1990.* Hamburg: Institut für Afrika-Kunde, 1991, 221pp

Medical

3732 van der Pol, H, Type of feeding and infant mortality in Yaoundé, in van der Walle E et al (eds), *Mortality and society (entry 771)*, 303–18

Natural resources

3733 Köhlhoff, D, Schilling, C, Water for Gouzda - a project to improve water supply in north Cameroon, *Applied geography and development*, 37, (1991) 68–77

3734 Rietsch, B J, *Nutzung und Schutz natürlicher Ressourcen in Kamerun.* Hamburg: Institut für Afrika-Kunde, 1992, 422pp

3735 Rietsch, B J, Périodisation des logiques de gestion des ressources naturelles et fondement d'une politique environnementale au Cameroun, *Afrika spectrum*, 26, 3 (1991) 351–373

Planning

3736 Njoh, A, Institutional impediments to private residential development in Cameroon, *Third World planning review*, 14, 1 (1991) 21–37

Politics

see also: 805, 896, 3687, 3728
3737 Awung, D T, The economic bases of the current political crisis in Cameroon, in Caron B et al

(eds), *Democratic transition in Africa (entry 817)*, 349–58

3738 Bassomb, N, *Le quartier special: détenu sans proces au Cameroun.* Paris: Harmattan, 1992, 191pp

3739 Eyinga, A, *L'UPC: une révolution manquée?* Paris: Harmattan, 1992, 191pp

3740 Gaillard, P, Pluralisme et régionalisme dans la politique camerounaise, *Afrique 2000*, 11 (1992) 97–109

3741 Kuoh, C T, *Le Cameroun de l'après-Ahidjo.* Paris: Karthala, 1992, 160pp

3742 Kuoh, C T, *Mon témoignage sur le Cameroun de l'indépendance. 2: une fresque du régime Ahidjo (1970–1982).* Paris: Karthala, 1991, 203pp

3743 Kuoh, C T, *Une fresque du régime Ahidjo.* Paris: Karthala, 1991, 208pp

3744 Mbembe, A, Power and obscenity in the post-colonial period: the case of Cameroon, in Manor J (ed), *Rethinking Third World Politics (entry 889)*, 166–82

3745 Mbembe, A, Provisional notes on the postcolony, *Africa*, 62, 1 (1992) 3–37

3746 Owona, T, *Die Souveränität und Legitimität des Staates Kamerun.* Munich: Tuduv, 1991, 351pp

3747 Various authors, *Le Cameroun éclaté? Une anthologie commentée des revendications ethniques.* Yaounde: Editions C3, 1992, 595pp

Religion, philosophy

No entry, see also: 3677

Rural economy

see also: 3704, 3706
3748 Barreteau, D, Dieu, M, Linguistique et développement rizicole dans le nord du Cameroun,

Cahiers des sciences humaines, 27, 3/4 (1991) 367–387

3749 Engola Oyep, J, Du jumelage à la péréquation au Cameroun: assurer la survie des périmètres hydro-rizicoles à l'heure de l'ajustement structurel, *Cahiers des sciences humaines,* 27, 1/2 (1991) 53–63

3750 Goheen, M, Chiefs, subchiefs ands local control: negotiations over land, struggles over meaning, *Africa,* 62, 3 (1992) 389–412

3751 Nana-Fabu, R, Mobilising savings in Cameroon, in Frimpong-Ansah J H & Ingham, B (eds), *Saving for economic recovery (entry 142),* 181–97

3752 Santoir, C, *Sous l'empire de cacao: étude diachronqie de deux terroirs camerounais.* Paris: ORSTOM, 1992, 192pp

3753 Seignobos, C, L'igname dans les monts Mandara (Nord Cameroun), *Geneva-Africa,* 30, 1 (1992) 77–96

Science & technology

No entry, see also: 1073

Urban studies

3754 Dongmo, J L, *L'approvisionnement alimentaire de Yaoundé.* Yaoundé: Yaoundé University, 1990, 229pp

CENTRAL AFRICAN REPUBLIC

Anthropology

No entry, see also: 3676

Arts

3755 Saulnier, P P, Chants d'orchestres en République

centrafricaine, *Politique africaine,* 45 (1992) 135–41

Current affairs

3756 Le Bris, E, Quantin, P, Les barricades, sont-elles anticonstitutionelles?, *Politique africaine,* 48 (1992) 142–45

CONGO

Economic and social history

3757 Samarin, W J, 'La politique indigène' in the history of Bangui, *Revue française d'histoire d'outre-mer,* 79, 294 (1992) 53–86

3758 Cantournet, J, *Des affaires et des hommes: Noirs et blancs, commerçants et fonctionnaires dans l'Oubangui du début du siècle.* Paris: Société d'ethnologie, 1991 (i.e. 1992), 233pp

Food

3759 Gruénais, M-E Delpuech, F, Du risque au développement: nutritionnelle: à propos d'une enquête, *Cahiers des sciences humaines,* 28, 1 (1992) 37–55

3760 Trèche, S, Massamba, J, Demain, le manioc sera-t-il encore l'aliment de base des Congolais?, *Food, nutrition and agriculture,* 1, 1 (1991) 19–26

History, C20th

3761 Thystère-Tchicaya, J P, *Itinéraire d'un africain vers la démoratie.* Geneva: Tricorne, 1992, 173pp

Industry & trade

see also: 3829
3762 Leplaideur, A, Moustier, P,

Dynamique du vivrier à Brazzaville: les mythes de l'anarchie et de l'inefficace, *Cahiers des sciences humaines*, 27, 1/2 (1991) 147–149

International relations

3763 **Mobonda, H,** Which American past for Congolese audiences?, *Journal of American history*, 79, 2 (1992) 472–476

Literature

3764 **Kashombo Ntompa,** 'Antoine m'a vendu son destin' de Sony Labou Tansi: une parabolede l'échec, *Zaïre-Afrique*, 259, (1991) 473–484

3765 **Luce, L F,** Passages: the women of Sony Labou Tansi, *Frech review*, 64, 5 (1991) 739–746

Media

3766 **Miyouna, L-R,** Télévision et développement? L'exemple du Congo, *Mondes en développement*, 19, 73 (1991) 57–61

Politics

3767 **Fayolle, A,** Les collectivités locales en république populaire du Congo, *Revue congolaise de droit*, 9 (1991) 61–90

Urban studies

3768 **Carozzi, C,** Il corrido urbano fra Brazzaville e Pointe Noire, in Beguinot C (ed), *Progetto strategico 'Aree metropolitane e innovazione': progress di ricerca* (Rome: Consiglio Nationale delle Ricerche, 1991), 15–34

EQUATORIAL GUINEA

Anthropology

3769 **Creus, J,** *Cuentos de los Ndowe de Guinea Ecuatorial.* Madrid: Edigrafos, 1991, 285pp

3770 **Creus, J,** Los cuentos de Ndjambu y el pensiamneto tradicional Ndowe, *Africa 2000*, 15 (1991) 37–43

3771 **Mampel, A B,** Iniciacion a la cocina Fang, *Africa 2000*, 15 (1991) 46–50

History, C20th

3772 **Ligero Morote, A,** Un episodio para la historia de Guinea ex-española, *Estudios africanos*, 5, 8/9 (1990) 7–20

3773 **Neves, C A das,** A reacção dos habitantes de Fernando Pó e Ano Bom à dominação estrangeira, *Studia*, 50, (1991) 199–214

Politics

No entry, see also: 3774

Sociology

3774 **Sepa Bonaba, E,** La Guinea de la Diáspora, *Estudios africanos*, 5, 8/9 (1990) 21–32

GABON

General

3775 **Barnes, J F,** *Gabon: beyond the colonial legacy.* Boulder: Westview, 1992, 163pp

Economy - Development

3776 **de Mowbray, P,** *Gabon to 1995: will oil secure economic transformation?* London: Economist Intelligence Unit, 1991, 93pp

History, C19th

3777 Gardinier, D E, The American Presbyterian mission in Gabon: male Mpongwe converts and agents, 1870–1883, *American Presbyterians,* 69, 1 (1991) 61–70

Library - documentation

3778 Gardinier, D, *Gabon.* Oxford: Clio, 1992, 178pp

Politics

see also: 3573

3779 Dorabji, E V, Coup, withdrawal and economic development in Gabon, in Danopoulos C P (ed), *From military to civilian rule* (London: Routledge, 1992), 195–213

3780 Pochon, J F, Ajustement et démocratisation: l'atypisme du Gabon, *Geopolitique africaine,* 15, 1 (1992) 59–70

CENTRAL AFRICA

Agriculture, scientific

3800 Voss, J, Conserving and increasing on-farm genetic diversity: farmer management of varietal bean mixtures in central Africa, in Moock J L & Rhoades, R E (eds), *Diversity (entry 1038)*, 34–51

Anthropology

3801 Gladstone, J, Luhrmann, T M, Audrey I Richards (1899–1984): Africanist and humanist, in Ardener S (ed), *Persons and powers (entry 31)*, 13–28, 51–57

Economy - Development

No entry, see also: 4210

Economic and social history

3802 Lunn, J, The political economy of primary railway construction in the Rhodesias, 1890–1911, *Journal of African history*, 33, 2 (1992) 239–54

Geography, human

No entry, see also: 3674

Health & welfare services

3803 Fisher, M, *Nswanga - the heir: the life and times of Charles Fisher, a surgeon in central Africa.* Ndola:

Mission Press, 1991, 247pp

History, general

3804 Wrigley, C, The *longue durée* in the heart of darkness, *Journal of African history*, 33, 1 (1992) 129–34 (review article)

History, C19th

3805 Cornelis, S, et al, *H M Stanley, explorateur au service du roi.* Tervuren: Musée de l'Afrique centrale, 1991, 88pp

Industry & trade

3806 Kitchen, R, Sarkey, D, Industrial efficiency and policy reform: the Central African Customs and Economic Union (UDEAC), *Industry and development*, 30, (1991) 57–80

International economic relations

3807 Gleave, M B, The Dar es Salaam transport corridor: an appraisal, *African affairs*, 91, 363 (1992) 249–67

Politics

3808 De Smedt, S, Presidentiële instituties en presidentialische praktijken postkoloniale Centraalafrikaninaanse politiek, *Res publica*, 33, 2 (1991) 303–26

Sociology

3809 Ndongko, T, The Lagos Plan and social development in central Africa: an evaluation, in Mohammed D (ed), *Social development in Africa (entry 1093)*, 25–106

ANGOLA

General

3810 Sogge, D, *Sustainable peace: Angola's recovery.* Harare: Southern African Research and Documentation Centre, 1992, 152pp

Anthropology

3811 Estermann, C, Die Twa im südwesten von Angola, *Journal (Namibia scientific society),* 42, (1990) 47–62
3812 Millet, J, Aspectos de religiosidad popular angolana, *Africa (São Paulo),* 12/13 (1989/90) 159–80
3813 Serrano, C, Angola: o discurso do colonialismo e a antropologia aplicada, *Africa (São Paulo),* 14/15 (1991/92) 15–36

Arts

3814 Gouveia, H C, Alarcïo, A, Museus e património cultural de Angola, *Revista internacional de esudos africanos,* 12/13, (1990) 421–451

Current affairs

3815 Beaudet, P, Fin de guerre en Angola: crise économique, crise de société, *Politique africaine,* 45 (1992) 148–53
3816 Coulson, A, Arms dump, *Focus on Africa,* 3, 3 (1992) 11–14

3817 Kurzweg, H U, Angola am Anfang einer neuen Periode, *Internationales Afrikaforum,* 28, 3 (1992) 273–283
3818 Smith, P, Angola: free and fair elections, *Review of African political economy,* 55 (1992) 101–106

Economy - Development

3819 Aguilar, R, Zejan, M, *Angola 1991: the last stand of central planning.* Stockholm: SIDA, 1992, 43pp
3820 Freitas, A J, Angola: economic recovery, *SADCC Energy,* 8, 20 (1990) 37–40
3821 Roque, F M, *Economia de Angola.* Libon: Bertrand, 1991, 335pp
3822 Roque, F M, *Wirtschaftsdemokratie in Angola: Gedenken sur Wirtschaftsreform.* Bonn: UNITA Freundskreis, 1991, 29pp
3823 UNIDO, *Angola: economic reconstruction and rehabilitation.* Vienna: UNIDO, 1990, 75pp

Economic and social history

3824 Pitcher, A, Lançar as sementes do fracasso: as primeiras tentativas de cultivo de algodão em Angola e Moçambique, *Revista internacional de estudos africanos,* 12/13, (1990) 99–135

History, general

3825 Thornton, J K, Miller, J C, A crónica como fonte, história e hagiografia: o *Catálogo dos governadores de Angola, Revista internacional de estudos africanos,* 12/13, (1990) 9–55

History, C6–18th

3826 Esteves, M L, Para o estudo

do tráfico de escravos de Angola
(1640–1668), *Studia,* 50, (1991)
79–107

History, C20th

3827 Birmingham, D, *Frontline
nationalism in Angola and
Mozambique.* London: Currey,
1992, 122pp

3828 Mourïo, F A A, O contexto
histórico-cultural da criação literária
em Agostinho Neto: memória dos
anos cinquenta, *Africa (São Paulo),*
14/15 (1991/92) 55–68

Industry & trade

see also: 521

3829 Kress, A, Conceptions and
reality of industrialisation based on
agricultural development in Angola
and in Congo, *African development
perspectives yearbook,* 2, (1990/91)
479–487

International relations

see also: 3846

3830 Rothchild, D, Conflict
management in Angola, *Transafrica
forum,* 8, 1 (1991) 77–101

3831 Tvedten, I, US policy toward
Angola since 1975, *Journal of
modern African studies,* 30, 1 (1992)
31–52

3832 Weitz, R, The Reagan doctrine
defeated Moscow in Angola, *Orbis,*
36, 1 (1992) 57–68

3833 Windrich, E, *The cold war
guerrilla: Jonas Savimbia, the US
media and the Angolan war.* New
York: Greenwood, 1992, 183pp

Law

3834 Amnesty International,
*Angola: human rights guarantees in
the revised constitution.* London:
Amnesty International, 1991, 33pp

Library - documentation

3835 Black, R, *Angola.* Oxford:
Clio, 1992, 176pp

Literature

3836 Baccega, M A, O movimento
entre a ficção e a história a caso
Mayombe, Africa (São Paulo),
12/13 (1989/90) 137–48

3837 Carter, J, Colonial literature in
Angola: a problem of taxonomy, in
Nethersole R (ed), *Emerging
literatures (entry 726),* 81–90

3838 Laban, M, *Angola: encontro
com escritores.* Porto: Fundação
Eng. Antonio de Almeida, 1991, 2
vols, 925pp

3839 Mensah, A M, Gender
relations in Perpetela's *Mayombe,
Marang,* 9 (1991) 121–32

Politics

see also: 3830, 3833

3840 Alvarez, D A, Angola: punto
de viraje, *Africa (São Paulo),* 14/15
(1991/92) 37–54

3841 Beaudet, P, (ed), *Angola: bilan
d'un socialisme de guerre.* Paris:
Harmattan, 1992, 131pp

3842 Beaudet, P, et al, *Angola and
southern Africa: uncertain futures.*
Bellville: University of the Western
Cape, Centre for Southern African
Studies, 1991, 17pp

3843 Conteh-Morgan, E, Civil and
external conflict interface: violence,
militarisation, and conflict
management in the Angolan civil
war, in Rupesinghe K (ed), *Internal
conflict (entry 932),* 187–207

3844 Gonzalez, D, Changes in
Angola: a viewpoint, *Revista de
Africa y Medio Oriente,* 3, 1 (1991)
101–134

3845 Kalflèche, J M, *Jonas Savimbi:
une autre voie pour l'Afrique.* Paris:
Criterion, 1992, 265pp

3846 Matlosa, K, The post-independence war in Angola and prospects for a negotiated settlement, *Taamuli*, NS 2, 1/2 (1991) 28–45

3847 Webber, M, Angola: continuity and change, *Journal of communist studies*, 8, 2 (1992) 126–44 (also in *entry 860*)

Rural economy

3848 Ramazzotti, M, Il problema dell'acqua nel sud dell'Angola, *Africa (Rome)*, 46, 3 (1991) 375–402

Science & technology

No entry, see also: 1082

MALAWI

General

3849 Skjønsberg, E, *Malawi: et ukjent land for Norge?* Oslo: Senter for Utvikling og milj, 1991, 22pp

Agriculture, scientific

3850 MacColl, D, Climate, weather and yields of maize at Bunda college, *Bunda journal of agricultural research*, 2, (1990) 58–84

Anthropology

3851 Nazombe, A, The text and the social context: witchcraft and death in Nantongwe songs, *Religion in Malawi*, 3 (1991) 34–38

3852 Soko, B J, The Vimbuza phenomenon: dialogue with the spirits, *Religion in Malawi*, 3 (1991) 28–33

Arts

3853 Nambote, M, An integrated approach to the study of traditional African dance, *Tizame*, 2 (1990) 41–48

Current affairs

3854 Kalipeni, E, Political development and prospects for democracy in Malawi, *Transafrica forum*, 9, 1 (1992) 27–40

3855 Lawyers Committee for Human Rights, *Malawi: ignoring calls for change.* New York: the Committee, 1992, 13pp

Demography

3856 House, W J, Zimalirana, G, Rapid population growth and poverty generation in Malawi, *Journal of modern African studies*, 30, 1 (1992) 141–61

Economy - Development

3857 Adam, C, et al, Malawi, in Adam C et al *Adjusting privatisation* (London: Currey, 1992), 352–75

3858 Chilowa, W, *Structural adjustment and poverty: the case of Malawi.* Bergen: CMI, 1991, 14pp

Economic and social history

3859 Makambe, E P, The impact of the 1907 agreement on Malawi labour migration to the Zimbabwean colonial market, *Scandinavian journal of development alternatives*, 11, 2 (1992) 95–123

3860 Phiri, K M, Precolonial migrations and agricultural change on the western side of Lake Malawi, *Eastern African social science research review*, 6,2 & 7/1, (1990/91) 157–70

Education

see also: 3868, 3889
3861 Fuller, B, Kapakasa, A,

What factors shape teacher quality: evidence from Malawi, *International journal of educational development,* 11, 2 (1991) 119–28

Environment

3862 Büchner, B, et al, *Gender, environmental degradation and development: the extent of the problem.* London: London Environmental Economics Centre, 1991, 37pp

3863 Mearns, R, *Environmental implications of structural adjustment: reflections on scientific method.* Brighton: Sussex University, IDS, 1991, 73pp

Finance

3864 Chaka, C S R, The experience of Malawi, in Roe A R et al (eds) *Instruments of economic policy (entry 341),* 52–61

3865 Chipeta, C, Mkandawire, M K, Interest rates, financial savings and macroeconomic adjustment in Malawi, in Frimpong-Ansah J H & Ingham, B (eds), *Saving for economic recovery (entry 142),* 119–38

Food

see also: 3882

3866 Chilowa, W, *Food insecurity and coping strategies among the low income urban households in Malawi.* Bergen: CMI, 1991, 22pp

3867 Chilowa, W, *Liberalisation of agricultural produce marketing and household food security in Malawi: preliminary results from baseline survey.* Bergen: CMI, 1991, 26pp

Gender

see also: 3895

3868 Davidson, J, Kanyuka, M, Girl's participation in basic

education in southern Malawi, *Comparative education review,* 36, 4 (1992) 446–66

3869 Hirschmann, D, The Malawi case: enclave politics, core resistance and 'Nkhoswe no. 1', in Staudt K (ed), *Women, international development, and politics* (Philadelphia: Temple UP, 1990), 163–79

3870 Nkunika, A I Z, The integration of women in development in Malawi: the role of the Ministry of Community Services, *Tizame,* 2 (1990) 24–30

Geography, human

3871 Kalipeni, E, Population redistribution in Malawi since 1964, *Geographical review,* 82, 1 (1992) 13–26

History, C6–18th

3872 Schoffeleers, M, *River of blood: the genesis of a martyr cult in southern Malawi, c. AD 1600.* Madison: University of Wisconsin Press, 1992, 325pp

History, C19th

3873 Ncozana, S S, Livingstonia Mission attitude to spirit possession, *Religion in Malawi,* 3 (1991) 43–51

3874 Sindima, H J, *The legacy of Scottish missionaries in Malawi.* Lewiston: Mellen, 1992, 152pp

History, C20th

3875 Kamlongera, C F, A species of pantomime to be deprecated: the case against Beni dance in colonial Malawi, *Tizame,* 2 (1990) 31–37

3876 McCracken, J, Authority and legitimacy in Malawi: policing and politics in a colonial state, in

Anderson D M & Killingray, D (eds), *Policing and decolonisation* (Manchester: Manchester UP, 1992), 158–86

3877 Power, J, 'Individualism is the antithesis of indirect rule': cooperative development and indirect rule in colonial Malawi, *Journal of southern African studies,* 18, 2 (1992) 317–47

3878 Woods, T, 'Bread with freedom and peace...': Rail workers in Malawi, 1954–1975, *Journal of southern African studies,* 18, 4 (1992) 727–38

Industry & trade

3879 Chipeta, M, Status of the informal sector in Malawi, *Southern Africa political & economic monthly,* 3, 12 (1990) 9–14

3880 Garrod, B, *The ferrocement boatbuilding project, Karonga, Malawi.* Portsmouth: Portsmouth Polytechnic, Centre for Marine Resource Economics, 1991, 15pp

3881 Kishindo, P, Land rights and fish farming in Malawi, *Eastern anthropologist,* 44, 2 (1991) 145–153

3882 Scarborough, V, *Domestic food market liberalisation in Malawi: a preliminary assessment.* Ashford: Wye College, 1990, 54pp

Law

see also: 688

3883 Kamchedzera, G S, The rights of the child in Malawi: an agenda for research, *International journal of law and the family,* 5, 3 (1991) 241–57

3884 Law Society, *Human rights in Malawi.* London: Law Society, 1992, 80pp

Natural resources

3885 Chapman, J D, Mpita

Nkhalango, a lowland forest relic unique in Malawi, *Nyala,* 12, 1/2 (1988) 3–26

Planning

3886 McClintock, H, Widening the role of physical planning in Africa: the experience of the National Physical Development Plan in Malawi, *Third World planning review,* 14, 1 (1991) 75–97

Politics

see also: 3884

3887 Blackwell, G, L'évolution politique du Malawi, *Afrique contemporaine,* 163 (1992) 17–25

Religion, philosophy

3888 Chiona, J, et al, Pastoral letter: the Catholic Bishops speak out, *Index on censorship,* 21, 5 (1992) 15–17

3889 Matiki, A J, Problems of Islamic education in Malawi, *Journal, Institute of muslim minority affairs,* 12, 1 (1991) 127–134

3890 van Dijk, R A, Young puritan preachers in post-independence Malawi, *Africa,* 62, 2 (1992) 159–81

Rural economy

see also: 1020

3891 Cromwell, E, Malawi, in Duncan A & Howell, J (eds), *Structural adjustment and the African farmer (entry 1017),* 113–57

3892 Dickerman, C W, Bloch, P C, *Land tenure and agricultural productivity in Malawi.* Madison: University of Wisconsin, Land Tenure Center, 1991, 56pp

3893 Dorward, A, Integrated decision rules as farm management tools in smallholder agriculture in

Malawi, *Journal of agricultural economics*, 42, 2 (1991) 146–160

3894 Nankumba, J S, Resource-use efficiency in selected farming systems in Malawi: implications for Agricultural Development Division (ADDs), *Bunda journal of agricultural research*, 2, (1990) 125–145

3895 Rauch, T, et al, *Small-scale processing at rural centres in Malawi: possibilities of development and promotion.* Weikersheim: Margraf, 1990, 217pp

3896 Sahn, D E, Arulpragasam, J, *Development through dualism? Land tenure, policy and poverty in Malawi.* Ithaca: Food and Nutrition Policy Program, Cornell University, 1991, 53pp

Science & technology

No entry, see also: 1073

Social welfare

3897 Simukonda, H P M, Creating a national NGO council for strengthening social welfare services in Africa: some organisational and technical problems experienced in Malawi, *Public administration and development*, 12, 5 (1992) 417–31

Urban studies

3898 Myburgh, D W, van Zyl, J A, Size relationships in the urban system of Malawi, *Africa insight*, 22, 2 (1992) 128–33

MOZAMBIQUE

General

3899 Pachelque, C, *Bibliografia, 1976-Junho de 1990.* Maputo: CEA,

Universidado Eudardo Mondlane, 1990, 38pp

Agriculture, scientific

3900 Silva, C da, Em Moçambique gado bovino em risco de extinção, *Extra*, 6 (1991) 12–18

Anthropology

see also: 3954

3901 da Gama Amaral, M G, *O povo Yao (mtundu wayao): (subsidios para o estudo de um povo do noreste de Moçambique).* Libson: Instituto de Invstigacão Cientifica Tropical, 1990, 493pp

Economy - Development

see also: 3924

3902 Hermele, K, Stick and carrot: political alliances and nascent capitalism in Mozambique, in Gibbon P & Bangura, Y (eds), *Authoritarianism, democracy and adjustment (entry 850)*, 169–87

3903 Mittleman, J H, Marginalisation and the international division of labour: Mozambique's strategy of opening the market, *African studies review*, 34, 3 (1991) 89–106

3904 Neves, A C, Breve apontamento sobre a situação actual na Província de Tete, *Arquivo*, 10 (1991) 209–220

3905 Utting, P, Mozambique, in his *Economic reform and Third World socialism* (Basingstoke: Macmillan, 1992, 49–82

Economic and social history

3906 Chilundo, A, Subsidos para o estudo do transporte rodoviario na Província de Nampula (1930–54), *Cadernos de historia*, 8 (1990) 73–90

3907 Coelho, J P B, Tete,

1900–1926, o estabelecimento de uma reserva da mão-de-obra, *Arquivo,* 10 (1991) 103–132

3908 Covane, L, A emigração clandestina de Moçambicanos para as minas e plantaçoes sul-africanas, 1897–1913, *Cadernos de historia,* 8 (1990) 91–102

3909 Isaacman, A, Coercion, paternalism and the labour process: the Mozambican cotton regime 1938–61, *Journal of southern African studies,* 18, 3 (1992) 487–526

3910 Isaacman, A, Isaacman, B, Os prazeiros como trans-raianos: um estudo sobre transformação social e cultural, *Arquivo,* 10 (1991) 5–48

3911 Mbwiliza, J F, *A history of commodity production in Makuani, 1600–1900: mercantilist accumulation to imperialist domination.* Dar es Salaam: Dar es Salaam University Press, 1991, 163pp

3912 Neves, J das, Tete e o trabalho migratório para a Rodésia do Sul, 1890–1913, *Arquivo,* 10 (1991) 83–102

3913 Tullner, M, Apontamento sobre a greve de 1917 no porto e caminho de ferro de Lourenço Marques, *Arquivo,* 9 (1991) 45–58

3914 Vieira, S, Os electricos de Lourenço Marques. Pt. 1, 1900–1920, *Arquivo,* 9 (1991) 5–44

Education

see also: 3924

3915 Macabi, G, Community education in Mozambique, *Convergence,* 24, 1–2 (1991) 40–45

3916 Pereira, L P, Visser, J, *The role of education in the process of cultural and socio-economic reintegration of children and teachers in the war zones of Mozambique.* The Hague: CESO, 1990, 13pp

Environment

3917 Cherrett, I, et al, *Norwegian aid and the environment in Mozambique: the issues.* Bergen: CMI, 1990, 82pp

3918 Rafael, F, Pouca sensibilidade no sector empresarial, *Economia,* 4 (1991) 13–19

Food

3919 Adam, Y, Guerra, fome, seca e desenvolvimento: liçoes de Changara, Moçambique, *Arquivo,* 10 (1991) 185–207

3920 Orr, D, Goncalves, F, Mozambique's rivers of sand, *Choices,* 1, 3 (1992) 4–10

Gender

3921 Berg, N, Gundersen, A, Legal reform in Mozambique: equality and emanicipation for women through popular justice, in Stlen K A & Vaa, M (eds), *Gender and change (entry 399),* 247–72

3922 Sheldon, K E, *The women's organisation in Mozambique.* East Lansing: Michigan State University, 1990, 11pp

Geography, human

3923 Kuder, M, Die Raumstrukturen Moçambiques, *DASP-Hefte,* 6, 30/31 (1991) 57–74

Health & welfare services

3924 Marshall, J, *War, debt and structural adjustment in Mozambique: the social impact.* Ottawa: North-South Institute, 1992, 94pp

3925 Romagnoli, L, Appunti geografica sulla salute nella capitale del Mozambico: fattori ambientali, condizionamenti sociali, sopravivenze tradizionali, *Rivista*

geografica italiana, 98, 3 (1991) 455–71

History, C19th

3926 Rzewuski, E, Origins of the Tungi sultanate (northern Mozambique) in the light of local traditions, in Pilaszewicz S & Rzewuski, E (eds), *Unwritten testimonies (entry 447)*, 193–213

History, C20th

see also: 3827

3927 Chitlango Khambane, Clerc, A D, *Chitlango: filho de chefe.* n.p.: Cadernos Tempo, 1990, 218pp

3928 Coelho, J P B, Entrevista com Celestino de Sousa: a actividade da FRELIMO em Tete, 1964–1967, *Arquivo,* 10 (1991) 133–168

3929 Liesegang, G, José Fernandes Jr, ca 1872–1965: testemunho do período mercantil e da implantação do imperialismó colonial na antiga zona de influéncia de Tete, *Arquivo,* 10 (1991) 49–82

3930 Silva, T C, Jose, A, Eduardo Mondlane: pontos para uma periodização da trajectoria de um nacionalista (1940–1961), *Cadernos de historia,* 8 (1990) 5–52

Industry & trade

3931 Weinmann, C D, *The making of wooden furniture in Mozambique.* Berlin: Free University, 1991, 35pp

3932 Weiss, J, Industrial policy reform in Mozambique in the 1980s, in Adhikari R et al (eds), *Industrial and trade policy reform in developing countries* (Manchester: Manchester UP, 1992), 111–119

International economic relations

3933 Adam, Y, *Foreign aid to Mozambique, needs and effects: a*

preliminary study. Bergen: CMI, 1990, 27pp

3934 Croll, P, Referat über die programme der technischen zusammenarbeit mit Mosambik anlässlich, *DASP-Hefte,* 6, 30/31 (1991) 37–56

3935 Head, J, Paying the piper, *Journal of southern African studies,* 18, 2 (1992) 430–38 (review article)

3936 O'Brien, P, et al, *Evaluation of Norway's non-project financial assistance to Mozambique.* Bergen: CMI, 1990, 52pp

International relations

3937 Du Preez, E, Südafrikas verbindungen zum südlichen Afrika unter besonderer berücksichtigung Mosambiks, *DASP-Hefte,* 6, 30/31 (1991) 21–36

Labour & manpower

3938 Cumbe, S P, O desemprego em Moçambique, que soluções?, *Economia,* 4 (1991) 29–33

Language

3939 Leiste, D, Zur sprachpolitik der Frelimo, *DASP-Hefte,* 6, 30/31 (1991) 89–95

Law

3940 Camurça, B, Kommentar zur neuen Verfassung der Republik Mozambik - die Grundrechte und Staatsziele, *DASP-Hefte,* 6, 30/31 (1991) 109–122

Literature

3941 Müller-Bochat, E, Rassische und kulturelle identität als Thema der portugiesischsprachigen literatur in Afrika, besonders in

Moçambique, *DASP-Hefte*, 6, 30/31 (1991) 75–88

3942 Serauky, C, Modernität in der moçambikanischen lyrik, *DASP-Hefte*, 6, 30/31 (1991) 96–108

Politics

see also: 835, 4309

3943 Africa Watch, *Conspicuous destruction: war, famine and the reform process in Mozambique*. New York: Africa Watch, 1992, 216pp

3944 Andersson, H, *Mozambique: a war against the people*. Basingstoke: Macmillan, 1992, 191pp

3945 Askin, S, Missão a RENAMO: a militarização da religão, *Cadernos de historia*, 8 (1990) 53–72

3946 Finnegan, W, *A complicated war: the harrowing of Mozambique*. Berkeley: University of California Press, 1992, 325pp

3947 Hansma, T, (ed), *Mozambique: a tale of terror told by ex-participants of Renamo and other refugees*. Amsterdam: African-European Institute, 1990, 71pp

3948 Hoile, D, *The 1992 Africa Watch report on Mozambique: disappointing, stereotyped and fragmentary*. London: Mozambique Institute, 1992, 15pp

3949 Muller-Blattau, B, *Julieta und die Stille des Todes. Mosambik- vom Krieg gegen die Kinder*. Reinbek bei Hamburg: Rowohlt, 1990, 133pp

3950 Nordstrom, C, The dirty war: civilian experience of conflict in Mozambique and Sri Lanka, in Rupesinghe K (ed), *Internal conflict (entry 932)*, 27–43

3951 O'Laughlin, B, Interpretations matter: evaluating the war in Mozambique, *Southern Africa report*, Jan. 1992 23–33

3952 Siddaway, J, Mozambique: destabilisation, state, society and space, *Political geography quarterly*, 11, 3 (1992) 239–58

3953 Vieira, S, Democracy and development: themes for a reflection on Mozambique, *Southern Africa political and economic monthly*, 4, 5 (1991) 17–22

3954 Wilson, K B, Cults of violence and counter-violence in Mozambique, *Journal of southern African studies*, 18, 3 (1992) 527–82

3955 Zacarias, A M, Mozambique on the road to peace?, *Southern Africa political and economic monthly*, 4, 5 (1991) 8–11

Religion, philosophy

No entry, see also: 3945

Rural economy

3956 Adam, Y, *Aid under fire: an evaluation of Mozambique-Nordic Agricultural Programme*. Stockholm: SIDA, 1991, 123pp

3957 Bowen, M L, Beyond reform: adjustment and political power in contemporary Mozambique, *Journal of modern African studies*, 30, 2 (1992) 255–79

3958 Caballero, L, *The Mozambican agricultural sector: background information*. Uppsala: Sveriges Lantbruksuniversitet, 1990, 104pp

3959 Eliseu, A B, Medeiros, E, Formas de cooperação e ajuda-mútua nas comunidades Nyungwe de Tete, *Arquivo*, 10 (1991) 169–184

3960 Quental-Mendes, C B, Monocultura do algodao contra agricultura camponesa sustentável, *Extra*, 7 (1991) 3–11

3961 Santos, P C dos, Empresas agrárias estatais: um problema, muitas soluçöes, *Extra*, 6 (1991) 20–26

3962 Tickner, V, Structural adjustment and agricultural pricing in Mozambique, *Review of African political economy*, 53 (1992) 25–42

3963 Viegas, W, Moçambique constrói a sua experiência, *Extra*, 7 (1991) 17–21

Sociology

3964 Cochan, AB, Scott, C V, Class, state and popular organisations in Mozambique and Nicaragua, *Latin American perspectives*, 19, 2 (1992) 105–24

3965 Elkoury, M, Mozambique: the next Somalia?, *Refugees*, 91 (1992) 30–33

3966 Almquist, A, Divination and the hunt in Pagibeti ideology, in Peek P M (ed), *African divination (entry 48)*, 101–111

ZAIRE

Anthropology

see also: 4083

3967 Bibi Lufenge, Bolakonga Bobwo, Opinions des femmes de Kisangani dur les interdits traditionnels de grossesse, *Africa (São Paulo)*, 12/13 (1989/90) 201–208

3968 Bolakonga Bobwo, Les tabous de grossesse chez les femmes Sakata, *Africa (São Paulo)*, 12/13 (1989/90) 188–200

3969 Bontinck, F, L'ethnonyme mng, *Annales aequatoria*, 12, (1991) 462–470

3970 Das, M, Kolack, S, Hunters and foragers of the rainforest: pygmies, in their *Technology, vales and society* (New York: Lang, 1990), 13–36

3971 Devisch, R, Mediumistic divination among the northern Yaka of Zaire: etology and ways of knowing, in Peek P M (ed), *African divination (entry 48)*, 112–32

3972 Duvieusart, L, Cas de

recherche de sorcellerie en milieu rural au Zaïre: suggestions sur la conduite à tenir par les autorités de l'État, *Zaïre-Afrique*, 268, (1992) 457–471

3973 Klein, H, (ed), *Leo Frobenius: ethnographische Notizen aus den Jahren 1905 und 1906*. Stuttgart: Steiner, 1990,

3974 Lobo Bundwoong Bope, *Afrikanische Gesellschaft im Wandel: soziale Mobilität und Landflucht am Beispiel der Region Mweka in Zaire*. Frankfurt: Brandes & Apsel, 1991, 204pp

3975 Mack, J, *Emil Torday and the art of the Congo 1900–1909*. London: British Museum, 1991, 96pp

3976 Mbonyinkebe Sebahire, Le tradipraticien dans la ville: le cas des Yaka à Kinshasa, *Cahiers des religions africaines*, 23, 45/46 (1989) 49–85

3977 Mubuy Mubay Mpier, Dreams among the Yansi, in Jedrej M C & Shaw, R (eds), *Dreaming, religion and society (entry 42)*, 100–110

3978 Ngub'Usim Mpey-Nka, Idiocosmognosies des paysans sans frontières du fleuve Zaïre et actions de développement de leurs sites, *Zaïre-Afrique*, 263, (1992) 163–171

3979 Pagezy, H, Fatness and culture among the southern Mongo (Zaire): the case of the primiparous nursing woman, *African study monographs*, 12, 3 (1991) 149–60

3980 Watanabe, K, La royauté et la chefferie: un essai de comparaison au sein d'un royaume (Kuba Zaïre), *Senri ethnological studies*, 31 (1992) 275–301

Arts

see also: 3975

3981 Kamba, S, *Production cinématographique et parti unique:*

l'exemple du Congo. Paris: Harmattan, 1992, 106pp

Current affairs

see also: 4060

3982 Ciervide, J, Zaïre 1990–1992: éveil du peuple, *Zaïre-Afrique,* 264, (1992) 219–226

3983 Gbabendu Engunduka, A, Efolo Ngobaasu, E, *Volonté de changement au Zaire. Vol. 1: de la consulation populaire vers la conférence nationale.* Paris: Harmattan, 1991, 216pp

3984 Gbabendu Engunduka, A, Efolo Ngobaasu, E, *Volonté de changement au Zaire. Vol. 2: archives 1990–91.* Paris: Harmattan, 1991, 223pp

3985 Willame, J C, *Zaire, années 90 (vers la troisième République). Vol. 1: de lka démocratie 'octroyé' à la démocratie enrayée (24 avril 1990 - 22 septembre 1991).* Brussels: CEDAF, 1991, 318pp

Demography

see also: 3993

3986 Ngondo a Pitshandenge, S, et al, la population du Zaïre à la veille des élections de 1993 et 1994, *Zaïre-Afrique,* 268, (1992) 487–506

Economy - Development

see also: 4036

3987 Kabarhuza, H, Development NGOs in Zaire: experiences and challenges, in NGLS (ed), *Voices from Africa 2 (entry 195),* 29–37

3988 MacGaffey, J, Initiatives from below: Zaire's other path to social and economic restructuring, in Hyden G & Bratton, M (eds), *Governance and politics (entry 864),* 243–61

3989 Maton, J, *Measuring the*

sensitivity of the income of the poor to changes in sectoral outputs and changes in income distribution: simulations by means of a simplified SAM for Zaire. Gent: ISVO, Rijksuniversiteit, 1992, 64pp

Economic and social history

3990 Depelchin, J, *From the Congo Free state to Zaire (1885–1974).* Dakar: Codesria, 1992, 235pp

3991 Kalele-ka-Bila, La culture obligatoire du coton au Congo belge, *Africa (Rome),* 47, 1 (1992) 83–92

3992 Kimoni, I, Kikwit et son destin: aperçu historique et sociologique, *Pistes et recherches,* 5, 2/3 (1990) 155–182

3993 Lyons, M, *A colonial disease: a social history of sleeping sickness in northern Zaire.* Cambridge: CUP, 1992, 335pp

3994 Lyons, M, Medecine and empire: the funding of sleeping sickness research in the Belgian Congo, in Twaddle M (ed), *Imperialism (entry 464),* 136–52

3995 Tshibangu Kabet Musas, L'experience coopérative au Congo (Zaire) dans le contexte coloniale: forme de duperie internationale et de devoyement des colonisés, *Africa (São Paulo),* 12/13 (1989/90) 43–55

3996 Tshibangu Kabet Musas, P, Contribution à l'histoire du commerce et des crises économiques au Zaïre: cas du Haut-Katanga Industriel de 1910 à 1937, *Zaïre-Afrique,* 259, (1991) 503–522

Education

3997 Cnockaert, A, Examens d'État au Kivu - Session 1991: éléments pour une analyse, *Zaïre-Afrique,* 266, (1992) 363–375

3998 Ekwa bis Isal, M, C.N.S.:
l'école zaïroise de demain,
Zaïre-Afrique, 266, (1992) 357–362

3999 Gege, K, Consciousness
raising literacy: the experience of
the Elimu Association of Zaire,
*Journal of the African Association for
Literacy and Adult Education*, 5, 3
(1991) 6–11

4000 Isango idi Wanzila,
Avènement de la démocratie et
avenir de l'enseignement
universitaire au Zaïre, *Zaïre-Afrique*,
267, (1992) 428–440

4001 Maboloko Ngulambangu,
Problématique de l'enseignement
de la géographie (locale et
nationale) au Zaïre, *Géokin*, 1/2,
2/1 (1990/1991) 249–265

4002 N'Gakegui, P M, Etudes
congolaises: education et
colonialisme, in Irele A (ed),
*African education and identity (entry
268)*, 88–108

**4003 Nteba Bakumba, Katana
Buruku Gege,** The experience of
the Elimu Assocation of Zaire,
Convergence, 24, 1–2 (1991) 25–31

Environment

see also: 1900

4004 Lubini, A, Kusehuluka, K,
Aperçu préliminaire sur les
groupements des jachères des
environs de Kikwit, *Pistes et
recherches*, 5, 2/3 (1990) 397–414

4005 Mbala, Z, et al, La lutte
anti-érosive et l'aménagement de
l'espace urbain de Kikwit, *Pistes et
recherches*, 5, 2/3 (1990) 219–237

Finance

4006 Banque du Zaire, The
Zairean experience, in Roe A R et
al *Instruments of economic policy
(entry 341)*, 133–36

4007 Jewsiewicki, B, Jeux d'argent
et de pouvoir au Zaire: la

'bindomanie' et le crépuscule de la
Deuxième République, *Politique
africaine*, 46 (1992) 55–70

**4008 Makumaya Nsamba
Kiambamba,** Les coopératives
d'epargne et de crédit du Zaïre:
banques et instruments de
capitalisation populaires: cas de la
Caisse populaire de crédit Luymas
(C.P.C.L.-CPZO), *Géokin*, 1/2, 2/1
(1990/1991) 217–231

4009 Ndele Bamu, A, Les grandes
leçons de l'histoire monétaire,
financière et économique du
Congo-Zaïre, *Zaïre-Afrique*, 267,
(1992) 395–403

Food

4010 Hilderbrand, K, et al,
Angolan refugees in Shaba, Zaire,
1984–1990, *Journal of refugee
studies*, 5, 3/4 (1992) 336–42

4011 Tollens, E, Cassava marketing
in Zaire: an analysis of its structure,
conduct and performance, in
Cammann L (ed), *Traditional
marketing systems (entry 113)*,
113–27

Gender

see also: 3979, 4089

4012 Shapiro, D, Tambashe, O,
*Women's employment, education and
contraceptive behaviour in Kinshasa.*
Philadephia: Pennsylvania State
University, Dept. of Economics,
1991, 30pp

Geography, human

**4013 Mashini Dhi Mbita
Mulenghe,** Niveau de vie des
ménages urbains et semi-urbains
dans une région du Zaïre
occidental: quelques éléments de
'bien-être' ou de 'mal-être' dans le
Kwango-Kwilu, *Géokin*, 1/2, 2/1
(1990/1991) 137–161

4014 Mpasi Ziwa Mambu, Le Zaïre en cartes: la "mouvance" des provinces de 1960 à 1988: un essai d'analyse géopolitique sur la territoriale du Congo-Zaïre, *Géokin*, 2, 2 (1991) 341–349

Geography, physical

4015 Fehr, S, La pluviométrie de Kikwit, *Pistes et recherches*, 5, 2/3 (1990) 183–217

Health & welfare services

4016 Bertrand, J T, Brown, J E, *Family planning success in two cities in Zaire.* Washington: World Bank, 1992, 37pp

History, general

4017 Hulstaert, G, L'épopée Lianja et l'histoire, *Annales aequatoria*, 12, (1991) 163–177

History, C6–18th

4018 Toso, C, Il contributo dei religiosi italiani al pacifico sviluppo dell'antico Congo (Sec. 17–18), *Africa (Rome)*, 47, 2 (1992) 184–220

History, C19th

4019 Brion, E, La fondation de poste de l'etat à Dèkèsè, *Annales aequatoria*, 12, (1991) 143–161

4020 Newbury, D, *Kings and clans: Ijwi Island and the Lake Kivu rift, 1780–1840.* Madison: University of Wisconsin Press, 11992, 371pp

4021 Yoder, J C, *The Kanyok of Zaire: an institutional and ideological history to 1895.* Cambridge: CUP, 1992, 213pp

History, C20th

see also: 4042

4022 Asui, O E, *L'administration coloniale et la question de la succession de Ngongo Leteta au Sankuru (1893–1956).* Brussels: CEDAF, 1991, 119pp

4023 Boelaert, E, *Mbandaka, hier et aujourd'hui: éléments d'historiographie locale.* Bamanya-Mbandaka: Centre Aequatoria, 1990, 270pp

4024 Hulstaert, G, Les débuts de la mission de Btèka, *Annales aequatoria*, 12, (1991) 509–524

4025 Kacza, T, *Die Kongo-Krise 1960–65.* Pfaffenweiler: Centaurus, 1990, 201pp

4026 Kalonda Djessa, J G, *Du Congo prospère au Zaire en débâcle.* Paris: Harmattan, 1991, 239pp

4027 Kapita Mulopo, P, *Patrice Lumumba: justice pour les heroes.* Paris: Harmattan, 1992, 306pp

4028 Olela Engombe Asui, L'administration coloniale et la question de la succession de Ngongo Leteta au Sankuru (1893–19560, *Cahiers du CEDAF*, No. 4 (1991) 1–119

4029 Pinlau, B, *Congo-Zaire, 1874–1981: la perception du lointain.* Paris: Harmattan, 1992, 285pp

4030 Willame, J C, *Patrice Lumumba: la crise congolaise revisitée.* Paris: Karthala, 1990, 496pp

Industry & trade

4031 Alliez, J-L, Réflexions sur l'approvisionnement en carburants au Zaïre, *Zaïre-Afrique*, 261, (1992) 19–27

4032 Fairhead, J, Paths of authority: roads, the state and the market in eastern Zaire, *European journal of development research*, 4, 2 (1992) 17–35

4033 Lederer, A, Évolution des transports à l'Onatra de 1976 à 1986, *Bulletin des séances,* 36, 2 (1990) 299–230

4034 Noti N'sele-Zoze, La recrudescence des métiers urbains traditionnels: quelques aspects de pauvreté dans les villes du Zaïre, *Géokin,* 1/2, 2/1 (1990/1991) 191–201

4035 Vanderlinden J, *A propos de l'uranium congolais.* Brussels: Académie Royale des Sciences d'Outre-Mer, 1991, 117pp

International economic relations

4036 Crowley, B L, Inside the whale: reflections on the UNDP in Zaire, *Canadian journal of development studies,* 12, 1 (1991) 199–212

4037 Gasibirege, R S, Quelle nouvelle coopération entre la Belgique et la Communauté économique des pays des grands lacs (CEPGL)? Bilan critique et prospective, *Au coeur de l'Afrique,* 59, 2/3 (1991) 391–420

4038 Kapena Katshinga, *Die Auswirkungen von ausländischen Direktinvestitionen auf die wirtschaftliche Entwicklung Zaires.* Frankfurt: Lang, 1990, 322pp

International relations

see also: 4025
4039 Dropkin, N, Israel's diplomatic offensive in Africa: the case of Zaire, *Transafrica forum,* 9, 1 (1992) 15–26

4040 Fafowara, O O, *Pressure groups and foreign policy: a comparative study of British attitudes and policy towards secessionist moves in the Congo (1960–63) and in Nigeria (1966–69).* Ibadan: Heinemann, 1990, 220pp

4041 Gibbs, D N, *The political*

economy of Third World intervention: mines, money and US policy in the Congo crisis. Chicago: University of Chicago Press, 1991, 322pp

4042 Leimgruber, W, *Kalter Krieg um Afrika: die amerikanische Afrikapolitik unter Präsident Kennedy 1961–1963.* Stuttgart: Steiner, 1990, 563pp

4043 Schatzberg, M G, *Mobutu or chaos? The United States and Zaire, 1960–1990.* Lanham: University Press of America, 1991, 114pp

Labour & manpower

4044 Makengo, M M, Vandeville, V, Ajustement du marché du travail au Zaire: le cas du secteur structuré, *Mondes en développement,* 19, 75/76 (1991) 93–107

4045 Nlandu Ndonani, P, L'an 24 du Conseil National du Travail, *Zaïre-Afrique,* 268, (1992) 473–486

Language

4046 Mbulamoko Nzenge Movoambe, État des recherches sur le Lingala comme groupe linguistique autonome: contribution aux études sur l'histoire et l'expansion du Lingala, *Annales aequatoria,* 12, (1991) 377–405

Law

4047 Mutoy Mubialal, L'individu devant la justice au Zaïre (de l'arbre à palabres aux cours et tribunaux), *Penant,* 102, 809 (1992) 182–196

4048 Ntumba Luaba-Lumu, La cessation des fonctions présidentielles en droit constitutionnel zaïrois, *Zaïre-Afrique,* 261, (1992) 5–18

Library - documentation

4049 Bibliotheque Nationale du Zaire, *Bibliographie du Zaire 1987–1988. Tome 1: imprimés.* Kinshasa: Bibliotheque Nationale du Zaire, 1990, 89pp

Literature

4050 Kalonji, M T Z, *Une écriture la Passion chez Ngandu Nkashama.* Paris: Harmattan, 1992, 134pp

Media

4051 Bitangilayi wa Mpoyi Mutombo, La politique agricole au Zaïre et ses paradoxes de 1970–1980, *Africa (Rome),* 46, 3 (1991) 440–446

4052 Cnockaert, A, La revue Zaïre-Afrique: 30 ans de chronique littéraire, *Zaïre-Afrique,* 260, (1991) 551–562

Natural resources

4053 Harroy, J P, Cinquante ans de la vie du parc national de la Garamba au Zaïre, *Bulletin des séances,* 36, 2 (1990) 193–210

4054 Terashima, H, et al, Ethnobotany of the Lega in the tropical rain forest of eastern Zaire. Part 1, zone de Mwenga, *African study monographs: supplementary issue,* 15 (1991) 1–61

Politics

see also: 4000, 4032

4055 Amnesty International, *The Republic of Zaire: outside the law, security force repression of government opponents, 1988–1990.* London: Amnesty International, 1990, 15pp

4056 Banga Bane, J, Pourquoi la violence? Réflexions sur des moments douloureux de la transition démocratique au Zaïre, *Zaïre-Afrique,* 263, (1992) 133–141

4057 Boissonade, E, *Le mal zairois.* Paris: Ed. Hermé, 1990, 495pp

4058 Boissonade, E, *Le mal zairois.* Paris: Herme, 1990, 495pp

4059 Bola, N B, Le bilan du Conseil de Ville de Kikwit (1982–1988), *Pistes et recherches,* 5, 2/3 (1990) 281–304

4060 Braeckman, C, *Le dinosaure: le Zaire de Mobutu.* Paris: Fayard, 1992, 382pp

4061 Braekman, C, *Le dinosaure: le Zaire du Mobutu.* Paris: Fayard, 1992, 382pp

4062 Djelo Empenge-Osako, L'évolution politique et constitutionnelle du Zaïre, *Bulletin des séances,* 36, 2 (1990) 137–163

4063 Dungia, E, *Mobutu et l'argent du Zaire: révélations d'un diplomate, ex-agent des services secrets.* Paris: Harmattan, 1992, 215pp

4064 Epee Gambwa, Otemikongo Mandefu Yahisule, Entités territoriales décentralisées et financement publique du développement local au Zaïre, *Zaïre-Afrique,* 266, (1992) 347–356

4065 Isango Idi Wanzila, Décentralisation territoriale et pratiques centralisatrices au Zaïre, *Zaïre-Afrique,* 258, (1991) 421–437

4066 Isango idi Wanzila, La présence des chefs coutumiers dans l'administration territoriale au Zaïre: quelle opportunité?, *Zaïre-Afrique,* 263, (1992) 151–162

4067 Kalala Bwabo, L'heure de la démocratie: se départir d'une mentalité d'irresponsabilité, *Zaïre-Afrique,* 258, (1991) 413–420

4068 Mashini Dhi Mbita Mulenghe, Encadrement territorial et développement socio-économique du Zaïre, *Géokin,* 2, 2 (1991) 295–304

4069 Mbaya, K, *Le Zaire: vers quelles*

destinées? Dakar: Codesria, 1992, 392pp

4070 Mouvance progressiste du Congo (Zaire), *Congo (Zaire): démocratie neocoloniale ou deuxième indépendance?* Paris: Harmattan, 1992, 192pp

4071 Mpati ne Nzita, N, L'Épiscopat zaïrois face à la démocratie naissante au Zaïre, *Zaïre-Afrique,* 265, (1992) 268–274

4072 Mwaliya Tsiyembe, Mayele Bukasa, *Invention de l'état de droit et projet de société démocratique en Afrique: le cas de Zaire.* Paris: Diane de Selliers, 1992, 220pp

4073 Mwanza wa Mwanza, La pauvreté des institutions administratives au Zaïre: les zones urbaines de Kinshasa, *Géokin,* 1/2, 2/1 (1990/1991) 175–189

4074 Ngondo a Pitshandenge Iman, Chiffre de population et enjeux politiques sous la 2ème République: les élections législatives de 1987, *Zaïre-Afrique,* 264, (1992) 227–248

4075 Obotela Rashidi, Problématique des rôles électoraux au Zaïre, *Zaïre-Afrique,* 262, (1992) 85–95

4076 Otemikongo Mandefu Yarisule, Le multipartisme au Zaïre: mythe et réalité, *Zaïre-Afrique,* 260, (1991) 541–548

4077 Perez, M C, Zaire: continuism versus multi-partyism, *Revista de Africa y Medio Oriente,* 3, 1 (1991) 51–74

4078 Saint-Moulin, L de, Histoire de l'organisation administrative du Zaïre, *Zaïre-Afrique,* 261, (1992) 29–54

4079 Willame, J C, *L'automne d'un despotisme: pouvoir, argent et obeissance dans le Zaire des années quatre-vingt.* Paris: Karthala, 1992, 232pp

Religion, philosophy

see also: 4071

4080 Kabongo Mbaya, P, *L'Eglise du Christ au Zaire: formation et adaptation du protestantisme, situation de dictature.* Paris: Karthala, 1992, 467pp

4081 Simbandumwe, S S, *A socio-religious and political analysis of the judeo-christian concept of prophetism and modern Bakongo and Zulu African prophet movements.* Lewiston: Mellen, 1992, 434pp

Rural economy

4082 Bwalala, J, Le rôle des centres de développement en milieu rural: le cas du CDR de Djuma-Bandundu, *Zaïre-Afrique,* 267, (1992) 421–427

4083 Fairhead, J, Representing knowledge: the 'new farmer' in research fashions, in Pottier J (ed) *Practicing development: social science perspectives* (London: Routledge, 1992), 187–104

4084 Marysse, S, Waeterloos, E, L'homogenéité socio-économique d'un milieu rural: un apparence trompeuse: exemples au Zimbabwe et au Rwanda, *Zaire Afrique,* 267 (1992) 405–415

4085 Mavungu Khonde, et al, Projet de développement et transformations socio-économique en milieu rural zaïrois: expérience du Bureau de Projet Ituri (B.P.I.) dans la zone d'Irumu (Haut-Zaïre), *Zaïre-Afrique,* 263, (1992) 173–187

4086 Mpasi Ziwa Mambu, La diversification des ricizultures pourrait constituer l'un des moyens pour augmenter la production, souvent insuffisante, dans la majeure partie des régions du Zaïre: quelques réflexions sur le Bas-Zaïre, *Géokin,* 1/2, 2/1 (1990/1991) 203–215

4087 **Musitu wu Maba,** Problèmes agraires de la sous-région du Kwilu: cas de l'acquisition de terrains de culture par les paysans citadins de Kikwit, secteur nord-ouest, *Pistes et recherches,* 5, 2/3 (1990) 335–362

4088 **Shapiro, D, Tollens, E,** *The agricultural development of Zaire.* Aldershot: Avebury, 1992, 201pp

4089 **Shapiro, D,** Farm size, household size and composition, and women's contribution to agricultural production: evidence from Zaire, *Journal of development studies,* 27, 1 (1990) 1–21

4090 **Tshibaka, T B,** *Labour in the rural household economy of the Zairian basin.* Washington: IFPRI, 1992, 64pp

Sociology

see also: 4012

4091 **Bailey, R C, et al,** The ecology of birth seasonality among agriculturalists in central Africa, *Journal of biosocial science,* 24, 3 (1992) 393–412

4092 **Bertrand, J T, et al,** Sexual behavior and condom use in 10 sites of Zaire, *Journal of sex research,* 28, 3 (1991) 347–364

4093 **Ngondo a Pitshandenge Iman,** Réflexions sur la problématique de la fécondité des adolescentes au Zaïre, *Zaïre-Afrique,* 260, (1991) 571–581

Urban studies

see also: 4005

4094 **Kabamba Kabata,** Réflexion sur quelques aspects de niveau de vie de la population de Kananga (Zaïre), *Géokin,* 1/2, 2/1 (1990/1991) 163–173

4095 **Maton, J,** *How do the poor in Kinshasa survive: miracle, enigma or black box?* Gent: ISVO,

Rijksuniversiteit, 1992, 40pp

4096 **Mutungu, K, Sangibala, N'K,** Essai d'une étude de l'habitat dans une ville du tiers-monde: l'exemple de Kikwit (Zaïre), *Pistes et recherches,* 5, 2/3 (1990) 309–334

4097 **Nzuzi, L,** Kinshasa: mutations contemporaines et perspectives d'aménagement, *Géokin,* 2, 2 (1991) 305–337

4098 **Vinck, H,** Boende, *Annales aequatoria,* 12, (1991) 534–553

ZAMBIA

Anthropology

see also: 4165

4099 **Geisler, G,** *Moving with tradition: the politics of marriage among the Toka of Zambia.* Bergen: CMI, 1990, 24pp

4100 **Kangwa, M M,** The Chisungu initiation rite among the Bemba of Zambia, *Occasional research papers,* 34, (1990) 49–73

4101 **van Binsbergen, W J M,** *Kazanga: etnicitiet in Afrika tussen staat en traditie.* Amsterdam: Free University, 1992, 44pp

4102 **van Binsbergen, W,** *Tears of rain: ethnicity and history in central western Zambia.* London: Kegan Paul, 1992, 495pp

4103 **Yoshida, K,** Masks and transformation among the Chewa of eastern Zambia, *Senri ethnological studies,* 31 (1992) 203–273

Current affairs

4104 **Chan, S,** *Prospects for the1991 elections in Zambia.* Braamfontein: SAIIA, 1991, 13pp

4105 **Constantin, F, Quantin, P,** Zambie: fin de parti, *Politique africaine,* 45 (1992) 123–28

4106 **Kibble, S,** Zambia: problems for the MMD, *Review of African*

political economy, 53 (1992)
104–108

4107 Rawlins, R, The people's will,
Focus on Africa, 3, 1 (1992) 5–11

Demography

**4108 Osei-Hwedie, K,
Osei-Hwedie, B,** Reflections on
Zambia's demographic profile and
population policy, *Journal of social
development in Africa*, 7, 1 (1992)
87–97

Economy - Development

see also: 173, 4125

4109 Fardi, M A, King, B, Zambia:
reform and reversal, in Thomas V
et al (eds), *Restructuring economies in
distress: policy reform and the World
Bank* (Oxford: OUP, 1992),
332–58

4110 Kayizzi-Mugerwa, S,
Zambia: a note of the
macroeconomic impacts of copper
prices, *Eastern Africa economic
review*, 6, 2 (1990) 143–147

4111 Mulenge, C, (ed), *Institutional
capacity building, economic
liberalisation and challenges for the
Third Republic: workshop proceedings.*
Lusaka: Institute of African
Studies, 1991, 75pp

4112 Mwanza, A M, (ed), *The
structural adjustment programme in
Zambia: lessons from experience.*
Harare: SAPES Books, 1992,
47pp

4113 Seshamani, V, Thee conomic
policies of Zambia in the 1980s:
towards structural transformation
with a human focus?, in Cornia A
G et al (eds), *Africa's recovery (entry
124)*, 93115

**4114 Sumaili, F K M,
Lungwangwa, G,** (eds), *Zambia in
the 1990s.* Lusaka: Professors'
World Peace Academy of Zambia,
1991, 182pp

Economic and social history

4115 Biermann, W, *Zambia,
unterminierte Entwicklung:
Weltmarkt und Industrialisierung ca.
1900–1986.* Saarbrucken:
Breitenbach, 1990, 318pp

4116 Kanduza, A M, History and
agricultural change in Zambia,
*Eastern African social science research
review*, 6,2 & 7/1, (1990/91) 1–13

4117 Kanduza, A M, History and
agricultural change in Zambia,
Transafrican journal of history, 20
(1991) 97–109

4118 Mulongo, A H, The decline of
the Bangweulu economy:
1880–1964, *Zambia journal of
history*, 4, (1991) 2–20

4119 Waite, G, *A history of medecine
and health care in pre-colonial
east-central Africa.* Lewiston:
Mellen, 1992, 187pp

Education

see also: 4128, 4160

4120 Lungwangwa, G, Saasa, O,
(eds), *Educational policy and human
resource development in Zambia.*
Lusaka: Institute for African
Studies, University of Zambia,
1991, 70pp

4121 Manyelele, M, The
introduction of Western education
among the Barotse of western
Zambia, *Occasional research papers*,
34, (1990) 83–105

Environment

No entry, see also: 297

Finance

No entry, see also: 1901

Food

4122 Black, R, Mabwe, T,

Planning for refugees in Zambia: the settlement approach to food self-sufficiency, *Third World planning review*, 14, 1 (1991) 1–20

Gender

see also: 4147, 4167

4123 Geisler, G, Who is losing out? Structural adjustment, gender and the agricultural sector in Zambia, *Journal of modern African studies*, 30, 1 (1992) 111–39

4124 Hansen, K T, Gender and housing: the case of domestic service in Lusaka, Zambia, *Africa*, 62, 2 (1992) 248–65

4125 Keller, B, Mbewe, D C, Policy and planning for the empowerment of Zambia's women farmers, *Canadian journal of development studies*, 12, 1 (1991) 75–88

4126 Longwe, S H, Clarke, R, *A gender perspective on the Zambian general election of 1991.* Lusaka: Zambia Association for Research and Development, 1991, 18pp

4127 Luig, V, Besessenheit als Ausdruch von Frauenkultur in Zambia, *Peripherie*, 47/48 (1992) 111–28

4128 Mumba, E, Adult literacy and learning opportunities for women and girls in Zambia, *International journal of university adult education*, 30, 3 (1991) 12–31

Geography, human

4129 Henkel, R, Bevölkerungswachstum, Wanderungsströme und Mobilität in Lusaka - jüngste Veränderungen und innerstädtliche Differenzierung, *Zeitschrift für Wirtschaftlichsgeographie*, 36, 1/2 (1991) 32–48

Geography, physical

4130 Korowski, S, Copperbelt ore minerals, *Zambian journal of applied earth sciences*, 5, 2 (1991) 1–9

4131 Korowski, S, Copperbelt minerals, *Zambian journal of applied earth sciences*, 5, 1 (1991) 1–17

4132 Menenti, M, et al, Early warning on agricultural production with satellite data and simulation models for Zambia, in Gastellu-Etchegorry J P (ed), *Satellite remote sensing (entry 412)*, 187–206

Health & welfare services

4133 Pillai, V K, Conaway, M, Immunisation coverage in Lusaka, Zambia: implications of the social setting, *Journal of biosocial science*, 24, 2 (1992) 201–209

History, general

No entry, see also: 450

History, C20th

4134 Ipenburg, A, *'All good men':* The development of Lubwa Mission, Chinsali, Zambia, 1905–67. Frankfurt: Lang, 1992, 345pp

Industry & trade

4135 Kaunga, E C, Privatisation in Zambia, in Ramanadham V V (ed), *Privatisation (entry 203)*, 373–95

4136 Mbewe, A, Rural electrification in Zambia, in Ranganathan V (ed), *Rural electrification (entry 1046)*, 17–66

4137 Milner-Gulland, E J, Leader-Williams, N, A model of incentives for the illegal exploitation of black rhinos and elephants: poaching in Luangwa Valley, Zambia, *Journal of applied ecology*, 29, 2 (1992) 388–401

4138 Muyunda, C M, Chimoto, C H, Sulphuric acid situation in Zambia, *Zambian journal of applied earth sciences,* 5, 2 (1991) 38–42

International relations

4139 Chan, S, *Kaunda and southern Africa: image and reality in foreign policy.* Kondon: British Academic Press, 1992, 231pp

Labour & manpower

4140 Fosh, P, Kazi, Z, The industrial relations systems of two ex-British colonies: Zambia and Singapore, *Round table,* 319 (1991) 299–312

4141 Mulenga, F E, Advancement, trade unionism and politics on the railways to 1992, *Zambia journal of history,* 4, (1991) 31–57

Law

see also: 688

4142 Coldham, S, Customary marriage and the urban local courts in Zambia, *Journal of African law,* 34, 1 (1990) 67–75

4143 Hamalengwa, M, The legal system of Zambia, *Rechtstheorie,* 12, (1991) 3–31

4144 Hamalengwa, M, The legal system of Zambia: law, politics and development in historical perspective, in Bondzi-Simpson P E (ed), *The law and economic development in the Third World* (New York: Prager, 1992), 21–41

Media

4145 Mhlaba, L, Press freedom in Zambia, or the right of the political opposition to be heard, *Legal forum,* 3, 4 (1991) 22–27

4146 Moore, R C, *The political reality of freedom of the press in Zambia.* Lusaka: Multimedia, 1991, 188pp

Medical

4147 Mwale, G, Burnard, G, *Women and AIDS in rural Africa: rural women's views of AIDS in Zambia.* Aldershot: Avebury, 1992, 127pp

Natural resources

see also: 4137

4148 Borsch, L, Gold prospecting, *Zambian journal of applied earth sciences,* 5, 1 (1991) 43–51

4149 Schmid, R M, Water balance, Luampa River, Zambia, *Zambian journal of applied earth sciences,* 4, 1 (1990) 62–66

Planning

4150 Mwape, B L, Party and local government in Zambian decentralised planning, in de Valk P & Wekwete, K H (eds), *Decentralising (entry 5485),* 176–91

4151 Noppen, D, Decentralisation and the role of district and provincial planning units in Zambia, in de Valk P & Wekwete, K H (eds), *Decentralising (entry 5485),* 192–205

Politics

see also: 903, 904, 4126, 4146

4152 Andreasson, B A, et al, *Setting a standard for Africa?: lessons from the 1991 Zambian elections.* Bergen: CMI, 1992, 137pp

4153 Baylies, C, Szeftel, M, The fall and rise of multi-party politics in Zambia, *Review of African political economy,* 54 (1992) 75–91

4154 Bjornlund, E, Bratton, M, et al, Observing multiparty elections in Africa: lessons from Zambia,

African affairs, 91, 364 (1992) 405–31

4155 Joseph, R, Zambia: a model for democratic change, *Current history*, 91, 565 (1992) 199–201

4156 Mbikusita-Lewanika, A, *Milk in a basket! The political-economic malaise in Zambia.* Lusaka: Zambia Research Foundation, 1990, 181pp

4157 Muwena, R M, Zambia's Local Administration Act, 1980: a critical appraisal of the integration objective, *Public administration and development*, 12, 3 (1992) 237–47

4158 Plattard, Y, Zambie: échec de l'expérience socialiste, *Revue des deux mondes*, (1992) 107–115

4159 Rakner, L, *Trade unions in processes of democratisation: a case study of labour-party relations in Zambia.* Bergen: Chr Michelesen Institute, 1992, 177pp

Religion, philosophy

4160 Carmody, B P, *Conversion and Jesuit schooling in Zambia.* Leiden: Brill, 1992, 179pp

4161 Rader, D A, *Chrisian ethics in an African context: a focus on urban Zambia.* New York: Lang, 1991, 201pp

4162 ter Haar, G, *Spirit of Africa: the healing ministry of Archbishop Milingo of Zambia.* London: Hurst, 1992, 286pp

Rural economy

see also: 1008, 1020, 4123, 4136

4163 Chinene, V R N, The Zambia land evaluation system and its preliminary validation in three agroecological zones, *Zambian journal of agricultural science*, (1990) 27–29

4164 Crehan, K, Structures of meaning and structures of interest: peasants and planners in northwestern Zambia, in Kaarsholm P (ed), *Cultural struggle (entry 4200)*, 185–208

4165 Gatter, P, Anthropology in farming systems research: a participant observer in Zambia, in Pottier J (ed), *Practising development: social science perspectives* (London: Routledge, 1992), 153–86

4166 Jansen, D J, Rukuvo, A, *Agriculture and the policy environment: Zambia and Zimbabwe.* Paris: OECD Development Centre, 1992, 63pp

4167 Jiggins, J, et al, *Seeds: breaking new ground - reaching out to women farmers in western Zambia.* Decatur: Seeds, 1992, 20pp

4168 Kasalu, E, et al, An economic/financial feasibility study of wheat production in Zambia, *Zambian journal of agricultural science*, (1990) 40–52

4169 Kean, S A, Agricultural policy reform in Zambia: the dynamics of policy formulation in the Second Republic, *Food policy*, 17, 1 (1992) 65–74

4170 Meyer, R E, A cross-cultural examination of organisational structure and control: the Zambian agricultural sector, *Journal of Asian and African studies*, 27, 3/4 (1992) 244–62

4171 Mwape, F, Kraft, D F, An econometric evaluation of the prospects for increased maize production in Zambia, *Zambian journal of agricultural science*, (1990) 17–26

4172 Ogura, M, Rural-urban migration in Zambia and migrant ties to home villages, *Developing economies*, 29, 2 (1991) 145–65

4173 Sugiyama, Y, The development of maize cultivation and changes in the village life of the Bemba of northern Zambia, *Senri ethnological studies*, 31 (1992) 173–201

Science & technology

4174 Chanda, D, Science and technology policies in Zambia, in Thomas-Emeagwali G (ed), *Science and technology in African history (entry 450)*, 147–64

Sociology

4175 Epstein, A L, *Scenes from African urban life: selected Copperbelt essays*. Edinburgh: Edinburgh University Press, 1992, 264pp

4176 Geisler, G, *Die politik der Geschlechterbezeihungennin einer landlichen Gemeinde in Zambia: 'Be quiet and suffer'*. Hamburg: Institut für Afrika-Kunde, 1990, 251pp

4177 Walubita, M S, *Zambia sporting score*. Lusaka: Multimedia, 1990, 192pp

Urban studies

see also: 2423

4178 Gaebe, W, Wirtschaftliche Probleme der Städte Schwarzafrikas am Beispiel von Lusaka, Sambia, *Zeitschrift für Wirtschaftlichsgeographie*, 36, 1/2 (1991) 21–31

4179 Hansen, K T, After *Copper town* : the past in the present in urban Zambia, *Journal of anthropological research*, 47, 4 (1991) 441–456

SOUTHERN AFRICA

General

4200 Kaarsholm, K, (ed), *Cultural struggle and development in southern Africa.* Harare: Baobab, 1991, 258pp

4201 Maasdorp, G, Whiteside, A (eds), *Towards a post-apartheid future: political and economic relations in Southern Africa.* Basingstoke: Macmillan, 1992, 226pp

4202 Potts, D, The changing geography of southern Africa, in Chapman G P & Baker, K M (eds), *The changing geography of Africa (entry 405),* 12–51

4203 Whiteside, A, Labour flows, refugees, AIDS and the environment, in Maasdorp G & Whiteside, A (eds), *Towards a post-apartheid future (entry 4201),* 155–73

Anthropology

4204 Groenewald, H C, (ed), *Oral traditions in southern Africa.* Pretoria: HSRC, 1990, 174pp

4205 Lewis-Williams, J D, Ethnographic evidence relating to 'trance' and 'shamans' among Northern and Southern Bushmen, *South African archaeological bulletin,* 47, 155 (1992) 56–60

4206 Spiegel, A D, McAllister, P A, (eds), *Tradition and transition in southern Africa.* New Brunswick: Rutgers UP, 1992, 274pp

Current affairs

4207 Rifrac, S, Evolutions recentes dans quelques pays de l'Afrique australe, *Cahiers du communisme,* 67, 4 (1991) 78–86

Demography

4208 Calitz, J M /Grove, M J, *A regional profile of the southern African population and its urban and non-urban distribution 1970–1990.* Sandton: Development Bank of Southern Africa, Centre for Information Analysis, 1991, 164pp

4209 Calitz, J M, *Southern African population projections 1995–2005 .* Sandton: Development Bank of Southern Africa, Centre for Information Analysis, 1991, 164pp

Economy - Development

see also: 1890, 1982, 4311, 4313

4210 Hawkins, A M, Economic development in the SADCC countries, in Maasdorp G & Whiteside, A (eds), *Towards a post-apartheid future (entry 4201),* 105–31

4211 Maasdorp, G, Economic prospects for South Africa in southern Africa, *South Africa international,* 22, 3 (1991/92) 121–127

4212 Mazur, R E, *Breaking the links: development theory and practice in southern Africa. A festschrift for Ann*

W Seidman. Trenton: Africa World Press, 1990, 329pp

4213 **Santho, S,** (ed), _Southern Africa after apartheid._ Harare: SAPES Trust, 1990, 240pp

4214 **Van der Merwe, D,** Economic cooperation in southern Africa: stuctures, policies, problems, _The comparative and international law journal of southern Africa,_ 24, 3 (1991) 386–404

Economic and social history

4215 **Edgecombe, R,** Dannhauser (1926) and Wankie (1972): two mining disasters. Some safety implications in historical perspective, _Journal of Natal and Zulu history,_ 13 (1990–91) 71–90

4216 **Posel, R,** Amahashi: Durban's ricksha pullers, _Journal of Natal and Zulu history,_ 13 (1990–91) 51–70

Education

see also: 1898

4217 **International Foundation for Education with Production,** _Defusing the time-bomb?: report on a seminar on education and training for employment and employment creation in the SADCC countries._ Gaborone: IIFP, 1990, 328pp

4218 **van Rijn, A J, Smit, C P,** (eds), _Proceedings of the regional workshop on computers in education._ Amsterdam: Centre for Development Cooperation Services, Free University, 1992, 172pp

Environment

4219 **Dube, P O,** Notes on ecology and society in southern Africa, in Irele A (ed), _African education and identity (entry 268),_ 358–68

Food

4220 **Annan, A,** Seeds of despair, _Focus on Africa,_ 3, 3 (1992) 30–33

Gender

see also: 4278

4221 **Johnson, C,** _Women on the front line: voices from southern Africa._ Basingstoke: Macmillan, 1992, 197pp

4222 **Kaale, B K,** Women dominate rural industries in the SADCC region, _SADCC Energy,_ 8, 22 (1990) 53–57

4223 **Rwezaura, B A,** _Perspectives on research methodology._ Harare: Women and Law in Southern Africa Rsearch Project, 1990, 204pp

Geography, human

4224 **Drakakis-Smith, D,** (ed), _Urban and regional change in southern Africa._ London: Routledge, 1992, 227pp

4225 **Foreign and Commonwealth Office,** _Drought in southern Africa: background brief._ London: FCO, 1992, 10pp

Geography, physical

4226 **Birkenhauer, J,** _The great escarpment of southern Africa and its coastal forelands: a reappraisal._ Munich: Universität München, Institut für Geographie, 1991, 419pp

4227 **Tyson, P D,** Climatic change in southern Africa: past and present conditions and possible future scenarios, _Climatic change,_ 18, 2/3 (1991) 241–58

Health & welfare services

4228 **Morgan R,** Social security in

the SADCC states of southern Africa: social welfare programmes ands the reduction of household vulnerability, in Ahmed E et al (eds), *Social security in developing countries* (Oxford: Clarendon, 1991), 415–65

History, general

4229 Beinart, W, Political and collective violence in southern African historiography, *Journal of southern African studies,* 18, 3 (1992) 455–86

History, early

4230 Dowson, T A, *Rock engravings of southern Africa.* Johannesburg: Witswatersrand University Press, 1992, 124pp

4231 Pwiti, G, Trade and economies in southern Africa: the archaeological evidence, *Zambezia,* 18, 2 (1991) 119–29

History, C19th

4232 Eldredge, E A, Sources of conflict in southern Africa, c. 1800–30: the 'Mfecane' reconsidered, *Journal of African history,* 33, 1 (1992) 1–35

History, C20th

4233 Neocosmos, M, Agrarian history and nationalist politics in southern Africa: notes towards a critique of conventional wisdom, *Eastern African social science research review,* 6,2 & 7/1, (1990/91) 96–140

4234 Vail, L, White, L, *Power and the praise poem: southern African voices in history.* London: Currey, 1992, 345pp

Industry & trade

4235 Jourdan, P, Mining in southern Africa, *Chamber of mines journal,* 34, 1 (1992) 33–41

4236 Kennedy, T L, *Southern African transport: an analytical model.* Pretoria: Africa Institute, 1990, 81pp

4237 Maasdorp, G, Trade relations in southern Africa: changes ahead?, in Maasdorp G & Whiteside, A (eds), *Towards a post-apartheid future (entry 4201),* 132–54

4238 Schmid, R M, SADCC mining sector, *Zambian journal of applied earth sciences,* 5, 1 (1991) 25–29

International economic relations

see also: 4280

4239 Balch, J A, Roskam, K L, (eds), *Southern Africa at the crossroads: new priorities for European cooperation.* Amsterdam: African-European Institute, 1990, 52pp

4240 Balch, J A, Roskam, K L, (eds), *Europe, SADCC and Africa: from conflict to cooperation.* Amsterdam: African-European Institute, 1991, 64pp

4241 Davies, R, *Integration or cooperation in a post-apartheid southern Africa: some reflections on an emerging debate.* Bellville: Centre for Southern African Studies, University of the Western Cape, 1992, 23pp

4242 Green, R H, SADCC: into the 1990s. Achievement in adversity and realistic hopes, *Africa contemporary record 1988/89,* (1992) A34–43

4243 Kumar, U, *Southern African Customs Union: lessons for the southern African region.* Cape Town: Centre for Southern African

Studies, University of the Western Cape, 1992, 25pp

4244 Leistner, E, Designing the framework for a Southern African Development Community, *Africa insight,* 22, 1 (1992) 4–13

4245 Maasdorp, G, *Economic cooperation in southern Africa: prospects for regional integration.* London: Research Institute for the Study of Conflict and Terrorism, 1992, 30pp

4246 Pirie, G H, Southern African air transport after apartheid, *Journal of modern African studies,* 30, 2 (1992) 341–48

4247 Russell, J, *Das südliche Afrika und die Europäische Gemeinschaft.* Brussels: Commission of the European Community, 1990, 91pp

4248 Stoneman, C, Thompson, C B, *Southern Africa after apartheid: economic repercussions of a free South Africa.* New York: United Nations, 1992, 12pp

4249 Tjonneland, E N, *Southern Africa after apartheid: the end of apartheid, future regional cooperation and foreign aid.* Bergen: Michelsen Institute, 1992, 216pp

4250 van Nieuwkerk, A, (ed), *Southern Africa at the crossroads: prospects for the political economy of the region.* Braamfontein: SAIIA, 1990, 267pp

4251 van Standen, G, *The theory and practice of regional economic integration in southern Africa.* Leicester: University of Leicester, Dept. of Politics, 1992, 73pp

4252 Viinikka, K Yrjö-Koskinen, E, *Import policies towards developing countries: import promotion and restriction mechanisms within the Nordic countries and the European Community - with special reference to the SADCC countries.* Helsinki: Kelsinki University, Institute of Development Studies, 1991, 117pp

4253 Viinikka, K, Yrjö-Koskinen,

E, SADCC and its export possibilities, in their *Import policies towards developing countries* (Helsinki: Helsinki University, IDS, 1991), 85–97

4254 Weisfelder, R F, SADCC after apartheid, *Transafrica forum,* 8, 3 (1991) 3–17

International relations

see also: 4286, 4294, 4297, 4828, 4837, 5447

4255 Adam, H, Moodley, K, Southern African regional relations and development policies, *Geneva-Africa,* 30, 2 (1992) 165–76

4256 Baynham, S, The new world order: regional and international implications for southern Africa, *Africa insight,* 22, 2 (1992) 84–94

4257 Benjamin, L, Sidiropoulos, E, The quest for security: Southern Africa at the crossroads, *Journal for contemporary history,* 16, 2 (1991) 96–122

4258 Beveridge, G R, The superpowers and southern Africa, in Allison R & Williams, P (eds), *Superpower competition and crisis prevention in the Third World* (Cambridge: CUP, 1990), 206–26

4259 Brill, H, *Die Republik Südafrika in Spannungsfeld interner, regionaler und globaler Konflikte.* Baden-Baden: Nomos, 1991, 346pp

4260 Clough, M, The superpowers in southern Africa: from confrontation to cooperation, in Breslauer G W et al (eds), *Beyond the Cold War: conflict and cooperation in the Third World* (Berkeley: Institute of International Studies, 1991), 85–100

4261 Crocker, C, *High noon in southern Africa - making peace in a rough neighbourhood.* New York: Norton, 1992, 533pp

4262 da Silva, A O, *Afrique australe:*

a la recherche d'une identité. Paris: Harmattan, 1991, 171pp

4263 du Pisani, A, South Africa and SADCC: into the 1990s, in Maasdorp G & Whiteside, A (eds), *Towards a post-apartheid future (entry 4201),* 174–86

4264 Grundy, K W, Southern Africa: the revolution prolonged, in Harbeson J W & Rothchild, D (eds), *Africa in world politics (entry 625),* 95–118

4265 Gutteridge, W, Prospects for regional security in southern Africa, *South Africa international,* 22, 3 (1991/92) 128–132

4266 Kühne, W, Southern Africa and the end of the East-West conflict, in Breslauer G W et al (eds), *Beyond the Cold War: conflict and cooperation in the Third World* (Berkeley: Institute of International Studies, 1991), 119–42

4267 Maasdorp, G, Whiteside, A, The 1990s and beyond, in Maasdorp G & Whiteside, A (eds), *Towards a post-apartheid future (entry 4201),* 201–215

4268 Macfarlane, S N, Superpower conflict and cooperation in southern Africa: Soviet Union, in Breslauer G W et al (eds), *Beyond the Cold War: conflict and cooperation in the Third World* (Berkeley: Institute of International Studies, 1991), 101–118

4269 Nkomo, S, After the Cold War: what is the US policy towards southern Africa?, *Transafrica forum,* 7, 4 (1991) 51–67

4270 Thompson, L, Of myths, monsters and money: regime conceptualisation and theory in the southern African context, *Journal of contemporary African studies,* 10, 2 (1991) 57–83

4271 Tikhomirov, V I, The Soviet Union and southern Africa: Soviet policy towards Africa since perestroika, *Africa contemporary record 1988/89,* (1992) A164–68

4272 Vale, P, External pressure for change in South and Southern Africa, in Maasdorp G & Whiteside, A (eds), *Towards a post-apartheid future (entry 4201),* 187–200

4273 Vasilkov, V, Great powers and southern Africa: rivalry or cooperation?, in Harbeson J W & Rothchild, D (eds), *Africa in world politics (entry 625),* 307–23

4274 Wardrop, J, Continuity and change in South Africa and in South Africa's relations with its neighbours, in Bruce R H (ed), *Prospects for peace: changes in the Indian Ocean region* (Perth: Indian Ocean Centre for Peace Studies, 1992), 253–72

4275 Weiss, T G, (ed), *The suffering grass: superpowers and regional conflict in southern Africa and the Caribbean.* Boulder: Lynne Reinner, 1992, 182pp

Labour & manpower

4276 Beukes, E P, (ed), *Development, employment and the new South Africa.* Innesdale: Development Society of Southern Africa, 1990, 374pp

4277 Thahane, T T, International labour migration in southern Africa, in Papademetriou D G & Martin, PL (eds), *The unsettled relationship* (Westport: Greenwood, 1991), 65–87

Law

see also: 4214, 4223, 4286, 4472

4278 Armstrong, A K, *Struggling over scarce resources: women and maintenance in southern Africa.* Harare: University of Zimbabwe Publications, 1992, 157pp

4279 Labuschagne, J M T, van den Heever, J A, Theft in

rudimentary legal systems: do universal characteristics exist?, *The comparative and international law journal of southern Africa*, 24, 3 (1991) 352–364

4280 **Mhone, K,** Law as a factor for regional integration: SADCC - problems and prospects, *The comparative and international law journal of southern Africa*, 24, 3 (1991) 379–385

Library - documentation

see also: 1915

4281 **State Library,** (ed), *Structures and roles of national library services in an evolving southern Africa. Proceedings of the sixth conference of national librarians of southern Africa.* Pretoria: State Library, 1992, 115pp

Media

4282 **Paterson, C,** Television news from the Frontline states, *Transafrica forum*, 8, 1 (1991) 59–75

Medical

4283 **Whiteside, A,** *AIDS in southern Africa.* Durban: University of Natal, Economic Research Unit, 1990, 35pp

Natural resources

4284 **Horvei, T,** Economic evaluation of SADCC energy projects, a means of establishing priorities, *SADCC Energy*, 8, 21 (1990) 5–9

4285 **Horvei, T,** Update on the SADCC energy situation, *SADCC Energy*, 8, 22 (1990) 33–39

4286 **Maluwa, T,** Towards an internationalisation of the Zambezi River regime: the role of

international law in the common management of an international watercourse, *The comparative and international law journal of southern Africa*, 25, 1 (1992) 20–43

4287 **Stiles, G,** Strategies for energy conservation in the SADCC countries. Pt 1, Background and current activities, *SADCC Energy*, 8, 21 (1990) 10–15

4288 **Stiles, G,** Strategies for energy conservation in the SADCC countries. Pt 2, Programme opportunities., *SADCC Energy*, 8, 22 (1990) 6–11

4289 **Tebicke, H L,** The transition to long-run sustainable energy supplies and utilization in the SADCC region, *SADCC Energy*, 8, 20 (1990) 29–32

Politics

see also: 4213, 4315

4290 **Alvaro, S,** *Afrique australe: à la recherche d'une identité.* Paris: Harmattan, 1991, 171pp

4291 **Anglin, D,** *International monitoring as a mechanism for conflict resolution in southern Africa.* Cape Town: Centre for Southern African Studies, University of the Western Cape, 1992, 42pp

4292 **Anglin, D G,** *International monitoring as a mechanism for conflict resolution in southern Africa.* Bellville: Centre for Southern African Studies, University of the Western Cape, 1992, 42pp

4293 **Baregu, M,** Armed struggle: the final phase in the liberation of southern Africa, *Maji Maji*, 47 (1990) 77–93

4294 **Baregu, M L,** Prospects for peace and security in southern Africa after Namibia's independence, *Taamuli*, NS 2, 1/2 (1991) 2–17

4295 **Bengu, S,** Destabilisation in southern Africa, in NGLS (ed),

Voices from Africa 3 (entry 913), 97–110

4296 Botha, T, et al, *Report on intergovernmental relations in Zimbabwe, Botswana and Namibia.* Bellville: Centre for Southern African Studies, University of the Western Cape, 1992, 84pp

4297 Chande, D, Changing faces in southern Africa, *Taamuli,* NS 2, 1/2 (1991) 18–27

4298 Davies, R, *Implications for southern Africa of the current impasse in the peace process in Mozambique.* Bellville: Centre for Southern African Studies, University of the Western Cape, 1991, 14pp

4299 Derens, J, Une double tâche pour le Parti communiste sud-africain, *Cahiers du communisme,* 68, 4 (1992) 103–107

4300 Glickman, H, (ed), *Towards peace and security in southern Africa.* New York: Gordon and Breach, 1990, 259pp

4301 Hastings, A, Church and state in southern Africa, *African affairs,* 91, 362 (1992) 134–37

4302 Legum, C, The southern African crisis: the tide begins to turn, *Africa contemporary record 1988/89,* (1992) A3–33

4303 Mandaza, I, The state and democracy in southern Africa, in Anyang' Nyong'o P (ed), *30 years of independence (entry 101),* 62–85

4304 Meyns, P, *The historical process of change: political outlook and economic prospects for southern Africa - a view from thew outside.* Cape Town: Centre for Southern African Studies, University of the Western Cape, 1992, 20pp

4305 Ohlson, T, Stedman, S J, *Trick or treat? The end of bipolarity and conflict resolution in southern Africa.* Cape Town: Centre for Southern African Studies, University of the Western Cape, 1992, 30pp

4306 Patel, H H, *Peace and security in a changing southern Africa: a frontline view.* Cape Town: Centre for Southern African Studies, University of the Western Cape, 1992, 22pp

4307 Patel, H H, The SADCC states, their international environment and change in South Africa, in Maasdorp G & Whiteside, A (eds), *Towards a post-apartheid future (entry 4201),* 45–61

4308 Richter, R, *Flüchtlingsbewegungen und Zwangsmigrationen im südlichen Afrika.* Munich: Forschungsstelle Dritte Welt, 1991, 45pp

4309 Saul, J S, *Socialist ideology and the struggle for southern Africa.* Trenton: Africa World Press, 1990, 199pp

4310 Seegers, A, War in southern Africa, *Africa,* 62, 2 (1992) 271–79

4311 Seidman, A, *The roots of crisis in southern Africa.* Trenton: Africa World Press, 1990, 209pp

4312 Umeh, O J, Determinants of administrative development in seven Southern African countries, *Indian journal of public administration,* 37, 1 (1991) 47–61

4313 Weimer, B, *Das Ende der weissen Vorherrschaft in südlichen Afrika.* Baden-Baden: Nomos, 1992, 380pp

Religion, philosophy

see also: 4301, 4326

4314 Esack, K, Islam in southern Africa: a rejoinder to Nkrumah, *Review of African political economy,* 53 (1992) 75–78

4315 Gifford, P, *The new crusaders: Christianity and the new right in southern Africa.* London: Pluto, revised edition, 1991, 131pp

4316 Hofmeyr, J W, et al, (eds), *A select bibliography of periodical articles*

on southern African church history.
Vol. 1, 1975–1989. Pretoria:
University of South Africa, 1991,
305pp

4317 **Hofmeyr, J W, et al,** (eds),
*History of the church in South Africa:
a document and source book.*
Pretoria: University of South
Africa, 1991, 436pp

4318 **Institute of Reformational
Studies,** *Cultural diversity in Africa:
embarassment or opportunity?*
Potchefstroom: Institute of
Reformational Studies,
Potchefstroom University, 1991,
261pp

4319 **Verstraelen-Guilhuis, G,** *A
new look at christianity in Africa:
essays on apartheid, education and a
new history.* Gweru: Mambo, 1992,
109pp

Rural economy

see also: 1930

4320 **Otzen, U,** *Stabilisation of
agricultural resources: concept,
requirement and measures to ensure
sustainable agricultural development,
with examples from southern Africa.*
Berlin: Geman Development
Institute, 1992, 143pp

4321 **Seidman, A, Baltzerson, A,**
(eds), *Transforming southern African
agriculture.* Trenton: Africa World
Press, 1992, 266pp

4322 **Spurling, A, et al,** *Agricultural
research in southern Africa: a
framework for action.* Washington:
World Bank, 1992, 61pp

Sociology

4323 **Beittel, M,** Southern Africa:
introduction, in Smith J &
Wallerstein, I (eds), *Creating and
transforming households* (Cambridge:
Cambridge UP, 1992), 189–96

4324 **Kaarsholm, P,** (ed), *Cultural
struggle and development in Southern*

Africa. London: Currey, 1991,
258pp

4325 **Quinlan, T,** Conservation in
southern Africa: a sociological
critique, *South Africa journal of
sociology,* 22, 4 (1991) 124–127

4326 **Raum, O K,** Can the
independent churches of southern
Africa be interpreted with Max
Weber's conceptual apparatus?,
Sociologus, 41, 2 (1991) 97–117

BOTSWANA

General

4327 **Weimer, B,** (ed), *Botswana:
vom Land der Betschuanen zum
Frontstaat. Wirtschaft, Gesellschaft,
Kultur.* Munster: Lit, 1991,
358pp

Anthropology

4328 **Botswana Society,** *Kalanga
retrospect and prospect.* Gaberone:
Botswana Society, 1991, 113pp

4329 **Gulbrandsen, V,** Material and
symbolic aspects of changing
property relations is Tswana
society, in Baxter P T W & Hogg,
R (eds), *Property, poverty and people
(entry 1000),* 164–81

4330 **Hitchcock, R K,** Kuacaca: an
early case of ethnoarchaeology in
the northern Kalahari, *Botswana
notes and records,* 23, (1991) 223–33

Demography

No entry, see also: 4342

Economy - Development

4331 **Claus, O, Weimer, B,**
Changing southern Africa: what
role for Botswana?, *Afrika spectrum,*
26, 3 (1991) 315–334

4332 **Good, K,** Interpreting the
exceptionality of Botswana, *Journal*

of modern African studies, 30, 1 (1992) 69–95

4333 Harvey, C, *Botswana: is the economic miracle over?* Brighton: Sussex University, IDS, 1992, 40pp

4334 Harvey, C, Lewis, S R, *Policy choice and development performance in Botswana.* Basingstoke: Macmillan, 1990, 341pp

4335 Hudson, D J, Booms and busts in Botswana, *Botswana notes and records*, 23, (1991) 47–67

4336 Mhozya, X, *The specification and estimation of an econometric model for Botswana.* Braunton, Devon: Merlin Books, 1992, 170pp

4337 Molutsi, P P, The political economy of Botswana: implications for democracy, in Molomo M G & Mokopakgosi, B T (eds), *Multi-party democracy (entry 4387)*, 29–37

4338 Nordås, H K, *Den konomiskeog politiske utvikling i Botswana.* Bergen: CMI, 1992, 28pp

4339 Parkinson, J R, Botswana: adjustment to wealth, in Milner C & Rayner, A J (eds), *Policy adjustment (entry 184)*, 197–219

Economic and social history

4340 Jones-Dube, E, The influences of entrepreneurs on rural town development in Botswana, *Botswana notes and records*, 23, (1991) 11–32

4341 Mushinge, C, The impact of colonial policies on ecological control and African cattle production in Botswana, 1885–1954, *Eastern African social science research review*, 6,2 & 7/1, (1990/91) 65–77

4342 Pennington, R, Harpending, H, How many refugees were there? History and population change among the Herero and Mbanderu of northwestern Botswana,

Botswana notes and records, 23, (1991) 209–21

Education

4343 Adam, S, *Education with production: a case study of Botswana.* Bremen: Universität Bremen, Nord-Süd Forum, 19991, 64pp

4344 Hinchliffe, K, The returns to vocational education in Botswana - research note, *Economics of education review*, 9, 4 (1990) 401–404

4345 Kahn, M J, Attitudes of Botswana senior secondary school pupils towards agriculture, *International journal of educational development*, 11, 3 (1991) 201–208

4346 Mautle, G, An exploratory study of primary school teachers' views on the social studies curriculum, *BOLESWA Educational research journal*, 7, (1990) 34–48

4347 Mokgwathi, G M G, Financing higher education in Botswana, *Higher education*, 23, 4 (1991) 425–31

Environment

see also: 4328

4348 Segosebe, E M, Van der Post, C, *Urban industrial solid waste pollution in Botswana: practice, attitudes and policy recommendations.* Gaberone: NIDR, 1991, 43pp

Food

4349 Simmons, C, Lyons, S, Rhetoric and reality: the management of Botswana's 1982–88 drought relief programme, *Journal of international development*, 4, 6 (1992) 607–631

Gender

see also: 4374

4350 Griffiths, A, The 'women's question' in Kwena family disputes, *Journal of legal pluralism and unofficial law,* 30/31 (1990/1991) 223–254

4351 Hasenjürgen, B, Female labour in the process of transformation: seen in the example of Botswana, *African development perspectives yearbook,* 2, (1990/91) 695–708

4352 Madisa, M, Women and politics, in Molomo M G & Mokopakgosi, B T (eds), *Multi-party democracy (entry 4387),* 55–59

History, early

4353 Campbell, A, The riddle of the stone walls, *Botswana notes and records,* 23, (1991) 243–49

4354 van Waarden, C, Stone Age people of Makalambedi Drift, *Botswana notes and records,* 23, (1991) 251–75

4355 Walker, N, Game traps: their importance in southern Africa, *Botswana notes and records,* 23, (1991) 235–42

History, C19th

4356 Mgodla, P T, *Missionaries and western education in the Bechuanaland Protectorate 1859–1904.* Gaborone: University of Botswana, Dept of Theology, 1991, 47pp

4357 Ramsay, J, The Batswana-Boer war of 1852–53: how the Batswana achieved victory, *Botswana notes and records,* 23, (1991) 193–207

History, C20th

4358 Parsons, N, Colonel Rey and

the colonial rulers of Botswana: mercenary and missionary traditions in administration, 1884–955, in Ajayi J F A & Peel, J D Y (eds), *Peoples and empires (entry 429),* 197–215

4359 Roberts, S, Tswana government and law in the time of Seepatitso, 1910–1916, in Mann K & Roberts, R (eds), *Law in colonial Africa (entry 684),* 167–84

Industry & trade

see also: 4340

4360 Fountain International, *Norad and the productive sector development in Botswana.* Gaborone: Fountain International, 1992, 191pp

4361 Pfotenhauer, L, (ed), *Tourism in Botswana.* Gaberone: Botswana Society, 1991, 412pp

4362 Ramasedi, B R, Rural electrification in Botswana, in Ranganathan V (ed), *Rural electrification (entry 1046),* 112–40

International economic relations

No entry; see also: 4360

International relations

4363 Claus, O, *Botswana: südafrikanisches Homeland oder unabhängiger Frontstaat?* Hamburg: Institut für Afrika-Kunde, 1992, 259pp

4364 Zaffiro, J J, Botswana's foreign policy and the exit of superpowers from southern Africa, *Africa insight,* 22, 2 (1992) 95–104

4365 Zaffiro, J J, The U S and Botswana in the 1990s: eroding continuity in a changing region, *Journal of contemporary African studies,* 10, 1 (1991) 18–44

Labour & manpower

4366 Higgins, K M, Management team training for local government: Botswana in the vanguard, *Botswana notes and records,* 23, (1991) 33–45

4367 Mugisha, R X, Mwamwenda, T S, Job mobility for graduates in Botswana, *South African journal of sociology,* 22, 4 (1991) 128–131

4368 Pfau, R H, The culture of the workplace in Botswana, *Botswana notes and records,* 23, (1991) 1–10

Language

4369 Andersson, L G, Janson, T, Languages and language use among students at the University of Botswana, *Marang,* 9 (1991) 42–51

Law

see also: 4350

4370 Love, C, Court sentencing in Botswana: a role for probation?, *Journal of social development in Africa,* 7, 2 (1992) 5–17

4371 Molokomme, A, *'Children of the fence':* the maintenance of extra-marital children under law and practice in Botswana. Leiden: Afrika Studiecentrum, 1991, 302pp

4372 Molokomme, A, Disseminating family law reforms: some lessons from Botswana, *Journal of legal pluralism and unofficial law,* 30/31 (1990/1991) 303–329

4373 Otlhogile, B, Drug control and the law in Botswana, *The comparative and international law journal of southern Africa,* 24, 2 (1991) 248–259

4374 Pfotenhauer, L, Interview with Unity Dow, *Botswana notes and records,* 23, (1991) 101–105

Library - documentation

4375 Brothers, S C, The development of Botswana's national library service, *Botswana notes and records,* 23, (1991) 69–81

4376 Parsons, Q N, Hitchcock, R K, *Index to publications 1969–1989.* Gaberone: Botswana Society, 1991, 72pp

4377 Wiseman, J A, *Botswana.* Oxford: Clio, 1992, 187pp

Literature

4378 Ménager-Everson, V S, *Maru* by Bessie Head: the Dilepe quartet or From drought to beer, *Commonwealth : essays and studies,* 14, 2 (1992) 44–48

4379 Séverac, A, Beyond identity: Bessie Head's spiritual quest in *Maru, Commonwealth : essays and studies,* 14, 1 (1991) 58–64

Media

4380 Zaffiro, J, *From police network to station of the nation: a political history of broadcasting in Botswana.* Gaberone: Botswana Society, 1991, 109pp

Natural resources

4381 Diphaha, J, Promoting alternative energy in Botswana: the case for subsidies, in Bhagavan M R & Karekezi, S (eds), *Energy for rural development* (London: Zed,1992), 108–118

4382 Gilbert, A, Natural resource accounting: a case study of Botswana, in Dixon J A et al (eds), *Dryland management (entry 1012),* 307–29

Planning

4383 Gasper, D R, Development

planning and decentralisation in Botswana, in de Valk P & Wekwete, K H (eds), *Decentralising (entry 5485)*, 224–54

4384 van Hoof, P, Rural development policy, regional development planning, and decentralisation in Botswana, in Drakakis-Smith D (ed), *Urban and regional change (entry 4224)*, 147–79

Politics

see also: 4338, 4352

4385 Holm, J D, Molutsi, P, State-society relations in Botswana: beginning liberalisation, in Hyden G & Bratton, M (eds), *Governance and politics (entry 864)*, 75–95

4386 Molomo, M G, Botswana's political process, in Molomo M G & Mokopakgosi, B T (eds), *Multi-party democracy (entry 4387)*, 11–22

4387 Molomo, M G, Mokopakgosi, B T, (eds), *Multi-party democracy in Botswana.* Harare: SAPES Trust, 1991, 63pp

4388 Molutsi, P P, Political parties and democracy in Botswana, in Molomo M G & Mokopakgosi, B T (eds), *Multi-party democracy (entry 4387)*, 5–9

4389 Nengwekhulu, R, The electoral process, in Molomo M G & Mokopakgosi, B T (eds), *Multi-party democracy (entry 4387)*, 39–47

4390 Otlhogile, B, How free and fair?, in Molomo M G & Mokopakgosi, B T (eds), *Multi-party democracy (entry 4387)*, 23–28

4391 Tsie, B, Election, democracy and hegemony in Botswana, in Molomo M G & Mokopakgosi, B T (eds), *Multi-party democracy (entry 4387)*, 49–53

Rural economy

see also: 1020, 4345, 4362

4392 Arntzen, J, A framework for economic evaluation of collective fencing in Botswana, in Dixon J A et al (eds), *Dryland management (entry 1012)*, 138–52

4393 Brhaug, K, *Politics, administration and agricultural development: the case of Botswana's Accelerated Rainfed Arable Programme.* Bergen: CMI, 1992, 158pp

4394 Braat, L G, Opschoor, J B, Risks in the Botswana range-cattle system, in Dixon J A et al (eds), *Dryland management (entry 1012)*, 153–74

4395 Helle-Valle, J, *New perspectives on old themes: diversity and change in Letlhakeng village, Botswana.* Oslo: Senter for Utvikling og Milj, Oslo University, 1992, 25pp

4396 Hitchcock, R K, Socioeconomic development among remote area dwellers: a note, *Botswana notes and records,* 23, (1991) 278–82

4397 Mazonde, I, From commercial water points to private wells and boreholes in Botswana's communal areas, in Baxter P T W & Hogg, R (eds), *Property, poverty and people (entry 1000)*, 182–91

4398 Milazi, D, The social implications of land policy and rural development in Botswana, *African journal of sociology,* 3, 2 (1989/1990) 61–69

4399 Peters, P E, Manoeuvers and debates in the interpretation of land rights in Botswana, *Africa,* 62, 3 (1992) 413–34

4400 van der Maas, H, *Effects of agricultural development programmes on the arable productivity of rural households in the North East District CFDA.* Utrecht: Institute of Geography, Utrecht University, 1991, 76pp

Science & technology

4401 Yates, R, et al, *Solar-powered desalination: a case study from Botswana.* Ottawa: IDRC, 1990, 55pp

Sociology

4402 Otlhogile, B, Infanticide in Bechuanaland: a footnote to Shapera, *Journal of African law,* 34, 2 (1990) 159–62

Urban studies

4403 Jones-Dube, E, The influence of entrepreneurs on rural town development in Botswana, in Baker J & Pedersen, P O (eds), *Rural-urban interface (entry 1111),* 148–70

LESOTHO

Current affairs

4404 Sejanamane, M, The politics of intrigue, *Southern Africa political and economic monthly,* 4, 3/4 (1990/1991) 6–9

Economy - Development

4405 Gay, J, et al, *Poverty in Lesotho: a mapping exercise.* Maseru: Sechaba Consultants, 1991, 189pp
4406 Matlosa, K, Impact of IMF structural adjustment programmes on Lesotho, *Southern Africa political and economic monthly,* 4, 3/4 (1990/1991) 12–15
4407 Petersson, L, *Lesotho: adjustment and liberalisation in Lesotho.* Srockholm: SIDA, 1992, 47pp
4408 Setai, B, Structural adjustment programme in Lesotho, *Africa development,* 16, 1 (1991) 5–22

Economic and social history

4409 Showers, K B, Malahlela, G M, Oral evidence in historical environmental impact assessment: soil conservation in Lesotho in the 1930s and 1940s, *Journal of southern African studies,* 18, 2 (1992) 276–96

Environment

see also: 4409
4410 Bojo, S, Benefit-cost analysis of the farm improvement with soil conservation project in Maphutseng, Mohale's Hoek District, Lesotho, in Dixon J A et al (eds), *Dryland management (entry 1012),* 98–112

Gender

4411 Ntimo-Makara, M, The women's response to the missionary initiative in the provision of education for women in Lesotho: a brief historical overview, *BOLESWA Educational research journal,* 7, (1990) 49–57

History, early

4412 Ambrose, D, *A tentative history of Lesotho palaeontology.* Roma: NUL Journal of research, 1991, 38pp

History, C19th

4413 Ambrose, D, Brutsch, A, (eds), *Thomas Arbousset, missionary excursion into the Blue Mountains.* Morija: Morija Archives, 1991, 219pp

Industry & trade

4414 Khalema, L M, Rural electrification in Lesotho, in

Ranganathan V (ed), *Rural electrification (entry 1046)*, 141–61

International relations

4415 **Tsikoane, T,** Lesotho Highlands Water Project and the implications for conflict resolution: a preliminary projection, *Taamuli*, NS 2, 1/2 (1991) 46–60

4416 **Weisfelder, R F,** Lesotho and the inner periphery in the new South Africa, *Journal of modern African studies*, 30, 4 (1992) 643–68

Labour & manpower

4417 **Guy, J, Thabane, M,** Basotho miners, oral history and workers' strategies, in Kaarsholm P (ed), *Cultural struggle (entry 4200)*, 239–58

Law

4418 **Kafula, R,** The role of law in the developing countries: the case of Lesotho, *Student law review*, 1, (1991) 1–12

4419 **Maqutu, W C M,** The meaning of African or European in the dual system of laws in Lesotho, *Student law review*, 1, (1991) 63–78

4420 **Sethathi, I T,** Is the rule of law the essence of constitutional government: the judicial independence and protection of human rights in Lesotho, *Student law review*, 1, (1991) 25–38

4421 **Sethathi, I T,** The plight of customary law practice in Bohali: past experience, present realities, and future possibilities, *Student law review*, 1, (1991) 54–62

Medical

4422 **Herman, D,** Maternal and child health data for 1989, *Lesotho epidemiological bulletin*, 5, 1 (1990) 35–39

4423 **Herman, D,** Notifiable disease reports for 1989, *Lesotho epidemiological bulletin*, 5, 1 (1990) 40–47

4424 **Herman, D,** Reflections on AIDS in Lesotho, *Lesotho epidemiological bulletin*, 5, 1 (1990) 4–7

4425 **Rombouts, L, Huurnink, A,** Mother and child health evaluation, Tebellong Health Service Area, *Lesotho epidemiological bulletin*, 5, 1 (1990) 8–19

4426 **Tracey, D, Makakole, B,** Tuberculosis in Lesotho, 1989, *Lesotho epidemiological bulletin*, 5, 1 (1990) 48–52

Natural resources

see also: 4415

4427 **Barrett, C, Senaoana, M,** *The price of water under the Lesotho Highlands Water Project.* Birmingham: Birmingham University, Dept. of Economics, 1991, 19pp

Politics

4428 **Makoa, F K,** Lesotho's military kingdom: an undemocratic political experiment, *Southern Africa political and economic monthly*, 4, 3/4 (1990/1991) 3–6

4429 **Matlosa, K,** Multi-partyism versus democracy in southern Africa: 'whither Lesotho?', *Verfassung und Recht in Ubersee*, 25, 3 (1992) 327–40

Rural economy

see also:4410, 4414

4430 **Mashinini, J,** Lesotho's traditional land tenure system has been blamed for low agricultural productivity, is this a fair criticism?, *Student law review*, 1, (1991) 39–47

Sociology

4431 Martin, W G, Lesotho: the creation of the households, in Smith J & Wallerstein, I (eds), *Creating and transforming households (Cambridge: Cambridge UP, 1992),* 231–49

4432 Matsela, Z A, An investigation of Sesotho traditional games: a preliminary study, *BOLESWA Educational research journal,* 7, (1990) 75–87

NAMIBIA

General

4433 Cubitt, G, Joyce, P, *This is Namibia.* Cape Town: Struik, 1992, 158pp

Anthropology

see also: 4445
4434 Barnard, A, *Hunters and herders of southern Africa: a comparative ethnography of the Khoisan peoples.* Cambridge: CUP, 1992, 349pp

4435 Gordon, R J, *The Bushman myth: the making of a Namibian underclass.* Boulder: Westview, 1992, 304pp

Current affairs

4436 Pisani, A, Rumours of rain: Namibia's post-independence experience, *Africa insight,* 21, 3 (1991) 171–79

Economy - Development

see also: 4489
4437 Châtel, B, et al, Namibie, *Marchés tropicaux et méditerranéens,* 48, 2421 (1992) 833–856

4438 Freeman, L, Contradictions of independence: Namibia in transition, *Transformation,* 17 (1992) 25–47

4439 Lamping, H, Jäschke, U, (eds), *Aktuelle Fragen der Namibia-Forschung.* Frankfurt: Institut für Wirtschafts- und Sozialgeographie, Goethe University, 1991, 315pp

4440 Murray, R, *Namibia through the 1990s: turning rich resources into growth.* London: Economist Intelligence Unit, 1992, 146pp

Economic and social history

see also: 4342, 4496
4441 Mokopakgosi, B T, Labour utilization and capitalist production in Namibia, 1907–1915, *Mohlomi,* 6, (1990) 97–138

Education

4442 Mkandawire, D S J, The academic achievement in liberal arts and science subjects of a fragmented Namibian secondary school system prior to independence, *Zimbabwe journal of educational research,* 4, 1 (1992) 17–31

Finance

4443 Harvey, C, Isaksen, J, (eds), *Monetary independence for Namibia.* Windhoek: Namibian Economic Policy Research Unit, 1990, 122pp

Gender

4444 Becker, H, Zwischen Parteipolitik und Autonomie: Erfahrungen der namibischen Frauenbewegung, *Peripherie,* 47/48 (1992) 49–73

4445 Shostak, M, *Nisa: the life and words of a !Kung woman.* London: Earthscan, 1990, 412pp

Geography, human

4446 Schnieder, K G, Richter, W, *Kavango und Ostcaprivi: periphere Wirtschaftsräume im Entwicklungsland Namibia.* Leverkusen: Selbstverf. d. Verf., 1991, 249pp

Health & welfare services

4447 Dropkin, G, Clark, D, *Past exposure: revealing health and enviromental risks of Rössing Uranium.* London: Namibia Support Committee, 1992, 134pp

History, general

4448 Enquist, R J, *Namibia: land of tears, land of promise.* Selinsgrove: Susquehanna UP, 1990, 174pp
4449 Fourie, D J, Reflections on Owambo origins and early movements, *Afrika und Übersee,* 74, 2 (1991) 205–221

History, early

4450 Leser, H, *Paläoklima und pleistozän-holozäne Entwicklung Nambias.* Basle: Basler Afrika Bibliographen, 1991, 213pp

History, C6–18th

4451 Guelke, L, Shell, R, Landscape of conquest: frontier water alienation and Khoikhoi strategies of survival 1652–1780, *Journal of southern African studies,* 18, 4 (1992) 803–24

History, C19th

4452 Eirola, M, *The Ovambogefahr: the Ovamboland reservation in the making.* Rovaniemi: Historical Association of Northern Finalnd, 1992, 309pp

History, C20th

4453 Brodersen-Manns, H, *Wie alles anders kam in Afrika: Südwester Erinnerungen aus den Jharen 1914/15.* Windhoek: Kuiseb, 1991, 77pp
4454 Mokopakgosi, B T, Conflicxt and collaboratiion in southeastern Namibia: missionaries, concessionaires and the Nama's war against German imperialism, 1880–1908, in Ajayi J F A & Peel, J D Y (eds), *Peoples and empires (entry 429),* 185–96
4455 Pyck, F Schwartze, A, *Namibia: der lange Weg in die Unabhängigkeit: von kolonialer Fremdherrschaft zur staatlichen Souveränität.* Bochum: Universität Bochum, Institut für Entwicklungsforschung und Entwicklungspolitik, 1991, 126pp
4456 Shamena, M, Namibia, in NGLS (ed), *Voices from Africa 3 (entry 913),* 111–117

Industry & trade

see also: 4447
4457 Moorsom, R, *Namibia's economy at independence: report on potential Norwegian-Namibian industrial cooperation.* Bergen: CMI, 1990, 81pp
4458 Sandlund, O T, Tvedten, I, *Pre-feasibility study on Namibian freshwater fish management.* Trondheim/Bergen: Norwegian Institute for Nature Research/CMI, 1992, 51pp
4459 UNIDO, *Namibia: industrial development at independence.* Vienna: UNIDO, 1990, 79pp

International economic relations

see also: 4457
4460 Balch, J A, et al, (eds), *Development for the Namibian people:*

new challenges for SADCC and the
international community.
Amsterdam: African-European
Institute, 1991, 104pp

**4461 Morris, D, van den Busche,
I,** *The state of EC-Namibia relations:
cooperation ion the fishing industry.*
London: CIIR, 1992, 24pp

4462 Odén, B, *Namibia's economic
links to South Africa.* Uppsala:
SIAS, 1991, 43pp

4463 Pilgrim, C M, Some legal
aspects of trade in the natural
resources of Namibia, *British
yearbook of international law,* 61,
(1990) 249–278

International relations

see also: 3285, 4489

4464 Adeoye, A O, The OAU and
the Namibian crisis 1963–1988,
African review, 16, 1/2 (1989)
98–112

4465 Dale, R, The United Nations
and African decolonisation:
UNTAG in Namibia, *Transafrica
forum,* 8, 3 (1991) 31–48

4466 De Klerk, P, Die
Walvisbaai-enklawe: 'n koloniale
oorblyfsel?, *Journal for
contemporary history,* 15, 3 (1990)
72–90

4467 Wood, B, Preventing the
vacuum: determinants of the
Namibia settlement, *Journal of
southern African studies,* 17, 4
(1991) 742–769

Labour & manpower

4468 Norval, D, Namoya, R, *The
informal sector within Greater
Windhoek: a profile study and needs
assessment of the informal sector as an
employment creator.* Windhoek: First
National Development
Corporation, 1991, 145pp

Language

4469 Lombard, J, Kirchner, E,
Afrikaans in Namibië, *Fasette,* 10, 2
(1991) 7–14

4470 Meyer, A, Afrikaans kom in
beweging in Namibië, *Fasette,* 10, 2
(1991) 26–33

Law

4471 Balch, J A, (ed), *Namibia's
constitution: framework for
democracy.* Amsterdam:
African-European Institute, 1990,
15, 72pp

4472 Cadoux, C, La République de
Namibie: un modèle
constitutionnel pour l'Afrique
australe?, *Revue du droit public,* 108,
1 (1992) 5–35

4473 Chantebout, B, La
constitution namibienne du 9
février 1990: enfin un vrai régime
semi-présidentiel!, *Revue française
de droit constitutionnel,* 1, 3 (1990)
539–49

4474 Gordon, R J, Vernacular law
and the future of human rights in
Namibia, *Acta juridica,* 1991
86–103

4475 Van Wyk, D, The making of
the Namibian constitution: lessons
for Africa, *The comparative and
international law journal of southern
Africa,* 24, 3 (1991) 341–351

4476 Van Wyk, D, et al, (eds),
*Namibia: constitutional and
international law issues.* Pretoria:
Centre for Public Law Studies,
University of South Africa, 1991,
227pp

Media

4477 Gorelick, N J, The challenges
of democratic television, in *Voices
from Africa 4 (entry 1064),* 79–88

Natural resources

4478 Lau, R, Stren, A, *Namibian water resources and their management: a preliminary history.* Windkoek: National Archives, 1990, 79pp

Planning

4479 Eele, G, Greener, R, *Issues in the development of statistical services in Namibia.* Bergen: CMI, 1990, 31pp

Politics

see also: 4467

4480 Ansprenger, F, *Freie Wahlen in Namibia: der Übergang zur staatlichen Unabhängigkeit.* Frankfurt: Lang, 1991, 156pp

4481 Clegg, M, Monitoring the vote: elections in Namibia in 1989 – a retrospective, *Parliamentarian,* 72, 4 (1991) 287–91

4482 Fritz, J C, *La Namibie indépendante: les coûts d'une décolonisation retardée.* Paris: Harmattan, 1991, 287pp

4483 Nathan, L, Human rights, reconciliatiion and conflict in independent Namibia: the formation of the Namibian army and police force, in Rupesinghe K (ed), *Internal conflict (entry 932),* 152–68

4484 Pabst, M, *Frieden für Südwest? Experiment Namibia.* Wesseling: Gesamtdeutscher, 1991, 309pp

4485 Putz, J, et al, *Namibia handbook and political who's who: post-election edition 1990.* Windhoek: Magus, 1990, 448pp

4486 Saunders, C, Transition in Namibia 1989–90 and the South African case, in Etherington N (ed), *Peace, politics and violence (entry 5047),* 213–30

4487 Saunders, C, Transition in Namibia 1989–1990: and the South African case, *Transformation,* 17 (1992) 12–24

4488 Saxena, S C, *Namibia and the world: the story of the birth of a nation.* Delhi: Kalinga, 1991, 382pp

4489 Sparks, D L, Green, D, *Namibia: the nation after independence.* Boulder: Westview, 1992, 204pp

4490 Tötemeyer, G, The regional reconstruction of the state: the Namibian case, *Politikon,* 19, 1 (1991) 66–82

4491 Weiland, H, *Namibia, wohin?: Perspektiven des Entkolonisierungsprozesses.* Bonn: Deutsches Kommission 'Justitia et Pax', 1990, 28pp

Religion, philosophy

No entry; see also: 4448

Rural economy

4492 Adams, M, Namibia: land reform: who will be the beneficiaries?, in Dudley N et al (eds), *Land is life: land reform and sustainable agriculture* (London: Intermediate Technology, 1992), 102–106

4493 Elkan, W, et al, *Namibian agriculture: policies and prospects.* Paris: OECD Development Centre, 1992, 66pp

4494 Erkkilä, A, Siiskonen, H, *Forestry in Namibia 1850–1990.* Joensuu: Joensuu University, 1992, 244pp

4495 Hinz, M O, Agriculture and its contribution to development in Namibia, *African development perspectives yearbook,* 2, (1990/91) 524–545

4496 Schneider, M B, *Bewässungslandwirtschaft in Namibia und ihre Gundlangen in der*

Kolonialzeit. Widhoek: Meinert, 1990, 179pp

4497 Tapscott, C, *The social economy of livestock production in the Ovambo region.* Windhoek: Nambian Institute for Social and Economic Research, 1990, 23pp

Urban studies

4498 Frayne, B, *Urbanisation in post-independence Windhoek: with special emphasis on Katatura.* Windhoek: NISER, 1992, 186pp

4499 Pendleton, W C, du Bois, B C, *Health and daily living survey of Windhoek, Namibia (1988–89).* Windhoek: Namibia Institute for Social and Economic Research, 1990, 70pp

SOUTH AFRICA

General

see also: 4201

4500 Clingman, S, (ed), *Regions and repertoires: topics in South African politics and culture.* Braamfontein: Ravan, 1991, 222pp

4501 Educational Resources Information Service, *Directory of South African resource centres.* Durban: University of Natal, Education Dept., 1992, unpagpp

4502 Jansen, J D, (ed), *Knowledge and power in South Africa: critical perspectives across the disciplines.* Johannesburg: Skotaville, 1991, 336pp

4503 Mamdani, M, Research and transformation: reflections on a visit to South Africa, *Economic and political weekly,* 27, 20/21 (1992) 1055–1062

4504 Moss, G, Obery, I, *South African review 6: from 'red Friday' to Codesa.* Johannesburg: Ravan, 1992, 508pp

4505 Tucker, R, Scott, B R, *South*

Africa: prospects for successful transition. Cape Town: Juta, 1992, 314pp

Anthropology

see also: 5090

4506 Bill, M, Literature, language and politics: a case study of Tsonga, in Nethersole R (ed), *Emerging literatures (entry 726),* 107–21

4507 Callaway, H, The initiation of a Zulu diviner, in Peek P M (ed), *African divination (entry 47),* 27–35

4508 Danskardt, R, 'Urban herbalism': the restructuring of informal survival in Johannesburg, in Preston-Whyte E & Rogerson, C (eds), *South Africa's informal economy (entry 4567),* 87–100

4509 Evans, J, On brûle bien les sorcières: les meutres *muti* et leur répression, *Politique africaine,* 48 (1992) 47–57

4510 Fernandez, J W, Afterword, in Peek P M (ed), *African divination (entry 48),* 213–21

4511 Hammond-Tooke, W D, Twins, incest and mediators: the structure of four Zulu folk tales, *Africa,* 62, 2 (1992) 203–220

4512 Thuynsma, P, Xhosa *ntsomi:* tailoring the tall tale, in Nethersole R (ed), *Emerging literatures (entry 726),* 145–54

Arts

4513 Botha, M, van Answegen, A, *Images of South Africa: an alternative film revival.* Pretoria: HSRC, 1992, 199pp

4514 Chapman, M, The sculptor and the citizen, *Theoria,* 80 (1992) 77–86

4515 Davis, G V, "Repainting the damaged canvas": the theatre of Matsemela Manaka, *Commonwealth : essays and studies,* 14, 1 (1991) 84–96

4516 Ménager-Everson, S V, The Albie Sachs debate, *Research in African literatures,* 23, 4 (1992) 59–66

4517 Rycroft, D K, Black South African urban music since the 1890s: some reminiscences of Alfred Assegai Kumalo (1879–1966), *African music,* 7, 1 (1991) 5–31

Current affairs

4518 Aicardi de St Paul, M, Afrique du Sud: le référendum du 17 mars 1992, *Afrique contemporaine,* 163 (1992) 26–29

4519 Cullinan, K, Moving the masses, *Work in progress,* 84 (1992) 7–10

4520 Du Plessis, B, Afrique du Sud: bilan et perspectives, *Revue des deux mondes,* Dec. 1990 154–61

4521 Faure, V, Afrique du Sud: référendum 92. Le passage, *Politique africaine,* 46 (1992) 126–31

4522 Jeffery, A, (ed), *Forum on mass mobilisation.* Johannesburg: SAIRR, 1991, 105pp

4523 Roth, T, *Südafrika: die letzte Chance.* Stuttgart: Erdmann, 1991, 316pp

Demography

4524 Preston-Whyte, E M, *Teenage pregnancy in selected Coloured and Black communities.* Pretoria: HSRC, 1991, 58pp

Economy - Development

see also: 4680

4525 Abedian, I, Standish, B (eds), *Economic growth in South Africa: selected policy issues.* Cape Town: OUP, 1992, 239pp

4526 Abedian, I, Standish, B, The way forward: policy guidelines for the 1990s, in Abedian I &

Standish, B (eds), *Economic growth in South Africa (entry 4525),* 215–30

4527 Anderson, M, *Productive investments for economic growth: proposal for a National Investment Board.* Salt River: Labour Research Service, 1991, 19pp

4528 Bethlehem, R, Economic development in South Africa, in Maasdorp G & Whiteside, A (eds), *Towards a post-apartheid future (entry 4201),* 62–82

4529 Bethlehem, R W, *Economic restructuring in post-apartheid South Africa.* Braamfontein: SAIIA, 1992, 17pp

4530 Broomberg, J, Masobe, P, *The economic impact of the AIDS epidemic in South Africa.* Cape Town: Economic Trends Research Group, University of Cape Town, 1991, 60pp

4531 Buys, J, South Africa's economic prospects 1992–1995, *South Africa international,* 22, 4 (1991/92) 161–168

4532 Coetzee, S, Development economics and policies to promote peace in South Africa, *Africa insight,* 22, 2 (1992) 121–27

4533 Coleman, K, *Nationalisation: beyond the slogans.* Johannesburg: Ravan, 1991, 179pp

4534 COSATU, *Our political economy: understanding the problems. A handbook for COSATU shop stewards.* Johannesburg: COSATU, 1992, 76pp

4535 Davies, R, South Africa and the SADCC: regional economic cooperation after apartheid, in Moss G & Obery, G (eds), *South African review 6 (entry 4504),* 436–44

4536 du Plessis, J E, *Methods of wealth and income redistribution: a classification.* Stellenbosch: The Stellenbosch Economic Project, 1992, 17pp

4537 Eckert, J B, et al, Sharpening

the tools: a provisional 1988 social accounting matrix for South Africa, *Development Southern Africa*, 9, 2 (1992) 243–255

4538 Fernandez, J I, Dismantling apartheid: counterproductive effects of continuing economic sanctions, *Law and policy in international business*, 22, 3 (1991) 571–602

4539 Gruber, R, South Africa's economic prospects - some assessments, *South Africa international*, 22, 3 (1992) 140–142

4540 Harris, L, The economic strategy and policies of the African National Congress, in McGregor A (ed), *McGregors' economic alternatives (entry 4560)*, 23–73

4541 Hawkins, A, Corporate strategy in South Africa, *South Africa international*, 22, 3 (1992) 133–136

4542 Honey, M, NGO and public sector cooperation, *Africa insight*, 22, 2 (1992) 116–120

4543 Howe, G, Le Roux, P, *Transforming the economy: policy options for South Africa.* Durban/Bellville: Indicator Project, University of Natal/Institute for Social Development, University of the Western Cape, 1992, 273pp

4544 ILO, *Study of the embargo of coal exports from South Africa.* Geneva: ILO, 1992, 28pp

4545 Innes, D, Privatisation versus nationalisation, in Innes D et al (eds), *Power and profit (entry 4546)*, 96–122

4546 Innes, D, et al, (ed), *Power and profit: politics, labour and business in South Africa.* Cape Town: OUP, 1992, 310pp

4547 Jenkins, C, Sanctions and their effect on employment in South Africa, *International labour review*, 130, 5/6 (1991) 657–71

4548 Kahn, B, Exchange rate policy and industrial restructuring, in

Moss G & Obery, G (eds), *South African review 6 (entry 4504)*, 493–508

4549 Keeton, M, et al, Gearing up for the long road: the challenge of poverty in South Africa, *Optima*, 38, 3 (1992) 122–36

4550 Kirsten, M, A quantitative assessment of the informal sector, in Preston-Whyte E & Rogerson, C (eds), *South Africa's informal economy (entry 4567)*, 148–60

4551 Lachman, D, Economic challenges facing South Africa, *Finance and development*, 29, 2 (1992) 6–9

4552 Lachman, D, (ed), *Economic policies for a new South Africa.* Washington: IMF, 1992, 42pp

4553 Leape, J, *South Africa's foreign debt and the standstill, 1985–1990.* London: London School of Economics, Centre for the Study of the South African Economy and International Finance, 1991, 34pp

4554 Lee, R, No perfect path: cooperation for development, *Africa insight*, 22, 2 (1992) 110–115

4555 Lewis, D, *The character and consequences of conglomeration in the South African economy.* Cape Town: Economic Trends Research Group, University of Cape Town, 1991, 18pp

4556 Loots, L J, Budgeting for post-apartheid South Africa, in Moss G & Obery, G (eds), *South African review 6 (entry 4504)*, 459–77

4557 Lundahl, M, *Apartheid in theory and practice: an economic analysis.* Boulder: Westview, 1992, 375pp

4558 MacCarthy, C, *Stagnation in the South African economy: where did things go wrong?* Stellenbosch: Stellenbosch University, Centre for Contextual Hermeneutics, 1991, 21pp

4559 McCarthy, C, *Stagnation in the*

South African economy: where did things go wrong? Stellenbosch: The Stellenbosch Economic Project, 1991, 21pp

4560 McGregor, A (ed), *McGregor's economic alternatives.* Kenwyn: Juta, 1992, 394pp

4560a McGregor, R W G, McGregor, G, Competition policy, in McGregor A (ed), *McGregors' economic alternatives (entry 4560),* 305–94

4561 McRae, I, Un rôle à jouer dans l'économie sud-africaine, *Revue des deux mondes,* Dec. 1990 146–53

4562 Moll, P G, The decline of discrimination against Coloured people in South Africa 1970 to 1980, *Journal of development economics,* 371, 1/2 (1991) 289–307

4563 Moll, P G, *The great economic debate: the radical's guide to the South African economy.* Johannesburg: Skotaville, 1990, 154pp

4564 Motsueyane, S M, et al, *Towards an economic and development policy framework for a post-apartheid South Africa.* Johannesburg: National African Federated Chamber of Commerce and Industry, 1991, 28pp

4565 Nattrass, N, Controversies about capitalism and apartheid in South Africa: an economic perspective, *Journal of southern African studies,* 17, 4 (1991) 654–677

4566 Padayachee, V, *The IMF and World Bank in post-apartheid South Africa: prospects and dangers.* Cape Town: Economic Trends Research Group, University of Cape Town, 1991, 31pp

4567 Preston-Whyte, E, Rogerson, C, (eds), *South Africa's informal economy.* Cape Town: OUP, 1991, 410pp

4568 Rogerson, C, Tracking the urban informal sector, in Moss G &

Obery, G (eds), *South African review 6 (entry 4504),* 378–87

4569 Rogerson, C, Preston-Whyte, E, South Africa's informal economy: past, present and future, in Preston-Whyte E & Rogerson, C (eds), *South Africa's informal economy (entry 4567),* 1–7

4571 Streeten, P, *Paul Streeten in South Africa: reflections on a journey.* Innesdal: Development Society of Southern Africa, 1992, 108pp

4572 Torr, C, Privatisation of the second kind, in Moss G & Obery, G (eds), *South African review 6 (entry 4504),* 450–58

4573 van den Berg, S, *The post-apartheid economy: an agenda for debate.* Stellenbosch: Stellenbosch University, Centre for Contextual Hermeneutics, 1991, 28pp

4575 Weimer, B, *Socio-economic transformation in South Africa: a comparative perspective.* Bordeaux: Institut d'études politiques, Université de Bordeaux, 1992, 20pp

4576 Zarenda, H, *An evaluation of the IMF mission document on economic policies for a new South Africa.* London: Dept. of Economics, School of Oriental and African Studies, 1992, 18pp

Economic and social history

4577 Abedian, I, Standish, B, The South African economy: an historical overview, in Abedian I & Standish, B (eds), *Economic growth in South Africa (entry 4525),* 1–24

4578 Allen, V L, *The history of Black mineworkers in South Africa. Vol. 1, The techniques of resistance 1871–1948.* Johannesburg: Moor Press, 1992, 491pp

4579 Baines, G, From populism to unionism:the emergence and nature of Port Elizabeth's Industrial and Commercial

Workers Union, 1918–20, *Journal of southern African studies*, 17, 4 (1991) 679–716

4580 Banks, A, *The decline of urban slavery in the Cape, 1806 to 1843.* Cape Town: University of Cape Town, Centre for African Studies, 1991, 246pp

4581 Cobley, A G, 'Far from home': the origins and significance of the Afro-Caribbean community in South Africa to 1930, *Journal of southern African studies*, 18, 2 (1992) 349–70

4582 Da Costa, Y, Assimilatory processes amongst the Cape muslims in South Africa during the 19th century, *South African journal of sociology*, 23, 1 (1992) 5–11

4583 Davenport, R, Historical background of the apartheid city to1948, in Swilling M et al (eds), *Apartheid city (entry 5328)*, 1–18

4584 Frankel, S H, *An economist's testimony: the autobiography of Professor S Herbert Frankel.* Oxford: Centre for Postgraduate Hebrew Studies, 1992, 354pp

4585 Heidenrych, H, Martin, B, *The Natal mainline story.* Pretoria: HSRC, 1992, 185pp

4586 Kennedy, B, Missionaries, Black converts and separatists on the Rand, 1886–1910: from accomodation to resistance, *Journal of imperial and Commonwealth history*, 22, 2 (1992) 196–222

4587 Minkley, G, Class and culture in the workplace: East London, industrialisation, and the conflict over work, 1945–57, *Journal of southern African studies*, 18, 4 (1992) 739–60

4588 Morrell, R, (ed), *White but poor: essays on the history of poor whites in southern Africa 1880–1940.* Pretoria: University of South Africa, 1992, 224pp

4589 Murray, C, *Black mountain: land, class and power in the eastern*

Orange Free State, 1880s to1980s. Edinburgh: Edinburgh UP, 1992, 354pp

4590 Nasson, B, 'Messing with Coloured people': the 1918 police strike in cape Town, South Africa, *Journal of African history*, 33, 2 (1992) 301–19

4591 Parnell, S, Sanitation, segregation and the Natives (Urban Areas) Act: African exclusion from Johannesburg's Malay Location, 1897–1925, *Journal of historical geography*, 17, 3 (1991) 271–88

4592 Pirie, G H, Rolling segregation into apartheid: South African railways, 1948–53, *Journal of contemporary history*, 27, 4 (1992) 671–93

4593 Zaal, F N, The ambivalence of authority and secret lives of tears: transracial child placements and the historical development of South African law, *Journal of southern African studies*, 18, 2 (1992) 372–404

Education

see also: 4689, 4716

4594 Archer, S, Moll, P, Education and economic growth, in Abedian I & Standish, B (eds), *Economic growth in South Africa (entry 4525)*, 147–86

4595 Chisholm, L, South African education in the era of negotiations, in Moss G & Obery, G (eds), *South African review 6 (entry 4504)*, 279–93

4596 Christie, P, Black education: the role of the state and business, in Innes D et al (eds), *Power and profit (entry 4546)*, 278–94

4597 Christie, P, *Open schools: racially mixed Catholic schools in South Africa, 1976–1986.* Johannesburg: Ravan, 1990, 182pp

4598 Christie, P, Gordon, A,

Politics, poverty and education in rural South Africa, *British journal of the sociology of education*, 13, 4 (1991) 399–418

4599 Flanagan, W, et al, Authority and emancipation in South African schools, *Education and society*, 10, 1 (1992) 13–21

4600 Frederikse, J, *All schools for all children: lessons for South Africa from Zimbabwe's open schools*. Oxford: OUP, 1992, 135pp

4601 Hartshorne, K, *Crisis and challenge: Black education 1910–1990*. Cape Town: OUP, 1992, 394pp

4602 Holdshock, T, Violence in schools: discipline, in McKendrick B & Hoffman, W (eds), *People and violence (entry 5270)*, 341–72

4603 Macdonald, C A, *Ballpoint pens and braided hair: an analysis of reasoning skills and the curriculum*. Pretoria: HSRC, 1990, 142pp

4604 Macdonald, C A, *Crossing the threshold into Standard Three in Black education*. Pretoria: HSRC, 1990, 196pp

4605 Macdonald, C A, *How many years do you have? English language skills evaluation*. Pretoria: HSRC, 1990, 122pp

4606 Macdonald, C A, *Swimming up the waterfall: a study of school-based learning experiences*. Pretoria: HSRC, 1990, 122pp

4607 Maqsud, M, Khalique, C M, Relationship of some socio-personal factors to mathematics achievement of secondary school and university students in Bophuthatswana, *Educational studies in mathematics*, 22, 4 (1991) 377–90

4608 Maqsud, M, Khalique, C M, Socio-personal correlates of mathematics achievement among secondary school pupils in Bophuthatswana, *International journal of educational development*, 11, 1 (1991) 31–40

4609 Meyer, S, *Erziehung als Schlüssel geselschaftlicher Veränderung: 'Bantu education' und People's education' in Südafrika*. Saarbrucken: Breitenbach, 1991, 136pp

4610 Motala, S, *Training for transformation: research training survey and workshop proceedings*. Johannesburg: Educational Policy Unit, Witwatersrand University, 1991, 118pp

4611 Muller, J, Education, *South African human rights and labour law yearbook*, 1, (1990) 92–109

4612 Nkomo, M, (ed), *Pedagaogy of domination: toward a democratic education in South Africa*. Trenton: Africa World Press, 1990, 474pp

4613 Orbach, E, A development perspective on the role and function of black colleges of education in South Africa, *Development Southern Africa*, 9, 2 (1992) 199–212

4614 Pouris, A, Scientific literacy, in Innes D et al (eds), *Power and profit (entry 4546)*, 295–303

4615 Pretorius, F, Comparative education: perspectives in a changing South Africa, *Prospects*, 22, 81 (1992) 102–111

4616 Prinsloo, J, Criticos, C, (eds), *Media matters in South Africa*. Durban: University of Natal, Education Dept., 1992, 301pp

4617 Samuel, J, Education in South Africa: strategic issues for the future, in Innes D et al (eds), *Power and profit (entry 4546)*, 270–77

4618 Shalem, Y, Teacher's struggle: the case of white English-speaking teachers in South Africa, *British journal of the sociology of education*, 13, 4 (1991) 307–28

4619 Soniden, C, Colyn, W, The safety of theory: working with educators in a squatter community, *Journal of educational thought*, 26, 3 (1991) 258–71

4620 Spangenberg, J B, *A comparative education profile of the population groups in South Africa.* Sandton: Information Clearing House, Development Bank of Southern Africa, 1991, 18pp

4621 Tilton, D, Creating an 'educated workforce': Inkatha, big business and educational reform in Kwazulu, *Journal of southern African studies,* 18, 1 (1992) 166–89

4622 Tjonneland, E N, *Universoitet og forsking i sr-Afrika: utfordringar utter apartheid og akademisk boikott.* Bergen: CMI, 1992, 16pp

4623 Van Zyl, C, *De Lange report: 10 years on.* Pretoria: HSRC, 1990, 178pp

4624 Wood-Robinson, C, Science education in South Africa: an outsider's view of the future, *Science, technology and development,* 10, 2 (1992) 265–74

4625 Wright, L, Some thoughts on African nationalism, literary education and the university, *Theoria,* 80 (1992) 25–30

Environment

see also: 4918

4626 Association for Rural Advancement, The Tembe Elephant Park, in Cock J & Koch, E (eds), *Going green (entry 4629),* 223–27

4627 Clarke, J, Tampering with the atmosphere, in Cock J & Koch, E (eds), *Going green (entry 4629),* 139–57

4628 Cock, J, The environment as a political issue, in Cock J & Koch, E (eds), *Going green (entry 4629),* 1–17

4629 Cock, J, Koch, E, (eds), *Going green: people, politics and environment in South Africa.* Cape Town: OUP, 1991, 262pp

4630 Coetzee, H, Cooper, d, Squandering a precious resource, in Cock J & Koch, E (eds), *Going green (entry 4629),* 129–38

4631 Cooper, D, Land use in South Africa, in Cock J & Koch, E (eds), *Going green (entry 4629),* 176–92

4632 Crompton, R Erwin, A, Labour and the environment, in Cock J & Koch, E (eds), *Going green (entry 2395),* 78–91

4633 Cunningham, A, The herbal medicine trade: resource degradation and environmental management for a 'hidden economy', in Preston-Whyte E & Rogerson, C (eds), *South Africa's informal economy (entry 4567),* 196–206

4634 Felix, M, The story of an asbestos-polluted community, in Cock J & Koch, E (eds), *Going green (entry 4629),* 33–43

4635 Fig, D, Community struggles in Namaqualand, in Cock J & Koch, E (eds), *Going green (entry 4629),* 112–28

4636 Gandar, M, Energy and the environment, in Cock J & Koch, E (eds), *Going green (entry 4629),* 94–109

4637 Jocobsohn, M, Conservation and development, in Cock J & Koch, E (eds), *Going green (entry 4629),* 210–22

4638 Klugman, B, Overpopulation and environmental degradation, in Cock J & Koch, E (eds), *Going green (entry 4629),* 66–77

4639 Koch, E, Community struggles around ecological problems, in Cock J & Koch, E (eds), *Going green (entry 4629),* 20–32

4640 Koch, E, Recent issues in environmental politics, in Moss G & Obery, G (eds), *South African review 6 (entry 4504),* 254–66

4641 Lawson, L, The environmental crisis in the urban areas, in Cock J & Koch, E (eds), *Going green (entry 4629),* 44–63

4642 Lukey, P, et al, South Africa

and the global waste problem, in Cock J & Koch, E (eds), *Going green (entry 4629)*, 160–73

4643 **Manuel, F, Glazewski, J,** Our common heritage, in Cock J & Koch, E (eds), *Going green (entry 4629)*, 193–207

4644 **Preston-Whyte, R,** (ed), *Rotating the cube: environmental strategies for the 1990s.* Durban: Centre for Social and Development Studies, Natal University, 1990, 117pp

4645 **Ramphele, M,** (ed), *Restoring the land: environment and change in post-apartheid South Africa.* London: Panios, 1991, 216pp

4646 **Ramphele, M, McDowell, C,** *Restoring the land: environment and change in post-apartheid South Africa.* London: Panos, 1992, 216pp

4647 **Ryan, B,** Venetia: a mine at the forefront of sustainable development, *Optima*, 38, 3 (1992) 100–107

Finance

4648 **Abedian, I,** Fiscal policy and economic growth, in Abedian I & Standish, B (eds), *Economic growth in South Africa (entry 4525)*, 25–54

4649 **Addleson, M,** Monetary policy in the 1970s and 1980s, in Jones S (ed), *Financial enterprise in South Africa (entry 4654)*, 33–61

4650 **Anon,** South Africa: rush to judgement, *Banker*, Aug 1992 38–45

4651 **Falkena, H B, et al,** *Financial institutions.* Cape Town: Tafelberg, 1992, 150pp

4652 **Holston, L,** Dabbling in derivatives, *Euromoney*, Dec. 1991 63–72

4653 **Jammine, A,** Monetary and fiscal policy, in McGregor A (ed), *McGregors' economic alternatives (entry 4560)*, 75–191

4654 **Jones, S,** (ed), *Financial enterprise in South Africa since 1950.* Basingstoke: Macmillan, 1992, 316pp

4655 **Jones, S,** From building society to to bank: the Allied, 1970–89, in Jones S (ed), *Financial enterprise in South Africa (entry 4654)*, 236–62

4656 **Jones, S,** Introduction: the growth of the financial sector, 1950–1988, in Jones S (ed), *Financial enterprise in South Africa (entry 4654)*, 1–19

4657 **Jones, S,** The Johannesburgh stock market and stock exchange, 1962–1987, in Jones S (ed), *Financial enterprise in South Africa (entry 4654)*, 273–301

4658 **Jones, S,** South Africa's first development bank: the Development Bank of South Africa, in Jones S (ed), *Financial enterprise in South Africa (entry 4654)*, 263–72

4659 **Jones, S,** Union acceptances: the First Merchant Bank, 1955–73, in Jones S (ed), *Financial enterprise in South Africa (entry 4654)*, 154–91

4660 **Jones, S, Scott, G W,** Wesbank: South Africa's leading hire purchase bank, 1968–90, in Jones S (ed), *Financial enterprise in South Africa (entry 4654)*, 213–35

4661 **Kahn, B,** Foreign exchange policy, capital flight and economic growth, in Abedian I & Standish, B (eds), *Economic growth in South Africa (entry 4525)*, 74–98

4662 **Kahn, B,** *South Africa's exchange rate policy: lessons from the past.* Cape Town: Economic Trends Research Group, University of Cape Town, 1992, 20pp

4663 **Kahn, B,** *South Africa's exchange rate policy, 1979–1991.* London: London School of Economics, Centre for the Study of the South African Economy and

International Finance, 1992, 28pp

4664 Kell, S, The Discount House of South Africa, 1957–88: profile of a market force, in Jones S (ed), *Financial enterprise in South Africa (entry 4654)*, 192–212

4665 Reichardt, M, The budgetary limits to borrowing for development in South Africa, *Africa insight,* 21, 3 (1991) 190–93

4666 Skinner, I, Osborn, E, Changes in banking in South Africa since the 1980s, in Jones S (ed), *Financial enterprise in South Africa (entry 4654)*, 62–79

4667 Solomon, V, Fiscal policy, 1974–89, in Jones S (ed), *Financial enterprise in South Africa (entry 4654)*, 20–32

4668 Verhoef, G, Afrikaner nationalism in South African banking: the case of Volkskas and Trust Bank, in Jones S (ed), *Financial enterprise in South Africa (entry 4654)*, 115–53

4669 Verhoef, G, Nedbank, 1945–89: the continenta;l approach to banking in South Africa, in Jones S (ed), *Financial enterprise in South Africa (entry 4654)*, 80–114

4670 Whittaker, J, Monetary policy for economic growth, in Abedian I & Standish, B (eds), *Economic growth in South Africa (entry 4525)*, 55–73

4671 Young, G, *The price for apartheid: the wealth tax and how it can pay for the reconstruction of Black communities.* Salt River: Labour Research Service, 1992, 20pp

Gender

see also: 4754, 4881, 4965, 5253

4672 Bazilli, S, (ed), *Putting women on the agenda.* Johannesburg: Ravan, 1991, 290pp

4673 Berger, I, *Threads of solidarity: women in South African industry.* Bloomington: Indiana UP, 1991, 368pp

4674 Bozzoli, B, The meaning of informal work: some women's stories, in Preston-Whyte E & Rogerson, C (eds), *South Africa's informal economy (entry 4567)*, 15–33

4675 Budlender, D, Rural women: the 'also-rans' in the development stakes, *Agenda,* 12 (1992) 27–40

4676 Budlender, D, Women in economic development, in Moss G & Obery, G (eds), *South African review 6 (entry 4504)*, 352–63

4677 Cock, J, *Colones & cadres: war and gender in South Africa.* Cape Town: OUP, 1991, 253pp

4678 Cock, J, *Women and war in South Africa.* London: Open Letters, 1992, 254pp

4679 Friedman, M, Hambridge, M, The informal sector, gender and development, in Preston-Whyte E & Rogerson, C (eds), *South Africa's informal economy (entry 4567)*, 161–80

4680 Ginwala, F, et al, *Gender and economic policy in a democratic South Africa.* Milton Keynes: Open University, Development Policy and Practice Group, 1991, 29pp

4681 Griesel, H, et al, *Simbambene: the voices of women at Mboza.* Johannesburg: Ravan, 1992, 64pp

4682 Gwagwa, N N, Women in local government: towards a future South Africa, *Agenda,* 10 (1991) 67–76

4683 Gwagwa, N N, Women in local government: towards a future South Africa, *Environment and urbanization,* 3, 1 (1991) 70–78

4684 Hannson, D, *'Strolling" as a gendered experience : a feminist analysis of young females in greater Cape Town.* Cape Town: University of Cape Town, Institute of Criminology, 1991, 26pp

4685 Hassim, S, *Conservative politics and the construction of gender in South Africa.* Montreal: University of Montreal, Centre for Developing-Area Studies, 1991, 27pp

4686 Horn, P, The way forward towards the emancipation of women, *Agenda,* 10 (1991) 53–66

4687 Kritzinger, A, van Aswegen, W F, Gender role attitudes of white female students enrolled in traditionally female and traditionally male university courses: a comparison, *South African journal of sociology,* 23, 2 (1992) 33–39

4688 Manicom, L, Ruling relations: rethinking state and gender in South African history, *Journal of African history,* 33, 3 (1992) 441–65

4689 Morrell, R, Gender in the transformation of South African education, *Perspectives in education,* 13, 2 (1992) 1–26

4690 Murray, C, O'Regan, C, Women's rights, *South African human rights and labour law yearbook,* 1, (1990) 262–272

4691 Preston-Whyte, E, Nene, S, Black women and the rural informal sector, in Preston-Whyte E & Rogerson, C (eds), *South Africa's informal economy (entry 4567),* 229–42

4692 Ramphele, M, The dynamics of gender within Black Consciousness organisations: a personal view, in Pityana N B et al. (ed), *Bounds of possibility (entry 5154),* 214–27

4693 Russel, D, et al, *A select bibliography on male violence against women and girls in South Africa.* Cape Town: University of Cape Town, Institute of Criminology, 1992, 15pp

4694 Seekings, J, Gender ideology and township politics in the 1980s, *Agenda,* 10 (1991) 77–88

4695 Segel, T, Labe, D, Family violence: wife abuse, in McKendrick B & Hoffman, W (eds), *People and violence (entry 5270),* 251–87

4696 Strebel, A, "There's absolutely nothing I can do, just believe in God": South African women with AIDS, *Agenda,* 12 (1992) 50–62

4697 Vogelman, L, Violent crime: rape, in McKendrick B & Hoffman, W (eds), *People and violence (entry 5270),* 96–134

4698 Wells, J, *We have done with pleading: the women's 1913 anti-pass campaign.* Johannesburg: Ravan, 1991, 43pp

Geography, human

4700 Baticle, Y, *L'espace sud-africain.* Paris: Masson, 19990, 222pp

4701 Jürgens, U, *Gemischtrassige Wohngebiete in südafrikanischen Städten.* Kiel: Universität Kiel, Geographischen Institut, 1991, 299pp

4702 Mabin, A, Comprehensive segregation: the origins of the Group Areas Act and its planning apparatuses, *Journal of southern African studies,* 18, 2 (1992) 405–29

4703 McCaul, C, The commuting conundrum, in Swilling M et al (eds), *Apartheid city (entry 5328),* 230–57

Health & welfare services

4704 Chetty, K S, Urbanisation and health: evidence from Cape Town, in Smith D M (ed), *Apartheid city (entry 5324),* 216–27

4705 de Beer, C, Health policy in transition? The limits to reform, in Moss G & Obery, G (eds), *South African review 6 (entry 4504),* 267–78

4706 Freeman, M, Motsei, M, Planning health care on South Africa: is there a role for traditional healers?, *Social science and medicine,* 34, 11 (1992) 1183–90

4707 Giles, C, Violence in group

care, in McKendrick B & Hoffman, W (eds), *People and violence (entry 5270)*, 373–404

4708 Kelly, J, *Finding a cure: the politics of health in South Africa.* Johannesburg: SAIRR, 1990, 57pp

4709 Lund, F, 'Reshaping old designs': South African welfare policy into the nineties, in Moss G & Obery, G (eds), *South African review 6 (entry 4504)*, 309–21

4710 Piyan, N B, Medical ethics and South Africa's security forces: a sequel to the death of Steve Biko, in Pityana N B et al. (ed), *Bounds of possibility (entry 5154)*, 78–98

4711 Simon, C, From the patient's viewpoint: the value of studying micro-level support systems in the development of rural health care, *Journal of contemporary African studies,* 10, 1 (1991) 2–17

History, general

see also: 4688

4712 Bozzoli, B, Les intellectuels et leurs public face à l'histoire: l'expérience sud-africaine du *History Workshop* (1977–1988), *Politique africaine,* 46 (1992) 15–30

4713 Broodryk, M, Die stand van eietydse geskiedenis in die RSA, *Journal for contemporary history,* 15, 3 (1990) 91–116

4714 Brown, J, (ed), *History from South Africa: alternative visions and practices.* Philadelphia: Temple University Press, 1991, 469pp

4715 Coquerel, P, *L'Afrique du sud: l'histoire séparée.* Paris: Gallimard, 1992, 176pp

4716 Cuthbertson, G, Grundlingh, A, Some problematical issues in the restucturing of history education in South African schools, *South African historical journal,* 26 (1992) 154–71

4717 Davidson, A, The study of South African history in the Soviet Union, *International journal of African historical studies,* 25, 1 (1992) 2–13

4718 Filatova, I, Some thoughts on Soviet South African studies under 'stagnation' and perestroika, *International journal of African historical studies,* 25, 1 (1992) 15–23

4719 Kallaway, P, L'éducation et la construction nationale dans l'Afrique du Sud des années 1990. Comment réformer l'enseignement de l'histoire pour l'après-apartheid, *Politique africaine,* 46 (1992) 84–98

4720 Liebenberg, B J, et al, *A bibliography of South African history, 1978–1989.* Pretoria: University of South Africa, 1992, 401pp

4721 Minnaar, A, et al, *Conflict and violence in Natal/Kwazulu: historical perspectives.* Pretoria: HSRC, 1991, 97pp

4722 Mostert, N, *Frontiers. The evolution of South African society and its central tragedy: the agony of the Xhosa people.* London: Cape, 1992, 1355pp

4723 Nxumalo, J, The national question in the writing of South African history: a critical survey of some of the major tendencies, *Journal of social studies (Dhaka),* 58, (1992) 17–91

4724 Southey, N, T R H Davenport: liberal historian of South Africa (and interview), *South African historical journal,* 26 (1992) 3–28

4725 Thompson, L, The study of South African history in the United States, *International journal of African historical studies,* 25, 1 (1992) 25–37

History, early

4726 Barham, L S, Let's walk before we run: an appraisal of historical materialist approaches to the Later Stone Age, *South African archaeological bulletin*, 47, 155 (1992) 44–51

History, C19th

4727 Crais, C C, *White supremacy and Black reistance in pre-industrial South Africa: the making of the colonial order in the eastern Cape.* Cambridge: CUP, 1992, 284pp

4728 De Beer, M, (ed), *A vision of the past: South Africa in photographs 1943–1910.* Cape Town: Struik, 1992,

4729 Edgecombe, D R, et al, (eds), *The debate on Zulu origins: a selection of papers on the Zulu kingdom and early colonial Natal.* Pietermaritzburg: Dept. of Historical Studies, University of Natal, 1992, 168pp

4730 Gump, J, *The formation of the Zulu kingdom in South Africa, 1750–1840.* Lewiston: Mellen, 1990, 207pp

4731 Hamilton, C A, 'The character and objects of Chaka': a reconsideration of the making of Shaka as 'Mfecane' motor, *Journal of African history*, 33, 1 (1992) 37–63

4732 Hofmeyr, I, Jonah and the swallowing monster: orality and literacy on a Berlin Mission Station in the Transvaal, *Journal of southern African studies*, 17, 4 (1991) 633–653

4733 Hummel, C, (ed), *Rev. F G Kayser: journal and letters.* Cape Town: Maskew Miller Longman, 1990, 216pp

4734 Laband, J, *Kingdom in crisis: the Zulu response to the British invasion of 1879.* Manchester: Manchester University Press, 1992, 272pp

4735 Manson, A, The Hurutshe and the formation of the Transvaal State, 1835–1875, *International*

journal of African historical studies, 25, 1 (1992) 85–98

4736 Sévry, J, *Chaka, empereur des Zoulous: histoire, mythes et legendes.* Paris : Harmattan, 1991, 251pp

4737 Thompson, P S, A fighting retreat: the Natal Native Mounted Contingent after Isandlwana, *Journal of Natal and Zulu history,* 13 (1990/91) 27–32

4738 Wylie, D, Textual incest: Nathaniel Isaacs and the development of the Shaka myth, *History in Africa,* 19 (1992) 411–33

History, C20th

see also: 4698, 47002

4739 Barnard, L, Kriek, D, (eds), *Sir de Villiers Graaff.* Pretoria: Digna, 1990, 175pp

4740 Barnard, S L, Groenewald, W L, Die stigting van die Bloemfonteinse Aksiekomitee vir Munisipale Kiesers in 1946: 'n kritiese evaluering, *Journal for contemporary history,* 16, 2 (1991) 76–95

4741 Buthelezi, S, The emergenceof Black Consciousness: an historical appraisal, in Pityana N B et al. (ed), *Bounds of possibility (entry 5154),* 111–29

4742 Crais, C C, Representation and the politics of identity in South Africa: an Eastern Cape example, *International journal of African historical studies,* 25, 1 (1992) 99–126

4743 du Pre, R H, *The making of racial conflict in South Africa.* Johannesburg: Skotaville, 1990, 139pp

4744 du Pre, R H, *The making of racial conflict in South Africa.* Johannesburg: Skotaville, 1992 (2nd, revised, edition), 276pp

4745 Everatt, D, Alliance politics of a special type: the roots of the ANC/SACP alliance, 1950–54,

Journal of southern African studies, 18, 1 (1992) 19–39

4746 Forman, S, Odendaal, A, (eds), *A trumpet from the housetops: the selected writing of Lionel Forman.* Cape Town: Philip, 1992, 230pp

4747 Gangal, S C, Gandhi and South Africa, *International studies,* 29, 2 (1992) 187–197

4748 Grunligh, L, Prejudices, promises and poverty: the experiences of discharged and demobilised Black South African soldiers after the Second World War, *South African historical journal,* 26 (1992) 116–35

4749 Haasbroek, J, Moll, J C, Wessels vs Wessels: Die omstrede Bethlehem-tussenverkiesing van 1914, *Journal for contemporary history,* 15, 2 (1990) 74–95

4750 Henshaw, P J, The transfer of Simonstown: Afrikaner nationalism, South African strategic dependence, and British global power, *Journal of imperial and Commonwealth history,* 22, 3 (1992) 419–44

4751 Laband, J P C, Mathere, J, *Isandlwana.* Pietermaritzburg: Centaur, 1992, 98pp

4752 Liebenberg, J C R, Van der Merwe, P J, Die wordingsgeskiedenis van apartheid, *Journal for contemporary history,* 16, 2 (1991) 1–24

4753 Limb, P, The ANC and the Black workers, in Etherington N (ed), *Peace, politics and violence (entry 5047),* 284–305

4754 Mager, A, 'The people get fenced': gender, rehabilitation and African nationalism in the Ciskei and Border region, 1945–55, *Journal of southern African studies,* 18, 4 (1992) 761–82

4755 Marais, A H, Louis Botha en P.W. Botha: 'n Vergelykende studie, *Journal for contemporary history,* 15, 2 (1990) 96–126

4756 Marks, S, The origins of ethnic violence in South Africa, in Etherington N (ed), *Peace, politics and violence (entry 5047),* 121–46

4757 Marks, S, Trapido, S, Lord Milner and the South African state reconsidered, in Twaddle M (ed), *Imperialism (entry 464),* 80–94

4758 Mouton, F A, Margaret Ballinger: opponent of apartheid or collaborator?, *South African historical journal,* 26 (1992) 136–53

4759 Ntantala, P, *A life's mosaic: the autobiography of Phyllis Ntantala.* Cape Town: Philip, 1992, 237pp

4760 Resha, M, *My life in the struggle.* Johannesburg: Congress of South African Writers, 1992, 269pp

4761 Rich, P B, *Hope and despair: English speaking intellectuals and South African politics.* London: British Academic Press, 1992, 269pp

4762 Rive, R, Cousins, T, *Seme: the founder of the ANC.* Johannesburg: Skotaville, 1991, 91pp

4763 Weinberger, G, Moritz Julius Bonn und sein Beitrag zur Wirtschaftsgeschichte Südafrikas, *Asien Afrika Lateinamerika,* 19, 2 (1991) 338–342

4764 White, B, The United Democratic Front in Natal, 1952–1953, *Journal of Natal and Zulu history,* 13 (1990/91) 1–26

4765 Woodson, D C, *Decade of discontent: an index to 'Fighting talk', 1954–1963.* Madison: Wisconsin University, African Studies Program, 1992, 86pp

Industry & trade

see also: 4647

4766 Alperson, N, Contemporary trends in corporate social responsibility, in Innes D et al (eds), *Power and profit (entry 4546),* 257–68

4767 Alperson, N, Empowerment in the informal sector: a long and winding road, in Innes D et al (eds), *Power and profit (entry 4546),* 143–62

4768 Andrews, A, et al, Business and social change, in Innes D et al (eds), *Power and profit (entry 4546),* 240–49

4769 Bank, L, A culture of violence: the migrant taxi trade in QwaQwa, in Preston-Whyte E & Rogerson, C (eds), *South Africa's informal economy (entry 4567),* 124–41

4770 Black, A, *Current trends in South African industrial policy: selective intervention, trade orientation and concessionary industrial finance.* Cape Town: Economic Trends Research Group, University of Cape Town, 1992, 20pp

4771 Economist Intelligence Unit, *Diamonds: a cartel and its future.* London: the Unit, 1992, 89pp

4772 Ellis, S, Défense d'y voir: la politisation de la protection de la nature, *Politique africaine,* 48 (1992) 7–21

4773 Ellison, A P, South Africa's transport policies, *Journal of transport economics and policy,* 26, 3 (1992) 313–18

4774 Grant, L J, Butler-Adam, J, Tourism and development needs in the Durban region, in Smith D M (ed), *Apartheid city (entry 5324),* 205–15

4775 Hartzenburg, T, Leiman, A, The informal sector and its growth potential, in Abedian I & Standish, B (eds), *Economic growth in South Africa (entry 4525),* 187–214

4776 Joffe, A, Ngoasheng, M, Industrial restructuring in the de Klerj era, in Moss G & Obery, G (eds), *South African review 6 (entry 4504),* 478–92

4777 Jourdan, P, *Mineral beneficiation: some refections on the*

potential for resource-based industrialisation in South Africa. Cape Town: Economic Trends Research Group, University of Cape Town, 1992, 23pp

4778 Kaplinsky, R, The manufacturing sector and regional trade in a democratic South Africa, in Maasdorp G & Whiteside, A (eds), *Towards a post-apartheid future (entry 4201),* 83–104

4779 Khosa, M, Capital accumulation in the Black taxi industry, in Preston-Whyte E & Rogerson, C (eds), *South Africa's informal economy (entry 4567),* 310–25

4780 Khosa, M M, Changing state policy and the Black taxi driver industry in Soweto, in Smith D M (ed), *Apartheid city (entry 5324),* 182–92

4781 Khosa, M, Routes, ranks and rebels: feuding in the taxi revolution, *Journal of southern African studies,* 18, 1 (1992) 232–51

4782 Kirby, D A, Opportunities for the promotion of enterprise among students - the South African case, *Small enterprise development,* 3, 2 (1992) 47–52

4783 Krafchik, W, Leiman, A, Inward industrialisation and petty enterpreneurship: recent experience in the construction industry, in Preston-Whyte E & Rogerson, C (eds), *South Africa's informal economy (entry 4567),* 345–64

4784 Lewis, D, The character and consequences of conglomeration in the South African economy, *Transformation,* 16 (1991) 29–48

4785 Louw, L, Privatisation, deregulation and nationalisation, in McGregor A (ed), *McGregors' economic alternatives (entry 4560),* 193–304

4786 Lupton, M, Worker producer cooperatives: restructuring for capital or for labour?, in

Preston-Whyte E & Rogerson, C (eds), *South Africa's informal economy (entry 4567)*, 380–98

4787 Mann, M, The rise of corporate social responsibility, in Innes D et al (eds), *Power and profit (entry 4546)*, 250–56

4788 McCaul, C, Trends in commuting, in Moss G & Obery, G (eds), *South African review 6 (entry 4504)*, 294–308

4789 Meth, C, *SA's Thatcherite miracle, 1979–89.* Cape Town: Economic Trends Research Group, University of Cape Town, 1992, 37pp

4790 Morris, M L, Stavrou, S E, *Telecommunication needs and provision to underdeveloped Black areas.* Durban: University of Natal, Centre for Social and Development Studies, 1992, 15pp

4791 Mosdell, T, Power, patronage and control: ambiguities in the deregulation of street trading in Pietermaritzburg, in Preston-Whyte E & Rogerson, C (eds), *South Africa's informal economy (entry 4567)*, 326–35

4792 Nicol, M, *Gold mining in South Africa: priorities for restructuring.* Cape Town: Economic Trends Research Group, University of Cape Town, 1991, 28pp

4793 Pirie, G H, Travelling under apartheid, in Smith D M (ed), *Apartheid city (entry 5324)*, 172–81

4794 Preston-Whyte, E, Petty trading at Umgababa: mere survival or the road to accumulation?, in Preston-Whyte E & Rogerson, C (eds), *South Africa's informal economy (entry 4567)*, 262–78

4795 Rogerson, C M, The absorptive capacity of the informal sector in the South African city, in Smith D M (ed), *Apartheid city (entry 5324)*, 161–71

4796 Rogerson, C, Deregulation, subcontracting and the '(in)formalisation' of small scale manufacturing, in Preston-Whyte E & Rogerson, C (eds), *South Africa's informal economy (entry 4567)*, 365–85

4797 Rogerson, C, Home-based enterprises of the urban poor: the case of spazas, in Preston-Whyte E & Rogerson, C (eds), *South Africa's informal economy (entry 4567)*, 336–44

4798 Standish, B, Resource endowments, constraints and growth policies, in Abedian I & Standish, B (eds), *Economic growth in South Africa (entry 4525)*, 99–127

4799 Stavrou, S E, *Future directions for the electicity supply industry.* Durban: University of Natal, Centre for Social and Development Studies, 1992, 13pp

4800 Thomas, E, Rotating credit associations in Cape Town, in Preston-Whyte E & Rogerson, C (eds), *South Africa's informal economy (entry 4567)*, 290–304

4801 Van der Merwe, B J, Van Seventer, D E N, The impact of a capital investment on a subregional level: research note on an extended input-output approach, *Development Southern Africa*, 9, 2 (1992) 233–241

4802 Zulu, P, Legitimating the culture of survival, in Preston-Whyte E & Rogerson, C (eds), *South Africa's informal economy (entry 4567)*, 115–23

International economic relations

see also: 4249, 4462, 4798, 5611

4803 Akinboye, S O, The sanctions debate and the challenges of the recent political reforms in South Africa, *Nigerian journal of international affairs*, 17, 1 (1991) 80–100

4804 Bell, T, *Should South Africa*

further liberalise its foreign trade?
Cape Town: Economic Trends
Research Group, University of
Cape Town, 1992, 41pp

4805 **Garner, J, Leape, J,** *South
Africa's borrowings on international
capital markets: recent developments
in historical perspective.* London:
London School of Economics,
Centre for the Study of the South
African Economy and International
Finance, 1991, 31pp

4806 **Garner, J, Thomas, L,** *South
Africa's trade partners, 1988–1991.*
London: London School of
Economics, Centre for the Study of
the South African Economy and
International Finance, 1992, 34pp

4807 **Hirsch, A,** *The external
environment and the South African
trade policy.* Cape Town: Economic
Trends Research Group, University
of Cape Town, 1992, 30pp

4808 **Hirsch, A,** Inward foreign
investment in a post-apartheid
South Africa: some policy
considerations, *South Africa
international*, 23, 1 (1992) 39–44

4809 **Jenkins, C,** *Assessing the
damage: the effects of sanctions on
South Africa.* Durban: Natal
University, Economic Research
Unit, 1992, 47pp

4810 **Krogh, D, et al,** *Prospects for
the global economy and their relevance
for South Africa.* Braamfontein:
SAIIA, 1991, 44pp

4811 **Lansing, Crane, J,** The
Comprehensive Anti-Apartheid Act
of 1986: a time to reconsider,
Journal of world trade, 25, 1 (1991)
89–104

4812 **Leistner, E,** Post-apartheid
South Africa's economic ties with
neighbouring countries,
Development Southern Africa, 9, 2
(1992) 169–185

4813 **Page, S, Stevens, C,** *Trading
with South Africa: the policy options
for the EC.* London: ODI, 1992, 78pp

4814 **Ruyter, T,** *Apartheid by air.*
Amsterdam: Holland Committee
on Southern Africa, 1990, 40pp

4815 **Shipping Research Bureau,**
*Fuel for apartheid: oil supplies to
South Africa.* Amsterdam: the
Bureau, 1990, 100pp

4816 **Shipping Research Bureau,**
*The oil embargo 1989–1991: secrecy
still rules.* Amsterdam: the Bureau,
1992, 16pp

4817 **Wright, S,** Sanctions and
strategic minerals, *Transafrica
forum*, 7, 4 (1991) 69–82

International relations

see also: 2742, 2865, 4259, 4267,
4272, 4425, 4416, 5111, 5448

4818 **Adam, H, Moodley, K,** The
background to Canada's policy
against apartheid; theoretical and
political implications, *Journal of
Commonwealth and comparative
politics*, 30, 3 (1992) 293–315

4819 **Anderton, N,** South Africa
and eastern Europe; the forging of
a new partnership, *South Africa
international*, 23, 1 (1992) 26–38

4820 **Barratt, J,** *Transition in South
Africa: the global context and the
international role.* Braamfontein:
SAIIA, 1992, 15pp

4821 **Belikov, I V, Belyaev, A V,**
Framing Soviet policy towards
South Africa: conflicting strategies,
South Africa international, 22, 2
(1991/1992) 86–96

4822 **Coetzer, P W, et al,** Relations
between South Africa and the
Soviet bloc, *Journal for contemporary
history*, 16, 2 (1991) 123–144

4823 **Evans, G,** *Continuity and
change in South Africa's present and
future foreign policy.* Braamfontein:
SAIIA, 1991, 18pp

4824 **Evans, G,** The struggle for
power in South Africa: the external
constituency, *World today*, 48, 12
(1992) 221–24

4825 Heino, T E, *Politics on paper: Finland's South Africa policy 1945–1991.* Uppsala: Scandinavian Institute of African Studies, 1992, 121pp

4826 Kamugisha, C A, Obnoxious alliance of destruction: zionism and apartheid in Africa and the Arab world, *Maji Maji,* 47 (1990) 1–13

4827 Karnik, S S, South Africa and the world: a select bibliography, *Africa quarterly,* 30, 1/2 (1990) 65–101

4828 Makinda, S M, South Africa as a regional great power, in Neumann I B (ed), *Regional great powers in international politics* (Basingstoke: Macmillan,1992), 151–78

4829 Nwokedi, E, South Africa and the United Nations: the dynamics of duplicity and defiance, *Quarterly journal of administration,* 25, 1 (1990/1991) 18–32

4830 Ohta, M, *The importance of Japan-South Africa relations.* Braamfontein: SAIIA, 1992, 9pp

4831 Owoeye, J, Changing trends in Afro-Asianism: a case study of Japan's attitudes towards apartheid South Africa, *Quarterly journal of administration,* 25, 1 (1990/1991) 5–17

4832 Payne, A, The international politics of the Gleneagles Agreement, *Round table,* 320 (1991) 417–30

4833 Reddy, E S, *India and South Africa: a collection of papers.* Durban-Westville: University of Durban-Westville, 1991, 29pp

4834 Sawant, A B, India's policy towards South Africa, *Africa quarterly,* 31, 1/2 (1991) 24–33

4835 Schoeman, E, *South Africa's foreign relations in transition 1985–1991: a select and annotated bibliography.* Johannesburg: SAIIA, 1992, 393pp

4836 Sharma, V, Apartheid and the United Nations, *Africa quarterly,* 30, 3/4 (1990) 96–111

4837 Vale, P, *Hoping against hope: the prospects for South Africa's post-apartheid regional policy.* Cape Town: Centre for Southern African Studies, University of the Western Cape, 1992, 42pp

4838 Vale, P, South Africa's 'new diplomacy', in Moss G & Obery, G (eds), *South African review 6 (entry 4504),* 424–35

4839 van Nieukerk, A du Pisani, A, *What do we think? A survey of white opinion on foreign policy issues.* Braamfontein: SAIIA, 1992, 469pp

4840 Van Wyk, K, Foreign policy orientations of the P W Botha regime: changing perceptions of State elites in South Africa, *Journal of contemporary african studies,* 10, 1 (1991) 45–65

4841 van Wyk, K, Radloff, S, South Africa's dyadic foreign policy behaviour: patterns of symmetry and reciprocity, *Politikon,* 19, 1 (1991) 83–101

4842 Young, T, South Africa's foreign relations in a post-apartheid era, *Rivista si studi politici internazionale,* 58, 3 (1991) 382–90

Labour & manpower

see also: 4632

4843 Albertyn, C, Freedom of association, *South African human rights and labour law yearbook,* 1, (1990) 297–316

4844 Cheadle, H, Strikes and lock-outs, *South African human rights and labour law yearbook,* 1, (1990) 349–355

4845 Crush, J, Power and surveillance on the South African gold mines, *Journal of southern African studies,* 18, 4 (1992) 825–44

4846 Davidson, J, Leslie, K, The life history of a Venda headman, in Preston-Whyte E & Rogerson, C (eds), *South Africa's informal economy (entry 4567)*, 54–67

4847 Dorrington, R E, *What are actuaries and who needs them anyway? The future of the profession in South Africa.* Cape Town: University of Cape Town, 1991, 18pp

4848 Flynn, L, *Studded with diamonds and paved with gold; miners, mining companies and human rights in South Africa.* London: Bloomsbury, 1992, 358pp

4849 Friedman, S, A new South African social contract?, in Innes D et al (eds), *Power and profit (entry 4546)*, 31–42

4850 Godfrey, S, Macun, I, The politics of centralised bargaining, in Moss G & Obery, G (eds), *South African review 6 (entry 4504)*, 388–402

4851 Godsell, B, Maphalala, J, Unemployment and the informal sector, in McGregor A (ed), *McGregors' economic alternatives (entry 4560)*, 1–22

4852 Hofmeyer, J F, *The rise in African wages in South Africa 1975–1985.* Durban: University of Natal, Economic Research Unit, 1990, 52pp

4853 Innes, D, The challenge of the participative movement, in Innes D et al (eds), *Power and profit (entry 4546)*, 219–33

4854 Innes, D, Empowerment in the workplace, in Innes D et al (eds), *Power and profit (entry 4546)*, 123–42

4855 Innes, D, Labour relations in the de Klerk era, in Moss G & Obery, G (eds), *South African review 6 (entry 4504)*, 338–51

4856 Innes, D, Labour relations in the 1990s, in Innes D et al (eds), *Power and profit (entry 4546)*, 184–93

4857 Jooma, A, *Migrancy after influx control.* Johannesburg: SAIRR, 1991, 120pp

4858 Kraak, A, Human resources development and organised labour, in Moss G & Obery, G (eds), *South African review 6 (entry 4504)*, 403–23

4859 Lyster, R, Swiss, S, Unemployment insurance and unemployment, *South African human rights and labour law yearbook*, 1, (1990) 383–392

4860 Maller, J, *Conflict and cooperation: case studies in worker participation.* Braamfontein: Ravan, 1992, 171pp

4861 McNamara, K, Discrimination in the workplace, in Innes D et al (eds), *Power and profit (entry 4546)*, 194–204

4862 Meth, C, *Income redistribution, productivity and trade union action in South Africa.* Cape Town: Economic Trends Research Group, University of Cape Town, 1991, 31pp

4863 Moodley, I, Mass dismissals, *South African human rights and labour law yearbook*, 1, (1990) 326–338

4864 Naicker, A, The transition from school to work of a group of Indian school-leavers, *South African journal of sociology*, 23, 3 (1992) 95–103

4865 Nupen, C, Class conflict and social partnership, in Innes D et al (eds), *Power and profit (entry 4546)*, 205–218

4867 Oosthuizen, M, Unfair dismissals - individual cases, *South African human rights and labour law yearbook*, 1, (1990) 356–370

4868 Pemberton, R, Disputes procedures (including private regulation of disputes), *South*

African human rights and labour law yearbook, 1, (1990) 289–296

4869 Pityana, S M, Orkin, M, (eds), *Beyond the factory floor: a survey of COSATU shop stewards.* Johannesburg: Ravan, 1992, 97pp

4870 Preston-Whyte, E, Invisible workers: domestic service and the informal economy, in Preston-Whyte E & Rogerson, C (eds), *South Africa's informal economy (entry 4567)*, 34–53

4871 Rudolph, D, Changes in Transkei labour relations, *South African human rights and labour law yearbook,* 1, (1990) 273–280

4872 Rycroft, A, Unfair discrimination in employment, *South African human rights and labour law yearbook,* 1, (1990) 371–381

4873 Sadie, J L, *The South African labour force 1960–2005.* Pretoria: University of South Africa, Bureau of Market Research, 1991, 186pp

4874 Tanner, C, Health, safety and workers' compensation, *South African human rights and labour law yearbook,* 1, (1990) 317–325

4875 Thompson, C, Collective bargaining, *South African human rights and labour law yearbook,* 1, (1990) 281–288

4876 Viljoen, D J, *Labour and employment in South Africa: a regional profile 1980–1990.* Sandton: Information Clearing House, Development Bank of Southern Africa, 1991, 128pp

4877 von Clausewitz, B, *Schattendasein: Farmarbeiter in Südafrika.* Hamburg: Evangelisches Missionwerk, 1990, 95pp

4878 Wood, G, The 1973 Durban strikes: of local and national significance, *Contree,* 31 (1992) 19–24

4879 Zondo, R, Redundancy and retrenchment, *South African human*

rights and labour law yearbook, 1, (1990) 339–348

Language

4880 de Kadt, E, Language, power and emancipation: a South African perspective, *Theoria,* 78 (1991) 1–15

Law

see also: 4593, 4611, 4690, 4843, 4844, 4867, 4868, 4872, 4874, 4879

4881 Albertyn, C, *Achieving equality for women: the limits of a bill of rights.* Johannesburg: Witswatersrand University, Centre for Applied Legal Studies, 1992, 31pp

4882 Bennett, T W, The compatibility of African customary law and human rights, *Acta juridica,* 1991 18–35

4883 Boister, N, The 'ius in bello' in South Africa: a postscript?, *The comparative and international law journal of southern Africa,* 24, 1 (1991) 72–87

4884 Burman, S, Illegitimacy and the African family in a changing South Africa, *Acta juridica,* 1991 36–51

4885 Chanock, M L, Law, state and culture: thinking about 'customary law' after apartheid, *Acta juridica,* 1991 52–70

4886 Colgan, D, *Review of the death penalty in 1991.* Johannesburg: Society for the abolition of the death penalty in South Africa, 1991, 20pp

4888 Currin, B, Capital punishment, *South African human rights and labour law yearbook,* 1, (1990) 1–23

4889 Dlamini, C R M, The role of customary law in meeting social needs, *Acta juridica,* 1991 71–85

4890 Dolny, H, Klug, H, Land

reform: legal support and economic regulation, in Moss G & Obery, G (eds), *South African review 6 (entry 4504)*, 322–37

4891 Dugard, J, Towards a democratic legal order for South Africa, *African journal of international and comparative law,* 2, 3 (1990) 361–383

4892 Ellmann, S J, *In time of trouble: law and liberty in South Africa's state of emergency.* Cape Town: OUP, 1992, 283pp

4893 Grant, B, Schwikkard, P J, People's courts?, *South African journal on human rights,* 7, 3 (1991) 304–316

4894 Haysom, N, *A constitutional court for South Africa.* Johannesburg: Centre for Applied Legal Studies, Witswatersrand University, 1991, 30pp

4895 Hoexter, C, Emergency law, *South African human rights and labour law yearbook,* 1, (1990) 110–126

4896 Kaganas, F, Murray, C, Law, women and the family: the question of polygyny in a new South Africa, *Acta juridica,* 1991 116–134

4897 Klug, H, Rethinking affirmative action in a non-racial democracy, *South African journal on human rights,* 7, 3 (1991) 317–333

4898 Luecke, J, Grundrechte in einer neuen südafrikanischen Verfassung, *Zeitschrift für ausländisches öffentliches Recht und Völkerechet,* 52, 1 (1992) 70–148

4899 MacQuoid-Mason, D, Legal representation and the courts, *South African human rights and labour law yearbook,* 1, (1990) 190–210

4900 Midgley, J R, Access to legal services: a need to canvass alternatives, *South African journal on human rights,* 8, 1 (1992) 74–83

4901 Mihalik, J, Expedient legal fiction and death sentences in Bophuthatswana, *The comparative and international law journal of southern Africa,* 24, 1 (1991) 105–120

4902 Mndaweni, C B, Limping marriages in the new South Africa?, *The comparative and international law journal of southern Africa,* 24, 2 (1991) 215–225

4903 Motala, Z, Independence of the judiciary, prospects and limitations of judicial review in terms of the United States model in a new South African order: towards an alternative judicial structure, *The comparative and international law journal of southern Africa,* 24, 3 (1991) 285–314

4904 Nhlapo, T R, The African family and women's rights: friends or foes?, *Acta juridica,* 1991 135–146

4905 Nicolson, D, Ideology and the South African judicial process: lessons from the past, *South African journal on human rights,* 8, 1 (1992) 50–73

4906 O'Regan, C, Forced removals, *South African human rights and labour law yearbook,* 1, (1990) 127–138

4907 Ramose, M B, et al, In search of a workable and lasting constitutional change in South Africa, *Quest,* 5, 2 (1991) 4–31

4908 Reichardt, M, *Koexistenz in Südafrika: eine kritische Nestandsaufname bestehender Verfassungsmodelle.* Frankfurt: Deutsch-Südafrikanische Gesellschaft, 1990, 22pp

4909 Robertson, M, Land and race (excluding group areas), *South African human rights and labour law yearbook,* 1, (1990) 171–189

4910 Rutsch, P, Group areas, *South African human rights and labour law yearbook,* 1, (1990) 139–151

4911 Sanders, A J G M, (ed), *The internal conflict of laws in South Africa.* Durban: Butterworths, 1990, 132pp

4912 Sarkin-Hughes, J, Changes to the security laws in South Africa, *Review [of the] International Commission of Jurists,* 47, (1991) 61–68

4913 Schiltz, C, *Republik Südafrika: die Verfassungsreform von 1984.* Hamburg: Institut für Afrika-Kunde, 1991, 183 + 90pp

4914 Seekings, J, The revival of 'people's courts': informal justice in transitional South Africa, in Moss G & Obery, G (eds), *South African review 6 (entry 4504),* 186–200

4915 Sloth-Nielsen, J, Legal violence: corporal and capital punishment, in McKendrick B & Hoffman, W (eds), *People and violence (entry 5270),* 73–95

4916 Stetler, N, (ed), *The Freedom Charter and beyond: founding principles for a democratic South Africa.* Cape Town: Wyvern, 1991, 296pp

4917 Van Niekerk, G J, Vorster, L P, (eds), *Field research in indigenous law.* Pretoria: University of South Africa, 1991, 91pp

4918 White, J, Law and environmental protection, in Cock J & Koch, E (eds), *Going green (entry 4629),* 244–51

4919 Wiechers, M, Reincorporation of the TBVC countries: international law practice and constitutional implications, *South African yearbook of international law,* 16, (1990/1991) 119–126

Library - documentation

4920 Napier, C J, Data-collection from government institutions in South Africa: a bibliographic note, *Journal of contemporary African studies,* 10, 1 (1991) 84–90

4921 Rossouw, F, *A South African bibliography to the year 1925. Vol. 5: supplement.* Pretoria: South African Library, 1991, 476pp

4922 State Library, (ed), *The relationship of national libraries to school and public library development. Proceedings of the fifth conference of national librarians of southern Africa.* Pretoria: State Library, 1991, 101pp

Literature

see also: 4625

4923 Abrahams, C, (ed), *The tragic life of Bessie Head and literature in South Africa.* Trenton: Africa World Press, 1990, 131pp

4924 Attwell, D, (ed), *Doubling the point: essays and interviews, J M Coetzee.* Cambridge, Mass.: Harvard UP, 1992, 438pp

4925 Barnard, I, The 'tagtigers'? The (un)politics of language in the 'new' Afrikaans fiction, *Research in African literatures,* 23, 4 (1992) 77–95

4926 Black, M, Alan Paton and the rule of law, *African affairs,* 91, 362 (1992) 53–72

4927 Botha, E, The emergence of the Afrikaans novel in the late nineteenth century, in Nethersole R (ed), *Emerging literatures (entry 726),* 53–61

4928 Brink, A, An ornithology of sexual'politics: Lewis Nkosi's *Mating birds, English in Africa,* 19, 1 (1992) 1–20

4929 Brown, D, Interview with Mongane Wally Serote, *Theoria,* 80 (1992) 143–49

4930 Brown, D, van Dyk, B, (eds), *Exchanges: South African writing in transition.* Pietermaritzburg: University of Natal Press, 1991, 125pp

4932 Butler, G, The emergence of South African literature in English:

comments of an ageing campaigner, in Nethersole R (ed), *Emerging literatures (entry 726)*, 35–52

4933 Carpenter, W, The scene of representation in Alex La Guma's later novels, *English in Africa*, 18, 2 (1991) 1–18

4934 Cartwright, J F, Bound and free: the paradox of the quest in Doris Lessing's *Children of violence*, *Commonwealth novel in English*, 4, 1 (1991) 46–61

4935 Chapman, M, et al, The function of literature in South Africa today, *Theoria*, 80 (1992) 155–70

4936 Coetzee, A, Polley, J, (eds), *Crossing borders: writers meet the ANC*. Bramley: Taurus, 1990, 207pp

4937 Couzens, T, *The ghostly dance: writing in a new South Africa (part 1)*. Mowbray: IDASA, 1990, 17pp

4938 de Jong, M, Dialogism as literary ethics, *Theoria*, 80 (1992) 39–53

4939 de Kok, I, (ed), *Spring is rebellious*. Cape Town: Philip, 1990, 150pp

4940 Foley, A, A sense of place in contemporary white South African poetry, *English in Africa*, 19, 2 (1992) 35–53

4941 Gallagher, S V, *A story of South Africa: J M Coetzee's fiction in context*. Cambridge, Mass.: Harvard UP, 1991, 258pp

4942 Gardner, C, Negotiating poetry: a new poetry for a new South Africa?, *Theoria*, 77 (1991) 1–14

4943 Goddard, K, Wessels, G, (eds), *Out of exile: South African writers speak*. Grahamstown: National English Literary Museum, 1992, 91pp

4944 Hart, D, The informal sector in South African literature, in Preston-Whyte E & Rogerson, C (eds), *South Africa's informal economy (entry 4567)*, 68–86

4945 Kearney, J A, Van der Post's response to *Turbott Wolfe*, *Theoria*, 80 (1992) 55–68

4946 Klopper, D, Francis Carey Slter and the 'Africanisation' of South African poetry, *English in Africa*, 19, 2 (1992) 1–13

4947 Knox-Shaw, P, On laying down the lore, *Theoria*, 80 (1992) 31–37

4948 Lazar, K, *Jump and other stories*: Gordimer's leap into the 1990s: gender and politics in her latest short fiction, *Journal of southern African studies*, 18, 4 (1992) 783–402

4949 Lazar, K R, 'Something out there'/something in there: gender and politcs in Gordimer's novella, *English in Africa*, 19, 1 (1992) 53–65

4950 Louvel, L, Nadine Gordimer's *My son's story* or the experience of fragmentation, *Commonwealth : essays and studies*, 14, 2 (1992) 28–33

4951 MacKenzie, C Woeber, C, *Bessie Head: a bibliography*. Grahamstown: National English Literary Museum, 1992, 105pp

4952 Maughan Brown, D, Adjusting the focal length: Alex La Guma and exile, *English in Africa*, 18, 2 (1991) 19–38

4953 Mkhize, J, Sexual politics 'and 'free' women in Achmat Dangor's *The Z Town trilogy*, *Staffrider*, 10, 1 (1992) 19–25

4954 Morphet, T, Ordinary - modern - post-modern, *Theoria*, 80 (1992) 129–41

4955 Mzamane, M V, The impact of Black Consciousness on culture, in Pityana N B (ed), *Bounds of possibility (entry 5154)*, 179–93

4956 Ndebele, N S, *Rediscovery of the ordinary: essays on South African literature and culture*. Johannesburg: Congress of Southern African Writers, 1991, 160pp

4957 Ogundele, W, Politics and the pastoral ideal in the poetry of Dennis Brutus, *Commonwealth : essays and studies,* 14, 2 (1992) 49–60

4958 Peck, R, Condemned to choose, but what? Existentialism in selected works by Fugard, Brink and Gordimer, *Research in African literatures,* 23, 3 (1992) 67–84

4959 Rasebotsa, N, Nadine Gordimer's 'Is there nowhere else we can meet?": a call to dialogue in a culture of silence, *Marang,* 9 (1991) 1–10

4960 Roberts, S, Cinderella's mothers: J M Coetzee's *In the heart of the country, English in Africa,* 19, 1 (1992) 21–33

4961 Rowe, M M, Mapping a way 'to offer one's self': Nadine Gordimer's *Burger's daughter, Commonwealth novel in English,* 4, 2 (1991) 45–54

4962 Sévry, J D, South Africa re-visited: 50 years of apartheid literature, *Commonwealth : essays and studies,* 14, 2 (1992) 19–27

4963 Smyer, R, *A sport of nature*: Gordimer's work in progress, *Journal of Commonwealth literature,* 27, 1 (1992) 71–86

4964 Sole, K, van Niekerk, M, *The ghostly dance: writing in a new South Africa (part 2).* Mowbray: IDASA, 1990, 8pp

4965 Stander, C, Willemse, H, Winding through nationalism, patriarchy, privilege and concern: a selected overview of Afrikaans women writers, *Research in African literatures,* 23, 3 (1992) 5–24

4966 Stephenson, G, Escaping the camps: the idea of freedom in J M Coetzee's *The life and times of Michael K, Commonwealth novel in English,* 4, 1 (1991) 77–88

4967 Strauss, J, *A select index to South African literature in English.* Grahamstown: National English Literary Museum, 1992, 169pp

4968 van Wyk, J, Afrikaans language, literature and identity, *Theoria,* 77 (1991) 79–89

4969 Van Wyk Smith, M, *Grounds of contest: a survey of South African English literature.* Kenwyn: Juta, 1990, 153pp

4970 Wilkinson, J, Dust and dew, moonlight and utopia: natural imagery in the first South African novel, *Commonwealth : essays and studies,* 14, 2 (1992) 34–43

4971 Wright, L, (ed), *Teaching English literature in South Africa: twenty essays.* Grahamstown: Institute for the Study of English in Africa, 1990, 286pp

Media

4972 Balch, J A, et al, (eds), *Violent stalemate: media perspectives on the South African negotiations.* Amsterdam: African-European Institute, 1990, 54pp

4973 Louw, R, (ed), *Media in a new South Africa.* Mowbray: IDASA, 1990, 21pp

4974 Marcus, G, Censorship under the emergency, *South African human rights and labour law yearbook,* 1, (1990) 24–35

4975 Martin, D C, En noir et blanc et couleur: que voir dans les clips sud-africaines?, *Politique africaine,* 48 (1992) 67–88

4976 Maswai, T, et al, *Mau-mauing the media: new censorship for the new South Africa.* Johannesburg: SAIRR, 1991, 66pp

4977 Mutloatse, M, Indigenous publishing in South Africa: the case of Skotaville publishers, in Altbach P (ed), *Publishing and development (entry 694)),* 211–22

4978 South African Library, *Book publishing in South Africa for the 1990s.* Cape Town: the Library, 1991, 117pp

4979 South African Library, (ed),
*Book publishing in South Africa for
the 1990s.* Cape Town: the Library,
1991, 117pp
4980 White, T, The Lovedale Press
during the directorship of R H W
Shepherd, *English in Africa,* 19, 2
(1992) 69–84

Medical

see also: 4696
4983 Lea, S, Foster, D, (eds),
*Perspectives on mental heath in South
Africa.* Durban: Butterworths,
1990, 304pp
4984 Marais, C, *Children of sorrow:
child sex abuse in South Africa.*
Rivonia: Ashanti Publishing, 1990,
135pp

Natural resources

see also: 4627, 4630, 4637
4985 Ledger, J, South Africa's
endangered species, in Cock J &
Koch, E (eds), *Going green (entry
4629),* 230–41
4986 Wyley, C, A bibliography of
contemporary writings on the
natural history of Natal and
Zululand in the 19th and early 20th
centuries, *Journal of Natal and Zulu
history,* 13 (1990/91) 91–110

Politics

see also: 834, 2943, 4487, 4621,
4628, 4635, 4639, 4692, 4710,
4721, 5193, 5218, 5222
4987 Adam, H, *Eastern Europe and
South African socialism: engaging Joe
Slovo.* Cape Town: IDASA, 1990,
15pp
4988 Adam, H, Eastern Europe and
South African socialism: engaging
Joe Slovo, *Theoria,* 76 (1990) 33–43
4990 Adam, H, Moodley, K,
Political violence, 'tribalism', and
Inkatha, *Journal of modern African
studies,* 30, 3 (1992) 485–510
4991 Adler, G, et al, Unions, direct
action and transition in South
Africa, in Etherington N (ed),
*Peace, politics and violence (entry
5047),* 306–43
4992 Ajulu, R, Political violence in
South Africa: a reply to Morris and
Hindson, *Review of African political
economy,* 55 (1992) 67–71
4993 Alexander, N, Black
Consciousness: a reactionary
tendency?, in Pityana N B et al.
(ed), *Bounds of possibility (entry
5154),* 238–53
4994 Alexander, N, National
liberation and socialist revolution,
in Callinicos A (ed), *Between
apartheid and capitalism (entry
5015),* 114–136
4995 Amnesty International, *South
Africa, state of fear: security force
complicity in torture and killing.*
London: Amnesty International,
1992, 100pp
4996 Amnesty International, *South
Africa: torture, ill treatment and
executions in ANC camps.* London:
Amnesty International, 1992, 26pp
4997 Anstey, M, Mediation in the
South African transition: a critical
review of the developments,
problems and potentials,
Geneva-Africa, 30, 2 (1992) 141–63
4998 Arnold, G, *South Africa:
crossing the Rubicon.* Basingstoke:
Macmillan, 1992, 29pp
4999 Atkinson, D, Rights, politics
and civil society in South Africa,
Theoria, 79 (1992) 43–55
5000 Atkinson, D, State and civil
society in flux: parameters of a
changing society, *Theoria,* 79
(1992) 1–28
5001 Atkinson, D, *The state, the city
and meaning: towards a new theory of
the South African state.* Durban:
University of Natal, Centre for
Social and Development Studies,
1990, 45pp

5002 Atkinson, D, The state, the city and political morality, *Theoria,* 78 (1991) 115–38

5003 Barrell, H, The turn to the masses: the ANC's strategic review of 1978–79, *Journal of southern African studies,* 18, 1 (1992) 64–92

5004 Beaudet, P, *Les grandes mutations de l'apartheid.* Paris: Harmattan, 1991, 199pp

5005 Bekker, S, Cities straddling homeland boundaries, in Swilling M et al (eds), *Apartheid city (entry 5328),* 108–118

5006 Bekker, S, (ed), *Capturing the event: conflict trends in the Natal region 1986–1991.* Durban: Natal University, Indicator Project, 1992, 76pp

5007 Bekker, S, et al, *Metropolitan government in Durban.* Durban: University of Natal, Centre for Social and Development Studies, 1990, 43pp

5008 Berhardt, I, Les Sud-Africains blancs et l'apartheid, *Revue des deux mondes,* Feb. 1991 204–15

5009 Bönneman, B, *'Die Weissen werden wir brauchen': südafrikanische Gespräche.* Hamburg: Lichterhand, 1992, 166pp

5010 Boraine, A, (ed), *Beyond apartheid: discussion papers on a democratic development in South Africa.* Copenhagen: CDR, 1992, 280pp

5011 Botes, L J S, et al, Aspekte van 'n post-apartheid Suid-Afrika uit die oogpunt van blanke Bloemfonteiners, *Journal for contemporary history,* 16, 2 (1991) 54–75

5012 Botha, T, Civic associations as autonomous organs of grassroots' participation, *Theoria,* 79 (1992) 57–74

5013 Budlender, G, Black Consciousness and the liberal tradition: then and now, in Pityana N B et al. (ed), *Bounds of possibility (entry 5154),* 228–37

5014 Bundy, C, Reform in historical perspective, in Callinicos A (ed), *Between apartheid and capitalism (entry 5015),* 91–104

5015 Callinicos, A, (ed), *Between apartheid and capitalism: conversations with South African socialists.* London: Bookmarks, 1992, 171pp

5016 Callinicos, A, et al, The agenda of the South African left, in Callinicos A (ed), *Between apartheid and capitalism (entry 5015),* 137–53

5017 Callinicos, A, Saul, J, Reform and revolution in South Africa: a reply to John Saul, *New left review,* 195 (1992) 111–117

5018 Carter, C, Community and conflict: the Alexandra rebellion of 1986, *Journal of southern African studies,* 18, 1 (1992) 115–42

5019 Cawthra, G, *South Africa's police: from police state to democratic policing?* London: CIIR, 1992, 40pp

5020 Cervenka, Z, *African National Congress meets eastern Europe: a dialogue on common experiences.* Uppsala: SIAS, 1992, 49pp

5021 Charney, C, Vigilantes, clientelism, and the South African state, *Transformation,* 16 (1991) 1–28

5022 Chidester, D, *Shots in the street: violence and religion in South Africa.* Boston, Mass.: Beacon Books, 1991, 220pp

5023 Cloete, F, Policy impact of democracy in South Africa, *Africa insight,* 21, 4 (1991) 222–32

5024 Cock, J, Political violence, in McKendrick B & Hoffman, W (eds), *People and violence (entry 5270),* 44–72

5025 Collinge, J-A, Launched on a bloody tide: negotiating the new South Africa, in Moss G & Obery, G (eds), *South African review 6 (entry 4504),* 1–25

5026 Coovadia, C, The role of the

civic movement, in Swilling M et al (eds), *Apartheid city (entry 5328)*, 334–49

5027 **Croeser, G,** Autonomy in local authority finance, in Swilling M et al (eds), *Apartheid city (entry 5328)*, 139–50

5028 **Cronin, J,** The CP and the left, in Callinicos A (ed), *Between apartheid and capitalism (entry 5015)*, 76–90

5029 **Cullinan, K, Malema, P,** Triangle of violence, *Work in progress*, 84 (1992) 11–14

5030 **Daphne, P, de Clercq, F,** Bophuthatswana: from 'independence' to regionalism, in Moss G & Obery, G (eds), *South African review 6 (entry 4504)*, 128–40

5031 **de Villiers, B,** *Democratic prospects for South Africa.* Pretoria: HSRC, 1992, 46pp

5032 **de Villiers, B,** *Regional government in the new South Africa.* Pretoria: HSRC, 1992, 90pp

5033 **de Villiers, B,** *Regional government in the new South Africa.* Prestoria: Human Sciences Research Council, 1992, 83pp

5034 **Devenish, G,** Constitutional reform, *South African human rights and labour law yearbook*, 1, (1990) 56–74

5035 **Diamond, L,** A constitution that works: some options, *South Africa international*, 23, 1 (1992) 45–48

5036 **Diseko, N,** The origins and development of the South African Student's Movement (SASM): 1968–70, *Journal of southern African studies*, 18, 1 (1992) 40–63

5037 **Döckel, J A, Somers, O,** A framework for intergovernmental fiscal relations in South Africa, *Development Southern Africa*, 9, 2 (1992) 139–152

5038 **Dreijmanis, J,** The Afrikaners, in Watson M (ed), *Contemporary minority nationalism* (London: Routledge,1991), 135–51

5039 **Drew, A,** Profile of the South African Communist Party, *Journal of communist studies*, 8, 2 (1992) 160–65

5040 **Drew, A,** *What makes peasants revolutionary? The case of South Africa.* Manchester: Manchester University, Dept. of Government, 1992, 33pp

5041 **Du Pisani, J A,** Die praktiese toepassing van die tuislandbeleid tydens die Vorsterera, *Journal for contemporary history*, 15, 2 (1990) 34–54

5042 **Du Pisani, J A, et al,** Teoretiese, historiese en politieke aspekte van protesoptogte in Suid-Afrika, *Journal for contemporary history*, 15, 3 (1990) 1–44

5043 **du Toit, B,** (ed), *Towards democracy: building a culture of accountability in South Africa.* Cape Town: IDASA, 1991, 217pp

5044 **du Toit, B M,** The far right in current South African politics, *Journal of modern African studies*, 29, 4 (1991) 627–67

5045 **Ellis, S,** The South African Communist Party and the collapse of the Soviet Union, *Journal of communist studies*, 8, 2 (1992) 145–59 (also in *entry 860*)

5046 **Ellis, S, Sechaba, T,** *Comrades against apartheid: the ANC and the South African Communist Party in exile.* London: Currey, 1992, 214pp

5047 **Etherington, N,** (ed), *Peace, politics and violence in the new South Africa.* Oxford: Zell, 1992, 352pp

5048 **Etherington, N,** Explaining the death throes of apartheid, in Etherington N (ed), *Peace, politics and violence (entry 5047)*, 102–20

5049 **Fine, R,** Civil society theory and the politics of transition in South Africa, *Review of African* political economy, 55 (1992) 71–83

5050 **Forder, J,** Conscription, *South African human rights and labour law yearbook,* 1, (1990) 36–55

5051 **Forsyth, P,** The past in the service of the present: the political use of history by Chief Buthelezi 1951–1991, *South African historical journal,* 26 (1992) 74–92

5052 **Forsyth, P, Maré, G,** Natal in the new South Africa, in Moss G & Obery, G (eds), *South African review 6 (entry 4504),* 141–51

5053 **Fox, R,** A piece of the jigsaw: the 1992 white referendum and South Africa's post-apartheid political geography, *Journal of contemporary African studies,* 10, 2 (1991) 84–96

5054 **Friedman, S,** Bonaparte at the barricades: the colonisation of civil society, *Theoria,* 79 (1992) 83–95

5055 **Friedman, S,** *The shapers of things to come?: National Party choices in the South African transition.* Johannesburg: Centre for Policy Studies, Witswatersrand University, 1992, 45pp

5056 **Friedman, S,** An unlikely utopia: state and civil society in South Africa, *Politikon,* 19, 1 (1991) 5–19

5057 **Fukuyama, F,** The next South Africa, *South Africa international,* 22, 2 (1991/1992) 71–81

5058 **Furlong, P J,** South Africa, in Gordon A & D (eds), *Understanding contemporary Africa (entry 9),* 283–316

5059 **Gastrow, S,** *Who's who in South Africa: number 4.* Johannesburg: Ravan, 1992, 333pp

5060 **Geldenhuys, D, Kotzé, H,** F W de Klerk: a study in political leadership, *Politikon,* 19, 1 (1991) 20–44

5061 **Giliomee, H,** Broedertwis: intra-Afrikaner conflict in the transition from apartheid 1969–91, in Etherington N (ed), *Peace,*

politics and violence (entry 5047), 162–95

5062 **Giliomee, H,** *Broedertwis:* intra-afrikaner conflicts in the transition from apartheid 1969–1991, *African affairs,* 91, 364 (1992) 339–64

5063 **Giliomee, H,** The last trek? Afrikaners in the transition to democracy, in Etherington N (ed), *Peace, politics and violence (entry 5047),* 28–45

5064 **Giliomee, H,** The last trek?: Afrikaners in the transition to democracy, *South Africa international,* 22, 3 (1991/92) 111–120

5065 **Ginwala, F,** Into and out of Codesa negotiations: the view from the ANC, in Etherington N (ed), *Peace, politics and violence (entry 5047),* 1–27

5066 **Gonzalez, C,** South African official and extra-parliamentary domestic strategy: decision-making mechanisms, *Revista de Africa y Medio Oriente,* 3, 1 (1991) 75–100

5067 **Govender, K,** Separate amenities, *South African human rights and labour law yearbook,* 1, (1990) 247–261

5068 **Grobbelaar, J,** 'Bittereinders': dilemmas and dynamics on the far right, in Moss G & Obery, G (eds), *South African review 6 (entry 4504),* 102–111

5069 **Gromyko, A, et al,** (eds), *The Moscow papers: the USSR and South Africa - similarities, problems and opportunities.* Johannesburg: SAIRR, 1991, 130pp

5070 **Halisi, C R D,** Biko and Black Consciousness philosophy: an interpretation, in Pityana N B et al. (ed), *Bounds of possibility (entry 5154),* 100–110

5071 **Hamill, J,** *South Africa; the rise and fall of 'total strategy'.* Leicester: University of Leicester, Dept. of Politics, 1992, 39pp

5072 **Haysom, N,** Negotiating a
political settlement in South Africa,
in Moss G & Obery, G (eds), *South
African review 6 (entry 4504)*, 26–43

5073 **Haysom, N,** Policing, *South
African human rights and labour law
yearbook*, 1, (1990) 228–246

5074 **Heymann, P B,** (ed), *Towards
peaceful protest in South Africa:
testimony of multinational panel
regarding lawful control of
demonstrations in the Republic of
South Africa.* Pretoria: HSRC,
1992, 197pp

5075 **Heymans, C,** Privatisation and
municipal reform, in Swilling M et
al (eds), *Apartheid city (entry 5328)*,
151–73

5076 **Howarth, D, Norval, A,**
*Subjectivity and strategy in South
African resistance politics: prospects for
a new imaginary.* Colchester: Essex
University, Dept. of Government,
1992, 38pp

5077 **Hudson, H,** Die rol en plek
van terrorisme in rewolusionêre
oorlogvoering: die ANC se
dilemma, *Journal for contemporary
history*, 15, 1 (1990) 31–46

5078 **Hughes, H,** Detentions, *South
African human rights and labour law
yearbook*, 1, (1990) 75–91

5079 **Humphries, R,** National Party
and state perspectives on
regionalism, *Africa insight*, 22, 1
(1992) 57–65

5080 **Humphries, R,** Wither
Regional Service Councils?, in
Swilling M et al (eds), *Apartheid
city (entry 5328)*, 78–90

5081 **Humphries, R, Shubane, K,**
*A delicate balance: reconstructing
regionalism in South Africa.*
Johannesburg: Centre for Policy
Studies, Witswatersrand
University, 1992, 34pp

5082 **Hyslop, J,** Polar night: social
theory and the crisis of apartheid,
in Moss G & Obery, G (eds), *South
African review 6 (entry 4504)*,
171–85

5083 **Innes, D, Kentridge, M,**
Violence on the Reef 1990–1991,
in Innes D et al (eds), *Power and
profit (entry 4546)*, 74–94

5084 **International Commission
of Jurists,** *Agenda for peace: an
independent survey of the violence in
South Africa.* Geneva: ICJ, 1992,
30pp

5085 **Jeffrey, A J,** *Riot policing in
perspective.* Johannesburg: SAIRR,
1991, 262pp

5086 **Jeffrey, A J,** *Spotlight on
disinformation about violence in South
Africa.* Braamfontein: SAIRR,
1992, 57pp

5087 **Jenny, H,** *Südafrika: vom
Chaos zur Versöhnung.* Herford:
Busse Seewald, 1992, 197pp

5088 **Kaiser, A, Müller, T O,** *Das
neue Südafrika: politische Portraits.*
Bonn: Dietz, 1992, 189pp

5089 **Karcher, G L,** Und das
Morden nimmt kein Ende: zur
Gewalt in den schwarzen
Townships Südafrikas,
Internationales Afrikaforum, 28, 1
(1992) 67–82

5090 **Kaschula, R,** Power and the
poet in contemporary Transkei,
*Journal of contemporary African
studies*, 10, 2 (1991) 24–43

5091 **Kentridge, M,** *An unofficial
war: inside the conflict in
Pietermaritzburg.* Cape Town:
Philip, 1990, 249pp

5092 **Kentridge, M,** War and peace
in Natal, in Innes D et al (eds),
Power and profit (entry 4546), 43–73

5093 **Kotzé, H, Greyling, A,**
*Political organisations in South Africa
A–Z.* Cape Town: Tafelberg, 1991,
255pp

5094 **Kriek, D J, et al,** (eds),
Federalism. Pretoria: HSRC, 1992,
344pp

5095 **Laurence, P,** South African
Communist Party strategy since
1990, in Moss G & Obery, G (eds),

South African review 6 (entry 4504), 79–94

5096 Lawrence, R, Shaping democracy in a future South Africa, *Theoria,* 76 (1990) 101–114

5097 Lee, R, (ed), *Values alive: a tribute to Helen Suzman.* Johannesburg: Ball, 1990, 236pp

5098 Legal Education Action Project, *Back to the laager: the rise of rightwing violence in South Africa.* Cape Town: University of Cape Town, Institute of Criminology, 1991, 159pp

5099 Legal Resource Centre, *Obstacles to peace: the role of the Kwazulu police in the Natal conflict.* Durban: the Centre, 1992, 211pp

5100 Lemon, A, Restucturing the local state in South Africa: regional services councils, redistribution and legitimacy, in Drakakis-Smith D (ed), *Urban and regional change (entry 4224),* 1–32

5101 Lodge, T, The African National Congress in the 1990s, in Moss G & Obery, G (eds), *South African review 6 (entry 4504),* 44–78

5102 Lodge, T, Post-modern bolsheviks: SA communists in transition, *South Africa international,* 22, 4 (1991/92) 172–179

5103 Lodge, T, Nasson, B, et al, *All, here and now: Black politics in South Africa in the 1980s.* London: Hurst, 1992, 412pp

5104 Louw, F K, *The heart of the nation: regional nd community government in the new South Africa.* Norwood: Amagi, 1991, 194pp

5105 Maake, N P, Multi-cultural relations in a post-apartheid South Africa, *African affairs,* 91, 365 (1992) 583–604

5106 Mabizela, T, et al, *Unfinished business: apartheid after apartheid.* Amsterdam: African-European Institute, 1990, 63pp

5107 Macdonald, M, The sirens'

song: the political logic of power-sharing in South Africa, *Journal of southern African studies,* 18, 4 (1992) 709–25

5108 Maistry, T, (ed), *Resistance cultural formations in South Africa: a directory.* Cape Town: Centre for Development Studies, 1991, 94pp

5109 Mallaby, S, *After apartheid.* London: Faber, 1992, 210pp

5110 Mandy, S, Local government finance and institutional reform, in Swilling M et al (eds), *Apartheid city (entry 5328),* 119–38

5111 Manzo, K, *Domination, resistance and social change in South Africa: the local effects of global power.* New York: Greenwood, 1992, 291pp

5112 Manzo, K, McGowan, P, Afrikaner fears and the politics of despair: understanding change in South Africa, *International studies quarterly,* 36, 1 (1992) 1–24

5113 Marais, E, et al, *Project for the study of violence.* Johannesburg: Dept. of Psychology, Witswatersrand University, 1992, 8 parts,

5114 Marais, H, The sweeping inferno: how can the violence be stopped?, *Work in progress,* 83 (1992) 14–17

5115 Marais, H Hani, C, What happened in the ANC camps?, *Work in progress,* 82 (1992) 14–20

5116 Maré, G, *Brothers born of warrior blood: politics and ethnicity in South Africa.* Braamfontein: Ravan, 1992, 121pp

5117 Martin, D C, (ed), *Sortir de l'apartheid.* Brussels: Complexe, 1992, 159pp

5118 Marx, A W, *Lessons of struggle: South African internal opposition 1960–1990.* Cape Town: OUP, 1992, 347pp

5119 Mathews, M, Human rights at Columbia University, *Theoria,* 75 (1990) 13–26

5120 **Mayekisa, M,** Socialists and trade unions, in Callinicos A (ed), *Between apartheid and capitalism (entry 5015)*, 105–113

5121 **McCarthy, J,** Local and regional government: from rigidity to crisis to flux, in Smith D M (ed), *Apartheid city (entry 5324)*, 35–36

5122 **McKenzie, E,** An unholy trinity? Big business, the Progressive Federal Party and the English press during the 1983 referendum, *Journal for contemporary history,* 15, 3 (1990) 55–71

5123 **Miller, S R,** Just war theory and the ANC's armed struggle, *Quest,* 4, 2 (1990) 80–102

5124 **Minaar, A, et al,** *Conflict and violence in Natal/Kwazulu: historical perspectives.* Pretoria: HSRC, 1992, 97pp

5125 **Minnaar, A,** (ed), *Patterns of violence - case studies of conflict in Natal.* Pretoria: HSRC, 1992, 264pp

5126 **Moodie, T D,** Ethnic violence on South African gold mines, *Journal of southern African studies,* 18, 3 (1992) 584–613

5127 **Moodley, K,** The continuing impact of Black Consciousness, in Pityana N B (ed), *Bounds of possibility (entry 5154)*, 143–52

5128 **Morphet, T,** 'Brushing history against the grain': oppositional discourse in South Africa, *Theoria,* 76 (1990) 89–99

5129 **Morris, M, Hindson, D,** The disintegration of apartheid: from violence to reconstruction, in Moss G & Obery, G (eds), *South African review 6 (entry 4504)*, 152–70

5130 **Morris, M, Hindson, D,** *Political violence and urban reconstruction in South Africa.* Cape Town: Economic Trends Research Group, University of Cape Town, 1991, 20pp

5131 **Morris, M, Hindson, D,**

South Africa: political violence, reform and reconstruction, *Review of African political economy,* 53 (1992) 43–59

5132 **Mosha, F G N,** (ed), *The challenges of post-apartheid South Africa.* Abeokuta: Africa Leadership Forum, 1991, 203pp

5133 **Moss, R,** *Shouting at the crocodile: Popo Molefe, Patrick Lekota and the freeing of South Africa.* Boston: Beacon Press, 1990, 200pp

5134 **Motlhabi, M,** *Towards a new South Africa: issues and objects in the ANC/Government negotiation for a non-racial democratic society.* Skotavile: 1992, 88pp

5135 **Motshabi, K B, Volks, S G,** Towards democratic cheiftaincy: principles and procedures, *Acta juridica,* 1991 104–115

5136 **Naidoo, G,** (ed), *Reform and revolution: South Africa in the nineties.* Johannesburg: Skotaville, 1990, 227pp

5137 **Naidoo, K,** The politics of youth resistance in the 1980s: the dilemmas of a differentiated Durban, *Journal of southern African studies,* 18, 1 (1992) 143–65

5138 **Nathan, L, Phillips, M,** 'Cross-currents': security developments under de Klerk, in Moss G & Obery, G (eds), *South African review 6 (entry 4504)*, 112–27

5139 **Nürnberger, K,** (ed), *A democratic vision for South Africa: political realism and Christian responsibility.* Pietermaritzburg: Encounter, 1991, 624pp

5140 **Nyatsumba, K M,** Azapo and the PAC: revolutionary watchdogs?, in Moss G & Obery, G (eds), *South African review 6 (entry 4504)*, 95–101

5141 **Olivier, J L,** *Eastern Europe and South Africa: implications for the future.* Pretoria: HSRC, 1990, 76pp

5142 Olivier, J L, State repression and collective action in South Africa, 1970–1984, *South African journal of sociology,* 22, 4 (1991) 109–117

5143 Olivier, N J J, ANC constitutional proposals and State reaction, *South Africa international,* 22, 2 (1991/1992) 55–64

5144 O'Meara, D, The new National Party and the politics of negotiation, in Innes D et al (eds), *Power and profit (entry 4546),* 10–30

5145 Onwu, N, et al, *A future South Africa in the African context: an African perspective.* Potchefstroom: Institute for Reformational Studies, 1992, 29pp

5146 Orkin, M, Beyond alienation and anomie: the emancipatory efficacy of liberation ideologies in South Africa, *International journal of sociology and social policy,* 11, 6/8 (1991) 195–211

5147 Orkin, M, 'Democracy knows no colour': rationales for guerrilla invovement among Black South Africans, *Journal of southern African studies,* 18, 3 (1992) 642–69

5148 Ottaway, M, Opposition parties and democracy in South Africa, *Issue,* 20, 1 (1992) 15–22

5149 Paolini, M, Le cooperative in Sudafrica: due differenti prospettive di sviluppo, *Africa (Rome),* 46, 3 (1991) 447–460

5150 Peirce, D L, *Post-apartheid South Africa: lessons from Brazil's 'Nova Republica'.* Johannesburg: Centre for Policy Studies, Witswatersrand University, 1992, 30pp

5151 Peiris, J B, The implosion of Transkei and Ciskei, *African affairs,* 91, 364 (1992) 364–87

5152 Pillay, D, von Holdt, K, Strategy and tactics, in Callinicos A (ed), *Between apartheid and capitalism (entry 5015),* 55–75

5153 Pillay, U, The Regional Services Council debacle in Durban, in Smith D M (ed), *Apartheid city (entry 5324),* 193–204

5154 Pityana, N B, et al, (eds), *Bounds of possibility: the legacy of Steve Biko and Black Consciousness.* London: Zed, 1992, 264pp

5155 Pityana, N B, Revolution within the law?, in Pityana N B et al. (ed), *Bounds of possibility (entry 5154),* 201–212

5156 PLANACT, Transition and development, in Moss G & Obery, G (eds), *South African review 6 (entry 4504),* 201–215

5157 Plaut, M, Debates in a shark tank: the politics of South Africa's non-racial trade unions, *African affairs,* 91, 364 (1992) 389–403

5158 Pretorius, L, Humphries, R, The Conservative Party and local government, in Swilling M et al (eds), *Apartheid city (entry 5328),* 309–21

5159 Raath, A W G, Waarom 'n Afrikanerstaat?, *Tydskrif vir Rasse-Aangeleenthede,* 42, 3/4 (1991) 55–62

5160 Ramphele, M, Empowerment and symbols of hope: Black Consciousness and community development, in Pityana N B (ed), *Bounds of possibility (entry 5154),* 154–78

5161 Rantete, J, *Room for compromise: the ANC and transitional mechanisms.* Johannesburg: Centre for Policy Studies, Witswatersrand University, 1992, 17pp

5162 Rantete, J, Giliomee, H, Transition to democracy through transaction? Bilateral negotiations between the ANC and NP in South Africa, *African affairs,* 91, 365 (1992) 515–42

5163 Reid, G, Cobbett, W, Negotiating in bad faith: local level negotiations and the Interim Measures for Local Government

Act, in Moss G & Obery, G (eds), *South African review 6 (entry 4504)*, 239–53

5164 **Reinecke, C J, et al,** *A future South Africa in the African context: a South African perspective.* Potchefstroom: Institute for Reformational Studies, 1992, 30pp

5165 **Rich, P,** Reviewing the origins of the Freedom Charter, in Etherington N (ed), *Peace, politics and violence (entry 5047)*, 254–83

5166 **Rickard, C,** Natal conflict, and strategies for peace, *South African human rights and labour law yearbook*, 1, (1990) 211–227

5167 **Roherty, J M,** *State security in South Africa: civil military relations under P W Botha.* New York: Sharpe, 1992, 227pp

5168 **Rosenke, W,** *Südafrika: Hoffnung auf die Ende der Apartheid.* Bonn: Die Grünen, 1990, 40pp

5169 **Sapire, H,** Politics and protest in shack settlements of the Pretoria-Witwaersrand-Vereeniging region, South Africa, 1980–1990, *Journal of southern African studies*, 18, 3 (1992) 670–97

5170 **Schlemmer, L,** *Dimensions of turmoil: position paper on current violence in South Africa.* Johannesburg: Witwatersrand University, Cente for Policy Studies, 1991, 17pp

5171 **Schlemmer, L,** The National Party constitutional proposals: stable democracy or minority imperialism?, *South Africa international*, 22, 2 (1991/1992) 65–70

5172 **Schmidt, S,** *Die Rolle des schwarzen Gewerkschaften in Demokratisierungprocess Südafrika.* Hamburg: Institut für Afrika-Kunde, 1991, 336pp

5173 **Schreuder, D,** The Commonwealth and peacemaking in South Africa, in Etherington N (ed), *Peace, politics and violence (entry 5047)*, 73–101

5174 **Schrire, R,** *Adapt or die: the end of white politics in South Africa.* London: Hurst, 1992, 243pp

5175 **Schrire, T,** White politics and strategies in the 1990s, in Maasdorp G & Whiteside, A (eds), *Towards a post-apartheid future (entry 4201)*, 10–28

5176 **Seegers, A,** Current trends in South Africa's security establishment, *Armed forces and society*, 18, 2 (1992) 159–74

5177 **Seekings, J,** Civic organisations in South African townships, in Moss G & Obery, G (eds), *South African review 6 (entry 4504)*, 216–38

5178 **Seekings, J,** Township resistance in the 1980s, in Swilling M et al (eds), *Apartheid city (entry 5328)*, 290–308

5179 **Seekings, J,** 'Trailing behind the masses': the UDF and township politics in the Pretoria-Witwatersrand-Vaal region, *Journal of southern African studies*, 18, 1 (1992) 93–114

5180 **Segal, L,** The human face of violence: hostel dwellers speak, *Journal of southern African studies*, 18, 1 (1992) 190–231

5181 **Shain, M, Frankental, S,** South African Jewry, apartheid and political change, *Survey of Jewish affairs*, (1991) 240–251

5182 **Shubane, K,** Black local authorities: a contradiction of control, in Swilling M et al (eds), *Apartheid city (entry 5328)*, 64–77

5183 **Shubane, K,** Civil society in apartheid and post-apartheid South Africa, *Theoria*, 79 (1992) 33–41

5184 **Shubane, K,** South Africa: a new government in the making?, *Current history*, 91, 565 (1992) 202–207

5185 **Sitas, A,** The making of the 'Comrades' movement in Natal, 1985–91, *Journal of southern African* *studies,* 18, 3 (1992) 629–41

5186 Smith, D M, Redistribution after apartheid: who gets what and where in the new South Africa, *Area,* 24, 4 (1992) 150–58

5187 Smith, T, *They have killed my children: one community in conflict 1983–1990.* Pietermaritzburg: Pietermaritzburg Agency for Christian Social Awareness, 1990, 28pp

5188 Spence, J E, The South African political process, *Government and opposition,* 26, 2 (1991) 316–28

5189 Suzman, H, *Holding the high ground.* Johannesburg: SAIRR, 1991, 19pp

5190 Swilling, M, The dynamics of reform, in Callinicos A (ed), *Between apartheid and capitalism (entry 5015),* 41–54

5191 Swilling, M, Quixote at the windmills: another conspiracy thesis from Steven Friedman, *Theoria,* 79 (1992) 97–104

5192 Swilling, M, Socialism, democracy and civil society: the case for associational socialism, *Theoria,* 79 (1992) 75–82

5193 Swilling, M, et al, Finance, electricity and the rent boycott, in Swilling M et al (eds), *Apartheid city (entry 5328),* 174–96

5194 Taylor, R, South Africa: a consociational path to peace?, *Transformation,* 17 (1992) 1–11

5195 Terreblanche, S, *The need for a transformation period towards a post-apartheid South Africa.* Stellenbosch: Stellenbosch University, Centre for Contextual Hermeneutics, 1991, 15pp

5196 Thede, N, Beaudet, P, De la lutte anti-apartheid aux mutations de la culture politique, *Politique africaine,* 48 (1992) 22–32

5197 Thomas, A, Violence and child detainees, in McKendrick B & Hoffman, W (eds), *People and*

violence (entry 5270), 436–64

5198 Turaki, Y, *An African response to the question of apartheid.* Potchefstroom: Institute for Reformational Studies, 1992, 22pp

5199 Uys, S, Can a democratic constitution take root in South Africa?, *South Africa international,* 22, 2 (1991) 82–85

5200 Van der Westhuizen, F G J, Die verwesenliking van 'n Afrikanervolkstaat: besetting, *Tydskrif vir Rasse-Aangeleenthede,* 42, 3/4 (1991) 63–74

5201 van Kessel, I, Inkatha: een beweging met een januskop, *Internationale spectator,* 45, 10 (1991) 640–647

5202 van Kessel, I, La révolte de la jeunesse dans le Sekhukhuneland, *Politique africaine,* 48 (1992) 33–46

5203 van Nieuwkerk, A, *Transitional politics in South Africa: from confrontation to democracy?* Braamfontein: SAIIA, 1992, 38pp

5204 van Zyl Slabbert, F, *The burden of democracy.* Braamfontein: SAIAA, 1992, 13pp

5205 Van Zyl Slabbert, F, Dilemmas for democracy in South Africa, *South Africa international,* 23, 1 (1992) 4–10

5206 Virmani, K K, *Nelson Mandela and apartheid in South Africa.* Delhi: Kalinga, 1991, 108pp

5207 Wardrop, J, The state, police and violence, 1989–91, in Etherington N (ed), *Peace, politics and violence (entry 5047),* 46–72

5208 Weinberger, G, Reformen in Südafrika und die Rolle der großen Kapitalgesellschaften, *Asien Afrika Lateinamerika,* Special issue (1991) 153–159

5209 Weitzer, R, Elite conflicts over policing in South Africa: 1980–1990, *Policing and society,* 1, 4 (1991) 257–68

5210 William, K, De Klerk and the security establishment: partner or

hostage?, *Work in progress,* 83
(1992) 10–13
5211 **Wilson, L,** Bantu Stephen
Biko: a life, in Pityana N B (ed),
Bounds of possibility (entry 5154),
15–77
5212 **Woker, T, Clarke, S,** Human
rights in the homelands, *South
African human rights and labour law
yearbook,* 1, (1990) 152–170
5213 **Zartman, I W,** Negotiation
and the South African conflict,
SIAS review, 11, (1991) 113–32
5214 **Zulu, P,** The
extra-parliamentary opposition in
South Africa, in Maasdorp G &
Whiteside, A (eds), *Towards a
post-apartheid future (entry 4201),*
29–44

Religion, philosophy

see also: 4081, 5022, 5070
5215 **Anderson, A,** *Bazalwane:
African pentecostals in South Africa.*
Pretoria: University of South
Africa, 1992, 181pp
5216 **Becken, H-J,** Mündliche
Überlieferung in Afrikanischer
Kirchengeschichte, *Neue Zeitschrift
für Missionswissenschaft,* 48, 1
(1992) 15–33
5217 **Bonzon, A,** Les églises dans la
tourmente politique, *Politique
africaine,* 48 (1992) 58–66
5218 **Dilger, M,** "Jesus is standing
beside us": the boycott of South
Africa by the Protestant Women's
Federation in Germany,
International review of mission, 81,
322 (1992) 281–285
5219 **Dubow, S,** Afrikaner
nationalism, apartheid and the
conceptualisation of 'race', *Journal
of African history,* 33, 2 (1992)
209–37
5220 **Enslin, P,** The limits of
community, *Theoria,* 75 (1990)
27–36
5221 **Esack, F,** Contemporary

religious thought in South Africa
and the emergence of Qur'anic
hermeneutical notions, *Islam and
Christian Muslim relations,* 2, 2
(1991) 206–226
5222 **Grobler, J E H,** Die rol van
bevrydingsteologie in politieke
aktivisme in Suid-Afrika en
Nicaragua: 'n
Histories-vergelykende analise,
Journal for contemporary history, 16,
1 (1991) 62–95
5223 **Haron, M,** Theses on Islam at
South African universities, *Islam et
sociétés au Sud du Sahara,* 5 (1991)
141–163
5224 **Lötter, H P P,** Some christian
perceptions of social justice in a
transforming South Africa,
Politikon, 19, 1 (1991) 45–65
5225 **Mokoape, K, et al,** Towards
the armed struggle, in Pityana N B
(ed), *Bounds of possibility (entry
5154),* 137–42
5226 **Nicol, W,** *A future South Africa
in the African context: a christian
perspective.* Potchefstroom: Institute
for Reformational Studies, 1992,
26pp
5227 **Pillay, G,** (ed), *The future of
religion.* Pretoria: HSRC, 1992,
215pp
5228 **Rossouw, D,** *Christen,
Kommunis en Sosialis in die nuwe
Suid Afrika.* Pretoria: HSRC, 1992,
162pp
5229 **Rothe, S,** *Der Südafrikanische
Kirchenrat (1968–1988): aus
liberaler Opposition zum radikalen
Widerstand.* Erlangen: Lutheran
Mission, 1990, 432pp
5230 **Sibisi, C D T,** The psychology
of liberation, in Pityana N B et al.
(ed), *Bounds of possibility (entry
5154),* 130–36
5231 **Villa-Vicenio, C,** *A theology of
reconstruction: nation-building and
human rights.* Cape Town: Philip,
1992, 300pp

Rural economy

see also: 4691

5232 Ault, D E, Rutman, G L, The effects of social, political and economic constraints on the black African's allocation of time: evidence from oscillating migrants in the Republic of South Africa, *Oxford economic papers,* 44, 1 (1992) 135–155

5233 Baber, R A A, Nieuwoudt, W L, Economic incentives in the subsistence areas of South Africa and the need for reform, *Development Southern Africa,* 9, 2 (1992) 153–168

5234 Brand, S S, What role should government play in agriculture in a new South Africa?, *Development Southern Africa,* 9, 2 (1992) 229–232

5235 Cunningham, A, Lean pickings: palm-wine tapping as a rural informal sector activity, in Preston-Whyte E & Rogerson, C (eds), *South Africa's informal economy (entry 4567),* 254–61

5236 de Klerk, M, *Prospects for commercial agriculture in the Cape.* Cape Town: Economic Trends Research Group, University of Cape Town, 1992, 28pp

5237 Green, R H, A possible strategy for land and agriculture in post-apartheid South Africa, in Matlhape A & Munz, A (eds), *Towards a new agrarian democratic order* (Amsterdam: SAERT Project, 1991), 68–82

5238 Hendricks, F T, *The pillars of apartheid: land tenure, rural planning and the chieftancy.* Uppsala: Almqvist and Wiksell, 1990, 187pp

5239 Honey, M, et al, The community support approach (CSA): an ABC for rural development, *Development Southern Africa,* 9, 2 (1992) 213–228

5240 Kröhne, H, Steyn, L, *Land use in Namaqualand.* Athlone: Surplus Peoples Project, 1991, 87pp

5241 Matlhape, S, (ed), *Towards a new agrarian democratic order: a reader on the South African land question.* Amsterdam: South Africa Economic Research and Training Project, 1991, 317pp

5242 May, J, *Transforming public expenditure on development: agricultural development intervention in the Bantustans.* Cape Town: Economic Trends Research Group, University of Cape Town, 1992, 34, 14pp

5243 McIntosh, A, Making the informal sector pay: rural entrepreneurs in KwaZulu, in Preston-Whyte E & Rogerson, C (eds), *South Africa's informal economy (entry 4567),* 243–53

5244 McIntosh, A, Rural income generating activities: collective responses, in Preston-Whyte E & Rogerson, C (eds), *South Africa's informal economy (entry 4567),* 279–89

5245 Segal, L, *A brutal harvest: the roots and legitimation of violence on farms in South Africa.* Johannesburg: Black Sash, 1991, 36pp

5246 Surplus Peoples Project, *'If one can live, all must live': a report on past, present and alternative land use in the Mier Rural Reserve in the northern Cape.* Athlone: Surplus Peoples Project, 1990, 36pp

5247 Vink, N, Fenyes, T, *The rural land question: a summary of papers from an IDASA workshop.* Cape Town: IDASA, 1990, 12pp

Sociology

see also: 4697, 4756, 5185

5248 Beittel, M, The Witswatersrand: Black households, white households, in Smith J &

Wallerstein, I (eds), *Creating and transforming households (Cambridge: Cambridge UP, 1992)*, 197–230

5249 Bekker, S, Wilson, C, *Project development in Durban and Pietermaritzburg: a survey of expert opinion.* Durban: University of Natal, Centre for Social and Development Studies, 1990, 38pp

5250 Bodis, J P, Les faux rebonds de l'ovale, *Politique africaine,* 48 (1992) 89–102

5251 Bryden, C, *Return of the prodigal son: South Africa's cricketing comeback.* Johannesburg: Ball, 1992, 208pp

5252 Campbell, C, Learning to kill? Masculinity, the family and violence in Natal, *Journal of southern African studies,* 18, 3 (1992) 614–28

5253 Cloete, E, Afrikaner identity: culture, tradition and gender, *Agenda,* 13 (1992) 42–56

5254 Coquerel, P, *L'Afrique du Sud des Afrikaners.* Brussels: Complexe, 1992, 303pp

5255 Da Costa, Y, The Muslim community in greater Cape Town: contemporary assimiliation processes, *South African journal of sociology,* 23, 3 (1992) 73–77

5256 De Haas, M, Of joints and jollers: culture and class in Natal shebeens, in Preston-Whyte E & Rogerson, C (eds), *South Africa's informal economy (entry 4567),* 101–114

5257 de Waal, M, Steyn, A F, Konseptualisering en operasionalisering van die ten verbintenis tot die huwelik, *South African journal of sociology,* 23, 1 (1992) 20–26

5258 du Toit, B M, *Cannabis, alcohol and the South African student: adolescent drug use 1974–1985.* Athens, Ohio: Ohio University, 1991, 166pp

5259 du Toit, S I, Family violence:

familicide, in McKendrick B & Hoffman, W (eds), *People and violence (entry 5270),* 288–300

5260 Eckley, S, Family violence: abuse of the elderly, in McKendrick B & Hoffman, W (eds), *People and violence (entry 5270),* 301–40

5261 Everatt, D, Sisulu, E, *Black youth in crisis: facing the future.* Braamfontein: Ravan, 1992, 89pp

5262 Glanz, L, Pretorius, R, Demographic correlates of self-reported delinquency among urban black youth, *South African journal of sociology,* 22, 4 (1991) 101–109

5263 Hannson, D, *We the invisible: a feminist analysis of the conception of 'street children' in South Africa.* Cape Town: University of Cape Town, Institute of Criminology, 1991, 21pp

5264 Hoffman, W, McKendrick, B, The nature of violence, in McKendrick B & Hoffman, W (eds), *People and violence (entry 5270),* 2–35

5265 Human Rights Commission, Violence in detention, in McKendrick B & Hoffman, W (eds), *People and violence (entry 5270),* 405–35

5266 Kistner, U, 'Talking rocks': conditions and problems of an emerging literature, in Nethersole R (ed), *Emerging literatures (entry 726),* 131–43

5267 Krumpholz, A, *Apartheid und Sport.* Munich: Florentz, 1991, 327pp

5268 Mahabeer, M, The influence of age and parent's marital status on Indian children's perceptions of self, family, teachers and school, *South African journal of sociology,* 23, 2 (1992) 60–65

5269 Malan, J S, *The aged in Lebowa and Venda.* Pretoria: HSRC, 1990, 70pp

5270 **McKendrick, B, Hoffman, W,** (eds), *People and violence in South Africa.* Cape Town: OUP, 1990, 495pp

5271 **McKendrick, B, Hoffman, W,** Towards the reduction of violence, in McKendrick B & Hoffman, W (eds), *People and violence (entry 5270)*, 466–82

5272 **Moller, V,** (ed), *Lost generation found: Black youth at leisure.* Durban: Centre for Social and Development Studies, Natal University, 1991, 61pp

5273 **Monsma, G N, et al,** *Poverty in South Africa.* Potchefstroom: Institute for Reformational Studies, 1991, 68pp

5274 **Peacock, R, Theron, A,** Die verband tussen swart straatkinders se biologiese en emosionele behoeftes en die tipe misdaad wat deur hulle gepleeg word, *South African journal of sociology,* 23, 1 (1992) 26–30

5275 **Sandler, H, Segel, N,** Violence against children: sexual abuse, in McKendrick B & Hoffman, W (eds), *People and violence (entry 5270)*, 211–50

5276 **Schurink, W J, et al,** (eds), *Victimisation: nature and trends.* Pretoria: HSRC, 1992, 606pp

5277 **Shuttleworth, J,** Sons of Shaka or sons of Umslopogaas?, in Etherington N (ed), *Peace, politics and violence (entry 5047)*, 147–61

5278 **Siff, M,** Violence in sport, in McKendrick B & Hoffman, W (eds), *People and violence (entry 5270)*, 135–61

5279 **Straker, G,** *Faces in the revolution: the psychological effects of violence on township youth in South Africa.* Cape Town: Philip, 1992, 156pp

5280 **Straker, G,** Violence against children: emotional abuse, in McKendrick B & Hoffman, W (eds), *People and violence (entry*

5270), 171–89

5281 **Van Wyk, A C, Steyn, A F,** Die werketiek en studentesubkulture, *South African journal of sociology,* 23, 3 (1992) 52–60

5282 **Winship, W,** Violence against children: physical abuse, in McKendrick B & Hoffman, W (eds), *People and violence (entry 5270)*, 190–210

5283 **Winslow, T J,** *Released into a prison without walls: a preliminary enquiry into the socioeconomic position of ex-political prisoners living in the Western Cape.* N.p.: Association of ex-Political Prisoners, 1991, 67pp

Social welfare

5284 **Friedman, S,** *Another elephant?: prospects for a South African social contract.* Johannesburg: Centre for Policy Studies, Witswatersrand University, 1991, 26pp

5285 **Jaffee, G,** Cooperative development in South Africa, in Moss G & Obery, G (eds), *South African review 6 (entry 4504)*, 364–77

5286 **Richards, R, Mller, V,** *The feasibility of a youth centre from Pinetown: a survey evaluation of young people's aspirations and expectations.* Durban: University of Natal, Centre for Social and Development Studies, 1990, 66pp

5287 **Steyn, J H,** Investment in human capital, *South Africa international,* 22, 3 (1992) 137–139

Urban studies

see also: 4641, 4989, 5001, 5169, 5178, 5180

5288 **Ardington, E M,** *Buckpassing in Canaan: an example of authorities' failure to address the needs of informal urban dwellers.* Durban: University of Natal, Centre for Social and Development Studies, 1992, 52pp

5289 Atkinson, D, One-city initiatives, in Swilling M et al (eds), *Apartheid city (entry 5328)*, 271–89

5290 Beavon, K S O, The post-apartheid city: hopes, possibilities and harsh realities, in Smith D M (ed), *Apartheid city (entry 5324)*, 231–42

5291 Beavon, K, Some alternativce scenarios for the South African city in the era of late apartheid, in Drakakis-Smith D (ed), *Urban and regional change (entry 4224)*, 66–99

5292 Bekker, S, et al, *Searching for stability: residential migration and community control in Mariannhill.* Durban: University of Natal, Centre for Social and Development Studies, 1992, 83pp

5293 Bernstein, A, The challenge of the cities, in Swilling M et al (eds), *Apartheid city (entry 5328)*, 322–33

5294 Bernstein, A, McCarthy, J, (eds), *Opening the cities: comparative perspectives on desegregation.* Durban: Centre for Social and Development Studies, Natal University, 1990, 67pp

5295 Boaden, B, Taylor, R, Informal settlement: theory versus practice in Kwazulu/Natal, in Smith D M (ed), *Apartheid city (entry 5324)*, 147–57

5296 Cameron, R, Managing the Coloured and Indian areas, in Swilling M et al (eds), *Apartheid city (entry 5328)*, 48–63

5297 Cloete, F, Greying and free settlement, in Swilling M et al (eds), *Apartheid city (entry 5328)*, 91–107

5298 Cook, G P, Khayelitsha: new settlement forms in the Cape Peninsula, in Smith D M (ed), *Apartheid city (entry 5324)*, 125–35

5299 Corbett, P, Post-apartheid housing policy, in Smith D M (ed), *Apartheid city (entry 5324)*, 255–65

5300 Crankshaw, O, et al, The road to 'Egoli': urbanisation histories from a Johannesburg squatter settlement, in Smith D M (ed), *Apartheid city (entry 5324)*, 136–46

5301 Cross, C, *Searching for stability: residential migration and community control in Marianhill.* Durban: Centre for Social and Development Studies, Natatl University, 1992, 83pp

5302 Dewar, D, Urbanisation and the South African city: a manifesto for change, in Smith D M (ed), *Apartheid city (entry 5324)*, 243–54

5303 Emmett, T, *Squatting in the Hottentots Holland Basin: perspectives on a South African social issue.* Pretoria: HSRC, 1992, 262pp

5304 Fassil Demissie, The urban African worker and the crisis of apartheid, *Africa development,* 16, 2 (1991) 121–26 (review article)

5305 Harrison, P, The policies and politics of informal settlement in South Africa: a historical perspective, *Africa insight,* 22, 1 (1992) 14–22

5306 Hendler, P, The housing crisis, in Swilling M et al (eds), *Apartheid city (entry 5328)*, 197–217

5307 Horn, S, et al, Winterveld: an urban interface settlement on the Pretoria metropolitan fringe, in Smith D M (ed), *Apartheid city (entry 5324)*, 113–24

5308 Lupton, M, Class struggle over the built environment in Johannesburg's coloured areas, in Smith D M (ed), *Apartheid city (entry 5324)*, 65–73

5309 Mabin, A, Dispossession, exploitation and struggle: an historical overview of South African urbanisation, in Smith D M (ed), *Apartheid city (entry 5324)*, 13–24

5310 Mabin, A, The dynamics of urbanisation since 1960, in Swilling

M et al (eds), *Apartheid city (entry 5328)*, 33–47

5311 **Maharaj, B,** The 'spatial impress' of the central and local states: the Group Areas Act in Durban, in Smith D M (ed), *Apartheid city (entry 5324)*, 74–86

5312 **McCarthy, J,** Class, race and urban locational relationships, in Swilling M et al (eds), *Apartheid city (entry 5328)*, 258–70

5313 **Minnaar, A,** *Squatters, violence and the future of the informal settlements in the greater Durban region.* Pretoria: HSRC, 1992, 84pp

5314 **Moller, V,** *Research into community needs and priorities: an overview.* Durban: Centre for Social and Developmental Studies, Natal University, 1990, 68pp

5315 **Parnell, S,** State intervention in housing provision in the 1980s, in Smith D M (ed), *Apartheid city (entry 5324)*, 53–64

5316 **Posel, D,** Curbing African urbanisation in the 1950s and 1960s, in Swilling M et al (eds), *Apartheid city (entry 5328)*, 19–32

5317 **Reddy, P S, Brijlal, P,** The role of pension funds in housing finance: the South African scenario, *Development Southern Africa*, 9, 2 (1992) 187–198

5318 **Reintges, C,** Urban (mis)management? A case study of the effects of orderly urbanisation on Duncan village, in Smith D M (ed), *Apartheid city (entry 5324)*, 99–109

5319 **Robinson, J,** Power, space and the city: historical refections on apartheid and post-apartheid urban orders, in Smith D M (ed), *Apartheid city (entry 5324)*, 292–302

5320 **Schlemmer, L Stack, S L,** *Black, white and shades of grey: a study of responses to residential segregation in the Pretoria-Witwatersrand region.* Johannesburg: Witwatersrand

Univeristy, Centre for Policy Studies, 1990, 250pp

5321 **Schlemmer, L,** Challenges of process and policy, in Swilling M et al (eds), *Apartheid city (entry 5328)*, 350–74

5322 **Scott, D,** The destruction of Clairwood: a case study on the transformation of communal living space, in Smith D M (ed), *Apartheid city (entry 5324)*, 87–98

5323 **Simon, D,** Reform in South Africa and modernisation of the apartheid city, in Drakakis-Smith D (ed), *Urban and regional change (entry 4224)*, 33–65

5324 **Smith, D M,** (ed) *The apartheid city and beyond: urbanisation and social change in South Africa.* London: Routledge, 1992, 322pp

5325 **Snyman, I,** (ed), *The housing challenge: options and means.* Pretoria: Human Sciences Research Council, 1991, 90pp

5326 **Soni, D V,** The apartheid state and Black housing struggles, in Smith D M (ed), *Apartheid city (entry 5324)*, 39–52

5327 **Steinberg, J, et al,** Contradictions in the transition from urban apartheid: barriers to gentrification in Johannesberg, in Smith D M (ed), *Apartheid city (entry 5324)*, 266–78

5328 **Swilling, M, et al,** (eds), *The apartheid city in transition.* Cape Town: OUP, 1991, 376 +19pp

5329 **Theron, P, et al,** *Public and private sector roles in the provision of electricity in urban areas of South Africa.* Cape Town: Economic Trends Research Group, University of Cape Town, 1991, 23pp

5330 **Tomaselli, K, Tomaselli, R,** 'Turning grey': how Westville was won, in Smith D M (ed), *Apartheid city (entry 5324)*, 279–91

5331 **Uys, T,** Belewenis van relatiewe deprivasie in 'n swart stedelike gemeenskap, *South African journal of sociology*, 22, 4 (1991) 117–124

5332 Van der Merwe, I J, In search of an urbanization policy for South Africa: towards a secondary city strategy, *Geography research forum*, 12, (1992) 102–127

5333 Voss, A E, The properties of paradise, *Theoria*, 80 (1992) 117–27

5334 Wolfson, T, Access to urban land, in Swilling M et al (eds), *Apartheid city (entry 5328)*, 230–57

SWAZILAND

General

5335 de Cocquereaumont-Gruget, A, *Le royaume du Swaziland: une état dans l'Afrique du Sud.* Paris: Harmattan, 1992, 286pp

Anthropology

5336 De Hen, F, Music and healers among the Swazi, *Bulletin des séances*, 36, 4 (1990) 665–677

Demography

5337 Warren, C W, et al, The determinants of fertility in Swaziland, *Population studies*, 46, 1 (1992) 5–18

Economic and social history

5338 Sikhondze, B B, The development of Swazi cotton cultivation: some theoretical problems, 1904–1985, *Mohlomi*, 6, (1990) 117–138

5339 Sikhonze, B A B, Monopoly commodity production in Swaziland: the case of cotton, *Eastern African social science research review*, 6,2 & 7/1, (1990/91) 171–81

5340 Simelane, H S, The colonial state, peasants and agricultutural production in Swaziland, *South African historical journal*, 26 (1992) 93–115

5341 Simelane, H S, Landlessness and imperial response in Swaziland 1938–1950, *Journal of southern African studies*, 17, 4 (1991) 717–741

Education

5342 Dlamini, B, Crop production skills possessed and taught by agricultural teachers in Swaziland, *BOLESWA Educational research journal*, 7, (1990) 23–33

5343 Wagana, J K S, An investigation in to factors that influence achievement in the English CDSC examination in Swaziland high schools, *NUL journal of research*, 1, (1991) 53–79

Gender

see also: 5351

5344 Booth, A R, 'European courts protect women and witches': colonial law courts as redistributors of power in Swaziland 1920–1950, *Journal of southern African studies*, 18, 2 (1992) 253–75

5345 McFadden, P, The impact of gender analysis on African development, *Southern Africa political and economic monthly*, 4, 3/4 (1990/1991) 39–42

5346 Rutabanzibwa-Ngaiza, J, *Participation of women in primary health care in Swaziland.* Washington: International Centre for Research on Women, 1990, 56pp

Geography, physical

5347 Van Regenmortal, G, On the differences in rainy season characteristics between extended dry and wet spells in Swaziland,

Eastern and southern Africa geographical journal, 3, 1 (1992) 35–49

History, C20th

5348 Fairlie, M, *No time like the past.* Ely : Pentland Press, 1992, 246pp

Industry & trade

5349 Harrison, D, Tradition, modernity and tourism in Swaziland, in Harrison D (ed), *Tourism and the less developed countries* (London: Belhaven, 1992), 148–62

5350 UNIDO, *Swaziland: enhancing industrial potential.* Vienna: UNIDO, 1992, 71pp

Law

see also: 5344

5351 Adinkrah, K O, Folk law is the culprit: women's 'non-rights' in Swaziland, *Journal of legal pluralism and unofficial law*, 30/31 (1990/1991) 9–31

5352 Adinkrah, K O, 'We shall take our case to the King': legitimacy and tradition in the administration of law in Swaziland, *The comparative and international law journal of southern Africa*, 24, 2 (1991) 226–239

Media

5353 McLean, P E, Radio and rural development in Swaziland, *Africa media review*, 6, 3 (1992) 51–64

Politics

5354 Abena, J, Swaziland, the beginning of the end of monarchist domination?, *Southern Africa political and economic monthly*, 4, 5

(1991) 30–33

5355 Levin, R, Swaziland's 'tinkhundla' and the myth of Swazi tradition, *Journal of contemporary African studies*, 10, 2 (1991) 1–23

5356 Rose, L L, *The politics of harmony: land dispute strategies in Swaziland.* Cambridge: Cambridge University Press, 1992, 234pp

5357 Walakita, P N L, (ed), *Swasiland.* Bad Honnef: Deutsche Stiftung für Internationale Entwicklung, 1990, 93pp

Rural economy

see also: 5342

5358 Russell, M, *African freeholders: a study of individual tenure farms in Swazi ownership.* Madison: University of Wisconsin, Land Tenure Center, 1990, 85pp

ZIMBABWE

General

5359 Baynham, S, (ed), *Zimbabwe in transition.* Stockholm: Almqvist & Wiksell, 1992, 284pp

5360 Lessing, D, *African laughter: four visits to Zimbabwe.* London: Harper and Collins, 1992, 416pp

Agriculture, scientific

5361 Chivinge, O A, A weed survey of arable lands of the small-scale farming sector of Zimbabwe, *Zambezia*, 15, 2 (1988) 167–179

Anthropology

5362 Jacobson-Widding, A, Pits, pots and snakes: an anthropological approach to ancient african symbols, *Nordic journal of African studies*, 1, 1 (1992) 5–27

5363 Ranger, T O, Religion and

witchcraft in everyday life in contemporary Zimbabwe, in Kaarsholm P (ed), *Cultural struggle (entry 4200)*, 167–81

5364 **Reynolds, P,** Dreams and the continuation of self among the Zezuru, in Jedrej M C & Shaw, R (eds), *Dreaming, religion and society (entry 42)*, 21–35

5365 **Schuthof, A, Boerenkamp, M,** *Spirits and survival: religion and crisis management within Tonga society, Zimbabwe.* Utrecht: Utrecht University, 1991, 91pp

Arts

5366 **Chaitanya, K,** The art situation in Zimbabwe, *Africa quarterly*, 30, 3/4 (1990) 112–118

5367 **Mubumbila, V M,** *Sciences et traditions africaines: les messages du Grand Zimbabwe.* Paris: Harmattan, 1992, 109pp

5368 **Williams, S,** Art in Zimbabwe: from colonialism to independence, in Kaarsholm P (ed), *Cultural struggle (entry 4200)*, 61–74

5369 **Winter-Irving, C,** *Stone sculptures in Zimbabwe: context, content and form.* Harare: Roblaw, 1991, 210pp

Economy - Development

see also: 2003, 5516

5370 **Coltart, D,** Economic liberalisation: political protectionism? Zimbabwe's economic outlook, *Legal forum*, 3, 3 (1991) 5–10

5371 **Davies, R, Sanders, D, et al,** Liberalisation for development: Zimbabwe's adjustment without the Fund, in Cornia A G et al (eds), *Africa's recovery (entry 122)*, 135–55

5372 **Friedrich, H J,** Strukturanpassung in Simbabwe: Perspektiven für formelle Ökonomie und Schattenwirtschaft,

Afrika spectrum, 27, 2 (1992) 159–85

5373 **Green, R H, Kahhani, X,** Zimbabwe: transition to economic crises 1981–83 - retrospect and prospect, in *The international monetary system and its reform, part 4* (Amsterdam: North Holland for UN, 1990), 315–57

5374 **Kadenge, P G, et al,** *Zimbabwe's structural adjustment programme: the first year experience.* Harare: SAPES Books, 1992, 26pp

5375 **Knight, V C,** Zimbabwe: the politics of economic reform, *Current history,* 91, 565 (1992) 219–223

5376 **Mlambo, K, Kayizzi-Mugera, S,** The macroeconomics of transition: Zimbabwe in the 1980s, *African development review,* 3, 1 (1991) 47–67

5377 **Riddell, R,** *Zimbabwe to 1996: at the heart of a growing region.* London: Economist Intelligence Unit, 1992, 123pp

5378 **Shreeve, G,** Zimbabwe: a time for cool heads, *Banker,* Sept 1992 21–25

Economic and social history

see also: 3859, 3912, 4588, 5420

5379 **Beach, D N,** Zimbabwean demography: early colonial data, *Zambezia,* 17, 1 (1990) 31–83

5380 **Bessant, L L,** Coercive development: land shortage, forced labour and colonial development in the Chiweshe reserve, colonial Zimbabawe, 1938–1946, *International journal of African historical studies,* 25, 1 (1992) 39–65

5381 **Burrett, R,** The optimistic years: the Ayrshire mine, 1892–1909 and beyond, *Heritage of Zimbabwe,* 10 (1991) 17–30

5382 **Chimhundu, H,** Early missionaries and the ethnolinguistic factor during the 'invention of tribalism'; in Zimbabwe, *Journal of African history,* 33, 1 (1992) 87–109

5383 Gronemeyer, R, (ed), *Der faule Neger: vom weissen Kreuzzug gegen den schwarzen Müssiggang.* Reinbek bei Hamburg: Rowohlt, 1991, 279pp

5384 Johnson, D, Settler farmers and coerced African labour in Southern Rhodesia, 1936–46, *Journal of African history,* 33, 1 (1992) 111–28

5385 Machigaidze, V E M, Land reform in colonial Zimbabwe: the Southern Rhodesia Land Husbandry Act and African response, *Eastern African social science research review,* 6,2 & 7/1, (1990/91) 14–46

5386 Makambe, E P, The Arab labour scheme for the Zimbabwean colonial market, 1900–1902: strategies towards bifurcating the work force, *Mohlomi,* 6, (1990) 55–96

5387 Molomo, L M, Gold mining in precolonial Zimbabwe, in Thomas-Emeagwali G (ed), *Science and technology in African history (entry 3487),* 79–100

5388 Mtisi, J, Relationship between government and private enterprise in the forestry and timber industry: the case of Zimbabwe, 1923–75, *Eastern African social science research review,* 6,2 & 7/1, (1990/91) 47–64

5389 Nyambura, P S, The origins and development of the cotton industry in colonial Zimbabawe, 1903–1935, *Eastern African social science research review,* 6,2 & 7/1, (1990/91) 141–56

5390 Phimister, I, Coal, crisis and class struggle: Wankie colliery, 1918–22, *Journal of African history,* 33, 1 (1992) 65–86

5391 Schmidt, E, *Peasants, traders and wives: Shona women in the history of Zimbabwe, 1870–1939.*

Harare: Boabab; London: Currey, 1992, 289pp

5392 Yoshikuni, T, African Harare, 1890–1925: labour migrancy and an emerging urban community, *African study monographs,* 12, 3 (1991) 133–48

Education

see also: 4600, 5423, 5544

5393 Chivore, B R S, Technical education in post-independent Zimbabwe: conditions of service, *Zimbabwe journal of educational research,* 4, 1 (1992) 71–88

5394 Dzvimbo, K P, Education for liberation and development: a comparison of Cuban and Zimbabwean educational practices, *Zimbabwe journal of educational research,* 3, 3 (1991) 281–308

5395 Dzvimbo, K P, The transition state and the dialectics of educational transformation in the Third World: the case of Zimbabwe, *International studies in the sociology of education,* 1, (1991) 43–58

5396 Edwards, G, Tisdell, C, Private versus government schools: race and the development of Zimbabwe's dual education system, *Scandinavian journal of development alternatives,* 11, 3/4 (1992) 31–49

5397 Jaji, G, Svardh, U, A study of teachers in technical drawing in Zimbabwe schools, *Zimbabwe journal of educational research,* 3, 3 (1991) 246–257

5398 Mandebvu, O S, Pupils' attitudes towards technical/vocational subjects: an exploratory study, *Zimbabwe journal of educational research,* 3, 2 (1991) 163–183

5399 Maposa, F, Problems within the dominant thinking in English language teaching in Zimbabwe today: the need for a new departure, *Zimbabwe journal of educational research*, 3, 2 (1991) 198–204

5400 Mberengwa, L, Integration of weaving into the home economics curriculum in Zimbabwean secondary schools, *Zimbabwe journal of educational research*, 2, 3 (1990) 274–286

5401 Moyana, R, Evidence of acquisition of the reading skill related to comprehension of the narrative passages: data from the international literacy study pilot testing in Zimbabwe, *Zimbabwe journal of educational research*, 3, 2 (1991) 125–143

5402 Mungazi, D A, *Colonial policy and conflict in Zimbabwe: a study of cultures in collision, 1890–1979.* New York: Crane Russak, 1992, 180pp

5403 Nhundu, T J, Interorganizational linkages and the success of cooperative educational programmes in Zimbabwe, *Zimbabwe journal of educational research*, 3, 3 (1991) 258–280

5404 Nkungula, A, Home economics teacher quality in Zimbabwean secondary schools, *Zimbabwe journal of educational research*, 2, 3 (1990) 239–249

5405 Nyagura, L M, A comparative analysis of the quality of primary education in Zimbabwe by school type, *Zimbabwe journal of educational research*, 3, 3 (1991) 208–224

5406 Nyagura, L M, Reece, J L, Teacher quality in Zimbabwe secondary schools, *Zimbabwe journal of educational research*, 2, 3 (1990) 211–238

5407 Schild, T, *Das Bildungssystem als Faktor im Entwicklungsprocess: eine Analyse des Bildungssystems in Zimbabwqe im sieten Jahr der Unabhängigkeit.* Frankfurt: Lang, 1990, 404pp

Environment

5408 Adjer, W N, Chigume, S, Methodologies and institutions in Zimbabwe's evolving environmental assessment framework, *Third World planning review*, 14, 3 (1991) 283–95

5409 Gore, C, et al, *The case for sustainable development in Zimbabwe.* Harare: Environment and Development Activities, 1992, 155pp

5410 Matownayika, J Z Z, Zimbabwe's national conservation strategy: a response to national and international stimuli to sustainable development, *Environment*, 20, 3 (1990) 31–39

5411 Moyo, S, (ed), *Zimbabwe's environmental dilemmas: balancing resource inequities.* Harare: Zimbabwe Environmental Research Organisation, 1991, 165pp

5412 Whitlow, R, Wetland use and abuse in Zimbabwe, *Transactions of the Zimbabwe scientific association*, 65, (1991) 24–33

Finance

5413 Moyo, J, *Politics of the national purse: public budgeting as public policy in Zimbabwe.* Harare: SAPES Books, 1992, 108pp

5414 Moyo, T, Trends of savings in financial intermediaries in Zimbabwe, in Frimpong-Ansah J H & Ingham, B (eds), *Saving for economic recovery (entry 142)*, 139–51

5415 Zhakata, R, Domestic debt management in Zimbabwe, in Roe A R et al (eds) *Instruments of economic policy (entry 341)*, 127–32

Food

5416 Christensen, G, Stack, J, *The*

dimensions of household food security
in Zimbabwe, 1980–1991. Oxford:
International Development Centre,
1992, 33pp

5417 Drakakis-Smith, D,
Strategies for meeting basic food
needs in Harare, in Baker J &
Pedersen, P O (eds), *Rural-urban
interface (entry 1111)*, 258–83

5418 Sachikonye, L M, Zimbabwe:
drought, food and adjustment,
Review of African political economy,
53 (1992) 88–93

5419 Weiner, D, Murphy, M,
Differential vulnerability to severe
agricultural drought in Zimbabwe,
*Eastern and southern Africa
geographical journal,* 3, 1 (1992)
13–33

Gender

see also: 5391

5420 Barnes, T, Win, E, *To live a
better life: an oral history of women in
the city of Harare, 1930–70.* Harare:
Baobab, 1992, 230pp

5421 Frese-Weghöft, G, *Frauen
tragen schwer: vom Alltag der Frauen
in Zimbabwe.* Reinbek bei
Hamburg: Rowohlt Taschenbuch,
1991, 183pp

5422 Gaidzanwa, R B, *The ideology
of domesticity and the struggles of
women workers.* The Hague: ISS,
1992, 15pp

5423 Ilon, L, Fitting girl's schooling
into existing economic paradigms:
confronting the complexities,
*International journal of educational
development,* 12, 2 (1992) 147–59

5424 van Dijk, M P, Women in the
informal sector in industrialising
Zimbabwe, *African development
perspectives yearbook,* 2, (1990/91)
709–720

5425 von Glehn, A, et al, *Sexual
and domestic violence: help, recovery
and action in Zimbabwe.* Harare:
Women and AIDS Support

Network, 1991, 312pp

Geography, human

5426 Heath, R A, Central place
theory and its application in
Zimbabwe, *Geographical
education magazine,* 14, 2 (1991)
53–73

Geography, physical

5427 Vogel, H, Effects of
conservation tillage on sheet
erosion from sandy soils at two
experimental sites in Zimbabwe,
Applied geography, 12, 3 (1992)
229–42

Health & welfare services

5428 Morgan, P, *Rural water
supplies and sanitation.* Basingstoke:
Macmillan, 1990, 358pp

5429 World Bank, *Zimbabwe:
financing health services.*
Washington: World Bank, 1991,
84pp

5430 Zinganga, A F, *Development of
the Zimbabwe family planning
program.* Washington: World Bank,
1992, 13pp

History, general

see also: 450

5431 Schmidt, B, *Zimbabwe: die
Entstehung einer Nation.*
Saarbrucken: Bretenbach, 1991,
185pp

5432 Zamponi, M, Gli stati dello
Zimbabwe pre-coloniale: problemi
di analisi storiografica, *Africa
(Rome),* 47, 2 (1992) 151–72

History, early

5433 Pwiti, G, The Iron Age in
northern Zimbabwe, *Mohlomi,* 6,
(1990) 165–174

History, C19th

5434 Molgård Jensen, S, *Our forefathers' blood: interviews from Zimbabwe.* Copenhagen: Mellomfolkelight Samvirke, 1992, 109pp

History, C20th

5435 Baumgertner, J, Beginn der Missionstätigkeit der SMB in Simbabwe: Johannes Beckmanns Erkundungsreise ins südliche Afrika 1938/39, *Neue Zeitschrift für Missionswissenschaft,* 48, 2 (1992) 81–114

5436 Sithole, M, Turmoil and tenacity: the road to the Unity Accord, *Zambezia,* 18, 2 (1991) 143–52

5437 West, M O, Ndabaniningi Sithole, Garfield Todd and the Dadaya School strike of 1947, *Journal of southern African studies,* 18, 2 (1992) 297–316

5438 Whyte, B, *Yesterday, today and tomorrow.* Harare: David Burke, 1990, 245pp

5439 Zvobgo, C J M, *The Wesleyan Methodist Missions in Zimbabwe 1891–1945.* Harare: University of Zimbabwe, 1991, 169pp

Industry & trade

see also: 521, 5424

5440 Bowen, B H, Nyemba, W R, Machine tool strategy for increased output to the export market, *Mining and engineering,* 56, 8 (1991) 11–15

5441 Lue-Mbizvo, C, (ed), *Proceedings of the ZERO workshop on energy, technology and rural industrial development: issues and prospects.* Harare: Zimbabwe Energy Research Organisation, 1991, 42pp

5442 Mair, S, Agricultural demand-led industrialisation: an option for Zimbabwe?, *African development perspectives yearbook,* 2, (1990/91) 556–576

5443 Rasmussen, J, Entreprenurial milieu in smaller towns: the case of Masvingo, Zimbabwe, in Baker J & Pedersen, P O (eds), *Rural-urban interface (entry 1111),* 171–86

5444 Rasmussen, J, *The entrepreneurial milieu: enterprise networks in small Zimbabwean towns.* Copenhagen: Roskilde University, Dept. of Geography, 1992, 299pp

5445 Riddell, R, Manufacturing sector development in Zimbabwe and the Côte d'Ivoire, in Stewart F et al (eds), *Alternative development strategies (entry 223),* 215–37

5446 Stoneman, C, Policy reform or industrialisation? The choice in Zimbabwe, in Adhikari R et al (eds), *Industrial and trade policy reform in developing countries* (Manchester: Manchester UP, 1992), 97–110

International economic relations

No entry, see also: 5440

International relations

5447 Barber, J, *Zimbabwe's regional role: prospects of a land-locked power.* London: Institute of Strategic Studies, 1991, 32pp

5448 Polhemus, J H, Zimbabwe's response to change in South Africa, in Etherington N (ed), *Peace, politics and violence (entry 5047),* 196–212

Labour & manpower

5449 Analoui, F, *Management development for senior officials: a study in Zimbabwe.* Bradford: Bradford University, Project Planning Centre, 1990, 20pp

5450 Cheater, A P, Industrial organisation in the first decade of

Zimbabwe's independence, *Zambezia,* 18, 1 (1991) 1–14

5451 Fallon, F R, Lucas, R E B, The impact of changes in job security regulation in India and Zimbabwe, *World bank economic review,* 5, 3 (1991) 395–413

5452 Gaidzanwa, R, Labour relations in a Zimbabwean mining enterprise established after independence, *Zambezia,* 18, 1 (1991) 49–67

5453 Gaidzanwa, R B, *An organisational study of five trade unions: final report.* Harare: Friedrich Ebert Foundation, 1990, 52, 33pp

5454 Maphosa, G J, Industrial democracy in Zimbabwe?, *Zambezia,* 18, 1 (1991) 15–24

5455 Mutizwa-Mangiza, D, An evaluation of workers' real participation in decision-making at enterprise level, *Zambezia,* 18, 1 (1991) 35–48

5456 Sachikonye, L M, Industrial relations crisis?: an anatomy of recent strikes in Zimbabwe, *Southern Africa political & economic monthly,* 3, 12 (1990) 37–44

5457 Shadur, M A, Labour relations in a Zimbabwean parastatal enterprise, *Zambezia,* 18, 1 (1991) 25–34

Language

5458 Mparutsa, C, et al, An investigation into language attitudes of secondary-school students in Zimbabwe, *Zambezia,* 17, 1 (1990) 85–100

Law

see also: 688

5459 Anon, The constitution and the economy: the Zimbabwe experience, *Legal forum,* 3, 4 (1991) 28–36

5460 Cutshall, C R, *Justice for the people: community courts and legal transformation in Zimbabwe.* Harare: University of Zimbabwe, 1991, 341pp

5461 Ncube, W, Dealing with inequities in customary law: action, reaction and social change in Zimbabwe, *International journal of law and the family,* 5, 1 (1991) 58–79

5462 Ncube, W, Nzombe, S, Continuity and change in the constitutional development of Zimbabwe, in Kaarsholm P (ed), *Cultural struggle (entry 4200),* 167–81

Library - documentation

see also: 666

5463 Chung, F, The growth and development of libraries in light of the changing current economic environment, *The Zimbabwe librarian,* 23, 1 (1991) 3–6

5464 Doust, R W, The problem of book supply in Zimbabwean libraries, *The Zimbabwe librarian,* 23, 1 (1991) 9–14

5465 Podmore, E A, Human resources in libraries in a developing Zimbabwe: a dual thrust, *The Zimbabwe librarian,* 23, 1 (1991) 19–22

Literature

5466 Caute, D, Marechera in black and white, in Kaarsholm P (ed), *Cultural struggle (entry 4200),* 95–111

5467 Flockemann, M, 'Not-quite insiders and not-quite outsiders': the 'process of womanhood' in *Beka Lamb, Nervous conditions,* and *Daughters of the twilight, Journal of Commonwealth literature,* 27, 1 (1992) 37–47

5468 Foster, K, Soul-food for the starving: Dambudzo Marechera's

House of hunger, Journal of Commonwealth literature, 27, 1 (1992) 58–70

5469 Kaarsholm, P, From decadence to authenticity and beyond: fantasies and mythologies of war in Rhodesia and Zimbabwe, 1965–1985, in Kaarsholm P (ed), *Cultural struggle (entry 4200)*, 33–60

5470 McLoughlin, T O, Ways of seeing the rural landscape in Zimbabwean fiction and painting, *Commonwealth : essays and studies*, 14, 2 (1992) 61–68

5471 Mutswaito, I S M, A Zimbabwean poet writing in English: a critical appraisal of Masaemun Bonas Zimunya's *Thought tracks, Zambezia*, 18, 2 (1991) 105–118

5472 Thomas, S, Killing the hysteric in the colonised's house: Tsitsi Dangarembga's *Nervous conditions, Journal of Commonwealth literature*, 27, 1 (1992) 26–36

5473 Viet-Wild, F, *Dambudzo Marechera: a sourcebook.* Oxford: Zell, 1992, 419pp

5474 Viet-Wild, F, *Teachers, preachers and non-believers: a social history of Zimbabwean literature.* Oxford: Zell, 1992, 408pp

Media

5475 Rusike, E T M, *The politics of the mass media.* Harare: Roblaw, 1990, 111pp

Medical

5476 Chandiwana, T, et al, Community control of schistosomiasis in Zimbabwe, *Central african journal of medecine*, 37, 3 (1991) 69–77

5477 Finkenflugel, H J M, Identifying people in need of rehabilitation in rural Zimbabwe, *Central African journal of medecine*,

37, 4 (1991) 105–109

5478 Moy, R J, et al, Recurrent and persistent diarrhoea in a rural Zimbabwean community: a prospective study, *Journal of tropical pediatrics*, 37, 6 (1991) 293–299

5479 Research Unit, *AIDS home care: a baseline survey in Zimbabwe.* Harare: School of Social Work, University of Zimbabwe, 1992, 48pp

5480 Tumwine, J K, Measles control in a rural area in Zimbabwe, *East African medical journal*, 68, 9 (1991) 694–701

5481 Whiteside, A, HIV infection and AIDS in Zimbabwe, *Industrial review (Zimbabwe)*, (1991) 29–35

Natural resources

5482 MacKenzie, J M, The natural world and the popular consciousness in southern Africa: the European appropriation of nature, in Kaarsholm P (ed), *Cultural struggle (entry 4200)*, 13–31

5483 Robertson, F, The natural resources of Hwedza Mountain Forest Reserve, *Zimbabwe science news*, 25, 7/9 (1991) 65–71

Planning

see also: 783

5484 de Valk, P, An analysis of planning policy with reference to Zimbabwe, in de Valk P & Wekwete, K H (eds), *Decentralising (entry 5485)*, 52–72

5485 de Valk, P, Wekwete, K H (eds), *Decentralising for participatory planning.* Aldershot: Gower, 1990, 283pp

5485a Rambanapasi, C, The political economy of public participation in planning in pluralist societies: the case of Zimbabwe, *Geoforium*, 23, 1 (1992) 95–104

5486 Wekwete, K H, Constraints to planning for socialism in Zimbabwe, in de Valk P & Wekwete, K H (eds), *Decentralising (entry 5485)*, 37–51

5487 Wekwete, K H, Mlalazi, A, Provincial/regional planning in Zimbabwe: problems and prospects, in de Valk P & Wekwete, K H (eds), *Decentralising (entry 5485)*, 73–85

5488 Wekwete, K H, Munswa, S, The role of external development agencies in district planning in Zimbabwe: a case study of districts in Masvingo province, in de Valk P & Wekwete, K H (eds), *Decentralising (entry 5485)*, 99–115

Politics

5489 Alexander, J, The unsettled land: the politics of land redistribution in Matabeleland, 1980–1990, *Journal of southern african studies,* 17, 4 (1991) 581–610

5490 Amin, N, State and peasantry in Zimbabwe since independence, *European journal of development research,* 4, 1 (1992) 112–62

5491 Chimanikire, D P, The significance of the unity accord between ZANU-PF and PF-ZAPU, *Taamuli,* NS 2, 1/2 (1991) 61–72

5492 Curriculum Development Unit, *Children of history.* Harare: Baobab, 1992, 91pp

5493 de Valk, P, Wekwete, K H, Challenges for local government in Zimbabwe, in de Valk P & Wekwete, K H (eds), *Decentralising (entry 5485)*, 86–98

5494 Döpcke, W, *Bauern und Guerillas in Zimbabwe: eine Literaturübersicht zu neuren Studien zum Befreiungskampf.* Stuttgart: Zimbabwe Netzwerk, 1991, 43pp

5495 Evans, M, Making an African army: the case of Zimbabwe, 1980–87, in Etherington N (ed), *Peace, politics and violence (entry 5047)*, 231–53

5496 Gowlland-Debbas, V, Collective responses to the unilateral declarations of independence of Southern Rhodesia and Palestine: an application of the legitimizing function of the United Nations, *British yearbook of international law,* 61, (1990) 135–153

5497 Gustaffson, L, et al, *Keeping the goals in sight: an evaluation of Swedish suport to public administration in Zimbabwe.* Stockholm: SIDA, 1991, 41pp

5498 Helmsing, A H J, et al, *Limits to decentralisation in Zimbabwe: essays on the decentralisation of government and p[lanning ni the 1980s.* The Hague: Institute of Social Studies, 1991, 177pp

5499 Kleinmeulman, D, *Income-generating projects of urban councils in Zimbabwe: contribution to socio-economic development and more financial autonomy?* The Hague: International Union of Local Authorities, 1991, 56pp

5500 Knight, V C, Growing opposition in Zimbabwe, *Issue,* 20, 1 (1992) 23–30

5501 Kriele, R, *Zimbabwe: von der Befreiungsbewegung zur Staatsmacht.* Saarbrucken: Brietenbach, 1990, 236pp

5502 Kriger, N, Popular struggles in Zimbabwe's war of national liberation, in Kaarsholm P (ed), *Cultural struggle (entry 4200)*, 125–48

5503 Kriger, N, *Zimbabwe's guerilla war: peasant voices.* Cambridge: Cambridge University Press, 1992, 303pp

5504 Manyungo, K D, The peasantry in Zimbabwe: a vehicle for change, in Kaarsholm P (ed), *Cultural struggle (entry 4200)*, 115–24

5505 Mhlaba, L, Local cultures and development in Zimbabwe: the case of Matabeleland, in Kaarsholm P (ed), *Cultural struggle (entry 4200)*, 209–25

5506 Moyo, J N, Democracy in the African reality: policy relevance of leftist intellectuals, *Africa quarterly*, 31, 1/2 (1991) 47–58

5507 Moyo, J, *Voting for democracy: a study of electoral politics in Zimbabwe.* Harare: University of Zimbabwe Publications, 1992, 244pp

5508 Mutizwa-Mangiza, N D, Rural local govenrment finance in Zimbabwe: the case of Gokwe District Council, *Public administration and development*, 12, 1 (1992) 111–22

5509 Nyathi, P T, Resettling ex-combatants: the experience of the Zimbabwe project, in NGLS (ed), *Voices from Africa 3 (entry 913)*, 118–25

5510 Quantin, P, *Qui gouverne le Zimbabwe? Esquisse d'un portrait de groupe.* Talence: Université de Bordeaux, CEAN, 1992, 19pp

5511 Raftopolous, B, Beyond the house of hunger: democratic struggle in Zimbabwe, *Review of African political economy*, 54 (1992) 59–74, & 55, 57–66

5512 Ranger, T, War, violence and healing, *Journal of southern African studies*, 18, 3 (1992) 698–707

5513 Skalnes, T, *Politisk liberalisering og konomisk reform.* Bergen: Chr. Michelsens Institute, 1992, 10pp

5514 Weitzer, R, *Transforming settler states: communal conflict and internal security in Northern Ireland and Zimbabwe.* Berkeley: University of California Press, 1990, 278pp

5515 Wekwete, K, Urban local government finance in Zimbabwe:

the case of Harare City Council, *Public administration and development*, 12, 1 (1992) 97–110

Religion, philosophy

see also: 4315

5516 Gasper, D, *Equity, equality and appropriate distribution: multiple interpretations and Zimbabwean usages.* The Hague: ISS, 1991, 23pp

5517 Marioti, L, *Il millennio in Africa. L'Apostolic Church of John Maranke': percorso storico-antropologico di sincretismo religioso e culturale nello Zimbabwe.* Tome: University of Rome, 1991, 226pp

5518 Mungazi, D, *The honoured crusade: Ralph Dodge's theology of liberation and initiatives for social change in Zimbabwe.* Gweru: Mambo, 1991, 142pp

Rural economy

see also: 1020, 4166, 5488

5519 Assefa Mehretu, Mutambirwa, C, Time and energy costs of distance in rural life space of Zimbabwe: a case study in the Chiduku Communal Area, *Social science and medicine*, 34, 1 (1992) 17–24

5520 Ayoub, Y, *Terre des hommes in Zimbabwe.* Osnabrück: Terre des hommes, 1991, 43pp

5521 Cousins, B, Weiner, D, Amin, N, Social differentiation in the communal lands of Zimbabwe, *Review of African political economy*, 53 (1992) 5–24

5522 Cusworth, J, Zimbabwe: issues arising from the Land Resettlement Programme, in Dudley N et al (eds), *Land is life: land reform and sustainable agriculture* (London: Intermediate Technology, 1992), 89–101

5523 Gasper, D, *What happened to*

the land question in Zimbabwe? *Rural reform in the 1980s.* The Hague: Institute of Social Studies, 1990, 41pp

5524 Gutto, S B O, Land and agrarian questions and problems of democratisation in Zimbabwe, in Rudebeck L (ed), *When democracy makes sense (entry 931),* 285–307

5525 Herbst, J, The dilemmas of land policy in Zimbabwe, *Africa insight,* 21, 4 (1991) 269–76

5526 Jamela, S, The challenges facing African NGOs: a case-study approach, in NGLS (ed), *Voices from Africa 2 (entry 195),* 17–27

5527 Loewenson, R, *Modern plantation agriculture: corporate wealth and labour squalor.* London: Zed, 1992, 147pp

5528 Mangwende, W, The land question in Zimbabwe: 10 years after, *Southern Africa political and economic monthly,* 4, 3/4 (1990/1991) 23–26

5529 Moyo, S Ngobese, P, *Issues for agricultural employment development in Zimbabwe.* Harare: ZIDS, 1991, 61pp

5530 Muir, A, Riddell, R, *Evaluating the impact of NGOs in rural poverty alleviation: Zimbabwe country study.* London: ODI, 1992, 126pp

5531 National Farmers Association of Zimbabwe, The Zimbabwean viewpoint, in Obasanjo O & d'Orville, H (eds), *Agricultural production and food security (entry 1040),* 77–81

5532 Ndiweni, M, *Involving farmers in rural technologies: case studies of Zimbabwean NGOs.* London: ODI, 1991, 54pp

5533 Pankhurst, D, Constraints and incentives in 'successful' Zimbabwean peasant agriculture: the interaction between gender and class, *Journal of southern African studies,* 17, 4 (1991) 611–632

5534 Pedersen, P O, Agricultural marketing and processing in small towns in Zimbabwe: Gutu and Gokwe, in Baker J & Pedersen, P O (eds), *Rural-urban interface (entry 1111),* 102–24

5535 Skålnes, T, Moyo, S, *Land reform and economic development strategy in Zimbabwe: state autonomy and the policy lobby.* Bergen: CMI, and Harare: ZIDS, 1990, 27pp

5536 Young, T, Hamdoh, A A, *The effects of change in household composition on consumption: Matabeleland South Province, Zimbabwe.* Manchester: Manchester University, Dept. of Agricultural Economics, 1992, 17pp

5537 Zinyama, L M, Local farmer organisations and rural development in Zimbabwe, in Taylor D R F & Mackenzie, F (eds), *Development from within (entry 1061),* 33–57

5538 Zinyama, L, Technology adoption and post-independence transformation of the small-scale farming sector in Zimbabwe, in Drakakis-Smith D (ed), *Urban and regional change (entry 4224),* 180–202

Science & technology

see also: 1082

5539 Robson, M, Introducing technology through science education: a case study from Zimbabwe, *Science, technology and development,* 10, 2 (1992) 203–21

Sociology

5540 Cheater, A P, *Industrial sociology in the first decade of Zimbabwean independence.* Harare: University of Zimbabwe, 1992, 88pp

5541 Cheater, A P, 'We are taken as shovels, used and put aside...'. Anthropological perspectives on the organisation of work and workers in Zimbabwean industry in the first decade of independence, *Zambezia*, 18, 1 (1991) 69–83

5542 Moyo, J N, State politics and social domination in Zimbabwe, *Journal of modern African studies*, 30, 2 (1992) 305–30

5543 Schmidt, K J, *Der Weg nach Zimbabwe oder: Versuche, die Fremde zu verstehen.* Hamburg: Ergebnisse, 1990, 284pp

5544 Siyakwazi, P D, Young people's attitudes towards household work: an analysis by age and its implications on home economics curriculum at secondary level, *Zimbabwe journal of educational research*, 4, 1 (1992) 32–48

5545 Zindi, F, Experimental substance use among rural and urban teenagers in Zimbabwe, *Zimbabwe journal of educational research*, 4, 1 (1992) 1–16

Urban studies

see also: 1939, 2423, 5426

5546 Davies, R J, Lessons from the Harare, Zimbabwe, experiment, in Smith D M (ed), *Apartheid city (entry 5324)*, 303–13

5547 Drakakis-Smith, D, Urbanisation and urban social change in Zimbabwe, in Drakakis-Smith D (ed), *Urban and regional change (entry 4224)*, 100–120

5548 Gervais-Lambony, M-A, Gervais-Lambony, P, Harare 10 years on, *Eastern and southern Africa geographical journal*, 3, 1 (1992) 75–84

5549 Mafico, C J C, *Urban low-income housing in Zimbabwe.* Aldershot: Avebury, 1991, 175pp

5550 Mutizwa-Mangiza, N D, *Planning suburban service centres in Harare, Zimbabwe. A study of structure, use patterns and needs with special reference to retaining in high-density residential areas.* Harare: University of Zimbabwe, 1991, 154pp

ISLANDS

General

5551 Houbert, J, The Mascareignes, the Seychelles and Chagos, islands with a French connection: security in a decolonised Indian Ocean, in Hintjens H M & Newitt, M D D (eds), *The political economy of small tropical islands* (Exeter: University of Exeter Press, 1992), 93–111

Environment

5552 Gable, F J, et al, Global environmental change issues in the western Indian Ocean region, *Geoforum,* 22, 4 (1991) 401–19

Geography, human

5553 Hébert, J C, L'équation dina morare = memorare = Zarin (Seychelles): (à partir des cartes de Cantino et de Çabot), *Études Océan Indien,* 13 (1991) 65–118

History, general

5554 Gerbeau, H, Les Indiens des Mascareignes: simples jalons pour l'histoire d'une reussite (XVIIe-XXe siècle), *Annulaire des pays de l'Océan Indien,* 12 (1990/91) 15–45

International relations

5555 Houbert, J, The Indian Ocean creole islands: geo-politics and decolonisation, *Journal of modern African studies,* 30, 3 (1992) 465–84

CAPE VERDE

Environment

5556 Courel, M F, Chamard, P C, Reforestation au Cap-Vert, *Afrique contemporaine,* 161 (1992) 238–247

History, general

5557 de Alberquerque, L, Santos, M E M, (ed), *História geral de Cabo Verde.* Lisbon: Centro des Estudos de História e Cartografia Antiga, 1991, 4 parts,

Literature

5558 Gomes da Silva, C A, An introduction to Capeverdean poetry of Portuguese expression, in Nethersole R (ed), *Emerging literatures (entry 726),* 91–105

5559 Nascimento, L G, The socio-political dimensions of Cape Verdean narrative, *Africa (Sïo Paulo),* 14/15 (1991/92) 81–89

Politics

5560 Cahen, M, La fortune changeante des Isles du Cap-Vert, *International journal of African historical studies,* 25, 1 (1992) 129–36

5561 Lima, A R, *Reforma politica em Capo Verde: do paternalismo a*

modernizaciö do estado. Praia:
Grafedito-Praia, 1991, 171pp

COMORES

General

5562 Blanchy-Daurel, S, *La vie
quotidienne à Mayotte.* Paris:
Harmattan, 1990, 239pp

Economy - Development

No entry: see also: 5636

Economic and social history

5563 Ottenheimer, M, Social
organisation and Indian Ocean
long distance trade, *Zetschrift für
Ethnologie,* 116, (1991) 125–24
5564 Wright, H T, Early Islam,
oceanic trade and town
development on Nzwani: the
Comorian Archipelago in the
11th-15th centuries AD, *Azania,*
27, (1992) 81–128

Finance

5565 Chacourou-Abal Anrabe, A,
*Le contrôle des finances publiques aux
Comores.* Paris: Harmattan, 1992,
368pp

Geography, human

5566 Couesnon, P, Mayotte: vers
quel avenir?, *Acta geographica,* 85,
(1991) 14–23

International relations

5567 Fasquel, J, *Mayotte, les
Comores et la France.* Paris:
Harmattan, 1991, 159pp
5568 Mahamoud, A, *Mayotte: le
contentieux entre France et les
Comores.* Paris: Harmattan, 1992,
304pp

Rural economy

5569 Anon, Découvrir Mayotte:
Boueni, commune du sud, *Jana na
Leo,* 24 (1991) 29–44
5570 Cheyssial, E, Qui a le courage
d'être agriculteur?, *Jana na Leo,* 24
(1991) 12–28

MADAGASCAR

Anthropology

5571 Beaujard, P, *Mythe et société à
Madagascar.* Paris: Harmattan,
1991, 611pp
5572 Lambek, M, Taboo as
cultutural practice among Malagasy
speakers, *Man,* 27, 2 (1992)
245–66
**5573 Vérin, P, Rajaonarimanana,
N,** Divination in Madagascar: the
Antemoro case and the diffusion of
divination, in Peek P M (ed),
African divination (entry 48),
53–68

Economy - Development

see also: 157
5574 Blardone, G, Stratégie de
développement et ajustements
structurels, une alternative à la
politique du FMI: application à
Madagascar et à la Tanzanie,
*Canadian journal of development
studies,* 13, 3 (1992) 433–442
5575 Rakotobe, F, *Pauvreté et
marché du travail à Antananarivo
(Madagascar).* Geneva:
International Institute for Labour
Studies, 1992, 61pp

Environment

5576 Raherimalala, E S, Les
enjeux de l'environnement, *Matoy,*
3 (1991) 19–20

Education

No entry: see also: 2310

Geography, physical

5577 Falloux, F, Institutional aspects of remote sensing and environmental data management issues and recommendations, in Gastellu-Etchegorry J P (ed), *Satellite remote sensing (entry 412)*, 207–215

History, general

5578 Jacob, G, (ed), *Regards sur Madagascar et la Révolution française.* Antananarivo: ed. CNAPMAD, 1990, 198pp

5579 Mantoux, C G, L'Islam noir et blanc de la côte des Zenj à Madagascar, d'après des écrits anciens et des manuscrits arabo-malagasy, *Recherches et documents,* 10 (1991) 1–77

5580 Wright, H, Fanony, F, L'évolution des systèmes d'occupation des sols dans la vallée de la rivière Mananara au nord-est de Madagascar, *Taloha,* 11 (1992) 16–64

History, C6–18th

5581 Molet-Sauvaget, A, Madagascar et les colonies d'Amérique pendent la grande période de la piraterie européenne (1680–1700): contexte et documents de base, *Études océan Indien,* 13 (1991) 7–63

History, C19th

5582 Raison-Jourde, F, *Bible et pouvoir à Madagascar au XIXe siècle: invention d'une identité chretienne et construction de l'Etat.* Paris: Karthala, 1991, 840pp

5583 Vérin, P, Etats ou cités-états dans le nord du Madagascar, *Taloha,* 11 (1992) 65–70

International economic relations

5584 Milner, C, Short- and long-run incidence of protection: the case of Madagascar, *Applied economics,* 24, 2 (1992) 257–63

5585 Rabetafika, R, Relance économique à Madagascar: code des investissements et zone franche industrielle: premier bilan et perspectives, *Annulaire des pays de l'Océan Indien,* 12 (1990/91) 469–511

International relations

5586 Zafimahova, S, Les enjeux régionaux, *Géopolitique africaine,* 14, (1991) 35–46

Natural resources

5587 Ghimire, K B, *Parks and people: livelihood issues in national parks management in Thailand and Madagascar.* Geneva: UNRISD, 1991,

Politics

5588 Deleris, F, Madagascar: la longue marche des pauvres, *Géopolitique africaine,* 14, (1991) 1–13

5589 Everts, N, Madagascar: historische achtergronden van een politieke opening, *Derde Wereld,* 11, 2 (1992) 19–30

5590 Manantenasoa, P, Foi chrétienne et engagement politique: clefs pour mieux comprendre le mouvement populaire, *Géopolitique africaine,* 14, (1991) 15–21

5591 Serpa, E, Madagascar: change and continuity, *Africa insight,* 21, 4 (1991) 233–45

5592 Zafimahova, S, Genèse d'une révolution, *Géopolitique africaine,* 14, (1991) 23–33

Religion, philosophy

see also: 5579
5593 Jaovelo-Dzao, R, La sagesse malgache, *Recherches et documents,* 11 (1991) 1–49

Rural economy

5594 Droy, I, La rehabilitation des petits périmètres irrigués à Madagascar: une réponse aux importations de riz?, *Cahiers des sciences humaines,* 27, 1/2 (1991) 117–127
5595 Hewitt, A, Madagascar, in Duncan A & Howell, J (eds), *Structural adjustment and the African farmer (entry 1017),* 86–112
5596 Velonantenaina, J W, et al, Petits périmètres irrigués, l'ire des paysans, *Matoy,* 4 (1991) 6–12

Sociology

5597 Gallon, T-P, Mythos oder Methode bei der Planung von Partizipation: die verklärte 'Fokonolona'- Tradition und 'soziale Integration' in einem madegassischen Dorf, *Afrika spectrum,* 26, 2 (1991) 181–197
5598 Rakotondrabe, M, La culture malgache face à la dialectique de la tradition et la modernité, *Recherches et documents,* 11 (1991) 51–79

Urban studies

No entry: see also: 1480

MAURITIUS

Demography

5599 Greenaway, D, Milner, C,

Did Mauritius really provide a 'case study in Malthusian economics'?, *Journal of international development,* 3, 4 (1991) 325–38

Economy - Development

see also: 5599
5600 Ecalle, F, et al, L'ajustement structurel de l'île Maurice, *L'économie de la Réunion,* 53 (1991) 13–19
5601 Shams, R, Mauritius: crisis and successful adjustment, *African development perspectives yearbook,* 2, (1990/91) 488–501
5602 Yin, P, et al, *L'Ile Maurice et sa zone franche: la deuxième phase de développement.* Rose Hill: Editions de l'Ocean Indien, 1992, 183pp

Economic and social history

5603 Bethelot, L, *Chambre de Commerce et d'Industries de Maurice: histoire de la plus ancienne institution du secteur privé mauricien.* Port Louis: La Sentinelle, 1991, 158pp
5604 Rouillard, G, *Historique de la canne à sucre à l'Ile Maurice 1639–1989.* n.p.: Mauritius Stationery Manufacturers, 1990, 50pp

Education

5605 Glover, V, et al, Commentaires critiques sur le Master Plan Education for the Year 2000, *Journal of the Mauritius Institute of Education,* 12 (1991/1992) 13–30
5606 Manrakhan, J, *The university in search of past and future.* Rose Hill: Ed. de l'Océan Indien, 1990, 90pp

Finance

5607 Paratian, R G, Ile Maurice:

les mutations en cours dans le système financière, *Annulaire des pays de l'Océan Indien,* 12 (1990/91) 533–44

Geography, human

5608 **Lebigre, J M,** Les marais maritimes de Mauritanie: protection et valorisation, *Les cahiers d'outre-mer,* 44, 176 (1991) 379–400

History, general

5609 **Sewtohul, N,** *L'Ile Maurice à travers ses villages: l'histoire du village de Triolet.* Port Louis: Proag Printing, 1990, 164pp

Industry & trade

5610 **Dordain, D, Hein, P,** Economie ouverte et industrialisation: le cas de l'île Maurice, *L'economie de la Réunion,* 53 (1991) 3–12

International economic relations

see also: 3548
5611 **Jeetun, A,** Trade with South Africa: future perspectives, *Eco,* 10 (1991) 18–32

Library - documentation

5612 **Bennett, P R,** *Mauritius.* Oxford: Clio, 1992, 200pp

Politics

5613 **Dukhira, C D,** *Mauritius and local government management.* Rose Hill: Editions de l'Océan Indien, 1992, 374pp
5614 **Eriksen, T H,** Containing conflict and transcending ethnicity in Mauritius, in Rupesinghe K (ed), *Internal conflict (entry 932),* 103–29

5615 **Mathur, H,** *Parliament in Mauritius.* Rose Hill: Editions de l'Ocean Indien, 1991, 321pp
5616 **Oodiah, M D /Teelock, A,** *Mouvement militant mauricien: 20 ans d'histoire (1969–1989).* Port Louis: Electronic Graphic Systems, 1990 (?), 221, 62pp

REUNION

Agriculture, scientific

5617 **Chastel, J M,** La mécanisation de la récolte de la canne à sucre à la Réunion: situation et perspectives, *L'agronomie tropicale,* 45, 4 (1990) 311–319

Demography

5618 **Pavageau, C,** Recensement: évolutions spatiales, l'ouest confirme, le sud surprend, *L'économie de la Réunion,* 49 (1990) 14–17

Finance

5619 **Callière, A, Pavageau, C,** La défiscalisation: quatre ans de défiscalisation pour les particuliers, *L'economie de la Réunion,* 53 (1991) 40–44

History, C6–18th

5620 **Wanquet, C,** *Les premiers députés de La Réunion à l'Assemblée Nationale.* Paris: Karthala, 1992, 240pp

History, C19th

5621 **Payet, J V,** *Histoire et escalavage à l'île Bourbon.* Parsi: Harmattan, 1990, 127pp

Industry & trade

5622 **Cheung Chin Tun, Y,** Les

petites entreprises industrielles à la Réunion en 1988, *L'economie de la Réunion*, 52 (1991) 21–29

5623 Cheung, Y C T, Tourisme à la Réunion, *L'economie de la Réunion*, 49 (1990) 19–23

Literature

5624 Sam-Long, J F, *Guide bibliographique de al poésie réunionnaie d'expression française et créole.* Saint Denis: Ed. du Travail, 1990, 102pp

Rural economy

5625 Guellec, A, L'aménagement des Hauts à la Réunion, *Annales de géographie*, 563, (1992) 1–27

Sociology

5626 Trotet, A, Le Cointre, G, Les terres agricoles: une modernisation en ordre dispersé, *L'economie de la Réunion*, 48 (1990) 7–12

5627 Cimbaro, P, Malgré une aggravation certaine la délinquance reste peu fréquente, *L'économie de la Réunion*, 58 (1992) 2–10

5628 Colliez, J P, La migration: croissance du courant issu de l'hexagone, *L'economie de la Réunion*, 53 (1991) 22–29

5629 Ghasarian, C, *Honneur, chance et destin: la culture indienne à la Réunion.* Paris: Harmattan, 1992, 255pp

Urban studies

5630 Boyer, J M, Jacod, M, Le logement à la Réunion: aujourd'hui et demain. [Pt. 1] Un parc de logements en extension inévitable, *L'economie de la Réunion*, 47 (1990) 2–5

5631 Boyer, J M, Jacod, M, Le logement à la Réunion: aujourd'hui

et demain. [Pt. 2] une amélioration rapide de l'habitat, *L'economie de la Réunion*, 47 (1990) 13–23

5632 Boyer, J M, Jacod, M, Le logement à la Réunion: aujourd'hui et demain. [Pt. 3] Un environnement économique difficile, *L'economie de la Réunion*, 47 (1990) 24–30

5633 Boyer, J M, Jacod, M, Le logement à la Réunion: aujourd'hui et demain. [Pt. 4] Des ménages aux possibilités financières limitées, *L'economie de la Réunion*, 47 (1990) 31–44

5634 Jacod, M, Pavageau, C, Aides au logement: un éventail de scénarios pour 1995, *L'économie de la Réunion*, 52 (1991) 3–19

SAO TOME

Economy - Development

5635 Ferreira, M E, Pobreza absoluta e desigualdades sociais, ajustamento estrutural e democracia na R.D. São Tomé e Príncipe, *Revista internacional de estudos africanos*, 12/13, (1990) 137–166

5636 Newitt, M D D, The perils of being a microstate: São Tomé and the Comoros Islands since independence, in Hintjens H M & Newitt, M D D (eds), *The political economy of small tropical islands* (Exeter: University of Exeter Press, 1992), 76–92

5637 Pinto da Costa, H, Towards an alternative development policy for São Tomé and Principe, in Hintjens H M & Newitt, M D D (eds), *The political economy of small tropical islands* (Exeter: University of Exeter Press, 1992), 112–22

Economic and social history

5638 Garfield, Robert, *A history of*

São Tome Island, 1470–1655: the key to Guinea. Lewiston: Mellen, 1992, 327pp

History, C20th

5639 Nascimento, A, Conflitos de europeus em S. Tomé e Príncipe em 1910, *Revista internacional de estudos africanos,* 12/13, (1990) 57–97

SEYCHELLES

Industry & trade

5640 Vorlaufer, K, Die Seychellen: Tourismus ais Entwicklungsoption für einen insularen Kleinstaat, *Afrika spectrum,* 26, 2 (1991) 221–255

AUTHOR INDEX

Bogonko, S N, 1895, 2020, 2021
Bohle, H G, 348
Böhmer, J, 109
Böhmer-Bauer, K, 1882
Bois, M, 1254
Boissier, A, 2905
Boissonade, E, 4057
Boister, N, 4883
Boisvert, J, 3724
Bojo, S, 4410
Bola, N B, 4059
Bolaji, A B O, 3488
Bolakonga Bobwo, 3967, 3968
Bolland, R, 2981, 2984
Bondzi-Simpson, P E, 537
Bonfils, J, 2643
Bongartz, M, 1730
Bonn, C, 1255, 1256
Bonnardel, R, 378
Bonnefous, M, 1168
Bönneman, B, 5009
Bontinck, F, 457, 3969
Bonzon, A, 5217
Boone, C, 3524
Booth, A R, 5344
Booth, D, 2286, 2390
Booth, M, 1360
Boraine, A, 5010
Borenane, N, 110
Bornstein, 1696
Borsch, L, 4148
Bosc, P M, 2528, 2608
Botes, L J S, 5011
Botha, E, 4927
Botha, M, 4513
Botha, P du T, 612
Botha, T, 4296, 5012
Bothomani, I B, 349
Botman, S, 1340
Botswana Society, 4328
Botte, R, 2907
Bou Ali, S 1474
Boudebaba, R, 1295
Boughton, J, 326
Boukar Massa, V, 3042
Boukharaoun, H, 1211, 1212
Bouraoui, H, 702
Bourdillon, M F C, 958
Bourenane, N, 1270
Bourgeot, A, 2606, 3008

Bourmaud, D, 1988
Bousfiha, N, 1432
Boutaleb, A, 1229
Boutet, R, 3239
Boutillier, J L, 2758
Boutrais, J, 298
Bouzar, W, 1257
Bove, R, 1963
Bowen, B H, 5440
Bowen, M L, 3957
Boyd, J, 3434
Boyd, R, 2425
Boyd-Buggs, D, 3556
Boyer, J M, 5630, 5631, 5632, 5633
Bozzoli, B, 4674, 4712
Braat, L G, 4394
Brabant, P, 299
Brachet, P, 1401
Bradley, J E, 2075
Braeckman, C, 4060, 4061
Braidwood, S J, 3616
Brand, S S, 5234
Brandon, A, 759
Brandt, H, 111
Brann, G, 1705
Brassuer, G, 2990
Bratton, M, 813, 814, 864, 4154
Braukamper, U, 1753
Braun, G, 1706
Braun, M, 3447
Brautigan, D, 2582
Bray, M, 2513
Bredeloup, S, 2738
Bregeon, J N, 1336
Brehun, L, 2926
Breitinger, E, 2430, 2431, 3728
Breman, H, 2529, 2595
Brenner, L, 3221
Brentjes, B, 1141
Breteau, C H 1468
Brett-Smith, S, 2952
Brijlal, P, 5317
Brill, H, 4259
Brink, A, 4928
Brion, E, 4019
British Consulate General, Casablanca, 1423
Brittain, V, 815
Broch-Due, V, 1972
Brodersen-Manns, H, 4453

de Clercq, F, 5030
de Cocquereaumont-Gruget, A, 5335
de Coninck, J, 2482, 3051
de Garine, I, 354
de Haan, L, 3640
de Haas, M, 5256
de Hen, F, 5336
de Jong, J, 660
de Jong, M, 4938
de Kadt, E, 4880
de Klerk, M, 5236
de Klerk, P, 4466
de Kok, I, 4939
de la Torre, I, 3634
de Latour, E, 3030
de Milly, H, 561
de Raulin, A, 2914
de Pinho, A T, 2572
de Ridder, N, 2595
de Rosny, E, 37
de Smedt, S, 3808
de Valk, P, 781, 782, 5484, 5485,
    5493
de Villiers, B, 5031, 5032
de Waal, A, 1786, 1846
de Waal, M, 5257
de Wilde, T, 2098, 2356, 3720
Deaton, A, 2714
Debreuille, M, 127
Decalo, S, 826, 827, 828
Decraene, P, 1390
Deeb, M, 1342
Defo, B C, 3683
Degand, J, 1964
Degefe, B, 1500
Deggs, M R 1381
Deheuvels, L W, 1290
Dei, G J S, 2833, 2888, 2889
Dejene Aredo, 1606
Déjeux, J, 1186
Del Pozo Manzano, E, 1414
Delage, P B, 2822
Delamasure, D, 1451
Delancey, V, 128
Deleris, F, 5588
Delobel, T, 2393
Delor-Vandueren, A, 1964
den Ouden, J H B, 2658
Deng, F M, 1787, 1847
Deng, L, 829

Denieuil, P N, 1478
Denis, P, 471
Dennis, C, 3179
Denzer, L, 2540
Depelchin, J, 3990
Derens, J, 4299
Derrick, J, 3684
Desfosses, H, 620
Desmazières, J F, 419
Desplanques, F, 1258
Dessalegn Rahmato, 1669
Devarajan, S, 329, 3688, 3722
Devenish, G, 5034
Devereux, S, 2834
Devey, M, 2992
Devineau, J L, 776
Devisch, R, 3971
Dewar, D, 4989, 5302
Dhadphale, M, 2139
Dhaouadi, M, 1476
Dia, A, 2966
Dia, I, 3588
Dia, S, 743
Diagne, A, 2620
Diallo, M, 2911
Diallo, S, 830
Diallo, T D, 3001
Diamond, L, 5035
Diarra, A, 129, 2979
Diarrah, C O, 3002
Diaw, A T, 3539
Diaw, B J, 2501
Diawara, G, 3009
Diawara, M, 55
Dibua, J I, 3449
Dickerman, C W, 3892
Dicko, A A, 2624
Diemer, G, 1011, 3589
Dieng, A A, 3541
Dieterlen, G, 2551
Dieu, M, 3748
Digre, B, 472
Dihm, M, 130
Diko, J, 2900
Dilger, M, 5218
Dilley, R, 3507
Dimkpa-Harry, S, 3083
Diop, A B, 3590
Diop, A O, 3516
Diop, B D, 2990

SUBJECT INDEX

Dreams, Berti, 1758
Dreams, Ingessana, 1761
Dreams, interpretation, 42
Dreams, Yansi, 3977
Dreams, Yoruba, 3065
Dress, women's, East Africa, 1935
Drinking, 2205
Drinking, Kenya, 2205
Drinking, South Africa, 5256
Drinking, Tanzania, 2345
Dromedary, and food, Horn of
  Africa, 1506
Drought relief, Botswana, 4349
Drought, and food security, Kenya,
  2047
Drought, and Lake Chad, 3460
Drought, and small towns, Sudan,
  1781
Drought, management, 366
Drought, Mozambique, 3920
Drought, northern Kenya, 2050
Drought, pastoralist response, Kenya,
  2051
Drought, Southern Africa, 4225
Drought, vulnerability, Zimbabwe,
  5419
Drought, Zimbabwe, 5418
Drug trade, 539, 551
Drugs, law, Botswana, 4373
Drugs, use, students, äigeria, 3488
Drugs, use, students, South Africa,
  5258
Drugs, use, Zimbabwe, 5545
Drumming, Mossi, 2670
Drumming, Yoruba, 3074
Drylands, 406, 1025
Drylands, and livelihood security,
  307, 365
Drylands, development constraints,
  East Africa, 1899
Drylands, Kenya, 2028
Drylands, management, 1012
Drylands, management, Kenya,
  2181, 2196
Drylands, management, Sudan, 1864
Drylands, output, Kenya, 2195
Drylands, research issues, 411
Drylands, resource management,
  1062
Drylands, resource use, 314

Duala, anticolonialism, 3712
Durban, image, 5333
Durban, Indian areas, 5322
Durban, local government, 5005,
  5007
Durban, Regional Services Council,
  5153
Durban, residential desegregation,
  5330
Durban, residential segregation, 5311
Durban, youth organisations, 5137
Dutch disease model, Nigeria, 3273
Dyula, and Islam, 2711
Earthquakes, and urban
  development, Egypt, 1381
East African Community, 563, 1911
East Europe, education of Africans,
  270
Eastern Cape (South Africa), history,
  4727
Eastern Europe, changes in, 842,
  5020
EC, 189, 237, 545, 546, 549, 564,
  578, 591
EC, and Horn, 1517
EC, and Maghreb, 1178
EC, and Mauritania, 1517
EC, and North Africa, 1142
EC, and Southern Africa, 4247
EC, import policy, 4252
EC, industrial cooperation, 514
EC, trade, South Africa, 4813
ECCAS, 174
Ecofarming, East Africa, 2532
Ecofarming, Sahel, 2532
Ecological crisis, 208
Ecomog, 2940, 3293
Econometric models, Botswana, 4336
Economic cooperation,
  Algeria-Cameroun, 1244
Economic crisis, 7, 11, 208
Economic integration, and trade
  policy, 542
Economic interdependence,
  Namibia-South Africa, 4462
Economic liberalisation,
  Mozambique, 3903
Economic modelling, Uganda, 2436
Economic reconstruction, Eritrea,
  1554

Subject Index

Women, and agriculture, Zaire, 4089
Women, and AIDS, 402
Women, and courts, Tanzania, 2368
Women, and customary law, colonial Eritrea, 1547
Women, and decorative painting, 54
Women, and development communication, 398
Women, and development projects, 373
Women, and education, colonial Sudan, 1780
Women, and education, northern Nigeria, 3190
Women, and educational performance, Ethiopia, 1586
Women, and equality, South Africa, 4881
Women, and fish trade, Tanzania, 2333
Women, and food production, 363
Women, and food production, Mali, 2969
Women, and independent churches, Nigeria, 3436
Women, and industrial work, South Africa, 4673
Women, and Islam, northern Nigeria, 3182
Women, and islamic education, Mamluk Egypt, 1304
Women, and land control, Swaziland, 5356
Women, and land use conflicts, Ciskei, 4754
Women, and law reform, Zimbabwe, 5461
Women, and law, Botswana, 4350
Women, and law, Southern Africa, 4223
Women, and liberation struggle, Southern Africa, 4221
Women, and liberation war, Algeria, 1221
Women, and liberation war, Eritrea, 1544
Women, and media, 374
Women, and politics, Egypt, 1320
Women, and politics, Malawi, 3869
Women, and power, C19 Bida, 3229

Women, and power, Yoruba, 3238
Women, and precolonial politics, 376
Women, and property, Mamluk Egypt, 1308
Women, and rural development, 382
Women, and rural development, Ethiopia, 1671
Women, and rural development, South Africa, 4675
Women, and rural trade, Kenya, 2053
Women, and state, South Africa, 4688
Women, and structural adjustment, Zambia, 4123
Women, and technology, history, 449
Women, and trade unions, South Africa, 4673
Women, biographies, Tanzania, 2340
Women, British, and colonialism, 481
Women, in rural household economy, Ethiopia, 1692
Women, land rights, Tanzania, 2365
Women, legal rights, Burkina Faso, 2687
Women, legal rights, South Africa, 4690
Women, legal rights, Swaziland, 5351
Women, legal status, Togo, 3653
Women, mental illness, Nigeria, 3359
Women, returns to education, Zimbabwe, 5423
Women, riots, 1950, Burundi, 1950
Women, rural, domestic work, Burkina Faso, 2678
Women, rural, Ghana, 2839
Women, rural, health, 388
Women, rural, informal sector, Tanzania, 2410
Women, rural, South Africa, 4681
Women, Shona, history, 5391
Women, singers, 1920s, Cairo, 1321
Women, slaves, Hausaland, 3183
Women, social history, Harare, 5420
Women, status, Nigeria, 3180
Women, violence against, South Africa, 5276
Woodfuel, Sahel, 2616
Woodlands, changes, East Africa, 1902
Work patterns, rural, persistence, Nigeria, 3457